Confucian Academies in East Asia

# Science and Religion in East Asia

*Series Editor*

Yung Sik Kim (*Seoul National University*)

*Editorial Board*

Benjamin Elman (*Princeton University*)
Jongtae Lim (*Seoul National University*)
Dagmar Schäfer (*Manchester University*)

VOLUME 3

The titles published in this series are listed at *brill.com/srea*

# Confucian Academies in East Asia

*Edited by*

Vladimír Glomb
Eun-Jeung Lee
Martin Gehlmann

BRILL

LEIDEN | BOSTON

This publication was supported by the Deutsche Forschungsgemeinschaft (DFG) through the Collaborative Research Center 980 "Episteme in Motion. Transfer of Knowledge From the Ancient World to the Early Modern Period" (SFB 980).

Cover illustration: Sohyŏn Academy, as depicted in North Korean map of famous cultural relics "Chosŏn myŏngsŭng yujŏk punp'odo," published by Kungnip ch'ulp'ansa, P'yŏngyang in 1956, second edition. (Private collection in Prague, Czech Republic.)

The Library of Congress Cataloging-in-Publication Data is available online at http://catalog.loc.gov

Typeface for the Latin, Greek, and Cyrillic scripts: "Brill". See and download: brill.com/brill-typeface.

ISSN 2214-8329
ISBN 978-90-04-42406-7 (hardback)
ISBN 978-90-04-42407-4 (e-book)

Copyright 2020 by Koninklijke Brill NV, Leiden, The Netherlands.
Koninklijke Brill NV incorporates the imprints Brill, Brill Hes & De Graaf, Brill Nijhoff, Brill Rodopi, Brill Sense, Hotei Publishing, mentis Verlag, Verlag Ferdinand Schöningh and Wilhelm Fink Verlag.
All rights reserved. No part of this publication may be reproduced, translated, stored in a retrieval system, or transmitted in any form or by any means, electronic, mechanical, photocopying, recording or otherwise, without prior written permission from the publisher.
Authorization to photocopy items for internal or personal use is granted by Koninklijke Brill NV provided that the appropriate fees are paid directly to The Copyright Clearance Center, 222 Rosewood Drive, Suite 910, Danvers, MA 01923, USA. Fees are subject to change.

This book is printed on acid-free paper and produced in a sustainable manner.

Printed by Printforce, the Netherlands

# Contents

Preface IX
Editors' Note XI
List of Illustrations and Tables XIII
Abbreviations XVI
Notes on Contributors XVII
Map of Relevant Academies XXI

Introduction 1

### PART 1
*Origins and Spread of Confucian Academies*

1 Some Reflections on Confucian Academies in China 21
   *Hoyt Cleveland Tillman*

2 An Enquiry into the Origins of Confucian Academies and the Mingtang in the Tang Period 45
   *Minamizawa Yoshihiko and Chien Iching*

3 The Nature and Educational Activities of Sungyang Academy in Kaesŏng 68
   *Chung Soon-woo*

4 Private Academies and Confucian Education in 18th-Century Vietnam in East Asian Context: The Case of Phúc Giang Academy 89
   *Nguyễn Tuấn-Cường*

5 Transmutations of the Confucian Academy in Japan: Private Academies of Chinese Learning (Kangaku Juku 漢学塾) in Late Tokugawa and Meiji Japan as a Reflection and a Motor of Epistemic Change 126
   *Margaret Mehl*

## PART 2
## *Curriculum of Confucian Academies*

6   Like Tea and Rice at Home: Lecture Gatherings and Academies during the Ming Dynasty   159
   *Deng Hongbo*

7   Books and Book Culture in Oksan Academy   197
   *Lee Byoung-Hoon*

8   Archery Ranges in the Educational Tradition of Confucian Academies in China   226
   *Thomas H.C. Lee*

9   Transmissions of the White Deer Grotto Academy Articles of Learning in Korea   252
   *Martin Gehlmann*

## PART 3
## *Social Role and Environment of Confucian Academies*

10   Confucian Academies and Their Urban Environments in Qing China   289
   *Steven B. Miles*

11   Shrines, Sceneries, and Granary: The Constitutive Elements of the Confucian Academy in 16th-Century Korea   319
   *Vladimír Glomb*

12   Disputes between Confucian Academies and Buddhist Monasteries from a Sociocultural View: The Case of the Wufeng Academy Litigation   359
   *Lan Jun*

## PART 4
## *From Religious Landscape to Cultural Heritage*

13 Songyang Academy in Time and Place: From Confucian Academy to Cultural Heritage   397
    *Linda Walton*

14 The Transmission and Transformation of Confucian Academy Rituals as Seen in Taiwanese Academies   437
    *Chien Iching*

15 Between Ruins and Relics: North Korean Discourse on Confucian Academies   456
    *Vladimír Glomb and Eun-Jeung Lee*

Index   493

# Preface

*Confucian Academies in East Asia* originated in an eponymous international conference at the Freie Universität Berlin held from May 4th to 6th, 2017. The conference was organized by the project "Knowledge Transfer in the Context of Differentiation and Institutionalization in 16th- and 17th-century Korea" within the framework of the Collaborative Research Center 980 "Episteme in Motion" in Berlin.[1] The motivation for the conference was to rethink the role of Confucian academies in both the premodern and modern contemporary societies of East Asia and to explore destinies of Confucian academies and their legacy in China, Korea, Japan, and Vietnam. For the first time international scholars were able to, at one time and one place, discuss together the topic of Confucian academies as a dynamic concept evolving over time in all countries concerned (People's Republic of China, Taiwan, Republic of Korea, Democratic People's Republic of Korea, Japan, and the Socialist Republic of Vietnam).[2] Studying Confucian academies as a shared historical memory of the region substantially contributes to an intercultural dialogue between the countries and political traditions, which until recently (and sometimes nowadays) had radically different views of Confucian heritage and its institutional background. The much discussed Confucian renewal[3] in the last three decades contributed to the growth of studies concerning Confucian academies, an inevitable companion of Confucian thought and social activities since Tang times until the present. Opening up questions about commonality and diversity of the academies across the disciplines and regions should enable us to embrace a fascinating heterogeneity subsumed under the common term of Confucian academies.

Thanks to the diligent work of all participants during and after the workshop,

---

1  For information on the concept and activities of the CRC 980, funded by the German Research Foundation (DFG), running since 2010, see the website <http://www.sfb-episteme.de>.
2  There have been regular exchanges between Chinese and South Korean researchers on Confucian academies since at least 2006 and individual co-operation between Taiwanese, Japanese, and Chinese Universities, but no conference on the history and status of Confucian academies in all countries of East Asia.
3  See, for example, Benjamin A. Elman, John B. Duncan, and Herman Ooms (eds.), *Rethinking Confucianism: Past and Present in China, Japan, Korea, and Vietnam* (Los Angeles: UCLA Asian Pacific Monograph Series, 2002); and Sébastien Billioud, Joël Thoraval, *The Sage and the People: The Confucian Revival in China* (Oxford: Oxford University Press, 2015), and recently Uri Kaplan, "Rebuilding the 'Eastern Country of Ritual Propriety': Decorum Camps, Sŏwŏn Stays, and the Confucian Revival in Contemporary Korea," *Sungkyun Journal of East Asian Studies* 18, no. 1 (2018): 59–84.

we are now able to bring the results of our debates to the reader; which would not be possible without the contributions of Namba Yukio (Fukuoka Jo Gakuin University), Park Kyung Hwan (Advanced Center for Korean Studies), Xiao Xiao (Hunan University), and Li Xinrui (Academy of Korean Studies) during the Berlin workshop sessions. Special thanks are also due to our commentators at the conference, Martina Deuchler (SOAS, Universität Zürich) and Marion Eggert (Ruhr-Universität Bochum), who helped us to navigate and make connections among the many diverse contributions. An important role in bringing this volume into being belongs to our colleagues who commented on the submitted contributions. Since the leitmotif of the conference was to problematize preconceived conceptions of Confucian academies and give free rein to individual scholars' interests it was not easy to find scholars able and willing to comment on topics of particular academies in 18th-century Vietnam; North Korean cultural preservation; or the practice of archery within the premises of Confucian academies: Christian Soffel (Universität Trier), Nathan Woolley (University of Glasgow), Liam Kelley (University of Hawai'i), Isabelle Sancho (EHESS-CNRS), Jan Sýkora (Charles University Prague), Felix Siegmund (Ruhr-Universität Bochum), Wang Sixiang (Stanford University), and Christina Moll-Murata (Ruhr-Universität Bochum) helped us with their positive criticism to incorporate new insights into the chapters of the volume. The difficult task of copy-editing the whole volume fell upon Bruce Tindall, to whose work we are grateful for. Crucial logistical support was given by management team of the CRC 980 Kristiane Hasselmann, Stefanie Fröhlich, and Anne Frederike Raschke. Lastly, we would like to thank Patricia Radder and Irene Jager at Brill for their patient assistance.

# Editors' Note

Regarding the editing of this volume we have imposed only a minimum of conformity and consistency on all contributions from the various backgrounds, since all authors must be free to find terms and translations befitting their topic, time, and space. Most of the technical vocabulary related to Confucian academies thus is rendered according to needs and conditions of the particular contribution. In order to accommodate our future readers, who may not be well versed in the specific jargon of the Confucian academies, we strived to reduce transliteration to a minimum. Translated terms often differ according to both author's choice and the historical context of its usage. Unlike some common terms, which are translated in a, more or less, fixed way, e.g. *shanzhang* 山長, rendered as director or headmaster of an academy, there is a wide range of terms, especially those connected to the inner structure of the academy, where English equivalents are hard to choose. Such is the case not only for obscure vocabulary of academic institutions or offices, but also for many well-known terms and concepts. A prime example is the frequently mentioned term of *jingshe* 精舍. In spite of Wing-tsit Chan's and later Thomas Lee's systematic efforts to find a universal translation for this term,[1] almost every scholar in this volume applies their own interpretation, depending on the context of his approach. Hoyt Tillman chose study lodge, Lan Jun preferred private study, Steven Miles translated it as retreat, Chien Iching reflected the Buddhist usage of the term by rendering it as hermitage, Vladimir Glomb applied study hall, and Deng Hongbo chose to rely on the transliteration of the original Chinese term.[2] In spite of such diversity, we hope the volume will be still easily readable. The same liberty was given to the authors in regard to

---

1  See Wing-Tsit Chan, *Chu Hsi: His Life and Thought* (Hongkong: The Chinese University Press, 1987), 163–169; and Thomas H.C. Lee, "Chu Hsi, Academies and the Tradition of Private Chiang-hsüeh," *Hanxue Yanjiu* 2, no. 1 (1984): 308–313. Wing-Tsit Chan uses the term "cottage," Thomas Lee gives a literary translation "residence or hut of essence" (see Thomas H.C. Lee, *Education in Traditional China. A History* [Leiden: Brill, 2000], 54), and John Meskill translates it as "sanctuary" (see John Meskill, *Academies in Ming China: A Historical Essay* [Tucson: University of Arizona Press, 1982], 11).
2  While the concept of Western academies is nowadays generally taken as a concept similar to Confucian academies and indeed bears some obvious similarities (see the Introduction to this volume), other educational institutions have been also suggested as applicable for comparison, e.g. Islamic madrasa schools or medieval European universities (see Linda Walton, *Academies and Society in Southern Sung China* [Honolulu: University of Hawai'i Press, 1999], 4–5; and Liu Heyan, *Songdai shuyuan yu ouzhou zhongshiji daxue zhi bijiao yanjiu* [Comparative Research between Song Dynasty Academies and Medieval European Universities] [Beijing: Renmin chubanshe, 2012], 1–22).

the specific phenomena of academy names. There were several methods how to name an academy ranging from ideological messages to simple toponyms or descriptions of the geographical features surrounding the institution. The situation is further complicated by the multiplicity of names often used for the same academy. Under such circumstances it would not be meaningful or even possible to find precise translations for many academy names. The decision whether to translate the academy name or not was thus left to the discretion of the authors.

# Illustrations and Tables

### Illustrations

0.1   Map of Relevant Academies   xix
2.1   Wangxiang Shrine. Yang Hongxun 楊鴻勛. "Mingtang fanlun: Mingtang de kaoguxue yanjiu 明堂泛論：明堂的考古學研究 (Survey of the Mingtang: An Archaeological Study of the Ming Tang)," *Tōhō gakuhō* 70 (1998): 86   50
2.2   The Jixian Shuyuan in Chang'an. Ikeda On 池田温. "Seitō no Shūken'in 盛唐之集賢院 (On Jixianyuan in the Mid-eighth Century)," *Hokkaidō daigaku bungakubu kiyō* 19 (1971): 55   59
3.1   Name plaque of Sungyang Academy. Photo Courtesy of Vladimír Glomb and Martin Gehlmann, 2018   80
3.2   Contemporary North Korean postcard of Sungyang Academy, part of the postcard set *Kaesŏng ŭi yujŏk, yumul/Historical Remains of Kaesong*. Pyongyang: Chosŏn up'yo sa, undated, around 2005   86
4.1   Map of the embassy's way to Beijing in 1766   103
4.2   Phụng sứ Yên Đài tổng ca 奉使燕臺總歌 (A General Song of the Embassy to Beijing). Stored in Vietnam National Library call number R.1375, page 20. <http://lib.nomfoundation.org/collection/1/volume/887/>   108
4.3   Page 5–6 of the *Thư viện quy lệ* 書院規例 (Academy Regulations) in woodblock, inverted. Photo Courtesy of Professor Nguyễn Huy Mỹ   111
6.1   Illustration of the lecture by Hui'an (Zhu Xi) and Nanxuan (Zhang Shi) at Yuelu (Hui'an Nanxuan Yuelu jiangdao zhi tu 晦庵南軒岳麓講道之圖). Deng Hongbo 邓洪波 (comp.), *Yuelu shuyuan zhi* (Records of Yuelu Academy), (Changsha: Yuelu Shushe, 2012), 48   161
7.1   *Mirror of the Tang Dynasty* (*Tangjian* 唐鑑) of Oksan Academy in 1562. Stored in the Oksan Academy vault. Photo courtesy of Lee Byoung-Hoon   203
7.2   Book case for the royal donation (*naesa* 內賜) of the *Royal Revised Version of a Hundred Chapters of Five Classics* (*Ŏjŏng ogyŏng paek p'yŏn* 御定五經百篇). Stored in the Oksan Academy vault. Photo courtesy of Lee Byoung-Hoon   206
7.3   *Record of Oksan Academy Books* (*Oksan sŏwŏn sŏch'aekki* 玉山書院書冊記) from 1713. Stored in the Oksan Academy vault. Photo courtesy of Lee Byoung-Hoon   210
7.4   Wooden board with the inscriptions "Academy books are not supposed to leave the academy gate" with explanations. Wooden board stored in the Oksan Academy vault. Photo courtesy of Lee Byoung-Hoon   214

| | | |
|---|---|---|
| 7.5 | Title page of *Sŏch'aek ch'agŏrok* 書冊借去錄 (*Record of Borrowed Books*) and page showing individual entries on borrowed books with check markings. Stored in the Oksan Academy vault. Photo courtesy of Lee Byoung-Hoon | 215 |
| 9.1 | Wooden hanging board containing the *White Deer Grotto Regulations* in the Myŏngnyundang of the Sŏnggyun'gwan in Seoul. Photo courtesy of Martin Gehlmann | 262 |
| 9.2 | Handwritten version of the *Diagram of the White Deer Grotto Regulations* (*Paengnoktong kyu to* 白鹿洞規圖) as included in the *Ten Diagrams of Sage Learning* (*Sŏnghak Sipto* 聖學十圖) by Yi Hwang, produced in the 18th or 19th century. Source: Private collection in Berlin | 269 |
| 9.3 | Academy rules from the *Records of Sŏak* (*Sŏak chi* 西岳志). Source: Private collection in Berlin | 275 |
| 9.4 | Wooden hanging board in P'iram Academy containing the *White Deer Grotto Regulations*, *Zhu Xi's Commentary*, and Kim Inhu's poem *Reading the White Deer Grotto Regulations* (*Tok paengnoktonggyu* 讀白鹿洞規). Photo courtesy of Martin Gehlmann | 280 |
| 10.1 | Map of Guangzhou. Adapted from the 1879 *Guangzhou fu zhi* 廣州府志 (*Guangzhou Prefectural Gazetteer*) | 292 |
| 11.1 | Current state of Ŭnbyŏng Study Hall. Photo courtesy of Vladimír Glomb and Martin Gehlmann, 2018 | 330 |
| 11.2 | Wooden nameplate of Ŭnbyŏng Study Hall in Sohyŏn Academy. Photo courtesy of Vladimír Glomb and Martin Gehlmann, 2018 | 350 |
| 12.1–2 | Map of the Wufeng area, adapted from Cheng Shangfei 程尙斐 (comp.), *Wufeng shuyuan zhi* 五峰書院志 (*Records of Wufeng Academy*), in: ZGLDSYZ, Volume 9, 162 | 364 |
| 13.1 | View of Mount Song from Songyang Academy today. Photo courtesy of Linda Walton | 398 |
| 13.2 | Songyang Academy in its Dengfeng County Setting. Geng Jie 耿介 et al. (eds.), *Songyang shuyuan zhi* 嵩陽書院志 (*Record of Songyang Academy*), [1701?], 1.24–25 | 408 |
| 13.3 | Drawing of Songyang Academy. Zhang Shenggao 張聖誥 et al. (comps.). *Dengfeng xian zhi* 登封縣誌 (*Records of Dengfeng County*), [1696 ed.] | 409 |
| 13.4 | Diagram of Songyang Academy. From UNESCO Submission, p. 349 at <http://whc.unesco.org/en/list/1395/documents/> | 422 |
| 15.1 | List of academies and shrines in P'yongan province located in Pyongyang. *Tongguk munhŏnnok* 東國文獻錄 (*List of Documents of the Eastern Country*), 1:32a, 1804, (Private collection in Prague) | 460 |

ILLUSTRATIONS AND TABLES　　　　　　　　　　　　　　　　　　　　　　　　　　　XV

15.2　　Japanese colonial postcard of Sungyang Academy with the tourist stamp, part of the postcard set *Kaijō keishu* 開城景趣 (*Kaesŏng sceneries*). Seoul: Hinode, undated　461

15.3　　North Korean postcard of Sungyang Academy. English caption: "Soongyang Suwon (a school in the feudal age) in Kaesong." Folk song "Kaesong Nambong Ka (Kaesong Gay Fellow), part of the postcard set *Chosŏn ŭi myŏngsŭng kojŏk* (*Scenic spots and historical relics of Korea*). Pyongyang: Kungnip misul ch'ulp'ansa, 1959　463

15.4　　Sungnyŏl Academy commemorative stela (Sungnyŏl sŏwŏn yuhŏ pi 崇烈書院遺墟碑) in Ch'ŏngjin. Photo courtesy of Jaroslav Bařinka　464

15.5　　Ryonggok Academy in 1959. Photo courtesy of Jaroslav Bařinka　468

15.6　　Cultural heritage information tablet in front of Ryonggok Academy installed by the People's Committee of Pyongyang City (P'yŏngyang si inmin wiwŏnhoe). Photo courtesy of Vladimír Glomb and Martin Gehlmann, 2018　475

## Tables

3.1　　List of Academies in the northern provinces according to the *Yŏllyŏsil kisul* 燃藜室記述 (*Narrative of Yŏllyŏsil*) (1806)　75

4.1　　Relevant terms in East Asia　90

4.2　　Schools in early modern East Asia. Source: Azuma Juji, "The Private Academies of East Asia: Research Perspectives and Overview," *A Selection of Essays on Oriental Studies of ICIS* (2011), 11　93

4.3　　Chinese academies visited by Nguyễn Huy Oánh in 1766　104

4.4　　Materials used in Phúc Giang Academy　115

6.1　　Selected academies and their educational gatherings　182

6.2　　Curriculum and course material of Hongdao Academy　184

10.1　　Prominent academies of 19th-century Guangzhou　291

15.1　　Founding of academies by royal reign. Source: O, Changhwan. "Sŏwŏne taehan yakkanŭi koch'al (Short Study on Confucian Academies)." *Ryŏksa kwahak* no. 6 (1956): 73　482

15.2　　The most frequently enshrined scholars. Source: O, Changhwan. "Sŏwŏne taehan yakkanŭi koch'al (Short Study on Confucian Academies)." *Ryŏksa kwahak* no. 6 (1956): 75　484

# Abbreviations

CBDB     *China Biographical Database*. Harvard University, Academia Sinica and Peking University, China Biographical Database. <https://projects.iq.harvard.edu/cbdb>.

CBMHPG     *Chŭngbo munhŏn pigo* 增補文獻備考 (*Augmented Reference Compilation of Documents*). Seoul: Hongmungwan, 1908.

SBCK     *Sibu congkan* 四部叢刊 (*Collectanea of the Four Categories*). Shanghai: Shangwu yinshuguan, 1919–1936.

SKQS     *Siku quanshu* 四庫全書 (*Complete Books of the Four Storehouses*). Reprint. Shanghai: Shanghai guji chubanshe, 1987. <http://db.ersjk.com>.

SKQSCM     *Siku quanshu cunmu congshu* 四庫全書存目叢書 (*Collectanea of works mentioned in the cunmu catalog*). Jinan: Jilu sushe, 1997.

SWCCS     *Sŏwŏn chi ch'ongsŏ* 書院誌叢書 (*Collection of Academy Records*). Volumes 1–9. Seoul: Minjok munhwasa, 1987.

TGCS     *T'oegye chŏnsŏ* 退溪全書 (*Complete Writings of T'oegye*). 1843. Kyujanggak #古3428–482. Database of Korean Classics. <http://db.itkc.or.kr>.

YGCS     *Yulgok chŏnsŏ* 栗谷全書 (*Complete Writings of Yulgok*). 1814. Sejong University Central Library #811.97–Yi I-Yul. Database of Korean Classics. <http://db.itkc.or.kr>.

ZGLDSYZ     *Zhongguo lidai shuyuan zhi* 中國歷代書院志 (*Historical Records of Chinese Academies*), edited by Zhao Suosheng 赵所生 and Xue Zhengxing 薛正兴, Volumes 1–16. Nanjing: Jiangsu jiaoyu chubanshe, 1995.

# Notes on Contributors

*Chien Iching*
簡亦精, Ph.D. from Kyushu University, is a researcher of Chinese philosophy at Kyushu University, Japan. She has studied Confucian academies of the Ming and Qing periods, and recently researches mainly about the relationship between rituals of Confucian academies and folk cults. Her special focus is on the relationship between the rituals of Confucian academies of Taiwan and Daoist gods of the civil service examinations and geomancy. She has published several articles about this topic, including in the well-known journal *Zhongguo shuyuan* (*Confucian Academies of China*) of Hunan University.

*Chung Soon-woo*
丁淳佑, is Professor at The Academy of Korea Studies in Seongnam, South Korea. He was a Visiting Professor at the University of British Columbia and the University of California, Berkeley, and served as Lecturing Professor at Paris Diderot University. His main fields of research are the educational history of the late Chosŏn dynasty and intellectual spaces. Some of his publications among many others are *Kongbu ŭi palgyŏn* (*The Discovery of Learning*), Seoul: Hyŏnamsa, 2007; *Sŏdang ŭi sahoesa* (*A Social History of the Sŏdang*), P'aju: T'aehaksa, 2013; *Sŏwŏn ŭi sahoesa* (*A Social History of the Academy*), P'aju: T'aehaksa, 2013; and articles in *Tosan sŏwŏn kwa chisik ŭi t'ansaeng* (*Tosan Academy and Birth of Knowledge*), edited by Chŏng Manjo, P'aju: Kul Hangari, 2012; and *Traditional Korean Philosophy: Problems and Debates*, edited by Youngsun Back, Philip J. Ivanhoe, and Halla Kim. London: Rowman & Littlefield, 2017.

*Deng Hongbo*
邓洪波, is Professor of history at the Yuelu Academy of Hunan University in Changsha. He is the director of the Chinese Academy Research Center at Hunan University and the vice-director of the Yuelu Academy Research Council. Since November 2015 he also serves as Leading Researcher for the project "Arrangement and Research of Chinese Academy Documents" funded by the Chinese National Planning Office of Philosophy and Social Science. Some of his publications include *Zhongguo shuyuan shi* 中国书院史 (*History of Chinese Academies*), revised edition, Wuhan: Wuhan daxue chubanshe, 2012; *Hunan shuyuan shigao* 湖南书院史稿 (Historical Manuscripts of Hunan Academies), Changsha: Hunan jiaoyu chubanshe, 2013; and as editor *Yuelu shuyuan zhi* 岳麓书院志 (*Records of Yuelu Academy*), Changsha: Yuelu shushe, 2013.

*Martin Gehlmann*
is a researcher in the fields of East Asian educational history and Confucian academies. Since 2014, he has been working at the Institute of Korean Studies of Freie Universität Berlin and since 2016 he is also a researcher within the framework of the project "Episteme in Motion: Transfer of Knowledge from the Ancient World to the Early Modern Period" at Freie Universität Berlin. He is also a member of the Yuelu Academy football team.

*Vladimír Glomb*
is a researcher in the fields of Korean philosophy, Confucianism in general, and premodern Korean language and thought. Since 2010, he has been lecturing as an assistant professor in the Department of Korean Studies at Charles University. Since 2016, he is a researcher within the framework of the project "Episteme in Motion: Transfer of Knowledge from the Ancient World to the Early Modern Period" at Freie Universität Berlin.

*Lan Jun*
兰军, is a member of the teaching staff at the Institute for History, Culture and Tourism at Jiangsu Normal University in Xuzhou. He received his M.A. degree at Wenzhou University and his Ph.D. degree at Hunan University. His research interests are the history and culture of Confucian Academies and he has published books and articles in the field.

*Lee Byoung-Hoon*
李炳勳, is a fellow at the Institute of Korean Culture at Yeungnam University in Kyŏngsan, where he also received his B.A. and Ph.D. degrees. He has been studying the history of Oksan Academy in Kyŏngju and has published several articles on its reconstruction and the community involved with the academy. Further research topics include the history of Confucian scholars and academies in the Yŏngnam region.

*Eun-Jeung Lee*
李恩政, is a political scientist and historian with research interests in modern and premodern intellectual, political, and diplomatic history and processes in Korea and East Asia. Since 2008, she has been Professor and head of Korean Studies in the Faculty for History and Cultural Studies at Freie Universität Berlin. She is the head of the project analyzing the role of Confucian academies in the transfer of knowledge during the sixteenth and seventeenth centuries within the framework of the project "Episteme in Motion. Transfer

of Knowledge from the Ancient World to the Early Modern Period" at Freie Universität Berlin.

*Thomas H.C. Lee*
李弘祺, Ph.D. (Yale, 1975), is Professor Emeritus of History and Asian Studies at The City College of New York. He has published broadly on Chinese education and intellectual history, including *Government Education and Examinations in Sung China*, London: Palgrave Macmillan, 1985; *Education in Traditional China, a History*, Leiden: Brill, 2001, and the Chinese version *Xue yi weiji, Chuantong Zhongguo de jiaoyu*, Hong Kong: The Chinese University of Hong Kong Press, 2015.

*Margaret Mehl*
is Associate Professor at the University of Copenhagen in the Department of Cross-Cultural and Regional Studies. In 1992 she received her Ph.D. Degree from the University of Bonn. She has worked at the University of Cambridge, University of Edinburgh, University of Stirling, and Freie Universität Berlin. Since 2001 she has been a member of the University of Copenhagen and her recent publications include *Private Academies of Chinese Learning in Meiji Japan: The Decline and Transformation of the Kangaku Juku*, Copenhagen: NIAS, 2005; *Not by Love Alone. The Violin in Japan 1850–2010*, Copenhagen: The Sound Book Press, 2014; and *History and the State in Nineteenth-Century Japan: The World, the Nation and the Search for a Modern Past*, Copenhagen: The Sound Book Press, 2017.

*Steven B. Miles*
is Professor in the Department of History at Washington University in Saint Louis. He specializes in the social and cultural history of early modern China. He is the author of *The Sea of Learning: Mobility and Identity in Nineteenth-Century Guangzhou* (2006) and *Upriver Journeys: Diaspora and Empire in Southern China, 1570–1850* (2017), and editor-in-chief of the journal *Late Imperial China*.

*Minamizawa Yoshihiko*
南澤良彦, Ph.D. at Kyoto University, is Professor of Chinese Philosophy at Kyushu University, Japan. He has researched about philosophy and the history of technology and science in premodern China, and recently has lectured and written on rituals, symbolisms, and the architecture of the Mingtang. He is the author of the book *Chūgoku meidō shisō kenkyū* 中国明堂思想研究 (A Study of Ideas about the Mingtang in China), Tokyo: Iwanami Shoten, 2018.

*Nguyễn Tuấn-Cường*
阮俊強, Ph.D. in Sino-Nom Studies (Vietnamese Sinology), Director of the Institute of Sino-Nom Studies at the Vietnam Academy of Social Sciences, Hanoi, Vietnam. He is also an Adjunct Professor of Sino-Nom Studies at Vietnam National University, Hanoi. He concentrates on Vietnamese Sinology, classical philology, Confucianism, and traditional education in Vietnam.

*Hoyt Cleveland Tillman*
田浩, Ph.D. in History and East Asian Languages from Harvard University, taught Chinese history at Arizona State University from 1976 until his retirement in 2019, and is now Special Appointed Professor at Hunan University's Yuelu Academy and a Research Affiliate at Peking University's Center for Research on Ancient Chinese History since 2004. In 2001, he was honored with the Alexander von Humboldt Prize. Most of his published books and articles focus on the history of Confucianism during the Song, Jin, and Yuan periods. His two most important monographs are: *Utilitarian Confucianism*; and *Zhu Xi de siwei shijie* (*Zhu Xi's World of Thought*), which is a greatly expanded and revised version of his *Confucian Discourse and Chu Hsi's Ascendancy*. He also coauthored with Christian Soffel *Cultural Authority and Political Culture in China*. Seeing diversity within Confucian thinking about social, political, and cultural issues, Tillman demonstrates greater complexity in Zhu Xi's philosophy and how it developed through borrowing from, or arguing against, his contemporaries.

*Linda Walton*
is Professor Emerita of History and International Studies at Portland State University, Portland, Oregon, USA. She received her B.A. degree from Wellesley College and her Ph.D. from the University of Pennsylvania. In addition to her book, *Academies and Society in Southern Sung China*, Honolulu: University of Hawai'i Press, 1999, she has published journal articles and book chapters on the social and intellectual history of Song and Yuan China (10th–14th centuries). Recent research includes a study of academies during the Mongol Yuan dynasty (1279–1368) and a project on the restoration of Confucian academies in contemporary China as sites of cultural heritage tourism.

ILLUSTRATION 0.1   Map of Relevant Academies

# Introduction

Speaking about Confucian academies in plural in the title of this book is not a reference to their vast number (which was never entirely counted) in the various countries of the Confucian world, but rather an allusion to their multiplicity in the sense of their heterogeneous nature. Understanding "The Confucian Academy" as a single uniform concept would probably not function for any period and culture where these institutions were present. When Matteo Ricci (1552–1610), during his time in south eastern China, most likely visited the legendary Bailudong shuyuan 白鹿洞書院 (White Deer Grotto Academy) in 1595 and described it as "an Academy of literati" (*una Academia di letterati*)[1] he gave to the standing term for the academies, *shuyuan* 書院, a more than appropriate rendering. Much like the Western semantics of the expression "Academy" that unites more than two thousand societies and institutions that are, to a certain degree, similar, yet incredibly diverse,[2] *shuyuan* or Confucian academies have never formed a simple linear tradition.

The development of Confucian academies in various countries to certain degree emulated Confucian teaching itself: while it appealed to common classical sources, the best form of the Confucian academy was actually the one

---

1  For a basic comparison of Italian and Chinese academies and Ricci's translation of the term see John Meskill, *Academies in Ming China: A Historical Essay* (Tucson: The University of Arizona Press, 1982), x–xii. Ricci also engaged in discussions with the Chinese literati and the director of the academy, Zhang Huang 章潢 (1527–1608), who was a good friend of his. Ricci actually never explicitly mentions that he visited White Deer Grotto Academy in his letters, but that he met with Zhang Huang and his disciples for discussions, from which most authors conclude that this must have been at the White Deer Grotto Academy. It could, however, also been at Zhang's Cixi Hall 此洗堂. See Xiao Lang, "Li Madou yu bailudong shuyuan ji qita: Yi wenxian zhengli shidu de kaocha (Matteo Ricci, the White Deer Grotto Academy and Others: A Literature Review)," *Jiangxi shehui kexue* 1 (2007): 100, For more sources on Ricci's contact with Chinese academies see Michela Fontana, *Matteo Ricci: A Jesuit in the Ming Court* (Lanham: Rowman & Littlefield Publishers, 2011), 138–139; Ronnie Po-Chia Hsia, *A Jesuit in the Forbidden City: Matteo Ricci 1552–1610* (Oxford: Oxford University Press, 2010), 157–163; Xu Haiyan and Bao Lili, *Li Madou zai Zhongguo* (Matteo Ricci in China) (Beijing: Zhongguo xiju chubanshe, 2006), 45.

2  For discussions on European academies see Tore Frängsmyr (ed.), *Solomon's House Revisited: The Organization and Institutionalization of Science* (Canton, MA: Science History Publications, 1990); Simone Testa, *Italian Academies and Their Networks 1525–1700, from Local to Global* (New York: Palgrave Macmillan, 2015); Sebastian Kühn, *Wissen, Arbeit, Freundschaft. Ökonomien und soziale Beziehungen an den Akademien in London, Paris und Berlin um 1700* (Göttingen: V&R unipress, 2011); Klaus Garber et al. (eds.), *Europäische Sozietätsbewegung und demokratische Tradition. Die europäischen Akademien der Frühen Neuzeit zwischen Frührenaissance und Spätaufklärung* (Tübingen: De Gruyter, 1996).

that reflected the needs of the scholars, pupils, or community running it. The fact that a Confucian academy was primarily not a building, but a living organism of scholars and students, on the one hand brought on an enormous diversity of academy types and curricula, but on the other hand also determined their innate fragility. Regardless of how influential and famous an academy might be, once its scholarly community dispersed, the academy disappeared and its specific curriculum, ethos, or structure vanished.[3] The history of Confucian academies is a story of a never-ending metamorphosis of the concept used (and often misused) until today.

Part of this publication is to treat both phenomena equally: the successful, i.e. long-lasting features of the academies as well as those less known or less successful characteristics that disappeared centuries or only decades ago. The narrative of Confucian academies is in the first place, as seen from our contemporary perspective, a retrospective of their wondrous survival ability and at the same time of regrettable losses. Nostalgia and hope for new revivals are making research on academies more personal than one would expect of this Confucian institution; seeing either the ruins or the extant buildings, we above all think about the scholars of the past. Such an aura was already embedded in the very genetic code of academies during their Song dynasty upsurge; the White Deer Grotto Academy, and many other academies, were not founded, but revived or restored at the places of their earlier Tang or earlier Song predecessors.[4] The emotions aroused by the image of a dead or decayed academy run like a red line through the centuries and are shared by both old and modern scholars. Lü Zuqian's 呂祖謙 (1137–1181) description of Zhu Xi 朱熹 (1130–1200) commenting sadly on the ruins of old White Deer Grotto Academy[5] pairs well with Wing-tsit Chan's (1901–1994) notes about his visit to the same academy in 1983, observing that it was remarkable to find it in a very good condition and

---

3   The most well-known academies are naturally the most long-lived, which counted their existence in centuries. This should not obscure the fact that neglect, wars, floods, or government suppression often limited academies' existence to mere decades. An example could be a sample of 118 Qing period academies in Guangdong, which had a median lifespan of 53.3 years; see Liu Boji, *Guangdong shuyuan zhidu yange* (History of the Guangdong Academy System) (Shanghai: Commercial Press, 1939), 116–117.
4   See Chen Wen-yi, *You guanxue dao shuyuan. Cong zhidu yu linian de hudong kan songdai jiaoyu de yanbian* (From Official School to Academy. Looking at the Evolution of Song Times Education from the Perspective of Interaction between Concept and Institution) (Taibei: Lianjing chubanshe, 2004), 28–45.
5   See Bailudong shuyuan ji (Account of White Deer Grotto Academy), in *Donglai ji* (Collected Writings of Donglai), Volume 6 (Jinhua: Xujinhua congshu, 1923), <http://db.ersjk.com> (accessed: 21 March 2018).

well taken care of after so many destructions and reconstructions over the centuries.[6]

The current promotion of Confucian academies in the PRC or the Republic of Korea should not obscure the fact that this latest revival is highly selective and many parts of the traditional world of the academies are missing and some are gone without trace. The 20th century was especially unforgiving to the academies; Wing-tsit Chan's surprise to see the White Deer Grotto Academy standing is, in the context of losses during the Cultural Revolution, well understandable. We are just a few decades away from Jaroslav Bařinka having to describe academies located in North Korea as "ruins of a formerly suggestive environment" and "subject of the scorn of the majority of modern Koreans."[7] The turbulent events of modernity greatly reduced the number of academies and sometimes wiped out whole centuries of their development: of the five big shrines and academies located in the current North Korean capital Pyongyang, none is extant today and almost no documents are available to trace their specific culture; archery ranges adjacent to Chinese academies are almost impossible to find; and even the most famous Qing-era city academies disappeared. Documenting the less-known or vanished features of Confucian academies is not solely motivated by the goal to add a few more details to the standing massive bulk of studies.[8] The neglected or forgotten aspect of academies shed much light on the very goal of these studies: to understand how to define the Confucian academy in the process of transformations through time and space.

## 1 Transfer of Knowledge

The possibility of regional comparisons brought on by the contributions covering China, Vietnam, Korea, and Japan in the volume is only magnifying the basic problem of a universal definition of Confucian academies. Rebekah Zhao

---

6  Wing-tsit Chan, "Chu Hsi and the Academies," in *Neo-Confucian Education: The Formative Stage*, ed. Wm. Theodore de Bary and John W. Chaffee (Berkeley: University of California Press, 1989), 405.
7  Jaroslav Bařinka, "Staré konfuciánské ústavy v Koreji," *Nový Orient* 23 (1968): 266.
8  There is no comprehensive bibliography of Confucian academy studies and given the magnitude of the research field in the last decades, it will be probably never compiled. During a joint conference in Taegu in October 2017 Yi Suhwan counted 101 monographs and edited volumes together with 179 studies published in the Republic of Korea in 2000–2017. Deng Hongbo indicates 3,349 articles and 197 books on academies published in PRC only in 2006–2016. Both papers presented at the conference *Han-Chung sŏwŏn yŏn'gu ŭi hyŏnjae wa mirae* (Present and Future of Korean-Chinese Academy Research), held on October 28, 2017 in Taegu, South Korea.

in 2003 described Confucian academies as "independent, or semi-independent educational institutions, primarily within the Confucian tradition. Their main function was to train students in classical studies and philosophical interpretation of Confucian doctrines, in addition to collecting, collating and publishing books."[9] In spite of the brevity of such a definition, we would have difficulty finding any single academy exactly corresponding to it. The binary oppositions defining the academy concept—private education vs. state schools, self-cultivation in contrast to official examinations, orthodox Confucianism opposing other religious and intellectual currents, independent scholarship in contrast to conservative elites, etc.—varied across time periods, philosophical schools, countries, or cultures. Even though a general adherence to Zhu Xi's model of the academy was often proclaimed, actual forms of academies often had very little in common with the White Deer Grotto Academy as it was designed during Zhu Xi's times. To understand the multiplicity of academy forms, it is necessary to leave the concept of a single model[10] and to focus on the transformations of academies according to their specific needs and environments.

As Hoyt Tillman reminds us in his contribution, Zhu Xi's model was not the only one to be followed in Song times; yet many Korean scholars employed ambiguous and quite personal images of Zhu Xi's White Deer Grotto Academy in order to form and legitimize their own academies (as Martin Gehlmann demonstrates). There were many scholars both in China and Korea who openly opposed participation in state examinations, which on the other hand was

---

9 See the entry by Rebekah X. Zhao, "Shu yuan (Confucian Academies)," in *The Encyclopedia of Confucianism*, ed. Yao Xinzhong (London: Routledge, 2015), 565.

10 The thesis that all academies were comparable units still has a strong influence resulting in a rather anachronistic view of traditional society and role of Confucian academies. Alexander Woodside, in *Lost Modernities: China, Vietnam, Korea, and the Hazards of World History*, 22–23, argues that "by the 1700s Choson Korea, with a population of perhaps seven to eight million people, had more than six hundred such academies; Qing dynasty China, with a population perhaps thirty times the size of Korea's in the eighteenth century, had little more than three times the number of Korea's academies (about nineteen hundred). Vietnam, with a probable population of four to five million people at the end of the 1700s, had no real tradition of academies at all." This by his opinion resulted in "Korea's superiority to China, let alone Vietnam, in the density of its academies may help to explain why polls taken even now, by East Asians themselves, show a greater predisposition to Confucian principles in Korea than in China." The different number of Korean academies is however a result of the different purpose and form of Korean academies compared to their Qing (or Vietnamese) counterparts. This flat comparison also ignores the fact that in 1871 had Chosŏn Korea only dozens of academies compared to hundreds of thriving Qing institutions. See Barry Keenan, *Imperial China's Last Classical Academies: Social Change in the Lower Yangzi, 1864–1911* (Berkeley: Institute of East Asian Studies, 1994).

the raison d'être of many Qing academies, as shown by Steven Miles. The archery exercises described by Thomas H.C. Lee are one of the least-expected activities associated with Confucian students in an academy. In order to answer the question of what has, in spite of such heterogeneity, guaranteed the status of Confucian academies or defined membership in this institutional category we have to shift our attention from the description of individual cases and particular agendas of individual academies to the concept of knowledge transfer[11] related to the concept of the Confucian academy itself.

Premodern cultures are often described as stable, both from an inside perspective as well as from the outside, and in particular their institutions are understood as attempts to cement certain "traditions." However, a long term perspective reveals that within these apparently stable systems of knowledge, epistemic change is constant.[12] Not only does the taught content in the academies change, but with each iteration and transfer the concept of the academy itself receives new impulses. The spread of academies in various countries of East Asia gives us ample evidence of how various scholars or groups studied, appropriated, and transformed the multiple traditions of Chinese academies, including in China itself. Korean scholars had a very good knowledge of academies since their first introductions to the Learning of the Way during Yuan times, yet the first academy explicitly declaring itself as a follower of Zhu Xi's model was established only in 1543. The Vietnamese scholar Nguyễn Huy Oánh 阮輝瑩 (1713–1789) visited southern China and took inspiration for his Phúc Giang Academy 福江書院 from the several Chinese academies he toured, yet careful research by Nguyễn Tuấn-Cường shows that he already *before* his trip to China had considerable experience with the founding of educational institutions. The knowledge of Chinese precedents surely inspired scholars from other countries, but could never answer the question of which model, if any, would be appropriate for the concrete local environment. Multiple traditions

---

11　Much of the concept of the knowledge transfer as it is understood in this volume is inspired by the joint project of Korean Studies from Ruhr-University Bochum and FU Berlin focusing on circulation, location, dynamics and integration of knowledge between Korea, China, Japan, and the West. For further details see *Space and Location in the Circulation of Knowledge (1400–1800): Korea and Beyond*, ed. Marion Eggert, Felix Siegmund, and Dennis Würthner (Bern: Peter Lang, 2014); *The Dynamics of Knowledge Circulation: Cases from Korea*, ed. Eun-Jeung Lee and Marion Eggert (Bern: Peter Lang, 2016); and *Integration Processes in the Circulation of Knowledge: Cases from Korea*, ed. Marion Eggert and Florian Pölking (Bern: Peter Lang, 2016).
12　See Eva Cancik-Kirschbaum and Anita Traninger, "Institution – Iteration – Transfer: Zur Einführung," in *Wissen in Bewegung: Institution – Iteration – Transfer*, ed. Eva Cancik-Kirschbaum and Anita Traninger (Wiesbaden: Otto Harrassowitz, 2015), 1–13; for more on the basic concept of the CRC 980 see <http://www.sfb-episteme.de/en>.

existed both in the synchronic and diachronic senses: late Chosŏn (1392–1910) scholars knew several radically different models of Chinese academies from Song, Yuan, Ming, and Qing times as well as various forms of academies from earlier periods of Korean tradition. However, to what degree they took them into consideration when devising new forms of their own curriculum or academy structures is an open question.[13]

The problem of what was studied in Confucian academies and how they structured their lecture activities, carefully documented for the Ming period in the volume by Deng Hongbo, is necessarily accompanied by the question what was studied *about* Confucian academies. Connections to the Song models could be very loose, as for example the Japanese private academies of Chinese Learning (*kangaku juku*) exhibit very different features compared to the Song models of the Confucian academy, yet even they have to be counted as the one branch of academy tradition. The concept of academy, besides an ideal plan for education, included a set of strategies necessary for running and administering such institutions, which could potentially (and often did) change whole communities in which the academies were established. The resonance of the academies and their environment is an important correlative in analyzing the academies' impact and significance. The very nature of the academies explicitly supposed an outward impact on local communities: students cultivating themselves should be able to cultivate their nearest environment as well, or at least this environment should respond to and be transformed by the academy's presence. Steven Miles's contribution is a crucial corrective to the idea of an isolated academy, where students enjoyed the natural beauty in solitude. It also very well shows that the construction and placing of an academy corresponded with the broader needs of the local community and that for the successful organization of the academy multiple social and economic factors had to be and were taken in consideration.[14]

Academy functions gradually evolved to an extent Zhu Xi could not have foreseen: networks of academies belonging to the same schools or political factions were able to generate considerable political and intellectual impact

---

13  Compare for example the case of Nguyễn Huy Oánh for whom the contemporary Yuelu Academy served as a model and inspiration to the situation in Korea, where Chosŏn scholars oriented themselves to the canonical example of the White Deer Grotto Academy under Zhu Xi. It is also important to know that Korean scholars could not have a firsthand experience of southern China academies since the movement of tributary missions was restricted only to visits of the imperial court.

14  A focus on the local role of academies can also be found in Xiao Yongming, *Ruxue, shuyuan, shehui: shehui wenhua shi shiye zhong de shuyuan* (Confucianism, Academies, and Society: a Sociocultural Historical Perspective on Academies) (Beijing: Shangwu yinshuguan, 2012).

both in China and Korea, and academies assumed crucial roles in many areas that were previously only loosely connected, as Vladimír Glomb shows by examining the view of Korean scholar Yulgok Yi I 栗谷李珥 (1536–1584) towards academies and their social role. The importance of Korean academies for the book publishing business and spread of Confucian publications is a prime example of how the academies were able to generate sources and capacities within the framework of local society not otherwise possible. Lee Byoung-Hoon's study on book collection of Oksan Academy 玉山書院 and its fame as an intellectual center of the whole province is a very fine example. Oksan Academy was not founded with the intention to become the center of book production, yet, forced by circumstance, acquired and executed this function.[15] Most of the strategies devised by the academies to ensure their optimal functioning and both an educational and a social impact were not derived from classical sources, but rather developed *ad hoc* during the process of their spread and development. Reconfigurations of the standing corpus of knowledge, derived mostly from Song precedents, were supplemented by a wide range of new techniques and strategies that academy scholars appropriated and adjusted. The student-selection process, the dissemination of academy publications, the role of academies in military conflicts, organizing lecture activities in connection with broader networks of scholars, etc., were broad areas where academies proved their flexibility and ability to adjust old models to the new challenges. This dynamic adaptability is well demonstrated by successful attempts to incorporate Western models of knowledge in Qing China (earlier described by Barry Keenan) and Meiji Japan or in early modern Korea as shown by Margaret Mehl and Chung Soon-woo in this volume.

## 2    Religious Function

One of the lasting legacies of the Jesuit (and to certain degree also the Enlightenment) interpretation of Confucianism was the tendency to stress rationalism and suppress all religious connotations, which could invoke notions of idolatry in the eyes of missionaries or backward superstitions in the eyes of

---

15    For further aspects on how Korean academies supplied a rather underdeveloped local book market see Vladimír Glomb and Eun-Jeung Lee, "No Books to Leave, No Women to Enter: Confucian Academies in Pre-Modern Korea and Their Book Collections," in *The Epistemic Legacy: Vehicles for the Collection and Transfer of Knowledge in Premodern Societies*, ed. Eva Canick-Kirschbaum, Jochem Kahl, Eun-Jeung Lee, and Michaela Engert (Wiesbaden: Otto Harrassowitz, 2020 (forthcoming)).

European intellectuals.[16] Yet there is no reason to suppose that the various forms of Chinese or Korean religiosity stopped at the academy gates. Since their very beginning academies were planned as a counterweight to the analogous institutions of Buddhist and Daoist temples and monasteries. As Linda Walton documents in her study, academies were located at, or later became, sacred places and entered into centuries-long struggles over spiritual influence on the local population.

The outward presence of Confucian institutions in the religious landscape is well documented in various records of interaction with the other agents of the local spiritual scene: Lan Jun's analysis of the scholarly network around Wufeng Academy 五峰書院 and its interactions with a Buddhist community show both hostile and amicable relations between monks and scholars. The heated ideological conflicts, often more or less fueled by local economic interests, should not turn attention away from the positive aspects of cross-religion neighborhood relations. Korean academies often employed the services of adjacent Buddhist monasteries for construction or book publishing projects; the director of Guangzhou's Yangcheng Academy 羊城書院 during the Dragon Boat Festival in 1823 received gifts from the four of the city's major Buddhist monasteries, and the Penghu Academy 蓬壺書院 in Taiwan hosts a temple dedicated to the God of the Sea. How does this image correspond with the alleged orthodoxy of academies and their scholars? Inevitable coexistence with the local population and other religious currents often resulted in certain accommodations on the side of the academy, which could materialize in the pantheon of the academy shrine.

As Ellen Neskar has demonstrated, Confucian shrines historically formed an important part of the Learning of the Way of Song times.[17] Shrines often became parts of new academies and in many cases (as for example in late Chosŏn Korea) they became the focal point of the academy. The establishment of a shrine and the selection of worthies to enshrine were often complicated and academies had to carefully decide who should become a spiritual patron and model worthy for both students and the local community. The building of shrines dedicated to the god Wenchang 文昌 (as analyzed by Chien Iching in this volume) or ancestors of powerful local families could forge important alliances with the local population, but could also evoke discontent among

---

16   See, for example, Eun-Jeung Lee, *Anti-Europa: Die Geschichte der Rezeption des Konfuzianismus und der konfuzianischen Gesellschaft seit der frühen Aufklärung* (Münster: Lit, 2003).

17   Ellen Neskar, "The Cult of Worthies: A Study of Shrines Honoring Local Confucian Worthies in the Sung Dynasty (960–1279)" (Ph.D. diss., Columbia University, 1993).

zealous literati, who were not willing to sacrifice the purity of Confucian ideals ruling the academy territory.

The impact of the academy presence on the local population presents a complicated question still to be described. Korean scholars organized assemblies within the academy precinct and read to the public aloud the Regulations of White Deer Grotto Academy, followers of Wang Yangming used open lectures hoping to transform the common folk in Ming China, and all strived to have an influence on the population participating in these indoctrinations. However, the belief of the common people and peasants in the Lushan area that Zhu Xi acquired his wisdom by swallowing a pearl of great value given to him by a miraculous fox[18] shows that the Confucian values presented by the academy were often understood in quite different ways. Connections between educational and religious activities in academies were manifested not only through the annual offerings to Confucius or the worthies of the academy shrine. The inquiry into Tang-dynasty inspirations of the academy concept by Minamizawa Yoshihiko and Chien Iching shows that the functions of the Tang *shuyuan*, besides preserving books and cultivating knowledge, also included strong religious overtones. The religious significance of Confucianism also proved to be a crucial factor for the turbulent destinies of academies in the 20th century. On the one hand it made them a key target in the fight of communist regimes against "old ways of thinking," but it has also helped them to survive in societies like Taiwan and South Korea, where with demise of the Confucian educational system, the academy shrines and related cults formed an important tool for keeping up otherwise obsolete and deserted institutions.

## 3 Modern Challenges

During its existence the academy system was exposed to several setbacks caused both by external and internal factors. Since their beginnings during Song times, when academies were often considered as suspicious novelties, they later evolved into respected institutions, which attracted both sympathy and enmity. The growth of the academies also enhanced the numbers of their adversaries, and the political networks they were able to command became occasionally targets of state repression. The case of Donglin Academy 東林書院 in the turbulent political events of the late Ming, or efforts of Korean kings

---

18  Chan Wing-tsit, "Chu Hsi and the Academies," 404. The story is recorded in in the chapter "The White Deer Hollow University," in Carl F. Kupfer, *Sacred Places in China* (Cincinnati: Western Methodist Book Co., 1911), 74.

to limit the number of the academies, culminating in a massive shut down during the rule of Taewŏngun 大院君 (1864–1873), are prime examples of the repressive stance the state sometimes took toward academies.

Attempts to curb dissenting academies or limit their numbers were on the other hand never entirely successful and often only strengthened the determination of academy scholars to continue their efforts. Furthermore, the state also acknowledged the role of the academies and often offered them patronage, as a useful and cheap augmentation to the existing educational system. The most substantial challenge to the very system of the academies came only with the advent of modernity and the dismantling of the traditional system of Confucian education. The abolition of state examinations in China (1905) and Korea (1894) to a large degree undermined the purpose of classical education, and the new focus on Western knowledge started to dominate the educational system in all countries of the region. Studies brought together in this volume challenge the common assumption that Confucian academies were not able to deal with those changes. The modern destinies of Sungyang Academy 崧陽書院 in North Korea, described by Chung Soon-woo, show that the academy community reacted to these changes and established a modern school within the premises of the academy without abolishing its Confucian activities, which continued without interruption. Just as with Japanese private academies, where many institutions were able to incorporate the needs of a modern curriculum into their activities, it is no accident that many modern Chinese universities emerged at the old precincts of Confucian academies.[19] Academies lost state support and often their land properties, but their communities often remained faithful to their original purpose and strived to keep the Confucian message alive.

In the period between the world wars academies were threatened by the transformation processes of Asian societies and often faced critique as relics of the past orders. On the other hand, it was also the time when the first modern studies devoted to the academies emerged[20] and they became the object of a scholarly debate concerning their role within the framework of traditional Asian society. The interwar decades were also marked by a transition to a new approach to the values of the academies as they started to be understood as a part of cultural heritage. For material and surveys from this period we are often indebted to a rather ambivalent source: the scholars of the Japanese Empire. In

---

19  Just to name a few: Hunan University, Zhejiang University, Shanxi University, Sichuan University, etc.
20  See for example famous Chinese intellectual Hu Shi's, "Shuyuan de lishi yu jingshen (History and Spirit of the Academies)," *Jiaoyu yu rensheng*, no. 9 (1923), or his "Shuyuan zhi shilüe (Brief History of the Academy system)," *Dongfang zazhi* 21, no. 9 (1924).

1918 the Japanese archaeologist and architectural historian Sekino Tadashi 関野貞 (1868–1935) visited Mount Song and the site of Songyang Academy 嵩陽書院 to document the valuable relics.[21] The very same Sekino Tadashi as a colonial bureaucrat documented several Korean academies in both private and government-sponsored publications.[22] The new colonial power had eminent interest to know the cultural property of both already occupied and planned colonies. The Second World War combined with civil wars both in China and Korea further reduced numbers of extant academies and dispersed their communities.

Emerging socialist states in China, Korea, and Vietnam liquidated academies and their supporters as the remnants of the traditional feudal order in a process of either direct destruction or nationalization, sometimes converting academy buildings to other uses, but mostly leaving them empty and deserted. The survival of the rest of academies was guaranteed by the protection of cultural heritage management: after all, academies were officially state property. Animosity toward feudal relics and simultaneous respect for cultural property are well demonstrated by conflict about Songyang Academy during the Cultural Revolution or in multiple cases of North Korean culture policy toward academies. The story of academies under communist regimes is not entirely free of curious moments, like Mao Zedong praising the education in Confucian academies as an educational alternative, which was to be combined with the strengths of modern education, in order to form the basis of a new university system,[23] or North Korean leader Kim Il-Sung enjoying visits to several academies.[24] Economic reforms in the PRC started a completely new approach toward academies and their legacy: the regime started to actively develop their economic potential as tourist sites and partially began to employ the academies in the propagation of its own interpretation of Confucian values.

The status of Confucian academies in almost all countries of the region at present has, to a certain degree, converged to the same point. Presented as a valuable cultural heritage they enjoy a high status best documented by

21  See Linda Walton, "Songyang Academy in Time and Place: From Confucian Academy to Cultural Heritage," in this volume, 397–436.
22  See Vladimír Glomb and Eun-Jeung Lee, "Between Ruins and Relics: North Korean Discourse on Confucian Academies," in this volume, 456–492.
23  See Mao Zedong, "Hunan zixiu daxue chuangli xuayuan (Proclamation for the Founding of the Hunan Self-study University)," in *Mao Zedong ji* (Writings of Mao Zedong), Volume 1, 1917.3–1924.4, ed. Minouro Takeguchi (Tokyo: Hokubasha, 1972), 81; also in: Ding Gang, "The Shuyuan and the Development of Chinese Universities in the Early Twentieth Century," in *East-West Dialogue in Knowledge and Higher Education*, ed. Ruth Hayhoe and Julia Pan (Armonk: Sharpe, 1996), 238.
24  See Glomb and Lee, "Between Ruins and Relics," in this volume, 467.

UNESCO status: in 2010 Songyang Academy achieved global recognition as part of the "Historical Monuments of Mount Song" UNESCO World Heritage Site; in 2016, UNESCO included 379 woodblocks of the Phúc Giang Academy in the "Memory of the World Asia-Pacific Regional Register"; and the unsuccessful Korean bid for the World Heritage List in 2016 is likely to be repeated.[25] This trend is paralleled in some countries by attempts to use restored academies for ideological purposes and as a tool for the propagation of various interpretations of Confucian values.[26] Attention and sudden availability of economic resources resulted, besides simple reconstruction, in the building of new infrastructure and facilities. Of the biggest importance are archives and preservation efforts concerning old documents and academies' memorabilia, which are becoming available to academic research.

## 4  Directions of Future Research

What can be learned from looking at the different trajectories of Confucian academies in East Asian countries? While it is difficult to compare academies of specific times and places, it is certainly possible to identify the patterns and forces behind processes of change shaping various forms of these Confucian institutions. Understanding academies rather as a constellation of various currents and forces, which have materialized into a distinct intellectual and material structure, opens doors to research on all variables constituting particular academies or parts of an academy movement. As many studies in this volume indicate, the state played an essential role correlating the changing destinies of academies through its involvement in the academy movement. In spite of their

---

25   On July 6th 2019 nine South Korean academies were included into the UNESCO World Heritage List at the 43rd Session of the World Heritage Committee in Baku, Azerbaijan. It is necessary to know that both Korean states already before have achieved acknowledgement for some individual academies. Sungyang Academy in Kaesong is a part of the UNESCO site "Historic Monuments and Sites in Kaesong," registered in 2013. The same phenomenon (protection of the particular academy within a broader project) is present also in the Republic of Korea, where Oksan Academy was registered in 2010 within the UNESCO World Heritage project "Historic Villages of Korea: Hahoe and Yangdong" (as part of the historical Yangdong Village).

26   See Sébastien Billioud and Joël Thoraval, *The Sage and the People: The Confucian Revival in China* (Oxford: Oxford University Press, 2015), 20–26; Uri Kaplan, "Rebuilding the 'Eastern Country of Ritual Propriety': Decorum Camps, Sŏwŏn Stays, and the Confucian Revival in Contemporary Korea," *Sungkyun Journal of East Asian Studies* 18, no. 1 (2018): 63–67; and Park Kyeong-hwan's presentation at the conference in Berlin titled *Current State of Confucian Academy Studies and the Restoration of Their Educational Function in the Andong Region*, May 5, 2017.

autonomous nature, academies were influenced by state policy and the various modes for spreading the Confucian message initiated by the central government. Possible modes of interaction could involve direct support, especially in early stages of academies in China and Korea; conflicts, as it often happened during Ming times; parallel coexistence, as was the case in late Chosŏn, when Korean academies operated almost without any state control; or incorporation into the educational system of the state, as it occurred during Qing times. Nonetheless, Confucian orientation of the central government was not always enough to create an environment suitable for the emergence of academies, as the cases of Tokugawa Japan and Vietnam show that even the existence of firmly Confucian government did not necessarily result in a surge of Confucian academies. The case of early Chosŏn Korea indicates that despite a strong propagation of Confucian values, academies emerged relatively late after the establishment of a rule that stood under the auspices of Zhu Xi's teaching. Another factor requiring an interdisciplinary approach is the position of academies vis-à-vis their alternatives or adversaries. Introduction and acceptance of academies within the local environment was based not only on the economic preconditions of the community, which was often essential, but also on competition with other religious currents and institutions that were competing for local resources. A society heavily spending on Buddhist monasteries was rather immune or averse to redirecting its attention to Confucian academies, and vice versa; the unopposed spread of academies in Korea was eased by the suppression of Buddhist temples and the absence of Daoist monasteries. The same can be said about the position of academies within the broader community of Confucian scholars and students. One of the most intrinsic questions is surely about the very need of Confucian scholars and communities to use and foster academies. Many schools and intellectual currents used different means to ensure their functioning and continuity. In the same way we study the motivation of academy founders it is necessary to focus on critiques of academies and scholars who stayed outside of the movement, often for good reasons. Ming scholars' extensive use of academies cannot hide the fact that their predecessor Lu Jiuyuan 陸九淵 (1139–1193) was not in favour of this instrument.[27] What was the relation of Qing evidential learning scholars to academies? Why were Korean scholars inspired by them not founding their own *sirhak* academies? Only a broader perspective that accounts the perspectives of scholars and currents not involved in the academies could answer the recurrent question

---

27   See Robert Hymes, "Lu Chiu-yüan, Academies, and the Problem of the Local Community," in *Neo-Confucian Education. The Formative Stage*, ed. Wm. Theodore de Bary and John W. Chaffee (Berkeley: University of California Press, 1989), 432–456.

running through all phases of their existence; the intellectual productivity of academies and their innovative or conservative nature. In the same way, asking for roles Confucian academies played, it is necessary to conversely detect which roles they regarded as unfulfilled or abandoned.

Confucian academies are well-suited to serve as a looking glass giving a precise picture of Confucian societies on a macro and micro level. Well-kept records and institutional memory are, in the case of academies, combined with the direct interaction of individual scholars and local environment. As economic and political units they played an important role on the local level, yet as a whole they periodically influenced even the higher echelons of state policy. A poor Confucian student could only dream about a way to the capital, but the local academy could give him the chance to hear famous scholars lecturing and thus be in touch with intellectual discourses of the day. In the same way the records of academy debates and lectures inform us about the knowledge, or often the lack thereof, of the very same local student, who otherwise passed through history unnoticed. The various roles of academies offer a wide range of possibilities to study this institution not as isolated entities, but rather as dynamic organisms in their multiple intellectual, economic, and social interactions.

## 5    Organization of This Book

The essays in this volume are arranged topically in four clusters, each focusing on different facet of Confucian academies. The first part, "Origins and Spread of Confucian Academies," consists of contributions analyzing the very process of founding and transforming the academies. The intentions and statements of academy founders often reveal how the conceptual unity of Confucian academies and connections to famous precedents of the past were understood and to which values they appealed by laying grounds for the new institutions.

The second cluster of contributions, "Curriculum of Confucian Academies," focuses on the most important, yet largely understudied, aspect of academies: the content of their educational activities. Unlike private tutoring or village schools, academy education was consciously based on a balance among teaching, disciplining, and self-cultivation. Educational methods, rules, or materials were often designed specifically for academy use and significantly differed from general Confucian education available beyond the walls of academy. Although keeping in touch with the demands of the state and society, the degree of independence the academies commanded enabled both teachers and disciples to pursue specific forms of a curriculum, possible to realize only in academies.

The third part of the volume, "Social Role and Environment of Confucian Academies," is devoted to the role of academies in the mundane world and their importance as social, political, and economic units. Academies, from the very beginning of their development, were trying to harmonize their roles as places of secluded study and strongholds of Confucian teaching. Closing the academy gates isolated academies from the noisy world, but academies never resigned the role of fulfilling their social obligations and acted as of defenders of Confucian values or their own academy interests (which academy scholars often understood as one).

The last part, "From Religious Landscape to Cultural Heritage," analyses overarching ideological discourses that have formed public opinion on Confucian academies. Singling out contributions on the religious function of academies highlights the fact the from their very beginning, academies played role of sacred places and as objects of popular pilgrimage. This aspect, to a certain degree, has survived until today. It would be rather impolite to compare Confucian scholars visiting famous academies with flocks of modern tourists, but both these categories of academy visitors were (and still are) attracted by the common appeal of these institutions.

As a whole, all contributions document both the diversity and the essential unity of the concept of "Confucian academy." The essays in this volume cannot cover all aspects of these fascinating institutions, but we hope it will encourage further studies in this field.

### References

Bařinka, Jaroslav. "Staré konfuciánské ústavy v Koreji." *Nový Orient* 23 (1968): 261–266.

Billioud, Sébastien, and Joël Thoraval. *The Sage and the People. The Confucian Revival in China*. Oxford: Oxford University Press, 2015.

Cancik-Kirschbaum, Eva, and Anita Traninger. "Institution – Iteration – Transfer: Zur Einführung." In *Wissen in Bewegung: Institution – Iteration – Transfer*, edited by Eva Cancik-Kirschbaum and Anita Traninger, 1–13. Wiesbaden: Otto Harrassowitz, 2015.

Chan, Wing-tsit. *Chu Hsi. His Life and Thought*. Hongkong: The Chinese University Press, 1987.

Chan, Wing-tsit. "Chu Hsi and Academies." In *Neo-Confucian Education: The Formative Stage*, edited by Wm. Theodore de Bary and John W. Chaffee, 389–413. Berkeley: University of California Press, 1989.

Chen, Wen-yi 陳雯怡. *You guanxue dao shuyuan. Cong zhidu yu linian de hudong kan songdai jiaoyu de yanbian* 由官學到書院. 從制度與理念的互動看宋代教育的演變 (From Official School to Academy. Looking at the Evolution of Song Times Education from the Perspective of Interaction between Concept and Institution). Taibei: Lianjing chubanshe, 2004.

Ding, Gang, and Ningsha Zhong (trans.). "The Shuyuan and the Development of Chinese Universities in the Early Twentieth Century." In *East-West Dialogue in Knowledge and Higher Education*, edited by Ruth Hayhoe and Julia Pan, 218–244. Armonk: Sharpe, 1996.

Eggert, Marion, Felix Siegmund, and Dennis Würthner (eds.). *Space and Location in the Circulation of Knowledge (1400–1800): Korea and Beyond*. Bern: Peter Lang, 2014.

Eggert, Marion, and Florian Pölking (eds.). *Integration Processes in the Circulation of Knowledge: Cases from Korea*. Bern: Peter Lang, 2016.

Elman, Benjamin A., John B. Duncan, and Herman Ooms (eds.). *Rethinking Confucianism: Past and Present in China, Japan, Korea, and Vietnam*. Los Angeles: UCLA Asian Pacific Monograph Series, 2002.

Frängsmyr, Tore (ed.). *Solomon's House Revisited. The Organization and Institutionalization of Science*. Canton, MA: Science History Publications, 1990.

Fontana, Michela. *Matteo Ricci: A Jesuit in the Ming Court*. Lanham: Rowman & Littlefield Publishers, 2011.

Garber, Klaus, Heinz Wismann, and Winfried Siebers (eds.). *Europäische Sozietätsbewegung und demokratische Tradition: Die europäischen Akademien der Frühen Neuzeit zwischen Frührenaissance und Spätaufklärung*. Tübingen: De Gruyter, 1996.

Glomb, Vladimír, and Eun-Jeung Lee. "No Books to Leave, No Women to Enter: Confucian Academies in Pre-Modern Korea and Their Book Collections." In *The Epistemic Legacy. Vehicles for the Collection and Transfer of Knowledge in Premodern Societies*, edited by Eva Canick-Kirschbaum, Jochem Kahl, Eun-Jeung Lee, and Michaela Engert. Wiesbaden: Otto Harrassowitz, 2020 (forthcoming).

Hsia, Ronnie Po-Chia. *A Jesuit in the Forbidden City: Matteo Ricci 1552–1610*. Oxford: Oxford University Press, 2010.

Hu, Shi 胡適. "Shuyuan de lishi yu jingshen 書院的歷史與精神 (History and Spirit of the Academies)." *Jiaoyu yu rensheng*, no. 9 (1923).

Hu, Shi 胡適. "Shuyuan zhi shilüe 書院制史略 (Brief History of the Academy system)." *Dongfang zazhi* 21, no. 9 (1924).

Hymes, Robert. "Lu Chiu-yüan, Academies, and the Problem of the Local Community." In *Neo-Confucian Education: The Formative Stage*, edited Wm. Theodore de Bary and John W. Chaffee, 432–456. Berkeley: University of California Press, 1989.

Kaplan, Uri. "Rebuilding the 'Eastern Country of Ritual Propriety': Decorum Camps, Sŏwŏn Stays, and the Confucian Revival in Contemporary Korea." *Sungkyun Journal of East Asian Studies* 18, no. 1 (2018): 59–84.

Keenan, Barry. *Imperial China's Last Classical Academies: Social Change in the Lower Yangzi, 1864–1911*. Berkeley: Institute of East Asian Studies, 1994.

Kupfer, Carl F. *Sacred Places in China*. Cincinnati: Western Methodist Book Co., 1911.

Kühn, Sebastian. *Wissen, Arbeit, Freundschaft: Ökonomien und soziale Beziehungen an den Akademien in London, Paris und Berlin um 1700*. Göttingen: V&R unipress, 2011.

Lee, Eun-Jeung, and Marion Eggert (eds.). *The Dynamics of Knowledge Circulation: Cases from Korea*. Bern: Peter Lang, 2016.

Lee, Eun-Jeung. *Anti-Europa: Die Geschichte der Rezeption des Konfuzianismus und der konfuzianischen Gesellschaft seit der frühen Aufklärung*. Münster: Lit, 2003.

Lee, Thomas H.C. "Chu Hsi, Academies and the Tradition of Private Chiang-hsüeh." *Hanxue Yanjiu* 2, no. 1 (1984): 301–329.

Lee, Thomas H.C. *Education in Traditional China: A History*. Leiden: Brill, 2000.

Liu, Boji 劉伯驥. *Guangdong shuyuan zhidu yange* 廣東書院制度沿革 (History of the Guangdong Academy System). Shanghai: Commercial Press, 1939.

Liu, Heyan 刘河燕. *Songdai shuyuan yu ouzhou zhongshiji daxue zhi bijiao yanjiu* 宋代书院与欧洲中世纪大学之比较研究 (Comparative research between Song dynasty academies and medieval European universities). Beijing: Renmin chubanshe, 2012.

Lü, Zuqian 呂祖謙. "Bailudong shuyuan ji 白鹿洞書院記 (Account of White Deer Grotto Academy)." In *Donglai ji* 東萊集 (Collected Writings of Donglai), Volume 6. Jinhua: Xujinhua congshu, 1923, <http://db.ersjk.com (accessed: 21 March 2018>).

Mao, Zedong 毛澤東. "Hunan zixiu daxue chuangli xuanyan 湖南自修大學創立宣言 (Proclamation for the Founding of the Hunan Self-study University)." In *Mao Zedong ji* 毛澤東集 (Writings of Mao Zedong), Volume 1, 1917.3–1924.4, edited by Minouro Takeguchi. Tokyo: Hokubasha, 1972.

Meskill, John. *Academies in Ming China: A Historical Essay*. Tucson: The University of Arizona Press, 1982.

Neskar, Ellen. "The Cult of Worthies: A Study of Shrines Honoring Local Confucian Worthies in the Sung Dynasty (960–1279)." Ph.D. diss., Columbia University, 1993.

Testa, Simone. *Italian Academies and Their Networks 1525–1700, from Local to Global*. New York: Palgrave Mcmillan, 2015.

Woodside, Alexander. *Lost Modernities: China, Vietnam, Korea, and the Hazards of World History*. Cambridge: Harvard University Press, 2006.

Xiao, Lang 肖朗. "Li Madou yu bailudong shuyuan ji qita: Yi wenxian zhengli shidu de kaocha 利玛窦与白鹿洞书院及其他．以文献整理视角的考察 (Matteo Ricci, the White Deer Grotto Academy and Others: A Literature Review)." *Jiangxi shehui kexue* 1 (2007): 95–101.

Xiao, Yongming 肖永明. *Ruxue, shuyuan, shehui: shehui wenhua shi shiye zhong de shuyuan* 儒学，书院，社会: 社会文化史视野中的书院 (Confucianism, Academies, and Society: A Sociocultural Historical Perspective on Academies). Beijing: Shangwu yinshuguan, 2012.

Xu, Haiyan 許海燕, and Bao Lili 包麗麗. *Li Madou zai zhongguo* 利玛窦在中国 (Matteo Ricci in China). Beijing: Zhongguo xiju chubanshe, 2006.

Zhao, Rebekah x. "Shu yuan 書院 (Confucian Academies)." In *The Encyclopedia of Confucianism*, edited by Yao Xinzhong, 565–568. London: Routledge, 2015.

## PART 1

## *Origins and Spread of Confucian Academies*

∴

CHAPTER 1

# Some Reflections on Confucian Academies in China

*Hoyt Cleveland Tillman* (田浩)

## 1  Introduction

My attention was first drawn to historic Confucian academies when I visited the Yuelu (Marchmount Hill) Academy (Yuelu Shuyuan 嶽麓書院) during August of 1983. The academy was being restored from abuse and neglect during the Cultural Revolution. Despite the extensive repairs and restoration at the time, the structures and especially the surviving cultural contents—such as Zhu Xi's 朱熹 (1130–1200) large characters carved into large black stone slabs—still conveyed its ancient dignity. On that occasion, I walked unaccompanied through the site with my family while the Academy's scholars were hosting Professor Wing-tsit Chan 陳榮捷 (1901–1994). In December of 2004, almost twenty years later, I returned at the invitation of Zhu Hanmin to give a lecture and to seek advice from him and other specialists, such as Xiao Yongming and Deng Hongbo.

I needed to return to the Yuelu Academy for advice because Christian Jacob in France had invited me to join a comparative project on sites of learning and to write a book chapter on Confucian academies in China as spaces and communities. My first impulse was to explore the daily life of students at Song academies and their experiences with their fellow students and teachers; however, Yuelu Academy specialists told me that extant research materials would be inadequate to such an ambitious inquiry into the daily lives of students there during the Song (960–1279). Instead, I utilized what I heard, saw, and read to write an essay that guided Western readers through the constructed spaces and uses of the academy. That essay was published in French in a massive comparative volume.[1] A Chinese version of my essay also appeared in the *Journal of Hunan University*,[2] but there was never an English version, so I will

---

[1] Hoyt Cleveland Tillman, "Les académies confucéennes dans en Chine au temps des Song (Xe–XIIIe siècle)," in *Les Lieux de savoir: Espaces et communautés*, eds. Christian Jacob et al. (Paris: Albin Michel, 2007), 323–342.

[2] Tian Hao (Hoyt Cleveland Tillman), "Songdai de rujia shuyuan (Confucian Academies during the Song Dynasty)," *Hunan daxue xuebao* 19, no. 6 (November 2005): 3–9.

include a few of its points in the present study. The underlying academic theme of that essay was how Zhu Xi used academies in his effort to ascend to be such an authoritative leader of *Daoxue* 道學 (Learning of the Way) Confucianism. During the Song era, this sociopolitical group or "fellowship" was more specific than Wm. Theodore de Bary's definition of "Neo-Confucianism" as something "broader" than the Chinese category *lixue* 理學; yet, *Daoxue* was far less narrow than Wing-tsit Chan's utilization of the term "Neo-Confucianism" to refer exclusively to the theories advanced by the Cheng brothers, Zhu Xi and their disciples. Many scholars still either inadequately realize these distinctions or simply focus on the more exclusive period of *Daoxue* beginning in 1181, and so conflate *Daoxue* with Chan's usage of "Neo-Confucianism" or continue to assume equivalence between Neo-Confucianism and *lixue*.[3] The editors in France probably invited me to contribute the chapter on Confucian academies because I had earlier included this theme about Zhu Xi and Confucian academies in my 1992 book on Confucian discourse and Zhu Xi's ascendency.

In my *Confucian Discourse*, I had highlighted the importance of academies in the rise of *Daoxue* and Zhu Xi's ascendancy. Early in that book's Introduction, I explained:

> Academies served as institutional centers for the group. Rituals performed at the academies enhanced bonding. Prostrating before a master, one ritually declared oneself a student and became part of a lineage for propagating certain texts. Services every morning that included burning incense before an altar for ancient sages and recent masters enhanced awareness among academy students of continuity and cohesiveness within the tradition.[4]

---

3 See explanations in Hoyt Cleveland Tillman, "A New Direction in Confucian Scholarship: Approaches to Examining the Differences between Neo-Confucianism and Tao-hsueh (Daoxue)," *Philosophy East and West*, 42, no. 3 (July 1992): 455–474; and "The Uses of Neo-Confucianism, Revisited," *Philosophy East and West* 44, no. 1 (January 1994): 135–142; as well as Wm. Theodore de Bary, "The Uses of Neo-Confucianism: A Response to Professor Tillman," *Philosophy East and West* 43, no. 3 (July 1993): 541–555; See also Tian Hao (Hoyt Cleveland Tillman), "Zhu Xi yu daoxue de fazhan zhuanhua (Zhu Xi and the Transformation of Learning of the Dao Confucianism)," in *Songdai xinruxue de jingshen shijie: yi zhuzixue wei zhongxin* (The Intellectual World of Neo-Confucianism in the Song Dynasty: Taking the Study of Zhu Xi as the Center of Discussion), ed. Wu Zhen (Shanghai: Huadong shifan daxue chubanshe, 2009), 10–23.

4 Hoyt Cleveland Tillman, *Confucian Discourse and Chu Hsi's Ascendancy* (Honolulu: University of Hawai'i Press, 1992), 3.

Later, in the first sentence in the book's separate section on academies, I asserted that in building a sense of community among literati in the *Daoxue* fellowship, "to Zhu Xi and Lü Zuqian 呂祖謙 (1137–1181), no institution was more important for this purpose than academies."[5] I also highlighted how much Zhu benefited from Lü Zuqian's earlier experience and guidelines for academies, as well as his connections to scholars and officials. Somehow, a scholar and friend overlooked all of my discussion of academies when she complained that my book reduced Zhu's ascendancy to his longevity alone and thus ignored the role of academies.[6] In response, I published a Chinese essay that succinctly set forth the various factors that I had given in the book for Zhu's ascendancy.[7] Since that scholar had difficulty seeing my discussion of academies in the thicket of my details in *Confucian Discourse*, I should take this opportunity to elaborate on my perspective on academies in the development of *Daoxue* Confucianism.

The institution of academies for Confucian classical learning had earlier roots; nevertheless, it was during the Song era that academies developed in ways that were to have enduring, yet intermittent, legacy in China, Korea, Japan, and Vietnam. Although the lists varied somewhat from time and personal vantage point, that Song legacy centered around four academies. Lü Zuqian recounted in 1180:

> At the beginning of the dynasty when people had just cast off the tribulations of warfare during the Five Dynasties period, scholars were still isolated. As things grew more settled, culture began to flourish. At first Confucian classicists made use of mountain retreats where they taught. The great teachers had as many as several thousand students. Songyang 嵩陽, Yuelu, Suiyang 睢陽, and the Bailudong 白鹿洞 (known as White Deer Grotto) were the most famous. They were known throughout the empire as the "four academies." The founders and their successors all honored the classicist profession. These academies were apportioned official books, allotted official salaries, and bestowed name plaques.[8]

---

5  Ibid., 108.
6  Linda A. Walton, *Academies and Society in Southern Sung China* (Honolulu: University of Hawai'i Press, 1999), see especially 40–41.
7  Tian Hao (Tillman), "Zhu Xi yu daoxue de fazhan zhuanhua."
8  Lü Zuqian, *Lü Donglai wenji* (Lü's Collected Short Writings), 6.138–139, Congshu jicheng edition; translation slightly altered from Walton, *Academies and Society*, 25–26; Another history of academies is by Deng Hongbo, *Zhongguo shuyuan shi* (History of Chinese Academies) (Shanghai: Dongfang chuban zhongxin, 2006). See also Tillman, "Les académies confucéennes," 323–342; and Tillman, "Either Self-Realization or Transmission of Received Wisdom in Confucian Education? An Inquiry into Lü Zuqian's and Zhu Xi's Constructions for Student

Writing in celebration of Zhu Xi's rediscovery of the site of the ruins of the White Deer Grotto Academy (Bailudong shuyuan 白鹿洞書院) and rebuilding the academy, Lü Zuqian drew attention both to the commitment by teachers to Confucian learning and to the crucial support extended by the government. (I will follow convention in referring to this academy by its better-known, standard English name.) Nevertheless, although government support was crucial to maintaining these academies, the relationship between Confucian teachers and the government was complex and contested—in part because intellectuals and the emperor were "counterpoised collaborators"[9] with often differing perspectives on priorities and means to achieve even the shared goal of a peaceful and harmonious social order. In this context, the tension was heightened by competition from government schools where even more attention was focused on preparing for the civil service examinations; moreover, tensions also arose between the local and the central, the ethical and the political. I will revisit my own and some others' research on such aspects of the academies, as well as briefly introduce some recent research by two graduate students at Arizona State University, in my effort to respond to the challenge from this conference's organizers for us to reflect on the history and diversity of academies in East Asia.

While I was completing the paper, I had the opportunity to hear a lecture at ASU by, and to have conversations with, Professor Park Young-Hwan 朴永煥, from the Chinese Department of Dongguk University, about the travels of a Chosŏn literatus in Fujian province in 1599. No In 魯認 (Lu Ren, 1566–1662) had lived in, and had discussions with Chinese in, a few costal academies, and I asked Professor Park about any differences the traveler noted about academies in Fujian and Korea. Professor Park replied that academies were the same throughout East Asia, and the only difference in Confucian culture was that Zhu Xi totally dominated in Korea with no influence from Buddhism and Daoism and not even any influence from other rival Confucians. I reported that the Institute of Korean Studies at the Freie Universität Berlin was hosting an international conference in May that would discuss diversity in Confucian academies; however, he simply replied, "interesting," but asked no questions and changed the subject. Thus, I was reminded about the need for this conference

---

Learning," in *Educations and Their Purposes: A Philosophical Dialogue among Cultures*, eds. Roger Ames and Peter Hershock (Honolulu: University of Hawai'i Press, 2008), 270–288. For the history and contemporary use of the Songyang Academy, see especially Linda Walton, "Songyang Academy in Time and Place: From Confucian Academy to Cultural Heritage," in this volume, 397–436.

9 Joseph R. Levenson and Franz Schurmann, *China: An Interpretive History from the Beginnings to the Fall of the Han* (Berkeley: University of California Press, 1975), 91.

to raise awareness among East Asian scholars about the actual history and diversity of Confucian academies.

## 2   Model Academies in Song China: The Yuelu Academy

The Yuelu (Marchmount Hill) Academy, situated on a slope at the foot of the Yuelu Mountain along the west bank of the Xiang River and across the river from the city of Changsha, was in 976 the first institution that the Song government officially called an "academy" (*shuyuan* 書院).[10] (I will follow common convention to refer to this academy by its Chinese name "Yuelu" instead of the rarely used literal gloss "Marchmount.") More importantly, it was rather unique in having originated as a government school established by the local prefect in cooperation with the local elite. Despite such promising beginnings, the academy soon declined. However, a new prefect in 996 successfully petitioned the Directorate of Education to provide resources to support his restoration of the academy and the approximately sixty students there. Academies soon attracted the attention and support of the new emperor, Song Zhenzong 宋真宗 (r. 998–1023), who even summoned the Yuelu Academy's headmaster, Zhou Shi 周式 (fl. early 11th century), to lecture at the capital's Directorate of Education. In response to Zhou Shi's request to return to Yuelu, the emperor presented him with sets of books, from the imperial collection, for the academy's library, which thus became renowned as the Pavilion of Imperial Books (Yushu lou 御書樓). Indeed, related to Nguyễn Tuấn-Cường's point that the Sinitic characters for "shuyuan" in Vietnam mean "library,"[11] we can observe, here in the case of the Yuelu Academy, *shuyuan* from the beginning functioned as a repository of important books. Emperor Zhenzong also gave Zhou Shi a four-character plaque with the name of the Yuelu Academy written in the emperor's calligraphy, and a replica of the name plaque hangs from the roof beams over the central entrance of the academy. Moreover, the emperor praised this academy as the principal place in the local area where talented scholars assembled. This imperial endorsement expressed in a couplet on the two doorposts: "State of

---

10   Unless otherwise noted, information about the Yuelu Academy is taken from Zhu Hanmin et al. (comp.), *Zhongguo shuyuan* (Chinese Academies) (Shanghai: Jiaoyu chubanshe, 2002); which includes Thomas Lee's introduction in English; the CD, "Qiannian xuefu," produced by Hunan University's Yuelu Academy Cultural Institute and distributed by Hunan Electronic and Audio-visual Publishing House; and my field research there in 2004.

11   Nguyễn Tuấn-Cường, "Private Academies and Confucian Education in 18th Century Vietnam in East Asian Context: The Case of Phúc Giang Academy," in this volume, 89–125.

Chu, unique home of talents" (*wei chu you cai* 惟楚有材) and "More abundant here than elsewhere" (*yu si wei sheng* 於斯爲盛). These statements were lifted out of context from the *Zuo Commentary* (*Zuozhuan* 左傳) and the Confucian *Analects* 8:20.

The Yuelu Academy became even more renowned when Hu Hong 胡宏 (1105–1161) and then Zhang Shi 張栻 (1133–1180) served as its principal masters and made it the center of their so-called Hunan School, i.e. the Huxiang branch of *Daoxue* Confucianism. Nonetheless, the academy needed another major restoration in 1165, which Zhang Shi celebrated in a record preserved on a stone stele at the academy. Zhang's record also proclaimed the guiding philosophy of the academy was grounded in the cardinal Confucian virtue of *ren* 仁, variously glossed as humaneness, human-heartedness, benevolence, and consummate person or conduct. Moreover, he asserted that the academy's educational mission was the cultivation of human talents through Confucian virtues, rather than merely training students to pass the civil service examinations and become officials:

> How could we allow students to gather here, boasting only of examination success and [the potential of] lucrative careers? How could we allow them to study only literary texts? Instead we desire to complete human talents in order to transmit this Way and to rescue our people. […] What exactly is this tradition? It is humaneness, [i.e.] the human heart. It is what regulates human nature, determines human destiny, orders the empire, and controls the myriad things.[12]

Like most *Daoxue* Confucians, Zhang also insisted upon discriminating clearly between integrity (*yi* 義) and self-interest (*si* 私). Even though Zhang Shi did not want students to be drawn to the academy only for training for the civil service examinations, he was a conscientious scholar-official who served admirably in office; therefore, he encouraged students to put learning to practical use in governance and cautioned them against becoming mired in abstract, speculative philosophy.

A famous intellectual exchange took place at the Yuelu Academy when Zhu Xi visited Zhang Shi for three months in 1167. Most of their discussions were engaged while sitting on the veranda of the headmaster's residence overlooking the academy's pool. One of the major topics was the *Doctrine of the Mean*

---

12   Zhang Shi, *Nanxuan xiansheng wenji* (Collected Writings of Master Nanxuan), in *Zhang Shi ji* (Zhang Shi's Works) (Beijing: Zhonghua shuju, 2015), 10:900; translation slightly modified from Walton, *Academies and Society*, 33–34.

(*Zhongyong* 中庸) which Zhu would later elevate to one of the key Four Books. Some of his comments on this classical text were inscribed in his calligraphy on a stele that still rests in the academy's stele gallery. Another major issue was the difference between the Hunan School and Zhu Xi's Fujian-based view regarding the role of the mind in self-cultivation, i.e. the debate over understanding self-cultivation in the relation between "already expressed" (*yifa* 已發) and "not yet expressed" (*weifa* 未發) states of the emotions. In that case, Zhu Xi became convinced during his visit about the superiority of the Hunan view over the Fujian view of his mentors; however, after returning to Fujian, Zhu Xi became increasingly uncomfortable with that decision and soon rejected the Hunan interpretation. Much of what we know about the debates are from the letters exchanged; unfortunately, Zhu did not preserve several of Zhang's key letters when Zhu edited his friend's collected short writings after Zhang's death in 1180.[13]

Regarding the more public forums at the academy, legends recount how over a thousand people came to hear Zhang Shi and Zhu Xi teach and debate in 1167. For the large audience, the two masters sat in chairs in the main hall facing eastward because the spillover crowds could see and hear from the courtyard without a wall separating them from the speakers. Such occasions at academies underscored efforts to reach larger audiences than Confucian teachers had been able to accommodate in earlier dynasties. Calligraphy ascribed to Zhu Xi was carved into large black stones that still adorn the inner walls of the lecture hall: Loyalty (*zhong* 忠), Filial Piety or Family Reverence (*xiao* 孝), Honesty and Purity (*lian* 廉), Moral Integrity and Ritual Propriety (*jie* 節). On another occasion during this visit, the two friends enjoyed watching the sunrise from their vantage point higher up Yuelu Mountain above the academy. They even had a covered platform erected there, and Zhu's stone inscription refers to it as the Hexitai 赫曦台 (Glorious Sunrise Stage). Centuries later when a real covered stage was constructed across from the main hall, it was named "Hexi Stage" to commemorate Zhu Xi and Zhang Shi's covered platform at the site where they viewed the sunrise.

After Zhang Shi's death, the Yuelu Academy declined until it was revitalized and restored yet again in 1194—this time by Zhu Xi when he served as the local prefect. This was the third major restoration within one hundred years; moreover, with the exception of Zhang Shi, who had been a student of the academy, it was in the other two cases the principal civil official sent to Changsha by the central government who initiated the restoration. This is an example of the

---

13   On the debates and exchanges of letters, as well as Zhu's editing of Zhang's collected short works, see especially my *Confucian Discourse*, 46–47, 59–82.

crucial role that the central government and its officials played in the viability of Song academies. Even though he had already significantly influenced the Hunan branch of *Daoxue* earlier, Zhu's role in restoring the Yuelu Academy and lecturing there while serving as the head of the prefecture enabled him to enhance his mark on this academy and its culture. As we will see below in other academies, although he continued to share Zhang Shi's attention to self-cultivation, Zhu Xi also made changes in rituals and discipline that served his ascendancy and authority over his students to an unprecedented degree.[14]

One way that the academies served to augment *Daoxue* orthodoxy was having students venerate earlier masters of the group. Even before its restoration by Zhu Xi, this academy had shrines paying homage not only to several founding teachers but also to major Northern Song *Daoxue* masters, such as Zhou Dunyi 周敦頤 (1017–1073), Cheng Hao 程顥 (1032–1086), and Cheng Yi 程頤 (1033–1107). According to comments of one of Zhu's students at the Zhulin Study Lodge (Zhulin jingshe 竹林精舍) in Fujian, he led students in paying daily homage to the Confucian worthies and sages:

> The master arose early every morning and would emerge from his chamber after all the students attending the academy had dressed, rung the bell, and gone to the image hall to await him. After they opened the door, the master ascended the hall, and led the students, in their proper ranks, in paying obeisance and lighting incense. He paid obeisance again and withdrew. One of the students would be sent to burn incense and pay reverence to the earth god's shrine. Afterwards, accompanying our Master and ascending into the chamber, we would pay reverence to the Former Sage/Former Teacher and then sit in the academy's study hall.[15]

The term "image hall" (*yingtang* 影堂) in relation to this account suggests that it was to portraits of the *Daoxue* worthies that homage was offered in a separate hall before Zhu and the students went to the main study hall where they venerated Confucius.

One of Zhu Xi's prayers to Confucius provides particularly impressive example of how Zhu Xi could utilize ritual memorials and prayers at academies to imprint orthodox thinking and instill reverent awe toward his particular

---

14  This is a major theme in my *Confucian Discourse* and especially its greatly expanded and revised Chinese version, under my Chinese name, Tian Hao, *Zhu Xi de siwei shijie: zengding ben* (Zhu Xi's World of Thought: Revised and Expanded Edition) (Taipei: Yunchen wenhua, 2008; Nanjing: Jiangsu Renmin chubanshe, 2009).

15  Zhu Xi, *Zhuzi yulei* (Zhu Xi's Classified Conversations) (Beijing: Zhonghua shuju, 1986), 107.2674.

understanding of the Dao and to his version of the *Daoxue* tradition. Again at the Zhulin Study Lodge, here called the Cangzhou Study Lodge (Cangzhou jingshe 滄州精舍), Zhu led the academy students in 1194 in addressing the spirits of the sages and particularly Confucius:

> I, the later student, Xi, venture to prayerfully entreat the Former and Ultimate Sage, the King of Promoting Culture [Confucius]. Let us celebrate the *dao* legacy [extending] back to Xi 羲 (Fu Xi 伏羲) and Xuan 軒 (Xuan Yuan 軒轅, i.e. the Yellow Emperor). Its achievements were all assembled by the Original Sage [Confucius], who transmitted the ancient [teachings], gave instructions, and set standards for ten thousand generations. His three thousand disciples were transformed as if [his instructions] had been a timely rain. Only Yan 顏 (Yanzi) and Zeng 曾 (Zengzi) were able to get the legacy of Confucius. It was not until Si 思 (Zisi) and Yu 輿 (Zengzi) that his legacy was made more lustrous and greater. Since then, subsequent followers lost the true transmission in the process of teaching and receiving. The legacy was not continued until more than one thousand years later. What Zhou [Dunyi] and the Cheng brothers learned and taught was that the myriad principles or patterns (*li* 理) had one single origin. As for Shao [Yong] 邵雍, Zhang [Zai] 張載, and Sima [Guang] 司馬光, even though their learning was diverse, they all arrived at the same conclusions about the *dao* 道 (Way). They facilitated us later generations, as if we were moving from a dark night into the dawning of a new day. When I, Xi, was a child, I received instruction from [my late father] because of my limitations. In my youth, standard teachers taught me, and in my mature years, I have met those who had the *dao*. Gazing upward respectfully, and even though nothing is heard, [I know that] due to the spirit consciousness (*ling* 靈) in the heavens (*tian* 天) above, we are fortunate that nothing [being passed down] has been lost. Now, I am old and retired [from government service], and those who are fond of the same things have gathered here, and we have built this study lodge. At the beginning of our living together, [I] look for the origins and deduce the roots [of our *dao*] because [I] do not dare obscure [our] minds. Presenting our offerings and praying respectfully, trust that the spirits, descending to this place, will draw nigh, communicate and bless with illumination. [We] will then faithfully and untiringly—without rejecting anything—transmit it [the *dao*] without interruption to those coming in the future. Now, as this is an auspicious day, I will lead the assembled students in

celebration, performing the rite of offering food to the spirits [of the sages and teachers named]. Please receive these food offerings![16]

Here, Zhu Xi explicitly utilizes a ritual to lead his students into pledging to accept and pass down the teachings that he had received from the sages; moreover, the promise made by the students was that they would not change anything regarding the *dao* that they had received from the sages through him.

Soon after his death in 1200, Zhu Xi himself was venerated in academy shrines, and the Southern Song in 1241 enshrined his spirit tablet in the Confucian Temple. In Nankang prefecture, where he had also taught and served as head of the prefecture, Zhu was enshrined jointly with Zhou Dunyi,[17] and Zhu shared a special shrine with Zhang Shi at the Yuelu Academy. By at least 1314, a small temple was erected adjacent to the Yuelu Academy's lecture hall to venerate both Zhang Shi and Zhu Xi together as famous teachers at this academy and as leaders of the orthodox tradition in Hunan. Significantly, 1314 was the year after the Mongol Yuan dynasty restored the civil service examinations and followed the 1241 Song precedent making Zhu Xi's selected Four Books, and his commentaries thereupon, the orthodox centerpiece of the educational and examination systems. The early 14th-century decision by the Yuan government was in sharp contrast to when the Mongol military subdued Changsha in 1275, and eighty to ninety percent of the teachers and students died defending the Yuelu Academy. The Mongol army destroyed the Song-era buildings, but restoration efforts during the Yuan and later dynasties followed the Song layout and style.

Because of the Yuelu Academy's rich legacy, it continued to be restored and honored in late imperial China. For example, both the Kangxi 康熙 (r. 1661–1722) and Qianlong 乾隆 (r. 1735–1796) emperors bestowed plaques as forehead boards to hang horizontally near the main entrance to the lecture hall. A replica of Kangxi's calligraphy reads, "Study Fulfills Natural Talents" (*xue da xing tian* 學達性天) while Qianlong's original still hangs to proclaim, "Orthodox Confucian Way in the South" (*dao nan zheng mai* 道南正脈). An adjacent building was built to house a new Confucian Temple in the Ming dynasty; moreover, a stone gate was erected to provide an entrance directly to this

---

16  Zhu Xi, *Zhuzi ji* (Zhu Xi's Works) (Chengdu: Sichuan jiaoyu chubanshe, 1996), 86.4446; translated and discussed in Tillman, "Zhu Xi's Prayers to the Spirit of Confucius and Claim to the Transmission of the Way," *Philosophy East and West* 54, no. 4 (October 1994): 503–504.

17  See Chen Xi and Hoyt Tillman, "Ghosts, Gods, and the Ritual Practice of Local Officials during the Song: With a Focus on Zhu Xi in Nankang Prefecture," *Journal of Song and Yuan Studies* 44 (2014): 291–327.

temple. Zhu Xi's titles and status were progressively elevated within the Confucian Temple in late imperial China to the point that in 1712, his spirit tablet was installed in the main Hall of Great Accomplishment as a correlate among the ten wise philosophers.[18] Thus, as students paid homage to Confucius there, they would also see the special prominence of Zhu Xi in the official rites, as well as in the tradition of their local academy. Although Zhu was initially Zhang Shi's guest at the academy, he progressively gained equal and then preferred status in the academy's tradition just as he did in the government's promotion of an orthodoxy constructed on his teachings.

## 3      Model Academies in Song China: The White Deer Grotto Academy

Among all the academies with which Zhu Xi is associated in a variety of roles (headmaster, teacher, founder, etc.), the academy most widely identified with Zhu Xi is the White Deer Grotto Academy. This is also the one for which Lü Zuqian wrote the celebratory record that listed the four greatest historic academies. The Grotto's site is at the foot of the Five Old Men Peaks of Mt. Lu in what was the Song-era prefecture of Nankang, but is now Xingzi county in Jiangxi province. Although the location originally had a Buddhist temple, it had fallen into ruins by the end of the 8th century when a scholar used the site as a retreat for studying the Classics and named the grotto after the white deer there.[19] Thus, Confucian education at the grotto had earlier roots than even the Yuelu Academy; however, the Grotto officially became an academy a year later in 977, when it received a name plaque and sets of books from the Song dynasty. However, given its quite remote, inconvenient location and the expansion of government schools in the Northern Song, this White Deer Grotto Academy had long been abandoned and had fallen into ruins by the time Zhu Xi sought to revive it as a symbol of Confucian learning in 1179. He even had to hire a woodcutter to locate the ruins within the forest. Upon arriving as the prefect in Nankang, Zhu Xi had begun lecturing at least once a week at the

---

18   See especially Huang Jinxing, *Youru shengyu: quanli, xinyang yu zhengdangxing* (Entering the Sage's Realm: Power, Belief, and Legitimacy) (Taipei: Yunchen wenhua, 1994); and Thomas A. Wilson (ed.), *On Sacred Grounds: Culture, Society, Politics, and the Formation of the Cult of Confucius* (Cambridge, MA: Harvard University Asia Center, 2002), 83, 85.

19   Unless otherwise noted, information about the White Deer Grotto Academy is taken primarily from the texts and photographs in Zhu Hanmin, *Zhongguo shuyuan*; and secondarily from Wing-tsit Chan, "Chu Hsi and Academies," in *Neo-Confucian Education: The Formative Stage*, eds. Wm. Theodore de Bary and John W. Chaffee (Berkeley: University of California Press, 1989), 389–413; and my 2011 fieldwork. See also my "Les académies confucéennes."

government school in the city, but expressed frustration about resistance to his efforts to shift attention away from career preparation for government examinations and toward personal cultivation of the virtues he expounded from the Confucian classics. Therefore, within a month, he petitioned the central government for assistance in restoring the White Deer Grotto Academy as a site of Confucian learning on a mountain otherwise totally dominated by Buddhist and Daoist temples. He pushed the project so relentlessly that within a year, the restoration project was completed. Having received Lü Zuqian's help in facilitating the central government's approval and resources, Zhu Xi had him write the official record of the restoration of the academy; moreover, Zhu had an abridged version of the record inscribed on a stele at the academy. Lü's record asserted that the restored academy was needed to respond to Buddhists and Daoists, to improve the educational system, and to promote *Daoxue* Confucianism.[20]

The goals that Lü Zuqian proclaimed for White Deer Grotto Academy could be illustrated in a practical way by the example of the lecture delivered there in 1181 by Lu Jiuyuan 陸九淵 (1139–1193), the most renowned public orator of the era. Having been invited by Zhu Xi, Lu choose to expound on *Analects* 4:16: "A superior person is persuaded by what is right, while the petty person is persuaded by what is profitable." He commented, in part:

> That which people understand arises from what they practice, and what they practice arises from the direction of the will. If your will cherishes rightness, what you practice must reside in rightness, and since you practice rightness, you shall understand what is right. If your will cherishes [personal] profit or benefit, what you practice surely resides [only] in advantages, and since you practice getting advantages, you shall [merely] understand what is advantageous. Therefore, the aspirations of learners must be determined.

While acknowledging the need for the civil service examination system, he cautioned students not to regard it as the standard for being a superior person. Allowing the will to embrace that false standard would betray the sages and leave one incapable of devoting one's mind to national affairs and rescuing the people. Thereupon, he challenged the students:

> I sincerely hope that you can deeply reflect about yourselves, that you not allow yourselves to become petty persons adrift amid desires and seeking

---

20  See my *Confucian Discourse*, 108–114.

advantages, and that you be fearful about this [selfish bent of will] and come to bitterly despise it. I further hope that you concentrate your will on rightness and daily exert yourselves in that direction—studying broadly, inquiring carefully, thinking comprehensively, and discriminating clearly to put rightness into practice honestly. If in this way you would enter the examination halls, your essays would certainly express your daily learning and the aspirations in your heart; furthermore, you would not be defying the sages. If in this way you were to accept an appointment to office, you would not be calculating for yourself, but certainly in all things you would be fulfilling your duties, devoting yourself to affairs, and having the country on your mind and the people in your hearts. Couldn't we call such a person a superior person![21]

Zhu Xi was reportedly so moved by the lecture that he had to fan himself on a cool day, and after the lecture, he exclaimed that he and his students would never forget Lu's instruction. Furthermore, having persuaded Lu to write up the lecture, Zhu had it engraved on stone at the academy.

The White Deer Grotto Academy is most famous for Zhu Xi's academy guidelines, *Bailudong Shuyuan Jieshi* 白鹿洞書院揭示, commonly referred to as his "Articles of Learning," which were first posted at this academy and in academies throughout the realm by the 1240s. He extorted students to follow Confucian virtues in their relationships with family members and friends. Reiterating explicitly the five cardinal human relationships, Zhu Xi went further by proclaiming that fulfilling these relationships in accord with the appropriate virtue was "all they needed to learn." Based upon the assumption that these virtues in human relationships were the content and goal of learning, Zhu identified five procedures for learning in what he regarded as their crucial sequence (as quoted from the *Zhongyong*): "Study it extensively, investigate it accurately, think it over carefully, sift it clearly, and practice it earnestly." Zhu Xi then quoted other classical passages as maxims providing the essentials for personal cultivation, handling affairs, and dealing with others. Thereupon, commenting on these principles, he asserted: "The sages and worthies of antiquity taught people to pursue learning with one intention only, which is to make students understand the meaning of moral principle through discussion, so that they can cultivate their own persons and then extend it to others."[22]

---

21   Lu Jiuyuan, *Lu Jiuyuan ji* (Works of Lu Jiuyuan) (Beijing: Zhonghua shuju, 1980), 23:275–276.
22   Zhu Xi, *Zhuzi ji* (Zhu Xi's Works) (Chengdu: Sichuan jiaoyu chubanshe, 1996), 74:3893–3895, translation in: Wm. Theodore de Bary and Irene Bloom (comp.), *Sources of Chinese Tradition*, 2nd edition (New York: Columbia University Press, 1999), 1:742–744.

Zhu Xi complained that although the sages did not want students merely to memorize texts and seek government office, students of his own day followed such priorities. Since students focused on such secondary matters to the neglect of moral cultivation, schools over the centuries had instituted regulations to control students; however, Zhu Xi's students could avoid such external restraints *if* they cultivated Confucian principles according to his Articles. Having posted these Articles on the crossbar or lintel over the doorway, he announced that students "should discuss them with one another, follow them, and take personal responsibility for their observance."[23]

In the 13th century, Zhu Xi's Articles for Learning were promoted by the Song government as a model for all academies; however, he had built upon the regulations and exhortations set forth earlier by Lü Zuqian. In addition to exhortations about cultivating Confucian virtues in one's relationships, Lü dealt with details regarding student behavior and study practices; moreover, Zhu apparently followed Lü's example of organizing group efforts to ensure that students corrected their faults.[24] Although Zhu's articles expounded general principles through a compilation of classical passages and thus some have suggested that he transcended traditional "rules" or discipline of students, he was surely in practice concerned with similar details about students' behavior and study discipline. For instance, in front of his students, one of the prayers to Confucius sought and gained insight into how to use sticks to corporally punish students whose bad behavior brought shame upon the academy.[25]

Zhu Xi's expectations about, and rules for, behavior are reflected in the extant 13th-century rules of the Illumined Way Academy (Mingdao Shuyuan 明道書院) in Jiankang (modern Nanjing), because these rules were reportedly based on the late 12th-century rules at the White Deer Grotto Academy. In addition to regular bi-monthly school rites, the rules set forth guidelines for academic study and behavioral life at the academy:

> Every ten days the headmaster entered the hall and gathered the students to receive lecture tallies. Lectures were repeated according to the regulations. There were thirty-eight lectures on the classics, and sixteen on the histories. They were all recorded on the lecture register. Each month there were three examinations: the first ten-day period [examination]

---

23   Ibid. For a discussion of the articles and their perception in Korea see Martin Gehlmann, "Transmissions of the White Deer Grotto Academy Articles of Learning in Korea," in this volume, 252–286.
24   Tillman, *Confucian Discourse*, 112–114; See also my "Either Self-realization or Transmission of Received Wisdom in Confucian Education?"
25   Zhu Xi, *Zhuzi ji*, 86.4423: translated and discussed in Tillman, "Zhu Xi's Prayers," 502.

was questions on the classics; the middle one was questions on histories; the final one was preparation for the examinations. Those who excelled were recorded in the dormitory record of moral achievement. The Rector was in charge of keeping records of whether or not students improved their moral achievement. When going out or coming in, the regular students always had to wear a long gown. There was a register for requests for leave. Those who went out without registering were punished. As soon as they were received by the academy, the scholars and colleagues were not allowed to go out or request visits. Those who transgressed were criticized and punished.[26]

Such rules provide a glimpse of the rigor of the academic program, discipline and moral training, as well as some of the dress codes and behavior requirements. This provides a concrete example that, contrary to some idealized accounts, even academies closely modeled upon Zhu Xi's Articles of Learning still required detailed rules and regulations for the students.

## 4  Sample Academies Later and Elsewhere

The influence of the Yuelu and White Deer academies extended beyond the Southern Song and even to the first academy that the Mongol conquerors authorized in Yanjing (modern Beijing). In his plea to the Mongol ruler to establish academies in the early 1240s, Yang Weizhong 楊惟中 (1206–1260) explained:

> Necessary general steps were: to seek appropriate men and give them positions as teachers; collect books to pursue their learning; build academies, like the ones at Yuelu and the White Deer Grotto, to serve as standards for All Under the Heavens; allow scholars to return to their prior abodes and work together lecturing and explicating.[27]

Yang's primary focus was the Great Ultimate Academy (Taiji Shuyuan 太極書院) centered on Zhou Dunyi as founding master of *Daoxue*, but also offering

---

26  Ma Guangzu and Zhou Yinghe (comp.), *Jingding Jiankang zhi* (Records of Jiankang during the Jingding Reign), Song Yuan difangzhi congkan edition (Beijing: Zhonghua shuju, 1990), 2:29.5b–6a; translation in Walton, *Academies and Society*, 2–3.

27  Hao Jing, "Taiji shuyuan ji (Record of the Great Ultimate Academy)," in *Quan Yuan wen* (Complete Prose of the Yuan Dynasty) (Nanjing: Jiangsu Renmin chubanshe, 1999), 4:339–340.

memorial sacrifices to the spirits of other *Daoxue* masters, especially the Cheng brothers, Shao Yong, and Zhu Xi.

Hao Jing's 郝經 (1223–1275) record of this academy elaborated on its historical and cultural significance. First, the naming of the academy was noteworthy: "The academy is not named for a place, but rather for the Supreme Ultimate, [because it] returns to the basics and values the origins. An academy is for studying the Dao, and the beginnings of the Dao are manifest in the Supreme Ultimate." Second, while highlighting the continuation of *Daoxue* from the Northern Song through the Jurchen Jin in North China, Hao Jing also emphasized the contributions of the books and teachers that the Mongol armies recently brought to North China and to the academy. He proclaimed, "This recently established Academy is to illuminate the Dao, and also marks [a new] beginning of the transmission of Yi-Luo 伊洛 learning [of the Cheng Brothers] to the North."[28] Third, Hao Jing proclaimed a special role for the Supreme Ultimate Academy and its students. Just as the Yuelu and White Deer Grotto academies in the South were exemplars of *Daoxue* teachings, so too would the Supreme Ultimate Academy become. He even predicted that this new academy would become an even more important standard for All Under the Heavens due to the fact that Yanjing was now the cultural center of the Central Plain and the administrative center of the new Mongol government in China. Elsewhere, as in his 1259 "Inscription for the Shrine Hall of the Two Cheng Masters of the Song" (Song liang xiansheng cidang ji 宋兩先生祠堂記) for the academy at Runan 汝南書院, Hao Jing struggled to balance his new allegiance to Zhu Xi's version of *Daoxue* Confucianism arriving from the Southern Song and his continuing commitment to his home area's and his family's grounding in a North China tradition of the Cheng brothers. Another noteworthy example of such efforts to reconcile the legacy of the Song academies with local culture in distant and distinct places would be the development of academies in the far south in Guangdong province during the Ming period.

The Guangdong example during the Ming also underscores our theme of the importance of government officials in the development of academies and of interactions with the imperial dynastic government. Here, I would like to briefly introduce David Tsz Hang Chan's May 2016 M.A. thesis at Arizona State University, where he focused on the case of Chen Xianzhang 陳獻章 (Chen

---

28  Ibid. For more discussion on Hao Jing's relationship to this academy, see Christian Soffel and Hoyt Cleveland Tillman, *Cultural Authority and Political Culture in China: Exploring Issues with the Zhongyong and the Daotong during the Song, Jin and Yuan Dynasties* (Stuttgart: Franz Steiner Verlag, 2012), 115–130.

Baisha 陳白沙, 1428–1500).[29] Chen first established the XiaoLu Mountain 小盧山 Academy and then the Chunyang Terrace 春陽台 Academy and eventually had even greater influence spreading and restoring private academies—usually with the help of local officials in Guangdong province. Along with Hu Juren 胡居仁 (1434–1484), and Wang Yangming 王陽明 (1472–1529), Chen was enshrined in the Confucian Temple in 1584. In contrast to most Confucian scholars who were enshrined in late imperial China, Chen Xianzhang had failed to pass the civil service examination or to serve as an official, and his writings were comparatively limited; yet, he was the first Cantonese thinker ever to be enshrined in the Confucian Temple. Somewhat similarly, Hu Juren even refused to take the examinations and declined invitations to office. However, David Chan explores Chen Xianzhang's and Hu Juren's significance as regional scholars and their contributions in promoting academies and the Ming tradition of *jianghui* 講會 (discussion gatherings).[30] While Hu's renown was enhanced by his service as master of the White Deer Grotto Academy, the difficulties of even such a famous academy may be seen not only when Chen Xianzhang declined to be its headmaster but also when the academy had to be rebuilt in the mid-16th century. We can perceive our theme of the importance of government support both in Chen's reliance on food and money given to his academy by local officials and in Chen's cooperation with local officials in suppressing local rebels. Given Thomas Lee's essay,[31] in this present volume, on archery training at Confucian academies, he will be happy to know that Chen insisted that his students practice archery. However, when such militarily useful training for his students evoked suspicions in the capital, Chen followed advice (from local officials and friends) to make a trip to Beijing to put such suspicions to rest by interacting with central government officials there.

The Guangdong case also highlights the growing importance of local culture in the development of academies and in the activities of scholars there. (This localization of academy culture is also a significant theme in Steven Miles's work on Guangdong.[32]) David Chan builds upon Dr. Lü Miaofen's extensive research that compares the philosophical ideas of Chen Xianzhang and

---

29    David Tsz Hang Chan, "Changing Political and Intellectual Landscapes during the Mid-Ming: Revival of Private Academies, Emergence of *jianghui*, and the Enshrinement Case of 1584," M.A. thesis, Arizona State University, 2016. That autumn, he began his Ph.D. program at the University of Michigan.
30    See Deng Hongbo, "Like Tea and Rice at Home: Lecture Gatherings and Academies during the Ming Dynasty," in this volume, 159–196.
31    Thomas H.C. Lee, "Archery Ranges in the Educational Tradition of Confucian Academies in China," in this volume, 226–251.
32    In addition to his essay in the present volume ("Confucian Academies and Their Urban Environments in Qing China," pp. 289–318), see Stephen B. Miles, *The Sea of Learning:*

Hu Juren,[33] but David Chan seeks to enhance the historical context and Chen Xianzhang's life. Moreover, David Chan acknowledges his debt to Lü Miaofen's explorations of the discussion gatherings held by Wang Yangming and his followers.[34] Whereas Lü Miaofen credits Wang Yangming with developing the new trend of academy discussions of issues in local politics and local society, David Chan draws attention to Chen Xianzhang's foreshadowing of this trend. Both Dr. Lü and David Chan thus echo and elaborate upon Professor Yü Ying-shih's 余英時 theme that Ming intellectuals, especially Wang Yangming and his followers, made a decisive turn to issues of local society as their primary focus for cultural reform and social activism.[35]

Confucian academies in the Chosŏn period of Korean history could further highlight our themes of the importance of both the government and the local culture of intellectuals, as well as the progressive emphasis on local society and issues. Here, I will draw upon the research paper which Liu Lidan wrote for one of my seminars at Arizona State University.[36] There is considerable evidence for the traditional claims for Zhu Xi's dominance of Confucian culture in Chosŏn Korea. Zhu Xi's learning was reportedly introduced into Korea by An Hyang 安珦 (1243–1306), and began to be more prominent after the founding of the Chosŏn dynasty in 1392. Beginning during King Sejong's 世宗 (r. 1418–1450) period, academies expanded their function from book storage to include educating students, and the National University of Korea, Sŏnggyun'gwan 成

---

*Mobility and Identity in Nineteenth-Century Guangzhou* (Cambridge, MA: Harvard University Asia Center, 2006).

33  Lü Miaofen, *Hu Juren yu Chen Xianzhang* (Hu Juren and Chen Xianzhang) (Taipei: Wenjin chubanshe, 1996).

34  Lü Miaofen, "Yangming xue jianghui (Discussion Gatherings of the Yangming School)," *Xin shixue* 9, no. 2 (1998): 45–87; and "Yangming xuezhe de jianghui yu you lun (Discussion Gatherings and Conversations Between Friends for Scholars of the Yangming School)," *Hanxue yanjiu* 17, no. 1 (1999): 79–104; and "Ming dai Ningguo fu de Yangming jianghui huodong (Discussion Gatherings and Activities in the Ningguo Prefecture during the Ming)," *Xin shixue* 12, no. 1 (2001): 53–113; and her culminating book, *Yangmingxue shiren shequn—lishi, sixiang yu shijian* (The Literati Fellowship of the Wang Yangming School—History, Thought and Practice)" (Taipei: Institute of Modern History of Academia Sinica, 2003).

35  Professor Yü presented his view as the keynote to the 1997 International Wang Yangming Conference in Kyoto; for the most recent version see, Ying-shih Yü, "Reorientation of Confucian Social Thought in the Age of Wang Yangming," in his *Chinese History and Culture* (New York: Columbia University Press, 2016), 1:273–320.

36  Liu Lidan, "Korea's White Cloud Grotto Academy's Receptivity to Zhu Xi's White Deer Grotto Academy," CHI 691 Seminar on Chinese Thought, spring 2014. A short version was presented at the panel, "Re-reading of Zhu Xi and Daoxue (Learning of the Way): Confucianism in the Song and Yuan Period," for the Western Conference of the Association for Asian Studies (October, 2014) at ASU, Tempe.

均館, suggested that Zhu Xi's guidelines at the White Deer Grotto Academy be followed in Korea. The government's role also extended to providing rewards and name plaques for the academies. The White Cloud Grotto Academy (Paegundong sowŏn 白雲洞書院) was established in 1543 by the local prefect of P'ungsŏng, Chu Sebung 周世鵬 (1495–1554), in An Hyang's hometown. Because prefect Chu Sebung had also built a shrine there for venerating not only such Chinese sages as Confucius and Mencius but also An Hyang and others, this was the first time that a Korean academy incorporated the key standard elements of Chinese Confucian academies, i.e. a library, shrines for sages, worthies, and academy leaders, and the education of students. As in Zhu Xi's case of the White Deer Grotto, Chu Sebung established his academy to promote *Daoxue* Confucianism and located it on a mountain that was dominated by Buddhist temples. Taking initiative as the chief official in the prefecture, Chu Sebung even justified his building of the academy during a drought by citing how Zhu Xi had similarly constructed the White Deer Grotto Academy while he served as a prefectural official during a drought in Nankang.

Nonetheless, Chu Sebung did not follow Zhu Xi's White Deer Grotto model in all aspects at the White Cloud Grotto. First, whereas Zhu Xi petitioned the dynastic court for authorization and resources to rebuild the academy in Nankang prefecture, Chu Sebung did not seek this degree of Chosŏn government involvement. However, around seven years later, Yi Hwang 李滉 (1501–1570), the local prefect and famous philosopher, requested books and a plaque. When the king bestowed the characters *sosu* 紹修 (i.e. inherit and cultivate), the academy's name was changed to Sosu Academy. Second, Zhu Xi had petitioned the imperial court to establish the position of headmaster with the salary to accord with other officials supervising memorial sacrifices; therefore, headmasters were sometimes local officials or teachers in government schools, especially after Song Lizong 宋理宗 (r. 1224–1264) endorsed Zhu's recommendation as a model for all academies in Song China. However, Chu Sebung emphasized the scholarly qualifications of the headmaster and the need for the headmaster to be in residence; moreover, the precedent of utilizing former (not current) officials was largely followed at least into the 18th century. Third, the White Deer Grotto Academy concentrated on academic discussions and self-cultivation and only secondarily allotted time to study for the civil service examinations, Chu Sebung stipulated a preference to admit students who had already passed the middle level of the examinations; moreover, this academy became famous for its successful training of students for the government's examinations. Fourth, Zhu Xi exalted Classical principles for behavior as his posted guidelines for students in their moral self-cultivation and de-emphasized the kind of regulations and discipline common in government schools. Chu

Sebung found it necessary to lay down more specific regulations to govern student behavior and the ongoing operation of the academy.

## 5    Conclusion

Of the 57 Korean academies which venerated a range of 19 Chinese sages and worthies, 25 (44 percent of the total) offered sacrifices to Zhu Xi, which surpassed the 8 academies where Confucius was so honored.[37] Although these percentages are impressive, the figures still reveal that a majority of Korean academies did not venerate Zhu Xi; thus, this framing opens a window for taking a second look at the White Cloud Grotto Academy in its relationship to Zhu Xi's White Deer Grotto Academy. Even this Korean case, which is widely assumed to copy Zhu Xi's model and orthodoxy closely, reveals some significant adjustments to accord with local culture and the political climate of the time and place. Indeed, I would suggest that compared to Chinese academies, there was a greater degree of localization in the case of Chosŏn academies. For example, local elites trying to enshrine their ancestors in the academies presented Zhu Xi's followers with a greater challenge than in China.

Scholars often praise Zhu Xi's focus on the general principles for learning and self-cultivation, rather than specific rules and regulations that characterized government schools; however, such conventional characterizations tend to overlook Zhu's warnings that deviant students would be dealt with according to standard regulations. Moreover, in at least one of his prayers to Confucius within the hearing of his students, he received authorization to inflict punishment with stokes of bamboo sticks. Zhu Xi expressed his gratitude to Confucius for leaving instructions in the classics to beat deviant students; moreover, Zhu's articulation of these statements within the hearing of the assembled students conveyed to them his authority as having come directly from Confucius. (For a more detailed analysis of how Zhu Xi enhanced his authority over his disciples in his claims to special access to the spirit of Confucius and in the prayers that he addressed to Confucius in front of his own students, please see my article in *Philosophy East and West* and the Chinese version included as an added chapter in the expanded version of my *Zhu Xi de siwei shijie*.[38])

---

37  Deng Hongbo, "Cong Chaoxian shuyuan kan Zhongguo shuyuan wenhua de chuanbo (Chinese Academy Culture's Transmission from the Perspective of Korean Academies)," *Yanbian daxue xuebao* 3 (1992): 79.

38  "Zhu Xi's Prayers to the Spirit of Confucius and Claim to the Transmission of the Way"; and the penultimate chapter only in the expanded and revised version of Zhu Xi de siwei shijie.

Lü Zuqian's earlier specific guidelines or rules for how students were to study and behave apparently also influenced Zhu Xi. How elite the students at academies were varied greatly not only according to such factors as the level of prosperity of the local area, but also the political climate of the particular country or ruling dynasty. Degree of government support and intervention reflected the political climate in time and place. Attitudes toward training students for the civil service examinations were of course influenced by whether or not the examinations were centered on the Four Books and Zhu Xi's commentaries. However, that ideological focus alone did not ensure that *Daoxue* masters and students would support the training for, and taking of, the state examinations.

Even though academies were institutions that were readily borrowed and instituted in new places across time, and thus had considerable similarities, there is a tendency (as illustrated by Professor Park Young-Hwan's comments) to assume blanket uniformity to the degree that all Chinese and Korean academies were the same. Indeed, in the *Brocade Brook Dairy* (*Kŭmgye ilgi* 錦溪日記), although No In noted the shared custom of students going outside of the lecture hall to welcome the master teacher, the Korean visitor did not make the same kind of remark in his more detailed description of the ritualized lecture and discussion session.[39] Hence, even Professor Park's source provides some hints of diversity between Chosŏn and Ming academies. Regardless of how one views those particular instances, I hope that scholars will further explore diversity among academies after considering the cases I have summarized. These examples point toward diversity among academies as changes reflected adjustments to local culture, political climate, prevailing philosophy or ideology.

### References

Chan, David Tsz Hang. "Changing Political and Intellectual Landscapes during the Mid-Ming: Revival of Private Academies, Emergence of *jianghui*, and the Enshrinement Case of 1584." M.A. thesis, Arizona State University, 2016.

Chan, Wing-tsit. "Chu Hsi and Academies." in *Neo-Confucian Education: The Formative Stage*, edited by Wm. Theodore de Bary and John W. Chaffee, 389–413. Berkeley: University of California Press, 1989.

---

39  In response to my draft paper, Liu Lidan graciously emailed me passages describing the *jianghui* which No In observed, which are described in the entries of the diary for the 24th and 25th day of the fifth month of 1599; see *Kŭmgye ilgi* 錦溪日記 (Brocade Brook Diary). Private collection. Database of Korean Classics, which she accessed from <http://db.itkc.or.kr> on Feb. 12, 2017.

Chen, Xi, and Hoyt Cleveland Tillman. "Ghosts, Gods, and the Ritual Practice of Local Officials during the Song: With a Focus on Zhu Xi in Nankang Prefecture." *Journal of Song and Yuan Studies* 44 (2014): 291–327.

De Bary, Wm. Theodore. "The Uses of Neo-Confucianism: A Response to Professor Tillman." *Philosophy East and West* 43.3 (July 1993): 541–555.

De Bary, Wm. Theodore, and Irene Bloom (comps.). *Sources of Chinese Tradition*, 2nd edition. New York: Columbia University Press, 1999.

Deng Hongbo 邓洪波. "Cong Chaoxian shuyuan kan Zhongguo shuyuan wenhua de chuanbo 从朝鲜书院看中国书院文化的传播 (Chinese Academy Culture's Transmission from the Perspective of Korean Academies)." *Yanbian daxue xuebao* 3 (1992): 76–85.

Deng Hongbo 邓洪波. *Zhongguo shuyuan shi* 中国书院史 (History of Chinese Academies). Shanghai: Dongfang chuban zhongxin, 2006.

Hao Jing 郝經. "Taiji shuyuan ji 太極書院記 (Record of the Great Ultimate Academy)." In *Quan Yuan wen* 全元文 (Complete Prose of the Yuan Dynasty). Nanjing: Jiangsu Renmin chubanshe, 1999.

Huang Jinxing 黃進興. *Youru shengyu: quanli, xinyang yu zhengdangxing* 優入聖域: 權力, 信仰與正當性 (Entering the Sage's Realm: Power, Belief, and Legitimacy). Taipei: Yunchen wenhua, 1994.

Levenson, Joseph R., and Franz Schurmann. *China: An Interpretive History from the Beginnings to the Fall of the Han.* Berkeley: University of California Press, 1975.

Liu Lidan 劉麗丹. "Korea's White Cloud Grotto Academy's Receptivity to Zhu Xi's White Deer Grotto Academy," CHI 691 Seminar on Chinese Thought, spring 2014. A short version was presented at the panel, "Re-reading of Zhu Xi and Daoxue (Learning of the Way): Confucianism in the Song and Yuan Period," for the Western Conference of the Association for Asian Studies (October 2014) at Arizona State University, Tempe.

Lu Jiuyuan 陸九淵. *Lu Jiuyuan ji* 陸九淵集 (Lu Jiuyuan's Works). Beijing: Zhonghua shuju, 1980.

Lü Miaofen 呂妙芬. *Hu Juren yu Chen Xianzhang* 胡居仁與陳獻章 (Hu Juren and Chen Xianzhang). Taipei: Wenjin chubanshe, 1996.

Lü Miaofen 呂妙芬. "Ming dai Ningguo fu de Yangming jianghui huodong 明代寧國府的陽明講會活動 (Discussion Gatherings and Activities in the Ningguo Prefecture during the Ming)." *Xin shixue* 12, no. 1 (2001): 53–113.

Lü Miaofen 呂妙芬. *Yangmingxue shiren shequn—lishi, sixiang yu shijian* 陽明學士人社群—歷史, 思想與實踐 (The Literati Fellowship of the Wang Yangming School—History, Thought and Practice). Taipei: Institute of Modern History of Academia Sinica, 2003.

Lü Miaofen 呂妙芬. "Yangming xue jianghui 陽明學講會 (Discussion Gatherings of the Yangming School)." *Xin shixue* 9, no. 2 (1998): 45–87.

Lü Miaofen 呂妙芬. "Yangming xuezhe de jianghui yu you lun 陽明學者的講會與友論 (Discussion Gatherings and Conversations between Friends for Scholars of the Yangming School)." *Hanxue yanjiu* 17.1 (1999): 79–104.

Lü Zuqian 呂祖謙. *Lü Donglai wenji* 呂東萊文集 (Lü's Collected Short Writings). Congshu jicheng edition.

Ma Guangzu 馬光祖, and Zhou Yinghe 周應合 (comp.). *Jingding Jiankang zhi* 景定建康志 (Song Jingding Period Local Gazetteer of Jiankang). Song Yuan difangzhi congkan 宋元方誌叢刊 edition. Beijing: Zhonghua shuju, 1990.

Miles, Stephen B. *The Sea of Learning: Mobility and Identity in Nineteenth-Century Guangzhou*. Cambridge: Harvard University Asia Center, 2006.

Soffel, Christian, and Hoyt Cleveland Tillman. *Cultural Authority and Political Culture in China: Exploring Issues with the Zhongyong and the Daotong during the Song, Jin and Yuan Dynasties*. Stuttgart: Franz Steiner Verlag, 2012.

Tian Hao 田浩 (Hoyt Cleveland Tillman). "Songdai de rujia shuyuan 宋代的儒家书院 (Confucian Academies during the Song dynasty)." *Hunan daxue xuebao* 19.6 (November 2005): 3–9.

Tian Hao 田浩 (Hoyt Cleveland Tillman). *Zhu Xi de siwei shijie (zengding ben)* 朱熹的思維世界 (增訂本) (Zhu Xi's World of Thought, revised and expanded edition). Taibei: Yunchen wenhua gongsi, 2008; Nanjing: Jiangsu Renmin chubanshe, 2009.

Tian Hao 田浩 (Hoyt Cleveland Tillman). "Zhu Xi yu Daoxue de fazhan zhuanhua 朱熹与道学的发展转化 (Zhu Xi and the Transformation of Learning of the Dao Confucianism)." In *Songdai xinruxue de jingshen shijie: yi Zhuzixue wei zhongxin* 宋代新儒学的精神世界：以朱子学为中心 (The Intellectual World of Neo-Confucianism in the Song Dynasty: Taking the Study of Zhu Xi as the Center of Discussion), edited by Wu Zhen 吳震, 10–23. Shanghai: Huadong shifan daxue chubanshe, 2009.

Tillman, Hoyt Cleveland. "A New Direction in Confucian Scholarship: Approaches to Examining the Differences between Neo-Confucianism and Tao-hsueh (Daoxue)." *Philosophy East and West* 42, no. 3 (July 1992): 455–474.

Tillman, Hoyt Cleveland. *Confucian Discourse and Chu Hsi's Ascendancy*. Honolulu: University of Hawai'i Press, 1992.

Tillman, Hoyt Cleveland. "The Uses of Neo-Confucianism, Revisited." *Philosophy East and West* 44, no. 1 (January 1994): 135–142.

Tillman, Hoyt Cleveland. "Zhu Xi's Prayers to the Spirit of Confucius and Claim to the Transmission of the Way." *Philosophy East and West* 54, no. 4 (October 2004): 489–513.

Tillman, Hoyt Cleveland. "Les académies confucéennes en Chine au temps des Song ($X^e$–$XIII^e$ siècle)." In *Les Lieux de savoir: Espaces et communautés* (Sites of Learning: Spaces and Communities), edited by Christian Jacob et al., 323–342. Paris: Albin Michel, 2007.

Tillman, Hoyt Cleveland. "Either Self-realization or Transmission of Received Wisdom in Confucian Education? An Inquiry into Lü Zuqian's and Zhu Xi's Constructions for Student Learning." In *Educations and Their Purposes: A Philosophical Dialogue among Cultures*, edited by Roger Ames and Peter Hershock, 270–288. Honolulu: University of Hawai'i Press, 2008.

Walton, Linda A. *Academies and Society in Southern Sung China*. Honolulu: University of Hawai'i Press, 1999.

Wilson, Thomas A. (ed.). *On Sacred Grounds: Culture, Society, Politics, and the Formation of the Cult of Confucius*. Cambridge: Harvard University Asia Center, 2002.

Yü, Ying-shih (Yu Yingshi). "Reorientation of Confucian Social Thought in the Age of Wang Yangming." In his *Chinese History and Culture*, 1: 273–320. New York: Columbia University Press, 2016. (He first presented this article as the keynote to the International Wang Yangming Conference in Kyoto, 1997).

Zhang Shi 張栻. "Nanxuan xiansheng wenji 南軒先生文集 (Zhang Nanxuan's Collected Short Writings)." In *Zhang Shi ji* 張栻集 (Zhang Shi's Works). Beijing: Zhonghua shuju, 2015.

Zhu Hanmin 朱汉民, et al. (comp.). *Zhongguo shuyuan* 中国书院 (Chinese Academies). Shanghai: Shanghai Jiaoyu chubanshe, 2002. (This included Thomas Lee's introduction in English, and the CD "Qiannian xuefu" 千年学府, produced by Hunan University's Yuelu Academy Cultural Institute and distributed by Hunan Electronic and Audio-visual Publishing House).

Zhu Xi 朱熹. *Zhuzi ji* 朱子集 (Zhu Xi's Works). Chengdu: Sichuan jiaoyu chubanshe, 1996.

Zhu Xi 朱熹. *Zhuzi yulei* 朱子語類 (Zhu Xi's Classified Conversations). Beijing: Zhonghua shuju, 1986.

CHAPTER 2

# An Enquiry into the Origins of Confucian Academies and the Mingtang in the Tang Period

*Minamizawa Yoshihiko and Chien Iching*

## 1       Introduction[1]

There is common agreement that the Tang period Jixian Shuyuan (Jixian shuyuan 集賢書院) was one of the first prototypes influencing the later development of Confucian academies (*shuyuan* 書院).[2] It is also well-known that the predecessor of the Jixian Shuyuan was the Lizheng Shuyuan (Lizheng shuyuan 麗正書院), which originated as to the Lizheng Compilatory Shuyuan (Lizheng xiushuyuan 麗正修書院) attached to Qianyuan Hall (Qianyuandian 乾元殿) in Luoyang, the eastern capital during the Tang.[3] In the first half of Emperor Xuanzong's 玄宗 (685–762) reign, known as the Kaiyuan 開元 era (713–741), he ordered the revision of books treasured by the imperial family in the east corridor of Qianyuan Hall. When this was completed the following year, the emperor showed the books, classified into the four traditional categories—classics (*jing* 經), histories (*shi* 史), masters (*zi* 子), and collected works (*ji* 集)—to a large numbers of officials.[4] This episode, which later led to the establishment of the Lizheng Compilatory Shuyuan, is well known in the history of Confucian academies.[5] Not many people, however, are aware that the

---

1   This work was supported by JSPS KAKENHI Grant Number JP15K02035.
2   See Yuan Mei, "*Suiyuan suibi* 14," in *Yuan Mei quanshu* (Complete Writings of Yuan Mei), Volume 5 (Nanjing: Jiangsu guji chubanshe, 1993); Zhu Hanmin, *Zhongguo de shuyuan* (Academies of China) (Taipei: Taiwan shangwu yinshuguan, 1993), 1–4; Fan Kezheng, *Zhongguo shuyuan shi* (History of Chinese Academies) (Taipei: wenjin chubanshe, 1995), 4; Deng Hongbo, *Zhongguo shuyuan shi* (History of Chinese Academies) (Shanghai: Dongfang chuban zhongxin, 2004), 1; Dai Shuhong and Xiao Yongming, "Tangdai Jixuan shuyuan yu 'Shuyuan' de ming he shi (Jixian Academy in the Tang Dynasty and the Name and True Meaning of the Term 'Academy')," *Daxue jiaoyu kexue* 2016–1 (2017): 63.
3   See Zhu Hanmin, *Zhongguo de shuyuan*, 3; Fan Kezheng, *Zhongguo shuyuan shi*, 3; Dai Shuhong and Xiao Yongming, "Tangdai Jixuan shuyuan," 66.
4   See *Yuhai* 27, "Guanshu," "Tang Qianyuandian guanshu," (Shanghai: Jiangsu guji chubanshe and Shanghai shudian [photofacsimile reprint of edition published by Zhejiang shuju in Guangxu 9 (1883)]), 533.
5   See Fan Kezheng, *Zhongguo shuyuan shi*, 3.

predecessor of Qianyuan Hall was the Mingtang 明堂 (Hall of Brightness) of Empress Wu Zetian (624–705) (Zetian Wuhou 則天武后 or Wu Zhao 武曌), and even fewer people know what sort of building the Mingtang actually was.[6]

The Mingtang does not have any direct connections with Confucian academies. However, if the Jixian Shuyuan, Lizheng Shuyuan, and Lizheng Compilatory Shuyuan were the among the main origins of Confucian academies, then, in order to probe the circumstances behind the birth of these shuyuan of Xuanzong, it becomes important to look back to Qianyuan Hall, in which they originated, and even further to Empress Wu's Mingtang, the predecessor of Qianyuan Hall, and examine the significance of the space that it occupied.[7] Empress Wu's Mingtang first was called Wanxiang Shrine, or Divine Palace of Myriad Images (Wanxiang shengong 萬象神宮), and then Tongtian Palace, or Palace for Communing with Heaven (Tongtian gong 通天宮). While these could be regarded as no more than grand names, it is quite obvious that they are a symbolic expression of the intent and fervent wishes of the person(s) who assigned these names. The terms *wanxiang* 萬象, *tongtian* 通天, and *qianyuan* 乾元 all have connotations of a center or source directly linked to Heaven. It was on a site of such significance that Xuanzong established a shuyuan.

Furthermore, Yixing 一行 (683–727), an eminent Esoteric Buddhist monk, resided in the Jixian Shuyuan and there compiled the Dayan calendar (*Dayan li* 大衍曆), yet there has been virtually no detailed research about Yixing's actual work in the shuyuan. Xuanzong installed leading officials, scholars, and literati of the time in his shuyuan, but Yixing differed considerably from such men since he was an astronomer and technician who produced astronomical instruments. Yixing's words and deeds, associated with the Jixian Shuyuan and with astronomy and the calendar, convey one aspect of the future of the first shuyuan and provide a valuable lead for gaining an idea on Xuanzong's ideas about shuyuan. Therefore a study of them will make a major contribution to the study of Confucian academies.

---

6  On the Mingtang, see Minamizawa Yoshihiko, *Chūgoku meidō shisō kenkyū* (A Study of Ideas about the Mingtang in China) (Tokyo: Iwanami shoten, 2018). For an English study of the Mingtang, see William Edward Soothill, *The Hall of Light: A Study of Early Chinese Kingship* (London: Lutterworth Press, 1951); for a description of Mingtang from the Zhou to the Northern Wei dynasties and a list of recent studies see David W. Pankenier, *Astrology and Cosmology in Early China: Conforming Earth to Heaven* (Cambridge: Cambridge University Press, 2013), 342–349.

7  On Empress Wu's Mingtang, see Antonino Forte, *Mingtang and Buddhist Utopia in the History of the Astronomical Clock: The Tower, Statue and Armillary Sphere Constructed by Empress Wu*, Serie Orientale Roma 59, PEFEO 145 (Rome/Paris: Istituto italiano per il Medio ed Estremo Oriente/EFEO, 1988); Minamizawa, *Chūgoku meidō shisō kenkyū*, 226–232.

In this essay, I focus on some peripheral topics such as the Mingtang, astronomy, and the calendar, which have not received adequate attention in past research on Confucian academies, and by doing so I hope to rectify some aspects of past research on the origins of Confucian academies and present some new observations.

## 2   Empress Wu Zetian's Removal of Qianyuan Hall and Her Establishment of the Mingtang

### 2.1   *The Origins of Qianyuan Hall*

In 688, Empress Wu removed Qianyuan Hall, which stood within the palace grounds in Luoyang, and built the Mingtang on its site. The predecessor of the Tang period Qianyuan Hall had been the Qianyang Hall (Qianyangdian 乾陽殿) of the Sui dynasty (581–618), which served as the State Chamber (*zhengdian* 正殿) and was the nerve center of government. During the Sui, the palace had been built in imitation of the celestial court known as the Enclosure of Purple Tenuity (Ziweiyuan 紫微垣) and was called the Citadel of Purple Tenuity (Ziweicheng 紫微城),[8] but Empress Wu renamed it Taichu Palace (Taichugong 太初宮). Qianyang Hall burnt down in 621, and Qianyuan Hall was erected on its site in 665.

Like Qianyang Hall, Qianyuan Hall was built as the State Chamber. Empress Wu renamed the city of Luoyang as Shendu, called its central palace Taichu Palace, and called the State Chamber inside Taichu Palace Qianyuan Hall. "Shendu 神都" means "Divine Capital," while *taichu*, literally "great beginning," refers to the original *qi* at the time of primordial chaos. The word *qianyuan* originates in the *Yijing* 易經 (*Book of Changes*) and signifies the motive force that gave birth to the myriad things and controls them.[9] From these designations it can be inferred that Empress Wu regarded Qianyuan Hall as a device that represented the root source within the Divine Capital and had the function of generating the myriad things.

In 674 Empress Wu changed the designation for "emperor" from *huangdi* 皇帝 to *tianhuang* 天皇 and that for "empress" from *huanghou* 皇后 to *tianhou* 天后. In traditional Chinese thinking, the emperor (*huangdi*) was the Son of Heaven (*tianzi* 天子). But because the term *tianhuang* was associated with the

---

8   See Ouyang Xiu and Song Qi, *Xin Tangshu* (New Book of the Tang), 38, "Dili zhi" 2 (Beijing: Zhonghua shuju, 1975), 981–982.
9   The *Yijing*, "Shangjing, Qiangua," in the *Shisanjing zhushu* (Commentaries and Explanations to the Thirteen Classics) (Beijing: Zhonghua shuju, 1980), 14.

title of the supreme deity Tianhuang Dadi 天皇大帝 (Great Emperor Celestial Sovereign), the emperor had now become a god on earth and the god of the Divine Capital was none other than the emperor himself. Qianyuan Hall was no mere chamber of state affairs, and its position as the root source of the universe was guaranteed by the supremacy and omnipotence of the emperor, now a living god.

## 2.2   What Was the Mingtang?

Empress Wu tore down this sacred palace and erected in its place the Mingtang, which she named Wanxiang Shrine. *Wanxiang* too is a word deriving from the *Yijing*[10] and signifies the myriad things that are generated by the workings of primordial state of heaven and that exist in harmony with each other. Therefore, Wanxiang Shrine was a shrine to the myriad things, a symbol of the genesis of all things and their harmony, and a temple to the myriad gods, who represented the essence and spirit of all things. Consequently, the act of tearing down Qianyuan Hall was not a negation of its meaning, and it may be supposed that Qianyuan Hall was opened up so as to actively affirm its special character and manifest its powers more effectively. Further, Empress Wu called the second Mingtang (erected in 696, a year after the first Mingtang burnt down) Tongtian Palace, a designation indicative of a perception that the Mingtang was an extension of Heaven, to which it was vertically connected.

But what exactly was the Mingtang? Among classical works, details of the Mingtang of the Xia, Yin, and Zhou are recorded in the *Zhouli* 周禮 (*Rites of Zhou*); and the *Liji* 禮記 (*Book of Rites*), *Dadai liji* 大戴禮記 (*Records of Ritual Matters by Dai the Elder*), *Xiaojing* 孝經 (*Classic of Filial Piety*), and *Shijing* 詩經 (*Classic of Poetry*) also include passages about the Mingtang of Zhou that are varied in content and mutually contradictory.

Marcel Granet (1884–1940), the eminent French Sinologist, has given a brief description of the Mingtang of Zhou, based on the *Liji*. According to Granet, "Mingtang" means a hall for clarifying things, was located in the capital, was built so that the Son of Heaven could perform on earth the celestial task of regulating the seasons, and was a building suitable for radiating the influence of the Son of Heaven throughout the entire country. It was a square, four-sided building with a conical roof and surrounded by a circular pond, since the cyclical task of the calendar was accomplished there, and its interior consisted of nine chambers.[11]

---

10   Kong Yingda's 孔穎達 (574–648) commentary on the *Yijing*, "Shangjing, Qiangua," 14.
11   Marcel Granet, *La religion des Chinois* (Paris: Gauthier-Villars et C[ie], 1922), 52–53.

Granet's description is by and large faithful to his source text. According to other texts, the Mingtang was a structure which, as well as having the function of managing the cycle of the seasons and the function of providing a venue for imperial audiences with feudal lords and vassal states, possessed the function of worshipping the gods of heaven and earth, of the sun, moon, and stars, of cold and heat, of wind and rain, and of mountains and rivers and also the ancestral spirits.

It is not certain whether the Mingtang of Zhou actually existed, and even if it did, its remains have not been discovered, nor is it known whether its descriptions in various works accord with its actual structure. Although the remains of the Mingtang erected by Wudi 武帝 (r. 141–87 BCE) of the Former Han dynasty (202 BCE–8 CE) on Taishan have also not been discovered, on the basis of textual research it is considered to have actually existed. The existence of the Mingtang built by Wang Mang 王莽 (45 BCE–23 CE) at the end of the Former Han has been archaeologically confirmed. In addition, excavations conducted at the site of the Mingtang built in Luoyang during the Later Han dynasty (25–220), have made it clear that, while the Mingtang underwent some modifications, it continued to be used during the subsequent Cao Wei (220–265), Western Jin (265–316), and Northern Wei (386–534) dynasties. Prior to the relocation of its capital to Luoyang, the Northern Wei had built a Mingtang in Pingcheng (present-day Datong, Shanxi province). Together with Wang Mang's Mingtang in Chang'an, the Later Han's Mingtang in Luoyang, and the Northern Wei's Mingtang in Pingcheng, it is Empress Wu's Mingtang of the Tang period that is counted as one of the four great embodiments of this institution.

## 3   The Use of Space in Empress Wu's Mingtang

### 3.1   *The Structure of Empress Wu's Mingtang*

A brief description of the Mingtang that Empress Wu had built to replace the Qianyuan Hall in 688 can be found in the "Liyi zhi" 禮儀志 (Monograph on Ritual) chapter of the *Jiu Tangshu* 舊唐書 (*Old Book of the Tang*). According to this description, the Mingtang was 294 *chi* 尺 (88.2m [1 *chi* = approx. 0.3 m]) high and each of its four sides was 300 *chi* long. It had three stories: the ground floor represented the four seasons, which were painted with the colour of the corresponding direction; the middle floor was based on the twelve months and had a cupola, on top of which there was a disc held up by nine dragons; and the upper floor was based on the twenty-four solar periods and also had a cupola. Inside the Mingtang there was an enormous log, the equivalent of ten pairs of outstretched arms in circumference, which served as the central pillar, being

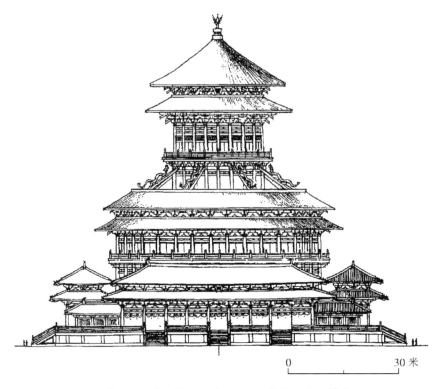

ILLUSTRATION 2.1   Conceptual architectural structure of Wangxiang Shrine
SOURCE: YANG HONGXUN. "MINGTANG FANLUN: MINGTANG DE KAOGUXUE YANJIU," 86

fastened with iron cables. The cupola was adorned with the figures of a pair of phoenixes that seemed to be flying. The Mingtang was called Wanxiang Shrine.[12]

The basic structure of Empress Wu's Mingtang represented an architectural style that overall gave concrete expression to the notion of "round above, square below" (*shangyuan xiafang* 上圓下方),[13] with the lower floor being square and corresponding to the four seasons, while the middle and upper floors had a cupola and were round (see ill. 2.1).[14] This architectural style coincides with that of the Mingtang of Zhou, described by Granet. In addition, the

---

12   Liu Xu, *Jiu Tangshu* (Old Book of the Tang) 22, "Liyi zhi" 2 (Beijing: Zhonghua shuju, 1975), 862.
13   On the notion of "round above, square below" as it relates to the Mingtang, see Minamizawa, *Chūgoku meidō shisō kenkyū*, 5–6, and Pankenier, *Astrology and Cosmology in Early China*, 346.
14   Yang Hongxun, "Mingtang fanlun: Mingtang de kaoguxue yanjiu" (An Archaeological Study of the Mingtang), *Tōhō gakuhō* 70 (1998): 86.

structure of each of its constituent parts gave concrete expression to the ideas of the five agents (*wuxing* 五行) and seasonal ordinances (*shiling* 時令), giving the building the characteristics that fully qualified it to be called a Mingtang.

## 3.2   *Religious Services at Empress Wu's Mingtang*

Once the Mingtang was completed, Empress Wu performed a comprehensive religious sacrifice (*daxiang* 大享), symbolically implemented executive commands and moral teachings (*buzheng* 布政), cared for the elderly (*yanglao* 養老), proclaimed a general amnesty, and changed the name of the regnal era. Our attention is drawn in particular to the rites of the religious sacrifice called *daxiang*. This was the largest in scale of the rites performed in the Mingtang, and celestial deities were worshipped together with ancestral spirits and various other spirits.

In the *daxiang* rite as it was performed up until 691, Haotian Shangdi 昊天上帝 (Supreme Thearch of Exalted Heaven) and Huang Diqi 皇地祇 (August God of Earth) were enshrined together inside the Mingtang, and King Wen of Zhou and Empress Wu's parents were worshipped together with them, while the spirits of the asterisms of the Enclosures of Purple Tenuity and Grand Tenuity and of the Five Mountains and Four Rivers were worshipped in the courtyard. Although this was a temporary measure taken because Luoyang's suburban altar was not yet ready to be used, Empress Wu's Mingtang represented a veritable pantheon befitting the name Divine Palace of Myriad Images. According to the directives governing the ceremonial ritual at the Mingtang as recorded in the *Zhenguan li* 貞觀禮 (*Rites of the Zhenguan Era*) completed in 637, the chief deities were the Five Celestial Thearchs, together with whom only the imperial ancestors, the Five Human Emperors, and the gods of the five offices were worshipped. The spirits of asterisms and the Five Mountains and Four Rivers were excluded from 691 onwards, but out of respect for Empress Wu's wishes the Supreme Thearch of Exalted Heaven and August God of Earth, and also the previous emperor and empress, were made objects of worship.[15] These directives governing religious services at Empress Wu's Mingtang were then reflected in the *Kaiyuan li* 開元禮 (*Rites of the Kaiyuan era*) of 732. We can surmise, with reference to the prescriptions of the *Kaiyuan li*,[16] that in the ceremonial space of Empress Wu's Mingtang the Supreme Thearch of Exalted Heaven and August God of Earth were enshrined inside the Mingtang. There

---

15   *Jiu Tangshu* 22, "Liyi zhi" 2, 864–865.
16   See Xiao Song et al., *Da Tang Kaiyuan li* (Rites of the Kaiyuan era of the Great Tang) 10, "Jili," "Huangdi jiqiu daxiang yu Mingtang," "Chenshe" (Tokyo: Kyūko shoin, 1972 [photofacsimile reprint of edition published by Hongshi Gongshantang in Guangxu 12 (1886)]), 75.

they were worshipped together with imperial ancestors, the previous emperor and empress, the Five Celestial Thearchs, and the Five Human Emperors, while the gods of the five offices were worshipped in the courtyard.

## 4 Xuanzong's Alternation between the Mingtang and Qianyuan Hall

### 4.1 The Switch from the Mingtang to Qianyuan Hall

Empress Wu died in 705, but the Mingtang continued to be maintained by her successors Zhongzong 中宗 (r. 684, 705–710) and Ruizong 睿宗 (r. 684–690, 710–712), and religious ceremonies and administrative rites were performed as they had been under Empress Wu. It was after the ascension of Xuanzong (r. 712–756) that this was changed. In 717 Xuanzong issued the following edict:

> Currently the Mingtang is adjacent to the imperial palace, and the services for worshipping my stern father together with Heaven are in some respects at variance with the connotations of filial duty. If it is not an established institution, it cannot be used as a standard. Therefore, the erudites of the Ministry of Rites, palace ministers, and grand masters consulted widely, respectfully followed precedents of yore, preserved the form of the State Chamber, and abolished the name "Mingtang." It is to be renamed Qianyuan Hall, and imperial visits are to accord with the ritual etiquette of the State Chamber.[17]

Xuanzong considered the close proximity of the Mingtang in Luoyang to the imperial palace to be inappropriate and therefore he revoked the designation "Mingtang," renamed it Qianyuan Hall, and ordered that henceforth the ceremonies performed there were to be based on the system of rites observed in the State Chamber.

### 4.2 The Switch from Qianyuan Hall Back to the Mingtang and Then Back Again to Qianyuan Hall

The subsequent events may be summarized as follows on the basis of the "Liyi zhi" of the *Jiu Tangshu*:

From 717 onwards, the rites of the Mingtang were abolished, new rites for the imperial audience at Qianyuan Hall on New Year's day and on the day of the winter solstice were instituted, and the venue of the *daxiang* rite in the third month of autumn was moved from the Mingtang to the Circular Altar.

---

17  *Jiu Tangshu* 22, "Liyi zhi" 2, 875.

In 722 Xuanzong changed the name of Qianyuan Hall back to Mingtang, but the *daxiang* rite was not performed.

In 737 Xuanzong ordered the chamberlain for palace buildings (*jiangzuo dajiang* 將作大匠) to pull down the Mingtang in Luoyang. However, because of the enormous expense it would entail, only the upper floor was pulled down, the central pillar was removed, and an octagonal tower was installed on the balcony substructure, on top of which the figures of eight dragons offering up a spherical gem were placed. The surrounding area was reduced in size, and standard tiles were used for the roof. The building's name too was changed back to Qianyuan Hall.[18]

## 5    The Use of Space in Xuanzong's Qianyuan Hall: The Birth of the Jixian Shuyuan

### 5.1    *Compilatory Work at Qianyuan Hall*

The first task carried out at the renovated Qianyuan Hall was the editing and copying of books. According to the "Zhiguan zhi" 職官志 (Monograph on Official Positions) chapter of the *Jiu Tangshu*, "in 717 books of the four categories were copied and edited below the east corridor of Qianyuan Hall and the palace storehouse was replenished. Four editorial officials were installed."[19] The "palace storehouse" (*neiku* 內庫) here refers to the libraries of the former emperors Taizong 太宗 (r. 626–649) and Gaozong 高宗 (r. 649–683). And because missing sections of these books had not been rectified and their chapters were in disarray, making it difficult to read them, Xuanzong ordered Chu Wuliang 褚無量 (646–720) and Ma Huaisu 馬懷素 (659–718) to sort and edit the books.[20] These were the origins and the original aim of the sorting of books at Qianyuan Hall.[21]

Chu Wuliang had accompanied Xuanzong during his visit to the eastern capital in 717, and once he was placed in charge of the copying and editing of books in the east corridor of Qianyuan Hall, he set up bookcases in front of Qianyuan Hall, arranged the books from the palace storehouse on them, carried out major revisions, and widely collected variant versions from throughout the

---

18    The above summary is based on *Jiu Tangshu* 22, "Liyi zhi" 2, 875–876.
19    *Jiu Tangshu* 43, "Zhiguan zhi" 2, "Zhongshusheng," Jixiandian shuyuan," 1851.
20    *Jiu Tangshu* 46, "Jingji zhi" 1, 1962.
21    See Wu Xiaping, *Tangdai zhongyang wenguan zhidu yu wenxue yanjiu* (Research on the Central Institutes and Literature in the Tang Dynasty) (Jinan: Qilu shushe, 2007), 50–51.

realm.[22] This took place in the eleventh month,[23] and because he replenished the storehouse's contents in a short span of time, on the 14th day of the eighth month of 718 Xuanzong ordered officials of the Secretariat and other civilian and military officials to view the books in the eastern corridor of Qianyuan Hall and gave Chu Wuliang and the storehouse officials rewards disbursed from the palace storehouse.[24] The place where this work had been carried out was called Qianyuanyuan 乾元院, which in the twelfth month of the same year was renamed Lizheng Compilatory Shuyuan.[25]

### 5.2   From Lizheng Compilatory Shuyuan to Jixian Shuyuan

When Xuanzong returned to Chang'an in the winter of 718, the books of the Lizheng Compilatory Shuyuan were transferred to the Lizheng Hall in the Eastern Palace (Donggong 東宮) in Chang'an and a Compilatory Shuyuan was established there, with Chu Wuliang again being put in charge of it by imperial order.[26]

Thereafter several more important events in the history of Confucian academies occurred during the Kaiyuan era. In particular, the establishment of shuyuan outside Guangshun Gate (Guangshunmen 光順門) in Chang'an and Mingfu Gate (Mingfumen 明福門) in Luoyang could be described as important events, in the sense that these shuyuan were located outside the imperial palace. This was not merely a geographical and spatial change, for it provided the occasion for the shuyuan to develop from a privileged asset of the imperial family and nobility, symbolized by their position inside the imperial palace, into a cultural asset open to the wider population, which had enormous cultural significance.

The establishment of shuyuan outside Guangshun and Mingfu Gates is recorded as follows in the official history of the Tang: "In 723 a shuyuan was also established outside Guangshun Gate in Chang'an. In 724 the Lizheng Shuyuan was established outside Mingfu Gate in Luoyang."[27] But different dates are given in another work, the *Jixian zhuji* 集賢注記 (*Notes on the Jixian Shuyuan*)

---

22  *Jiu Tangshu* 102, "Chu Wuliang zhuan," 3167.
23  Du You, *Tongdian* 21, "Zhiguan" 3, "Zhongshusheng," "Zhongshuling," "Jixian xueshi," (Beijing: Zhonghua Shuju, 1984), 126.
24  *Yuhai* 27, "Guanshu," "Tang Qianyuandian guanshu," 533.
25  *Xin Tangshu* 47, "Baiguan zhi" 2, "Zhongshusheng," "Jixiandian shuyuan," 1213. On the dating of the change in name to the twelfth month, see the *Jixian zhuji* quoted in *Yuhai* 52, "Yiwen," "Tang Qianyuandian sibushu Lizhengdian sikushu Jixianyuan dianji," 988.
26  *Xin Tangshu* 57, "Yiwen zhi" 1, 1422; *Xin Tangshu* 200, "Ruxue zhuan" 3, "Chu Wuliang," 5689.
27  *Xin Tangshu* 47, "Baiguan zhi" 2, "Zhongshusheng," "Jixiandian shuyuan," 1213.

by Wei Shu 韋述 (691–758) of the Tang.[28] Wei Shu belonged to a leading family of the Tang period, was well versed in literature and history, and was employed at the Jixian Academy during the Kaiyuan and Tianbao 天寶 (742–756) eras.[29] His *Jixian zhuji* was lost at an early stage, but it is quoted in works such as the *Yuhai* 玉海 (*Sea of Jade*) and the *Zhiguan fenji* 職官分紀 (*Official Positions Arranged Chronologically*), and it is held in high regard as a reliable source. The problem is that the *Jixian zhuji* gives the date of the establishment of the shuyuan outside Mingfu Gate as 722.

In the *Jixian zhuji*[30] as quoted in the *Zhiguan fenji* by Sun Fengji 孫逢吉 (1135–1199) of the Song it is stated that "in the spring of 722 the emperor visited the Eastern Capital and for the first time moved the shuyuan outside Mingfu Gate to the north of the Secretariat and named it Lizheng as hitherto."[31] The *Yuhai* (fasc. 52) by Wang Yinglin 王應麟 (1223–1296) of the Southern Song also quotes from the *Jixian zhuji*, stating that "in the spring of 722 they moved the shuyuan outside Mingfu Gate to the north of the Secretariat."[32] In the *Tang huiyao* 唐會要 (*Collection of Important Documents of the Tang*) too it is stated that "[the Jixian Shuyuan of] the Eastern Capital is to the west of the main street outside Mingfu Gate. It had originally been the residence of Princess Taiping 太平. The shuyuan was first moved here in the third month of 722."[33] *Yuhai* 167 too, citing the *Jixian zhuji* and *Tang huiyao*, states that "the Jixian Shuyuan of the Eastern Capital is to the west of the main street outside Mingfu Gate [...]. The Shuyuan was first moved here in the third month of 722."[34]

---

28  Wei Shu's dates are based on Tao Min (ed.), *Jinglong wenguan ji. Jixian zhuji* (Notes on the Jinglong wenguan. Notes on the Jixian Shuyuan), "Wei Shu jianpu" (Beijing: Zhonghua shuju, 2015).

29  *Jiu Tangshu* 102, "Wei Shu zhuan," 3183; see also Tao Min (ed.), *Jinglong wenguan ji: Jixian zhuji*, 198–199.

30  The *Zhiguan fenji* gives the title as *Jixian jizhu* 集賢記注. Many books give the title as *Jixian zhuji* 集賢注記, but no small number of books have *Jixian jizhu*. For example, both forms can be seen in the original notes of the *Yuhai*. In the present essay the form *Jixian zhuji* has been uniformly used. See also Tao Min (ed.), *Jinglong wenguan ji. Jixian zhuji*, 201.

31  Sun Fengji, *Zhiguan fenji* (Official Positions Arranged Chronologically) 15, "Jixian shuyuan," (Beijing: Zhonghua shuju, 1988), 376.

32  *Yuhai* 52, "Yiwen," "Tang Qianyuandian sibushu Lizhengdian sikushu Jixianyuan dianji," 989.

33  Wang Pu, *Tang huiyao* (Collection of Important Documents of the Tang) 64, "Shiguan" 2, "Jixianyuan," (Beijing: Zhonghua shuju, 1991), 1320.

34  *Yuhai* 167, "Gongshi," "Yuan" 1, "Tang Jixiandian shuyuan," 3060.

In the past, only the 724 thesis has been mentioned, but in recent research the 722 thesis has been gaining support.[35] However, the account given in the *Jixian zhuji* continues as follows: "In the spring of 723, the emperor made a tour of the north, worshipped Houtu 后土 (Sovereign Earth), and returned to Chang'an. He founded for the first time a shuyuan outside Guangshun Gate of the Daming Palace (Daminggong 大明宮) and called it the Lizheng Shuyuan in accordance with its former designation. In the winter of 724 the emperor went to Luoyang, separately established for the first time a shuyuan outside Mingfu Gate, and also called it the Lizheng Shuyuan."[36] The establishment of a shuyuan outside Mingfu Gate in 724 too is thus clearly mentioned. If one believes the account in the *Jixian zhuji*, a shuyuan was established twice outside Mingfu Gate, in 722 and in 724, and it may be supposed that this was indeed the case.

In 718 the Lizheng Compilatory Shuyuan had been relocated to Chang'an and since there would no longer be a shuyuan in Luoyang, it seems strange that the *Jixian zhuji* should state that a shuyuan was moved outside Mingfu Gate when the emperor visited the eastern capital of Luoyang in 722. But as is evident from Chu Wuliang's biography and the "Yiwen zhi" 藝文志 (Monograph on Literature) in the *Xin Tangshu* 新唐書 (*New Book of the Tang*),[37] it was the books that had been moved in 718 and not the building and its library functions. If this was the case, then in late 718 the books held by the Lizheng Compilatory Shuyuan of Qianyuan Hall in Luoyang were sent to Lizheng Hall in the Eastern Palace in Chang'an, but the building and library functions were maintained for visits by the emperor, and when Xuanzong visited Luoyang in 722 the shuyuan's functions as the emperor's private library were transferred from Qianyuan Hall to a building outside Mingfu Gate, with the name of the building being Lizheng Compilatory Shuyuan, the same name that had been used when it had been in Qianyuan Hall.

---

35　Works such as Xu Song, *Tang liangjing chengfang kao* (Research of the Two Capitals of the Tang) (Beijing: Zhonghua shuju, 1985) mention only the 724 thesis. Recent studies include Ikeda On, "Seitō no Shūken'in (On Jixianyuan in the Mid-8th Century)," *Hokkaidō daigaku bungakubu kiyō* 19 (1971); Zhao Yongdong, "Tangdai Jixiandian shuyuan kaolun (A Study of the Jixiandian Academy in the Tang Dynasty)," *Nankai xuebao* 4 (1986): 12–20; and Matsumoto Yasunobu, "Tōto Rakuyōkyū Meifukumon fukin ni tsuite (On the Vicinity of the Mingfu Gate of the Palace in the Eastern Capital of Luoyang)," in *Tō ōchō no kyūjō to gozen kaigi* (Imperial Palaces and Councils in the Imperial Presence during the Tang Dynasty) (Kyoto: Kōyō shobō, 2006). Ikeda mentions both theses, while Zhao and Matsumoto give the 722 thesis.

36　*Zhiguan fenji* 15, "Jixian shuyuan," 376.

37　*Xin Tangshu* 57, "Yiwen zhi," 1, 1422; *Xin Tangshu* 200, "Ruxue zhuan" 3, "Chu Wuliang," 5689.

The account given in the *Jixian zhuji* for the period from 723 onwards is not inconsistent with the official histories as regards historical facts *per se*, even though there are some subtle nuances in its choice of words. Let us take a brief look at the history of the shuyuan during the Kaiyuan era as recorded in the *Jixian zhuji*.

In the spring of 723, Xuanzong returned to Chang'an and founded a shuyuan outside Guangshun Gate of the Daming Palace, called the Lizheng Shuyuan in line with the earlier designation. The reason that Wei Shu uses the word "founded" (*chuangzao* 創造) is probably that he considered that, while the shuyuan was a successor to the earlier Compilatory Shuyuan, it was substantially different from it.

In the winter of 724, a shuyuan was for the first time established separately outside Mingfu Gate, and it too was called the Lizheng Shuyuan. "For the first time" means that it was the first time for it to be established there as a shuyuan proper rather than a compilatory shuyuan, and the statement that it was "established separately" would have been due to the perception that it was different from the Lizheng Compilatory Shuyuan established in 722.

In 725, the Lizheng Shuyuan was renamed Jixian Shuyuan by imperial command.[38] This represented the birth of the Jixian Shuyuan.

### 5.3  *The Revival of the Mingtang and the Growth of Shuyuan*

But why was it necessary to remove the Lizheng Compilatory Shuyuan from Qianyuan Hall in 722? What springs to mind in connection with this is the fact that in 722 Qianyuan Hall was once again converted back into the Mingtang. Although it is stated in the "Liyi zhi" of the *Jiu Tangshu* that the *daxiang* rite was not performed, according to the *Tongdian* 通典 (*Comprehensive Statutes*), "in the third month of autumn in 732 the *daxiang* ceremony was performed. The Supreme Thearch of Exalted Heaven was worshipped, offerings were also made to Ruizong, and the emperors of the five directions and gods of the five offices were also worshipped."[39] The description of this ceremony is faithful to the prescriptions of the *Kaiyuan li*. The year 732 was the year in which the *Kaiyuan li* was brought to completion, its compilation having been initiated in 722. In other words, the revival of the Mingtang had anticipated the establishment of new rites and was done with the aim of performing the Mingtang rites there.

As a result of the revival of the Mingtang, the Lizheng Compilatory Shuyuan within the former Qianyuan Hall, which did not befit the Mingtang, had to be relocated. Initially, the renovations to the building itself consisted of little

---

38   *Zhiguan fenji* 15, "Jixian shuyuan," 376.
39   *Tongdian* (Comprehensive Statutes) 44, "Daxiang Mingtang," "Da Tang," 254.

more than a change of name. But a vast number of ritual implements, offerings, and so on were used in the rites performed in the Mingtang, starting with the *daxiang* rite, and it was anticipated that the Mingtang would require an extensive area for their preparation, storage, and maintenance. It was probably for this reason that the Lizheng Compilatory Shuyuan, which occupied an area appropriate for a library and had little relationship with the religious rites of the Mingtang, was removed.

Although the Lizheng Compilatory Shuyuan was thus relocated because of unavoidable circumstances, when one considers its subsequent growth, this could be said to have been a good thing for the institution. The following excerpts are from the *Jixian zhuji* descriptions of the Jixian Shuyuan established in the twin capitals of Chang'an and Luoyang.

The Jixian Shuyuan of the Daming Palace in Chang'an: It lies to the west of the main street outside Guangshun Gate. [...] The shuyuan is 80 *bu* (approx. 125 m [1 *bu* 步 = 1.56 m]) from east to west and 69 *bu* (approx. 107 m) from north to south. It has living quarters for auxiliary Hanlin academicians, a guesthouse, a study, a library, a stationery storeroom, an east corridor where academicians live, a small hall in the northeast compound, a north compound, kitchens for academicians and copyists, more than one hundred fruit trees, a long corridor, a room where Yixing lived, with an observatory, and a small garden.

The Jixian Shuyuan in Luoyang: It lies to the west of the main street outside Mingfu Gate. [...] The shuyuan is 41 *bu* (approx. 64 m) from east to west and 58 *bu* (approx. 90 m) from north to south. It has a study, a scriptorium on the east side of the east compound, rooms attached to the south and north of the study, a covered walkway in the courtyard, a west hall in the south compound, a main hall to the south of the alley by the main gate, and a west compound. The covered walkway in the courtyard is rectangular and open to the south. There are also a small meditation chamber and a corridor within the hermitage. The canal outside the main gate flows south from Chongxian 崇賢 Gate in the north and reaches here.[40]

The area of the Jixian Shuyuan in Chang'an was 13,375 m² while that of the Jixian Shuyuan in Luoyang was 5,760 m². Xuanzong's Qianyuan Hall had originally been the Tongtian Palace, the size of which almost had been the same as that of Wanxiang Shrine. The length of each side of Wanxiang Shrine had been 300 *chi* (90 m), giving it an area of 8,100 m², which means that the Jixian Shuyuan in Chang'an was about 1.65 times as large and the Jixian Shuyuan in

---

40   *Zhiguan fenji* 15, "Jixian shuyuan," 376–378.

CONFUCIAN ACADEMIES AND THE MINGTANG 59

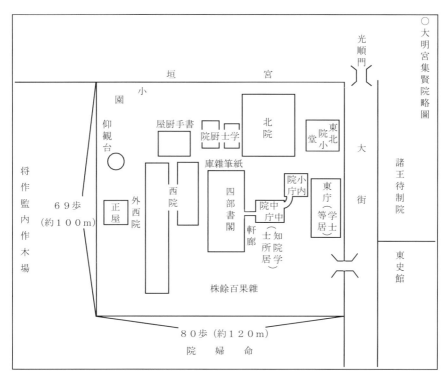

ILLUSTRATION 2.2    Floorplan of the Jixian Shuyuan in Chang'an.
SOURCE: IKEDA ON. "SEITŌ NO SHŪKEN'IN," 55

Luoyang about 0.7 times as large. But when one considers that they had been able to utilize only a small part of the palace grounds, by being moved outside the palace gates the shuyuan would no doubt have been able to enjoy a degree of space and freedom that would have been inconceivable when they had been located inside the palace grounds (ill. 2.2).[41]

Among the buildings scattered about the grounds of the two shuyuan, the studies (*shuge* 書閣 and *shutang* 書堂), library (*sibu shuge* 四部書閣), stationery storeroom (*zhibi zaku* 紙筆雜庫), and scriptorium (*xing xieshu lang* 行寫書廊) were for conducting the operations of the shuyuan; the living quarters of auxiliary Hanlin academicians (*zhongyuan zhongting* 中院中廳) and academicians (*donglang* 東廊) and the guesthouse (*tang dongxu* 堂東序) were related to everyday life; and the kitchens for academicians (*xueshi chuyuan* 學士厨院) and copyists (*shushou chuwu* 書手厨屋) provided support for the staff. These

41   Ikeda, "Seitō no Shūken'in," 55.

could all be said to have constituted the functions of the shuyuan's library and accessory facilities that had been carried over from the time when they had been located in the east corridor of Qianyuan Hall. In contrast, the observatory (*yangguantai* 仰觀臺) for observing the heavens and the meditation chamber (*chanzuo xiaotang* 禪坐小堂), a Buddhist facility, were not associated with the shuyuan's library functions and would have been built in the course of exploring new areas of development for the shuyuan. The more than one hundred fruit trees, small garden, covered walkway, and canal outside the main gate would have represented attempts to bring aspects of art and recreation into the shuyuan.

Xuanzong also built Jixian Shuyuan in the Xingqing Palace (Xingqinggong 興慶宮) and Huaqing Palace (Huaqinggong 華清宮) in Chang'an, the former in 736 and the latter in 740.[42] According to the *Jixian zhuji*, "the Jixian Shuyuan in the Xingqing Palace had more than ten trees of various kinds, a rock garden, and a bamboo grove in its grounds, and these provided cool shade," while "the Jixian Shuyuan in the Huaqing Palace had a hermitage inside the west wall for perambulating."[43] It can be inferred that these shuyuan too had elements of recreation and spiritual activity that diverged from the functions of a library.

Xuanzong's aim for the Jixian Shuyuan was not to leave them at the level of mere libraries but to develop them into comprehensive cultural spaces that encompassed science, technology, religion, art, recreation, and so on.

## 6     The Jixian Shuyuan in Chang'an and Yixing

### 6.1    *Yixing's Career and Shuyuan*

An especially striking feature of the Jixian Shuyuan in Chang'an was the presence of the monk Yixing and his observatory. Yixing was born as Zhang Sui 張遂, and as well as being an eminent monk of Esoteric Buddhism, he was also a renowned astronomer and calendrical scholar.[44] His biography is included in the "Fangji zhuan" 方伎傳 (Biographies of Magicians and Diviners) section of the *Jiu Tangshu*, which describes his upbringing, his education, and the circumstances leading to his ordination as a Buddhist monk as follows:

Yixing was gifted from an early age, read widely, and was especially well-versed in the calendar, astronomy, and the study of the five agents (*wuxing*). It

---

42   See *Yuhai* 167, "Gongshi," "Tang Jixiandian shuyuan," 3060.
43   *Zhiguan fenji* 15, "Jixian shuyuan," 377.
44   For a short biography of Yixing as well as a study of images and legends later associated with him see Jeffrey Kotyk, "Yixing and Pseudo-Yixing: A Misunderstood Astronomer-Monk," *Journal of Chinese Buddhist Studies* 31 (2018): 1–37.

is said that he borrowed the *Taixuan jing* 太玄經 by Yang Xiong 揚雄 (53 BCE–18 CE) from Yin Chong 尹崇 (?–?), a learned Daoist bibliophile, and mastered its secrets within a few days. Impressed, Yin Chong declared that Yan Yuan 顏淵 (521–490 BCE) had been reborn as Yixing, and as a result Yixing became quite famous.[45] Wu Sansi 武三思 (?–707) admired his learning and conduct and tried to cultivate a friendship with him, but Yixing rejected his approaches and went into hiding. He later took the tonsure, becoming a monk, and retired to Mount Song (Songshan 嵩山), where he became a disciple of the monk Puji 普寂 (651–739). In 717 Xuanzong summoned him to Chang'an, installing him in Guangtai Hall (Guangtaidian 光太殿; the *Leibian Chang'an zhi* mentions this wrongly as Guangdadian 光大殿), and often had candid conversations with him "about the way to bring peace to the land and pacify the people."[46]

Guangtai Hall stood to the north of Lizheng Hall. The fact that Yixing resided in Guangtai Hall is also recorded in the *Leibian Chang'an zhi* 類編長安志 (*Gazetteer of Chang'an Arranged by Subject Matter*) by Luo Tianxiang 駱天驤 (1223?–1300?) of the Yuan: "Guangda Hall: It lies to the north of Lizheng Hall. Xuanzong ordered the Chan master Yixing to compile the Dayan calendar in Guangda Hall. He later moved to Lizheng Hall."[47] Since the Compilatory Shuyuan was established in Lizheng Hall in 718, Yixing would have witnessed books being brought to Lizheng Hall as the Compilatory Shuyuan was being established.

According to the "Tianwen zhi" 天文志 (Monograph on Astronomy) of the *Jiu Tangshu*, the compilation of the Dayan calendar was initiated in 721. At the time, the occurrence of solar eclipses did not coincide with calculations based on the Linde calendar (*Linde li* 麟德曆) and it was for this reason that Yixing was ordered to produce a new calendar.[48] The new Dayan calendar produced by Yixing was presented to the emperor by Zhang Yue 張說 (667–730) in 728, the year after Yixing's death.[49]

In the *Leibian Chang'an zhi* we also read: "Cheng'en Hall (Cheng'endian 承恩殿): It stands within the grounds of Guangda Hall. It was built when Xuanzong was in the Eastern Palace. In 720 the Chan master Yixing was ordered by the emperor to compose a commentary on the *Yijing* here."[50] Yixing's commentary on the *Yijing* mentioned here probably corresponds to the *Zhouyi lun* 周易論

---

45  On this portrayal of Yixing see Kotyk, "Yixing and Pseudo-Yixing," 15.
46  See *Jiu Tangshu* 191, "Fangji zhuan," "Yixing," 5112.
47  Luo Tianxiang, *Leibian Chang'an zhi* (Gazetteer of Chang'an Arranged by Subject Matter) 2, "Donggong" (Beijing: Zhonghua Shuju, 1990), 62.
48  *Jiu Tangshu* 35, "Tianwen zhi" 1, 1293.
49  *Jiu Tangshu* 8, "Xuanzong ji" 1, 192.
50  *Leibian Chang'an zhi* 2, "Donggong," 62.

(*On the Zhouyi*) and *Dayan lun* 大衍論 (*On Great Expansion*) attributed to Yixing in the "Yiwen zhi" of the *Xin Tangshu*. The year 720 was a time when the personnel organization of the Compilatory Shuyuan of Lizheng Hall was progressing, and it is to be surmised that, chronologically speaking, Yixing first studied the "great expansion" (*dayan*) theory of the *Yijing*, set about producing the Dayan calendar in Guangtai Hall (Cheng'en Hall), and then moved to Lizheng Hall, where things had finally settled down, with a view to completing the Dayan calendar.

In order to compile the calendar, a special instrument was made at Lizheng Hall. This was an armillary sphere, called *huangdao youyi* 黃道游儀, which was an instrument for making astronomical observations that was indispensable for producing a calendar. Yixing had argued for the need for such an instrument in a memorial presented in 721 after he had been ordered to produce a new calendar, but there was no such instrument in any observatory at the time. However, Liang Lingzan 梁令瓚 (693–?), who was attached to the Military Service Section (*bingcao* 兵曹) of the Guard Command (*shuaifu* 率府), had built a wooden model of such an instrument in the Lizheng Shuyuan, and so Yixing made the following request:

> Although knowledge of the armillary sphere has existed since ancient times, there has not been any actual instrument. The ecliptic moves with the heavens, and it is difficult to observe with ordinary instruments. Therefore, people of yore thought deeply about the matter, but no one was able to make it a reality. Liang Lingzan has now created this instrument and smoothly observed the movements of the sun and moon. Because it is essential for calendrical calculations, it is my hope that one will be made of copper and iron in the Shuyuan so as to measure the positions of the stars without any errors. This proposal was then approved.[51]

The armillary sphere cast from copper and iron was completed in 725, the same year as the Lizheng Shuyuan was renamed Jixian Shuyuan. Although it was later moved to the imperial observatory, the armillary sphere was planned, developed, and produced in the shuyuan, and for a time it would no doubt have been kept there, where it would have been tested and experiments would have been conducted. Yixing also submitted a memorial proposing the construction of a water-driven celestial globe (*shuiyun huntian fushi tu* 水運渾天俯視圖), one of the greatest precision instruments in the history of astronomy. However, this was initially placed in front of Wucheng Hall (Wuchengdian

---

51   *Jiu Tangshu* 35, "Tianwen zhi" 1, 1294.

武成殿), and it was installed in the Jixian Shuyuan only after it stopped working.[52]

### 6.2   Xuanzong's Plans: The Shuyuan as a Comprehensive Cultural Space

Why was Liang Lingzan at the Lizheng Shuyuan? According to textual sources, he was serving at the Lizheng Shuyuan as an edict attendant (*daizhiguan* 待制官). Originally referring to someone who waited for imperial edicts, this was the title of a position that was institutionalized during the Tang and was found in the palace and government offices. Those appointed to this position were assigned to answer inquiries made by the emperor during his visits to the office in question, and during Xuanzong's reign it was customary for academicians of the Institute for the Advancement of Literature (Hongwenguan 弘文館) and élite officials (*qingguan* 清官) among capital officials (*jingguan* 京官) of the fifth rank and above to be appointed to this position.

There are few sources relating to Liang Lingzan, and little is known about his career. However, according to the *Xin Tangshu*, he wrote a commentary on the *Yukanding Liji yueling* 御刊定禮記月令 (*Monthly Ordinances of the "Book of Rites" Edited by Imperial Command*) together with Li Linfu 李林甫 (?–752) and others in his capacity as an edict attendant,[53] and in 721 he was promoted from court gentleman for ceremonial service (*jiangshilang* 將仕郎) and served at the shuyuan on account of his expertise in literature; thereafter he served as adjutant (*canjun* 參軍) in the Military Service Section of the Guard Command of the Right, and then retired, ending his official career as adjutant (*sima* 司馬) in the garrison of Prince Heng 恆.[54] In other words, Liang Lingzan seems to have been appointed edict attendant at the Lizheng Shuyuan on account of his scholarship and not because of his talent for producing astronomical instruments. Therefore, his making of a model of an astronomical instrument at the Lizheng Shuyuan was no more than a hobby and was a product of happenstance. It was also a coincidence that Yixing happened to learn of Liang Lingzan and his invention at the Lizheng Shuyuan. But these two coincidences were to bring about a major change in the character of shuyuan.

As a result of Yixing's becoming acquainted with Liang Lingzan, the Lizheng Shuyuan became a place for the study of astronomy and the calendar and for the development of astronomical instruments. The function of scientific and technological research and development was thus added to the functions of the Lizheng Shuyuan. Xuanzong was quite unaware of this. He had known

---

52   *Jiu Tangshu* 35, "Tianwen zhi" 1, 1294–1296.
53   *Xin Tangshu* 57, "Yiwen zhi" 1, "Lilei," 1434.
54   *Xin Tangshu* 199, "Ruxue zhuan" 2, 5682.

nothing about Liang Lingzan prior to Yixing's memorial, and although he had asked Yixing to produce a new calendar, he had no recollection of having asked him to manufacture any astronomical instruments. But for Xuanzong Yixing was a charismatic figure with whom he discussed at Guangtai Hall "the way to bring peace to the land and pacify the people"—that is, how to realize the ideal state—and whom he "revered as Heavenly Master."[55] Furthermore, the promulgation of a new calendar would be one of the greatest of honours for the emperor, and if the production of an astronomical instrument was deemed indispensable for this purpose, there would have been no reason for him to object.

We have to ask why the Lizheng Shuyuan became the site of these activities. For literary officials such as Chu Wuliang and Wei Shu, the shuyuan was a universe of books. Calendrical studies may have still fallen within its remit, but the smelting of metals and assembling of machinery in the manner of a blacksmith would no doubt have been completely unexpected. However, the shuyuan's ethos was one that attracted scholars and literati and welcomed free-ranging activities. It was for this reason that the hobby of an edict attendant was sanctioned. The aim of a universe of books is not to collect books, but to investigate the truth through books. The calendar produced by Yixing was called the Dayan calendar. *Dayan* is a term used in the *Yijing* and signifies the number corresponding to heaven and earth, or the universe.[56] For Yixing, the study of astronomy and the calendar represented nothing other than the investigation of the truth of the cosmos or the universe, and one facet of this was the production and use of astronomical instruments. Guided by Yixing, Xuanzong installed an observatory in the Lizheng Shuyuan, had an astronomical instrument constructed there, and so investigated the principles of the universe. In Xuanzong's understanding, the Lizheng Shuyuan had moved a step away from being a place for the collection and production of books to being a space for the praxis and realization of knowledge. The Jixian Shuyuan that subsequently took shape as a comprehensive cultural space encompassing science, technology, religion, art, recreation, and so on was one satisfactory outcome of these developments.

---

55  On Xuanzong's use of the title "Heavenly Master" (*tianshi* 天師), i.e. master of the Son of Heaven, to refer to Yixing, see Zanning, *Song gaoseng zhuan* 5, "Tang Zhongyue Songyangsi Yixing zhuan" (Beijing: Zhonghua Shuju, 1987), 94.

56  Wang Bi's commentary on the *Yijing*, "Xici zhuan" 1, in the *Shisanjing zhushu*, 80.

## 7 Concluding Remarks

Today the word *shuyuan*, denoting this institution of East Asia, is usually translated as "Confucian academy." The word "academy" derives from the Akademia, a school established by the ancient Greek philosopher Plato. Plato's pupil Aristotle later established his own school, the Lykeion, with the patronage of Alexander the Great. As is well known, the Ptolemaic dynasty in Egypt subsequently established the Mouseion, modelled on the Lykeion, in its capital Alexandria.

The Mouseion in Alexandria was a major research center with a large library. It formed part of the royal palace and had various facilities, like the Lykeion, which had a shrine dedicated to the Muses (Mouseion) and adorned with statues of these goddesses of literature and the arts and a bust of Aristotle, a covered walkway or portico (*stoa*), an altar, gardens, a walkway (*peripatos*), and living quarters. It was here that the very latest scholarly research on science, mathematics, natural philosophy, and philosophy was being conducted in the contemporary Mediterranean world.[57]

Xuanzong's shuyuan were born out of Qianyuan Hall and subsequently continued to form part of the imperial palace. They had a library, and diverse branches of scholarship, including the very latest developments in science and technology, in the case of Yixing, were studied there, while within their grounds there were gardens, walkways, living quarters, kitchens, and so on. Furthermore, Qianyuan Hall had originally been Empress Wu's Mingtang, which had, moreover, been a Pantheon, or temple dedicated to all deities, directly connected to heaven. Although Xuanzong turned this Mingtang into Qianyuan Hall, the passageway to heaven was not cut off, as is indicated by the meaning of the word *qianyuan*. The fact that the shuyuan originated in a shrine or temple should not be overlooked. While I do not object to the use of the word "academy" as a translation for shuyuan, it could be said that the Jixian Shuyuan created and owned by the emperor was rather a space suggestive of the Mouseion.

The shuyuan at the time of Qianyuan Hall was a library for organizing the emperor's book collection. But once the stage shifted to the Lizheng Shuyuan in the Eastern Palace in Chang'an, the shuyuan gradually began to change its character and diversify its functions. This was occasioned by its encounter with Yixing and by his selection of the Lizheng Shuyuan as the locus for his activities. And from the time when Xuanzong acknowledged Yixing's wishes and granted him permission to act freely at the Lizheng Shuyuan, the shuyuan

---

57  See Mostafa El-Abbadi, *Life and Fate of the Ancient Library of Alexandria* (Paris: Unesco/UNDP, 1990).

broke free from the constraints of a library and became a comprehensive cultural space where all manner of books accumulated and intellectuals from many disciplines and of the highest caliber thronged to engage freely in scholarship, science, technology, religion, art, recreation, and so on. It became, in other words, a paradise for intellectuals.

### References

Dai Shuhong 戴书宏, and Xiao Yongming 肖永明. "Tangdai Jixuan shuyuan yu 'Shuyuan' de ming he shi" 唐代集贤书院与'书院'的名和实 (Jixian Academy in the Tang Dynasty and the Name and True Meaning of Term 'Academy')." *Daxue jiaoyu kexue* 2016–1 (2017): 63–67.

Deng Hongbo 邓洪波. *Zhongguo shuyuan shi* 中国书院史 (History of Chinese Academies). Shanghai: Dongfang chuban zhongxin, 2004.

Du You 杜佑. *Tongdian* 通典 (Comprehensive Statutes). Beijing: Zhonghua shuju, 1984.

Fan Kezheng 樊克政. *Zhongguo shuyuan shi* 中國書院史 (History of Chinese Academies). Taipei: Wenjin chubanshe 1995.

El-Abbadi, Mostafa. *Life and Fate of the Ancient Library of Alexandria*. Paris: Unesco/UNDP, 1990.

Forte, Antonino. *Mingtang and Buddhist Utopia in the History of the Astronomical Clock: The Tower, Statue and Armillary Sphere Constructed by Empress Wu*. Rome/Paris: Instituto italiano per il Medio ed Estremo Oriente/EFEO, 1988.

Granet, Marcel. *La religion des Chinois*. Paris: Gauthier-Villars et C[ie], 1922.

Ikeda On 池田温. "Seitō no Shūken'in 盛唐之集賢院 (On Jixianyuan in the Mid-eighth Century)." *Hokkaidō daigaku bungakubu kiyō* 19 (1971): 47–98.

Kotyk, Jeffrey. "Yixing and Pseudo-Yixing. A Misunderstood Astronomer-Monk." *Journal of Chinese Buddhist Studies* 31 (2018): 1–37.

Liu Xu 劉昫. *Jiu Tangshu* 舊唐書 (Old Book of the Tang). Beijing: Zhonghua shuju, 1975.

Luo Tianxiang 駱天驤. *Leibian Chang'an zhi* 類編長安志 (Gazetteer of Chang'an Arranged by Subject Matter). Beijing: Zhonghua shuju, 1990.

Matsumoto Yasunobu 松本保宣. "Tōto Rakuyōkyū Meifukumon fukin ni tsuite 東都洛陽宮明福門付近について (On the Vicinity of the Mingfu Gate of the Palace in the Eastern Capital of Luoyang)." In *Tō ōchō no kyūjō to gozen kaigi* 唐王朝の宮城と御前会議 (Imperial Palaces and Councils in the Imperial Presence during the Tang Dynasty), 203–224. Kyoto: Kōyō shobō, 2006.

Minamizawa Yoshihiko 南澤良彦. *Chūgoku meidō shisō kenkyū* 中国明堂思想研究 (A Study of Ideas about the Mingtang in China). Tokyo: Iwanami shoten, 2018.

Ouyang Xiu 歐陽修, and Song Qi 宋祁. *Xin Tangshu* 新唐書 (New Book of the Tang). Beijing: Zhonghua shuju, 1975.

Pankenier, David W. *Astrology and Cosmology in Early China: Conforming Earth to Heaven.* Cambridge: Cambridge University Press, 2013.

Soothill, William Edward. *The Hall of Light: A Study of Early Chinese Kingship.* London: Lutterworth Press, 1951.

Sun Fengji 孫逢吉. *Zhiguan fenji* 職官分紀 (Official Positions Arranged Chronologically). Beijing: Zhonghua shuju, 1988. [Photofacsimile reprint of edition included in Wenyuan Pavilion 文淵閣 copy of SKQS].

Tao Min 陶敏 (ed.). *Jinglong wenguan ji. Jixian zhuji* 景龍文館記集賢注記 (Notes on the Jinglong wenguan. Notes on the Jixian Shuyuan). Beijing: Zhonghua shuju, 2015.

Wang Pu 王溥. *Tang huiyao* 唐會要 (Collection of Important Documents of the Tang). Beijing: Zhonghua shuju, 1991.

Wu Xiaping 吳夏平. *Tangdai zhongyang wenguan zhidu yu wenxue yanjiu* 唐代中央文館制度与文学研究 (Research on the Central Institutes and Literature in the Tang Dynasty). Jinan: Qilu shushe, 2007.

Xiao Song 蕭嵩, et al. *Da Tang Kaiyuan li* 大唐開元禮 (Rites of the Kaiyuan Era of the Great Tang). Tokyo: Kyūko shoin, 1972. [Photofacsimile reprint of edition published by Hongshi Gongshantang in Guangxu 12 (1886)].

Xu Song 徐松. *Tang liangjing chengfang kao* 唐兩京城坊考 (Research on the Two Capitals of the Tang). Beijing: Zhonghua shuju, 1985.

Yang Hongxun 楊鴻勛. "Mingtang fanlun: Mingtang de kaoguxue yanjiu 明堂泛論: 明堂的考古學研究 (An Archaeological Study of the Mingtang)." *Tōhō gakuhō* 70 (1998): 1–94.

Yuan Mei 袁枚. *Yuan Mei quanshu* 袁枚全集 (Complete Writings of Yuan Mei). Nanjing: Jiangsu guji chubanshe, 1993.

*Yijing* 易經 (Book of Changes). In the *Shisanjing zhushu* 十三經注疏 (Commentaries and Explanations to the Thirteen Classics). Beijing: Zhonghua shuju, 1980.

*Yuhai* 玉海 (Sea of Jade). Volume 27, "Guanshu" 觀書, "Tang Qianyuandian guanshu" 唐乾元殿觀書. Shanghai: Jiangsu guji chubanshe and Shanghai shudian. [Photofacsimile reprint of edition published by Zhejiang shuju, in Guangxu 9 (1883)].

Zanning 贊寧. *Song gaoseng zhuan* 宋高僧傳 (Biographies of Eminent Monks Compiled during the Song Period). Beijing: Zhonghua shuju, 1987.

Zhao Yongdong 赵永东. "Tangdai Jixiandian shuyuan kaolun 唐代集贤殿书院考论 (A Study of the Jixiandian Academy in the Tang Dynasty)." *Nankai xuebao: Zhexue shehui kexue ban* 4 (1986): 12–20.

Zhu Hanmin 朱漢民. *Zhongguo de shuyuan* 中國的書院 (Academies of China). Taipei: Taiwan shangwu yinshuguan, 1993.

CHAPTER 3

# The Nature and Educational Activities of Sungyang Academy in Kaesŏng

*Chung Soon-woo*

## 1   Introduction

The northern regions of Korea—which today are part of the territory of the Democratic People's Republic of Korea (DPRK)—belonged to the sphere of Confucian culture already in 372, when the Koguryŏ kingdom (37 BCE–668 CE) established T'aehak 太學, its first higher education institution. During the 16th century the first Confucian academies were established in Korea, including some located in the northern regions. From this time onward these academies assumed a crucial role in the dissemination of the Confucian message within local environments. During the first centuries of the Chosŏn dynasty (1392–1910), education and scholarship in northern areas were, compared to the capital area and the southern parts of the peninsula, backward and far less prosperous. A quite similar situation can be found in the later periods of the dynasty as well. There were always more Confucian academies in southern provinces than in the northern regions. However, the ancient capital cities of Pyongyang and Kaesŏng, located in the northern region, did come over the course of time to host several Confucian academies. Understanding how the Confucian academies in these two areas functioned gives us important insight into the character of the Confucian culture in the region and into the specific features of northern academies. Sungyang Academy 崧陽書院, located in the former Koryŏ (918–1392) capital of Kaesŏng, was the most powerful academy in the northern region and therefore deserves special attention. Unfortunately, research on northern academies (which are now located in DPRK) has been hampered by several obstacles. First among them is the scarcity of materials available. We have only short mentions or brief descriptions in the royal annals and other official records at our disposal, apart from scattered parts of local gazetteers and a few academies' chronicles (*sŏwŏn chi* 書院誌). Academies located in the Republic of Korea are readily accessible and retain a wide range of well-preserved documents, which illustrate their history and various aspects of their existence. In contrast, documents on the preservation, education, and management of northern academies are largely limited and it is nearly impossible to perform any field research. Basic research on northern academies was recently done by South Korean scholars within the framework of the cultural heritage agenda. However, there is still need for further in-depth studies. In the circles of South Korean academia, only a few North Korean studies of Confucian academies are known: *Chosŏn kyoyuksa* (History of Education in Korea) by Yi Man'gyu, Chŏng Sŏngch'ŏl's *Chosŏn ch'ŏrhaksa* (History of Korean Philosophy),[1] and some general works touching on the subject. This study of Sungyang Academy aims to stimulate an interest concerning Confucian academies located in North Korea, and in a broader sense to contribute to the understanding of Confucian culture heritage in the DPRK.

## 2    Chosŏn State Policy toward Confucian Academies in the Northern Provinces

Traditionally, the northern provinces, consisting of the Haesŏ 海西 (Hwanghae province), Kwandong 關東 (Kangwŏn province), Kwansŏ 關西 (P'yŏngan province) and Kwanbuk 關北 (Hamgyŏng province)[2] regions, were relatively backward in regards to education and scholarship when compared to other regions of Korea. The only exceptions were some of the southern parts of the Haesŏ region. The North-South gap is well visible in the numbers of Confucian academies in respective areas. The main reason for the North's cultural backwardness was the official court policy mostly focused on military priorities when it came to the government of northern provinces. A typical example of the official attitude toward the issue of education and scholarship in northern provinces is a statement made by King Yŏngjo 英祖 (r. 1724–1776), in a conversation with Hong Ponghan 洪鳳漢 (1713–1778), the governor of P'yŏngan province: "The court has no intention of inculcating culture to the northeastern region and educating it. As I have heard, in Kwansŏ there are a lot of local schools. These must be removed."[3] The same attitude is visible in Yŏngjo's rejection of a proposal by the governor of Hamgyŏng province, Yi Chŏngbo 李鼎輔 (1693–1766), to dispatch teachers to every district of his province and to grant each teacher sufficient support using tax revenue in the form of crop

---

1   Yi Man'gyu, *Chosŏn kyoyuksa* 1 (*History of Korean Education*) (Seoul; Ŭryu munhwasa, 1947); Chŏng Chinsŏk et al., *Chosŏn ch'ŏrhaksa* 1 (History of Korean Philosophy 1) (Pyongyang: Kwahagwŏn ch'ulp'ansa, 1960). Both were republished in South Korea during the 1980s.
2   In the current administrative division of the DPRK P'yŏngan and Hamgyŏng provinces are divided into North and South P'yŏngan, Chagang province, Ryangan province, and North and South Hamgyŏng.
3   *Yŏngjo sillok* 32/10/4#2.

yields.[4] This policy was also continued by Yŏngjo's heir, the otherwise very cultured King Chŏngjo 正祖 (r. 1776–1800). In 1781 we find records expressing his reasons for the restrictive policy toward educational activities in the northern provinces: "In the whole Ŭiju prefecture are dozens of local schools. When civil virtues and education thrive, martial virtues and military skills decline. Such are the circumstances."[5] The king discussed the topic with Border Defense Command (Pibyŏnsa 備邊司) in 1783, and from the excerpt below we can observe that he also insisted on the strict limitation of the educational policies in northwestern regions.

> Recently all the customs in Kwansŏ have changed, and its people no longer revere archery and horsemanship. They pretend to strive for Confucian teaching and fame, and schools and scholars' studies surround every village. In every county local shrines and altars are erected without due considerations, recklessly breaking the law prohibiting such activities. They drain resources, and none can suppress their enormous evil. The number of students in every province, prefecture, county, and district are determined according to law. Schools without permit became hideouts of idlers. Local magistrates are too afraid of slanders and unruly behaviour to report this matter. It is the duty of local officials to prohibit all such cases.[6]

The royal policy was motivated by an old bias that the support of education and civil virtues in the northwest region would lead to the weakening of military preparedness that was necessary to guard the state border. Another factor was the concerns of the central government about creating an independent class of educated northwestern elites, which could form alliances with foreign powers across the border in case of potential conflicts. This concern became even more serious after a string of peasants' rebellions in the region, which were often joined and led by local teachers. Academies, which were the main sources of independent Confucian education, were also subject to royal disapproval. The excessive proliferation of Confucian academies in the southern provinces led the government, during the reigns of Sukchong 肅宗 (r. 1674–1720) and Yŏngjo, to impose restrictions on the establishment of new academies, which further hindered the introduction of academies into the northern

---

4  *Sŭngjŏngwŏn ilgi*, Yŏngjo 25/4/20.
5  *Chŏngjo sillok* 5/11/2#3.
6  *Chŏngjo sillok* 7/10/29#3.

regions.[7] Dynasty annals or the *Sŏwŏn tŭngnok* 書院謄錄 (Register of Academies) often spoke about the poor state of education in the region, which was directly linked to the repressive royal policy. Despite the negative attitude of the central government, local scholars were continually striving to build academies in their region, and such efforts were often successful. An analysis of northern academies appearing in the *Sŏwŏn tŭngnok* shows some patterns and pretexts for building academies in the region.

The first models were examples of academies or shrines built in order to venerate a person or scholar born in the area. Such constructions were however often controlled, restricted, or revoked by the central government. A good example is the request of local scholars to establish an academy in honor of the famous Confucian Sŏnu Hyŏp 鮮于浹 (1588–1653), who was from Pyongyang. Sŏnu Hyŏp was famous for his knowledge of classics and rituals, as well as of the *Book of Changes*. He was held in the high esteem by the local population, which often called him the "Confucius of Kwansŏ Province." His scholarly qualities were also acknowledged by the court, which even had him invited to lecture in the National University (Sŏnggyungwan 成均館). In spite of his widely recognized status, when Pyongyang literati proposed the establishment of an academy to venerate Sŏnu Hyŏp, the government insisted that in such a case the simple shrine that had been erected by the local people was already sufficient and there was no need to further extend it into an academy.[8] From 1680 onward, the local population continued to petition the court with requests to establish the academy. The first plea was rejected on the grounds that P'yŏngan province is a military area and the shrine therefore could not be modified into an academy.[9] Finally in 1683, the court consented and approved the establishment of the academy, bestowing a royal plaque with the name Yonggok 龍谷 (Dragon Valley).[10] Yonggok Academy later became one of the most representative academies in the region.

Another way to attempt to build an academy was to establish one in order to venerate a worthy figure who was already included in the national Confucius Shrine (Munmyo 文廟) in the capital. As you can see in Table 3.1, there was among the northern academies a relatively high number of academies

---

7   King Yŏngjo in 1725 issued a strict ban on building new academies and between 1738–1741 in Hamgyŏng and P'yŏngan provinces ordered a thorough investigation of such cases. In case of violation heavy penalties like the demotion of the province governor could be imposed. See *Sŏwŏn tŭngnok* (Register of Academies), Yŏngjo 14/8/27 and 14/12/17, as well as 17/7/4.
8   See *Sŏwŏn tŭngnok*, Hyŏnjong 13/7/3.
9   See *Sŏwŏn tŭngnok*, Sukchong 6/3/8; 7; 8/10/23, etc. all successively mention this case.
10  The academy is located at the foot of the Mt. Yonggak 龍角山 (Mt. Dragon Horn).

venerating Cho Kwangjo 趙光祖 (1482–1519), Kim Koengp'il 金宏弼 (1454–1504), Yi Hwang 李滉 (1501–1570), and Yi I 李珥 (1536–1584). In these cases, the founding of the academy was justified by the symbolic power of the venerated scholars, who exemplified the will of the local scholars to plant the values of the officially sanctioned Genealogy of the Way (*daotong* 道統) of Korean Confucianism in the area. For most of the northern academies, the selection of a worthy scholar from the Munmyo pantheon was also quite specific: they predominantly selected those held in esteem by the Noron faction, which had been holding the political upper hand in central politics for decades: Yi I, Sŏng Hon 成渾 (1535–1598), Kim Changsaeng 金長生 (1548–1631), Song Siyŏl 宋時烈 (1607–1689), and so on. However, this strategy did not always prove successful. A central establishment for the Northeastern literati, Tohoe Academy 都會書院 in Hamhŭng, venerated scholars who belonged to the thoroughly orthodox line of the Korean transmission of the Way (Chŏng Mongju 鄭夢周 [1337–1392], Cho Kwangjo, Yi I, Yi Hwang and Sŏng Hon), but it never succeeded in being conferred a royal approval.

On the other hand, there were also some cases where the central government purposefully supported the building of shrines and academies as political means to create a connection with the local population. One such example could be chartering of Ichesa 夷齊祠, a shrine dedicated to legendary Chinese heroes Bo Yi 伯夷 and Shu Qi 叔齊, which was located at Suyang Mountain 首陽山[11] in Hwanghae province.[12] The foundation of Inhyŏn Academy 仁賢書院 in Pyongyang belongs to the same category as well, as it was venerating the legendary Kija/Jizi 箕子. This also holds true for the foundation of academies and shrines venerating Koryŏ scholar Chŏng Mongju, who was simultaneously venerated as a principled loyalist to the Koryŏ dynasty and as the founding figure of the Korean Learning of the Way. Chŏng Mongju was venerated not only in the aforementioned Sungyang Academy; there were also attempts to establish other academies to venerate him. In 1664 a petition was sent to the court to establish an academy for Chŏng Mongju in Pungnyŏng, Sunan county, but it was rejected on the grounds that there were already enough academies dedicated to him in other regions.[13] A petition for a joint enshrinement of famous Koryŏ minister Pak Sangch'ung 朴尙衷 (1332–1375) in Chŏng Mongju's academy was thwarted as well.[14] On the other hand, the symbolic value of

---

11   The same name as Mount Shouyang, which was the Mountain where Bo Yi and Shu Qi sought seclusion in protest to King Wu of Zhou.
12   See *Sŏwŏn tŭngnok*, Sukchong 27/3/15.
13   See *Sŏwŏn tŭngnok*, Hyŏnjong 4/4/20.
14   See *Sŏwŏn tŭngnok*, Sukchong 7/3/3.

Chŏng Mongju's figure and the court's respect for him could be well seen in the bestowing of a royal calligraphy to Sungyang Academy by King Yŏngjo.[15]

The third type of pretext for the founding of an academy was through the commemoration of the banishment destinations (exiled scholars were frequently sent to the northern provinces as punishment) or the places of assignment of important Confucians during their official career. These kinds of academies were inevitably connected with the central government's political orientation and there is a relatively large number of institutions which gained official recognition this way. The prime example is Kyŏnghyŏn Academy 景賢書院, which was established and chartered in Kanggye, the place of banishment of the famous scholar Yi Ŏnjŏk 李彥迪 (1491–1553).[16] There were several other requests to establish academies to commemorate famous Confucians who were either exiled to northern regions or served there as local officials. Such figures include Chŏng Yŏch'ang 鄭汝昌 (1450–1504), Ki Chun 奇遵 (1492–1521), Yu Hŭich'un 柳希春 (1513–1577), and so on.[17] In many cases, the establishment of these academies was led by their relatives or members of their political faction. Hangnyŏ Academy 鶴翎書院 in Sŏngch'ŏn was established to venerate the Namin scholars[18] Cho Hoik 曺好益 (1545–1609) and Chŏng Ku 鄭逑 (1543–1620).[19] The ruling Noron faction,[20] on the other hand, strived to enlarge its influence in the region by the founding of Pyŏktong Academy 碧潼書院 in Chŏngju, where Min Yujung 閔維重 (1630–1687) and his brother Min Chŏngjung 閔鼎重 (1628–1692) were enshrined.[21] These strategies are in certain contrast to the situation in southern regions, where during this period the tendency to establish academies along family lines to venerate one's own ancestor was the norm.

The last form of academies peculiar to the northern regions comprised those established to venerate famous generals or other military figures. The symbolic purpose of such shrines and academies was to stress the geopolitical identity of northern regions as part of the realm. A good example is Koguryŏ general Ŭlchi Mundŏk 乙支文德 (?–after 618?) who was venerated in Inhyŏn Academy.[22] With the support of the ancient general's cult followers, dormitories that held reading lectures were established, and in Pyongyang a Sŏgŏmjae

---

15  See *Sŏwŏn tŭngnok*, Yŏngjo 17/1/12.
16  See *Sŏwŏn tŭngnok*, Hyŏnjong 5/12/19.
17  See *Sŏwŏn tŭngnok*, Hyŏnjong 11/7/15; and Sukchong 11/2/2.
18  Namin scholars or Southerners was a political faction of Korean scholars and officials.
19  See *Sŏwŏn tŭngnok*, Hyŏnjong 13/11/28.
20  Noron or Old learning was a political faction of Korean scholars and officials.
21  See *Sŏwŏn tŭngnok*, Sukchong 26/10/23.
22  See *Sŏwŏn tŭngnok*, Hyŏnjong 12/11/20; and Sukchong 2/5/5 as well as 32/10/30.

書劍齋 (Pavilion of Letters and Sword) was built, where students from local schools and academies participated in lectures followed by military training.[23] Another instance of stressing the martial values of a region was the donation of crop fields and labour forces to Ch'unghyŏn Academy 忠賢書院 in Kŭmch'ŏn, which venerated Kang Kamch'an 姜邯贊 (948–1031), Sŏ Kyŏn 徐甄 (fl. 15th century) and Yi Wŏnik 李元翼 (1547–1634), all known for their military merits. All these cases are results of adaptive strategies of local literati to establish local academies while circumventing by the government regulations on northern provinces.[24]

### 3  Sungyang Academy: Its Worthies and Problems of the Genealogy of the Way

Sungyang Academy is a chartered academy in Kaesŏng and can be considered as one of the best documented academies preserved in DPRK. During Chosŏn times, Sungyang Academy wielded significant social and political influence. The main figure enshrined in the academy was Chŏng Mongju, the Koryŏ loyalist as well as eminent figure of Korean Confucianism. Chŏng Mongju gained respect and veneration through his adherence to Confucian principles as well as his moral integrity and in the history of Korean Confucianism is understood as a martyr to these values. It is also important to note the symbolic and intellectual meaning of the location of the academy. Kaesŏng, the former royal capital, still kept its spirit and the intellectual environment of the previous dynasty, and only slowly absorbed the then-new Chosŏn culture.

The origins of the academy can be traced to the sixth year of King Sŏnjo (1573, r. 1567–1608), when local governor Nam Ŭngun 南應雲 (1509–1587) conferred with the local literati and decided to establish Munch'ung tang 文忠堂 (Cultivated Loyalty Hall) in order to venerate the moral integrity and scholarship of Chŏng Mongju and Hwadam Sŏ Kyŏngdŏk 花潭 徐敬德 (1489–1546). In 1575 the facilities received a royal plaque naming it Sungyang,[25] and Chŏng Mongju was chosen as the main enshrined figure while Sŏ Kyŏngdŏk served as a collateral enshrined worthy. Over the course of centuries, other scholars were also enshrined in the academy. For instance, Kim Sanghŏn 金尙憲 (1570–1657), a figure favored by the Noron faction, started to be venerated in 1668. In 1681,

---

23  See *Sŏwŏn tŭngnok*, Sukchong 2/1/26.
24  See *Sŏwŏn tŭngnok*, Sukchong 15/4/16.
25  Sungyang is the old name of Kaesong. Sungyang Academy 崧陽書院 in Kaseong and the Chinese Songyang Academy 嵩陽書院 are homophonic in Korean.

TABLE 3.1  List of Academies in the northern provinces according to the *Yŏllyŏsil kisul* 燃藜室記述 (Narrative of Yŏllyŏsil) (1806)

| Academy | Place | Founding year | Enshrined person |
|---|---|---|---|
| *Hwanghae Province* | | | |
| Todong Academy 道東書院 | Songhwa | 1617 | Zhu Xi, Cho Kwangjo, Yi Hwang, Yi I |
| Ch'uibong Academy 鷲峯書院 | Anak | 1589 | Zhu Xi, Yi I |
| Paengnokt'ong Academy 白鹿洞書院 | Hwangju | 1588 | Zhu Xi, Kim Koengp'il, Yi I |
| Yulgok Academy 栗谷書院 | Ŭllyul | 1613 | Zhu Xi, Kim Koengp'il, Yi I |
| Tosan Academy 道山書院 | Kimch'ŏn | 1682 | Yi Chehyŏn, Yi Chonghak 李種學, Cho Sŏgyun 趙錫胤 |
| Tongyang Academy 東陽書院 | P'yŏngsan | 1642 | Sin Sunggyŏm 申崇謙, Yi Saek 李穡 |
| Kubong Academy 九峯書院 | P'yŏngsan | 1696 | Pak Sech'ae 朴世采 |
| Kyŏnghyŏn Academy 景賢書院 | Chaeryŏng | 1655 | Zhu Xi, Yi I |
| Yonggye Academy 龍溪書院 | Suan | 1662 | Han Kwannyŏng 漢管寧, Yi Unsong 李連松, Kang Paengnyŏng 姜栢年 |
| Pibong Academy 飛鳳書院 | Yŏnan | 1656 | Zhu Xi, Ch'oe Ch'ung 崔冲, Kim Koengp'il, Sŏng Hon, Yi I, Pak Sech'ae |
| Ponggang Academy 鳳崗書院 | Munhwa | 1656 | Zhu Xi, Cho Kwangjo, Yi Hwang, Yi I |
| Chŏnggye Academy 程溪書院 | Munhwa | 1669 | Ryu Kwan 柳寬 |
| Chŏngwŏn Academy 正院書院 | Sinch'ŏn | 1580 | Zhu Xi, Cho Kwangjo, Yi Hwang, Yi I |
| Sohyŏn Academy 紹賢書院 | Haeju | 1586 | Zhu Xi, Cho Kwangjo, Yi Hwang, Yi I, Sŏng Hon, Kim Changsaeng, Song Siyŏl |

TABLE 3.1 List of Academies in the northern provinces according to the *Yŏllyŏsil* (*cont.*)

| Academy | Place | Founding year | Enshrined person |
|---|---|---|---|
| Munhŏn Academy 文憲書院 | P'yŏksŏng | 1549 | Ch'oe Ch'ung, Ch'oe Yusŏn 崔惟善 |
| Pongyang Academy 鳳陽書院 | Changyŏn | 1695 | Pak Sech'ae |
| Munhoe Academy 文會書院 | Paech'ŏn | 1568 | Yi I, Sŏng Hon, Cho Hŏn, Pak Sech'ae (Eastern Shrine), An Tang, Sin Ŭngsi, O Ŏngnyŏng, Kim Tŏksŏng (Four local worthies, Western Shrine) |
| Munjŏng Academy 文井書院 | Pongsan | 1681 | Yi I, Kim Changsaeng, Kim Chip, Kang Sŏkki |
| Hwagok Academy 花谷書院 | Sŏhŭng | 1584 | Kim Koengp'il, Yi I, Kim Kyul 金橘 |
| Yongyam Academy 龍巖書院 | Changyŏn | 1589 | Zhu Xi, Yi I |

*P'yŏngan Province*

| Academy | Place | Founding year | Enshrined person |
|---|---|---|---|
| Ch'ŏngch'ŏn Academy 清川書院 | Anju | ?, year *kyehae* | Ŭlchi Mundŏk, Ch'oe Yundŏk 崔潤德, Yi Wŏnik, Kim Tŏksŏng |
| Haktong Academy 鶴洞書院 | Kangsŏ | 1590 | Kim Pan 金泮 |
| Ch'ŏnggye Academy 清溪書院 | Kangdong | 1672 | Yi Hwang, Cho Hoik, Kim Yuk |
| Sanghyŏn Academy 象賢書院 | Hŭich'ŏn | 1576 | Kim Koengp'il, Cho Kwangjo |
| Kŭmsan Academy 鰲山書院 | Yonggang | 1664 | Kim An'guk 金安國, Kim Chŏngguk 金正國 |
| Pongmyŏng Academy 鳳鳴書院 | Chŏngju | 1663 | Kin Sangyong 金尚容, Kim Sanghŏn 金尚憲 |
| Sinan Academy 新安書院 | Chŏngju | 1712 | Zhu Xi |
| Sŏngsan Academy 星山書院 | Sunan | 1647 | Chŏng Mongju, Han Usin 韓禹臣 |

TABLE 3.1　List of Academies in the northern provinces according to the *Yŏllyŏsil* (cont.)

| Academy | Place | Founding year | Enshrined person |
|---|---|---|---|
| Kyŏnghyŏn Academy 景賢書院 | Kanggye | 1609 | Yi Ŏnjŏk |
| Hangnyŏng Academy 鶴翎書院 | Sŏngch'ŏn | 1607 | Cho Hoik, Chŏng Ku, Pak Taedŏk |
| Ch'ungjŏng Academy 忠正書院 | Pyongyang | ?, year *chŏnghae* | Hong Ikhan 洪翼漢, Hong Myŏnggu 洪命耈 |
| Yonggok Academy 龍谷書院 | Pyongyang | 1658 | Sŏnu Hyŏp |
| Inhyŏn Academy 仁賢書院 | Pyongyang | 1576 | Kija |
| Kubong Academy 九峯書院 | Pyŏktong | 1697 | Min Chŏngjung 閔鼎重, Min Yujung 閔維重 |
| Yakpong Academy 藥峯書院 | Yŏngbyŏn | 1688 | Cho Kwangjo |
| Chuja Academy 朱子書院 | Sŏnch'ŏn | ?, year *sinsa* | Zhu Xi, Yi I |
| Kimch'ang Academy 金昌書院 | Sŏkch'ŏn | 1707 | Kim Ikho |
| Wŏlp'o Academy 月浦書院 | Kwaksan | 1707 | Yi Wŏn 李黿, Hong Kyŏngu 洪儆禹 |
| Tonam Academy 遯庵書院 | T'aech'ŏn | 1718 | Sŏnu Hyŏp, Kim Ikho 金翼虎 |

*Hamgyŏng Province*

| Munhoe Academy 文會書院 | Hamhŭng | 1575 | Yi Kyeson, Yu Kang 兪絳, Yi Hubaek 李後白, Han Chungyŏm 韓浚謙, Yi Kwangha 李光夏, Nam Kuman, Mun Tŏkkyo 文德敎 |
|---|---|---|---|
| Unjŏn Academy 雲田書院 | Hamju | 1667 | Chŏng Mongju, Cho Kwangjo, Yi Hwang, Yi I, Sŏng Hon, Song Siyŏl, Cho Hŏn, Min Chŏngjung |

TABLE 3.1   List of Academies in the northern provinces according to the *Yŏllyŏsil* (*cont.*)

| Academy | Place | Founding year | Enshrined person |
|---|---|---|---|
| Hŭnghyŏn Academy 興賢書院 | Yŏnghŭng | 1612 | Chŏng Mongju, Cho Kwangjo, Yi Kyeson |
| Myŏngch'ŏn Academy 溟川書院 | Kilju | 1670 | Cho Hŏn |
| Chongsan Academy 鍾山書院 | Chongsŏng | 1667 | Chŏng Yŏch'ang 鄭汝昌, Ki Chun, Yu Hŭich'un, Chŏng Yŏp 鄭曄, Kim Sanghŏn, Chŏng Hongik, Chŏng On 鄭蘊, Cho Sŏgyun, Yu Kye, Min Chŏngjung, Nam Kuman 南九萬 |
| Ch'unggok Academy 忠谷書院 | Onsŏng | 1606 | Ki Chun, Kim Tŏksŏng, Yu Kye 俞棨 |
| Yongjin Academy 龍津書院 | Tŏkwŏn | 1695 | Song Siyŏl |
| Munp'o Academy 文浦書院 | Munch'ŏn | ?, year *kapsul* | Song Siyŏl, Min Chŏngjung |
| Nodŏk Academy 老德書院 | Pukjŏng | 1627 | Yi Hangbok 李恒福, Kim Tŏksŏng, Chŏng Hongik 鄭弘翼, Yi Sangjin 李尙眞, O Tuin 吳斗寅, Yi Sehwa 李世華 |
| Oktong Academy 玉洞書院 | Anbyŏn | 1608 | Yi Kyeson 李繼孫, Kim Sangyong, Cho Sŏkyun |

two other Noron scholars, Kim Yuk 金堉 (1580–1658) and Cho Ik 趙翼 (1579–1655) were added to the list, and in 1784 U Hyŏnbo 禹玄寶 was co-enshrined as well. During this time, Sungyang Academy played a central role in the Kaesŏng area. The most peculiar feature of the academy is its primary figure of veneration, Chŏng Mongju, who steadfastly remained loyal to the fallen Koryŏ dynasty until the moment he was murdered by the prince Yi Pangwŏn 李芳遠 (1367–1422)—the later King T'aejong (r. 1418–1422). He was well-known for his support of Confucian teaching and the later generation of Confucians gave him the epithet "founding patriarch of the Learning of Principle (*ihak chi cho* 理學之祖)." The movement for conferring posthumous honors to him grew together with the activities of the *sarim* 士林 ("forest of scholars"), who interpreted his life as a symbol of unsubdued moral integrity during the bloody literati purges. Chŏng Mongju was introduced into Confucius Shrine[26] and became part of the official Confucian pantheon during the beginning of the 16th century, as the court's gesture of recognition of the literati sacrifices during the political purges of the 15th and early 16th centuries, and also as a signal of state support for Confucian virtues. Chŏng Mongju was later venerated in Yŏngch'ŏn Imgo Academy 臨皐書院, Ch'unghyŏn Academy 忠賢書院, and thirteen other academies, thereby becoming one of the emblematic figures of Korean Confucianism. This eventually resulted in the bestowal of a royal plaque to Sungyang Academy in 1575. At the same time, King Sŏnjo directly expressed acknowledgement for Chŏng Mongju, declaring him to be a "founding ancestor of Confucians in the Eastern Country, whose moral integrity shines more than the Sun and Moon."[27] The special status of Chŏng Mongju could be seen in the rather ambiguous statement by King Sŏnjo concerning the arrangement and inscription of Chŏng's spirit tablet in the shrine: "Would an official of Koryŏ desire to receive ranks and honors of a different dynasty? Write on the tablet not his name, but simply write Master P'oŭn." This meant that Chŏng Mongju finally gained, with some reservations, royal respect by the dynasty against which he had desperately resisted. Poet Kŏ Ch'ŏllo 車天輅 (1556–1615), from Kaesŏng, once expressed the general admiration in which the literati of his generation held Chong Mongju through his poem titled "Sungyang Academy":

> Local people erected the shrine, whose sight resembles a high hill.
> His name was written in the state history, glowing tall above.
> Writings in the Six Classics show the works of the Sage.
> Morals set for the people shall last for ten thousand years.[28]

These verses reveal the high esteem of Kaesŏng literati for Chŏng Mongju. The accentuating of his moral integrity and placing him at the beginning of the Korean version of the genealogy of the Way (*daotong*) indeed can be traced back to the reign of King Sŏnjo, when Korean literati started to reinterpret Chŏng Mongju's legacy as not only a loyal subject, but also a Confucian martyr. There were, however, also dissenting voices, especially concerning Chŏng Mongju's relation to the Learning of the Way, and whether if he was actually a Confucian thinker in the proper sense. An example is T'oegye Yi Hwang, who

---

26   Chŏng Mongju was introduced to the Confucian shrine in 1517.
27   See *P'oŭn chip*, P'oŭn sŏnsaeng nyŏnbo koi (Investigation of Discrepancies in the Chronological Biography of Master P'oŭn), 17b.
28   *Osan chip*, Sokchip 2:2b, Sungyang sŏwon.

ILLUSTRATION 3.1  Name plaque of Sungyang Academy.
SOURCE: COURTESY OF VLADIMÍR GLOMB AND MARTIN GEHLMANN, 2018

had his doubts about Chŏng Mongju's scholarly credentials: "In our Eastern Country, the founder of Learning of the Principle is said to be Chŏng Mongju, and Kim Koengp'il and Cho Kwangjo are regarded as leaders (*su* 首). But it is just so that writings of these three masters are not preserved and we cannot see the actual depth of their scholarship."[29] This shows an alternative attitude, considering Chŏng Mongju to be man of superior moral qualities possessing certain merits in spreading the Confucian message, but ultimately lacking the in-depth scholarship associated with the later generations of Korean Learning of the Way teaching. A similar phenomena can be witnessed inside the terminology of the so-called "Four Worthies of the Eastern Country" (Tongbang sahyŏn 東方四賢)," which emerged during the middle Chosŏn period. The four scholars representing the development of Korean Confucianism, Kim Koengp'il, Chŏng Yŏch'ang, Cho Kwangjo, and Yi Ŏnjŏk were later joined by Yi

---

29  T'oegye sŏnsaeng ŏnhaengnok 5. See Chung Soon-woo, "T'oegye tot'ongnonŭi yŏksachŏk ŭimi (Historical Meaning of T'oegyes Debate on the Genealogy of the Way)," *T'oegye hakpo* 111 (2002): 1–42; and Kim Yŏngdu, "Sŏnjo ch'o Munmyo chongsa nonŭiwa tot'ongnonŭi pyŏnhwa (Discussions on the introductions to the Confucius shrine during the early reign of King Sŏnjo and the transformation on the debate of the genealogy of the Way)," *Han'guk sasang sahak* 31 (2008).

Hwang and formed the Five Worthies of the Eastern Country, which together were introduced into the Confucius Shrine. Chŏng Mongju, the predecessor of this group, and Yi Hwang, the last member of the line, form the two poles of the transition from a focus on moral integrity during early Chosŏn Confucianism to a focus on scholarship and philosophical knowledge in the later times.[30]

During the later parts of the Chosŏn dynasty, Sungyang Academy was once again in the middle of controversies on reinterpretations of the history of the transmission of the Way in Korea. It was the third attempt to establish new criteria for the question of who was to be venerated as an exemplary Confucian scholar, and the controversy now revolved around the second main figure enshrined in the Sungyang Academy, Hwadam Sŏ Kyŏngdŏk. His life was surrounded by numerous legends, such as the well-known birth dream of his mother in the Confucius shrine and other stories. He was awarded the highest rank in the state examinations, but refused to take office and instead continued to live freely, retired to a life amidst nature and residing in seclusion. His philosophical thought was inspired by Song thinkers Shao Yong 邵雍 (1011–1077) and Zhang Zai 張載 (1020–1077) and focused predominantly on the role of *qi* and its transformation processes. Because of this focus, Sŏ Kyŏngdŏk was criticized as neglecting moral issues and, because of fierce critique by Yi Hwang, he was denied official acknowledgement as an exemplary scholar in Confucius Shrine or as part of the Korean Genealogy of the Way.[31]

In spite of this setback, the Kaesŏng literati never abandoned ambitions to gain state recognition for Sŏ Kyŏngdŏk and exerted considerable efforts to change his official status. Wang Sŏngsun 王性淳 (1869–1923), disciple of the great scholar Ch'anggang Kim T'aegyŏng 滄江 金澤榮 (1850–1927), developed a new concept of the genealogy of Korean Confucianism, which now put emphasis on Sŏ Kyŏngdŏk, and included him in what Kim called the Five Worthies of Chosŏn (Chosŏn ohyŏn 朝鮮五賢). In this new concept, the real beginning of in-depth philosophical studies in Korea was traced back to Sŏ Kyŏngdŏk, later followed and further developed by Yi Hwang and Yi I. The genealogy Sŏ Kyŏngdŏk–Yi Hwang–Yi I strived to emulate the classical Song *daotong* genealogy Zhou Dunyi–Shao Yong–Brothers Cheng–Zhu Xi and attempted to establish a new interpretation of the history of Korean Confucianism.[32] Kaesŏng scholars in this way reacted to the challenges their country was facing with the coming of modernity and attempted to reformulate grounds for the

---

30  On the contrary Hwadam was highly valued by Yulgok Yi I.
31  No Kwanbŏm, "Chosŏn hugi kaesŏngŭi yuhak chŏnt'ong (Confucian Traditions in Late Chosŏn Kaesong)," *Han'guk Munhwa* 66 (2014): 316.
32  See *Chunggyŏng chi* 中京誌 (Gazetteer of Middle Capital) 5, Hakkyo cho.

renewal of Confucianism based on their own, local scholarly background. In the eyes of the Kaesŏng literati, the official Confucian genealogy, which was formulated for centuries among the academia of the capital, was not relevant anymore, and the historical situation demanded its revision.

## 4 Sungyang Academy's Lectures

Since the foundation of the academy up until the 17th century, Sungyang Academy was under the strong influence of Sŏ Kyŏngdŏk's school. In 1609 Hwagok Academy 花谷書院 was founded, where Sŏ Kyŏngdŏk was enshrined as the main worthy, together with his most famous disciples Pak Sun 朴淳 (1523–1589), Min Sun 閔純 (1519–1591), Hŏ Yŏp 許曄 (1517–1580), and others. The academy thus functioned as an academic rally point for local scholars and adherents of the Sŏ Kyŏngdŏk school. Next to Hwagok Academy a separate shrine was established, where the disciples of Sŏ Kyŏngdŏk and other scholars from the Kaesŏng area related to him, like Ma Ŭigyŏng 馬羲慶 (1525–1589), Yi Kyŏngch'ang 李慶昌 (1554–1627), and others, were worshipped.[33] In this way, the literati of the Sŏ Kyŏngdŏk's circle were able to continue their studies of numerology and the *Changes* and keep the legacy of the Kaesŏng thinker alive. However, during the 18th century the Kaesŏng scholars started to drift apart under the influence of the Rak 洛 school, which was influential in the capital and was represented by scholars like Toam Yi Chae 陶菴 李縡 (1680–1746) or Miho Kim Wŏnhaeng 渼湖 金元行 (1702–1772).

Since this time Kaesŏng and Seoul cultures started to merge into one single current. Representatives of this new tendency were scholars who connected both the capital scholars of the Rak school and Kaesŏng literati, like the renowned Confucian Kim Sit'ak 金時鐸 (1713–1751), a scholar from a Kaesŏng merchant family, or Cho Yusŏn 趙有善 (1731–1809), who was well connected to Kim Wŏnhaeng's school.[34] In particular, Cho Yusŏn was widely praised for the perfection of local scholarship which had started with Chŏng Mongju's "learning of the ancient capital" (*kodo chi hak* 古都之學). Cho Yusŏn also elaborated on Sŏ Kyŏngdŏk's numerological speculations and was ultimately said to have arrived at a complete understanding of the principle of *li*.[35] The close connection between Sungyang Academy and capital literati circles started when

---

33   For a detailed discussion see No Kwanbŏm, "Chosŏn hugi kaesŏng ŭi yuhak chŏnt'ong," 325–327.
34   *Maesan chip* 42: 11a.
35   See *Chunggyŏng chi* 5, Hakkyo cho; and *Sunggyŏng chi* 4, Hakkyo cho.

Kim Wŏnhaeng consented to the plea of Kaesŏng Confucians and became the director of Sungyang Academy. Kim Wŏnhaeng accepted the position in the hope to create an ideal academy focused not on worldly success, but on pure Confucian education devoted to study of Learning of the Way. Kim Wŏnhaeng compiled various academy regulations authored by Yi Hwang and Yi I, and composed new rules for Sungyang Academy. He devoted a significant part of the rules to the critique of state examinations. According to Kim Wŏnhaeng, scholarship striving for success in the examinations degenerated into the mere useless training of literary abilities and blind memorization of classical texts. Besides compiling the rules, Kim Wŏnhaeng also composed dozens of articles concerning lectures and educational activities, which were collected in his *Kanghoe chŏlmok* 講會節目 (*Articles for Lectures*). Kim Wŏnhaeng believed that Kaesŏng literati were not inferior to their colleagues in the capital, but at the same time criticized their focus on literary composition instead of serious study of the classics. In order to enhance such studies, Kim Wŏnhaeng organized reading sessions every month where local literati read and discussed the Four Books and Six Classics.[36] The relatively free culture of the Kaesŏng literati circle thus attained a more academic hue of Learning of the Way. Unfortunately, we have no detailed records about Kim Wŏnhaeng's lectures and educational courses during his time in Sungyang Academy. Some information on the characteristics of these activities can be won from the records of Sŏksil Academy 石室書院, where Kim taught as well. According to the Rules of Sŏksil Academy and its prescribed course of lectures, meetings were to be held on the sixteenth day of every month. The course of lectures was as follows: 1) assignment of parts of a chosen text, 2) reading in front of teachers and memorizing it, 3) raising questions and discussion, 4) recitation of the Bailudong Rules and the Hakkyo mobŏm, and 5) conclusion of the lecture. For every lecture a protocol was required, which was to be sent to the director of the academy. Kim Wŏnhaengs strict and rigorous pedagogical system in Sŏksil Academy (close to the capital) was also transmitted to Kaesŏng, and gave rise to the demand for a more elaborate teaching curriculum in Sungyang Academy. Towards his students, Kim Wŏnhaeng emphasized the importance of establishing an earnest intention to study above all else. In this sense, he continued the traditional approach coined by Yi I and his successors in the Noron faction. The most integral parts of his admonitions were warnings against interest in literary composition or heterodox teachings, as well as an emphasis on the need for a solid basis for scholarship: studies of advanced curriculum, which were represented

---

36  See Cho Junho, "Sŏksil sŏwŏn ŭi kŏllipkwa Andong Kimssi (Construction of Sŏksil Academy and Andong Kim Clan)," *Han'guk kyebo yŏn'gu*, no. 5 (2014): 93–118.

by the *Great Learning* (*Taehak* 大學), must be preceded by a knowledge of the basics, represented by the *Lesser Learning* (*Sohak* 小學). Unlike Yi Chae, who pleaded for an approach of broad learning, Kim Wŏnhaeng put emphasis on the practical application of the Confucian teachings, inspired by his favourite chapter of the *Lesser Learning* focusing on respecting oneself (Chin. *jingshen*, Kor. *kyŏngsin* 敬身). He was deeply convinced that superfluous learning motivated by the state examinations was ultimately harmful and led to heresies. In this sense, he considered learning for state examinations as the lowest form of study. In his triadic classification, Kim viewed the study of classics as the highest form and the middle ground was reserved for literary studies.[37]

Kim Wŏnhaeng came of a notable background of a well-known family. Among his ancestors were Kim Sanghŏn, who earned lasting fame and spiritual influence through his resistance to the Manchu threat, and Kim Ch'anghyŏp 金昌協 (1651–1708), the most famous scholar of his times. Kim Wŏnhaeng also considered himself to be follower of the great scholar and influential politician Song Siyŏl, whom he respected for his enduring Ming loyalism and for upholding the virtues of the ideal government. Kim Wŏnhaeng expressed his deep conviction about the historical significance of Song Siyŏl in an exclamative statement that "generally, if a student wants to study the way of Confucius and Mencius, how he could avoid studying Master Zhu? If he wants to study the way of Master Zhu, how he could avoid studying Venerable Uam [Song Siyŏl]?"[38] His views on teaching were by a large degree shaped according to Song Siyŏl's ideas. Kim Wŏnhaeng continued Song Siyŏl's line via Yi Chae and through him quite naturally inherited Song's ideas on the issues in late Chosŏn Confucianism, an example of which is his view on the debate on the difference between the human and the animal nature. Kim Wŏnhaeng considered, following the theory of the Rak School, the nature of all beings to be fundamentally the same. The differences between human beings and other creatures were, in his opinion, caused only by their *qi* endowment, which in the case of humans could be easily reversed through cultivation and education. Unlike the opposing opinion, which stated that differences between beings are based not only on individual *qi* endowment, but also on the level of principle, Kim Wŏnhaeng's interpretation was universalist and had far-reaching political consequences. The seemingly scholastic debate was in reality deeply connected to the political debate on relation to Manchu China, since it led to differing answers to the diplomatic question of whether northern barbarians could, like other true human beings, be considered as a part of the civilized world, and deserved to be

---

37  *Miho sŏnsaeng ŏnhaengnok* 4.
38  *Miho sŏnsaeng ŏnhaengnok* 1.

a partner in the intellectual exchange. Universalist approaches logically acknowledged the Qing's right to its own voice and therefore enabled cultural dialogue with prosperous Manchu China. This interpretation was fitting for the worldview of cosmopolitan Kaesŏng merchants and enabled Sungyang Academy scholars to study the currents of contemporary Chinese scholarship in more depth.

## 5   Sungyang Academy New Education

As time passed, Sunyang Academy became the most influential academy in the area, as well as a symbol of Kaesŏng culture. Kings Sukchong, Yŏngjo, and Kojong 高宗 (r. 1863–1907)[39] always dispatched officials to perform sacrifices in the academy shrine during their inspection tours to the province, and Yŏngjo even donated his personal calligraphy to the academy. The continued interest of reigning monarchs naturally enhanced the political importance of the academy. Owing to its privileged position, the academy was spared in the wake of abolition of academies during the rule of Taewŏngun and continued to exist in the last days of the dynasty.[40] An interesting fact is that the academy reacted positively to new trends brought on by the modern education movement in the 20th century. According to *Chunggyŏng chi* 中京誌 (*Gazetteer of the Middle Capital*), the Poch'ang School (Poch'ang hakkyo 普昌學校) was founded by Yi Tonghwi 李東輝 (1873–1935) in the year *pyŏngo* of the Kwangmu era (1906) in Sungyang Academy's precincts. The significance of this event was marked by the gift of a name plaque written personally by an imperial prince. Disciples of the great Confucian scholar Kim T'aegyŏng started the new era of modern scholarship in the Kaesŏng area in this school. At the same time, they also formed Kaesŏng kyoyuk ch'onghoe 開城教育總會 (Kaesŏng Society for Education) in order to support new trends in the private education. Im Kyuyŏng 林圭永 (?–?), Kim T'aegyŏng's main disciple, organized a gathering to commemorate the heroic death of Chŏng Mongju, in which speeches of famous local personalities were shared to praise educational efforts of the Kaesŏng community.[41] During the Japanese colonial period, academy scholars continued lecturing and organizing joint sessions of local scholars in order to promote

---

39   In the years 1897 to 1907 Kojong ruled as Korean Emperor.
40   Other academies, besides Sungyang Academy, that were spared in the northern provinces include Ch'ungnyŏl Academy 忠烈書院, Pongyang Academy 鳳陽書院, Munhŏn Academy 文會書院, and Nodok Academy 老德書院.
41   See No Kwanbŏm, "Kŭndae ch'ogi kaesŏng munindŭl ŭi chiyŏk undong (Local Movements of Kaesong Literati in the Early Modern Period)," *Han'guk sasang sahak* 9 (2015): 258.

ILLUSTRATION 3.2   Contemporary North Korean postcard of Sungyang Academy.
SOURCE: PART OF THE POSTCARD SET KAESŎNG ŬI YUJŎK, YUMUL/ HISTORICAL REMAINS OF KAESONG

universal Confucian values in the modernized society. Sungyang Academy reacted in various ways to the coming modernity, mostly in accord with the attitudes of the Kaesŏng merchant community, which put its independent spirit into new ways of both economic and intellectual production.

## 6   Conclusion

Sungyang Academy is one of the prime examples of Confucian Academies located in northern Korean regions. Although there is still a necessity for further studies from more aspects, the case of Sungyang Academy certainly illustrates several crucial features specific to northern Korean academies. The crucial determinant for founding and operating Confucian academies in the northern provinces was the government policy of maintaining the military spirit and culture of the area and suppressing civil forms of education. The second feature of northern academies is their focus on military figures or banished scholars venerated in their shrines. This indigenous academic culture mirrors the national tradition of regarding the region as a frequent battlefield and the remote corner of the country used for exiled convicts. As seen in the case of Sungyang Academy, northern academies were not an expression of local decentralization, but were still under strong influence of the central government. Academies in the northern regions served as an instrument of central government ideology, even though they had little in common with their southern counterparts and had strong autonomous tendencies. On the other hand, during the demise of the old socioeconomic order, Sungyang Academy showed progressive tendencies toward new trends: Sungyang Academy scholars proposed a new interpretation of Korean genealogy of the Way and established a school following trends of modern education.

Up to this point, we have gained introductory understanding of the characteristics of Confucian academies in the northern Korean regions. In the future, further studies investigating not only academies, but also other aspects of the educational environment in the north including local schools, scholar studios, and other traditional educational institutions are needed. Only then can a more comprehensive picture of the educational as well as cultural situation in the north be achieved, which can help put the historical and contemporary emphasis on the southern academies into a broader perspective. This however presupposes the accessibility of relevant documents and data, which today still remains limited.

## References

Chŏng Chinsŏk, Chŏng Sŏngch'ŏl, and Kim Ch'angwŏn. *Chosŏn ch'ŏrhaksa 1* (History of Korean Philosophy), 2nd edition. Pyongyang: Kwahagwŏn ch'ulp'ansa, 1962.

Cho Junho. "Sŏksil sŏwŏn ŭi kŏllip kwa Andong Kimssi (Construction of Sŏksil Academy and the Andong Kim Clan)." *Han'guk kyebo yŏn'gu*, no. 5 (2014): 93–118.

Chung Soon-woo. "T'oegye tot'ongnon ŭi yŏksa chŏk ŭimi (Historical Meaning of T'oegye's Debate on the Genealogy of the Way)." *T'oegye hakpo* 111 (2002): 1–42.

*Chunggyŏng chi* 中京誌 (Gazetteer of Middle Capital). Kaesong 1875, Kyujanggak #奎 4462, Database of Korean Classics, <http://www.db.itkc.or.kr> (accessed: 1 May 2017).

Kim Yŏngdu. "Sŏnjo ch'o Munmyo chongsa nonŭi wa tot'ongnonŭi pyŏnhwa (Discussions on the Introductions to the Confucius Shrine during the Early Reign of King Sŏnjo and the Transformation in the Debate of the Genealogy of the Way)." *Han'guk sasang sahak* 31 (2008): 329–364.

*Maesan sŏnsaeng munjip* 梅山先生文集 (Collected Writings of Master Maesan). 1866. Kyujanggak #古3428–322. Database of Korean Classics. <http://www.db.itkc.or.kr> (accessed: 1 May 2017).

*Miho chip* 渼湖集 (Collected Writings of Miho). 1799 Kyujanggak #奎 7028. Database of Korean Classics. <http://www.db.itkc.or.kr> (accessed: 1 May 2017).

No Kwanbŏm. "Chosŏn hugi kaesŏngŭi yuhak chŏnt'ong (Confucian Traditions in late Chosŏn Kaesong)." *Han'guk Munhwa* 66 (2014): 307–359.

No Kwanbŏm. "Kŭndae ch'ogi kaesŏng munindŭl ŭi chiyŏk undong (Local Movements of Kaesong Literati in the Early Modern Period)." *Han'guk sasang sahak* 9, (2015): 253–299.

*Osan chip* 五山集 (Collected Writings of Osan). 1791. Kyujanggak #奎 2822. Database of Korean Classics. <http://www.db.itkc.or.kr> (accessed: 1 May 2017).

*P'oŭn sŏnsaeng munjip* 圃隱先生文集 (Collected Writings of Master P'oŭn). 1607. Yonsei University central library 811.96-Chŏng mongju-p'o-ra. Database of Korean Classics. <http://www.db.itkc.or.kr> (accessed: 1 May 2017).

*Sŏwŏn tŭngnok* 書院謄錄 (Register of Academies). After 1746, Kyujanggak #奎12905, Database of Korean Classics, <http://www.db.itkc.or.kr> (accessed: 1 May 2017).

*Toam sŏnsaeng chip* 陶菴先生集 (Collected Writings of Master Toam). 1803. Kyujanggak #古 3428-27. Database of Korean Classics. <http://www.db.itkc.or.kr> (accessed: 1 May 2017).

*T'oegye chŏnsŏ* 退溪全書 (Complete Writings of T'oegye). 1843. Kyuchanggak #古3428–482. Database of Korean Classics. <http://www.db.itkc.or.kr> (accessed: 1 May 2017).

Yi Man'gyu. *Chosŏn kyoyuksa I* 朝鮮教育史 (History of Korean Education). Seoul: Ŭryu munhwasa, 1947.

*Yŏllyŏsil kisul* 燃藜室記述 (Narrative of Yŏllyŏsil). Chosŏn kosŏ kanhaeng hoe 朝鮮古書刊行會. Seoul: 1912. Database of Korean Classics. <http://www.db.itkc.or.kr> (accessed: 1 May 2017).

CHAPTER 4

# Private Academies and Confucian Education in 18th-Century Vietnam in East Asian Context: The Case of Phúc Giang Academy

*Nguyễn Tuấn-Cường*

## 1    Thư Viện/Shuyuan/書院 in Vietnam: Library and Academy

The foundations of Vietnam's civil service examination system were laid during the Lí 李 dynasty (1009–1225) with the first examination being administered in 1075; examinations would continue to be held until the end of the Nguyễn 阮 dynasty (1802–1945) with the last examination being administered in 1919. Based on extant Classical Chinese records, we know that 184 examinations were administered throughout Vietnamese history, resulting in the granting of the Metropolitan Laureate (*tiến sĩ, jinshi* 進士) degree to 1,894 people.[1] On average, every five years (4.5 to be exact) an examination for the Metropolitan Laureate degree was administered with each examination resulting in about ten (10.3) new graduates. Before its replacement with a European-based education system, the civil service examination was the means by which people were selected to fill intellectual and political occupations.[2]

The present-day Vietnamese language still contains vocabulary which has roots in the civil service examination. For example, the academic term "bachelor" is translated into Chinese, Japanese, and Korean as 學士 (*xueshi, gakushi, haksa*), whereas Vietnamese renders it as *cử nhân* 舉人, a Sinitic title carried over from the civil service examination. Similarly, "Ph.D." is translated into Chinese, Japanese, and Korean as 博士 (*boshi, hakase, paksa*) whereas Vietnamese uses *tiến sĩ* 進士 for Ph.D. and *bác sĩ* 博士 primarily for medical doctors. The term for "library" also follows a similar pattern: while other East Asian countries have a united term 圖書館 (*tushuguan, toshokan, tosŏgwan*), Vietnam uses a different Sinitic term *thư viện* 書院.

---

[1] Ngô Đức Thọ et al., *Các nhà khoa bảng Việt Nam 1075–1919* (Metropolitan Laureates in Vietnam 1075–1919) (Hà Nội: Nhà xuất bản Văn học, 2006).

[2] Phan Trọng Báu, *Nền giáo dục Pháp – Việt* (The French-Vietnamese Education System) (Hà Nội: Nhà xuất bản Khoa học xã hội, 2015).

TABLE 4.1   Relevant terms in East Asia

| English | Chinese | Japanese | Korean | Vietnamese |
| --- | --- | --- | --- | --- |
| Doctor (Ph.D.) | 博士 bóshì | 博士 hakase はかせ | 博士 paksa 박사 | 進士 tiến sĩ |
| Bachelor | 學士 xuéshì | 學士 gakushi がくし | 學士 haksa 학사 | 舉人 cử nhân |
| Library | 圖書館 túshūguǎn | 圖書館 toshokan としょかん | 圖書館 tosŏgwan 도서관 | 書院 thư viện |

Historically speaking, the usage of the term Thư viện/shuyuan in Vietnam was primarily limited to meaning library, while its other meaning—academy—was used only rarely.

Thư viện 書院, as in library, refers to a location where books and other texts are stored *sans* any organized educational function/program. The use of the term "書院" can be traced to the Zhenyuan 貞元 (785–805) era of the Tang dynasty, during which it began to appear in the names of various state founded centers such as the Lizheng shuyuan 麗正書院 and the Jixiandian shuyuan 集賢殿書院. The purpose of these two centers was to collect, edit, compare, amend, and annotate various books, to advise the court, and to function as a royal library in which the emperor could read and study.[3] This was the original meaning of *shuyuan*, which has gradually disappeared in China, but which continues to be used in Vietnam. As evidenced by extant records extending back 1,000 years, Vietnam has a long history of storing books. In pre-1945 Vietnam, there were many terms to describe what could be described as a library: 1) Tạng 藏, e.g. Đại Hưng tạng 大興藏 (1023), Bát Giác kinh tạng 八覺經藏 (1021), Trung Hưng tạng 中興藏 (1034). These were all libraries which stored Buddhist and Confucian texts; 2) Thư các 書閣, e.g. Bí thư các 秘書閣 (1087); 3) Thư lâu 書樓, e.g. Tàng thư lâu 藏書樓 (1825); 4) Thư viện 書院 (as library), e.g.

---

3   Wang Bingzhao, *Zhongguo gudai shuyuan* (Ancient Academies of China) (Beijing: Zhongguo guoji guangbo chubanshe, 2009), 2. See Minamizawa Yoshihiko and Chien Iching "An Enquiry into the Origins of Confucian Academies and the Mingtang in the Tang Period," in this volume, 45–67.

Tụ Khuê thư viện 聚奎書院 (1852),[4] Tân thư viện 新書院 (1909–1923),[5] Bảo Đại thư viện 保大書院 (1923–1947), Long Cương thư viện 龍崗書院 (private), etc.[6] The only exception is that 圖書館 has never been used in Vietnam to describe a "library" as it is commonly used throughout East Asia. This is possibly because the tradition of "shuyuan" as an academy was never prominent enough in Vietnam to conflict with the usage of *thư viện* 書院 as in library. Hence, 書院 was and continues to be mainly used in Vietnamese with the meaning of library.

*Thư viện/shuyuan* is more commonly used throughout East Asia to describe an academy, that is, a place to organize educational and research activities. These centers also functioned as places to store books and make woodblock printings, and served as areas for worship. During the disordered transitional period between the Tang dynasty and the Five Dynasties period (907–960), many scholars fled to the mountains to study, eventually establishing centers to gather books and teach.[7] These centers were often called *shuyuan*; hence Confucian academies began to take on the meaning of a place for organized education. Although such academies began to appear during the Tang dynasty, it wasn't until the Song dynasty that they truly flourished. During the Southern Song dynasty, Neo-Confucian scholars established academies across China. The academy tradition continued all the way to the Qing dynasty, at which point it had lasted over thousand years, spread all over China, and extended its influence over neighboring East Asian countries.[8] Academies played an important role throughout East Asia as centers of Confucian education, printing and

---

4   For the catalog of Tụ Khuê thư viện see *Tụ Khuê thư viện tổng mục* 聚奎書院總目, Institute of Sino-Nom Studies Catalog number: A.110/1-3, comprising approximately 4,000 titles with almost 9,000 individual works from Vietnam, China, and Europe.

5   For the catalog of Tân thư viện see *Tân thư viện thủ sách* 新書院守冊, catalog number A. 2645/1-3, 2,640 titles are recorded with 51,371 books.

6   For the history of Vietnamese libraries see Dương Bích Hồng, *Lịch sử sự nghiệp thư viện Việt Nam trong tiến trình văn hoá dân tộc* (A History of the Field of Library in Vietnam during Its National Cultural Progress) (Hà Nội: Vụ Thư viện – Bộ văn hoá Thông tin, 1999), 45–71.

7   Wang Bingzhao, *Zhongguo gudai shuyuan*, 2.

8   See "Shuyuan 书院" in Ji Xiaofeng (ed.), *Zhongguo shuyuan cidian* (Dictionary of Chinese Academies) (Hangzhou: Zhejiang jiaoyu chubanshe, 1996), 686–687; Margaret Mehl, *Private Academies of Chinese Learning in Meiji Japan: The Decline and Transformation of the Kangaku Juku* (Copenhagen: NIAS Press, 2003); Namba Yukio, "Riben shuyuan de yanjiu xianzhuang yu keti (Situation and Issues of Japanese Academy Research)," *Hunan daxue xuebao* 3 (2007): 19–22; Milan Hejtmanek, "The Elusive Path to Sagehood: Origins of the Confucian Academy System in Korea Chosŏn Korea," *Seoul Journal of Korean Studies* 26, no. 2 (December 2013): 233–268; Chung Man-jo, "Hanguo shuyuan yanjiu dongxiang zongshu (Summary of Trends of Korean Academy Research)," *Hunan daxue xuebao* 6 (2005): 29–38.

storing books, academic research, syncretism of the Three Teachings (Confucianism, Buddhism, Daoism), architecture, archiving, and cultural exchange between countries.[9] They also contributed to the formation of a public sphere and civil society in the East even from the early modern period.[10]

## 2  No Academies in Vietnam?

The Japanese scholar Azuma Juji has sketched a table of various schools/academies in East Asia in the early modern period (see table 4.2; Sinographs added by Nguyễn Tuấn Cường):[11]

According to Azuma, Vietnam had only the model of private schools and not private academies, a model which was present in all other East Asian countries. This premise is not completely accurate. Although Vietnam doesn't share the same rich academy tradition with China, Japan, and Korea, in Vietnamese history there have been at least three such centers with the characters *thư viện* 書院 included in their names (this does not include other centers with the same function that operated under different names).

The earliest usage of the term *thư viện* meaning academy in Vietnamese history is a record of the founding Lạn Kha Academy 爛柯書院 (literally "the Academy of the Decayed Axe") in Lạn Kha Mountain (located in present day Bắc Ninh province in the North) during the Trần 陳 dynasty (1226–1400). In the *Annan zhiyuan* 安南志原 (*The Original Accounts of Annan*) by Ming-dynasty scholar Gao Xiongzheng 高熊徵 (1636–1706), we find this note about Lạn Kha Mountain:

> The Trần dynasty established an academy (*shuyuan* 書院) here, promoted the well-known Confucian scholar Trần Tôn 陳蓀 to be the Head of the Mountain (山長),[12] and to teach *sinh đồ* 生徒.[13] The Trần King often

---

9   Yang Busheng and Peng Dingguo, *Zhongguo shuyuan yu chuantong wenhua* (Chinese Academies and Traditional Culture) (Changsha: Hunan Jiaoyu Chubanshe, 1992).
10  Koo Jeong-Woo, "The Origins of the Public Sphere and Civil Society: Private Academies and Petitions in Korea, 1506–1800," *Social Science History* 3 (2007): 381–409.
11  Azuma Juji, "The Private Academies of East Asia: Research Perspectives and Overview," *A Selection of Essays on Oriental Studies of ICIS* (2011), 12.
12  This expression in China and Korea is a common appellation for the director of the academy.
13  *Sinh đồ* 生徒 is equivalent to *tú tài/xiucai* 秀才 and refers to students who had already passed three out of four local examinations.

TABLE 4.2    Schools in early modern East Asia

|  | China | Korea | Vietnam | Japan |
|---|---|---|---|---|
| *Civil-service examination* | Yes | Yes | Yes | No |
| *Government schools* | School for Sons of the State 國子監; prefecture, department, and district schools 府縣學校 | Sŏnggyun'gwan 成均館, local schools 鄉校 | School for Sons of the State 國子監; province, prefecture, and district schools 府縣學校 | Shōheizaka School 昌平坂学問所, domain schools 藩校, local schools 鄉校 |
| *Private schools 1* | Private academies 書院 | Private academies 書院 | Private schools 私塾 | Private schools 私塾 and private academies 書院 |
| *Private schools 2 (for commoners)* | Elementary schools 小學, free private schools 義学, family schools 家塾 | Writing schools 書堂 | Private schools 私塾 | Local schools 鄉校, schools attached to temples 寺子屋 (writing schools 手習所) |

SOURCE: AZUMA JUJI, "THE PRIVATE ACADEMIES OF EAST ASIA," 11

visited for sightseeing, and gave a banquet on the festival of the Double Ninth [9th day of 9th lunar month].[14]

The official historical annals of the Nguyễn dynasty in Vietnam, *Khâm định Việt sử thông giám cương mục* 欽定越史通鑑綱目 (*The Imperially Ordered Annotated Text Completely Reflecting the History of Việt*) copied this information as follows:

> According to the *Annan zhi* 安南志 (*An Account of Annan*) of Ming-dynasty scholar Gao Xiongzheng, the Trần dynasty established Lạn Kha Academy, and promoted the well-known Confucian scholar Trần Tôn to

---

14   Gao Xiongzheng and Anonymous, *An Nam chí nguyên* (The Original Records of Annan), translated, annotated, and introduced by Hoa Bằng, ed. Lộc Nguyễn (Hà Nội: Nhà xuất bản Đại học Sư phạm Hà Nội, 2017), 268. Translated text in Vietnamese: "Họ Trần từng lập thư viện Lạn Kha ở đây, dùng danh nho Trần Tôn làm sơn trưởng, dạy dỗ các sinh đồ. Vua Trần thỉnh thoảng cũng đến vãn cảnh, mở yến ăn tết Trùng dương."

be the Administrator (院長) of the academy and to teach *sinh đồ*. The King often visited the academy.[15]

Aside from these two short excerpts, there are currently no other records of Lạn Kha Academy. However, this is clearly a model of an academy specializing in the education of *sinh đồ* 生徒, complete with a renowned scholar functioning as Head of the Mountain (山長) or Administrator (院長).

The second example of an academy is that of Sùng Chính Academy 崇正書院 during the Tây Sơn 西山 dynasty (1778–1802), founded by Emperor Quang Trung 光中 (r. 1788–1792) in Nghệ An province. Although Phú Xuân was the capital, Quang Trung founded this academy in Nghệ An in honor of Nguyễn Thiếp 阮浹 (1723–1804), a renowned scholar who had rusticated in Nghệ An. The emperor founded the Sùng Chính Academy in Nguyễn Thiếp's place of retirement and invited him to become the head of the academy. Quang Trung also approved plans to relocate the capital of his dynasty to Nghệ An; however, he passed away before this could be realized. The Sùng Chính Academy reprinted, translated, woodblock-printed, and distributed a number of Confucian classics. Notably, many of these classics were translated and printed in Nôm script[16] in order to facilitate the use of Vietnamese in education. Unfortunately, the Tây Sơn dynasty was short lived and the Sùng Chính Academy had only little over a decade to function as a central academy.[17]

If Lạn Kha and Sùng Chính were representative of academies with a central status and education sponsored on a national scale, Phúc Giang Academy 福江書院 (Phúc Giang thư viện) was representative of a private academy in Nghệ Tĩnh (present day Nghệ An and Hà Tĩnh provinces in central Vietnam)—a relatively remote area during the 18th century. Despite this, Phúc Giang Academy produced enormous results in the formation of students and the compilation, editing, printing, and distribution of Confucian teaching materials. The success of Phúc Giang Academy has not been matched by any other private academy in Vietnamese history. The investigation of Phúc Giang Academy's

---

15 Historiography Institute of the Nguyễn Dynasty, *Khâm định Việt sử thông giám cương mục* (Imperially Ordered Annotated Text Completely Reflecting the History of Việt), Vol. 1 (Hà Nội: Nhà xuất bản Giáo dục, 2007), 648. Translated text in Vietnamese: "Theo sách *An Nam chí* của Cao Hùng Trưng đời Minh, nhà Trần có dựng ra Lạn Kha thư viện, dùng danh nho Trần Tôn làm viện trưởng, dạy các sinh đồ. Nhà vua thường đến chơi."
16 Nôm script (*chữ Nôm*, 喃字) is a kind of "square script" to record Vietnamese language, used in Vietnam from around the 10th to the early 20th centuries.
17 As for Sùng Chính thư viện, see Hoàng Xuân Hãn, *La Sơn phu tử* (Master La Sơn), in *La Sơn Yên Hồ Hoàng Xuân Hãn*, Vol. 2 (Hà Nội: Nhà xuất bản Giáo dục, 1998), 1067–1073. In the decrees issued by Quang Trung to Nguyễn Thiếp both Sùng Chính thư viện 崇正書院 and Sùng Chính viện 崇正院 are used to refer to this academy.

sudden success as a model of a private academy has pushed the author of this paper to examine the foundation and activities of this Confucian academy in 18th-century central Vietnam in the context of the movement of East Asian academies prior to the 20th century.

## 3  Civil Service Examinations and Education in 18th-Century Vietnam

After gaining independence from China at the beginning of the 10th century, the next 500 years of Vietnamese leading up to the 15th century witnessed the rise and fall of the Đinh 丁 (968–980), Former Lê 前黎 (980–1009), Lí 李 (1009–1225), and Trần 陳 (1226–1400) dynasties. During this time, Buddhism was the primary philosophical system in the country, whereas Confucianism did not yet play a key role in government and society. Despite this, the civil service examination developed early on a national scale. From the beginnings of the examination in 1075 through the 15th century the contents of the exam included portions on Buddhism and Daoism in addition to Confucianism. In 1070, under the rule of Lí Thánh Tông 李聖宗 (r. 1054–1072), the Temple of Confucius (Văn Miếu 文廟) was built in the capital Thăng Long, in order to venerate Confucius, along with other famous Confucians, and to function as an academy for the royal princes. Just six years later, in 1076, Lí Nhân Tông 李仁宗 (r. 1072–1128) ordered the construction of the Directorate of Education (Quốc Tử Giám 國子監, literally "School for Sons of State") next to Temple of Confucius—this could be regarded as the first "national university" of Vietnam. At first, the Directorate of Education was reserved for members of the royal family and the sons of top ranking officials—however, in 1253 King Trần Thái Tông 陳太宗 (r. 1225–1258) allowed for scholars of exceptional talent and potential to enroll, even if they came from commoner families. At the same time, the school system—both public and private—remained primitive. Education on a local basis was most often organized by local Confucian scholars and Buddhist monks, who offered classes in their villages.[18]

It was not until the foundation of the Lê dynasty in 1428 that Confucianism replaced Buddhism as the driving force behind government and culture. Confucian education was strongly promoted and schools, both private and public, were founded in greater numbers than before. Vietnam's Lê dynasty had two periods: the Initial Lê dynasty 黎初 (Lê Sơ, 1428–1527) and the Restored Lê

---

18  Nguyễn Đăng Tiến et al., *Lịch sử giáo dục Việt Nam trước Cách mạng Tháng Tám 1945* (A History of Vietnamese Education before the August Revolution in 1945) (Hà Nội: Nhà xuất bản Giáo dục, 1996), 12–45.

dynasty 中興黎朝 (Lê Trung Hưng, 1533–1789); the interruption was due to an usurpation of the throne by the short-lived Mạc 莫 dynasty (1527–1592). The final years of the Lê dynasty were marked by the Trịnh-Nguyễn wars, which lasted from 1627 through the end of the 18th century, with the Trịnh Lords (Chúa Trịnh 鄭主), along with the puppet Lê emperors in the north and the Nguyễn Lords (Chúa Nguyễn 阮主) in the south of the Gianh River (present day Quảng Bình province in central Vietnam), which served as a border. This long civil war caused a detrimental effect on the development of government, economy, culture, and education in Vietnam—most especially in the central region including the provinces of Nghệ An, Hà Tĩnh, and Quảng Bình, which were often the location of battles and extremely unstable, causing a poor situation for education.

During the Trịnh-Nguyễn wars of the 17th and 18th centuries, the Vietnamese school system could be divided between public and private schools. The largest public school was the Directorate of Education in the capital Thăng Long, at which the sons of elites were educated alongside exceptionally talented commoners. The formation and preparation took three years and students were held to rigorous standards. Also located in the capital were other schools reserved for sons of official families such as Chiêu Văn quán 昭文館 (Institute for the Glorification of Literature), Sùng Văn quán 崇文館 (Institute for the Veneration of Literature), Tú Lâm cục 秀林局 (Department of the Forest of Cultivated Talents), Trung thư giám 中書監 (Office of the Secretariat Supervisor), and Ngự tiền cận thị cục 御前近侍局 (Palace Attendants Service). In the provinces (then called Phủ 府 and Lộ 路), schools were opened following the model of the Directorate of Education, to teach Confucian classics, writing skills, and literary commentary. The private school system followed a model of moderate and small size and was organized around villages by local scholars. The instructors were often retired officials; those who had been a local laureate (*cử nhân* 舉人) or a metropolitan laureate (*tiến sĩ* 進士), but had not yet received an assignment; or those who had failed the local examination and had to wait until the next examination, often three years later. Whereas the instructors at public schools received a salary from the court, those at private schools had to collect tuition fees from their students. Some villages set aside a plot of land called *học điền* 學田 (literally "study field") to be communally tended in order to pay for hiring educators for the local private school. The actual curriculum of private and public schools was essentially identical—no distinction was made between students of private and public schools when it came time to take the civil service examination.[19]

---

19   Đinh Khắc Thuân, *Giáo dục và khoa cử Nho học thời Lê ở Việt Nam qua tài liệu Hán Nôm* (Confucian Education and Examination during the Lê Dynasty in Vietnam through Sino-

All famous schools from this period (17th–18th centuries) were located in northern Vietnam—in particular, they were centered around Thăng Long (present day Hanoi). Each school was connected with a famous scholar. For example, Nguyễn Đình Trụ's (1627–1703) school in the Thanh Trì district helped form over one thousand scholars, 70 of whom graduated as metropolitan laureates. Vũ Thạnh's (1664–?) school in Hào Nam village was similarly crowded and graduated just as many metropolitan laureates. These two schools were the most famous in Thăng Long. Aside from these two, other famous schools included the school of the Nguyễn clan from Phú Thị village (late 18th century), the school of Nguyễn Công Thịnh (1757–1824) in Quan Hoa village, and that of Đỗ Văn Luân (?–?) in Thượng Yên Quyết village.[20] Seventeenth-century central Vietnam did not have a developed education system—hence, students had to travel north to find teachers and schools. This was representative of the divide between the capital region (here meaning northern Vietnam) as opposed to the outer region (central and southern Vietnam) in terms of the developing of the Vietnamese education system during the 18th century.

Examined from a purely geographical perspective, Vietnam belongs entirely to the region of Southeast Asia. However, when other major elements—such as government and culture—are taken into consideration alongside religion (Confucianism) and script (Sinographs), it becomes clear that Vietnam is an East Asian country—a member of the Sinosphere. Keith Taylor expresses a moderate viewpoint when he observes that if Vietnam were cut in half at the Hải Vân mountain pass, the northern half of Vietnam would tend towards East Asia whereas the southern half would tend towards Southeast Asia.[21] The reason behind this geographical divide are the multiple "Southern Expansions" in Vietnamese history. The current boundaries of unified present-day Vietnam are the result of multiple dynasties ceaselessly working to expand their territory southward.

It is evident that the Confucian education system in northern Vietnam came into existence and was solidified earlier than in the central and southern parts of the country. This divide was apparent even in the civil service examination system. During the Trần dynasty examinations of 1256 and 1266, there was a unique instance in Vietnamese history in which one examination awarded the highest top scholar honors to two individuals—one called the Kinh trạng nguyên 京狀元 (literally, first-ranked Laureate of the capital region), the other called the Trại trạng nguyên 寨狀元 (literally, first-ranked Laureate of the

---

Nom Materials) (Hà Nội: Nhà xuất bản Khoa học xã hội, 2009), 49–53.

20  Bùi Xuân Đính, *Giáo dục và khoa cử Nho học Thăng Long – Hà Nội* (Confucian Education and Examination in Thăng Long – Hà Nội) (Hà Nội: Nhà xuất bản Hà Nội, 2010), 84–91.

21  Keith W. Taylor, "Surface Orientations in Vietnam: Beyond Histories of Nation and Region," *The Journal of Asian Studies* 4 (1998): 972–973.

outer region). This division was also repeated in the conferring of the Thái học sinh 太學生[22] (metropolitan laureates) degree. The *Đại Việt sử kí toàn thư* 大越史記全書 (*The Complete Annals of the Great Việt*, 1697) mentions these two examinations as follow:

> In spring, the second month, an examination was opened. Trần Quốc Lặc was awarded first-ranked laureate of the capital region, Trương Xán was awarded first-ranked Laureate of the outer region. Chu Hinh was awarded second-ranked laureate (榜眼), Trần Uyên was awarded third-ranked laureate (探花郎). There were 43 successful metropolitan laureates (42 from the capital region and 1 from the outer) with different positions due to their examination results.[23]
>
> The third month, an examination was opened. Trần Cố was awarded First-ranked laureate of the capital region; Bạch Liêu was awarded first-ranked Laureate of the outer region; the second-ranked laureate (name unclear); Hạ Nghi was awarded third-ranked laureate. There were 47 successful metropolitan laureates with different positions due to their examination results.[24]

The early 19th-century Vietnamese scholar Phan Huy Chú 潘輝注 (1782–1840) wrote in his famous work *Lịch triều hiến chương loại chí* 歷朝憲章類誌 (*Categorized Records on Administrative Systems of Successive Dynasties*):

> In the 6th year of Nguyên Phong [1256], there was an examination in the second month. One first-ranked Laureate of the capital region (Kinh trạng nguyên) and one first-ranked Laureate of the outer region (Trại trạng nguyên) were awarded. Previously there was no distinction made between Kinh 京 (the capital or the center) and Trại 寨 (the outer)—only one first-ranked Laureate was awarded. Thanh Hoá and Nghệ An were then classified as Trại, hence the distinction made between Kinh and Trại.[25]

---

22  Thái học sinh 太學生 is the equivalent of the metropolitan laureate (*tiến sĩ* 進士) degree and was used in Vietnam from 1232 (Trần dynasty) to 1400 (Hồ dynasty).

23  Hoàng Văn Lâu (trans.), *Đại Việt sử kí toàn thư* (Complete Annals of The Great Việt), Vol. 2 (Hà Nội: NXB Khoa học xã hội, 1993), 26.

24  Hoàng Văn Lâu (trans.), *Đại Việt sử kí toàn thư*, 36.

25  Phan Huy Chú, *Lịch triều hiến chương loại chí* (Categorized Records on Administrative Systems of Successive Dynasties 歷朝憲章類誌), Vol. 2, translated and annotated by The Translation Group of the Institute of History (Hà Nội: Nhà xuất bản Giáo dục, 2007), 10.

Citing the 15th-century Lê dynasty historian Ngô Sĩ Liên 吳士連 (the editor in chief of the *Đại Việt sử kí toàn thư*), Phan Huy Chú explains further:

> Trần dynasty examinations differentiated between Kinh and Trại just as the Qing differentiated between Manchu and Han. However, it isn't that this was a regional prejudice in selecting talented individuals. The Trần dynasty took into account that Hoan Châu and Ái Châu were remote regions without a pervasive education system and with less talented scholars compared to metropolitan regions—hence, at the examination, the most talented individual from those remote regions was awarded Trại trạng nguyên, an honor equal to that of the Kinh trạng nguyên, as an encouragement.[26]

The differentiation between Kinh (in northern Vietnam) and Trại (from Thanh Hoá southward) reveals that until the end of the 13th century, after 200 years of civil service examinations in Vietnam, the center of education remained in the north, revolving around Thăng Long, while the remainder of the country from Thanh Hoá, Nghệ An, and Hà Tĩnh southward, produced few graduates. In 1256, 45 metropolitan laureates were awarded, but only one was from the Trại regions, because regions distant from Thăng Long lacked a solid system of Confucian education and students lacked both schools and competent teachers. Prospective students were forced to travel to neighboring provinces to pursue their studies. The defective state of education in the central and southern regions did not end in the 13th century, but rather continued well into the 18th century. During the Restored Lê Dynasty (1533–1789) revolts and unrest pervaded the countryside, especially during the Trịnh-Nguyễn wars, which lasted almost 200 years (from the 17th century to the end of the 18th century). The central regions in particular were ravaged by war, causing education, economy, and culture to remain undeveloped.

During the 18th century, Phúc Giang Academy was founded in Hà Tĩnh, a province in the central region, in these difficult circumstances. In spite of tremendous difficulties, the success of Phúc Giang Academy became legendary in monarchical Vietnam. The foundation and activities of Phúc Giang Academy are connected with Nguyễn Huy Oánh, a famous cultural figure of Vietnam.

---

26   Phan Huy Chú, *Lịch triều hiến chương loại chí*, 10.

## 4   Nguyễn Huy Oánh: Official, Scholar, and Diplomat

Nguyễn Huy Oánh 阮輝瑩 (1713–1789) was born in Trường Lưu village, Lai Thạch commune, La Sơn district, Nghệ An prefecture—trấn Nghệ An (present day Trường Lộc commune, Can Lộc district, Hà Tĩnh province). His clan records, written in classical Chinese, span the 15th century through the 19th century, a total of twelve generations, among which were 16 individuals with extant works (along with 18 other individuals with non-extant works) numbering in the hundreds.[27] Such a family is rare in Vietnam. This shows that Nguyễn Huy Oánh was born into a family famous for its history of scholarship, official status, and literary output.

Nguyễn Huy Oánh met with good fortune throughout his examinations and official career. He graduated at the top in both the local examination of 1732 in Nghệ An and the metropolitan examination of 1748 in Thăng Long. The examination of the latter year awarded 13 metropolitan laureates, without the first-ranked (*trạng nguyên* 狀元) and the second-ranked (*bảng nhãn* 榜眼) laureates, hence although graduating at the top, Nguyễn Huy Oánh was graduated as the third-ranked (*thám hoa* 探花).[28] Throughout his official career, he was constantly promoted and never once demoted. He was assigned to many different government posts belonging to various ministries. His highest position was Minister of Ministry of Works (Công bộ Thượng thư 工部尚書), equivalent to a minister today. However, most significantly, he had experience with multiple assignments related to education and scholarship: Hanlin Academy Edict Attendant (Hàn lâm viện đãi chế 翰林院待製, 1748), Proofreader of the East Hall (Đông Các hiệu thư 東閣校書, 1753), Proctor (Giám khảo 監考) of the 1757 examinations, Grand Academician of the East Hall (Đông Các đại học sĩ 東閣大學士, 1757), and Chancellor of the Directorate of Education (Tế tửu Quốc tử giám 國子監祭酒, 1759).[29]

---

27  Trần Hải Yến, "Nghiên cứu văn hoá văn học nhìn từ di sản một tộc họ (Cultural and Literary Studies: A Look from the Heritage of a Family)," in *Nguyễn Huy Oánh và dòng văn Trường Lưu trong môi trường văn hoá Hà Tĩnh* (Nguyễn Huy Oánh and Trường Lưu Literary School in the Cultural Environment of Hà Tĩnh) (Hà Nội: Nhà xuất bản Lao Động 2014).

28  "Bi kí bia Tiến sĩ khoa Mậu Thìn niên hiệu Cảnh Hưng 9 (1748)" [景興九年戊辰科進士題名記], in Ngô Đức Thọ, *Văn bia Tiến sĩ Văn miếu Quốc tử giám Thăng Long* (Metropolitan Laureate Inscriptions in the Temple of Confucius and Directorate of Education in Thăng Long) (Hà Nội: Nhà xuất bản Hà Nội, 2010), 817–823.

29  Nguyễn Đức Nhuệ, "Về các chức quan của Nguyễn Huy Oánh" (About the Official Titles of Nguyễn Huy Oánh), in *Kỉ yếu hội thảo khoa học Danh nhân văn hoá Nguyễn Huy Oánh* (Proceedings of the Conference on the Cultural Figure Nguyễn Huy Oánh) (Hà Tĩnh: Sở Văn hoá, Thể thao và Du lịch Hà Tĩnh xuất bản, 2008), 117–139.

According to the records, Nguyễn Huy Oánh authored 13 books with 37 volumes,[30] only 10 books (20 volumes) of which, written in Sinographs and/or Nôm script, are extant: 1) *Bắc dư tập lãm* 北輿集覽 (*Reading the Collection of Chinese Geography and Custom*; catalog number A.2009 in Vietnam Institute of Sino-Nom Studies), a record of the geography and customs of 15 Chinese provinces, originally excerpted from the *Mingsheng Quanzhi* 名勝全志 (*Complete Records of Famous Spots*); 2) *Hoàng hoa sứ trình đồ* 皇華使程圖 (*A Map of the Embassy to China*, text kept by the Nguyễn Huy family), a map and notes about the envoy mission to China; 3) *Phụng sứ Yên Đài tổng ca* 奉使燕臺總歌 (*A General Song of the Embassy to Beijing*, A.373, R.1375), a collection of poetry along with journals describing the envoy trip in detail; 4) *Sơ học chỉ nam* 初學指南 (*Guides for Primary Learning*, A.1634), a manual for beginner students; 5) *Quốc sử toản yếu* 國史纂要 (*A Brief Survey of National History*, A.1923) a Vietnamese history book which ends with the Trần dynasty; 6) *Huấn nữ tử ca* 訓女子歌 (*A Song for Teaching Daughters*, AB.85) a 632-line Nôm text written in the six-eight meter verse instructing girls in traditional virtue and duties according to Confucian teaching; 7) *Dược tính ca quát* 藥性歌括 (*A General Song of Medicine*), a Nôm text written in the six-eight meter verse describing various medicinal plants and procedures; 8) *Thạc Đình di cảo* 碩亭遺稿 (*The Manuscripts Left by Thạc Đình*, A.3133), a collection of Nguyễn Huy Oánh's poetry collected by his grandson Nguyễn Huy Vinh;[31] 9) *Phúc Giang thư viện quy lệ* 福江書院規例 (*The Regulations of Phúc Giang Academy*) in woodblocks archived in Trường Lưu; 10) *Ngũ kinh toản yếu đại toàn* 五經纂要大全 (*A Concise Compilation of the Great Collection of Works on the Five Classics*), 9 volumes in woodblocks. Based on a catalogue of both his extant and lost works, it can be seen that Nguyễn Huy Oánh had an expansive knowledge of multiple fields: Confucian classics, geography, history, medicine, literature, foreign relations, and education. This model of the polymath intellectual versed in multiple fields was representative of Vietnamese Confucian scholars before the 20th-century switch to Western influenced scholarship, which focused on a specific concentration.

---

30  Including: *Ngũ kinh Tứ thư toản yếu* 四書五經撮要 (15 volumes), *Trường Lưu Nguyễn thị* 長流阮氏 (10 volumes), *Hoàng hoa sứ trình đồ* 皇華使程圖 (2 volumes), *Bắc dư tập lãm* 北輿集覽 (1 volume), *Phụng sứ Yên Đài tổng ca* 奉使燕臺總歌 (1 volume, also entitled *Phụng sứ Yên Kinh tổng ca* 奉使燕京總歌), *Sơ học chỉ nam* 初學指南 (1 volume), *Tiêu Tương bách vịnh* 瀟湘百詠 (1 volume), *Quốc sử toản yếu* 國史纂要 (1 volume), *Châm cứu toát yếu* 針灸撮要 (1 volume), *Thạc Đình di cảo* 碩亭遺稿 (2 volumes), *Huấn nữ tử ca* 訓女子歌 (1 volume), and *Phúc Giang thư viện quy lệ* 福江書院規例 (1 volume in woodblocks).

31  Lại Văn Hùng et al., *Tuyển tập thơ văn Nguyễn Huy Oánh* (Selected Literary Works of Nguyễn Huy Oánh) (Hà Nội: Nhà xuất bản Hội Nhà văn, 2005), 11–16.

Because of his talents and contributions to the court, Nguyễn Huy Oánh was selected to be head ambassador on a tribute mission to Qing China. His entourage began their journey in 1766 and arrived in Beijing (former name Yanjing) at the end of that same year. In the beginning of 1767, they began their journey back to Vietnam, arriving at the end of the year. Time on the road took up most of the journey. This provided Nguyễn Huy Oánh with opportunities to socialize and exchange poetry with Chinese officials and scholars from various backgrounds and social strata, from provincial to metropolitan, visit the Temple of Confucius in Beijing, and visit other famous sites in China. Aside from official duties related to foreign relations with China, Nguyễn Huy Oánh also engaged in cultural exchange and poetry with Chosŏn and Japanese ambassadors in Beijing, helping to build cordial relations between East Asian countries in the 18th century.[32]

During his journey to Beijing, Nguyễn Huy Oánh composed various materials that could be used as a sort of guide for other ambassadors—fortunately, these works, including *Bắc dư tập lãm* 北輿集覽, *Hoàng hoa sứ trình đồ* 皇華使程圖, and *Phụng sứ Yên Đài tổng ca* 奉使燕臺總歌, and a part of *Thạc Đình di cảo* 碩亭遺稿, are still extant. After reading these documents, I have determined that Nguyễn Huy Oánh visited eleven Chinese academies. In my opinion, visiting these shuyuan did have influence on Nguyễn Huy Oánh's management of Phúc Giang Academy after returning to Vietnam.

The following is a list of the eleven academies in Guangxi, Hunan, Shandong, and Hebei that Nguyễn Huy Oánh visited from the 9th of the second month to the 14th of the twelfth month of 1766 (lunar calendar) on the way to Beijing. There are no records of visits on the return trip to Vietnam although the same route was taken.

Nguyễn Huy Oánh's mission visited more academies than any other missions from Vietnam. For instance, Lý Văn Phức 李文馥 (1785–1849) on his way to Yanjing in 1841 visited only two academies: Hengshan 衡山 (in Hunan province) and Yingzhou 瀛洲 (in Anhui province);[33] Nguyễn Văn Siêu 阮文超 (1799–1872) while heading for Yanjing in 1849 also passed by just two academies: Pingshan 屏山 (in Guangxi) and Ziyang 紫陽 (in Henan).[34] This might

---

32 Nguyễn Thanh Tùng, "Nguyễn Huy Oánh: Nhà ngoại giao (Nguyễn Huy Oánh: A Diplomat)," in *Kỉ yếu hội thảo khoa học Danh nhân văn hoá Nguyễn Huy Oánh* (Proceedings of the Conference on the Cultural Figure Nguyễn Huy Oánh) (Hà Tĩnh: Sở Văn hoá, Thể thao và Du lịch Hà Tĩnh xuất bản, 2008), 172–190.

33 Lý Văn Phức, *Chu Nguyên tạp vịnh thảo* (A Manuscript of Miscellaneous Verses of China), 1841.

34 Nguyễn Thị Thanh Chung, *Phương Đình vạn lý tập của Nguyễn Văn Siêu: Văn bản và giá trị thi ca* (*Phương Đình vạn lý tập* by Nguyễn Văn Siêu: The Text and the Poetric Values) (Hà Nội: Nhà xuất bản Giáo dục Việt Nam, 2015), 149, 162.

PRIVATE ACADEMIES IN 18TH-CENTURY VIETNAM 103

ILLUSTRATION 4.1   Map of the embassy's way to Beijing in 1766

TABLE 4.3  Chinese Academies visited by Nguyễn Huy Oánh in 1766

| Academies | Location | Nguyễn Huy Oánh's descriptions and activities at the academies | Lunar date (d/m/y) |
|---|---|---|---|
| Lijiang Academy 麗江書院 | Taiping 太平, Guangxi 廣西 | "There was also Lijiang Academy, elaborately constructed" (又有麗江書院製極華艷).[a] | 9/2/1766 |
| Yangming Academy 陽明書院 | Nanning 南寧, Guangxi 廣西 | "There was also Yangming Academy, inscribed *Jinglun Canzan* (Contributions to Politics). This was the old school of Duke of Wencheng [Wang Yangming]" (又有陽明書院，扁：經綸參贊。是文成公舊講學處)[b] | 17/2/1766 |
| Wucheng Academy 武成書院 | Pingnan 平南, Guangxi 廣西 | "Under the walls was Wucheng Academy, inscribed: *Xue Hai Guan Lan* (Watching the Waves of the Ocean of Scholarship)." (城下有武成書院，扁：學海觀瀾)[c] | 22/3/1766 |
| Cangwu Academy 蒼梧書院 | Cangwu 蒼梧, Guangxi 廣西 | "Within the city was Cangwu Academy inscribed: *Hui Feng Qi Wu* (The Flying Phoenix Stops on the Cangwu Area)." (城內有蒼梧書院，扁：翽鳳棲梧)[d] | The end of 3/1766 |
| Guyan Academy 古岩書院 | Wuzhou 梧州, Guangxi 廣西 | "Guyan Academy was inscribed *Shuangkui Tang* (Chamber of Two Cinnamon Trees)." (城頭有古岩書院，扁：雙桂堂)[e] | The end of 3/1766 |
| Airi Academy 愛日書院 Liuen Academy 流恩書院 | Kuilin 桂林, Guangxi 廣西 | "There was also Airi Academy and Liuen Academy." (又有愛日、流恩書院)[f] | 18/5/1766 |
| Shigu Academy 石鼓書院 | Hengzhou 衡州, Hunan 湖南 | "Atop the mountain was Shigu Academy wherein seven eminent men, including Zhou Dunyi, Zhu Xi, and Han Yu, Huang Gan were venerated"; inscribed *Ming Jiao Le Di* (The Happy Land of Names and Teachings – namely the Confucian ethical code). (崙上是石鼓書院，祀周子、朱子、昌黎、黃幹等七賢。扁：名教樂地)[g] Nguyễn Huy Oánh also wrote a poem entitled *Đề Thạch Cổ thư viện* 題石鼓書院 (Writing on the Shigu shuyuan). | The end of 6/1766 |

TABLE 4.3    Chinese Academies visited by Nguyễn Huy Oánh in 1766 (*cont.*)

| Academies | Location | Nguyễn Huy Oánh's descriptions and activities at the academies | Lunar date (d/m/y) |
|---|---|---|---|
| Yuelu Academy 嶽麓書院 | Changsha 長沙, Hunan 湖南 | Detailed descriptions of the shuyuan including three poems: *Đề thư viện* 題書院 (Writing on the [Yuelu] shuyuan), *Đề lục quân tử từ* 題六君子祠 (Writing on the Temple of the Six Gentlemen), *Tặng Nhạc Lộc giáo chủ Vương Văn Thanh* 贈岳麓教主王文清 (Presented to Yuelu Academy's headmaster Wang Wenqing).[h] | 1/7/1766 |
| Longshan Academy 龍山書院 | Dongping 東平, Shandong 山東 | "Within the city was Longshan Academy, inscribed *Jiang Zhang Chun Feng* (Spring Wind Blowing into the Red Curtain)." (城中有龍山書院，扁：絳帳春風)[i] Nguyễn Huy Oánh also wrote a poem entitled *Long Sơn thư viện* 龍山書院 (The Longshan Academy). | 5/12/1766 |
| Yingzhou Academy 瀛洲書院 | Hejian 河間, Hebei 河北 | "Within the city was Yingzhou Academy, founded to teach the Tai family. The district opened to teach children." (城有瀛洲書院，立教泰姓人。縣所延以授生童)[j] | 14/12/1766 |

a   Nguyễn Huy Oánh, *Phụng sứ Yên Đài tổng ca* (A General Song of the Embassy to Beijing), trans. Lại Văn Hùng et al. (Hà Nội: Nhà xuất bản Khoa học xã hội, 2014), 26–27 (for the translated text into Vietnamese), 322 (for the original Literary Chinese).
b   Nguyễn Huy Oánh, *Phụng sứ Yên Đài tổng ca*, 31, 324.
c   Nguyễn Huy Oánh, *Phụng sứ Yên Đài tổng ca*, 54, 331.
d   Nguyễn Huy Oánh, *Phụng sứ Yên Đài tổng ca*, 59, 334. There is a mistake in the punctuation of the Vietnamese translation.
e   Nguyễn Huy Oánh, *Phụng sứ Yên Đài tổng ca*, 59, 334. "Cinnamon trees" refers to metropolitan laureates in civil service examinations.
f   Nguyễn Huy Oánh, *Phụng sứ Yên Đài tổng ca*, 84, 343. The Vietnamese translation mistakenly identifies this as a single shuyuan, "Ái Nhật Lưu Ân" [Airi Liuen].
g   Nguyễn Huy Oánh, *Phụng sứ Yên Đài tổng ca*, 110, 354. The Vietnamese translation mistakenly translates: "Trên đỉnh núi có Thư viện Thạch Cổ thờ Chu Tử (Đôn Di), Chu Tử (Hi), Xương Lê, Hoàng Cán và bảy vị hiền" [Atop the mountain was Shigu (a place) to venerate Zhou Dunyi, Zhu Xi, Han Yu, Hoang Jin, and seven worthies].
h   Nguyễn Huy Oánh, *Phụng sứ Yên Đài tổng ca*, 115–116, 355-356.
i   Nguyễn Huy Oánh, *Phụng sứ Yên Đài tổng ca*, 208–209, 386–387. "Red curtain" means the classroom.
j   Nguyễn Huy Oánh, *Phụng sứ Yên Đài tổng ca*, 223, 392.

have been simply because Nguyễn Huy Oánh was an official of education; hence, his mission focused much more on educational situation in localities and spent more time visiting Chinese academies both for sightseeing and for investigating the private training models.

Among these eleven academies, Nguyễn Huy Oánh gave a detailed description of Yuelu Academy 嶽麓書院, wrote three poems inspired by it, and met with the headmaster of the academy. He also wrote one poem each for the Longshan Academy 龍山書院 and Shigu Academy 石鼓書院. The other eight academies were merely given a sketchy description by the envoy. This implies Nguyễn Huy Oánh's particular concentration on Yuelu Academy.

Yuelu Academy was among the most famous shuyuan both in China and all of East Asia. Building on the previous foundations of a Buddhist temple, in 967 during the Northern Song, Zhu Dong 朱洞 (?–?), prefect of Tanzhou 潭州太守, founded the Yuelu Academy at Yuelu Mountain 嶽麓山, in Changsha district of Hunan province. For the next thousand years, Yuelu Academy would be a center of education, compiling and archiving books, and developing Confucian thought. Later generations also called Yuelue Academy "the School of A Thousand Years" (Qian nian xuefu 千年學府).[35]

The fame of the Yuelue Academy was quick to catch the attention of Vietnamese diplomats. Nguyễn Trung Ngạn 阮忠彥 (1289–1370) of the Trần dynasty (1226–1400) visited Yuelu Mountain during the 1314–1315 tribute to the Yuan 元 dynasty (1271–1368). His poetry collection, *Giới Hiên thi tập* 介軒詩集 (*The Poetry Collection of Giới Hiên*), is the earliest extant collection of envoy poetry in Vietnam. In this collection, there are two poems which mention the Buddhist temple at Yuelu, located close to Yuelu Academy. In the poem titled *Hồ Nam* 湖南 (Hunan) there is the line: "Hidden in the clouds, the bells of Yuelu toll faintly in the distance" (雲藏嶽麓疏鐘遠). Another poem is prefaced *Du Nhạc Lộc tự* 遊嶽麓寺 (Visiting Yuelu Temple).[36] There is a good chance that Nguyễn Trung Ngạn visited Yuelu Academy during this trip.

Nguyễn Huy Oánh's *Phụng sứ Yên Đài tổng ca* records this event from the seventh lunar month of 1766 when his group visited Yuelu Academy on the way to Beijing:

---

[35] "Yuelu shuyuan 岳麓书院," *Zhongguo shuyuan lansheng* (Splendors of Chinese Academies), in ed. Deng Hongbo and Peng Aixue (Changsha: Hunan daxue chubanshe, 2000), 205–247. See also, for information on the Yuelu Academy, Hoyt Tillmann, "Some Reflections on Confucian Academies in China," in this volume, 21–44.

[36] Bùi Huy Bích, *Hoàng Việt thi tuyển* (A Collection of Vietnamese Poetry) (Hà Nội: Nhà xuất bản Văn học, 2007), 132–137.

On the first day of the seventh month, we passed the temple of Bao Ye, which had a plaque inscribed "One laugh and the river was made clear." Having passed through Niutou zhou, on the left was Yuelu Academy. During the Song dynasty, Zou Hao took up residence here after being demoted. After that, Zhang Shi built a pavilion in remembrance of Zou Hao; Zhu Xi inscribed this pavilion "Home of the Way"; Emperor Song Lizong bestowed a plaque inscribed "Yuelu Academy." From Zibei pavilion, we held up our robes and ascended into Chengde Hall, which had a plaque inscribed "Transcendent Comprehension of the Supreme Ultimate." Behind all this was Yushu Tower. Further up the mountain is Sizhen Pavilion, where the poem-lessons of Master Cheng on Seeing, Hearing, Speaking, and Doing, along with the poem-lesson of Master Fan on the Heart-mind, are inscribed on rocks. The highest point on the mountain is called Goulu, where the Da Yu Stele is located, inscribed with seventy-three characters; beneath is Canglang cave, once the hiding place of Minister Zhong Xianchao; Chuixiang Pavilion is situated on the mountaintop.[37]

Faced with the scholarly tradition and scenery surrounding Yuelu Academy, Nguyễn Huy Oánh also wrote three seven-character regulated verse poems on Yuelu. The poem *Đề thư viện* 題書院 (Writing on the [Yuelu] Academy) opens with the lines:

I gaze up upon the origins of the Learning of the Principle (*Lixue*)
On this envoy trip, visiting this academy.[38]

The first four lines of the second poem *Đề lục quân tử từ* 題六君子祠 (Writing on the Temple of the Six Gentlemen) are:

From Yuelu looking into the distance, cranes descend from the sky
[Down to] the hazy river which will prove good for bathing.

---

37  Nguyễn Huy Oánh, *Phụng sứ Yên Đài tổng ca*, 115–116, 355–356. The English quotations in this paper differ from the Vietnamese translation in this book. Original text in Classical Chinese: "七月初一日, 經包爺廟, 扁 "一笑河清." 過牛頭冊[洲], 左边山腰有岳麓書院; 宋時邾[鄒]浩貶官居此; 後張栻愛公築臺, 朱子書額曰 "道鄉," [宋]理宗御扁曰 "岳麓書院." 自自卑亭摳衣而上, 入成德堂, 扁 "超然会太極"; 最後爲御書樓. 登山一級是四箴亭, 石刻程子 "視, 咱[聽], 言, 動" 箴及范氏 "心" 箴. 山之最高處名岣嶁山, 有大禹碑, 七十三字; 下有蒼筤谷, 是尚書鐘仙巢舊隐; 上有吹香亭."

38  Nguyễn Huy Oánh, *Phụng sứ Yên Đài tổng ca*, 116, 356. The English quotations in this paper differ from the Vietnamese translation in this book. Original text in Classical Chinese: "理學淵源仰主張; 曾因覲闕詣書堂."

ILLUSTRATION 4.2  *Phụng sứ Yên Đài tổng ca* 奉使燕臺總歌 (A General Song of the Embassy to Beijing).
SOURCE: VIETNAM NATIONAL LIBRARY CALL NUMBER R.1375, PAGE 20

Knowing well that high positions in examination only result in low official positions

I remember that worthy men of old also found themselves in this situation.[39]

The Temple of the Six Gentlemen (Liujunzi ci 六君子祠), originally called the Hall of the Six Gentlemen (Liujunzi tang 六君子堂), is a temple located within Yuelu Academy built in 1526 during the Jiajing 嘉靖 era (1521–1567) of the Ming dynasty. It is built for the worship of six scholars who helped build and develop Yuelu Academy: Zhu Dong as prefect of Tanzhou; Li Yunze 李允則 (953–1028) also as prefect of Tanzhou 潭州知州; Zhou Shi 周式 (?–?) as first headmaster of Yuelu (shouren shanzhang 首任山長); Liu Gong 劉珙 (1122–1178) as grand academician of the Hall for Aid in Government (Zizhengdian daxueshi 資政殿大學士); Chen Gang 陳鋼 (?–?); and Yang Maoyuan 楊茂元 (1450–1516) as subordinate prefect of Changsha (Changsha fu tongzhi 長沙府同知). The third and fourth lines of the above poem reveal Nguyễn Huy Oánh's discontent with his relatively minor sixth and fourth rank assignments[40] despite having graduated with top distinction in the 1748 examinations (only in 1782 immediately before retirement was he promoted to subordinate second rank assignment). Nguyễn Huy Oánh was able to relate to the scholars honored in the Temple of the Six Gentlemen, for they also found themselves in minor positions despite their high academic distinctions. Amidst their lowly assignments, their images would be forever engraved in people's memory due to the devoting of their energy to developing education through a private academy. Surely, it was this identification with the Six Gentlemen that led Nguyễn Huy Oánh to develop his own academy based on the model of Yuelu Academy after returning to Vietnam.

The third poem is titled *Tặng Nhạc Lộc giáo chủ Vương Văn Thanh* 贈岳麓教主王文清 (Presented to Yuelu Shuyuan's Headmaster Wang Wenqing). Wang Wenqing 王文清 (1688–1779) attained the Metropolitan Laureate degree in 1724 under the Yongzheng 雍正 era (1722–1735). Along with Wang Fuzhi 王夫之 (1619–1692), Wang Kaiyun 王闓運 (1833–1916), and Wang Xianqian 王先謙 (1842–1917), he was part of a group known as the Four Wangs of Hunan. Wang Wenqing was the 37th headmaster of Yuelu Academy, and held this post twice

---

39   Nguyễn Huy Oánh, *Phụng sứ Yên Đài tổng ca*, 117, 356. The English quotations in this paper differ from the Vietnamese translation in this book. Original text in Classical Chinese: "嶽麓遙遙鶴下空; 滄茫一水浴常豐. 極知高第能卑宦; 曾憶先賢有此風."
40   The rule of official assignments in monarchical Vietnam included totally nine 'ranks' (品), ascending from the ninth to the first, each with 'subordinate' (從) and 'official' (正) status.

from 1745 and 1763. In 1766, Nguyễn Huy Oánh visited Yuelu Academy and, impressed by Wang Wenqing, presented him with a poem (handwritten in the *Thạc Đình di cảo* 碩亭遺稿, A.3133) which begins:

> Ninety years old[41] and still strong, you are an impressive talent;
> I gaze upon you as high as the Tai Mountain and the northern star.[42]

While passing through Hunan, Nguyễn Huy Oánh visited Yuelu Academy, observed and wrote about the architecture and surrounding scenery, and met the headmaster of the academy. Although his descriptions of the other eight academies were rather brief, Nguyễn Huy Oánh described Yuelu Academy in great detail because it was such a major academy in China. He was noticeably impressed by the scenery, history, and educational activities during this visit. His admiration was not limited to past renowned scholars connected with Yuelu Academy, but also extended to the man he met there in person. Along with the Six Gentlemen, Wang Wenqing made significant contributions to Yuelu Academy and the promulgation of Confucian teachings. These were the pedagogical models which inspired Nguyễn Huy Oánh's admiration. Is it possible that these good impressions from Yuelu Academy had a strong influence on Nguyễn Huy Oánh's educational philosophy and inspired him to create a private academy after returning to Vietnam? At the very least, we know that when his envoy arrived in Beijing, Nguyễn Huy Oánh was already making regulations for an academy, which he named Phúc Giang, after a river in his home in Trường Lưu village.

Currently in the Nguyễn Huy family woodblock collection is a set of woodblocks for a work titled *Thư viện quy lệ* 書院規例 (*Academy Regulations*). This set is composed of six one-sided woodblocks with totally 12 pages, of which 10 are extant (page 3–4 missing). The first page is titled *Phúc Giang thư viện khải mông* 福江書院啟蒙 (Initiation into Phúc Giang Academy). This informs us that the name of the academy is taken from the Phúc Giang 福江 (River of Good Fortune). At the conclusion of this work there is a note: "Đinh Hợi/ *dinghai* 丁亥 year, Cảnh Hưng era [1767], written by the envoy Nguyễn Lưu Trai at the Huitong lodging in Beijing" (時, 皇朝景興強圉大淵獻, 奉使大陪臣阮榴齋書于北京會同館). "Lưu Trai" 榴齋 was a penname of Nguyễn Huy Oánh.

---

41 Wang Wenqing was 78 years old in that year (1766). Nguyễn Huy Oánh might have used "ninety years old" to stress on Wang's longevity.

42 Nguyễn Huy Oánh, *Thạc Đình di cảo* (The Manuscripts Left by Thạc Đình), trans. Lại Văn Hùng et al. (Hà Nội: Nhà xuất bản Khoa học xã hội, 2014), 151–153, 487–488. The English quotations in this paper differ from the Vietnamese translation in this book. Original text in Classical Chinese: "九十康彊屬巨髦; 泰山北斗仰彌高."

# PRIVATE ACADEMIES IN 18TH-CENTURY VIETNAM 111

ILLUSTRATION 4.3    Page 5–6 of the *Thư viện quy lệ* 書院規例 (Academy Regulations) in woodblock, inverted.
SOURCE: COURTESY OF PROFESSOR NGUYỄN HUY MỸ

This indicates that he wrote this draft at the beginning of 1767 while still in Beijing. According to the schedule of the mission, they would depart Beijing on the afternoon of the 16th day of the second lunar month in 1767.[43] This places the dating of this draft within the first one and a half lunar months of 1767. It isn't clear when these woodblocks were made, and the only information on the printer is the name Nguyễn Huy Vượng 阮輝旺 (second half of the 18th century)—a student of Nguyễn Huy Oánh in Phúc Giang Academy.

The content of the regulations includes: 1) rituals for beginning education (followed by two missing pages); 2) model writing for celebratory notices for graduates and exemplary students; 3) ritual rubrics and model writing samples for various rituals that took place in the academy from the first month to the last month of the lunar calendar; 4) moral requirements for students; 5) selected aphorisms related to education and morality taken from Chinese Confucians.[44] Descriptions of ritual take up about four-fifths of the work. Moral and educational instructions take up the remaining fifth. The work is comprised of approximately 2,000 characters, of which 1,600 are extant.

---

43   Nguyễn Huy Oánh, *Phụng sứ Yên Đài tổng ca*, 253.
44   Hoàng Ngọc Cương, "Về sách *Thư viện quy lệ* của Thư viện Phúc Giang (About the *Academy Regulations* of Phúc Giang Academy)," in *Nghiên cứu bảo tồn mộc bản Trường Lưu* (Research and Preservation of Trường Lưu Woodblocks) (Hà Tĩnh: Hà Tĩnh Press, 2015), 173–186.

We are aware that most Chinese academies had educational regulations (xuegui 學規).[45] Is it possible that Nguyễn Huy Oánh referenced an existing document to compose his own *Phúc Giang Academy Regulations*? Having visited Yuelu Academy in person, Nguyễn Huy Oánh certainly must have been familiar with the *Yuelu shuyuan xuegui* 岳麓書院學規 (*Educational Regulations of Yuelu Academy*), a famous document written by Li Wenzhao 李文炤 (1672–1735) comprising 8 regulations and edited by Wang Wenqing into 18 short regulations totaling only 108 characters. However, the *Phúc Giang Academy Regulations* has nothing in common with the *Yuelu shuyuan xuegui*. Nguyễn Huy Oánh's regulations are also very different from Zhu Xi's famous *Bailudong shuyuan xuegui* 白鹿洞書院學規 (*Educational Regulations of Bailudong Shuyuan*)[46] which had gained popularity in Chosŏn and Japan.[47] It can be inferred that, although Nguyễn Huy Oánh favored the academy model of China, he did not follow their regulations, but instead sought to create his own according to his own philosophy and goals.

## 5 Nguyễn Huy Oánh as Educator and Phúc Giang Academy

Based on *Nguyễn thị gia tàng* 阮氏家藏,[48] the classical Chinese family records of the Nguyễn Huy clan, and on the history of his official assignments,[49] it can confirmed that Nguyễn Huy Oánh underwent three different periods as an educator: 1) From the time he passed the local examination 鄉試 (1732) until he graduated top rank laureate in the metropolitan examination (1748), he opened a school in Cồn Lều (present day Chợ Quan in Trường Lưu), gathering over a thousand pupils and attracting the solicitation of many officials, who invited him to their residences as a private teacher; 2) from 1756–1757 while he was on official assignment in Sơn Nam, when at leisure, he would teach students, who

---

45  Deng Hongbo (ed.), *Zhongguo shuyuan xuegui jicheng* (Compilaton of Chinese Academy Regulations) (Shanghai: Zhongxi shuju, 2011).

46  Another title is *Bailudong Shuyuan Jieshi* 白鹿洞書院揭示.

47  Li Bangguo, "Zhuxi yu Bailudong shuyuan zai Chaoxian Riben de yingxiang (The Influence of Zhu Xi and the White Deer Grotto Academy in Korea and Japan)," *Hubei shifan xueyuan xuebao* 1 (1995): 98–101; Zhang Pinduan, "Zhuxi *Bailudong Shuyuan Jieshi* zai Riben de liuchuan ji yingxiang (Influence and Transmission of the Zhu Xi's White Deer Grotto Articles of Learning in Japan)," *Nanping shizhuan xuebao* 3 (2004): 35–37; and Martin Gehlmann, "Transmissions of the White Deer Grotto Academy Articles of Learning in Korea," in this volume, 252–286.

48  Nguyễn Huy Vinh, *Nguyễn thị gia tàng* (阮氏家藏 Family Records of the Nguyễn Huy Clan), (Vinh: Nhà xuất bản Đại học Vinh, 2019), 222–238.

49  Nguyễn Đức Nhuệ, "Về các chức quan của Nguyễn Huy Oánh," 117–139.

came from all over to study in great numbers. After this, he returned to Thăng Long and oversaw metropolitan examinations, was assigned to positions such as vice chancellor of the Directorate of Education (Tư nghiệp Quốc tử giám 國子監司業) and then chancellor of the Directorate of Education (Tế tửu Quốc tử giám 國子監祭酒) until 1766 when he left for China—a total of approximately 10 years. Having been assigned to such high ranking posts related to education on a national scale, it is certain that Nguyễn Huy Oánh had many responsibilities related to preparing advanced teaching and lecture materials; 3) after returning from his envoy mission in 1767, Nguyễn Huy Oánh's multiple achievements led to his promotion and a series of posts in different areas—it is certain that he would not have had much time in any one place to start a lasting school. However, after declining the assignment of grand councilor (Tham tụng/Cancong 參從 in the Lê dynasty's official titles system), Nguyễn Huy Oánh resigned from service and retired in 1783 and spent the rest of his days in retirement until his death in 1789. During those six years, Nguyễn Huy Oánh devoted his time to the private school that he opened in Trường Lưu, Hà Tĩnh.[50] He spent a total of 20–30 years involved in education, interrupted several times by changes in assignment, concentrated around his home of Trường Lưu, but also with brief periods spent in Sơn Nam and Thăng Long.

### 5.1 Founding Phúc Giang Academy

The name "Phúc Giang thư viện" 福江書院 (Phúc Giang Academy) first appeared in the draft of the academy regulations written by Nguyễn Huy Oánh in 1767 while in Beijing. However the Nguyễn Huy clan's family tradition of opening schools can be traced to Nguyễn Huy Tựu 阮輝俶 (1690–1750), the father of Nguyễn Huy Oánh. Nguyễn Huy Tựu achieved the local laureate degree during the Lê dynasty, held an official post as Huấn đạo 訓導 (overseeing education in a district), and was posthumously honored with the post of Công bộ Tả Thị lang 工部左侍郎 (senior vice minister of Department of Public Works). According to the *Nguyễn gia trang khoa danh điền bi kí* 阮家莊科名田碑記 (Stele on the Study Field of the Nguyễn Clan's Farm) written by Nguyễn Huy Oánh in 1760, Nguyễn Huy Tựu "took pleasure in teaching students. A total of 1,218 students from all directions came to receive instruction."[51] This shows that Nguyễn Huy Oánh's father had already opened a school of considerable size at this relatively early date. Nguyễn Huy Oánh carried on his father's legacy and

---

50　Lại Văn Hùng, *Tuyển tập thơ văn Nguyễn Huy Oánh*, 9–10.
51　Nguyễn Huy Mỹ (ed.), *Các tác giả dòng văn Nguyễn Huy Trường Lưu: Cuộc đời và tác phẩm [tuyển chọn]* (Writers of Nguyễn Huy Literary School in Trường Lưu: Their Lives and Their Selected Works) (Hà Nội: Nhà xuất bản Lao Động, 2012), 189–190.

opened a school in Cồn Lều in 1732, immediately after acquiring the local laureate degree. These two schools can be considered as predecessors of Phúc Giang Academy.

Phúc Giang Academy was also known by the name of Thạc Đình học hiệu 碩亭學校 (Thạc Đình School) and Trường Lưu học hiệu 長留學校 (Trường Lưu School). However, Phúc Giang Academy was the official name used in the *Academy Regulations* as well as in the official decrees from the emperor. There are currently no extant documents which provide an exact date for Phúc Giang Academy's foundation, but we can tentatively estimate that its foundation could not have happened later than 1783, when Nguyễn Huy Oánh retired, because the term Phúc Giang Academy appeared twice in a 1783 decree in which the court authorized him to be worshipped even when he was still alive.[52] After his retirement Nguyễn Huy Oánh was able to gather all his resources together to start his "educational revolution" in Trường Lưu. These resources included an erudite and diverse intellectual foundation, real life experience teaching at different levels during previous periods, renown and respect among contemporary scholars, and familiarity with the models of other academies, particularly Yuelu Academy.

### 5.2   *Editing and Woodblock-Printing Educational Materials*

One activity common to Chinese shuyuan was the editing and woodblock printing of books for educational purposes—this activity was called *shuyuan keshu* 書院刻書—woodblock printing in academy.[53] This tradition began during the Tang dynasty and expanded widely during the Song dynasty. The term "academy copy" (*shuyuan ben* 書院本) was used to refer to editions of books printed by academies.[54] Nguyễn Huy Oánh received this tradition of printing in academies from China and used it to organize the educational materials used in Phúc Giang Academy. He used one of his studio names, Thạc Đình 碩亭, for his printing house. For this reason, several extant books from Phúc Giang Academy are marked Thạc Đình tàng bản 碩亭藏板 (woodblocks archived by the Thạc Đình printing house), or Thạc Đình chính bản 碩亭正本 (official version of the Thạc Đình printing house).

---

52   Đinh Khắc Thuân, "Về các đạo sắc phong cho Nguyễn Huy Oánh (About Imperial Edicts for Nguyễn Huy Oánh)," in *Nguyễn Huy Oánh và dòng văn Trường Lưu trong môi trường văn hoá Hà Tĩnh* (Nguyễn Huy Oánh and Trường Lưu Literary School in the Cultural Environment of Hà Tĩnh) (Hà Nội: Nhà xuất bản Lao Động, 2014).

53   Cheng Gujia and Deng Hongbo (eds.), *Zhongguo shuyuan zhidu yanjiu* (Research on the Chinese Academy System) (Hangzhou: Zhejiang jiaoyu chubanshe, 1997), 232–326.

54   Ji Xiaofeng (ed.), *Zhongguo shuyuan cidian,* 687–688.

TABLE 4.4    Materials used in Phúc Giang Academy

| No. | Title | Author | Format | Content |
|---|---|---|---|---|
| 1. | *Phúc Giang thư viện quy lệ* 福江書院規例 | Nguyễn Huy Oánh | 5 woodblocks, compiled in 1767 | School regulations for Phúc Giang Academy, written in 1767 in Beijing. |
| 2. | *Sơ học chỉ nam* 初學指南 | Nguyễn Huy Oánh | A.1634, 80 pages handwritten in 1773 | Standards for beginning students. |
| 3. | *Huấn nữ tử ca* 訓女子歌 | Nguyễn Huy Oánh | AB.85, 18 pages, printed | 632 lines in luc bat meter instructing girls in traditional Confucian virtues and values. |
| 4. | *Quốc sử toản yếu* 國史纂要 | Nguyễn Huy Oánh | A.1923, 194 pages, printed | Vietnamese history from beginnings to the Tran dynasty, excerpted from the *Đại Việt sử kí toàn thư* 大越史記全書 (The Complete Annals of the Great Việt) of Ngô Sĩ Liên. |
| 5. | *Thi kinh toản yếu đại toàn* 詩經纂要大全 | Nguyễn Huy Oánh | 2 volumes, 63 woodblocks | This series is collectively titled *Ngũ kinh toản yếu đại toàn* 五經纂要大全 (A Concise Compilation of the Great Collection of Works on the Five Classics), comprised of 9 volumes compiled by Nguyễn Huy Oánh over a period of a decade and completed by 1756 at the latest; in 1758 it was printed and widely distributed; summarized and excerpted from the *Wujing daquan* 五經大全 of Ming dynasty scholar Hu Guang 胡廣 (1369–1418) et al. |
| 6. | *Thư kinh toản yếu đại toàn* 書經纂要大全 | Nguyễn Huy Oánh | 2 volumes, 81 woodblocks | |
| 7. | *Lễ kinh toản yếu đại toàn* 禮經纂要大全 | Nguyễn Huy Oánh | 2 volumes, 46 woodblocks | |
| 8. | *Dịch kinh toản yếu đại toàn* 易經纂要大全 | Nguyễn Huy Oánh | 1 volume, 43 woodblocks | |
| 9. | *Xuân Thu toản yếu đại toàn* 春秋纂要大全 | Nguyễn Huy Oánh | 2 volumes, 53 woodblocks | |
| 10. | *Tính lí toản yếu đại toàn* 性理纂要大全 | Nguyễn Huy Tựu | 2 volumes, 81 woodblocks | Summary of the *Xingli daquan* 性理大全 by Hu Guang et al. There is an addition containing information on Vietnamese history. Nguyễn Huy Oánh handwrote this work with Nguyễn Huy Tự as proofreader. |

As mentioned above, Nguyễn Huy Oánh authored 37 volumes of 13 books, of which 10 books are extant. Based on the content of these extant works, we can confirm that the following works were materials used in Phúc Giang Academy—we are also lucky to have paper printings and/or woodblocks (木板 mộc bản) of these works:[55]

As for the method of organizing these teaching materials, the works can be divided into two groups: 1) Original works which include *Phúc Giang thư viện quy lệ* 福江書院規例, *Sơ học chỉ nam* 初學指南, *Huấn nữ tử ca* 訓女子歌; 2) abridgements of existing works such as *Quốc sử toản yếu* 國史纂要, the content of which is two-fifths of the *Đại Việt sử kí toàn thư* 大越史記全書;[56] *Ngũ kinh toản yếu đại toàn* 五經纂要大全, selected and abridged from the *Wujing daquan* 五經大全 (*Great Compendia of the Five Classics*) of Hu Guang's 胡廣 (1369–1418) group of Ming-dynasty scholars (this abridgment contains only about 6–7% of the original work);[57] *Tính lí toản yếu đại toàn* 性理纂要大全, edited by Nguyễn Huy Tựu, taken from the *Xingli daquan* 性理大全 (*Great Compendia of Nature and Principle*) by this same Ming-dynasty group and shortened from 70 volumes to 2. All of the works belonging to these two groups are brief and aimed at elementary education rather than advanced studies to develop scholarship, unlike most materials produced by Chinese academies.

The content of these materials is broad—they include classroom regulations, study methods, education for girls, Vietnamese history, Confucian classics, and Song-Ming Neo-Confucianism. The content also includes instructions on ritual rubrics, practicing writing characters, and morality. The "regionalization" reflected in these materials is noteworthy—the knowledge represented in *Phúc Giang thư viện quy lệ* 福江書院規例, *Sơ học chỉ nam* 初學指南, and *Huấn nữ tử ca* 訓女子歌 is all on Vietnam. Even in abridgements from Chinese works like *Tính lí toản yếu đại toàn* 性理纂要大全, Nguyễn Huy Tựu added content on Vietnamese rulers.[58]

---

55  See Phạm Văn Ánh, "Lược khảo về các bản ván gỗ hiện lưu tại gia tộc họ Nguyễn Huy Trường Lưu (A Preliminary Research on the Existing Woodblocks in Nguyễn Huy Family in Trường Lưu)," in *Nghiên cứu bảo tồn mộc bản Trường Lưu* (Research and Preservation of Trường Lưu Woodblocks) (Hà Tĩnh: Hà Tĩnh Press, 2015), 119–136; see also *Phuc Giang School Woodblocks (8th–20th centuries)*, Nomination form–Asia/Pacific Memory of the World Register, 2015, provided by Professor Nguyễn Huy Mỹ—the 16th descendant of the Nguyễn Huy clan.

56  Nguyễn Huy Oánh, *Quốc sử toản yếu* (A Conscise History of the State) (Huế: Nhà xuất bản Thuận Hoá, 2004), 6.

57  Phạm Văn Ánh, "Lược khảo về các bản ván gỗ hiện lưu tại gia tộc họ Nguyễn Huy Trường Lưu," 132.

58  Thái Huy Bích, "Lược thuật sách *Tính lí toản yếu đại toàn*, quyển hạ (Brief Relation of the *Tính lí toản yếu đại toàn*, second volume)," in *Nghiên cứu bảo tồn mộc bản Trường Lưu*

Among the participants in the compiling and editing of these works were: Nguyễn Huy Tựu (9th generation) edited *Tính lí toản yếu đại toàn* 性理纂要大全; Nguyễn Huy Oánh (10th generation, son of Nguyễn Huy Tựu) edited and wrote the base text for many woodblocks; Nguyễn Huy Cự and Nguyễn Huy Quýnh (both Nguyễn Huy Oánh's younger brothers) helped write characters for carving of woodblocks; Nguyễn Huy Tự (11th generation, son of Nguyễn Huy Oánh) wrote characters and proof-read; Nguyễn Huy Vượng (student of Nguyễn Huy Oánh) oversaw the production process of the woodblocks. Obviously, the most significant role was that of Nguyễn Huy Oánh. This is not to mention the details surrounding the workmen who actually carved and printed the works (there is no information on these individuals).

The number of extant woodblocks is 379. This is certainly not reflective of the total number of blocks produced by the Thạc Đình printing house. Due to various circumstances, it is certain that many woodblocks have been lost or damaged. Aside from the texts printed for use in the Confucian education mentioned above, the printing house also printed at least one other book—*Phụng sứ Yên Đài tổng ca* 奉使燕臺總歌, totaling one hundred pages, printed after 1767. Aside from that, "Tứ thư toản yếu tự" 四書纂要序 (Foreword to the Concise Compilation of the Four Books) written in 1773 in the *Thạc Đình di cảo* 碩亭遺稿 records: "[This edition of] *Tứ thư toản yếu* 四書纂要 (*Concise Compilation of the Four Books*) follows after *Ngũ kinh toản yếu* 五經纂要, *Tính lí toản yếu* 性理纂要 (*Concise Compilation of Nature and Principle*), and *Quốc sử toản yếu* 國史纂要—all of which have been previously printed."[59] This means that the *Tứ thư toản yếu* was compiled and printed by Nguyễn Huy Oánh in 1773, but, unfortunately, there are no extant editions of it in print or woodblock form. Despite this, from this bit of information, we know that the Thạc Đình printing house operated for 16 years (1758–1773) and printed at least 1,700 pages of publications. The dates of these printings show that Nguyễn Huy Oánh and the other teachers at Trường Lưu had already begun printing before he left on his envoy mission (1766–1767), meaning that the printing of books wasn't necessarily directly influenced by the envoy mission. However, the envoy mission seems to have influenced the printing activity in terms of the works printed after the mission such as *Phúc Giang thư viện quy lệ*, *Phụng sứ Yên Đài tổng ca* (printed after 1767) and *Tứ thư toản yếu* (1773).

---

(Research and Preservation of Trường Lưu Woodblocks) (Hà Tĩnh: Hà Tĩnh Press, 2015), 137–142.

59  "Tứ thư toản yếu tự 四書纂要序," in Nguyễn Huy Oánh, *Thạc Đình di cảo*, 414–416.

### 5.3   Tuition Fees: Tuition and Study Fields

In *Nguyễn Gia trang khoa danh điền bi kí* 阮家莊科名田碑記 (Stele on the Study Field of the Nguyễn Clan's Farm, 1760), Nguyễn Huy Oánh records that his father, Nguyễn Huy Tựu, "collected the money given as gifts and purchased a plot of land in Cồn Hến. With additional purchases, the area eventually exceeded one acre."[60] This was called a *keming tian* 科名田 (*khoa danh điền*, literally fields for names of the laureates, or study fields), that is, a plot of land used to pay for expenses related to education. Nguyễn Huy Oánh followed his father's example and purchased twenty acres of top quality land (*nhất đẳng điền* 一等田) in order to help pay the expenses of Phúc Giang Academy.[61] The parents of poor students who did not have enough money to pay expenses were allowed to use a part of this land to help provide for their needs.[62] This tradition of study fields also existed in several Chinese academies and was called academy study fields (*shuyuan xuetian* 書院學田).[63] Yuelu Academy also had a famous tradition of study fields. Within the duration of the Ming dynasty alone, Yuelu Academy acquired 2,222.9 acres of land for this purpose.[64]

### 5.4   Educational Achievements

Although the greatest credit belongs to Nguyễn Huy Oánh, all three generations of the Nguyễn Huy clan (from Nguyễn Huy Tựu through Nguyễn Huy Oánh to Nguyễn Huy Tự) made contributions to Phúc Giang Academy; this isn't to mention the following generations which continued the academy, albeit with less success. Nguyễn Huy Oánh and his son Nguyễn Huy Tự were the principal lecturers, who oversaw and managed Phúc Giang Academy successfully. The official records of the Nguyễn dynasty record that Phúc Giang Academy had "a collection of tens of thousands of books" and had students "numbering in the thousands, among which many were successful graduates."[65] Bùi Dương Lịch 裴楊瓅 (1757–1828) wrote: "The students [of Nguyễn Huy Oánh] numbered in

---

60   Nguyễn Huy Mỹ (ed.), *Các tác giả dòng văn Nguyễn Huy Trường Lưu: Cuộc đời và tác phẩm*, 189–190.
61   Đinh Khắc Thuân, "Nguyễn Huy Oánh với Trường Lưu học hiệu (Nguyễn Huy Oánh and the School of Trường Lưu)," in *Nghiên cứu bảo tồn mộc bản Trường Lưu* (Research and Preservation of Trường Lưu Woodblocks) (Hà Tĩnh: Hà Tĩnh Press, 2015), 38–44.
62   Hà Quảng, "Nguyễn Huy Oánh: Nhà giáo dục lỗi lạc (Nguyễn Huy Oánh: An Outstanding Educator)," in *Kỉ yếu hội thảo khoa học Danh nhân văn hoá Nguyễn Huy Oánh* (Proceedings of the Conference on the Cultural Figure Nguyễn Huy Oánh) (Hà Tĩnh: Sở Văn hoá, Thể thao và Du lịch Hà Tĩnh xuất bản, 2008), 162–171.
63   Ji Xiaofeng, *Zhongguo shuyuan cidian*, 688.
64   Chen Gujia and Deng Hongbo (eds.), *Zhongguo shuyuan zhidu yanjiu*, 417.
65   Historiography Institute of the Nguyễn Dynasty, *Đại Nam nhất thống chí* (The Unification Records of the Great South), Vol. 2 (Huế: Nhà xuất bản Thuận Hoá, 1997), 237.

the thousands, over thirty of whom graduated as metropolitan laureates and had official assignments in the same court. Those who graduated with local laureate degrees and received appointments were too numerous to count."[66] Phúc Giang Academy became the top center of education in the entire nation, threatening even the status of the schools in Thăng Long, the capital and center of Confucian studies. Phúc Giang Academy contributed greatly to Confucian education in the central and southern regions of Vietnam and helped in the formation of several prominent scholar families in the central region, expanding private education beyond Thăng Long.

With all these outstanding achievements, Nguyễn Huy Oánh received multiple promotions and decrees from both the Lê and Nguyễn courts. Already in 1783, the Lê dynasty gave permission for him to be venerated at Phúc Giang Academy even while he was still alive.[67] The *Phượng Dương Nguyễn tông thế phả* 鳳陽阮宗世譜 (*Family Chronicle of the Nguyễn Clan in Phượng Dương*)[68] records that in 1824, 1843, and 1920 Nguyễn Huy Oánh was promoted, by the Nguyễn dynasty, as a demigod to be worshipped in Phúc Giang Academy. For example, in 1824 he was given the title of The Erudite Demigod of Phúc Giang Academy 福江書院淵博之神.[69] Among the populace, Nguyễn Huy Oánh became known as the Demigod of the Academy (*Thần thư viện*) and Phúc Giang Academy became known as the Academy Temple (*Đền thư viện*). Phúc Giang Academy was the only school that received an imperial edict promoting the worship of a demigod.

Today, some of Phúc Giang Academy's collection has been archived, transliterated, translated, researched, and promoted by descendants of the Nguyễn Huy family, receiving the attention and praise of researchers and society at large. In 2016, UNESCO listed 379 woodblocks of the Phúc Giang Academy on the "Memory of the World Asia-Pacific Regional Register." This was a unique event, because it was the first time for Vietnam that UNESCO listed a regional heritage (as opposed to a national one) as world heritage class.

---

66   Bùi Dương Lịch, *Nghệ An kí* (A Record of Nghệ An), trans. Nguyễn Thị Thảo (Hà Nội: Nhà xuất bản Khoa học xã hội, 1993), 309.
67   Đinh Khắc Thuân, "Về các đạo sắc phong cho Nguyễn Huy Oánh," 27.
68   Catalog number VHv.1354, Nguyễn Huy Giáp 阮輝甲 compiled 1894, Nguyễn Huy Chương 阮輝璋 transcribed in 1942.
69   Nguyễn Huy Mỹ (ed.), *Các tác giả dòng văn Nguyễn Huy Trường Lưu: Cuộc đời và tác phẩm*, 45.

## 6 Conclusions

Academies have been an educational tradition in East Asian countries since about the 9th century. Although the first academy in Vietnam was founded quite early (no later than by the end of the 14th century with the Lạn Kha Academy in Trần dynasty, possibly over 150 years earlier than the first academy in Chosŏn Korea), and the model of the Phúc Giang Academy received great attention in 18th century Vietnam, it must be admitted that the academy tradition in Vietnam is much less rich than that of other East Asian countries and territories such as China, Japan, Korea, and Taiwan. What was the reason for this? In my opinion, there are two main reasons. First, Confucianism in Vietnam was not strong enough to develop different schools of thoughts whereas the promotion of different strains of thought within Confucianism were central to the development of the academy system in order to delve more deeply into key issues in Confucian philosophy. Private academies in general seem to not only provide knowledge for participating in civil service examinations, but even more established forums for debating, criticizing, and digging deeply into Confucian philosophy. Yet Vietnam did not boast many Confucians who had enough education or inspiration to contribute creatively to East Asian Confucianism as a whole. The second reason is that Vietnamese Confucians did not often adhere to the concept of receiving the teachings of one's teacher in order to further develop and pass these teachings on. That is to say, the idea of having a student carry on the teachings of his teacher was not regarded as important, aside from a few notable exceptions among five generations of teachers-students during the 18th to early 19th centuries,[70] none of which was able to start a large movement. This led to the proliferation of a system, including Phúc Giang Academy, wherein a particular academy only exists inasmuch as it is connected with a particular teacher—hence the academy ceases to exist once that particular teacher ceases teaching or relocates. Regardless, Phúc Giang Academy existed for about 80 years, including its primitive state in the form of a school founded by Nguyễn Huy Tựu (9th generation) and the school in Cồn Lều founded by

---

[70] These five generations of teacher-disciples refer to Vũ Công Đạo 武公道 (1629–1714), Vũ Thạnh 武晟 (1664–?), Nguyễn Tông Quai 阮宗乖 (1692–1767), Lê Quý Đôn 黎貴惇 (1726–1784), and Bùi Huy Bích 裴輝璧 (1744–1818), all famous and top rank scholars in their own time who boasted success in government, scholarship, and education. They represented the beginning and end of a Confucian renaissance in 18th-century Vietnam. See Nguyễn Kim Sơn, "Năm thế hệ thầy trò nổi tiếng trong lịch sử Nho học Việt Nam (Five Famous Generations of Masters and Students in the History of Vietnamese Confucianism)," in Một số vấn đề về Nho giáo Việt Nam (Issues in Vietnamese Confucianism), ed. Phan Đại Doãn, 252–274 (Hà Nội: Nhà xuất bản Chính trị Quốc gia, 1999).

Nguyễn Huy Oánh (10th generation) in the 1730s all the way until the death of Nguyễn Huy Tự (11th generation) in 1790. There was no other private academy in Vietnam prior to the 20th century with a similarly long existence. Obviously, the Nguyễn Huy clan's emphasis on transmission of tradition between teacher and student (*shifa/sư pháp* 師法), and transmission of family (*jiafa/gia pháp* 家法) tradition, were significant in the continuation of their schools in Trường Lưu, creating an "educational revolution" in this remote area. It is hard to find such a tradition of family transmission in the history of Chinese academies.

In the case of Nguyễn Huy Oánh and his Phúc Giang Academy, although his interactions with Chinese academies during his envoy mission of 1766–1767 (specifically his interactions with Yuelu Academy) left him deeply impressed, in reality, Nguyễn Huy Oánh had already organized activities similar to those commonly found in Confucian academies even *before* his trip to China. These included: opening a school, organizing, woodblock-printing, distributing, and archiving teaching materials, buying study fields. Despite this, it must also be affirmed that, after returning from his envoy mission, Nguyễn Huy Oánh selectively adopted various aspects from the model of Yuelu Academy in order to push education, centered around the development of Phúc Giang Academy into the largest center of private education in Vietnam, located in the poor and undereducated central region of Vietnam, where Confucianism was not nearly as strong as in the north. This means that, although the model taken from Yuelu Academy had an *indirect* impact, nevertheless it played a significant role in pushing and developing the model of private schools in Vietnam.

### Acknowledgements

This research is funded by Vietnam National Foundation for Science and Technology Development (NAFOSTED) under grant number 602.02-2016.03. The author would like to thank the following scholars for their comments to revise this paper: Professor Nguyễn Huy Mỹ (the 16th descendant of the Nguyễn Huy clan), Professor Nguyễn Thanh Tùng (Hanoi University of Education), Professor Deng Hongbo 鄧洪波 (Hunan University), Professor Liam Kelley (University of Hawai'i at Mānoa). All of the existing mistakes belong to the author.

### References

Azuma, Juji. "The Private Academies of East Asia: Research Perspectives and Overview." *A Selection of Essays on Oriental Studies of ICIS* (2011): 1–18.

Bùi Dương Lịch 裴楊瓑. *Nghệ An kí* 乂安記 (A Record of Nghệ An). Translated by Nguyễn Thị Thảo. Hà Nội: Nhà xuất bản Khoa học xã hội, 1993.

Bùi Huy Bích 裴輝璧. *Hoàng Việt thi tuyển* 皇越詩選 (A Collection of Vietnamese Poetry). Hà Nội: Nhà xuất bản Văn học, 2007.

Bùi Xuân Đính. *Giáo dục và khoa cử Nho học Thăng Long – Hà Nội* (Confucian Education and Examination in Thăng Long – Hà Nội). Hà Nội: Nhà xuất bản Hà Nội, 2010.

Chen Gujia 陈谷嘉, and Deng Hongbo 邓洪波 (eds.). *Zhongguo shuyuan zhidu yanjiu* 中国书院制度研究 (Research on the Chinese Academy System). Hangzhou: Zhejiang jiaoyu chubanshe, 1997.

Chung Man-jo 郑万祚. "Hanguo shuyuan yanjiu dongxiang zongshu 韩国书院研究动向综述 (Summary of Trends of Korean Academy Research)." *Hunan daxue xuebao* 6 (2005): 29–38.

Deng Hongbo 邓洪波. "Zhongguo shuyuan yanjiu zongshu (1923–2007) 中国书院研究综述 1923–2007 (Summary of Chinese Academy Research 1923–2007)." *Higashi-Ajia bunka kōshō kenkyū: bessatsu 2* (2008): 21–35.

Deng Hongbo 邓洪波 (ed.). *Zhongguo shuyuan xuegui jicheng* 国书院学规集成 (Compilaton of Chinese Academy Regulations). Shanghai: Zhongxi shuju, 2011.

Deng Hongbo 邓洪波, and Peng Aixue 彭爱学 (eds.). *Zhongguo shuyuan lansheng* 中国书院揽胜 (Splendors of Chinese Academies). Changsha: Hunan daxue chubanshe, 2000.

Đinh Khắc Thuân. *Giáo dục và khoa cử Nho học thời Lê ở Việt Nam qua tài liệu Hán Nôm* (Confucian Education and Examination during the Lê Dynasty in Vietnam through Sino-Nom Materials). Hà Nội: Nhà xuất bản Khoa học xã hội, 2009.

Đinh Khắc Thuân. "Về các đạo sắc phong cho Nguyễn Huy Oánh (About Imperial Edicts for Nguyễn Huy Oánh)." In *Nguyễn Huy Oánh và dòng văn Trường Lưu trong môi trường văn hoá Hà Tĩnh* (Nguyễn Huy Oánh and Trường Lưu Literary School in the Cultural Environment of Hà Tĩnh), 27–29. Hà Nội: Nhà xuất bản Lao Động, 2014.

Đinh Khắc Thuân. "Nguyễn Huy Oánh với Trường Lưu học hiệu (Nguyễn Huy Oánh and the School of Trường Lưu)." In *Nghiên cứu bảo tồn mộc bản Trường Lưu* (Research and Preservation of Trường Lưu Woodblocks), 38–44. Hà Tĩnh: Hà Tĩnh Press, 2015.

Dương, Bích Hồng. *Lịch sử sự nghiệp thư viện Việt Nam trong tiến trình văn hoá dân tộc* (A History of the Field of Libraries in Vietnam during Its National Cultural Progress). Hà Nội: Vụ Thư viện – Bộ văn hoá Thông tin, 1999.

Gao Xiongzheng 高熊徵, and Anonymous. *An Nam chí nguyên* 安南志原 (The Original Accounts of Annan). Translated, annotated, and introduced by Hoa Bằng, edited by Lộc Nguyên. Hà Nội: Nhà xuất bản Đại học Sư phạm Hà Nội, 2017.

Hà Quảng. "Nguyễn Huy Oánh: Nhà giáo dục lỗi lạc (Nguyễn Huy Oánh: An Outstanding Educator)." In *Kỉ yếu hội thảo khoa học Danh nhân văn hoá Nguyễn Huy Oánh* (Proceedings of the Conference on the Cultural Figure Nguyễn Huy Oánh)," 162–171. Hà Tĩnh: Sở Văn hoá, Thể thao và Du lịch Hà Tĩnh xuất bản, 2008.

Hejtmanek, Milan. "The Elusive Path to Sagehood. Origins of the Confucian Academy System in Korea Chosŏn Korea." *Seoul Journal of Korean Studies* 26, no. 2 (December 2013): 233–268.

Historiography Institute of the Nguyễn Dynasty. *Đại Nam nhất thống chí* 大南一統志 (The Unification Records of the Great South), Volume 2. Huế: Nhà xuất bản Thuận Hoá, 1997.

Historiography Institute of the Nguyễn Dynasty. *Khâm định Việt sử thông giám cương mục* 欽定越史通鑑綱目 (Imperially Ordered Annotated Text Completely Reflecting the History of Việt), Volume 1. Hà Nội: Nhà xuất bản Giáo dục, 2007.

Hoàng Ngọc Cương. "Về sách *Thư viện quy lệ* của Thư viện Phúc Giang (About the *Academy Regulations* of Phúc Giang Academy)." In *Nghiên cứu bảo tồn mộc bản Trường Lưu* (Research and Preservation of Trường Lưu Woodblocks), 173–186. Hà Tĩnh: Hà Tĩnh Press, 2015.

Hoàng Văn Lâu (trans). *Đại Việt sử kí toàn thư* 大越史記全書 (Complete Annals of The Great Việt), Volume 2. Hà Nội: NXB Khoa học xã hội, 1993.

Hoàng Xuân Hãn. *La Sơn phu tử* (Master La Sơn). In *La Sơn Yên Hồ Hoàng Xuân Hãn*, Volume 2, 1067–1073. Hà Nội: Nhà xuất bản Giáo dục, 1998.

Ji Xiaofeng 季啸风 (ed). *Zhongguo shuyuan cidian* 中国书院辞典 (Dictionary of Chinese Academies). Hangzhou: Zhejiang jiaoyu chubanshe, 1996.

Koo, Jeong-Woo. "The Origins of the Public Sphere and Civil Society: Private Academies and Petitions in Korea, 1506–1800." *Social Science History* 3 (2007): 381–409.

Lại Văn Hùng, et al. *Tuyển tập thơ văn Nguyễn Huy Oánh* (Selected Literary Works of Nguyễn Huy Oánh). Hà Nội: Nhà xuất bản Hội Nhà văn, 2005.

Li Bangguo 李邦国. "Zhuxi yu Bailudong shuyuan zai Chaoxian Riben de yingxiang 朱熹与白鹿洞书院在朝鲜日本的影响 (The Influence of Zhu Xi and the White Deer Grotto Academy in Korea and Japan)." *Hubei shifan xueyuan xuebao* 1 (1995): 98–101.

Lý Văn Phức 李文馥. *Chu Nguyên tạp vịnh thảo* 周原雜詠草 (A Manuscript of Miscellaneous Verses of China). 1841. Institute of Sino-Nom Studies call number A.1188, Hanoi, Vietnam.

Mehl, Margaret. *Private Academies of Chinese Learning in Meiji Japan: The Decline and Transformation of the Kangaku Juku*. Copenhagen: NIAS Press, 2003.

Namba Yukio 难波征男. "Riben shuyuan de yanjiu xianzhuang yu keti 日本书院的研究现状与课题 (Situation and Issues of Japanese Academy Research)." *Hunan daxue xuebao* 3 (2007): 19–22.

Ngô Đức Thọ. *Văn bia Tiến sĩ Văn miếu Quốc tử giám Thăng Long* (Metropolitan Laureate Inscriptions in the Temple of Confucius and Directorate of Education in Thăng Long). Hà Nội: Nhà xuất bản Hà Nội, 2010.

Ngô Đức Thọ, et al. *Các nhà khoa bảng Việt Nam 1075–1919* (Metropolitan Laureates in Vietnam 1075–1919). Hà Nội: Nhà xuất bản Văn học, 2006.

Nguyễn Đăng Tiến, et al. *Lịch sử giáo dục Việt Nam trước Cách mạng Tháng Tám 1945* (A History of Vietnamese Education before the August Revolution in 1945). Hà Nội: Nhà xuất bản Giáo dục, 1996.

Nguyễn Đức Nhuệ. "Về các chức quan của Nguyễn Huy Oánh (About the Official Titles of Nguyễn Huy Oánh)." In *Kỉ yếu hội thảo khoa học Danh nhân văn hoá Nguyễn Huy Oánh* (Proceedings of the Conference on the Cultural Figure Nguyễn Huy Oánh), 117–139. Hà Tĩnh: Sở Văn hoá, Thể thao và Du lịch Hà Tĩnh xuất bản, 2008.

Nguyễn Huy Mỹ (ed.). *Các tác giả dòng văn Nguyễn Huy Trường Lưu: Cuộc đời và tác phẩm (tuyển chọn)* (Writers of Nguyễn Huy Literary School in Trường Lưu: Their Lives and Their Selected Works). Hà Nội: Nhà xuất bản Lao Động., 2012.

Nguyễn Huy Oánh 阮輝瑩. *Quốc sử toản yếu* 國史纂要 (A Conscise History of the State). Huế: Nhà xuất bản Thuận Hoá, 2004.

Nguyễn, Huy Oánh 阮輝瑩. *Phụng sứ Yên Đài tổng ca* 奉使燕臺總歌 (A General Song of the Embassy to Beijing). Translated by Lại Văn Hùng et al. Hà Nội: Nhà xuất bản Khoa học xã hội, 2014.

Nguyễn Huy Oánh 阮輝瑩. *Thạc Đình di cảo* 碩亭遺稿 (The Manuscripts Left by Thạc Đình). Translated by Lại Văn Hùng et al. Hà Nội: Nhà xuất bản Khoa học xã hội, 2014.

Nguyễn Kim Sơn. "Năm thế hệ thầy trò nổi tiếng trong lịch sử Nho học Việt Nam (Five Famous Generations of Masters and Students in the History of Vietnamese Confucianism)." In *Một số vấn đề về Nho giáo Việt Nam* (Issues in Vietnamese Confucianism), edited by Phan Đại Doãn, 252–274. Hà Nội: Nhà xuất bản Chính trị Quốc gia, 1999.

Nguyễn Thanh Tùng. "Nguyễn Huy Oánh: Nhà ngoại giao (Nguyễn Huy Oánh: A Diplomat)." In *Kỉ yếu hội thảo khoa học Danh nhân văn hoá Nguyễn Huy Oánh* (Proceedings of the Conference on the Cultural Figure Nguyễn Huy Oánh), 172–190. Hà Tĩnh: Sở Văn hoá, Thể thao và Du lịch Hà Tĩnh xuất bản, 2008.

Nguyễn Thị Thanh Chung. *Phương Đình vạn lý tập của Nguyễn Văn Siêu: Văn bản và giá trị thi ca* (*Phương Đình vạn lý tập* 方亭萬里集 by Nguyễn Văn Siêu: The Text and the Poetric Values). Hà Nội: Nhà xuất bản Giáo dục Việt Nam, 2015.

Phạm Văn Ánh. "Lược khảo về các bản ván gỗ hiện lưu tại gia tộc họ Nguyễn Huy Trường Lưu (A Preliminary Research on the Existing Woodblocks in the Nguyễn Huy Family in Trường Lưu)." In *Nghiên cứu bảo tồn mộc bản Trường Lưu* (Research and Preservation of Trường Lưu Woodblocks), 119–136. Hà Tĩnh: Hà Tĩnh Press, 2015.

Phan Huy Chú 潘輝注. *Lịch triều hiến chương loại chí* (Categorized Records on Administrative Systems of Successive Dynasties 歷朝憲章類誌), Volume 2, translated and annotated by The Translation Group of the Institute of History. Hà Nội: Nhà xuất bản Giáo dục, 2007.

Phan Trọng Báu. *Nền giáo dục Pháp – Việt* (The French-Vietnamese Education System). Hà Nội: Nhà xuất bản Khoa học xã hội, 2015.

*Phượng Dương Nguyễn tông thế phả* 鳳陽阮宗世譜 (Family Chronicle of the Nguyễn Clan in Phượng Dương). Institute of Sino-Nom Studies catalog number VHv.1354.

*Tân thư viện thủ sách* 新書院守冊 (Handbook of the New Library). Institute of Sino-Nom Studies catalog number A. 2645/1–3.

Taylor, Keith Weller. "Surface Orientations in Vietnam: Beyond Histories of Nation and Region." *The Journal of Asian Studies* 4 (1998): 949–978.

Thái Huy Bích. "Lược thuật sách *Tính lí toản yếu đại toàn*, quyển hạ (Brief Relation of the *Tính lí toản yếu đại toàn* 性理纂要大全, second volume)." In *Nghiên cứu bảo tồn mộc bản Trường Lưu* (Research and Preservation of Trường Lưu Woodblocks), 137–142. Hà Tĩnh: Hà Tĩnh Press, 2015.

Trần Hải Yến. "Nghiên cứu văn hoá văn học nhìn từ di sản một tộc họ (Cultural and Literary Studies: A Look from the Heritage of a Family)." in *Nguyễn Huy Oánh và dòng văn Trường Lưu trong môi trường văn hoá Hà Tĩnh* (Nguyễn Huy Oánh and Trường Lưu Literary School in the Cultural Environment of Hà Tĩnh), 139–154. Hà Nội: Nhà xuất bản Lao Động 2014.

*Tụ Khuê thư viện tổng mục* 聚奎書院總目 (General Catalog of Tụ Khuê Library). Institute of Sino-Nom Studies catalog number: A.110/1–3.

Wang Bingzhao 王炳照. *Zhongguo gudai shuyuan* 中国古代书院 (Ancient Academies of China). Beijing: Zhongguo guoji guangbo chubanshe, 2009.

Yang Busheng 杨布生, and Peng Dingguo 彭定国. *Zhongguo shuyuan yu chuantong wenhua* 中国书院与传统文化 (Chinese Academies and Traditional Culture). Changsha: Hunan jiaoyu chubanshe, 1992.

Zhang Pinduan 张品端. "Zhuxi 'Bailudong Shuyuan Jieshi' zai Riben de liuchuan ji yingxiang 朱熹'白鹿洞书院揭示'在日本的流传及其影响 (Influence and Transmission of Zhu Xi's White Deer Grotto Academy Articles of Learning in Japan)." *Nanping shizhuan xuebao* 3 (2004): 35–37.

CHAPTER 5

# Transmutations of the Confucian Academy in Japan: Private Academies of Chinese Learning (Kangaku Juku 漢学塾) in Late Tokugawa and Meiji Japan as a Reflection and a Motor of Epistemic Change

*Margaret Mehl*

## 1 Introduction

The Chinese First Vice Premier Deng Xiaoping 邓小平 (1904–1997) reportedly told the former Japanese statesman Saionji Kinkazu 西園寺公一 (1906–1993) in a conversation in June 1974 that China had inflicted two great and lasting burdens on Japan: the Chinese characters (*kanji* 漢字) and Confucianism. According to the newspaper *Asahi shinbun* 朝日新聞, Deng stated that while the suffering inflicted on China by the Japanese lasted only decades, the influence of Confucian philosophy in Japan had lasted for over 1,700 years and that he regretted this.[1]

It is true that to this day the Japanese have a writing system that uses thousands of Chinese characters and that the influence of Confucianism can still be felt (whether it is stronger than in China, as Deng asserted, is open to debate, particularly in the light of China's apparent Confucian revival). On the institutional level, however, Japan presents a different picture from China: the Chinese Confucian Academy (*shūyuàn*, Jpn. *shoin* 書院) described in most of the chapters in this volume has never existed in Japan, despite early efforts to establish such an institution. Chinese texts, particularly the Confucian canon, formed the basis of learning. This kind of text-based study learning is generally described as *kangaku* 漢学, usually rendered in English as "Chinese learning." The term *kangaku*, although used by Japanese scholars today for Chinese learning throughout history, did not gain general currency until well into the

---

1  "Tō Shōhei fuku shushō naigai jōsei o kataru 鄧小平副首相 内外情勢を語る (Prime Minister Deng Xiaoping Talks about the Domestic and International Situation," *Asahi shinbun* 6 June 1974, morning edition, p. 4 "Kokusai"; the report uses "meiwaku o kaketa" a phrase commonly used by Japanese representatives to express regret for Japan's misdeeds during WW2. The episode was reported again on 20 July 1977, morning edition, page 7.

19th century. Before the end of the 18th century the culture of knowledge, dominated as it was by Chinese influences, was perceived as universal. Only with the changing geopolitical situation from the in the late 18th century and the newly emerging fields of knowledge that came to be known as ancient studies (*kogaku* 古学), Japanese or national studies (*wagaku* 和学, *kokugaku* 国学) and Dutch (later Western) studies (*rangaku* 蘭学, *yōgaku* 洋学), did Chinese learning gradually transform into a distinct field of knowledge, and as such an object of criticism by representatives of the new fields.[2]

The institutions where Chinese learning was transmitted were adapted to local circumstances almost from the beginning. The *juku* 塾 discussed here is just one such institution, but it will be at the center of this chapter both because of its importance for education in the early modern and into the modern period and because its form can be said to be at the core of most other forms of schooling in traditional Japan. This will be clear from the following, very brief survey of education in Japan from establishment of the centralized imperial state in ancient times to the late Tokugawa period.

## 2 Confucianism and Educational Institutions in Japan until 1871

When the Japanese first imported Chinese ideas and institutions, and from the sixth century onwards began to establish an imperial bureaucratic state modelled on the Tang state, the new laws, codified in the Taihō Code 大宝律令 of 701, included the provision of a State Academy (Daigakuryō 大学寮) modelled on the Tang state's Directorate of Education (Guozijian 國子監) and influenced by similar institutions in Paekche on the Korean mainland.[3] The core curriculum consisted of Chinese classics and there was an examination system. Japan's high-ranking nobles, however, had little incentive to study at the Academy, since rank rather than passing examinations was and remained the key to advancement. As a result, the Daigakuryō "continued to function primarily as a technical school for low- and mid-level functionaries in the ministries, bureaus, and provincial offices of the state."[4]

The structure of the Academy also changed. By the middle of the Heian period (794–1185), attending lectures in the Academy proper was less important than were personal relationships with recognized scholars, who as often as not

---

[2] Michael Facius, *China übersetzen: Globalisierung und Chinesisches Wissen im Japan im 19. Jahrhundert* (Frankfurt a.M.: Campus, 2017), 10, 29, 84–95, 108.

[3] For this and the following, see Brian Steininger, *Chinese Literary Forms in Heian Japan: Poetics and Practice* (Cambridge, MA: Harvard University Asia Center, 2017), 125–172.

[4] Ibid., 131.

taught in their own homes. Even within the Academy, as well as outside it, rank and personal connections were decisive for advancement. By the late Heian period, the Academy was a "loose collective of scholarly households" who had privileges over curriculum and nomination to posts.[5] The content of education at the Academy is less well documented than the structure, but some general trends are discernible, which suggest an increasing distancing from the Chinese model. Pronunciation, initially closely modelled on contemporaneous Chinese pronunciation and taught by scholars from the mainland, gave way to *kundoku* 訓読, with Chinese words pronounced in a fashion closer to Japanese and fixed Japanese words and phrases for paraphrasing the Chinese narrowing the scope of possible meanings. Meanwhile an "alternative body of knowledge centered on court ritual" emerged and challenged the authority of the Academy scholars.[6]

In sum, in the course of the Heian period, "practices of examinations, ceremonies, and Sinitic pronunciation" give way to "personal nominations, private tutoring, and *kundoku* recitation," with a corresponding change in the "lived experience of the classical canon's meaning."[7] Classical (Chinese) learning (*gakumon* 学問) did, however, remain important and the Academy model spread to both private tuition among the nobility and, in medieval Japan, to warrior education and education in the Buddhist temples.[8] Even in the late medieval period, when the imperial state had largely disintegrated and new models had been introduced from the continent in the form of Song learning, the legacy of Heian Japan remained significant. The history of education in the medieval period is not too well documented. This is even true of the most famous institutions of the time, the Kanezawa Bunko 金沢文庫 and the Ashikaga Gakkō 足利学校. The Kanezawa Bunko, which still exists today, is a collection of books assembled by members of the Hōjō military clan in the Kamakura period (1185–1333). It is not clear who first established the Ashikaga Gakkō or Ashikaga College in what is now Tochigi prefecture, but after a period of decline it was revived in the 15th century and Uesugi Norizane 上杉憲実 (1410–1466) from another prominent warrior family became its head. Its curriculum consisted of Chinese learning and military studies and it was the most important school of the period.[9]

---

5   Ibid., 137.
6   Ibid., 161.
7   Ibid., 171.
8   Ibid., 166, 168.
9   Suzuki Hiroo, *Genten/kaisetsu Nihon kyōikushi* (Sources and Commentaries on the History of Education in Japan) (Tokyo: Nihon Tosho Bunka Kyōkai, 1994 [1985]), 38–39.

Scholarship and learning in medieval Japan were centered on the Buddhist temples, but in the early 17th century, at the beginning of the Tokugawa period, Fujiwara Seika 藤原惺窩 (1561–1619) contributed decisively to the secularization of learning and the development of the Neo-Confucian orthodoxy that became the cornerstone of Tokugawa ideology.[10] Tokugawa Ieyasu 德川家康 (1543–1616) appointed Fujiwara's pupil Hayashi Razan 林羅山 (1583–1657) as his advisor. In 1630, the third shogun, Iemitsu 家光 (1604–1651), had Razan found a school to train bakufu officials. This would eventually become the Shōheizaka Gakumonjo 昌平坂学問所 or Shōheikō 昌平黌, the highest institution of learning in Tokugawa Japan; but initially it amounted to little more than a private academy in Hayashi's home. In 1690 this became the semi-official school of the shogunate, which continued to support the Hayashi family. In the 1790s, under Matsudaira Sadanobu 松平定信 (1779–1829), it came fully under the auspices of the shogunate (although successive members of the Hayashi family continued as heads of the school) and was completely reorganized. It provided training mainly for the shogun's direct vassals; though during the last decades of the bakufu students came from all over Japan.

In some ways the Shōheikō bears a striking resemblance to the Daigakuryō of the Nara (710–794) and Heian periods, introduced above. It likewise had a sort of dual structure consisting of formal sessions at the college proper private tuition at the homes of well-known scholars. And at the Shōheikō too, examinations existed, but were of minor significance for most of the students, because in the government of the Tokugawa, as at the imperial court of ancient Japan, rank mattered more than scholastic achievement.

In the course of the Tokugawa period and especially from the latter half of the eighteenth century, the domains followed the example of the shogunate and established their own schools. Some of these domain schools (*hankō* 藩校) like the Shōheikō started as private establishments, and "personal discipleship, rather than institutional membership" continued to dominate in most of these schools.[11] By the end of the Tokugawa period most domains had their own schools and the larger ones more than one.[12] Usually they were exclusively for samurai, but toward the end of the period some were opened to commoners. Other domains established separate community schools for commoners

---

10   Since much has been written about education and scholarship in Tokugawa Japan a very brief summary will suffice here. The most comprehensive introduction to education in English is still Ronald P. Dore, *Education in Tokugawa Japan* (London: The Athlone Press, 1984).

11   Ibid., 73.

12   Naramoto Tatsuya, *Nihon no hankō* (The Domain Schools of Japan) (Kyoto/Tokyo: Tankōsha, 1970).

(*gōgaku* 郷学). The most famous of these is Shizutani Gakkō 閑谷学校 in Okayama domain, which existed, with interruptions, well into the 20th century. The shogunate and lords of the domains established schools for commoners partly in response to their demand for education, but also in an effort to control commoner education.[13]

The content of samurai education at the Shōheikō and the *hankō* is usually summarized as *bun-bu* 文武, that is, literary and military training, a combination prevalent already in medieval Japan. The former was based on the Song canon of texts and strongly emphasized moral education as a means to maintaining peace. Matsudaira Sadanobu, who reorganized the Shogunate's school, also issued the infamous "ban on heresy" in 1790 in order to strengthen Song orthodoxy; but in practice heterodox scholars were not repressed, although they did lose students. The extent of standardization and formalization of the curriculum in the domain schools varied considerably, as well as the extent to which demands were made on proficiency. In general, the fact that academic achievement was not a major criterion for advancement as well as the close relationship between teacher and student made it difficult to fail students, at least as long as they were diligent. Nor was there a fixed age for graduation; rather than leaving school abruptly, students tended to gradually cease attending.

Confucian ceremonies were conducted at most schools at least twice a year, in the spring and in the autumn, and at least 59 of the over 200 schools had a Confucian shrine. Dore calls Confucianism "the nearest thing Tokugawa Japan had to a 'religion.'"[14] But it was never exclusive, and in military training, perceived to be exclusively Japanese, ceremonies were more likely to center on Shinto deities.

In sum, the schools associated with the Tokugawa political system often originated in private academies and retained much of their personal character. They varied considerably in relation to attendance, organization, and examinations and although they provided vocational training for future officials, standards tended to be vague and social advancement depended on rank, not on examination results. In fact, the differences between these schools and the private academies, which like the domain schools increased dramatically in the latter half of the Tokugawa period, are fluid. Not only did some scholars who ran a *juku* also teach at the school of their domain, but some *juku* also

---

13   Ishikawa Matsutarō, "The Meiji Restoration and Educational Reforms," *Acta Asiatica* 54 (1988): 24–47.
14   Dore, *Education in Tokugawa Japan*, 92. Bellah, on the other hand, treats the Ishida Baigan 石田 梅岩 (1685–1744) and his eclectic teaching in his discussion of Tokugawa Religion.

received financial support from their domain. Examples include Kan Chazan's 菅茶山 (or Sazan, 1748–1827) Renjuku 廉塾 in Fukuyama domain,[15] and Hirose Tansō's 広瀬淡窓 (1787–1856) Kangien 咸宜園 in Hita (Ōita prefecture). Tansō, as a result, had to resist official attempts to influence the running of his *juku*.[16]

Collectively, the private academies are generally known as *juku*. Many of them have the word *juku* in their names. Occasionally the name includes the term *shoin* 書院;[17] other names include *en* 園 (as in Kangien), *dō* 堂, *kan* 館 and *gakusha* 学舎.[18] Although the master of a *juku* no doubt chose the name with care, it is difficult to draw any general conclusions about the *juku* from the names alone. The dictionary defines it as an educational institution, where in his own home an individual teaches students who are attracted because of his scholarship and character, and study his personal brand of learning.[19] Students could come from most social classes and geographical regions and their age varied. The earliest *juku* existed in the 8th century, but from the 17th century they greatly increased in number. The subjects taught at a *juku* belonged to the field of *kangaku* (Chinese learning) in the widest sense, that is, the study of classical written Chinese and the literature, history and philosophy of China, the composition of Chinese poetry (*kanshi* 漢詩) and, from the late Edo period, the study of Japanese works written in Sino-Japanese (*kanbun* 漢文). A canon of classical Chinese texts, beginning with the *Classic of Filial Piety* (*Kōkyō* 孝経) and continuing with the *Four Books and Five Classics* (*Shisho Gokyō* 四書五経), was central to the curriculum of most *juku*. In the second half of the Edo

---

15   Hiroshima-ken Rekishi Hakubutsukan (ed.), *Fukuyama-han no kyōiku to bunka: Edo jidai kōki o chūshin ni* (Education and Culture in Fukuyama Domain in the Edo Period) (Fukuyama: Hiroshima-ken Hakubutsukan Tomonokai, 1994).

16   On Kangien see for example Richard Rubinger, *Private Academies of Tokugawa Japan* (Princeton: Princeton University Press, 1982). For Kangien as a model for today's schools see Tanaka Kayo, "Kangien. Hirose Tansō no shijuku kyōiku ga konnichi ni ataeru imi (Hirose Tansō's *juku* Education and its Meaning for Today)," *Katei kagaku* 61, no. 3 (1994): 54–58; Inoue Yoshimi, *Nihon kyōiku shisō no kenkyū* (Research on Educational Thought in Japan) (Tokyo: Keisō Shobō, 1978). Inoue Yoshimi briefly treats the history of the Kangien between 1868 and 1871, but says little about the following period.

17   For example, Seikei Shoin 青谿書院, one of the case studies in Margaret Mehl, *Private Academies of Chinese Learning in Meijji Japan: The Decline and Transformation of the Kangaku Juku* (Copenhagen: NIAS Press, 2003), 89–98.

18   Examples include Suisaien, Zōshun'en, the *juku* opened by Murakami Butsusan and Tsunetō Seisō respectively; Shijōdō; Nishō Gakusha Suishō Gakusha; Shijōdō.

19   Hosoya Toshio, *Shin kyōikugaku daijiten = New encyclopedia of education*, ed. Shohan, 8 vols. (Tokyo: Daiichi Hōki Shuppan, 1990), 415; Umihara Tōru, *Nihonshi shōhyakka: Gakkō* (A Little Encyclopedia of Japan: Schools) (Tokyo: Kondō Shuppansha, 1979), 70–71; The *Shin kyōikugaku daijiten* cites "private academy" as the standard English translation, but here *juku* will be used for conciseness.

period *juku* for other fields of learning, including Western learning, emerged. These gained importance in the Meiji period, but the *kangaku juku* were still the most numerous for several years.

## 3  Continuity and Change in Meiji Japan and the *Kangaku Juku*

Despite the significance of the *kangaku juku* for the development of education in Meiji Japan, they have long been neglected. In histories of education in Japan after the Meiji Restoration of 1868, *juku* rarely receive much of a mention; the emphasis is on the public school system modelled on Western systems, formally introduced by the Education Law of 1872. Even though modernization theory has long been criticized and often explicitly rejected, we still see the persistence of what John Tosh calls "a naïve antithesis between 'traditional' and 'modern,' at odds with any sense of process in history."[20] The traditional/modern binary has been and is enormously powerful in both Japanese and Chinese studies. As one sinologist (Theodore Huters) expressed it: "The pull of historical teleology has proved relentless, particularly in light of the traditional/modern binary that just does not seem to go away as a characteristic of Chinese studies, whether inside or outside of China."[21]

The fall of the shogunate in 1867 was, at least initially, legitimated as a restoration of the imperial bureaucratic state of the Nara and Heian periods, hence the term *fukko* 復古, which lingers on in the English designation of the events as the Meiji Restoration. The Restoration has even been described as "an attempt to inherit China."[22] In the early Meiji period, China still provided the model for political institutions and laws. The first government institutions were modelled on those of the Nara period, including the Daigaku 大学, but they were short-lived.

For education, the decisive reform was heralded by the Education Law of 1872, which laid the foundation of a state-controlled public education system with compulsory schooling for all and a network of modern schools. Already in 1871 the domain schools had been abolished together with the domains as part of the centralization of government (*haihan chiken* 廃藩置県). Many of them were reopened, most often as schools teaching Western subjects, which were

---

20  John Tosh, *The Pursuit of History (Revised Third Edition)* (London: Longman, 2002), 215.
21  Theodore Huters, *Bringing the World Home: Appropriating the West in Late Qing and Early Republican China* (Honolulu: University of Hawai'i Press, 2005), 5. For Japanese studies, most recently Facius, *China übersetzen*, 15–21.
22  Ben-Ami Shillony, "The Meiji Restoration: Japan's Attempt to Inherit China," in *War, Revolution & Japan*, ed. Ian Neary (Sandgate, Folkestone, Kent: Japan Library, 1993).

eventually absorbed into the mainstream. With the law of 1872, private schools of all kinds, including the *kangaku juku*, were formally abolished. This, however, did not mean that the older institutions disappeared overnight: education was high on the government's agenda, but the government lacked the resources to immediately introduce the education system stipulated in the law, and traditional institutions filled the gap for several years. Many domain schools continued in some form or other as private schools or remodeled into modern, local authority public schools. They often adopted a curriculum of Western subjects; the Confucian classics, if taught at all, became just one subject of many.

Private schools had to apply for permission to reopen, including *juku* and *terakoya* 寺子屋, which were essentially *juku* that offered elementary education.[23] Although there were *juku* that specialized in national learning (*kokugaku*) or Western subjects, the majority were *kangaku juku*. Many of them existed into the 1880s. The *juku* were particularly significant at the secondary level. In the course of the Meiji period, several *juku* adapted themselves to changed circumstances; they broadened the curriculum, charged fees and strove for official recognition. Some erected purpose-built buildings. A significant number became private schools within national education system, usually as lower secondary schools (*chūgakkō* 中学校).

The expansion of schooling in Meiji Japan was in part a continuing trend from the Tokugawa period as well as a result of the Meiji government's modernization program. The continuing importance of the *kangaku juku*, moreover, was not solely due to their practical function of filling a gap in government provision. Another reason, or rather group of related reasons, has to do with the continuing importance of *kanbun* and *kangaku:* knowledge of *kanbun* (Sino-Japanese) continued to be essential, since official documents were written in a heavily sinicized style, and a subject of entrance examinations for the government schools. Besides, *kanbun* was still the language of scholarship, including the language for studying the West. In fact, scholarship itself did not, at first, shed the legacy of *kangaku,* and the Sinocentric world view that *kangaku* reflected (I will return to this point later). Moreover, the local population often preferred *juku* to the new schools, because they were tried and trusted and

---

23  Meiji documents often refer to *juku* as *shijuku* 私塾, although the *shi* is redundant, since *juku* are by nature private. There is no clear demarcation between *juku* and *terakoya*, and historians of education prefer to distinguish between *gakumon juku* and *tenarai juku*, although the reality is more a continuum than a clear distinction. For a treatment in English of the Meiji government's policy concerning the *juku*, see Richard Rubinger, "Education: From One Room to One System," in *Japan in Transition: From Tokugawa to Meiji,* ed. Marius B. Jansen and Gilbert Rozman (Princeton: Princeton University Press, 1986).

what they taught was more relevant to their needs; this was particularly true of rural communities, where the fabric of society did not change much until well into the 20th century.[24]

## 4   What Were the *Kangaku Juku* Like?

The essentially private and individual nature of the *juku* meant that they varied widely with regard to who attended and for how long, curriculum, their master's style, their ability to survive beyond the founding master's death, etc. In *Private Academies in Meiji Japan*, I include a number of case studies in an effort to show different types of *juku* and their masters: a representative of the scholars of late Tokugawa Japan who continued to be active into the Meiji period (Yasui Sokken 安井息軒, 1799–1876); a scholar who founded a new institution in the Meiji period to cater for the continuing demand for expertise in *kanbun* and *kangaku* (Mishima Chūshū 三島中洲, 1830–1919); a female *kangaku* scholar who began by running a conventional *kangaku juku*, but eventually specialized in female education when the demand for this grew and whose *juku* transformed into a school that exists to this day (Miwada Masako 三輪田眞佐子, 1843–1927); and three scholars in rural areas, far from Tokyo, whose *juku* spanned the transition period from Tokugawa into Meiji (Ikeda Sōan 池田草庵, 1813–1878; Tsunetō Seisō 恒遠醒窓, 1803–1861, and Murakami Butsusan 村上仏山, 1810–1879).[25]

Despite the diversity of *kangaku juku*, some generalizations are possible. The majority were located in former castle towns and were run by former samurai. Study was predominantly self-study and consisted mainly of reading works from the Confucian canon (most commonly the *Four Books* and *Five Classics*) and Japanese histories in written in *kanbun*. Other forms of study were lectures and group reading sessions. Rules issued by the masters most commonly exhort students to study hard, behave in a decorous fashion, and maintain discipline; to strive for harmonious relationships and not to leave without authorization. The students most often came from the surrounding areas and from the local elite, except in large towns. Almost all of them were male. Most were in their teens. Some of them—or all of them in Tokyo—were boarders. Multiple attendance, either simultaneous or consecutively, was common in large towns.

---

24   An example is Shijōdō in Akita prefecture: see Mehl, *Private Academies*, 173–181.
25   Mehl, *Private Academies*, Chapter 3, 62–116.

Only one *juku* will be described in detail here (two more will be discussed in the following chapter): Ikeda Sōan's Seikei Shoin 青谿書院, the only *juku* I examined that included the term *shoin* in its name. Despite its name, Seikei Shoin had more in common with other *juku* of its time than with the Chinese and Korean *shuyuan* and *sŏwŏn*.[26]

Ikeda Sōan, "the Sage of Tajima" (*Tajima seijin* 但馬聖人) was a respected scholar, who spent most of his life in his home province of Tajima (now part of Hyogo prefecture), a remote region with few educational opportunities. Sōan established Seikei Shoin in 1847, after having taught three years in Kyoto and four in his home region. Most of his students came from the surrounding area, but many came from further afield. His death spelt the end of Seikei Shoin.

Born as the third son of a wealthy farmer in the village of Shukunami 宿南 in Yabu 養父 district (now Yabu city), Sōan lost his parents as a child and was sent to a temple in a neighbouring village to be brought up as a priest.[27] An encounter with the Confucian scholar Sōma Kyūhō 相馬九方 (1801–1879), who came from Takamatsu (Shikoku) to teach in the village for a while, led Sōan to give up the study of Buddhism for that of Confucianism. He followed Sōma to Kyoto in 1831 and studied with him until 1835. During this time the scholar Kasuga Sen'an 春日潜庵 (1811–1878) became his mentor and friend. Sōan then continued to study privately, earning his living by teaching. From 1836 to 1840 he led the life of a recluse in Matsuo on the western outskirts of Kyoto, devoting himself solely to his studies. Returning to Kyoto in summer 1840, he opened a *juku* as did many Confucian scholars in Kyoto at the time. His fame grew and the people of his native district asked him to come home to teach there and promised their support.[28] In the spring of 1843 Sōan returned to Tajima and took over a building in the village of Yōka 八鹿. Sōan started with 15 students, the number increasing to 35 in his first year. Soon he had so many students that in 1845 he had to have a new building erected. Sōan seems to have been content with life in Tajima, although he did miss the intercourse with other scholars.

---

26   The following is based on Mehl, *Private Academies*, 89–98.
27   The most important publications on Ikeda Sōan are: Toyoda Shōhachirō, *Tajima no Seijin* (The Sage of Tajima) (Yōkachō: Seikei Shoin, 1983 (1907)); Okada Takehiko, *Edoki no jūgaku* (Confucianism in the Edo Period) (Tokyo: Mokujisha, 1982); Hikita Seiyū, "Ikeda Sōan," in *Kasuga Sen'an, Ikeda Sōan* (*Sōsho Nihon no shisōka*, 44), ed. Ōnishi Harutaka and Hikita Seiyū (Tokyo: Meitoku Shuppansha, 1986); Ueda Hirao, *Tajima Seijin Ikeda Sōan* (Ikeda Sōan, the Sage of Tajima) (Kasei: Fuji Shoō/Tajima Bunka Kyōkai, 1993). Unless otherwise stated, the following is based on Ueda's book.
28   Hiroshi Watanabe, "Jusha, Literati and Yangban, Confucianists in Japan, China and Korea," *Senri Ethnological Studies* 28 (1990): 13–30.

The number of students continued to grow, and Sōan acquired his own premises in his native village and built Seikei Shoin in 1847. Here he continued to teach for the next three decades until his death. For some years he lectured at the domain schools of the neighbouring domains of Toyooka and Fukuchiyama, but he always returned to Shukunami. His fame grew and pupils came to study from further and further afield. Soon Seikei Shoin too had to be extended. A new boarding house built in 1858 was named Shōfūdō 松風洞 and in 1863 a new extension named Seigiryō 精義寮 was built.

Occasionally, Sōan took his nephew and a few students on lengthy trips to visit other scholars. In 1845 they went to Shikoku to meet the scholars Hayashi Ryōsai 林良斎 (1807–1849) and Kondō Tokuzan 近藤篤山 (1766–1846) and others, as well as to Kyoto to meet his old scholar friends. In 1851 they travelled to Edo to study with Satō Issai 佐藤一斎 (1772–1859). During this trip Sōan had the chance to meet with other scholars, including Ōhashi Totsuan 大橋訥庵 (1816–1862), and to copy rare books from the Shōheikō. In early 1858 Sōan took two pupils to Kyoto and Osaka.[29]

In the last years of his life Sōan was beset by misfortune, losing several family members. In 1877 he became ill himself and travelled first to Kyoto, then to Tokyo for treatment. In May 1878, feeling slightly better, he returned home, but died in September.

Ikeda Sōan's scholarship was derived from *yōmeigaku* 陽明学, that is the scholarship based on the philosophy of Wang Yangming 王陽明 (1472–1528), which emphasized the unity of knowledge and action and the role of the human heart (*kokoro* 心) in understanding. But his ideas developed from a mixture of different schools. His first teacher in *kangaku*, Sōma Kyūhō, was a disciple of Ogyū Sorai 荻生徂徠 (1666–1728), one of the foremost representatives of the *kogaku* school that aimed to return to the original texts of Confucius and Mencius and to define fundamental Confucian terms. Besides *yōmeigaku*, Sōan studied *shushigaku* 朱子学, the school based on the philosophy of Zhu Xi 朱熹 (1130–1200), during his studies in Kyoto. During his lifetime Sōan published a commentary on the *Greater Learning*. His commentaries on the *Doctrine of the Mean* and the *Book of Changes* were published posthumously.

One strand of *yōmeigaku* emphasized political action and several of its adherents became well known, such as Yoshida Shōin 吉田松陰 (1830–1859) and Saigō Takamori 西郷隆盛 (1828–1877). Sōan's friend Kasuga Sen'an was another representative of this branch of *yōmeigaku*. Sōan himself, however, represented the contemplative strand. He did not encourage political activism in his

---

29  On Sōan's exchanges with scholars and friends, see Ueda, *Tajima Seijin Ikeda Sōan*, 114–122.

pupils either. When some of them wanted to take part in the Ikuno rising in 1863, he dissuaded them, but when unsuccessful, he expelled one student and cautioned the others. He then assembled all his other students and warned them not to be swayed by the events of the times.[30]

Sōan's penchant for contemplation and introspection is reflected in journals, entitled *Sansō kōka* 山窓功課 and *Igyō yokō* 肄業餘稿. *Sansō kōka* is a kind of study journal, begun in 1847. The journal was intended as a daily reflection on his diligence (or otherwise) in his studies, teaching and actions, for his own encouragement. Sōan recorded what he read and taught, the time he spent in silent meditation, events, and visitors.[31] The record shows that Sōan studied whenever his other commitments allowed it.

*Igyō yokō* is a collection of maxims Sōan recorded between 1860 and 1877.[32] They are a mixture of general observations and personal reflections. Many stress the importance of study, especially of reading the classics and the histories (*keishi* 経史; e.g. nos. 1, 104, 166) and of following the Way without being swayed by the ways of the world. Sōan's teaching flowed from his own study and pursuit of self-improvement.[33] He attached great importance to training in self-discipline and moral education as well as observance of correct forms. The day began and ended with a short ceremony in which the pupils, after tidying their persons and putting their writing utensils in order, would sit lined up according to age to greet their teacher. Lessons themselves were informal. There were no desks, so pupils could not hide behind them and fool about; the texts were spread on fans. There were no formal ranks; pupils were grouped together roughly by ability, so group sizes varied. The older pupils taught the younger ones after being thoroughly briefed by Sōan. Lectures based on the Confucian classics were held in the morning and in the afternoon. There was not much teaching of composition and none of poetry. Sōan sometimes gave special lessons to slow or to exceptionally enthusiastic students.

---

30    Hikita, "Ikeda Sōan," 314–315.
31    Hikita, "Ikeda Sōan," 235–239.
32    Some of them are quoted and discussed in Ueda, *Tajima Seijin Ikeda Sōan*, 152–223, published with annotations in: Seikei Shoin Hozonkai, ed. *Seikei Shoin kaijuku 150 shūnen kinen (1): Igyō yokō/ Tajima seijin/Ikeda Sōan* (The 150th Anniversary of Seikei Shoin; Hyōgo-ken Yabu-gun Yōka-chō) (Seikei Shoin Hozonkai, 1998). For a sample, see Yabu city's homepage: <http://www.city.yabu.hyogo.jp/6637.htm> (accessed 22 December 2017).
33    Information on Sōan's teaching from the biographical sources, especially Toyoda, *Tajima no Seijin*, 62–71. Also Ueda Hirao, "Ikeda Sōan no kyōiku ni tsuite (About Ikeda Sōan's Education)," *The Himeji Gakuin Review* 11 (1980): 1–10; Hyōgo-ken Kyōikushi Henshū Iinkai, ed. *Hyōgo-ken kyōiku shi* (History of Education in Hyōgo Prefecture) (Kobe: Hyōgo-ken Kyōiku Iinkai, 1963), 343–348.

A formal curriculum, rules for student behavior and fixed fees were only specified after 1871, when the Ministry of Education demanded this from all who wished to continue running a private school. In autumn 1873, in answer to government orders, Sōan reluctantly submitted a formal application to run a *juku*. In a memorandum drawn up at the same time he laments the fact that he is forced to take this step.[34] The question of fees in particular disturbed him, since for him teaching was not something one did for the money.

The list of texts prepared for submission then contains the usual Confucian classics, grouped in order of priority:

> *Shōgaku* 小学 [*Xiaoxue*; *Elementary Learning*]; *Daigaku* 大学 [*Daxue*; *The Great Learning*]; *Rongo* 論語 [*Lunyu*; *Analects*]; *Mōshi* 孟子 [*Mengzi*; *Mencius*]; *Chūyō* 中庸 [*Zhongyong*; *Doctrine of the Mean*]; *Kinshiroku* 近思録 [*Jinsilu*; *Reflections on Things at Hand*].
> *Shikyō* 詩経 [*Shijing*; *Book of Odes*]; *Shokyō* 書経 [*Shujing*; *Book of Documents*]; *Ekikyō* 易経 [*Yijing*; *Book of Changes*].
> *Jūhatsu shiryaku* 十八史略 [*Shiba shilüe*; *Outlines of the Eighteen Histories*]; *Shunjū Sashiden* 春秋左氏伝 [*Chunqiu Zuo shi zhuan*; *Mr. Zuo's Commentary on the "Spring and Autumn Annals"*].
> *Bunsho kihan* 文章軌範 [*Wenzhang guifan*; *Model Compositions*]; *Tōsō hatsukabun* 唐宋八家文 [*Tang-Song ba da jia wen*; *Texts of the eight masters of Tang and Song prose*].[35]

Other texts were used according to students' needs.

Teaching was described as consisting of lectures and individual reading and texts named were the *Four Books* and *Five Classics* and the *Elementary Learning*; others ranged from the *Kinshi roku* to the collections of writers from the Song to the Ming as well ancient and modern Chinese and Japanese histories and European and Korean texts. The only *juku* regulation mentioned in the application is that seating order was to be independent of rank or ability, solely according to age, with the exception of students from the nobility, who were to be seated at the top of the class.

Outside lessons, pupils were encouraged to exercise and made to work in the fields and take part in the daily chores; this Sōan considered part of their education. Those students whom Sōan deemed suitable were given responsibility for maintaining discipline. He dealt with delinquents by talking to them and making them sit in silent meditation to reflect upon their misdeeds. If they

---

34   Both quoted in Seikei Shoin 9 (1982.11.25): 2–3.
35   As quoted in *Hyōgo ken kyōikushi*, 346.

offended a second time he notified the parents and if they offended a third time they had to leave; this happened rarely.

Who were Sōan's students? A total of 673 names are recorded in the student register from the time of Sōan's return to Tajima to the end of his life.[36] In the first five years, while he was teaching at Risseisha 立誠舎, Sōan taught a total of 62 pupils, most of whom came from Tajima and many from the surrounding Yabu district. Local students continued to be in the majority; 390, or 58 percent from the register, were from Tajima province. But the years 1865 to 1872 saw an increase in the number of students from outside Tajima. The overall number of entrants varied from year to year, but rose significantly from the 1860s. The highest number of 46 students is recorded for 1868 and after 1868 the number of entrants was between 20 and 40, except for 1873 (10) and 1878, the year of Sōan's death (12). Apart from Tajima, many pupils came from neighbouring provinces, such as Inaba, Harima, Tanba, and Tango, places where Sōan had personal connections. A significant number also came from Sanuki, including Tadotsu domain, where Sōan had visited Hayashi. Some came from as far afield as Hizen and Shimotsuke, including Utsunomiya domain, which had invited Sōan to an official post.

The increase of students from outside the locality after 1868 contrasts with the *juku* of Tsunetō Seisō and Murakami Butsusan in northern Kyushu, where students from outside the area tended to decrease.[37] Sōan, on the other hand, even received students from regions that had not previously been represented at Seikei Shoin, such as Hitachi, with two from Mito domain entering in 1871, and Kaga, with two pupils from Kanazawa domain entering in 1870 and one in 1871. Often several students from one province would come from the same district, suggesting that Sōan's name became known among a group of people, perhaps after one pupil had gone to Seikei Shoin. Most students were commoners, but many, especially among those that came from other regions, were samurai. In the years 1868 and 1869 the majority of entrants were samurai. Overall, out of the 673 named in the registers, 174 were samurai, 445 commoners, eight physicians, three Shinto priests, three Buddhist priests, and two members of the nobility.

The registers tell us only when a pupil entered, not how long he stayed, so it cannot be said precisely how many pupils were there at any one time. Moreover, many students came from local farming families and their attendance

---

36  Entrance registers in Toyoda, *Tajima no Seijin*, 1 (new pagination after page 87)–18. For an analysis see Maeshima Masamitsu, "Meiji ishin to hōken kyōgaku: Ikeda Sōan o chūshin ni (The Meiji Restoration and the Scholarship and Education of Feudalism)," *Shinwa joshi daigaku kenkyū ronsō* 26 (1993): 100–124, 104–108.

37  Mehl, *Private Academies*, 108.

would have varied with the seasons. In 1862 Sōan recorded that he had 30 boarders and eight to nine day pupils. In 1868 the number sank to around 10, but the same year saw a record number of entrants, and the buildings had to be extended. In 1869 he noted that he had about 50 in his *juku*.[38] At times up to 60 pupils are said to have lived in the *juku*, in two boarding houses of two floors each. Students cooked their own meals, buying their own rice, salt, firewood, and coal, fetching water and using vegetables grown in the fields nearby. Sōan ate with his students. The students also did their own cleaning and prepared their bath six times a month.[39]

The numbers show that Seikei Shoin thrived even after the introduction of the Education Law in 1872; it remained high until 1877, the year before Sōan's death, and many entrants came from outside Tajima. The isolation of the region and the lack of alternatives may well be the main reason, but the high number of students from other regions suggests that Sōan's person and teaching attracted students and contributed to the enduring success of Seikei Shoin.

After Sōan's death there was no one to take over Seikei Shoin, so it ceased to exist as a *juku*. His memory, on the other hand has been preserved to this day, thanks to the efforts of his former students.[40] In 1880 a memorial to Ikeda Sōan was erected and 1887 the Society to Preserve Seikei Shoin (*Seikei Shoin Hozon Kai* 青谿書院保存会) was formed, which became a foundation (*zaidan hōjin* 財団法人) in 1910.[41]

Seikei Shoin reflected the distinct personality and philosophy of its Master Ikeda Sōan, who despite his tendency towards reclusiveness and contemplation attracted may students from quite far afield. At the same time, it shared characteristics with other *juku*, such as the combination of reading Confucian classics and emphasis on discipline and moral training as well as the boardinghouse life as an extension of home life with students sharing in household work.

Because of Seikei Shoin's location in an isolated region one might speculate that Sōan's *juku* might well have continued for several more years, at least as a *juku* for local students, if a successor to Sōan had presented himself. The 1880s

---

38   Maeshima, "Meiji ishin to hōken kyōgaku," 107–108.
39   The architecture of Seikei Shoin is described in Kinki Daigaku Rikō Gakubu Kensetsu Gakka Kenchikushi Kenkyūshitsu (Sakurai Toshio and Matsuoka Toshirō), ed. *Kyōiku shisetsu no kenchikuteki kenkyū, Shijuku Kansanrō no chōsa kenkyū o chūshin to shite* (Research on the Architecture of Educational Institutions) (Osaka: Hachioshi Bunkazai Chōsa Kenkyūkai, 1983), 48–49; information on daily life from Toyoda, *Tajima no Seijin*, 68–70.
40   The following is from Ueda, *Tajima Seijin Ikeda Sōan*, 226–236.
41   It is still preserved and a local tourist spot: see <https://yabu-kankou.jp/sightseeing/seikei> (10 February 2020).

even saw the establishment of a few new *juku* in places where there was still a gap in educational provision. But many *juku* disappeared when their master died and most of those that did not, lasted no longer than another generation or two. By the 1890s the *juku* in its traditional form was becoming obsolete. The Education Law of 1872 laid down the principle of education as a route to worldly success and created the basis for a social order based on academic achievement rather than birth (*gakureki shakai*). It was this and other social changes rather than direct government intervention that caused the *juku* to disappear. There is no direct, institutional continuity from the historical *juku* to the present day *juku*, which many Japanese school children attend in addition to their regular school. This pattern of attendance, regular school and present-day *juku*, may, however, be an example of indirect continuity, which may also manifest itself in the proliferation of informal study groups, still a common feature in Japan.

One of the most remarkable legacies can be found in what I have described as the "*juku* myth," which was formed even as the *juku* themselves were dying out, and perhaps because they were dying out. This myth stresses the strong personal influence of the teacher, the deep ties between teacher and students, the community of students, and the emphasis on moral as well as intellectual training. Essentially, it is a specific expression of nostalgia; certain historical traits are exaggerated and elevated to evoke a vanishing way of life and a more intimate and humane way of education. Often this is motivated by dissatisfaction with the current school system, and in some cases the myth has inspired educators to create their own version of a *juku*.[42]

The *juku* myth, however, often has more to do with the *juku* as an institution rather than with the Confucian heritage. The changing significance of this heritage and especially the epistemological change that occurred in the course of the late 19th century were another major reason for the decline of the *kangaku juku*.

---

42   On myths and memories as a significant historical force, see Raphael Samuel and Paul Thompson, "Introduction," in *The Myths We Live By*, ed. Raphael Samuel and Paul Thompson (London: Routledge, 1990), 1–22. So prevalent is this myth that it is very difficult for the historian, not to see the *juku* through the lens of the myth. In *Private Academies*, I therefore decided to make the lens part of my study rather than to try and avoid it, see Mehl, *Private Academies*. On the *juku* ideal as an inspiration for educators in the twentieth century, see also Margaret Mehl, "N.E.S. Grundtvig, Niels Bukh and Other 'Japanese' Heroes. The Educators Obara Kuniyoshi and Matsumae Shigeyoshi and Their Lessons from the Past of a Foreign Country," *European Journal of East Asian Studies* 6.2 (2007): 155–184; and my "Lessons from history? Obara Kuniyoshi (1887–1977), new education and the role of Japan's educational traditions," *History of Education* 38.4 (2009): 525–543.

## 5 The *Kangaku Juku* and Epistemic Transformation[43]

During their continued existence, the *kangaku juku* may well have contributed to some of the achievements that are generally credited to the modern school system; they transmitted a common cultural heritage, including a common written language, which bound those that attended them together and contributed to a common identity. Even as the *juku* began to dwindle away from the late 1880s onwards, Confucianism was revived as the basis for moral education in all schools. In fact, these years saw general revival of Japanese traditions, including organized Confucianism.[44] A number of Confucian societies were created, while attention was also given to the study of Japanese and Chinese classics in higher education. At the Imperial University of Tokyo, a special department for Chinese and Japanese classical studies (Koten Kōshūka 古典講習科) was established in 1882 and in the same year an institute for Japanese philology was founded (Kōten Kōkyūsho 皇典講究所; the present Kokugakuin University).

These new institutions reflect the changing place of China and of *kangaku* in the intellectual world of Meiji Japan. *Kangaku*, from being the basis of both intellectual and moral training, was reconfigured: education in Confucian morals was separated from the scholarly study of China, which from the 1890s was carried out within the newly-emerging specialist disciplines of *tōyōshi* 東洋史 (Eastern history), *tōyō bungaku* 東洋文学 (Eastern literature) and *tōyō tetsugaku* 東洋哲学 (Eastern philosophy). While *kangaku* was the philological study of China, which stressed close reading of the classics in order to determine the truth that they defined, the new academic disciplines employed methods of textual criticism combined with Western scientific methods and comparative approaches to distinguish true facts.[45] All this was part of a major transformation, in which the

---

43   In the following I refer to the project "Episteme in Motion" at the Collaborative Research Center at Freie Universität Berlin, examination of processes of knowledge change (CRC 980). See also Eva Cancik-Kirschbaum and Anita Traninger, "Institution – Iteration – Transfer: Zur Einführung," in *Wissen in Bewegung: Institution – Iteration – Transfer*, ed. Eva Cancik-Kirschbaum and Anita Traninger (Wiesbaden: Harrassowitz, 2015). Chinese learning as knowledge that until the 19th century could claim universality gradually transformed into a field of study defined in relation to other fields and then, from the late 19th century into a series of modern academic disciplines dedicated to producing knowledge about China: see Facius, *China übersetzen*.

44   Warren Smith, *Confucianism in Modern Japan: A Study of Conservatism in Japanese Intellectual History* (Tokyo, Hokuseido Press, 1959), 56; Margaret Mehl, "Chinese Learning (*kangaku*) in Meiji Japan," *History* 85 (2000): 48–66.

45   Miura Kanai, "Meiji no shin kangakusha (akamon bunshi) to sono katsudō (The New Kangaku Scholars of Meiji (the Akamon Literati) and their Activities)," *Tōyō bunka, fukkan* 63

West replaced China as a universal and a normative reference. The Meiji government's program of modernization based on Western models entailed the adoption of the conceptual language of the West and the redrawing of Japan's cognitive map. The impact of the West's version of universalism was comparable to the large-scale adoptions of Confucian concepts in ancient Japan and of Neo-Confucianism in late medieval and early modern Japan.

The process of this profound transformation, however, was more gradual and more complex than past research has acknowledged. The continuing significance of "China" as a universal and a normative reference (in contrast to empirical China) is highlighted in a recent article by David Mervart. As Mervart (citing recent research by Japanese scholars) argues, "The fact that Western countries became the new frame of reference from the mid-19th century did not immediately change this: the West was worth emulating because it excelled in '"Chinese" normative virtues.'"[46] The continuing existence of the *kangaku juku* in Meiji Japan thus constitutes evidence of the continuing significance of China and Chinese learning.[47] At the same time the *juku* played a significant part in the process of transformation. This is perhaps best illustrated by the examples of two of the most eminent *kangaku* scholars of their time: Mishima Chūshū and Shigeno Yasutsugu 重野安繹 (Seisai 成斎, 1827–1910). They were two of the so-called "three literary masters of the Meiji era" (*Meiji no Sandai bunsō* 明治の三大文宗), and it is significant that all three of them were *kangaku* scholars.[48]

Shigeno was a vassal of the lord of Satsuma and taught at the school of his domain in the last years of the Tokugawa bakufu. After the Restoration, in summer 1869, he opened a *juku* in Osaka. In 1871 he moved it to Tokyo, at the end of that year he entered the Ministry of Education. In 1875 he became a member of the Office of Historiography.[49] Little is known about his *juku*, but in the Metropolitan Archives in Tokyo there are two applications by Shigeno, dated 1873 and

---

(1989): 51–64; Stefan Tanaka, *Japan's Orient: Rendering Past into History* (Berkeley: University of California Press, 1993). For a comprehensive study, see Smith, *Confucianism in Modern Japan*, 56.

46 David Mervart, "Meiji Japan's China Solution to Tokugawa Japan's China Problem," *Japan Forum* 27.4 (2015): 544–558, 555. See also Shillony, "The Meiji Restoration: Japan's Attempt to Inherit China."

47 For a comprehensive study of the changing place of Chinese and China-related knowledge in the 19th century, see Facius, *China übersetzen*.

48 Smith, *Confucianism in Modern Japan: A Study of Conservatism in Japanese Intellectual History*, 54. The third one was Kawada Takeshi 川田剛 (Ōkō 甕江, 1830–1896), official in the office of historiography and then in the imperial household.

49 On Shigeno as a historian, see Margaret Mehl, *History and the State in Nineteenth-Century Japan: The World, the Nation and the Search for a Modern Past* (Second edition with new

1888.⁵⁰ Comparing them with each other is interesting, as they show how Shigeno changed the character of what he offered in accordance with the times.

The first document, dated 1873, is an application for the *juku* opened in 1871. It offered *kangaku*, but there is a paragraph about Shigeno's principles for education, and it stresses that young people must also study Western learning and that all learning should be of practical use. The study of history is mentioned as being particularly important—hardly surprising, given Shigeno's work as a historian. The *juku* had two classes, for reading and training; in the first the students learned to read *kanbun* and do arithmetic, while in the second they studied political affairs and learned to write essays discussing current affairs and to compose memoranda to rulers. Thus the *juku* offered elementary education at a time when the state school system was only just beginning to be established; the importance given to the study of political affairs suggests that the *juku* catered for men wishing to enter government service. A few years later, Itō Hirobumi 伊藤博文 (1841–1909) denounced students from *kangaku juku*, who spent too much time debating world affairs.⁵¹

The statements about education are followed by rules relating to boarding, curfew, eating and drinking, and other aspects of student life. Remarkably, one clause explicitly permitted students to study Western learning as long as it did not interfere with their regular studies at the *juku*. This contrasts with Hayashi Kakuryō 林鶴梁 (1806–1878), for whom interest in things Western was a reason for expelling a student.⁵²

Shigeno's second application was made in 1888. We do not know the fate of Shigeno's *juku* between 1873 and 1888; presumably he at least taught informally. Again, the subject is *kangaku*. *Yōgaku* and arithmetic are left for students to study in their own time. Unlike the earlier *juku*, pupils are expected to have completed elementary school; by this time elementary schools were well established. The aim of the *juku* was to teach knowledge of *kangaku* writings necessary for the Japanese and to provide moral and ethical training. The curriculum of Seitatsu Shoin 成達書院 spelt out the textbooks for each semester, mostly Chinese classics and histories of Japan in *kanbun*. Advancement depended on passing exams. The

---

*preface*) (Copenhagen: The Sound Book Press, 2017). On his *juku*, see Mehl, *Private Academies*, 122–123, 161.

50  The documents relating to the opening of private schools are in the archives in the Metropolitan Library in Tokyo (Kaigaku gansho 開学願書). The applications for opening schools in Tokyo are printed in Tōkyō-to, ed. *Meiji 6 nen kaigaku meisaisho*, 7 vols. (Tokyo: Tōkyō-to, 1961–1963), Vol. 1, 377–76; 1888 application: *Tōkyō kyōiku shiryō taikei* (10 vols., Tōkyō Toritsu Kyōiku Kenkyūsho, 1971–4), Vol. 7 (1973), 667–668. The printed version of the 1888 application is incomplete.

51  Byron K. Marshall, *Learning to be Modern* (Boulder: Westview Press, 1994), 55.

52  Mehl, *Private Academies*, 49.

study of *kangaku* had largely been canonized in the Edo period, but including histories of Japan in *kanbun* was an innovation of the Meiji period. The rules for the boarding house were the usual ones,[53] but—interestingly in the light of Shigeno's previous application—included the prohibition of discussions about current affairs. This presumably reflects the tightening of controls on freedom of expression in the latter half of the Meiji era.

The number of students is given as 50, although a pupil who entered the following year later said there were only 34 pupils in his time. Most of them were also studying elsewhere. Shigeno himself was the only teacher named in the application, but, presumably, he devoted most of his time to his work as a historian. Lessons were mostly taught by others, presumably older pupils. Apparently the *juku* closed only two years later, possibly for financial reasons and because Shigeno could not devote enough time to it, but he continued to lecture regularly on the Confucian classics in his own home. The application of 1888 shows that Shigeno tried to set up something formal and permanent, but ultimately he failed. Those *juku* which were more successful were gradually absorbed into the formal education system.

Shigeno's *juku* may well have been typical of a *juku* in the capital at the time; Mishima Chūshū's was not, although the two men had a few things in common. Like Shigeno, Mishima had taught at the school of his domain (Matsuyama) and had opened a *juku* in the early years of Meiji, before moving to the capital to become a government official. He retired in 1877, however, and devoted all his time to teaching.[54]

Nishō Gakusha 二松学舎 was founded in October 1877. That month, Mishima submitted a formal application.[55] *Kangaku* is named as the only subject. The number of students is given as 50. The school rules begin with a list of the texts to be studied: the *Four Books* and *Five Classics*, histories of China, collections of models for writing, histories of Japan (*Nihon shi, Nihon gaishi, Koku-*

---

53  Examples in ibid., 135–145.
54  The following is largely based on ibid., 71–82. The principal sources on Mishima's biography and Nishō Gakusha are: Yamaguchi Kakuyō, *Mishima Chūshū: Nishō Gakusha no sōritsusha* (Mishima Chūshū: The Founder of Nishō Gakusha) (Tokyo: Nishō Gakusha, 1977); Yamada Taku and Umejirō Ishikawa, *Yamada Hōkoku/Mishima Chūshū* (*Sōsho Nihon no shisōka 41*) (Yamada Hōkoku and Mishima Chūshū) (Tokyo: Meitoku Shuppansha, 1977); Nishō Gakusha (ed.), *Nishō Gakusha hyakunenshi* (One Hundred Years' History of Nishō Gakusha; Tokyo: Nishō Gakusha, 1977); Nishō Gakusha (ed.), *Nishō Gakusha kyūjūnenshi* (Ninety Years' History of Nishō Gakusha) (Tokyo: Nishō Gakusha, 1967). On his thought, see also, Nakata Masaru, *Mishima Chūshū* (*Shiriizu Yōmeigaku 34*) (Tokyo: Meitoku Shuppansha, 1990).
55  Printed in Tōkyō Toritsu Kyōiku Kenkyūsho ed. *Tōkyō kyōikushi shiryō taikei*, 10 vols. (Tokyo: Tōkyō Toritsu Kyōiku Kenkyūsho, 1971–1974), 3: 248–249.

*shiryaku*) and "histories of all the Western countries," as well as "translations of texts on economics, law, and so forth." The school regulations continue: "This school makes training in *kanbun* its main aim, but since it is impossible to compose texts without being well read, we will, in addition to meetings for writing and discussing compositions, prescribe time for the Japanese, Chinese, and Western texts mentioned above and teach them by means of lectures (*kōshaku* 講釈), group reading (*kaidoku* 会読), giving opportunities for questions (*shitsumon* 質問) and simple reading aloud (*sodoku* 素読)."

In 1879 new regulations were printed.[56] They include a statement on the aims of Nishō Gakusha, entitled *Kangaku tai'i* 漢学大意 [The Main Purpose of Chinese Learning] with the following text:

> The aim of *kangaku* is to cultivate oneself, to govern other people, and to become a person who will be useful in their lifetime; it is not to become merely a Confucian scholar whose learning and literary skills are without practical application. Therefore, the foundations have to be laid by justice and humanity and morality. This is the reason for lessons in the Confucian classics. Furthermore, it is necessary to know the changes of the times (*jisei*) and the development of institutions and laws and to excel in the talent of adapting to the changing environment. This is the reason for lessons in history. But in order to put this learning into practice it is necessary to employ writing to expand and cultivate learning. Also, even if one cannot put it into practice because it is not suited to the times, that learning can be transmitted by writing and made available for future generations. Therefore, since writing becomes a tool to activate what has been learnt, that is not dependent on circumstances, it must certainly be studied. This is the reason for lessons in writing. To learn them it is necessary to employ old and new models. This is the reason for lessons to study the sages and the collections of model writings. To include poetry may not be necessary, but nevertheless this is a part of composition, and since it has a use for expressing one's will, these lessons must not be dispensed with.

> Thus we offer the subjects Confucian classics, history, collections of the sages, and poetry, and it is our purpose to produce people who are useful to the world, who read books, but do not fall into investigating texts to the smallest detail and pick out individual phrases, who compose

---

56 *Nishō Gakusha shasoku* (School Regulations of Nishō Gakusha) (Tokyo: Nishō Gakusha 1879 [June]). Digital collection of the National Diet Library, <http://dl.ndl.go.jp/info:ndljp/pid/813322>.

poetry but do not get carried away into whittling away at every word. Moreover, although the overabundance of Chinese works cannot be exhausted with the few works we read in our lessons, in this age *yōgaku* [Western learning] is widely practiced, and *kangaku* does not extend to reach the minuteness of *yōgaku*'s final truths, laws, technology, and so forth. At least those who want to study learning that is of practical use have to study Western works as well. That is why we make the *kangaku* lessons simple, and just leave space to study Western writings. If people wish to make *kangaku* their sole object of study and hope from the start to read widely, that is a reason for setting up the opportunity for questions. We hope that all who enter this school to study will understand this "import" and then study the lessons one by one and become useful in their lifetime.[57]

Evidently, Mishima read the signs of the times. His approach was pragmatic. He did not offer anything but *kangaku* in his school, but he realized that his students needed to become proficient in Western learning as well and provided space for them to acquire it.

This is also reflected in the curriculum given in the regulations; it is among the most comprehensive for a *kangaku juku* and includes nearly all the works mentioned the curricula of other *kangaku juku* of the period. It was divided into four ranks, of which the fourth was subdivided into two courses, the rest into four. Twenty-three works are listed, beginning with the *Four Books* and the *Five Classics*. Most of them are Chinese, but some Japanese works in *kanbun* are included, such as the *Nihon gaishi* 日本外史 (*The Extra History of Japan*) by Rai San'yō 頼山陽 (1780–1832), which was widely read, and the *Dainihonshi* 大日本史 (*The History of Great Japan*), which was more unusual. Teaching methods are also mentioned: reading (*sodoku*), translating classical Japanese back into classical Chinese in class, descriptive compositions in class, and composing argument and poetry in class. The regulations stated that apart from the texts named, anything in Japanese or Chinese or translations from Western works could be read that did not do damage to good conduct or contradict national prohibitions. Moreover, students who were older, perhaps already pursuing a career or studying elsewhere and not able to follow the regular curriculum, could, if they provided an explanation from their guarantor, study whatever they chose.

The curriculum was adjusted several times. According to the one-hundredth anniversary history of Nishō Gakusha, the following curriculum applied from 1879 to 1882; it mentioned 39 works, more than the curriculum in the printed

---

57   Author's translation. See Mehl, *Private Academies*, 74.

regulations, but omitted some works included previously. It is quoted here as an example of one of the most comprehensive kangaku curricula:[58]

*3rd rank*
COURSE 3: *Nihon gaishi* 日本外史 [*The Extra History of Japan*]; *Nihon seiki* 日本政記 [*A Record of Japanese Government*]; *Jūhatsu shiryaku* 十八史略 [*Shiba shi lue; Outlines of the Eighteen Histories*]; *Kokushiryaku* 国史略 [*Outline of Our National History*], *Shōgaku* 小学 [*Xiaoxue; Elementary Learning*].
COURSE 2: *Seiken igon* 靖献遺言; *Mōgyū* 蒙求 [*Mengqiu*]; *Bunsho kihan* 文章軌範 [*Wengzhang guifan*].[59]
COURSE 1: *Tōshisen* 唐詩選 [*Tang shi xuan; Selection of Poetry from the Tang Dynasty*]; *Kōchō shiryaku* 皇朝史略 [*Historical Outline of Japan*]; *Kobun shinpō* 古文真宝 [*Guwen zhenbao*]; *Fukubun* 複文 [*Fuwen*].

*2nd rank*
COURSE 3: *Mōshi* 孟子 [*Mengzi; Mencius*]; *Shiki* 史記 [*Shiji; Historical Records by Sima Qian*]; *Bunsho kihan* 文章軌範; *Santaishi* 三体詩 [*San ti shi*], *Rongo* 論語 [*Lunyu; Analects*].
COURSE 2: *Rongo* 論語; *Tōsō hatsukabun* 唐宋八家文 [*Tang-Song ba da jia wen*]; *Zenkōkansho* 前後漢書 [*Qianhou Han shu; Histories of the Han Dynasty*].
COURSE 1: *Shunju Sashiden* 春秋左氏伝 [*Chunqiu Zuo shi zhuan; Zuo commentary on the "Spring and Autumn Annals"*]; *Kōkyō* 孝経 [*Xiaojing; Classic of Filial Piety*]; *Daigaku* 大学 [*Daxue; The Great Learning*]

*1st rank*
COURSE 3: *Kanpishi* 韓非子 [*Han fei zi*]; *Kokugo* 国語 [*Guoyu; Conversations of the States*]; *Sengokusaku* 戦国策 [*Zhanguo ce; Intrigues of the Warring States*]; *Chūyō* 中庸 [*Zhongyong; Doctrine of the Mean*]; *Sōshi* 荘子 [*Zhuangzi*].
COURSE 2: *Shikyō* 詩経 [*Shijing; Book of Odes*]; *Sonshi* 孫子 [*Sun zi*]; *Bunsen* 文選 [*Wenxuan*]; *Sōshi* 荘子 [*Zhuangzi*]; *Shokyō* 書経 [*Shujing; Book of

---

58   *Nishō Gakusha Hyakunenshi*, 124–126, presumably, the curriculum cited here is the later one of the two, but this is not quite clear.

59   *Seiken igen*: by Asami Keisai, 1689; collection of final sayings by famous Chinese heroes with biographical notes and Japanese loyalists' acts. *Mōgyū*: 746, textbook for beginners; collection of sayings and anecdotes from the ancients with four-character phrases as titles; used in Japan since the Heian period. *Bunshō kihan*: 13th century; for preparing for examinations; models for essays; widely read in Japan since the mid-Edo period.

*Documents*]; *Kinshiroku* 近思録 [*Jinsilu*; *Reflections on Things at Hand*]; *Junshi* 荀子 [*Xunzi*].

COURSE 1: *Shūeki* 周易 [*Zhouyi*; *Book of Changes*]; *Reiki* 礼記 [*Liji*; *Book of Rites*]; *Rōshi* 老子 [*Laozi*]; *Bokushi* 墨子 [*Mozi*]; *Meiritsu* 明律 [*Minglü*; *Penal Code of the Ming Dynasty*]; *Ryōnogige* 令義解.[60]

Over the years, details changed, but the essence remained the same. Mishima aimed to provide an education in the Chinese classics and in Chinese and Japanese history, while at the same time making concessions to the fact that most of his students would not be devoting all their time to *kangaku*. Like Shigeno, Mishima aimed to educate future statesmen and bureaucrats. In fact, as a result of Mishima's connections with the Ministry of Justice many students came to him to prepare for the Ministry's entrance examination or for entry into the law school attached to the Ministry. Others prepared for entry into the Army's school.

When it was established, Nishō Gakusha had 32 students, which had increased to close to 300 two years later. The 1880s saw a decline in numbers, probably a result of government measures to curtail private education, economic depression (which caused student numbers to drop everywhere), and the increasing dominance of Western education. But in the more favorable economic climate after the Sino-Japanese War, student numbers increased again. Like Shigeno, Mishima was not opposed to his students pursuing other studies besides *kangaku*; it even appears that many students studied mainly elsewhere, using Nishō Gakusha as a boarding house, since it was reputed to be cheap. Mishima probably needed such students to make his school financially viable, but he did insist that they at least come to his morning lectures. An example is Kanō Jigorō 嘉纳治五郎 (1860–1938), educator and founder of Kōdōkan jūdō, who boarded at Nishō Gakusha while studying politics and economics at Tokyo University.

Mishima's *juku* had the status of an equivalent to middle school (*hensoku chūgakkō* 変則中学校), but Mishima aimed to make it a regular middle school (*seisoku chūgakkō* 正則中学校). At that time there were only 31 public middle schools, none of them in Tokyo, where the first one opened in 1878, so Mishima was filling a gap in provision. The following year, however, the government changed the goalposts by introducing a new curriculum for middle schools; schools offering only a limited range of subjects were classed among the

---

60   A Japanese work by Kiyohara Natsuno 清原夏野, 833; official commentary on the Yōrō Code of 718; like the histories of Japan this did not figure in conventional *kangaku* curricula.

private schools of miscellaneous types (*shiritsu kakushu gakkō* 私立各種学校). Still there were only three regular middle schools in Tokyo and thus there was little pressure for private schools to conform. Nishō Gakusha continued to provide specialized education in *kangaku* in the best *juku* tradition. Even when restrictions for private schools did increase, Mishima managed to secure a niche for his *juku* by filling a gap in the provision of education; his *juku* catered for students preparing for exams requiring *kanbun*. Mishima aimed to establish Nishō Gakusha as a permanent institution and in order to achieve this made good use of his connections in government and the imperial house. Successful alumni actively secured financial support. Just after Mishima's death, Nishō Gakusha became a foundation (*zaidan hōnin* 財団法人); its existence beyond the lifetime of its founder was thus secured.

Mishima founded his *juku* in a climate favourable to *kangaku*. By the late 1870s reaction against the excesses of Westernization had begun to set in and attempts were made to revive Japanese traditions including *kangaku*. The value of Confucianism for moral education was recognized. Nishō Gakusha with its emphasis and moral education and character training fitted well into this trend.[61] The fact that some of the most prominent *kangaku* scholars of the previous generation died around 1877 (such as Hayashi Kakuryō and Yasui Sokken) may also have benefited Nishō Gakusha. At the same time, Nishō Gakusha, while showing many characteristics of traditional *kangaku juku*, gradually took on the role of a modern school providing training in one specialized field of study and thus both reflecting and contributing to the changing position of *kangaku*.

## 6   Conclusion

Shigeno Yasutsugu's and Mishima Chūshū's *juku*, for all the differences between them both illustrate the epistemic change that occurred in the two scholars' lifetime as well as the way the *kangaku juku* helped bring this change about (although the change eventually rendered them obsolete), by transmitting the *kangaku* from one era to the other, enabling it to transform in the process.

Shigeno Yasutsugu was one of the most important scholars of the Meiji period. He is particularly interesting in our context, because he is credited with being one of the pioneers of modern historical scholarship, although in his time he was equally (if not more) well known as a *kangaku* scholar. His

---

61   *Nishō Gakusha shasoku* (Tokyo: Nishō Gakusha, 1879 [June]).

writings show him as being deeply rooted in the tradition of Chinese learning and even a world view characterized by China as the normative reference.[62] Although in his lectures he stressed that Japan must go with the times (*jisei*), combining Western achievements with Japanese traditions,[63] he himself continued to look upon China as the source of true learning. A good example of this is his lecture "On the Methods of Historical Compilation" (1879), in which Chinese historiography, especially the definitive standard history (*zheng shi*, Jpn. *seishi* 正史) is treated as the standard by which he measures all works of history.[64] Another example is his lecture "All Scholarship is Ultimately *Kōshō* 考証 Textual Criticism."[65] *Kōshōgaku* 考証学 (Chin. *kaozhengxue*; "school of verifications and proofs") originated in China (at the time of the Qing dynasty [1644–1912], when Neo-Confucian studies in China were at their height). The new school of textual criticism was characterized by its close examination and interpretation of Confucian classics. In Japan, the same methods were applied to the study of Japanese texts. Scholars have credited *kōshōgaku* as being a major influence in the emerging modern humanities disciplines.[66] Shigeno himself equated *kōshō* with the Western concept of induction. He explained this term with the etymology of the Sino-Japanese *kinō* 帰納, with which "induction" was translated, and does not seem to have distinguished this from the meaning of "induction" in the Western sense of inferring a general law from particular instances.

This is just one of many examples of how using Chinese terms to translate Western concepts could blur the distinction between different cultural and epistemological traditions. Another would be the use of the word *ongaku* 音楽 to translate the Western concept of "music," which had no equivalent in Japan. It had connotations of serious, official, predominantly instrumental

---

62 Mehl, "Chinese Learning (*kangaku*) in Meiji Japan." He did, however, contribute to the transformation of *kangaku*; see, for example, Demin Tao, "Shigeno Yasutsugu as an Advocate of 'Practical Sinology' in Meiji Japan," in *Nihon kangaku shisō ronkō* (Suita: Kansai Daigaku Shuppanbu, 1999).

63 Shigeno Yasutsugu, "Rekishi to kyōiku (History and Education)," in *Zōtei Shigeno hakushi shigaku ronbunshū* (Revised and extended collection of articles by Shigeno Yasutsugu), ed. Ōkubo Toshiaki (Tokyo: Meicho Fukyūkai, 1989 [1890]).

64 Shigeno Yasutsugu, "'Rekishi hensan no hōhō o ronzu (On the Methods of Historical Compilation)," in *Zōtei Shigeno hakushi shigaku ronbunshū*, ed. Ōkubo, Toshiaki (Tokyo: Meicho Fukyūkai, 1989 [1879]).

65 Shigeno Yasutsugu, "Gakumon wa tsui ni kōshō ni ki su (All Scholarship is Ultimately *kōshō* Textual Criticism)," in *Zōtei Shigeno hakushi shigaku ronbunshū*, ed. Ōkubo Toshiaki (Tokyo: Meicho Fukyūkai, 1989 [1890]).

66 Most recently, from a comparative perspective, Takemura Eiji, *Edo kōki jusha no firorogi* (Philology by Confucian Scholars in the Late Edo Period) (Kyoto: Shibunkaku, 2016).

music—in other words, the sort of music that could be part of "rites and music" (*reigaku* 礼楽). Another connotation of *ongaku* is "foreign," which in ancient Japan meant Chinese and in the Tokugawa and Meiji periods increasingly meant "Western."[67] In a recent work by a Japanese music scholar, Shigeno is credited with having moved the *kokugaku* scholar Konakamura Kiyonori 小中村清矩 (1822–1895), the author of the first book-length comprehensive history of music, to change the title of his book to *Kabu ongaku ryakushi* 歌舞音楽略史 (*A Brief History of Singing and Dancing and Music*, published in 1888). Konakamura had previously used the term *ongyoku* 音曲 rather than *ongaku*.[68]

Not only did Shigeno's scholarship both reflect and contribute to the transformation of Chinese knowledge and of knowledge in general in 19th-century Japan, revealing him as a scholar rooted in the idea of a universal China as well as a pioneer of modern science (here used in the broad sense of *Wissenschaft*) that built both on practices developed in the Tokugawa period and—as far as possible with his limited knowledge of them—practices introduced from the West.[69] The fact that Shigeno, after 1868, ran a *kangaku juku* even while pursuing a career first in government offices and then at the Imperial University, likewise shows him as a scholar straddling two worlds—or perhaps, more appropriately, two types of institutions in one world that was undergoing a profound transformation.[70] The institutional transition to modernity was a long, uneven, winding path rather than the straight flat road it has often been

---

67  See Hosokawa Shuhei, "Ongaku, Onkyō/Music, Sound," in *Working Words: New Approaches to Japanese Studies* (Center for Japanese Studies, UC Berkeley, 2012).

68  Saitō Kei, <*Ura*> *Nihon ongakushi: ikei no kindai* (The "Other Side" of the History of Music in Japan: a strange-looking modernity) (Tokyo: Shunjūsha, 2015). Saitō also credits Shigeno with having authored the very first history of music that treated music comprehensively, across the genres, published in two parts in 1881 and 1883 with the title, *Fūzoku kabu genryū kō* 風俗歌舞源流考 (Considerations about the Origin of Popular Music and Dance). Shigeno also contributed a preface in *kanbun* to Konakamura's work.

69  For the field of historiography, see Mehl, *History and the State in Nineteenth-Century Japan*, 2–3, 15–16, 77–18, 101–102.

70  This is not the place for an extensive treatment of the concept of modernity, but I have drawn on newer discussions that pay attention to different forms modernity takes in different times and places. These different forms result from the "plurality of pasts" and the "plurality of futures" or, in other words, the variations in "preexisting conditions" and "available modernities." In the realm of education in Japan after 1868, the "preexisting conditions" include the educational institutions of the Tokugawa period and the dominance of *kangaku* as the basis of learning. See Sudipta Kaviraj, "An Outline of a Revisionist Theory of Modernity," *European Journal of Sociology* 46, no. 3 (2005): 497–526, 498, 500; Carol Gluck, "The End of Elsewhere: Writing Modernity Now (AHR Roundtable)," *American Historical Review* 116, no. 3 (2011): 676–687, 679, 681.

represented as in the past. Chinese learning continued to be part of the baggage as Japan travelled along this path, and was reconfigured in the process. In the course of the transition the cognitive and epistemological map was redrawn in response to the geopolitical shift that characterized the 19th century. The history of the *kangaku juku* sheds light on these changes.

### References

Bellah, Robert N. *Tokugawa Religion: The Values of Pre-Industrial Japan*. Glencoe, IL: The Tree Press, 1957.

Cancik-Kirschbaum, Eva, and Anita Traninger. "Institution – Iteration – Transfer: Zur Einführung." In *Wissen in Bewegung: Institution – Iteration – Transfer*, edited by Eva Cancik-Kirschbaum and Anita Traninger, 1–13. Wiesbaden: Harrassowitz, 2015.

Dore, Ronald P. *Education in Tokugawa Japan*. London: The Athlone Press, 1984.

Facius, Michael. *China übersetzen: Globalisierung und Chinesisches Wissen im Japan im 19. Jahrhundert*. Frankfurt a.M.: Campus, 2017.

Gluck, Carol. "The End of Elsewhere: Writing Modernity Now (AHR Roundtable)." *American Historical Review* 116, no. 3 (2011): 676–687.

Hikita Seiyū 疋田啓佑. "Ikeda Sōan 池田草庵." In *Kasuga Sen'an, Ikeda Sōan* 春日潜庵・池田草庵 (*Sōsho Nihon no shisōka, 44*), edited by Ōnishi Harutaka 大西晴隆 and Hikita Seiyū 疋田啓佑, 181–344. Tokyo: Meitoku Shuppansha, 1986.

Hiroshima-Ken Rekishi Hakubutsukan 広島県歴史博物館 (ed.). *Fukuyama-han no kyōiku to bunka: Edo jidai kōki o chūshin ni* 福山藩の教育と文化: 江戸時代後期を中心に (Education and Culture in Fukuyama Domain in the Edo Period). Fukuyama: Hiroshima-ken Hakubutsukan Tomonokai, 1994.

Hosokawa, Shuhei. "Ongaku, Onkyō/Music, Sound." In *Working Words: New Approaches to Japanese Studies*, 1–22. Center for Japanese Studies, UC Berkeley, 2012.

Hosoya Toshio 細谷俊夫. *Shin kyōikugaku daijiten* 新教育大事典 (*New Encyclopedia of Education*). Edited by Shohan. 8 vols. Tokyo: Daiichi Hōki Shuppan, 1990.

Hyōgo-Ken Kyōikushi Henshū Iinkai 兵庫県教育史編集委員会 (ed.). *Hyōgo-ken kyōiku shi Hyōgo-ken kyōiku shi* 兵庫県教育史 (History of Education in Hyōgo Prefecture). Kobe: Hyōgo-ken Kyōiku Iinkai, 1963.

Inoue Yoshimi 井上義巳. *Nihon kyōiku shisō no kenkyū* 日本教育思想の研究 (Research on Educational Thought in Japan). Tokyo: Keisō Shobō, 1978.

Ishikawa, Matsutarō. "The Meiji Restoration and Educational Reforms." *Acta Asiatica* 54 (1988): 24–47.

Kaviraj, Sudipta. "An Outline of a Revisionist Theory of Modernity." *European Journal of Sociology* 46, no. 3 (2005): 497–526.

Kinki Daigaku Rikō Gakubu Kensetsu Gakka Kenchikushi Kenkyūshitsu 近畿大学理工学部建築学科建築史研究室 (Sakurai Toshio and Matsuoka Toshirō) (ed.). *Kyōiku shisetsu no kenchikuteki kenkyū, Shijuku Kansanrō no chōsa kenkyū o chūshin to shite* 教育施設の建築的研究，私塾・環山楼の調査研究を中心として− (Research on the Architecture of Educational Institutions). Osaka: Hachioshi Bunkazai Chōsa Kenkyūkai, 1983.

Maeshima Masamitsu 前嶋雅光. "Meiji ishin to hōken kyōgaku: Ikeda Sōan o chūshin ni 明治維新と封建教学: 池田草庵を中心に (The Meiji Restoration and the Scholarship and Education of Feudalism)." *Shinwa joshi daigaku kenkyū ronsō* 26 (1993): 100–124.

Marshall, Byron K. *Learning to be Modern*. Boulder: Westview Press, 1994.

Mehl, Margaret. "Chinese Learning (*kangaku*) in Meiji Japan." *History* 85 (2000): 48–66.

Mehl, Margaret. *History and the State in Nineteenth-Century Japan: The World, the Nation and the Search for a Modern Past (Second edition with new preface)*. Copenhagen: The Sound Book Press, 2017.

Mehl, Margaret. "Lessons From History? Obara Kuniyoshi (1887–1977), New Education and the Role of Japan's Educational Traditions." *History of Education* 38, no. 4 (2009): 525–543.

Mehl, Margaret. "N.E.S. Grundtvig, Niels Bukh and Other 'Japanese' Heroes: The Educators Obara Kuniyoshi and Matsumae Shigeyoshi and Their Lessons from the Past of a Foreign Country." *European Journal of East Asian Studies* 6, no. 2 (2007): 155–184.

Mehl, Margaret. *Private Academies of Chinese Learning in Meiji Japan: The Decline and Transformation of the Kangaku Juku*. Copenhagen: NIAS Press, 2003.

Mervart, David. "Meiji Japan's China Solution to Tokugawa Japan's China Problem." *Japan Forum* 27, no. 4 (2015): 544–558.

Miura Kanai 三浦叶. "Meiji no shin kangakusha (akamon bunshi) to sono katsudō 明治の新漢学者「赤門文士」とその活動 (The New Kangaku Scholars of Meiji [the Akamon Literati] and Their Activities)." *Tōyō bunka, fukkan* 63 (1989): 51–64.

Nakata Masaru 中田勝. *Mishima Chūshū* 三島中洲 (*Shiriizu Yōmeigaku* シリーズ陽明学 34). Tokyo: Meitoku Shuppansha, 1990.

Naramoto Tatsuya 奈良本辰也. *Nihon no hankō* 日本の藩校 (The Domain Schools of Japan). Kyoto/Tokyo: Tankōsha, 1970.

Nishō Gakusha 二松學舍 (ed.). *Nishō Gakusha hyakunenshi* 二松學舍百年史 (One Hundred Years' History of Nishō Gakusha). Tokyo: Nishō Gakusha, 1977.

Nishō Gakusha 二松學舍 (ed.). *Nishō Gakusha kyūjūnenshi* 二松学舎九十年史 (Ninety Years' History of Nishō Gakusha). Tokyo: Nishō Gakusha, 1967.

Okada Takehiko 岡田たけひこ. *Edoki no jūgaku* 江戸期の儒学 (Confucianism in the Edo Period). Tokyo: Mokujisha, 1982.

Rubinger, Richard. *Private Academies of Tokugawa Japan.* Princeton: Princeton University Press, 1982.

Rubinger, Richard. "Education: From One Room to One System." In *Japan in Transition: From Tokugawa to Meiji,* edited by Marius B. Jansen and Gilbert Rozman, 195–230. Princeton: Princeton University Press, 1986.

Saitō Kei 斎藤桂. *<Ura> Nihon ongakushi: ikei no kindai*〈裏〉日本音楽史: 異形の近代 (The "Other Side" of the History of Music in Japan: A Strange-looking Modernity). Tokyo: Shunjūsha, 2015.

Seikei Shoin Hozonkai 青谿書院保存会 (ed.). *Seikei Shoin kaijuku 150 shunen kinen (1): Igyō yokō/ Tajima seijin/Ikeda Sōan* 青谿書院家塾150周年記念 (1): 肄業餘稿・但馬聖人・池田草庵 (The 150th Anniversary of Seikei Shoin. Hyōgo-ken Yabu-gun Yōkachō). Seikei Shoin Hozonkai, 1998.

Shigeno Yasutsugu 重野安繹. "Rekishi hensan no hōhō o ronzu 歴史編纂の方法を論ず (On the Methods of Historical Compilation)." In *Zōtei Shigeno hakushi shigaku ronbunshū* 増訂重野博士史学論文集, edited by Ōkubo Toshiaki 大久保利謙, 1–8. Tokyo: Meicho Fukyūkai, 1989 (1879).

Shigeno Yasutsugu 重野安繹. "Gakumon wa tsui ni kōshō ni ki su 学問は遂に考証に帰す (All Scholarship is Ultimately *Kōshō* Textual Criticism)." In *Zōtei Shigeno hakushi shigaku ronbunshū* 増訂重野博士史学論文集 (Revised and Extended Collection of Articles by Shigeno Yasutsugu), edited by Ōkubo Toshiaki 大久保利謙, 35–47. Tokyo: Meicho Fukyūkai, 1989 (1890).

Shigeno Yasutsugu 重野安繹. "Rekishi to kyōiku 歴史と教育 (History and Education)." in *Zōtei Shigeno hakushi shigaku ronbunshū* 増訂重野博士史学論文集, edited by Ōkubo Toshiaki 大久保利謙, 49–61. Tokyo: Meicho Fukyūkai, 1989 (1890).

Shillony, Ben-Ami. "The Meiji Restoration: Japan's Attempt to Inherit China." In *War, Revolution & Japan,* edited by Ian Neary, 20–32. Sandgate, Folkestone, Kent: Japan Library, 1993.

Smith, Warren. *Confucianism in Modern Japan: A Study of Conservatism in Japanese Intellectual History.* Tokyo: Hokuseido Press, 1959.

Steininger, Brian. *Chinese Literary Forms in Heian Japan: Poetics and Practice.* Cambridge, MA: Harvard University Asia Center, 2017.

Suzuki Hiroo 鈴木博雄. *Genten/kaisetsu Nihon kyōikushi* 原点・解説日本教育史 (Sources and Comentaries on the History of Education in Japan). Tokyo: Nihon Tosho Bunka Kyōkai, 1994 (1985).

Takemura Eiji 竹村英二. *Edo kōki jusha no firorogi-* 江戸後期儒者のフィロロギー (*Philology by Confucian Scholars in the Late Edo Period*). Kyoto: Shibunkaku, 2016.

Tanaka Kayo 田中加代. "Kangien. Hirose Tansō no shijuku kyōiku ga konnichi ni ataeru imi 広瀬淡窓の塾教育が今日に与える意味 (Hirose Tansō's *juku* Education and its Meaning for Today)." *Katei kagaku* 61.3 (1994): 54–58.

Tanaka, Stefan. *Japan's Orient: Rendering Past into History*. Berkeley: University of California Press, 1993.

Tao, Demin. "Shigeno Yasutsugu as an Advocate of 'Practical Sinology' in Meiji Japan." In *Nihon kangaku shisō ronkō*, 69–81. Suita: Kansai Daigaku Shuppanbu, 1999.

Tōkyō-To (ed.). *Meiji 6 nen kaigaku meisaisho* 明治6年開学明細書. 7 vols. Tokyo: Tōkyō-to, 1961–1963.

Tōkyō Toritsu Kyōiku Kenkyūsho 東京都立教育研究所 (ed.). *Tōkyō kyōikushi shiryō taikei* 東京教育史資料大系. 10 vols. Tokyo: Tōkyō Toritsu Kyōiku Kenkyūsho, 1971–1974.

Tosh, John. *The Pursuit of History (Revised Third Edition)*. London: Longman, 2002.

Toyoda Shōhachirō 豊田小八郎. *Tajima no Seijin* 但馬の聖人 (The Sage of Tajima). Yōkachō: Seikei Shoin, 1983 (1907).

Ueda Hirao 上田平雄. "Ikeda Sōan no kyōiku ni tsuite 池田草庵の教育について (About Ikeda Sōan's Education)." *The Himeji Gakuin Review* 11 (1980): 1–10.

Ueda Hirao 上田平雄. *Tajima Seijin Ikeda Sōan* 但馬聖人池田草庵 (Ikeda Sōan, the Sage of Tajima). Kasei: Fuji Shoō/Tajima Bunka Kyōkai, 1993.

Umihara Tōru 海原徹. *Nihonshi shōhyakka: Gakkō* 日本史小百科: 学校 (A Little Encyclopedia of Japan: Schools). Tokyo: Kondō Shuppansha, 1979.

Watanabe, Hiroshi. "Jusha, Literati and Yangban, Confucianists in Japan, China and Korea." *Senri Ethnological Studies* 28 (1990): 13–30.

Yamada Taku 山田琢, and Umejirō Ishikawa 石川梅次郎. *Yamada Hōkoku/Mishima Chūshū (Sōsho Nihon no shisōka 41* 叢書日本の思想家 *41)* 山田方谷・三島中洲 (Yamada Hōkoku and Mishima Chūshū). Tokyo: Meitoku Shuppansha, 1977.

Yamaguchi Kakuyō 山口角鷹. *Mishima Chūshū: Nishō Gakusha no sōritsusha* 三島中洲－二松学舎の創立者 (Mishima Chūshū: The Founder of Nishō Gakusha). Tokyo: Nishō Gakusha, 1977.

# PART 2

## *Curriculum of Confucian Academies*

CHAPTER 6

# Like Tea and Rice at Home: Lecture Gatherings and Academies during the Ming Dynasty

*Deng Hongbo*

## 1   Introduction

Confucian academies were cultural and educational institutions, run by scholars, that within their framework carried out various activities such as book collection, study, teaching, discussions, examination preparation, writing, and publishing. In the more than thousand-year-long history of the academies, their development during the Ming dynasty certainly stands out. While still inheriting models and concepts from the past, the academies underwent enormous transformations. One of the most important aspects of their development during this period was their extensive interactions with the state. Because the Ming government generally feared the intellectual autonomy of the academies, it sought to suppress their rise through different strategies. In the early years of the Ming, many academies were co-opted or transformed into state schools, ensuring their loyalty by integrating them into the educational system with the civil service examinations at its core. The state further refrained from providing financial support for more independent academies, making it challenging to sustain an institution outside the official system, which led to the decline of many academies. However, the financial burden of a comprehensive educational system proved too heavy for the state and the academies made a remarkable comeback as government-sponsored education gradually weakened. This, together with the rise of new intellectual trends promoted through the academies, brought about an unprecedented bloom of Confucian academies in middle and late Ming period.[1] As feared by the government the academies at this point began to provide space for dissenting voices and the struggle

---

[1]  For an overview of the development of Confucian academies in the Ming dynasty see Bai Xinliang, *Ming qing shuyuan yanjiu* (Study of Academies in the Ming and Qing Dynasties) (Baoding: Gugong chubanshe, 2012); for English sources see John Meskill, *Academies in Ming China* (Tucson: University of Arizona Press, 1982); and Thomas H.C. Lee, *Education in Traditional China. A History* (Leiden: Brill, 2000), 99–104. On the history of local state schools in the Ming dynasty see Sarah Schneewind, *Community Schools and the State in Ming China* (Stanford: Stanford University Press, 2006).

between state and academies led to a total of twelve crackdowns on the academies under three Ming emperors.[2]

All fifteen provinces of Ming China hosted academies, which amounted to a total of over two thousand and by far exceeded the number of academies during the Tang und Song dynasties. The academy system saw its extraordinary growth during the Ming dynasty due to popularity of Wang Yangming 王陽明 (1472–1529) and Zhan Ruoshui 湛若水 (1466–1560), whose followers established many academies in the roughly one hundred years of the Zhengde 正德 (r. 1505–1521), Jiajing 嘉靖 (r. 1521–1567), Longqing 隆慶 (r. 1567–1572), and Wanli 萬曆 (r. 1572–1620) emperors' reigns. 1,108 academies were revived or newly founded in this period, accounting for 56 percent of all known academies established during the whole of the Ming dynasty. In the fifty years of the Jiajing and Longqing reigns alone, 663 academies were built or revitalized, which shows the sudden as well as expansive momentum of the academy rise in a short period of time. A look at the annual average of new academies further underscores the prosperity of the academy system during this period; the Zhengde reign averages around nine, the Jiajing reign around thirteen, the Longqing reign around eleven, and the Wanli reign around six new academies a year.[3]

Many of these academies not only became involved in local culture by seeking to instill specific Confucian values and norms of behavior among the local population, but reversely also accommodated to local customs, which imbued the academies with individual characteristics. Moreover, they continued to serve as places to advance one's own erudition, to evaluate future talents, and to criticize and remonstrate against the court, instilling the academies with a social and political role. These characteristics and the popularity of the academies, as we will see, are all related to their lecture gatherings (*jianghui* 講會).

*Jianghui* has a long tradition of being connected to academy education,[4] but with the rise of the Yangming School in China and its advocacy by its disciples in the late 16th and early 17th centuries, lectures seemed to move beyond the academies.[5] The settings of gatherings changed so that people began to

---

2  See Deng Hongbo, *Zhongguo shuyuan shi* (History of Chinese Academies) (Wuhan: Wuhan University Press, 2015), 396–420.
3  For the complete numbers of the Ming dynasty see Deng Hongbo, *Zhongguo shuyuan shi*, 282.
4  For a short overview of the history of lecturing in the academies see Thomas H.C. Lee, "Chu Hsi, Academies and the Tradition of Private Chiang-hsüeh," *Hanxue yanjiu* 2, no. 1 (1984): 301–329.
5  See Lu Miaw-fen (Lü Miaofen), "Practice as Knowledge: Yang-ming Learning and Chiang-hui in Sixteenth-Century China" (Ph.D. diss., University of California. Los Angeles, 1997); also her *Yangmingxue shiren shequn—lishi, sixiang yu shijian* (The Literati Fellowship of the Wang

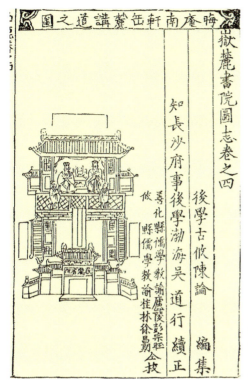

ILLUSTRATION 6.1
Illustration of the lecture by Hui'an (Zhu Xi) and Nanxuan (Zhang Shi) at Yuelu.
SOURCE: DENG HONGBO [COMP.], *YUELU SHUYUAN ZHI*, 48

come together anywhere to study among the like-minded, family, or friends. *Jianghui* sessions were organized everywhere and for every purpose and occasion. However, we should not assume that academies and *jianghui* became parallel but unrelated institutions or that they were actually mutually exclusive affairs. By looking at lecture gatherings with no designated space and no designated aim—here summarized under the phrase found in the literature, "to organize gatherings everywhere (*suidi juhui* 隨地舉會)"—and the later tendency of returning to the academies to lecture, we can reconstruct the circumstances of the *jianghui* and the relationship with the academies, and understand the academies' role in the Ming dynasty educational scene.

However, before this stands a necessary discussion of terms connected with the lecture gatherings, as these bear some problems of ambiguity and inconsistency.[6] While *jianghui* is the more common term in the Ming dynasty, we

---

Yangming School—History, Thought and Practice) (Taipei: Zhongyang yanjiuyuan jindaishi yanjiusuo, 2003).

6  This further also entails to the problem of choosing an appropriate English translation for the term. The aforementioned "lecture gatherings" is used by Thomas Lee and will be used in this article as it stands closest to the meaning of the original two characters. However, the wide

sometimes also encounter the term *huijiang* 會講 (gatherings for lectures) that historically had been used to describe academic discussion between scholars and in front of an audience, e.g. the famous meeting between Zhang Shi 張栻 (1133–1180) and Zhu Xi 朱熹 (1130–1200) at Yuelu Academy 嶽麓書院 in 1167.[7] By the time of the Ming dynasty the term was used to refer more generally to teaching activities in the academies, including daily discussions between teachers and students, as the study regulations of the Hongdao Academy 弘道書院 show:

> Every other day in the afternoon assemble at the hall for *huijiang*, and depending on status engage in reading. At first discuss the passage among yourselves, and if there are any difficult parts, further discuss among the students in the *huijiang* and visit the teacher to inquire about it. While searching to attain the meaning of the words by the former sages and worthies, do not fool yourself into understanding it.[8]

Yet, the use of *huijiang* is more ambiguous and often also appears in connection with lecture gatherings outside of the academies. There have been different explanations as how to understand the difference and usage of *jianghui* and *huijiang*. Li Caidong, an expert on the history of Confucian academies, considers both terms to stem from Southern Song tradition and to be connected to Zhu Xi, but with different meanings. He views *huijiang* as describing the activity of an academic gathering or discussion, while *jianghui* designates the organization, group, or institution behind the lectures, which in his opinion

---

range of activities and organization subsumed under the term makes many other translations plausible as well. In her English dissertation Lü Miaofen employs the quite similar translation of "lecture meetings," but mostly relies on the transcription of the Chinese term, surely to underscore the diversity of the concept. In his chapter in this volume Hoyt Tillman uses the term "discussion gatherings," which certainly includes the sometimes open, participatory aspects of the gatherings that are somewhat lost with the term "lecturing." John Meskill and Martin Huang both focus more on the term *jiangxue* 講學, which Meskill translates as "philosophical discussions" and Huang as "philosophical debates," thus specifying the contents the gatherings were concerned with. Martin Huang includes a short discussion of the terms and also mentions the translation in *The Cambridge History of China* of *jiangxue* as "discourse on learning." See also Wm. Theodore de Bary's discussion on the right translation of the term in his, *The Message of the Mind in Neo-Confucianism* (New York: Columbia University Press, 1989), 218–225.

7  See Zhu Hanmin and Deng Hongbo, *Yuelu Shuyuan shi* (History of the Yuelu Academy) (Changsha: Hunan jiaoyu chubanshe, 2013), 118–134.
8  ZGLDSYZ 6: 489.

are not to be confused.[9] A similar position was advocated by Chen Lai, professor of the history of philosophy.[10] However, this position has been challenged, doubting the theory that *jianghui* marks the organization behind the lectures. Wu Xuande maintains that there is no clear divide between the usage of *jianghui* and *huijiang*, and that meaning of *jianghui* as the activity of lecturing and gathering originated among Buddhist traditions of the Northern and Southern Dynasties period (420–589).[11] Having extensively studied the Yangming scholar community, Lü Miaofen generally considers that the term *jianghui* during the Ming period was used to describe a flurry of activities related to gatherings for discussion, such as daily lectures in the academies, friends making informal visits to discuss matters of scholarship, gatherings to educate the local population, public lectures related to community compacts, as well as formal lecture activities organized by local scholars. She considers a clear demarcation of the contents included as difficult, but also as unnecessary as she defines *jianghui* as "composed of scholars, gentry, and their kin that are connected to a locality and regularly organize for lecture activities, showing a modest level of institutionalization, but not necessarily being connected to an academy or other institution."[12] In Wu Zhen's opinion, stemming from his research of the disciples of Wang Yangming, *jianghui* cannot be considered to describe an academic organization in the strict sense, because it does not exhibit regulations limiting the number of participants or discriminating among them based on status.[13] Chen Shilong frames *jianghui* as lectures, but emphasizes their connection to the Yangming School and considers the spread of its ideas and the association with friends as the core of the *jianghui* idea. He states that "even though *jianghui* appeared in the Song and Yuan and the lecture movement continued in the early Qing, as a general trend we have to consider *jianghui* as a Ming dynasty phenomenon."[14]

9  Li Caidong, *Zhongguo shuyuan yanjiu* (Research on Chinese Academies) (Nanchang: Jiangxi gaoxiao chubanshe, 2005), 111–120; see also his *Jiangxi gudai shuyuan yanjiu* (Research on Ancient Academies in Jiangxi) (Nanchang: Jiangxi jiaoyu chubanshe, 1993), 318–320.
10  Chen Lai, *Zhongguo jinshi sixiangshi yanjiu* (Research on the History of Modern Thought in China) (Beijing: Shangwu yinshuguan, 2003), 339.
11  Wu Xuande, *Jiangyou wangxue yu ming zhonghouqi Jiangxi jiaoyu fazhan* (The Jiangxi Wang School and Educational Developments in Jiangxi in the Middle to Late Ming Period) (Nanchang: Jiangxi jiaoyu chubanshe, 1996), 302.
12  Lü Miaofen, "Yangming xue jianghui (Discussion Gatherings of the Yangming School)," *Xin shixue* 9, no. 2 (1998); see also her *Yangmingxue shiren shequn*, 73–74.
13  Wu Zhen, *Mingdai zhishijie jiangxue huodong xinian* (The System of Lecture Activities in Intellectual Circles in the Ming Dynasty) (Shanghai: Xuelin chubanshe, 2003), 37.
14  Chen Shilong, *Mingdai zhongwanqi jiangxue yundong qiaoyi* (The Lecture Movement during the Middle to Late Ming Dynasty) (Shanghai: Fudan daxue chubanshe, 2007), 2–16.

With these studies in mind and with further historical data it is possible to put forward some thoughts on this topic.[15] First, *huijiang* as lecturing activities of Confucian scholars began in the Tang dynasty and after the introduction of official schools and academies in the Song became a normal teaching activity in the successive dynasties. Not only as a teaching or lecture activity, but sometimes also as the matter of organizing the lectures, as a term moving between the noun "lecture" and its gerund "lecturing," not just having one meaning. Second, *jianghui* often appears as the verb to *huijiang*, meaning "to lecture"; however, both words overlap and can designate activities. *Jianghui* sometimes also appears as a general term, clearly identifiable as a noun, referring to the organization or institution behind the lectures, i.e. a lecture society or an academy. Therefore the idea of *jianghui* as an institution also has some ground. Further, *jianghui* being designed to spread ideas among friends and between teachers and students are not limited to the Ming dynasty or the Yangming School, but can also be observed among Zhu Xi's followers during the Song, Yuan, Ming, and Qing periods. Conclusively, *huijiang* and *jianghui* overlap in their meaning, which lies between an activity and its organization. In the following, this paper will therefore, if not specifically marked as otherwise, use the term *jianghui* as referring to both usages, the academic organization/institution and the activity of lecturing itself.

The paper will further propose that the *jianghui* sessions in the academies during the Ming dynasty can be generally divided into three types, which are categorized by the level of their academic depth and their target audience, namely: academic gatherings geared towards scholars (*xueshu jianghui* 學術講會), teaching gatherings for students (*jiaoxue jianghui* 教學講會), and gatherings to transform through education (*jiaohua jianghui* 教化講會) that were directed more towards the general population. These three types also reflect the functions of Confucian academies during the Ming dynasty, in creating, spreading, and popularizing Confucian culture. Although the academic and transformation type of the gatherings have not always been summarized under these terms, their contents, achievements, and contributions have been widely recognized by academics now and in the past. The teaching type of the gatherings usually received the scorn of "serious" Confucian scholars, as it ostensibly promoted useless rote-memorization in preparation for the civil service examinations for the sake of personal advancement. However, as a matter of fact, studying for the examinations and sagely learning were not two

---

15   A more detailed look at studies concerned with *jianghui* can be found in Deng Hongbo, "Mingdai shuyuan jianghui yanjiu de lishi yu xianzhuang (History and Present Situation of Ming Dynasty *Jianghui* Studies)," *Zhongguo wenhua yanjiu,* Spring 2009: 102–112.

completely different matters and neither could be considered as easy. From the libraries and the books listed in the reading curriculums of academies we can actually see that the knowledge system applied in learning for the civil service examinations in reality also covered most of the content considered as the traditional study canon at the time. Success in the official examinations therefore must be also understood as an important guarantee for the continuous transmission of traditional Confucian culture.

According to my own research, there were at least eighty *jianghui* communities based in Confucian academies in different parts of the country during the Ming dynasty.[16] Due to their facing different surroundings, conditions, and problems, and employing different policies, as well as due to the effects of differences in original customs, academic atmospheres, styles of administering the lectures by the hosts, audience, and academic level, all these lecture gatherings over time naturally developed quite dissimilar characteristics and took on more local identities. It needs to be also pointed out that, through rotations of the gatherings between different places, the assembly of large gatherings, or the organization of gatherings in remote places, etc., the actual characteristics of the gatherings were under constant change. One main development during the Ming period was understood as following the process of "gather for lectures, establish academies, so both can be seen everywhere" (*lian jianghui, li shuyuan, xiang wang yu yuanjin* 聯講會, 立書院, 相望於遠近),[17] which implied the continuous enlargement of the lecturing circle, from township to county, from county to prefecture, and from the prefecture to the province, sometimes even forming inter-provincial gatherings. Although sizes varied, we can see a constant expansion of the circle of the gatherings and with it the network of the associated academy. This process, under the influence of local culture, entered into a conversion, necessarily again leading to more cultural homogeneity in the organization of the lecture gatherings.

Yet this organizational homogeneity of gathering for lectures, establishing academies, and guiding students still possessed multiple cultural directions in its content and did not produce ideological uniformity. In combination with academic developments, it not only initiated the bloom of the Wang Yangming teachings and *jianghui* promoting Wang's ideas, but later also created the impetus for the late Ming dynasty dissent of the Donglin movement criticizing and rejecting the teachings of Wang's followers. It seems therefore safe to say

---

16  See Deng Hongbo, "Mingdai shuyuan jianghui yanjiu (Academy lecturing [Jianghui] in the Ming Dynasty)" (Ph.D. diss., Hunan University, 2007), Chapter 6, 103–132.
17  Zhang Tingyu, *Mingshi* (History of the Ming), Volume 231 (Beijing: Zhonghua Shuju, 1974), 6053.

that mutual relations and the search for the like-minded through lectures and associations is one of the main reasons for the flourishing of the gatherings.[18] Therefore, the concept of association academies (*shetuan shuyuan* 社團書院) must be put forward. The famous Donglin Academy 東林書院 was formed around a *jianghui* and became an association that also had the bearings of an early political organization. Lectures and discussing politics were the most prominent features of association academies, which often put them at odds with the authoritarian state and ultimately led to instances of violent suppression of academies by the court during the Ming dynasty.[19] In this sense, the relationship between lecture gatherings and academies from an organizational point of view has to be seen as parallel and independent. However, in reality, academies and *jianghui* often coexisted in the same body. The combination of lectures and academies was a sensible choice by Wang Yangming, Zhan Ruoshui, and their followers in seeking to establish places of academic freedom to discuss their ideas outside of state-enforced orthodoxy. It also imbued the academies and their lecture gatherings with a political spirit.

In the following this article will discuss the aforementioned three types of lecture gatherings connected to Confucian academies. However, a preliminary inquiry about the extent lecture gatherings attained in this period should help to understand the importance of the phenomenon of *jianghui* in the Ming dynasty as well as its connection to Confucian academies.

## 2  "Organize Gatherings Everywhere"

Among the disciples of Wang Yangming, there were some who found no pleasure in advancing their official careers and rather chose to spend their whole lives lecturing to students through *jianghui* sessions, like Qian Dehong 錢德洪 (1496–1574), who is said to have spent "thirty years in the fields [outside the cities], not one day without lecturing. In Jiangxi, Zhejiang, Xuan[cheng], She[xian] [both modern Anhui province], Chu [modern Hubei and Hunan provinces], and Guangdong, from famous districts to impassable places, in all

---

18  See Lu Miaw-fen, "Practice as Knowledge," Chapter 4, 222–266; and Martin W. Huang, "Male Friendship and *Jiangxue* (Philosophical Debates) in Sixteenth-Century China," in *Male Friendship in Ming China*, ed. Martin W. Huang (Leiden: Brill, 2007), 146–178.

19  For the history of suppression of the Donglin Faction and its academy see John W. Dardess, *Blood and History in China: The Donglin Faction and its Repression 1620–1627* (Honolulu: University of Hawai'i Press, 2002).

having a place to lecture."[20] Or Wang Ji 王畿 (1498–1583) who, in a quite similar statement, is said to have spent "more than forty years under trees, not one day without lecturing, from the two capitals [Beijing and Nanjing] to Wu [modern Jiangsu], Chu, Min [modern Fujian], Yue [modern Hangzhou, Shaoxing], Jiangxi, and Zhejiang, in all having a place to lecture."[21] It was their efforts that built the foundation for the spread of the Yangming School in various communities. However, there were also disciples of Wang Yangming that held official posts up to high-ranking ministers, even assuming office in the Grand Secretariat (*Zaixiang* 宰相) and lectured toward the court, like Xu Jie 徐階 (1512–1578), who in the ruling courts of the Jiajing and Longqing emperors "was simply called disciple of Yaojiang [Wang Yangming], taking extreme delight in the teachings of innate knowledge."[22] He built academies in all parts of the country, forming *jianghui* communities, "his reputation being known everywhere, he was admired by the court and the people."[23] This in turn gave the Yangming School and its academies a high social reputation. It was these efforts by Wang Yangming disciples to promote his teachings in every stratum of society that led to the boom of the academy movement during the Ming dynasty, ultimately casting off the stagnation the academies had experienced in the preceding one hundred years.

The teachings of Wang Yangming and Zhan Ruoshui put an emphasis on the initiative of the individual, believing that everyone, whether official, gentry, or farmer, with the right stimulus could become a sage like Yao or Shun. So as the streets were full of sages, then altars were to be everywhere, and through their great academic enthusiasm people were to establish lectures, gathering in groups of friends learning together, and subsequently forming *jianghui* associations. Not choosing a fixed place, people were to organize the lectures everywhere: in the family, in the clan, in the villages, in the towns, in the counties, among multiple counties, in the provinces, in the old capitals, in the current capital, there was to be no place without lectures; every ten days, every month, every season, every year, there was to be no time without a lecture.

The quotation "organize gatherings everywhere" itself can be found in the biography of Ming scholar Chen Qi'en 陳其蒽 (?–?) in the *Records of Wufeng Academy* (*Wufeng shuyuan zhi* 五峰書院志):

---

20   See Huang Zongxi, *Mingru xuean* (The Records of Ming Scholars), Volume 11, "Zhe zhong Wangmen xuean yi (Scholarly Annals of the Wang School in Zhejiang)" (Beijing: Zhonghua shuju, 1985), 225.
21   See Huang Zongxi, *Mingru xuean*, Volume 12, 238.
22   See Shen Defu, *Wanli yehuo bian* (Unofficial Matters of the Wanli Reign), Volume 8, "Jichan 嫉諂 (Envy and Flattery)" (Beijing: Zhonghua shuju, 1959), 215.
23   Ibid.

> The Master's personal name was Qi'en, his courtesy name was Shengnan (生南) and his style was Pingzhai (蘋齋). He was from Anwen in Dongyang. Among the students of his hometown he was known to be bold and chivalrous, and to enjoy drinking his fill. [...] When he came to pay a visit to his master Chunzhao, the master delightedly exclaimed: Shengnan is here, a man of our Way! [Qi'en] then changed and returned to measure, deeply contemplating and fully applying himself, attaining great courage, reaching the place of knowledge and practicing it in his acts without fail. [...] His places for lecture were Wufeng in Yongkang, Wenshan in Dongyang, and the western hermitage, organizing gatherings everywhere, guiding younger scholars, being sincere and meticulous. Where words weren't sufficient he would break into song. Among the stupid and wise, there was no one who was not moved. After Chunzhao disappeared, he [Qi'en] transmitted his teachings widely, but could not replace the master's strength.[24]

The abovementioned Chunzhao 春洲 is the style name of Chen Shifang 陳時芳 (1567–1642) from Dongyang, whose teacher was fellow countyman Du Weixi 杜惟熙 (1521–1601), himself a student of Wang Yangming's disciple Lu Kejiu 盧可久 (1503–1579) from Yongkang, making Cheng Qi'en a fourth-generation disciple of Wang Yangming. Cheng Qi'en's name cannot be found in the *Records of Ming Scholars* (*Ming ruxue an* 明儒學案). And while the biographies of Lu and Du are to be found in the attachment to this work, they are not included among the followers of Wang Yangming in Zhejiang, showing that Wufeng Academy 五峰書院, in Yongkang, was not considered as an important base of Yangming learning.[25] However, as this short biography states, Chen's lectures did not focus on one Confucian academy or a Buddhist hermitage, but were organized everywhere. It also provides us with a glimpse into the lectures, with Chen Qi'en employing song to convey his message to everyone, showing how the later students of the Yangming School embraced *jianghui* sessions as technique to promote their ideas.

A similar statement can be found in the epitaph inscription made by Lü Ben 呂本 (1504–1587) for Qian Dehong:

---

24  ZGLDSYZ 9: 177–178.
25  For information on Wufeng Academy and its scholar community, see Lan Jun, "Disputes between Confucian Academies and Buddhist Monasteries from a Sociocultural View: The Case of the Wufeng Academy Litigation," in this volume, 359–393.

[Qian Dehong] traveled all over Xuan[cheng], Jiangxi, and Guangdong, everywhere gathering for lectures. His reputation called out, even deep in the mountains and in remote valleys, his whole life there were those wishing to see and hear Xu's [Qian Dehong] words. When he was in Shao[zhou] [modern Guangdong), Chen Baogu 陳豹谷 invited him to head Mingjing Academy 明經書院, when in Linying the official Yu Yang 玉陽 sought to make him head of Jiayi Academy 嘉義書院, when in Wanling Liu Chuquan 劉初泉 employed him as head for Shuixi jingshe 水西精舍 at Lion rock, when he was in Qizhou Shen Gulin 沈古林 asked him to head Chongzheng Academy 崇正書院, when he was in Jiangxi provincial education commissioner Wang Jingsuo [Wang Zongmu 王宗沐] opened a lecture hall at Huaiyu mountain. Scholars of eight towns invited the master as director of their academies, like Chongxuan 沖玄, Doushan 斗山, Qingyuan 青原, Junshan 君山, Futian 福田, Qulu 衢麓 Fuzhen 復真 and Fugu 復古 Academies. For twenty years he traveled back and forth and all academies had regulations and lecture protocols, altogether becoming many volumes placed in the master's complete writings. When he was 70 years old he wrote a memorial of retiring (*yixianshu* 頤閒疏) and sent out that he couldn't travel far anymore. Every spring and autumn, he still stopped for lectures at Tianzhen Academy 天真書院, because the travel up the lake was only ten days.[26]

The popularity of the lectures at this time is also reflected in a statement by Li Maoming 李懋明 (?–?) found in the *Records of Bailuzhou Academy* (*Bailuzhou shuyuan zhi* 白鷺洲書院志): "In my village, lectures were as common as tea and rice at home, there was no place without them, no age not participating. At [Bai]Luzhou Academy, [re]built in the Wanli years, from the *jiawu* year (1594) to the *jiazi* year (1624) for more than thirty years the lectures did not stop."[27]

As can be seen in the above quotes, the gatherings had pervaded deep into distant villages and remote valleys and the high frequency of the lectures was considered normal. It also seems that they had achieved their desired effect of transforming the people and becoming customary, as Qian Dehong writes about the Xiyin gathering society (Xiyinhui 惜陰會): "In the *wushen* year (1548) Longxi [Wang Ji] came to Qingyuan and the Fugu lecture society. Now after nine years he has arrived again. In the farthest villages and remote valleys, all

---

26 Qian Ming, *Xu Ao, Qian Dehong, Dong Jian ji* (Collected Works of Xu Ao, Qian Dehong, Dong Jian) (Nanjing: Fenghuang chubanshe, 2007), 418.
27 ZGLDSYZ 2: 678.

the people know of the lectures and everyone respects and follows the teachings."[28] The growth of the lectures during this time also becomes more apparent from the audience numbers. Wang Ji himself recounts on how a new *jianghui* requested him to lecture and mentions its growth:

> When I arrived for the lecture in Shuixi, Du Zizhi 杜子質 together with about twenty other students came to the gathering place. They requested: "Zhi has heard the master's teaching before, he then returned to his village and established a gathering for several villages in Jiulong. First, there were only students preparing for the examinations. Then, hearing that everyone could study to become a sage, the farmers, workers, merchants, and shopkeepers all came to the lectures. Now that the master [Wang Ji] arrived here, we've come to ask him to teach us and strengthen our understanding." The disciples Gong Xuanlüe, Zhou Shunzhi, Wu Chongben, Wang Ruzhou from Lanshan came through Baofeng to Jiulong. The number of participants was more than three hundred. The village elders all respectfully came together and were elated. The scholars and monks said they had earlier seen an omen and prognosticated the lecture. The gathering went on for three days.[29]

Generally speaking, as the lectures could be organized everywhere, there could be up to several hundred people in attendance, which is a considerable number for a 16th-century small peasantry society. Several hundred people attending a lecture held for a few days, sometimes even for ten days or up to half a month, moreover moving from place to place often without break, even today in the 21st century, is not a common occurrence. The literature also presents us with several records mentioning numbers of close to a thousand, several thousand, or nearly ten thousand people attending lectures. Examples can be found in the writings of Zou Shouyi 鄒守益 (1491–1562) about the lecture gatherings at Qingyuan, recording that "the ones from far away gather once a year, those from closer by come once a month, small lectures have a hundred people, big lectures have a thousand."[30] And the Xinyin lecture society in Xiyuan headed by Wang Shihuai 王時槐 (1522–1605) also have been said to be attended by

---

28  Qian Ming, *Xu Ao, Qian Dehong, Dong Jian ji*, 177.
29  Wang Ji, *Wang Ji ji* (Collected Writings of Wang Ji), Volume 7, "Shu taiping jiulong huiji (Writing the Records of the Taiping Jiulong lectures)" (Nanjing: Fenghuang chubanshe, 2007), 172.
30  Shen Jia, *Mingru yanxing lü* (Records of Words and Deeds of Ming Confucians), "Zou Shouyi (Zou Shouyi)," in SKQS.

"hundreds of scholars coming from everywhere."[31] There are quite a few other sources mentioning high audience numbers, which sometimes surely were meant to underscore the popularity of certain gatherings rather than to give an accurate count. The head of Yongxin county, Yu Maoheng 余懋衡 (*jinshi* of 1592), for example, describes the audience of a lecture by Wang Shihuai, Zou Yuanbiao 鄒元標 (1551–1624), and Zou Deyong 鄒德泳 (?–?) as reaching up to ten thousand people.[32]

Of course, the main force behind the popularity of the lectures was the scholars, most of them associated with the Yangming School. They lectured at home, met in their hometowns, held, organized, and attended lectures, and traveled around the country in order to debate with fellow scholars. One of these scholars, well-known for his skills in the art of lecturing, was Luo Rufang 羅汝芳 (1515–1588), whose style name was Jinxi 近溪 (Nearby creek) and who was, together with Wang Ji whose style name was Longxi 龍溪 (Dragon creek), known as the "Two creeks (*erxi* 二溪)." The *Records of Ming Scholars* states about both that "while Longxi's tongue is surpassed by his writing, Jinxi's writing is surpassed by his tongue."[33] Throughout his life Luo enthusiastically held lectures and even while he was preparing for the court examinations in Beijing, he organized lecture gatherings in nearby Lingji Temple (Lingji gong 靈濟宮). While serving as prefect of Ningguo prefecture he continued his lecture activities and founded Zhixue Academy 志學書院 as place for this, attracting over a hundred scholars. After the death of his parents he returned to his hometown for mourning, but students from everywhere followed and came to visit and hear him lecture. Later he was appointed in Yunnan, where he organized lectures, for example in Wuhua Academy 五華書院 in Kunming. In 1577 he quit government service in order to completely concentrate on lecturing, especially in southeastern China. After his death several hundred of his disciples decided to hold monthly gatherings reading his collected writings.[34]

We have seen how the wide appeal of lectures came about through popular scholars,[35] the high frequency, wide availability, and accessibility of the lecture gatherings. However, the uncomplicated organization of lecture gatherings

---

31  "Xiyuan xiyin huixu (Order of the Xiyuan Lecture Gatherings)," in *Ji'an fuzhi* (Prefectural Gazetteer of Ji'an), Volume 19, Guangxu, in *Zhongguo fangzhi congshu huazhong difang* (Series of Chinese Local Records, Central China) (Taipei: Chengwen chubanshe, 1985).
32  See Ono Kazuko, *Mingji dangshe kao* (Study of Political Factions in the Ming Dynasty) (Shanghai: Shanghai guji chubanshe, 2006), 159.
33  Huang Zongxi, *Mingru xuean*, Volume 34, 762.
34  Fang Zuyou, Liang Yiqun, Li Qinglong, *Luo Rufang ji* (Collected Writings of Luo Rufang), Appendix, "Luo Jinxi shi xingshi (Brief Biography of Teacher Luo Jinxi)" (Nanjing; Fenghuang chubanshe, 2007), 833–851.
35  For more on this see Lü Miaofen, *Yangming xue jianghui*, 50.

and their informal nature, being conducted anywhere at any time, also made the threshold of what actually was considered a lecture relatively low and the contents sometimes arbitrary. This in turn became an obstacle for the development of the lectures as in the long run the absence of fixed places for the gatherings made them volatile and often unsustainable for a committed community around them. Looking at lecture gatherings in various parts of the Ming Empire an interesting phenomenon comes to light. Lecture gatherings without a stable institution to support them seldom existed for more than a short time and often are mentioned just once in historical records, while lectures that were institutionalized around an academy or another association building endured and remained in the historical annals. The Xiyin gathering society off the western banks of the Yangzi River, the Shuixi gathering society (Shuixihui 水西會) off the eastern banks of the Yangzi, as well as the Donglin gathering society (Donglinhui 東林會) and Feng Congwu's 馮從吾 (1556–1627) Guanzhong gathering society (Guanzhonghui 關中會), etc., all relied on an academy to persevere for several centuries. Therefore, we can speak of a tendency of the lecture gatherings to return to the academies.

An academy could become a place of lecture gatherings in two ways. First, an existing academy formed the practice of holding lecture gatherings on its grounds or supported them administrative and financially. An example of this was Bailuzhou Academy in Ji'an, which at the time was as famous as the White Deer Grotto Academy (Bailudong shuyuan 白鹿洞書院) or Ehu Academy 鵝湖書院, and since the Song and Yuan dynasties had been an educational and academic center. During Ming times it set up house regulations (*guanli* 館例) for holding lectures concerned either with examination preparation or with the teachings of the School of Principle (*lixue* 理學). While other lectures were not this fixed, they usually drew in a larger audience. During the Jiajing reign provincial education intendant Wang Zongmu 王宗沐 (1524–1592) invited Zou Shouyi for a lecture on the *Daxue* and *Zhongyong*, which drew in thousands of listeners. During the Wanli and Tianqi 天啟 (r. 1621–1627) years lecture gatherings under the title "orthodox learning gatherings" (*zhengxue hui* 正學會) were organized inside the academy. Later, in the final years of the Ming dynasty, government officials and students of the academy again organized lecture gatherings, this time named "following humanness gatherings" (*yiren hui* 依仁會). Thus the academy became home to the lecture gatherings, which were held on academy grounds, and all related administrative matters were also permanently fixed within the various academy regulations. The records of the reconstruction of Xuegu Academy 學古書院 summarize the developments as follows: "The academy indeed was a place where the Confucian scholars lectured to make the relationships of the people clear, and so transformed the people, corrected their customs, and produced talent."[36]

Another way was for new academies to be established out of already existing premises, originally created to facilitate the lecture gatherings. With the rising popularity of a lecture community its members and attendants naturally increased and with no designated space the organization of the gatherings became more difficult, which raised the need for a steady location that also could serve as an administrative fixture, i.e. for the collection of membership fees. A thriving lecturing community hence gave the impetus for the revival of an abandoned academy or the establishment of a new academy. One example among many is the establishment of Yide Academy 一德書院 by Liu Yuanqing 劉元卿 (1544–1609), who in this case complains about the multitude of lecture gatherings in one community. "Recently, how can one control the number of gatherings? They are called Lize gathering, Zhiren gathering, Chen family gathering, or Yang family gathering. Therefore, now the Wang, the Yan, the Zhang and the Xie family have banded together to form the Yide gathering [at Yide academy], this is how the number of lectures is controlled!"[37] Liu Yuanqing, a native of modern day Lianhua county, in his writings also recounts the circumstances that led to the construction of Fuli Academy 復禮書院 in his hometown.

> West from the town [Ji'an], about sixty miles from the city walls, the road is dangerous and long, blocking the message from being taught, and the people quibble and gossip about who's rich, as their customs are low. Therefore Wang Ziying 王子應, He Zongkong 賀宗孔, and Zhao Shikong 趙師孔 got the sons and elders of the village together for a gathering.... Every season there is one gathering, which always guides the youngsters in teaching [...] and changes could gradually be observed in the customs. So, they came together and planned: "The seasonal lecture is over after five days and sometimes it's very hot or cold, for which one cannot plan. Why not collect resources to build an academy?"[38]

Looking at Liu Yuanqing's explanations, another factor for the foundation of the academy becomes visible too:

---

36  Wang Shu, "Xuegu shuyuan ji (Records of Xuegu Academy)," in *Sanyuan xian xin zhi* (New Gazetteer of Sanyuan County) Volume 4, Guangxu. In *Zhongguo fangzhi congshu huabei difang* (Collection of Chinese Local Records, North China) (Taipei: Chengwen chubanshe, 1976), 168.
37  Liu Yuanqing, *Liu Pinjun quanji* (Complete Writings of Liu Pinjun), Volume 9, in SKQS.
38  Liu Yuanqing, *Liu Pinjun quanji*, Volume 7; also in *Ji'an fuzhi*, Volume 19.

> How can we now here in Anfu be more backward than Chaling? [...] We held the first gathering in Kuiqiu, and several scholars of the area have assembled in order to build Fuli Academy.[39]

In this case an academy was built in place of an existing lecture gathering in order to "save face" and to compete with the surrounding areas, but also to change the customs of the common folk. Whether it was due to inside needs or outside stimuli, *jianghui* associations increasingly relied on academies to maintain their activities.

Feng Congwu, who "first lectured at home and later at Baoqing temple"[40] and ultimately in Guanzhong Academy 關中書院 and Shoushan Academy 首善書院, institutionalized his lectures with the help of several officials as the *Records of Guanzhong Academy* (*Guanzhong shuyuan ji* 關中書院記) tell us:

> I, quite unworthy, together with some like-minded held lectures at the old Baoding temple for some years. In the thirty seventh year of the Wanli reign (1609), on the first day of the tenth month, Vice Minister Master Wang [Keshou 汪可受 (1559–1620)], Censor Master Li [Tianlin 李天麟], Vice Commissioner Master Chen [Ning 陳寧], and educational commissioner Master Duan [Youxian 段猷顯] came to a lecture. With about a thousand in attendance, we talked on the nature of the mind, being so joyful we only started to part at dusk. Getting ready to leave the masters told me: Lecturing in the temple can only be temporary and in the long run will only result in trouble, so there should be other plans for this. The next day, it was commanded, that the two counties would build Guanzhong Academy in the garden a little east of the temple, inviting me and Zhou Shuyuan 周淑遠 to lecture there for the younger scholars. Master Wang repeatedly set aside public fields for the academy, and invited Grand Coordinator Xu to attend and praise the lectures, using his salary to increase [the fields]. The lecture hall is six pillars wide, and its hanging board says: "Sincerely hold fast" (*yunzhi* 允執)[41] referring to the name of the academy.[42]

---

39  Liu Yuanqing, *Liu Pinjun quanji*, Volume 6.
40  Feng Congwu, *Shaoxu ji* (Collected Writings of Shaoxu), Volume 15, "Guanzhong shuyuan ke di ti ming ji (Record of Examination Results in Guanzhong Academy)," in SKQS.
41  "Sincerely hold fast the due Mean (*yun zhi qi zhong* 允執其中)" appears in *Lunyu* 20.1 and as 允執厥中 (*yun zhi jue zhong*) in the *Shangshu* 尚書 (Book of Documents), both implying moderation in one's actions.
42  Feng Congwu, *Shaoxu ji* (Collected Writings of Shaoxu), Volume 15, "Guanzhong shuyuan ji (Records of Guanzhong Academy)."

Not only is the large scale of the lectures at Baoding temple remarkable, but so is Feng Congwen's rise from lecturing at home to lecturing in an abandoned temple to lecturing in an academy.

The most famous academy of the late Ming dynasty, the Donglin Academy, also emerged out of a lecture gathering as can be seen in the funeral praise for Gao Panlong 高攀龍 (1562–1626), who had revived the academy during the Ming:

> At first [Gao Panlong] lectured in Jiangsu. A few friends always got together above Erquan; together with Master Guan Dongming they discussed the meaning of "no distinction between good and evil" (*wu shan wu e* 無善無惡).[43] The audience arrived toe to heel, there was no more space to fill. Therefore Master Jingyang [Gu Xiancheng 顧憲成 (1550–1612)[44]] suggested: "The mechanics have their shops to dwell in,[45] but we don't have a place to lecture?" Therefore several like-minded came together, collected money, and chose Master Yang Guishan's [Yang Shi 楊時 (1053–1135)] old lecturing place and continued to call it Donglin, providing a space for friends to rest. Every month the gentlemen from Wu and Yue gathered for three-day-long lectures and several hundred people came from near and far.[46]

As seen above, while *jianghui* could be maintained in family settings, in villages, shrines, or temples, many scholars consciously sought to institutionalize their gatherings in an academy in order to ensure longevity. However, it also needs to be emphasized that not all lecture gatherings ultimately became set in academies. Not only were there other ways to successfully institutionalize the gatherings, but some communities deliberately remained without a fixed

---

43  This refers to Wang Yangming's *Four Sentence Teaching* (*Sijujiao* 四句教): "In the substance of the heart/mind, there is no distinction between good and evil. When thoughts are activated, there is distinction between good and evil. The truly good knowledge is that which knows good and knows evil. *Gewu* involves doing good and removing evil." Translation by Shun Kwong-Loi, "Wang Yang-ming on Self-Cultivation in the Daxue," *Journal of Chinese Philosophy* 38 (December 2011): 105. Also Tu Wei-ming, "An Inquiry into Wang Yang-ming's Four-Sentence Teaching," *The Eastern Buddhist*, New Series 7, no. 2 (October 1974), 32–48.
44  Gu Xiancheng was the founder of the Donglin movement.
45  Quote from *Lunyu* 19.7; Translation by James Legge.
46  Xu Xiandeng, *Donglin shuyuan zhi* (Records of Donglin Academy)," Volume 7 (Beijing: Zhonghua shuju, 2004), 231.

place and chose to implement different forms for organizing their lecture gatherings like rotating lectures.[47]

## 3    Three Types of Lecture Gatherings

After understanding the extent of popularity lecture gatherings enjoyed in the Ming dynasty and their relation to Confucian academies, it is time to focus on the actual proceedings and aims of lecture gatherings in the academies. Because of the diverse nature of the many of these gatherings, it is difficult to dissect *jianghui* traditions along straight lines as they show several overlapping features and ambiguities in the usage of terms. Therefore the proposed distinction considers the main aim and target audience of a lecture and intends to give a framework for classification of the various forms of lectures.

### 3.1    Academic Lectures (*Xueshu Jianghui* 學術講會)

As mentioned above, the term *jianghui* had its origin in the Buddhist activities of discussing sutras and spreading Buddhist teachings.[48] During the Northern Song the term was already used by Confucian scholars to refer to gatherings discussing their ideas. Shao Baowen 邵伯溫 (1057–1134), son of Shao Yong 邵雍 (1011–1077), recounts a story about a certain Jiang Yu 姜愚 (?–?), a *boshi* 博士 (erudite) at the national college, who out of friendship raised money for his friend's marriage by holding lectures on the *Lunyu*.[49] This story relates how Confucian scholars at this time used the lectures not only to expound the meaning of certain texts, but also to draw in an audience willing to pay for attending. By the Southern Song the lectures had become a standard feature of education in the palace, government schools, and the academies.[50] In the Yuan dynasty the lecture system of the Song was mostly continued and academies

---

47    See Deng Hongbo, "Mingdai shuyuan jianghui zuzhi xingshi de xin tese (New Characteristics of Academy Lecture Organization Forms in the Ming Dynasty)," *Jiangxi jiaoyu xueyuan xuebao* 30, no. 1 (2009): 108–114.

48    The term *jianghui* is for example used in the Biography of Niu Sengru 牛僧孺 (780–849) in the *Old Book of the Tang* (*Jiu Tangshu* 舊唐書) describing the monk official opening a lecture to praise the words of Buddha. See *Jiu Tangshu* (Old Book of the Tang), Volume 72, "Niu Sengru zhuan (Biography of Niu Sengru)" (Beijing: Zhonghua shuju, 1975).

49    Shao Bowen, *Wen jian lü* (Records of Things Heard and Seen), Volume 18, in SKQS.

50    Zhu Xi himself lectured at White Deer Grotto academy and left a poem called "Bailu jianghui cibo zhangyun 白鹿講會次卜丈韻 (Poem in verse about the Bailu Lecture Gatherings)"; he also mentions lectures in letters to his friends more than once. See Zhu Xi, *Huian ji* (Collected Writings of Huian), Volume 42, "Da Hu Guangzhong (Answering Hu Guangzhong)," or ibid., Volume 53, "Da Liu Jizhang (Answering Liu Jizhang)."

constructed specific buildings for their lecture gatherings, such as Chengjiang Academy 澄江書院 in Jiangyin county.[51]

As discussed before, we can generally assume that these types of lectures were actual talks given by famous or well-spoken scholars and orators expounding a chapter or a phrase from the classics in front of students or other scholars, while also leaving some space for questions and debate. The most famous example of such a lecture can already be found during the Southern Song, when Zhu Xi invited Lu Jiuyuan 陸九淵 (1139–1193) to speak on Righteousness and Profit.[52] During the Ming dynasty it was not necessarily the master of a certain school who gave lectures to the students of associated academies, but sometimes his disciples would also spread out to relay and propagate the teachings of their specific school. Looking at the historical documents we can find 18 mentions of *jianghui* in the *History of the Ming* (*Mingshi* 明史) and the *Records of Ming Scholars*.[53] This seems like a rather small number; however, most of these mentions describe *jianghui* organization that sometimes organized lectures for more than forty years. Many academies became part of larger lecturing circles that moved their gatherings between different academies, of which some like the Xiyin gathering society or the Shuixi gatherings were already mentioned. Through individual biographies of Ming scholars and academy records produced during this period, we can have a brief glimpse into some of the lectures that were not part of these large lecturing circles.

In 1571 Luo Rufang while staying at a friends of his in the Hengxiang region also visited the famous Yuelu Academy in Changsha for a lecture. Some quotations of his lecture are preserved to us in the *Words of Yuelu Academy Gatherings* (*Yuelu shuyuan huiyu* 岳麓書院會語) written down by a member of the academy named Zeng Fengyi 曾鳳儀 (?–?):

> In life one has to value the establishment of one's will. Do not apply it to simple and slight matters. Observe the sages and worthies of the past: their achievements stand for several thousand years. In life one has to value the pleasure of learning. First study filial piety and deferentiality. If after a long time when one is on the level of the virtues and accomplishments of the ancestors, then one can begin to teach others. In life on has to value teachers and friends. Between Confucius and [his disciple] Zeng

---

51   Tong Shu, *Ji'an ji* (Collected Writings of Ji'an), Volume 6, "Mao Zhang guan muzhi ming (Funeral Inscription for Official Mao Zhang)," in SKQS.
52   See Hoyt Tillman, "Some Reflections on Confucian Academies in China," in this volume, 21–44, for translated parts of the lecture. See also John W. Chaffee, "Chu Hsi and the Revival of the White Deer Grotto Academy. 1179–1181 AD," *T'oung Pao* 71 (1985): 44, 58.
53   Deng Hongbo, *Mingdai shuyuan jianghui yanjiu*, 63.

Shen there was no special teaching. As for mastering the teachings of the master, daily examine yourself on the three points.[54] In life one has to value studying. The time spend studying is time well spent. Giving body and mind to family and country, his a heavy burden to carry.[55]

Luo also played an active part in the establishment of lectures in Wuhua Academy in Kunming. The academy was originally founded in 1524 and in 1574 already had to be rebuilt, but by then had become the biggest academy in Yunnan province. The recordings of a lecture gathering in the winter of 1574 contained in the *Words of Wuhua Gatherings* (*Wuhua huiyu* 五華會語) let us know of the program of this gathering: "At the gathering at Wuhua Academy three scholars were lecturing. The first spoke on [the quote from *Analects* 19.13] 'The officer, having discharged all his duties, should devote his leisure to learning,' the second spoke about the disciples [of Confucius] Yan Yuan 顏淵 and Jie Lu 季路, and the third spoke on the place of desire for wealth and nobility among men."[56]

Academic lectures often were very meticulously structured and organized around a quite strict schedule that included ritualistic performances before and after the lectures. The *huijiang* of Gongxue Academy 共學書院 in Fuzhou are an interesting example. Gongxue Academy was built in 1594 by Grand Coordinator (*xunfu* 巡撫) Xu Fuyuan 許孚遠 (1535–1604), an official who transformed the local school into an academy, intending to bring together the people of the area to study together, hence the name *Gongxue* 共學 (study together). Starting from 1618 Yue Hesheng 岳和聲 (?–?) served in the academy and organized the lectures, two large lectures every spring and autumn and two small lectures every month. It was also Yue Hesheng who left us with a text recording the concrete practice of a lecture, guided by the commands of the ritual officer, in his records of the academy:

> Ritual Officer: Stand according to one's status (visitors in east of the hall, masters in the west), bow (to the front), second bow; stand up, divide into lines, bow again; stand up, sit down in lines looking to the front. Ritual Officer: The bell for chanting. The bell players strike the bell three times. Ritual Officer: Start chanting. A poem and some verse. Chant in harmony

---

54  Reference to *Lunyu* 1.4.
55  Luo Rufang, "Luo Mingde gong shumu (Catalogue of Master Luo Mingde)," in *Luo Rufang ji* (Collected Works of Luo Rufang), ed. Fang Zutai, Liang Yiqun, Li Qinglong (Nanjing: Fenghuang chubanshe, 2007), 8. The first two topics are from the *Analects*, the third is from the *Mencius*.
56  Luo Rufang, *Luo Rufang ji*, 147.

with each other, to mark verses use bells or lithophones. Pause chanting. Ritual Officer: Chant again (mark verse and ending as before). Stop chanting. Sit down quietly. Ritual Officer: Drum sounds for the lecture. The drummer strikes the drum three times. Ritual Officer: Furnish writing desk. Fix writing desk, then the director will chant such and such's name, the lecturer gets out of his line, arriving at the writing desk he bows once before it and then the starts the lecture. The students stand and listen. After the lecture is over, the lecturer bows once more and returns to his line. The student in charge of reading the lecture recordings gets to the front. After the [re]reading of the lecture, cup hands and ask questions, again sit down quietly. Ritual Officer: Start chanting (again mark verse and ending like before). Stop chanting. Bring in tea and crackers. Ritual Officer: Move the writing desk. All rise. Ritual Officer: Stand according to status, bow, bow again; stand up, divide into lines, bow towards each other, bow again, stand up. When the ritual is over, according to status dignified see each other off.[57]

The collective chanting of poetry was common feature of many academies during the Ming dynasty and was incorporated into the gatherings to arouse the mind of the participants and built a bond between them.[58] The lectures in Gongxue Academies varied between large lectures and smaller ones. During large lectures an outside lecturer, most commonly a famous scholar would visit the academy to speak on a topic to the students. In smaller lectures that were more frequent a student, as seen above, or the director of the academy would speak on a phrase out of the classics, which would then be discussed. The former activity seems to be closer to pure lecture activity, while the latter tended to include more discussion.

### 3.2 Educational Lectures (*Jiaoxue Jianghui* 教學講會)

Academies were academic organizations, but in the Ming even more so they were educational institutions. Wang Yangming understood the role of academies as "assisting to redress the shortcomings of the schools."[59] Zhan Ruoshui advocated the combination of sagely learning and the civil service examinations. Reflecting their role in the early years of the dynasty, it was a commonly held view among scholars that academies served as an extension of the state

---

57  ZGLDSYZ 10: 177.
58  See Lu Miaw-fen, "Practice as Knowledge," 140–146.
59  Wang Shouren, "Wansong shuyuan ji (Records of Wansong Academy)," in *Wang Yangming quanji* (Complete Writings of Wang Yangming), Volume 7 (Shanghai: Shanghai guji chubanshe, 1992), 252–253.

school system and therefore also served to prepare students for the examinations. In a time when lecture gatherings were popular, the academies not only served as places for lectures, but also often provided a concrete curriculum to advance study by offering a diverse range of educational gatherings.

Most of the gatherings in the academies that had an educational background were concerned quite concretely with examination practice or preparation. These were called *huiwen* 會文 (gathering for writing) or *wenhui* 文會 (writing gathering), sometimes also *huikao* 會考 (gathering for examinations) and a few other names.[60] They were composition classes and a regular teaching activity in the academies. *The Yushan Academy Articles for Gatherings* (*Yushan shuyuan huiyue* 虞山書院會約) state:

> On third day of every month the students are to assemble for the gathering for writing in the *jingshe* 精舍 and the classics room as the teacher supervises. The student on duty prepares the test papers, and upon hearing the directors' command, it is used. All students write their names on the small note on the cover of the paper. When the gathering is over, after the student on duty has collected all [papers], the notes are taken off and the name is written in the corner of the back of the paper, which is then folded and sealed. On the same day, the teacher then enters the building with three *juren* [graduates of the provincial examinations], locks the door, and they check [the papers]. After they are finished, the magistrate of the county reads them again, then announces the top three papers and meets with the top student. [...] On the sixth day of every month the *juren* scholars are to assemble for *huiwen* in the Xiange building, the magistrate of the county personally inspects them. [...] For people coming from far away, everybody is provided with three pecks of rice and vegetables a month, and one silver coin is given each month, for individual use.[61]

Writing gatherings for students and for graduates of the provincial examinations were held on different days, at different venues, and were differently assessed. However, the amount of money and food provided was the same for everybody. Many academies constructed special halls for these gatherings for writing (*wenhui tang* 文會堂) as places to hold examination gatherings, e.g. the White Deer Grotto Academy,[62] Zhengxue Academy 正學書院 in Yancheng,[63]

---

60  See Table 6.1.
61  ZGLDSYZ 8: 70, 72.
62  See He Qiaoxin, "Zhongjian shuyuan ji (Records of the Reconstruction of the Academy)," in *Bailudong shuyuan guzhi wu zhong* (Five Old Records of White Deer Grotto Academy), edited by Li Maoyang et al., Volume 2 (Beijing: Zhonghua shuju, 1995), 1248.
63  See *Jiangnan tongzhi* (Local gazetteer of Jiangnan), Yongzheng ed., in SKQS.

Fengshan Academy 鳳山書院 in Puqi county (modern Hubei),[64] Dongshan Academy 東山書院 and Huangu Academy 環谷書院, both in Qimen county[65], or Ziyang Academy 紫陽書院 in Huizhou in where "flocks of scholars day in day out were grinding away the whetstone."[66] Because it was so common to find these "writing halls" in the academies, it is reasonable to assume that they were used for daily educational activities. The gatherings for examinations (*huikao* 會考) of Bailuzhou Academy display another feature of these educational activities. Held on the first and fifteenth day of each month, not only did the students take a test, but to attract participants, free meals were offered to students from in- and outside of the academy.[67] By maintaining contact with all aspiring students preparing for the civil service examinations the academy built a prefecture-wide network to rely on.

To view the writing gatherings only as preparation for the examinations would obscure the fact that these classes were also used to assess the general quality of the students and their progression in the curriculum. Looking at the organization of these gatherings in some academies we see their regular nature and high frequency, which were also implemented to ensure discipline and diligence among the members of the academy.

In most cases, examination-focused gatherings were held at least once a month, often three or more times, sometimes as many as eight or nine times in one month. It is quite well known that examination preparation was the main function of academies during the Ming dynasty. To this end, various academies designed different teaching curricula. Looking at the curriculum of Hongdao Academy the contents and the aim of these "classes" becomes clear. The academy was founded by Wang Chengyu 王承裕 (1465–1538). From its beginning it served as an institution focused on examination preparation and produced quite a few successful officials. Its study regulations (*xuegui* 學規) were set up by Wang in 1496.[68]

---

64  See Wang Yan, "Fengshan shuyuan ji (Records of Fengshan Academy)," in *Puqi xian zhi yi, er, san* (Puqi County Gazetteer 1–3), Volume 3, Daoguang ed., edited by Lao Guangtai (Taipei: Chengwen chubanshe, 1975), 249–259.
65  See Li Fan, "Dongshan shuyuan jilüe (Brief Records of Dongshan Academy)," in *Qimen xian zhi* (Qimen County Gazetteer) 1–4, Volume 18, ed. Wang Yunshan (Taipei: Chengwen chubanshe, 1975), 718, also Lü Nan, "Zhongxiu huangu shuyuan jilüe (Brief Records of the Restoration of Huangu Academy)," in *Qimen xian zhi* (Qimen County Gazetteer) 1–4, Volume 18, ed. Wang Yunshan (Taipei: Chengwen chubanshe, 1975), 720.
66  He Qixian, "Ziyang shuyuan ji (Records of Ziyang Academy)," in *Zhongguo difangzhi wencheng, Anhui fuxian zhiji 48, Daoguang Huizhou fuzhi* 1, ed. Ma Buchan (Nanjing: Jiangsu guji chubanshe, 1998), 216.
67  ZGLDSYZ 2: 585.
68  ZGLDSYZ 6: 489–490; A full translation of the study regulations of Hongdao Academy can be found in Meskill, *Academies in Ming China*, 58–61.

TABLE 6.1 Selected academies and their educational gatherings

| Academy name | Place | Name of the gatherings | Date and contents | Period (ca.)[a] |
|---|---|---|---|---|
| Chongwen Academy 崇文書院 | Hangzhou (Zhejiang) | Boat classes 舫課[b] | Every year spring and autumn on special days | 1572– till after 1644 |
| Zhengren Academy 證人書院 | Guiji (Zhejiang) | Gathering for classes 會課 | Every month after the 15th day | 1627– till after 1644 |
| Yingshan Academy 贏山書院 | Chunan (Zhejiang) | Gathering for writing 會文 | Every month three times: one gathering on the Four Books, one on the Five Classics, one on poems, memorials, documents, and questions | 1620–? |
| Renwen Academy 仁文書院 | Shaoxing (Zhejiang) | Gathering for classes 會課 | Every month three times, rotating in the prefecture | 1572–1620 |
| Yushan Academy 虞山書院 | Changshu (Jiangsu) | Gathering for writing 會文 | Normal students on the 3rd day of the month, *Juren* degree holders on the 6th day | 1572–1620 |
| Gongxue Academy 共學書院 | Fuzhou (Fujian) | Gathering for classes 會課 | Every month three times, rotating in the prefecture | 1572–1620 |
| White Deer Grotto Academy 白鹿洞書院 | Xingzi (Jiangxi) | Large gathering 大會 | Every 2nd and 16th day of the month | 1572–? |
| | | Small gathering 小會 | Four times a month | |
| Bailuzhou Academy 白鷺洲書院 | Ji'an (Jiangxi) | Gatherings for writing 會文 Gatherings for examinations 會考 | Every month six times, Every month 1st and 15th day | 1572–1620 |

182　　　　　　　　　　　　　　　　　　　　　　　　　DENG HONGBO

TABLE 6.1  Selected academies and their educational gatherings (cont.)

| Academy name | Place | Name of the gatherings | Date and contents | Period (ca.)[a] |
|---|---|---|---|---|
| Hunan Academy 湖南書院 | Jinan (Shandong) | Composition 作文 | Every month three times on the meaning of one of the Four Books or Five Classics, Every month 6th day on prose, Every 16th day on exam. questions Every 26th day on memorials | 1521–1567 |
| | | Examinations 考試 | Every month three times oral exams, | |
| | | Seasonal examinations 季考 | Every end of the season | |
| Baiquan Academy 百泉書院 | Huixian (Henan) | Gathering for writing 會文 | Every month three times | 1572–1620 |
| Lianxi Academy 濂溪書院 | De'an (Hubei) | Composition 作文 | Every month one or two times | 1572–1620 |
| Wenjin Academy 問津書院 | Huanggang (Hubei) | Monthly gathering 月會 | Every month 16th day | 1572–1620 |
| Yuyang Academy 玉陽書院 | Wenchang (Hainan) | Gathering for writing 會文 | Every month 16th day | 1572–1620 |
| Shangyou Academy 尚友書院 | Ding'an (Guangdong) | Gathering for writing 會文 | 2nd month of every season, 13th day | 1572–1620 |
| Dake Academy 大科書院 | Xiqiao (Guangdong) | Examination preparation 考業 | Every month six times | 1505–1521 |

TABLE 6.1　Selected academies and their educational gatherings (*cont.*)

| Academy name | Place | Name of the gatherings | Date and contents | Period (ca.)[a] |
|---|---|---|---|---|
| Hongdao Academy 弘道書院 | Sanyuan (Shaanxi) | Composition of old texts 作古文 | Every month 1st day publication of exam topic, end of month submission of drafts (poems, rhapsodies, petitions, memorials) | 1487–1567 |
| | | Composition of contemp. texts 作時文 | Every other day (Classics, Four Books, prose, questions, documents) | |
| | | Examinations 考試 | Every month 2nd and 16th day | |

[a]　We often have concrete evidence when study regulations and a curriculum were set up, but information on how it fell into disuse or was discarded is difficult to obtain. Sometimes it is possible to trace how the academy itself was abandoned. Therefore the periods here are just mentioned to give a general timeframe of when these gatherings took place, but cannot be precise.

[b]　The boat classes of Chongwen Academy in Hangzhou were special occasions during which the students of the academy would embark on boats on the West Lake and answer examination questions. This gathering became quite popular and attracted many visitors. See Deng Hongbo, *Mingdai shuyuan jianghui yanjiu*, 80–82.

TABLE 6.2　Curriculum and course material of Hongdao Academy

| Category of course | Name of course | Teaching materials |
|---|---|---|
| Compulsory Courses | Classics 經書 | *Yijing* 易經 (*Book of Changes*)<br>*Shijing* 詩經 (*Book of Poetry*)<br>*Shujing* 書經 (*Book of History*)<br>*Chunqiu* 春秋 (*Spring and Autumn Annals*)<br>*Liji* 禮記 (*Book of Rites*) |
| | Four Books 四書 | *Lunyu* 論語 (*Analects*)<br>*Daxue* 大學 (*Great Learning*)<br>*Zhongyong* 中庸 (*Doctrine of the Mean*)<br>*Mengzi* 孟子 (*Mencius*) |
| | Histories 史書 | *Tongjian gangmu* 通鑒綱目 (*Outlines and Details of the Comprehensive Mirror*) |

TABLE 6.2  Curriculum and course material of Hongdao Academy (cont.)

| Category of course | Name of course | Teaching materials |
|---|---|---|
|  |  | *Xu tongjian gangmu* 續通鑒綱目 (*Continuation of Outlines and Details of the Comprehensive Mirror*)<br>*Tongjian jieyao* 通鑑節要 (*Essential Excerpts of the Comprehensive Mirror*)<br>*Xu tongjian jieyao* 續通鑑節要 (*Continuation of Essential Excerpts of the Comprehensive Mirror*)<br>*Shilüe* 史略 (*Concise histories*)<br>*Shiduan* 史斷 (*Short histories*) |
| Elective Courses | Investigation [of the Learning of] Principle 察理 | *Xingli Daquan* 性理大全 (*Great Compendia of Nature and Principle*)<br>*Jinsilu* 近思錄 (*Reflections on Things on Hand*) |
|  | Ritual 學禮 | *Zhuzi jiali* 朱子家禮 (*Zhu Xi's Family Rituals*)<br>*Yili* 儀禮 (*Etiquette and Rites*)<br>*Zhouli* 周禮 (*Rites of the Zhou*) |
|  | Old texts 古文 | *Wenzhang guifan* 文章軌範 (*Model Compositions*)<br>*Tangyin* 唐音 (*Tang poems*) |
|  | Extensive studies 博觀 | *Zhenguan zhengyao* 貞觀政要 (*Essentials of Politics in the Zhenguan Reign*)<br>*Tangjian* 唐鑑 (*Mirror of the Tang*)<br>*Daxue yanyi* 大學衍義 (*Abundant Meanings of the Great Learning*) |
|  | Governance 明治 | *Wujing qishu* 武經七書 (*Seven Military Classics*)<br>*Wujing zonglei* 武經總類 (*Military Classics arranged topically*)<br>*Daming lü* 大明律 (*Penal Law of the Great Ming*)<br>*Xingtongfu* 刑統賦 (*Rhymed Essays of Punishments*)<br>*Jiuhuang huomin* 救荒活民 (*Disaster Relief and Saving the People*)<br>*Huangzheng beikao* 荒政備考 (*Reference Book for Disaster Relief Policy*)<br>*Hefang Tongyi* 河防通議 (*Comprehensive Discussions of River Management*)<br>*Jingqu Tushuo* 徑渠圖說 (*Maps and Explanations of the Jing Canal*)<br>*Wuzhong shuili* 吳中水利 (*Book on Water Conservancy in Wu*) |
|  | Calligraphy 作字 | Works of Ouyang Xun 歐陽詢<br>Works of Yu Shinan 虞世南<br>Works of Yan Zhenqing 顏真卿<br>Works of Liu Gongquan 柳公權 |

The compulsory courses mentioned here were designed for attending the civil service examinations, and all students had to participate in them. The teaching materials for these courses were the basic books of the Confucian tradition and reflect the core content of the traditional knowledge system. The study regulations of the academy stipulate that these materials were to be read and recited every day, interspersed with lectures and questioning by the teacher. Every other day there were writing exercises on the meaning of the classics and the four books, as well as on contemporary text forms, such as prose writing, memorials, etc. The goal of these exercises was to strengthen the students' understanding of the text and make it possible for them to use the sages' words to attain success in the examinations. As for the elective courses, only the course on rituals had no direct connection to the examinations. Topics and question in the examinations would often be selected out of the *Xingli daquan* 性理大全 (*Great Compendia of Nature and Principle*), the *Jinsilu* 近思錄 (*Reflections on Things at Hand*) or required knowledge of the penal systems of earlier dynasties. Even calligraphy can be understood as standing in relation to the examinations as the examinee had to be able to read different scripts. In a sense, the elective courses have to be viewed as being complementary to the compulsory courses, as all their contents could provide help during the examinations. We can also see, that in order to function as an institution preparing for the examinations an academy had to provide around thirty different books for its students.

### 3.3 Gatherings to Transform through Education (*Jiaohua Jianghui* 教化講會)

Lecture gatherings were not always aimed at students, other scholars, or trained officials, but also sought to educate people of lower classes. Such *jianghui* are in some points related to the two forms discussed above and in some points quite different. All academies sought to expand their audience, which would serve as basis of lectures and support all operations of the academy. The origins of lectures seeking to transform the customs of the people in the Ming dynasty can be ascribed to Wang Yangming founding five academies in the Ganzhou region (Jiangxi), which were mostly family or village academies.[69] Sometimes academies in prefectural cities would also open their grounds for lectures to the common folk. The aims of such lectures were to spread morality,

---

[69] See Deng, *Zhongguo shuyuan shi*, 306. For Wang Yangming's general view of the academies see Deng, *Zhongguo shuyuan shi*, 309–315; a short discussion in English can be found in George L. Israel, *Doing Good and Ridding Evil in Ming China: The Political Career of Wang Yangming* (Leiden: Brill, 2014), 33.

promote good behavior, and to generally change the customs of the people. As mentioned before, disciples of the Yangming School believed that everybody could attain the status of a sage and therefore sought to popularize the concept of Confucian academies by opening their doors to villagers, townsfolk, and even Buddhist monks to listen to lectures. This is something seen rather rarely in the preceding dynasties.

Renwen Academy 仁文書院 in the prefectural seat Jiashao (Zhejiang province) was founded in 1603 by Zheng Zhenxian 鄭振先 (1572–1628) on the urging of official Che Daren 車大任 (?–?). A lecture hall and a shrine, offering rites to Xuan Xue 薛瑄 (1389–1464), Chen Baisha 陳白沙 (1428–1500), Hu Juren 胡居仁 (1434–1484), and Wang Yangming, were constructed. A year later the Vice Commissioner of Education (*tixue fushi* 提學副使), Yue Yuansheng 岳元聲 (1557–1628), began to hold lectures there. Lecture regulations (*jianggui* 講規) that prescribed the lecture dates, but also regulated the income of the academy from its fields in order to guarantee the smooth operation of *jianghui* activities were set up. According to the regulations the lectures were to be conducted following a specific pattern:

> It is agreed upon that every visitor coming to pay respects, must first clean his hands and then can enter to gather in the Renwu hall. Every gathering starts at nine in the morning when the bell is sounded five times. Two student assistants of the academy guide the visitors inside [the shrine] with the appropriate demeanor and a clear mind. Arriving in front of the spirit tablets of the four gentleman, all chant, form lines, bow in lines, and stand up. After four bows, the ritual is complete. When first joining the gathering, the visitor must do the four bows by himself. Then all return to Renwu hall, standing on the eastern and western side, upon three drum strikes sit down solemnly at their place. After sitting silently for some time, the director first holds up Master Huiwengs *Academy Regulations* [White Deer Grotto regulations], Master Xiangshan's [Lu Jiuyuan] lecture *Expounding the Chapter on Righteousness and Profit* (*Yu yi li zhang* 喻義利章), reciting some parts and discussing some points, while the participants listen attentively. Again after a while, the participants discuss the meaning, using the six classics to discuss and raise question amongst each other. After three in the afternoon, upon seven strikes of the drum, the servants bring in tea and biscuits. After the gathering is over everyone bows once and departs.[70]

---

70    ZGLDSYZ 10: 112–113.

For the people seeking to attend such lectures, Renwen Academy adopted a broad and open attitude, inviting everyone who was seeking to study and listen to the lectures. The study regulations go on:

> Scholars who earnestly practiced self-cultivation often came out of a low status, like Wu Pingjun [Wu Yubi 吳與弼 (1391–1496)][71] or Wang Xinzhai [Wang Gen 王艮 (1483–1541)],[72] and therefore could not attend the government schools. When choosing students in this way, it may be that in the deep forests and lush wilderness there is talent lost, and how can one encourage the common people to take the cultivation of the self as fundamental? Therefore, on the day of the gathering, if some common people from the countryside, who are diligent and enjoy cultivating themselves, just want to listen to the lecture, do not obstruct them and let them enter. Those who harbor secret thoughts concerned with only themselves and rely on their name seeking to enter—those are all to be rejected, as they cannot attain anything.[73]

The aforementioned Yushan Academy 虞山書院 included the opening of the academy to the common people in its regulations as well. Visitors were divided according to their status. Higher classes, such as filial sons, people of high moral character, and hermits, could sit with the members of the academy and sign their names in the visitors' book. Lower class common people had to sit on the ground and would only sign their names in a register of the lecture. In the front of lecture register an introduction for the visitors was given and the reason of the lecture was explained:

> The Yushan lecture gatherings refuse nobody. Everyone can become a sage like Yao or Shun; how could we discuss what class they belonged to! All common people, whether of old age or young, know the principle of righteousness, no matter if a member of the community compact, an official, a grain tax collector or community head, a merchant in the market, a farmer, no matter if a monk, a Daoist, or a traveler, no matter if from this

---

[71] Wu Yubi came from an important family, but decided to give up on an official career and lived as a teacher. See Theresa Kelleher (trans.), *The Journal of Wu Yubi: The Path to Sagehood* (Indianapolis: Hackett Publishing Company, 2013).

[72] Wang Gen was a salt farmer's son, See Elizabeth J. Perry, *Challenging the Mandate of Heaven: Social Protest and State Power in China* (Armonk, M.E. Sharpe, 2002), 78–79; also Steven Miles, "Wang Gen," in *Encyclopedia of Confucianism*, ed. Xinzhong Yao (New York: Routledge, 2003), 633–634.

[73] ZGLDSYZ 10: 113.

or a different area, only those with the will to attend the lecture are allowed to sign, on the previous day or in the morning of the lecture day, their name in the lecture register. Host and guests wait together and the assistants should guide them in, look carefully at the regulations and make the ritual bows. If there is someone with something profound on their mind they are allowed to ascend the hall and lecture on it. Formerly, Wang Xinzhai spend time as a salt farmer, Han Shan 寒山[74] and Shide 拾得[75] were beggars together, Zhang Pingshu [Zhang Boduan 張伯端 (987–1082)][76] worked as a beadle in a yamen. How could our county dare to scrape away the talents-in-waiting? Only those are not allowed who use their name as an opportunity to meddle their way inside, do not abide by the rules, raise disorder with their words and cause the rites to be missed—these our county cannot let in.[77]

Such openness of lectures inside the academies was surely one reason for the wide popularization of the academies during the latter half of the Ming dynasty. Moreover, while academies in the towns were opening up to the common people, simultaneously family and village academies in the countryside also began to transform. Originally teaching mostly younger children, they extended their reach and included all male members of the families; their focus was not only on the teaching of writing any more, but also the study of ritual and lectures on the correct customs became daily lessons.

The last example concerns Anfu county in Ji'an prefecture, which was a hotbed of the Yangming School in the Ming dynasty and already many academies of the area have been mentioned. This region produced a row of scholars who studied with Wang Yangming himself, like Zou Shouyi, Liu Xiao 劉曉 (?–?), Liu Bangcai 劉邦採 (?–?), Liu Wenmin 劉文敏 (?–?), Liu Yangdeng 劉陽等 (?–?) and many more.[78] In 1526 Liu Bangcai and Liu Xiao 劉曉 (?–?) proposed the Xiyin lectures, a gathering held bi-monthly at last day of the month, in which scholars from four districts learned from each other and discussed the theories of their teachers. In 1536 Zou Shouyi and Cheng Wende 程文德 (1497–1559) founded the Fugu Academy 復古書院 in the county seat as a place for their

---

74  A legendary poet of the Tang dynasty.
75  A legendary Buddhist monk of the Tang dynasty, said to be good friends with Han Shan.
76  A famous Daoist and alchemist of the Northern Song period.
77  ZGLDSYZ 8: 91.
78  On this and the situation of Academies in Anfu county, including a map, see Meskill, *Academies in Ming China*, 87–92, 117–122. See also Anne Gerritsen's look at Ji'an in the successive dynasties of Song, Yuan and Ming: Anne Gerritsen, *Ji'an Literati and the Local in Song-Yuan-Ming China* (Leiden: Brill, 2007).

lectures.[79] In 1553 Lianshan Academy 連山書院 (also called Lianshan Study [*Lianshan shuwu* 連山書屋]) was founded in the region, and in 1558 Fuzhen Academy 復真書院, in 1572 Fuli Academy 復禮書院, in 1591 Shiren Academy 識仁書院, and in 1593 Daodong Academy 道東書院 followed. Among this cluster of academies Fugu Academy served as the center, while academies in all directions could be used for gatherings. Zou Shouyi described this development: "At this time the spirit has gathered, everyone is diligent in their thoughts, convincing to be good and correcting the wrongs. Was it not shameful before?"[80] Besides the above mentioned six academies there were several lecture halls, studies, mountain lodges, and also more academies scattered in the four districts.[81]

Fuzhen Academy was a small lecture academy in the village of Nanli, not comparable to large academies like the White Deer Grotto Academy or the Ehu Academy. However, during the Jiajing and Wanli periods many famous scholars converged there to study and its name became known beyond the area.[82] We can view Fuzhen Academy as illustrative of the academies in the area, founded to open remote regions for the spread of Confucian teachings and representing the ideal of the Confucian scholar pursuing academic life far off the power and distractions of the capital. The scholars who lectured in such village academies also sought to convey Confucian ideas and morals to the local population and instill into them their customs through their lectures.

One example for this is Wang Shihuai, who himself was from Anfu county. He left for Shaanxi to serve as an official in 1571, but returned when he was fifty years old to lecture at Fuzhen Academy and died there at the age of eighty-three. In his *Words of Fuzhen Gatherings* (*Fuzhen huiyu* 復真會語) we can find that he lectured on such topics as the relationship between sagehood and nature. His biography in the records of the academy illustrates the audience of his lectures as encompassing a large range of people from different backgrounds.

---

79    See Nie Bao, "Fugu shuyuan ji (Records of Fugu academy)," in *Nie Bao ji* (Collected Works of Nie Bao), Volume 5, ed. Wu Kewei (Nanjing: Fenghuang chubanshe, 2007), 134.
80    Zou Shouyi, "Zou Dongkuo xiansheng chuangjian shuyuan xu (Preface of Master Zou Dongkuo to the Construction of the Academy)," in *Bailuzhou shuyuan zhi* (Records of Bailuzhou Academy), ed. Gao Liren (Nanchang: Jiangsu renmin chubanshe, 2008), 229–230.
81    See Li Caidong, *Jiangxi gudai shuyuan yanjiu* (Research on Ancient Academies in Jiangxi) (Nanchang; Jiangxi jiaoyu chubanshe, 1993), 294–297, 342–343.
82    Meskill, *Academies in Ming China*, 89.

Our county [because of Wang Shihuai's efforts] has places for Confucian scholars to gather, the village has a shrine, a hall for lectures, and the people ascending it must defer to the master [Wang Shihuai]. Xiyuan, Fugu, are his rivers Zhu and Si,[83] Qingyuan is like the shrine in Luo.[84] Each time the master donned his robe and sat high to lecture, he spread righteousness. The worthy scholars understood, the wanting scholars smiled, the vulgar ones opened their narrow hearts, the stubborn ones fused it with what they had learned before, the village elders did not understand and just nodded, the children had no way to understand and played outside amongst themselves. He not only used words to move, but also managed this without speaking. The censor Lord Wu first honored his teachings, and provincial officers Lord Wang and other lords expounded it. His places were in Fuzhen, Fuli, Daodong 道東, Longhua 龍華, Xuantan 玄潭, Cuihe 翠和, Yunxing 雲興, Mingxin 明新 and Mingxue 明學 Academy.[85]

In short, we have evidence of Ming dynasty Confucian scholars employing public lectures as a tool to educate the general population and relying on the academies as fixtures for such efforts. Whether this was accomplished by opening up the academies in larger settlements for wider audiences, or by founding academies in remote villages, effectively creating community centers, depended on local circumstances. This shows the wide range of different institutional bearings an academy could take on according to scholarly and social needs, which reflected onto practice of the lecture gatherings. Yet it needs to be pointed out here that most lecture gatherings and organizations remained matters of the literati elites and participation or membership relied on extensive knowledge of the Confucian corpus of literature.

## 4     Conclusion

Looking at the history of Confucian academies, the Ming dynasty can be viewed as a somewhat transitionary phase. Academies, during the preceding dynasties, had been mostly associated with Zhu Xi and his teachings. As these were gradually embraced by the state and disseminated through the official educational system, including government schools and the civil service

---

83    The rivers Zhu and Si flow to the north and south Qufu, the hometown of Confucius.
84    The shrine of the two brothers Cheng in Luoyang.
85    Wang Ji et al., "Wang Tangnan xiansheng liezhuan (Biography of Master Wang Tangnan)," in *Fuzhen zhi* (Records of Fuzhen), Kangxi ed., stored in Guojia tushuguan, Beijing, Volume 3, 17.

examinations, the academy system somewhat lost its purpose and declined. However, academies again proved their value as spaces of critical thinking with the advent of Wang Yangming, Zhan Ruoshui, and their followers. Many academies were rejuvenated and experienced an unprecedented growth, by far surpassing their numbers during the Tang, Song, and Yuan dynasties. Concurrent with the decline of the state education system, academies started to take over the role of official schools offering classes for examination preparation and also serving as local educational institutions. Academies were still inheriting their roles and functions from earlier dynasties, while gradually becoming much more integrated in the official educational system—a characteristic academies would increasingly take on during the later Qing dynasty by mainly developing into institutions for examination preparation.

The history of lecture gatherings is closely connected to the history of the academies, but the two institutions were not necessarily dependent on each other. *Jianghui* and academies mutually influenced each other, which lead to the transformation of both concepts. Especially scholars of Yangming School, with their great enthusiasm for education, adapted the format of the lecture gatherings to local circumstances and strove to widen their audience. While they discovered that there were many spaces to lecture, they also realized that organization and upkeep of such activities became increasingly challenging, not to mention problems of housing and sheltering the participants in case of extreme weather conditions. The academies always had been places of scholarship and, equipped with lecturing halls, dormitories, school fields, and libraries, could guarantee the long-term existence of a lecture gathering. Therefore, during the Ming dynasty we can witness the trend of *jianghui* returning to the academies.

Lectures in the academies also diversified. Developing out of Buddhist tradition, lectures transformed from famous scholars discussing or giving talks in front of an audience to regular classes scheduled within a systematized curriculum. These classes not only served to prepare the members of the academy for the civil service examinations, but also still actively transferred the Confucian knowledge system to a new generation and therefore still carried on the original functions of *jianghui*. Furthermore, some scholars also attempted to use the lectures to reach a wide audience, including the common population, to spread their ideas. Confucian academies, by being able to unify the local community around a steady institution, proved to be the perfect tool. So, while *jianghui* activities and Confucian academies certainly have to be viewed as two separate and not subordinate concepts, during the Ming dynasty both were employed to create, spread, and popularize Confucian culture and therefore naturally overlapped and appeared together.

## References

Bai Xinliang 白新良. *Ming qing shuyuan yanjiu* 明清书院研究 (Study of Academies in the Ming and Qing Dynasties). Baoding: Gugong chubanshe, 2012.

Chaffee, John W. "Chu Hsi and the Revival of the White Deer Grotto Academy. 1179–1181 AD" *T'oung Pao* 71 (1985): 40–62.

Chen Lai 陈来. *Zhongguo jinshi sixiangshi yanjiu* 中国近世思想史研究 (Research on the History of Modern Thought in China). Beijing: Shangwu yinshuguan, 2003.

Chen Shilong, 陈时龙. *Mingdai zhongwanqi jiangxue yundong qiaoyi* 明代中晚期讲学运动巧一 (The Lecture Movement During the Middle to Late Ming Dynasty). Shanghai: Fudan daxue chubanshe, 2007.

Dardess, John W. *Blood and History in China: The Donglin Faction and its Repression 1620–1627*. Honolulu: University of Hawai'i Press, 2002.

de Bary, Wm. Theodore. *The Message of the Mind in Neo-Confucianism*. New York: Columbia University Press, 1989.

Deng Hongbo 邓洪波. "Mingdai shuyuan jianghui yanjiu 明代书院讲会研究 (Academy Lecturing [*Jianghui*] in the Ming Dynasty)." Ph.D. diss., Hunan University, 2007.

Deng Hongbo 邓洪波. "Mingdai shuyuan jianghui yanjiu de lishi yu xianzhuang 明代书院讲会研究的历史与现状 (History and present situation of Ming dynasty *jianghui* studies)." *Zhongguo wenhua yanjiu,* Spring (2009): 102–112.

Deng Hongbo 邓洪波. "Mingdai shuyuan jianghui zuzhi xingshi de xin tese 明代书院讲会组织形式的新特色 (New Characteristics of Academy Lecture Organization Forms in the Ming Dynasty)." *Jiangxi jiaoyu xueyuan xuebao* 30, no. 1 (2009): 108–114.

Deng Hongbo 邓洪波. *Zhongguo shuyuan shi* 中国书院史 (History of Chinese Academies). Revised edition. Wuhan: Wuhan daxue chubanshe, 2015.

Feng Congwu 馮從吾. *Shaoxu ji* 少墟集 (Collected Writings of Shaoxu). SKQS Wenyuan edition. Available at: <http://db.ersjk.com> (accessed: 01 February 2018).

Gerritsen, Anne, *Ji'an Literati and the Local in Song-Yuan-Ming China*. Leiden: Brill, 2007.

He Qiaoxin 何喬新. "Chongjian shuyuan ji 重建書院記 (Records of the Reconstruction of the Academy)." In *Bailudong shuyuan guzhi wu zhong* 白鹿洞书院古志五种 (Five Old Records of White Deer Grotto Academy), edited by Li Maoyang 李梦阳 et al., Volume 2. Beijing: Zhonghua Shuju, 1995.

He Qiaoxin 何喬新. "Ziyang shuyuan ji 紫陽書院記 (Records of Ziyang Academy)." In *Zhongguo difangzhi wencheng* 中国地方志集成 (Collection of Chinese Local Records), *Anhui fuxian zhiji* 安徽府县志辑 48 (Collection of Anhui Gazetteers 48), *Daoguang Huizhou fuzhi* 道光徽州府志 1 (Daoguang Era Huizhou Prefecture Gazetteer 1), edited by Ma Buchan 马步蟾, 216–217. Nanjing: Jiangsu guji chubanshe, 1998.

Huang, Martin W. "Male Friendship and *Jiangxue* (Philosophical Debates) in Sixteenth-Century China." In *Male Friendship in Ming China*, edited by Martin W. Huang, 146–178. Leiden: Brill, 2007.

Huang Zongxi 黃宗羲. *Mingru xuean* 明儒學案 (The Records of Ming Scholars). Beijing: Zhonghua shuju, 1985.

Israel, George L. *Doing Good and Ridding Evil in Ming China: The Political Career of Wang Yangming*. Leiden: Brill, 2014.

*Ji'an fuzhi* 吉安府志 (Prefectural Gazetteer of Ji'an). Volume 19, Guangxu edition. On *Zhongguo fangzhi congshu* 中國方志叢書華中地方 (Collection of Chinese Local Records, Central China). Taipei: Chengwen chubanshe, 1985.

*Jiangnan tongzhi* 江南通志 (Local Gazetteer of Jiangnan). Yongzheng ed. SKQS Wenyuan edition. Available at: <http://db.ersjk.com> (accessed: 01 February 2018).

Kelleher, Theresa (trans.). *The Journal of Wu Yubi: The Path to Sagehood*. Indianapolis: Hackett Publishing Company, 2013.

Lee, Thomas H.C. "Chu Hsi, Academies and the Tradition of Private Chiang-hsüeh." *Hanxue yanjiu* 2, no. 1 (1984): 301–329.

Lee, Thomas H.C. *Education in Traditional China. A History*. Leiden: Brill, 2000.

Li Caidong 李才栋. *Jiangxi gudai shuyuan yanjiu* 江西古代书院研究 (Research on Ancient Academies in Jiangxi). Nanchang: Jiangxi jiaoyu chubanshe, 1993.

Li Caidong 李才栋. *Zhongguo shuyuan yanjiu* 中国书院研究 (Research on Chinese Academies). Nanchang: Jiangxi gaoxiao chubanshe, 2005.

Li Fan 李泛. "Dongshan shuyuan jilüe 東山書院記略 (Brief Records of Dongshan Academy)." In *Qimen xian zhi* 祁門縣志 (Qimen County Gazetteer) 1–4, Volume 18, edited by Wang Yunshan 汪韵珊, 718–719. Taiwan: Chengwen chubanshe, 1975.

Liu Yuanqing 劉元卿. *Liu Pinjun quanji* 劉聘君全集 (Complete Writings of Liu Pinjun). SKQS Wenyuan edition. Available at: <http://db.ersjk.com> (accessed: 01 February 2018).

Liu Xu 劉昫. *Jiu Tangshu* 舊唐書 (Old Book of the Tang). Beijing: Zhonghua Shuju, 1975.

Lu Miaw-fen (Lü Miaofen). "Practice as Knowledge: Yang-ming Learning and Chianghui in Sixteenth-Century China." Ph.D. diss., University of California, Los Angeles, 1997.

Lü Miaofen 呂妙芬. "Yangming xue jianghui 陽明學講會 (Discussion Gatherings of the Yangming School)." *Xin shixue* 9, no. 2 (1998): 45–87.

Lü Miaofen 呂妙芬. *Yangmingxue shiren shequn—lishi, sixiang yu shijian* 陽明學士人社群—歷史, 思想與實踐 (The Literati Fellowship of the Wang Yangming School—History, Thought and Practice). Taibei: Zhongyang yanjiuyuan jindaishi yanjiusuo, 2003.

Lü Nan 呂柟. "Zhongxiu huangu shuyuan jilüe 重修環谷書院記略 (Brief Records of the Restoration of Huangu Academy)." In *Qimen xian zhi* 祁門縣志 (Qimen County Gazetteer) 1–4, Volume 18, edited by Wang Yunshan 汪韵珊, 719–720. Taiwan: Chengwen chubanshe, 1975.

Luo Rufang 羅汝芳. *Luo Rufang ji* 羅汝芳集 (Collected Works of Luo Rufang). Edited by Fang Zutai 方祖猷, Liang Yiqun 梁一群 and Li Qinglong 李庆龙. Nanjing: Fenghuang chubanshe, 2007.

Meskill, John. *Academies in Ming China*. Tucson: University of Arizona Press, 1982.

Miles, Steven. "Wang Gen" in *Encyclopedia of Confucianism*, edited by Xinzhong Yao, 633–634. New York: Routledge, 2003.

Nie Bao 聶豹. "Fugu shuyuan ji 復古書院記 (Records of Fugu Academy)." In *Nie Bao ji* 聶豹集 (Collected Works of Nie Bao), Volume 5, edited by Wu Kewei 吳可为, 133–134. Nanjing: Fenghuang chubanshe, 2007.

Ono Kazuko 小野和子. *Mingji dangshe kao* 明季黨社考 (Study on Political Factions in the Ming Dynasty). Shanghai: Shanghai guji chubanshe, 2006.

Perry, Elizabeth J. *Challenging the Mandate of Heaven: Social Protest and State Power in China*. Armonk: M.E. Sharpe, 2002.

Qian Ming 錢明 (ed). *Xu Ao, Qian Dehong, Dong Jian ji* 徐愛, 錢德洪, 董澐集 (Collected Works of Xu Ao, Qian Dehong, Dong Jian). Nanjing: Fenghuang chubanshe, 2007.

Schneewind, Sarah. *Community Schools and the State in Ming China*. Stanford: Stanford University Press, 2006.

Shao Bowen 邵伯溫. *Wen jian lü* 聞見錄 (Records of Things Heard and Seen). Volume 18. SKQS Wenyuan edition. Available at: <http://db.ersjk.com> (accessed: 01 February 2018).

Shen Defu 沈德符. *Wanli yehuo bian* 萬曆野獲篇 (Unofficial Matters of the Wanli Reign). Beijing: Zhonghua shuju, 1959.

Shen Jia 沈佳. *Mingru yanxing lu* 明儒言行錄 (Records of Words and Deeds of Ming Confucians). SKQS Wenyuan edition. Available at: <http://db.ersjk.com> (accessed: 01 February 2018).

Shun, Kwong-Loi. "Wang Yang-ming on Self-Cultivation in the Daxue." *Journal of Chinese Philosophy* 38 (December 2011): 96–113.

Tong Shu 同恕. *Ji'an ji* 集庵集 (Collected Writings of Ji'an). SKQS Wenyuan edition. Available at: <http://db.ersjk.com> (accessed: 01 February 2018).

Tu, Wei-ming. "An Inquiry into Wang Yang-ming's Four-Sentence Teaching." *The Eastern Buddhist*, New Series 7, no. 2 (October 1974): 32–48.

Wang Ji 王吉, et al. "Wang Tangnan xiansheng liezhuan 王塘南先生列傳 (Biography of Master Wang Tangnan)." In *Fuzhen zhi* 復真志 (Records of Fuzhen), Volume 3, Kangxi edition, 15–18, stored in Guojia tushuguan, Beijing.

Wang Ji 王畿. *Wang Ji ji* 王畿集 (Collected Writings of Wang Ji). Nanjing: Fenghuang chubanshe, 2007.

Wang Shouren 王守仁. *Wang Yangming quanji* 王陽明全集 (Complete Writings of Wang Yangming). Shanghai: Shanghai guji chubanshe, 1992.

Wang Shu 王恕. "Xuegu shuyuan ji 學古書院記 (Records of Xuegu Academy)." In *Sanyuan xian xin zhi* 三原縣新志 (New Gazetteer of Sanyuan county), Volume 4, Guangxu edition, in *Zhongguo fangzhi congshu huabei difang* 中國方志叢書華北地方 (Collection of Chinese Local Records, North China), 168–169. Taibei: Chengwen chubanshe, 1976.

Wang Yan 王儼. "Fengshan shuyuan ji 鳳山書院記 (Records of Fengshan Academy)." In *Puqi xian zhi yi, er, san* 蒲圻縣志 (Puqi County Gazetteer), Volume 3, Daoguang edition, edited by Lao Guangtai 劳光泰, 249–259. Taibei: Chengwen chubanshe, 1975.

Wu Zhen 吳震. *Mingdai zhishijie jiangxue huodong xinian* 明代知識界讲学活动系年 (The System of Lecture Activities in Intellectual Circles in the Ming Dynasty). Shanghai: Xuelin chubanshe, 2003.

Xu Xiandeng 許獻等. *Donglin shuyuan zhi* 東林書院志 (Records of Donglin Academy), edited by Liu Delin 刘德麟 and Zhu Hui 朱慧. Beijing: Zhonghua shuju, 2004.

Zhang Tingyu 張廷玉. *Mingshi* 明史 (History of the Ming). Beijing: Zhonghua shuju, 1974.

Zhu Hanmin 朱汉民, and Deng Hongbo 邓洪波. *Yuelu Shuyuan shi* 岳麓书院史 (History of the Yuelu Academy). Changsha: Hunan jiaoyu chubanshe, 2013.

Zhu Xi 朱熹. *Huian ji* 晦庵集 (Collected Writings of Huian), in SKQS Wenyuan edition. Available at: <http://db.ersjk.com> (accessed: 01 February 2018).

Zou Shouyi 鄒守益. "Zou Dongkuo xiansheng chuangjian shuyuan xu 鄒東廓先生創建書院序 (Preface of Master Zou Dongkuo to the Construction of the Academy)." In *Bailuzhou shuyuan zhi* 白鷺洲书院志 (Records of Bailuzhou Academy), edited by Gao Liren 高立人, 229–230. Nanchang: Jiangsu renmin chubanshe, 2008.

CHAPTER 7

# Books and Book Culture in Oksan Academy

*Lee Byoung-Hoon*

## 1       Introduction

In the second half of the 16th century Korean literati started to establish Confucian academies based on the model of the Chinese White Deer Grotto Academy (Chin. Bailudong shuyuan, Kor. Paengnoktong sŏwŏn 白鹿洞書院). Korean academies were predominantly established in order to venerate former Confucian worthies and sages, and to stimulate students to follow these models via study and self-cultivation. Academies not only served as educational institutions, but also played an important role in the development of the Korean version of the Learning of the Way and its dissemination in local society. During the second half of the 16th century the basic features of the architectural and ideological framework of Korean academies were defined: lecture hall and dormitories were accompanied by a ritual space reserved for a Confucian worthy enshrined in the academy and together served for lectures and educational activities, which were regulated by academy rules (*wŏn'gyu* 院規). During the 17th century the educational practice in academies further developed into a pattern in which lectures were led by famous scholars and academies started to adhere to particular scholarly lineages that transmitted, via master-disciple relationships, particular interpretations of the Confucian canon. Korean academies also became social and political centers, participating in both philosophical and political disputes of the day. Based on their geographical location, political adherence, or influence of the enshrined Confucian scholar, academies developed extensive networks serving to enhance their status and political influence. The spread and development of Korean academies reached its peak during the 18th century, but several structural and political problems caused by the academy boom finally resulted into attempts by the state to regulate and later to reduce their numbers, especially in order to curb their economic power. The final blow to the academy system came in 1868 when the government decided to abolish all academies and shrines that were without a royal charter (*saaek* 賜額), authorizing their existence.[1] Chartered

---

1   For general representative Korean discussions of the Korean Academy system see Chŏng Manjo, "Ch'oegŭn ŭi sŏwŏn yŏn'gu tongyang e kwanhan kŏmt'o (Review of General Research

academies were also subjected to a selection process, and in 1871 it was decreed that only those academies whose enshrined scholars were also venerated in the metropolitan Confucius Shrine (Munmyo 文廟) were allowed to continue their existence, albeit under the condition that there could always be only one academy dedicated to one particular scholar. With the exception of the twenty-seven academies fulfilling these criteria, all others were abolished. Because of the Korean War and the impacts of modernization on Korean society there are only ten remaining academies that can claim to have kept their original form and a continuous existence to the present time.[2] One of these is Oksan Academy 玉山書院 in Kyŏngju; its history and cultural tradition offer a unique example enabling us to understand the contours of Korean Confucian academy culture.

Oksan Academy was founded in 1572 and (unlike many other Korean academies) survived the 1592 Hideyoshi Invasions without any harm. Despite of several reconstructions it kept its original architectural features: its pavilion Mubyŏllu 無邊樓 (Pavilion of Boundlessness) is a prime example of the early academy pavilions. The construction of the academy complex follows the traditional pattern of Korean academies locating the teaching facilities in front and the shrine (often at an elevated place) in the rear part. As was mentioned, the status of an academy, manifested often by the royal charter, depended on the fame and prestige of the scholar venerated in the academy shrine. Hoejae Yi Ŏnjŏk 晦齋 李彥迪 (1491–1553), enshrined in Oksan Academy, was an influential thinker and official and his prestige, together with royal charter later bestowed on the academy, made Oksan academy most prominent among other academies in the Yŏngnam area.

---

Trends in Recent Academy Studies)," in *Chosŏn sidae sŏwŏn yŏn'gu* (Studies of Confucian Academies in the Chosŏn Period), ed. Chŏng Manjo (Seoul; Chimmundang, 1997); Chŏng Manjo, "Han'guk sŏwŏn ŭi yŏn'gu hyŏnhwang kwa chŏnmang (Present State and Prospects of Korean Academy Studies)," in *Han'guk ŭi sŏwŏn kwa hangmaek yŏn'gu* (Studies of School Ties and Academies in Korea), ed. Kyŏnggi taehakkyo sosŏng haksul yŏn'guwŏn (Seoul: Kukhak charyowŏn, 2002), 9–28; Yi Haejun, "Sŏwŏn yŏn'gu wa munjung sŏwŏn (Family Lineage Academies and Academy Studies)," in *Chosŏn hugi munjung sŏwŏn yŏn'gu* (Studies on Later Chosŏn Family Lineage Academies) (P'aju: Kyŏngin munhwasa, 2008), 1–18.

2   Korean academies are protected by the South Korean government as historical relics within the framework of cultural protection legislation. On March 8, 1967, Oksan Academy was acknowledged as Historical Relic Nr. 154. It was further (as a part of the historical Yangdong Village) registered in 2010 as the UNESCO World Heritage "Historic Villages of Korea: Hahoe and Yangdong." Oksan Academy is also, together with the Tosan, Sosu, Pyŏngsan, Todong, Namgye, Musŏng, Tonam, and P'iram academies, part of the pending UNESCO World Heritage proposal "Seowon, Confucian Academies of Korea"; see <http://whc.unesco.org/en/tentative lists/5648/> (accessed: 01 December 2017).

Since its very beginning Oksan Academy engaged in publishing and disseminating the works of Yi Ŏnjŏk and procured a large amount of books and materials for the education of its students. As a social and political center of activities in the area it also stored numerous documents related to its role. Its archives and library are well-preserved and today present one of the biggest library corpuses of Korean academies still extant. The book collecting, preserving, and publishing activities of Oksan Academy are the subject of this study.

## 2  History of Oksan Academy

Oksan Academy was founded by the joint efforts of Kyŏngju magistrate Yi Chemin 李齊閔 (1528–1608) and the local community in 1572. A royal plaque was bestowed in 1573 and officially endorsed its named as "Oksan Academy."[3] The royal favor toward the academy was further demonstrated by gifts of books: corpuses of the Four Books and Five Classics were donated in 1577, in 1588 the *Sohak ŏnhae* 小學諺解 (*Vernacular Explanation of the Lesser Learning*) and in 1590 several other Confucian works were gifted. The economic foundations of the academy were also secured by an endowment of fourteen slaves from the Kyŏngju prefecture. At the end of the 16th and beginning of the 17th century numerous visits and support by local officials further enhanced the reputation of the academy and in 1606 Yi Ŏnjŏk was included in the pantheon of the Confucius Shrine (in the capital). All these factors enabled the academy to publish several works of Yi Ŏnjŏk and through royal gifts, purchases, or printed volumes it established itself as the local publishing center and an important library. Because of its role as a storage place for the print woodblocks of the adjacent Kugang Academy 龜江書院 and Kyŏngju Prefecture, Oksan Academy also became the publishing center for the whole Kyŏngju area.[4] The publishing activities of the academy were, until a disastrous fire in 1834, also carried out by the dependent Chŏnghyesa Monastery 定惠寺, which belonged to the academy property.

The academy's wealth was mostly based on land and slaves, but it also possessed dependent properties, i.e. a Buddhist monastery and various businesses in the local area. Dependent peasants regularly provided tributes supplying

---

[3] For a history of Oksan Academy see Yi Suhwan, *Chosŏn hugi ŭi sŏwŏn. Oksan sŏwŏn ŭl chungsim ŭro* (The Academies of Late Chosŏn: With a Focus on Oksan Academy) (Kwach'ŏn: Kuksa p'yŏnch'an wiwŏnhoe, 1992).

[4] See Yi Suhwan, "Sŏwŏn kirok charyo chŏngni ŭi hyŏnhwang kwa kwaje (Present State and Tasks of the Organization of the Document Sources of the Academy)," in *Minjong munhwa nonch'ong*, Volume 52 (2012): 423–447.

the academy with necessary goods and the monks of Chŏnghyesa Monastery contributed to the academy economy by producing various products ranging from straw sandals to vegetables. There was, however, another distinctive economic feature of Oksan Academy: thanks to its location near the sea the academy also owned fishing enterprises and boats, which provided salt and sea products for both daily needs and sacrificial offerings.[5] The substantial wealth of the academy was used to promote its role within local literati and student community, providing students with lodging, preparing study materials, organizing lectures, preparing students for state examinations, etc. The influence of the academy remained unhampered even after the abolition of other academies and in 1884 it was still able to muster 8,849 signatures of local literati for the petition to the throne.[6]

## 3   The Academy and Its Library

Because of their librarian and publishing functions Confucian academies played an important role in the spread of Confucian culture in the local Korean society. Rural Korea of Chosŏn times was generally characterized by an almost nonexistent book market, and students who were not able to purchase books from the government publishing agency in the capital, Kyosŏgwan 校書館 or through the few booksellers in Seoul, had many difficulties accessing the books necessary for their studies. Countryside areas were dependent on the few books published by local magistrates or officials, but these were generally not available for individual acquisition. Expenses for books and the minimal distribution of volumes forced literati to rely on private archives and handwritten copies circulated from hand to hand.[7] In this context the book services offered by a local academy were a welcome remedy for this dire situation. Academies having a library or a storage for print woodblocks (usually called *changsŏgak* 藏書閣 and *changp'angak* 藏板閣) stored a large number of

---

5   *Oksan sŏwŏn chi* (Records of Oksan Academy) (Kyŏngsan: Yŏngnam taehakkyo ch'ulp'anbu, 1993), 147–158.
6   Lee Byoung-hoon, "19 segi ch'o kyŏngju oksan sŏwŏn kangdang chunggŏn kwa wisang pyŏnhwa (The Reconstruction of the Oksan Academy Lecture Hall in the Early 19th Century and Changes in Status)," *Han'gukhak yŏn'gu* 57 (2016): 267–270.
7   For general overview of Korean publishing culture and history see Ok Yŏngjŏng, "Han'guk sŏwŏn ŭi changsŏ wa ch'ulp'an munhwa (Publishing and Librarian Culture of Korean Academies)," *Han'guk ŭi sŏwŏn munhwa* (Korean Academy Culture), munsach'ŏl (2014): 345–368; and Son Kyeyŏng, "Ch'ulp'an munhwasa yŏn'gu hyŏnhwang kwa saengwalsa roŭi chŏpkŭn (Current State of Research on the Cultural History of Publishing and a Micro Historical Approach)," *Yŏngnamhak* 13 (2008): 369–397.

books and often published them as well. In fact, large and affluent academies like Tosan Academy 陶山書院 and Pyŏngsan Academy 屏山書院 in Andong, Sosu Academy 紹修書院 in Yŏngju, Oksan Academy or P'iram Academy 筆巖書院 in Changsŏng, and Tonam Academy 遯巖書院 in Nonsan were the only local institutions able to invest substantial amounts of money for the procurement of books and the expenses of their printing enterprises. A general feature of these academies was their important position within the local environment due to their status as chartered academies, the eminent scholars they venerated, and the extensive networks they were able to mobilize for their role of centers of book culture.[8] Their financial abilities often depended on the support of local elites, donations, and their tax-free status. With the resources accumulated by these means, such academies were able to establish facilities for both the storage and the production of books and other materials necessary for the spread of the Confucian message. The process of collecting and preserving books was deeply connected with the specific needs of the academies as educational institutions. In spite of local variations, the basic corpus of literature for the education of students remained largely the same: the *Xiaoxue* 小學 (*Lesser Learning*) together with the Four Books and Five Classics, Zhu Xi's 朱熹 (1130–1200) *Family Rituals* (*Jiali* 家禮), Zhen Dexiu's 真德秀 (1178–1235) *Xinjing* 心經 (*Classic of the Mind*), the *Jinsilu* 近思錄 (*Reflections on Things at Hand*), followed by the various historical books, etc.[9] The Rules of Oksan Academy stipulated the reading curriculum in the following way:

> All students should in their reading take the Four Books and Five Classics as original sources with the *Lesser Learning* and the *Family Rituals* serving as a gate to them. [...] While it is necessary to study various histories, philosophies, collective writings, literary works, and prose and poems and also to prepare for the civil service examinations, these should be studied as a matter of secondary importance.[10]

In order to meet the demands defined by the academy rules it was necessary to acquire books either by royal donation, individual gifts, or the support of local elites. Elites in the broader area of Kyŏngju city, via the Oksan Academy library, gained access to valuable sources of knowledge and the academy served as a crucial institution for the spread of Yi Ŏnjŏk's intellectual heritage (also raising

---

8   See Ok, "Han'guk sŏwŏn ŭi changsŏ wa ch'ulp'an munhwa," 345–346.
9   See Kim Yunsik, "Chosŏnjo sŏwŏn mun'go e kwanhan ilgoch'al (A Study on Early Chosŏn Academy Libraries)," *Sŏjihak yŏn'gu* 41 (2008): 298–299.
10  *Oksan sŏwŏn chi*, 36–37.

the prestige of his descendants and disciples living in the area). Both these factors contributed to the creation of extensive networks of alumni, readers, and supporters, further contributing to the growth of the academy and its book collection. Thanks to its long uninterrupted existence Oksan Academy acquired, via the above mentioned means, an unusual (compared to other private or academy libraries) number of rare books, many of them during the earliest period of the academy. During the first decades of its existence the academy was able to capitalize on the fame and influence of Yi Ŏnjŏk to attract a large number of book donations from the royal court, local officials, and individual literati.

The most prominent source of book donations from early on was Kyŏngju prefecture itself. The central government publishing office often delegated printing projects of Confucian and educational books to local government offices in order to share printing cost and reduce logistical problems. As the biggest town in the area and seat of the prefecture, Kyŏngju participated in many such undertakings. According to the local gazetteer *Tonggyŏng chapki* 東京雜記 (*Miscellaneous Records of the Eastern Capital*), the Kyŏngju Prefectural Office had published sixty-nine different titles by 1700.[11] Prefect Yi Kyebok 李繼福 (?–?) in 1512 ordered new editions of the *Samguk sagi* 三國史記 (*Historical Records of Three Kingdoms*) and the *Samguk yusa* 三國遺事 (*Memorabilia of the Three Kingdoms*) chronicles. The prefecture in 1543 published the *Chunqiu Hushi zhuan* 春秋胡氏傳 (*Commentary on the Chunqiu by Mr. Hu*), the *Shujing* 書經 (here called *Shuzhuan* 書傳) and the *Zijingpian* 自警編 (*Treatise on Self-Admonition*) and sent these volumes to Sosu Academy.[12]

One especially active prefect was Kwiam Yi Chŏng 龜巖 李楨 (1512–1571), who during his term from the ninth month of 1560 to the first month of 1563 commissioned several important publications: the *Yi-Luo yuanyuan lu* 伊洛淵源錄 (*Records of the Yi and Luo School*) in 1561, the *ErCheng cuiyu* 二程粹語 (*Selected Words of Two Chengs*) in 1562, the *Huangming lixue mingchen yanxinglü* 皇明理學名臣言行錄 (*Records of Words and Deeds of August Ming famous scholars of the Learning of Principle*) in 1562, the *Tangjian* 唐鑑 (*Mirror of the Tang Dynasty*) in 1562, etc.[13] All these books are recorded in the Oksan Academy book catalogue *Sŏch'aek chŏnyŏdorok* 書冊傳與都錄 (*Complete*

---

11  See *Tonggyŏng chapki* (Miscellaneous Records of the Eastern Capital), Volume 3, Sŏjŏk, Pujang ch'aekp'an.
12  See Nam Kwŏnhŭi, "Chosŏn sidae kyŏngju kanhaeng ŭi sŏjŏk (Publication and Books in Kyŏngju during the Chosŏn Period)," *Silla munhwa* 33 (2009): 7–9.
13  See U Chŏngim, "T'oegye Yi Hwang kwa kŭ ŭi mundo tŭrŭi sŏjŏk kanhaeng kwa sŏwŏn ŭi kinŭng (T'oegye Yi Hwang and Book Publishing and Academy Functions under His Disciples)," *Chiyŏk kwa yŏksa* 22 (2008): 217–220.

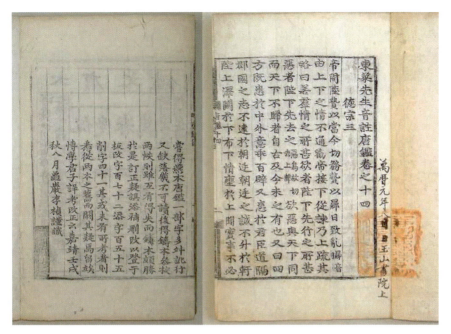

ILLUSTRATION 7.1  *Mirror of the Tang Dynasty* of Oksan Academy in 1562.
SOURCE: PHOTO COURTESY OF AUTHOR

*Records of Transmitted and Donated Books*) and we may presume that they were donated to the academy shortly after its foundation.[14] *Mirror of the Tang Dynasty* contains a preface by Yi Chŏng dated to the eight month of the year *imsul* of the Jiajing era (1562) and on the first page is a brush note "In the eight month of the first year of Wanli era (1573) given to Oksan Academy."[15]

Yi Chemin, who was the prefect of Kyŏngju in 1573 and had initiated the founding of the academy, besides fields and slaves also donated books to the new academy. In addition to the above mentioned book titles the prefecture furthermore published and disseminated the writings of academy patron Yi Ŏnjŏk. In 1575 for the first time the *Hoejae chip* 晦齋集 (*Collected Writings of Hoejae*) was published,[16] as well as other works of Yi Ŏnjŏk, i.e. the *Taehak changgu poyu* 大學章句補遺 (*Supplement to Commentary on the Great Learning in Phrases and Paragraphs*) and the *Sok Taehak hongmun* 續大學或問

---

14  The book catalogue *Sŏch'aek chŏnyŏdorok* is kept in the vault of Oksan Academy and has not been published yet.
15  See Illustration 7.1. This edition of the *Mirror of the Tang Dynasty* was printed in 1562 and is still stored in the vault of Oksan Academy.
16  See "Kan'gi 刊記 (Records of Printing)," in *Hoejae chip* 晦齋集 (Collected Writing of Hoejae).

(*Continuation of Questions on the Great Learning*). During the reign of King Sŏnjo 宣祖 (r. 1567–1608) the official interest in the works of Yi Ŏnjŏk became even more pronounced:[17] the *Chungyong kugyŏng yŏnŭi* 中庸九經衍義 (*Extended Meaning of Zhongyong and Nine Classics*) was edited in 1574 by royal order in the Office of the Special Councilors (Hongmungwan 弘文館) and the result was published in 1583 by Kyŏngju prefecture. The prefecture supported the publication of works by other famous scholars connected to the area as well. During the sixteenth century the works of Ikjae Yi Chehyŏn 益齋 李齊賢 (1287–1367), a Koryŏ scholar from Kyŏngju were published by the prefecture. Publications commissioned by the prefecture were one of the constituent parts of the newly established Oksan Academy.

A brief look into the oldest extant book catalogue of the Oksan Academy, the *Oksan sŏwŏn sŏch'aekki* 玉山書院 書冊記 (*Record of Oksan Academy Books*), from 1713 shows that many books from the academy collection were published before the establishment of the academy.[18] It is not possible to verify dates of their acquisition, but seals of the original owners at least reveal the original origin or the names of the donators. Colophons like "owned by the family archive of Yi family from Yŏgang" or "Tongnaktang" 獨樂堂 (Hall of Solitary Bliss), which was Yi Ŏnjŏk's studio, show that these books were donated to the academy by Yi Ŏnjŏk's descendants. Books donated to the academy also included rare manuscripts authored by Yi Ŏnjŏk or publications bestowed upon him during his official career by the king. The handwritten manuscripts of Yi Ŏnjŏk's works and royal gifts to him were the most treasured part of the academy book collection. The circle of supporters of the academy also provided other publications: descendants of Yi Ŏnjŏk's younger brother Yi Ŏn'gwal 李彥适 (1494–1553) for example donated his own copy of the *Tongguk t'onggam* 東國通鑑 (*Comprehensive Mirror of the Eastern Country*) and another gift was a copy of the *Hoeam sijip* 晦庵詩集 (*Poetry Collection of Hui'an*) originally owned by Chisan Kwŏn Ŭnghwa 智山 權應鋒 (1547–1610), as is attested by a note in the book. These donations show us that private book gifts were one of the crucial components of the new academy book collection.

A special section of the book donations were publications produced and donated by other academies. The fame and power of a particular academy derived from its ability to propagate the teachings of its scholarly affiliation and to create effective social and political networks. Tosan Academy published

---

17  See Yi Suhwan, "Hoejae Yi Ŏnjŏk kwa oksan sŏwŏn (Hoeja Yi Ŏnjŏk and Oksan Academy)," *Kyŏngju sahak* 16 (1997): 412–414.

18  The book catalogue *Oksan sŏwŏn sŏch'aekki* is as well stored in the vault of the academy and has not been published yet.

works of its founder, T'oegye Yi Hwang 退溪 李滉 (1501–1570), Chagye Academy 紫溪書院 in Ch'ŏngdo published the collected oeuvre of Kim Ilson 金馹孫 (1464–1498), who was venerated in the academy shrine, and Sŏak Academy 西岳書院 in Kyŏngju frequently published its chronicle *Sŏak chi* 西岳志 (*Records of the Western Mountain*)[19] in order to praise the Silla (57 BCE–935 CE) figures venerated there. Book publication and dissemination were not only effective means to increase power and influence for academies; the same phenomena can be seen looking at influential family lineages that relied on the same strategy. In 1606 the Ki family from Haengju donated the works of Ki Chun 奇遵 (1492–1521) to Oksan Academy. The reason for this donation was the fact, that Ki Chun was the uncle of Ki Taesŭng 奇大升 (1527–1572), the author of an eulogy for Yi Ŏnjŏk. Another offspring from the Ki family, high official Ki Chahŏn 奇自獻 (1567–1624), in 1609 performed a ritual homage in the academy shrine. The Ki family was obviously quite eager to promote its connection with the important academy, which was thankful for both the displayed respect and the book donations. On the other hand, the Ki Family could be sure that the books of its ancestor would be well preserved and accessible to scholars from the Kyŏngju area.

The trajectory of book donations was steadily growing with time and we may say that until the 18th century Oksan Academy enjoyed a continuous flow of book gifts from local officials and individual donators. In 1713 Kyŏngju prefecture donated the historical compendium *Saryak* 史略 (*Outline of History*), in 1743 the *Sahan ilt'ong* 史漢一統 (*Combined Shiji and Hanshu*) and in 1753 the *Jinsilu*. The Provincial Governor's Office in 1730 contributed the *Samgang haengsildo* 三綱行實圖 (*Real Illustrations of the Conduct Based on Three Moral Bonds*) and the *Iryun haengsildo* 二倫行實圖 (*Real Illustrations of the Conduct Based on Two Human Relations*) to the academy collection. It further published and donated the *Sŏjŏn taemun* 書傳大文 (*Great Compendium on Shujing*) in 1769. The influential local elites contributed many publications as well. Provincial governor Ch'oe Sŏkhang 崔錫恒 (1654–1724) in 1701 sent the *Kwangguk chigyŏngnok* 光國志慶錄 (*Record to Celebrate the Glory of the State*). From 1703 to 1709 Hayang magistrate Yi Pogin 李復仁 sent several copies of works of his famous ancestor Yi Tŏkhyŏng 李德馨 (1561–1613). In 1755 the Kyŏngju prefect Hong Samik 洪三益 (?–?) donated the published works of his father,

---

19  The *Sŏak chi* is probably one of the most circulated records of Confucian academies in Korea. For information on its publishing history see Rokutanda Yutaka, "A Survey of the Variant Versions of the Sŏakchi and their Taxonomy," *The Memoirs of Toyo Bunko* 73 (2005): 111–139.

ILLUSTRATION 7.2
Book case for the royal donation (*naesa* 內賜) of the *Royal Revised Version of Hundred Chapters of Five Classics*.
SOURCE: PHOTO COURTESY OF AUTHOR

*Naejae chip* 耐齋集 (*Collected Works of Naejae*).[20] This flow of donations only started to dissipate and disappeared after the second half of the 18th century when the academy system endured decline and the Korean book market was shaped more and more by commercial presses.

The most decisive factor for the existence of an academy certainly was, besides networks formed around an enshrined person, gaining royal support. The very act of chartering an academy (materialized in a gift of a royal plaque, often inscribed by the king himself) and the bestowal of land and slaves, or later on tax privileges, was often followed by further support through the court. Chartered academies were together with local schools supplied with goods necessary for annual offerings and various gifts, often in the form of book donations. Since the first such instances, like the donation of books to the first Korean academy, Sosu sŏwŏn, royal donations began to play an important role, through both their economical and symbolic function. Royal books donations, so-called *naesabon* 內賜本, were usually marked by the inscription *naesa*

---

20   Lee Byoung-hoon, "Kyŏngju oksan sŏwŏn ŭi changsŏ sujip mit kwalli silt'ae rŭl t'onghae pon tosŏgwan chŏk kinŭng (Library Functions Seen through the Collection and Management of Books in the Kyŏngju Oksan Academy)," *Han'guk minjok munhwa* 58 (2016): 8–17.

(bestowed by the court) and the date of the gift. These books were kept in special cases (sometimes called *kwe* 櫃) preventing possible damage.

Books donated by the king were also held in a separate building, often called Ŏsŏgak 御書閣 (Pavilion of Sovereign Books) or Chongyŏnggak 尊經閣 (Pavilion of Venerated Classics). Browsing of these books was customarily preceded by respectful bowing.[21] Royal donations belonged to the most treasured assets of the academy and naturally enhanced its position and influence.

Oksan Academy was chartered in the twelfth month of 1573, but the first royal book gift was bestowed only in 1577: consisting of two sets of the Four Books and Five Classics, the ninety-five volumes of the *Zhuzi daquan* 朱子大全 (*Complete Works of Master Zhu*), one hundred forty volumes of the *Zhuzi yulei* 朱子語類 (*Conversations of Master Zhu Arranged Topically*), and four volumes of the *Yusŏnnok* 儒先錄 (*Record of Outstanding Confucians*). The relatively late date of the book donation was caused by the delay on the side of Editorial Review Office, which had to, as a matter of priority, first supply the royal court. Royal donations to Oksan Academy followed also in 1588 (*Sohak ŏnhae*) and in 1590 (one set of the *Sasŏ ŏnhae*). Besides these gifts we also find an undated donation of fifteen volumes of the *Xingli daquan* 性理大全 (*Great Collection of Works on Human Nature and Principles*), probably given to the academy during the end of the 16th century. Together with other treasured documents like Yi Ŏnjŏk's manuscripts, a letter of King Myŏngjong 明宗 (1545–1567), lists of famous visitors, and rosters of academy leaders were kept in special boxes in the separate pavilion.[22]

Royal donations to Oksan Academy amass in two periods, during the 16th century pioneer times of the academy and from 1794 onwards. What were reasons for almost two hundred years' lacuna in royal support? The cessation of support was partially caused by a combination of simple economic reasons (the dire situation of the royal finances after the Japanese and Manchu invasion combined with overpopulation and other factors) and political decisions. The royal court was unable to support the growing number of academies equally and due to the adherence of the Oksan scholars to political factions that had been ousted from the central offices, there was a little will to support them on the side of government. As an academy venerating scholars enshrined in the Confucius temple, Oksan Academy theoretically had the right for royal supplies of books, but politically adversaries at the court successfully ignored

---

21  See Yun Hŭimyŏn, "Chosŏn sidae sŏwŏn ŭi tosŏgwan kinŭng yŏn'gu (Study on Library Functions of Academies during the Chosŏn Period)," *Yŏksa hakpo* (2005): 8.
22  See *Yŏrŭp wŏnu sajŏk* (Academies and Shrines Sites by District), Volume 5, Kyŏngsangdo, Kyŏngju, Oksan Sŏwŏn. [1759].

this rule.²³ The situation changed at the end of the 18th century and with the new politics of impartiality by King Chŏngjo 正祖 (r. 1776–1800), Yi Ŏnjŏk and his intellectual heritage guarded by Oksan Academy again found a royal favor which was materialized in a series of book donations. The string of gifts, including such works as the *Ŏjŏng Chusŏ paeksŏn* 御定朱書百選 (*Royal Edition of Master Zhu's Letters*) (1794), the *Ŏjŏng Sok Taehak hongmun* (*Royal Edition of Supplement to Questions on the Great Learning*) (1794), the *Ŏjŏng Kyujang chŏngun* (*Royal Edition of Sovereign Correct Rhymes*) (1796), and the *Hyangnye happ'yŏn* 鄉禮合編 (*Local Rites Compiled*) (1797) shows the extent of the renewed royal interest. The same reversal of the originally hostile policy toward dissenting academies is to be seen also in the case of Tosan, Imgo 臨皋書院, or Todong 道東書院 Academies, which started again enjoy royal support after long decades of the official neglect. Royal gifts were also accompanied by visits of high government officials, who performed sacrifices and often personally delivered royal gifts.

## 4 Purchase, Copy, Printing and Exchange of Books

In spite of all donations and support, the most reliable source of acquiring publications required for the academy education still was simple purchase. However, due to the high prices this usually required substantial investments. With books imported from China even more complications came into play: these were available for purchase only in the capital or via the regular mission to the Chinese court.²⁴ The further the distance from the capital as center of the book trade, the worse this situation grew. Oksan Academy in 1757 bought one hundred thirty volumes of the *Shiji pinglin* 史記評林 (*Forest of Comments on Shiji*) for 7 *liang* and in the following year for 1 *liang* bought four volumes of the *P'oŭn chip* 圃隱集 (*Collected Writings of P'oŭn*).²⁵ The *Shiji pinglin* was a Ming-times compendium on the *Shiji* and related historical problems; it was an indispensable book for students aspiring to participate in the state examinations. The academy obviously bought the book to meet its own members'

---

23  Kim Yunsik, "Chosŏnjo sŏwŏn mun'go e kwanhan ilgoch'al," 303–304.
24  General information about book imports from China can be found in Kang Myŏnggwan, "Chosŏn hugi sŏjŏk ŭi suip yut'ong kwa changsŏga ŭi ch'urhyŏn. 18, 19 segi kyŏnghwa sajok (Import and Circulation of Books in the Late Chosŏn Period and the Rise of the Book Collector)," *Minjok munhaksa yŏn'gu* 9 (1996): 171–194.
25  See *Kanso pyŏlbich'aek kajŏn chŏnyŏgi* (Record of Published, Procured, Bought, and Received Books), *pyŏngja* 丙子 (1756) to *chŏngch'uk* 丁丑 (1757), stored in the Oksan Academy vault.

demand. Same year the academy gained a copy of the *Liji* in ten volumes. Judging from the absence of records on related expenses, the copy was probably produced within the academy. In the case of other books, like the *Hakpong chip* 鶴峯集 (*Collected Writings of Hakpong*) and the *Ŏnhaeng t'ongnok* 言行通錄 (*Comprehensive Record of Words and Deeds* [*of Master T'oegye*]) we have at our disposal records of payments for ink and paper, suggesting that academy already owned the wooden matrices for the print. Oksan Academy also, on demand, printed the works of Yi Ŏnjŏk and sent them to various libraries and collectors. In 1762 the academy payed 11 *liang* for copying five books (thirty volumes) of the *Nosa yŏngŏn* 魯史零言 (*Fragments of Sayings from Lu History*), a historical compendium on the ancient Chinese state of Lu. Five *liang* were used to finance the paper and the rest of the amount were expenses for professional handwriting. Copying was certainly the cheaper way of acquisition. Although relatively rare, we can also find instances of books being exchanged between the academy and other collections. The record of received goods shows that in the second month of 1734 the academy exchanged the *Family Rites* for the *Jinsilu* and in the twelfth month of 1745 two volumes of historical compilation for *Yŏktae ch'ŏmnok* 歷代捷錄 (*Short Records of Historical Chronology*) were exchanged. Seen from the records, the most frequently bought book was certainly *Book of Rites*. It was copied in 1757, but in 1762 it was also bought for 11 *liang* in the capital. In 1782 the book was again purchased, this time in a Chinese edition (*t'angp'anbon* 唐板本).[26]

The book collection of Oksan Academy was primarily concerned with studies of Yi Ŏnjŏk's intellectual legacy and the general Confucian curriculum. The early 19th-century Roster of Lectures (*Kangan* 講案) and records of the students grades are witnesses of the reading practices and document the regular readings of and examinations on the *Zhongyong*, the *Great Learning*, the *Family Rituals* and the *Lesser Learning*.[27] Thorough knowledge of these classics (and especially of the *Liji*) was a necessary step for more advanced studies of Yi Ŏnjŏk works.

## 5   Book Collection Management

Oksan Academy among Korean Confucian academies stores an exceptionally high number of old books and documents. A 2004 survey registered 1,156 old

---

26   Ibid.
27   *Oksan sŏwŏn chi*, 675–676.

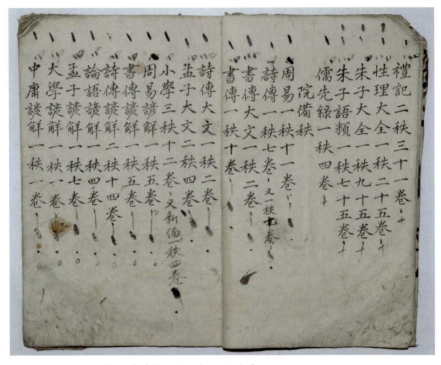

ILLUSTRATION 7.3   *Record of Oksan Academy Books* from 1713.
SOURCE: PHOTO COURTESY OF AUTHOR

documents and 943 titles comprising 3,977 volumes.[28] Thus Oksan Academy, together with the Tosan and Pyŏngsan academies, ranks among the academies in the Republic of Korea whose libraries contain more than three thousand books. The most valuable parts of the Oksan collection are a copy of the *Samguk sagi* chronicle, registered as National Treasure Nr. 525, and original manuscripts composed by Yi Ŏnjŏk during his stay in his adjacent studio from 1547 to 1553, registered as National Treasure Nr. 586.

The extant book catalogues reveals the trajectory of book acquisition during the centuries of the academy's existence. The collection, from 1572 to 1592, numbered 115 book titles in 1,239 volumes. The record for the year 1713 shows 161 titles in 1,446 volumes and in 1801 numbered the collection as being 253 titles in 1,905 volumes.[29]

28   See Munhwajae Ch'ŏng (Cultural Heritage Administration), *2004 nyŏn ilban tongsan munhwajae taryang sojangch'ŏ silt'ae chosa pogosŏ* (Report on the General Investigation of the State of Registered Cultural Assets in Holding Institutions in 2004), 2004.

29   See Lee Byoung-hoon, "Kyŏngju oksan sŏwŏn ŭi changsŏ sujip mit kwalli silt'ae rŭl t'onghae pon tosŏgwan chŏk kinŭng," Table 1.

The average growth by 0.4 volumes per year (i.e. one new title every 2–3 years) during the 17th century increased to one title per year in the 18th century, which demonstrates the advances of Korean book publishing. These advances were more structural than technical: most of the books were published by elite families in honor of their ancestor, often in the newly established academies. Due to the growth of these quasi-private academies, many families abandoned their relationship with Oksan Academy and established their own institutions.[30] This process is well visible in the documents as a significant loss of books during this time. Since the founding of the academy, not even one volume of its collection had been lost. However in 1752 seven titles donated by the king (in 67 volumes) and eleven other titles numbering to 132 volumes were taken out of the collection. All these titles had been loaned to the Kyŏngju prefect ten years before and then never returned. This event shows us two interesting details about the situation of 18th-century Oksan Academy: it was forced to follow the wishes of the local prefect and it broke the most important rule concerning the book collection. Academy elders were since its founding well aware of dangers threatening their book collections and included simple measures into the academy rules:

> First rule: be cautious performing the sacrifices.
> Second rule: venerate worthies by rituals.
> Third rule: maintain academy buildings.
> Fourth rule: prepare provisions for the academy.
> Fifth rule: catalogue ("mark") books.
> When you are not cautious performing the sacrifices it is as if there was no offering. When you do not venerate worthies according to the ritual it is as if worthies had not arrived. When you do not maintain buildings, they are sure to fall into ruins. When provisions are not supplied, there will for sure be a shortage. When books are not catalogued they are sure to be dispersed and lost. Of these five points, not one is to be ignored.
> Youngsters from district official families are not allowed to obstruct the functioning of the academy, behave improperly within the academy or arbitrarily appropriate academy books.
> Academy books, equipment and property are by no means allowed to leave the gate of the academy.[31]

---

30  See Yi Haejun, *Sŏwŏn yŏn'gu wa munjung sŏwŏn*, for a study on family lineage academies.
31  *Oksan sŏwŏn chi*, 36–37.

After the 1752 incident the academy decided to prevent further losses and stopped the lending of books, especially to local authorities, represented by the Kyŏngju prefect, but these efforts were not successful. The welfare of the academy depended to certain degree on local authorities and it was difficult to resist the local prefect, who decided about the allocation of local resources. On the other hand in 1752 the academy was able obtain an official notification about the loss of academy books acknowledging the affair, which shows that although the academy was unable to recover its property, the matter was not treated lightly. In fact, we cannot find any mentions of books being lent out of the academy to private individuals. All book loans were made in response to official requests and only after debate and internal sanctioning of the request did the academy lend out books or send printed copies. Records of the book collection for the period from 1796 to 1874 show the requests for the borrowing of certain books as well as the academy's reaction. In 1792 court official Yi Mansu 李晚秀 (1752–1820), who was dispatched to the academy to perform the annual offerings, attempted to borrow several publications for use in his court responsibilities but was refused. The king personally commented on this incident.

> The rule that Oksan Academy books cannot leave its gates has been already established and it is proper and auspicious being so. If we want to see them, we must follow this rule, and thereby help to preserve the books. It is certainly possible to see books which are held by local scholars but one must come for books with a humble request.[32]

Sure enough after this event there were no further requests from the Kyŏngju prefect or other officials to obtain academy books.

In spite of all regulations and efforts, losses of books continued to occur. In the catalogue we find an entry, made on of fifteenth day of the first month of the year *pyŏngsin* (1836), to check the inventory of books. The inspection (which lead to conflicts about responsibilities between the involved persons in charge of the collection) revealed several missing volumes, which had not been previously recorded. The list indicates nineteen damaged or lost books.

> *Mencius* (royal donation)—6 volumes missing, *Ŭirye kyŏngjŏn tohae* 儀禮經傳圖解 (*Diagrams and Explanations to Yili and its Commentaries*)—one volume out of 14 missing, *Ŭirye to* 儀禮圖 (*Diagrams to*

---

[32] See "Ch'i chesi yegwan kujŏn (As Told by an Official Arriving for the Sacrifices)," in *Sŏch'aek chŏnyŏdorok* (Complete Records of Transmitted and Donated Books).

*Yili*)—one volume out of 9 missing, *Chengshi waishu* 程氏外書 (*Outer writings of Brothers Cheng*), *Kongja t'onggi* 孔子通紀 (*Comprehensive Annals of Confucius*)—one volume out of 2 missing.[33]

We can see that even one of the most valuable royal gifts received by the academy, the *Mencius*, and books from the earliest period of the collection had vanished. During the 18th century there were no more demands for borrowing books by local officials, but a new phenomenon appeared; the private borrowing of books by persons connected with the academy. The reason behind this breach of academy rules was the transformation of the academy leadership to a more private, family structure; scholars coming from the same family background were less prone to report their misgivings and treated the academy as their own property. One attempt to improve the readers' discipline was to engrave a plaque with the quote of King Chŏngjo, "Academy books are not supposed to leave the academy gate."

This was done in the second month of 1840, but the situation did not improve. The *Tangjung wanŭi* 堂中完議 (*Inventory of the Institution's Property*), a report on the academy from eight day of fifth month 1856, states that in spite of such prohibitions descendants of mighty families connected to the academy were browsing and borrowing books without authorization, never returning them.[34] At the same time the record criticizes negligence on the side of personnel in charge of the library. Any reader wishing to browse academy books was supposed to meet the administrator (*yusa* 有司) in charge of the library, who would record the date, name of the book, and the name of the reader. The regulations for borrowing books forbade the carrying of books out of the academy premises, but apparently it was quite difficult to wage a conflict over this rule with members of powerful local families. An adjustment (or resignation) to such incidences is attested by a certain change of the rules: after 1862 the loan was to be recorded not only by name, date, and book title but also by destination. Three volumes of catalogue for the years from 1884 to 1936, *Sŏch' aek ch'agŏrok* 書冊借去錄 (*Record of Borrowed Books*) shows that the majority of readers were from families residing near the academy, from the various branches of Yi Ŏnjŏk descendants, or from the adjacent Kugang Academy. Oksan

---

[33] See "Kyŏnggakso changsŏ ch'aek (Books Stored in the Pavilion of Classics)," in *Sŏch'aek chŏnyŏdorok* (Complete Records of Transmitted and Donated Books), *pyŏngsin* 丙申 [1776] first month 15th day.

[34] See Yŏngnam charyo kwŏnyŏk sent'ŏ, <http://yn.ugyo.net/dir/list?uci=KSAC+Y08+KSM-XD.1856.4713-20160630.Y1650102005> (accessed: 01 December 2017).

ILLUSTRATION 7.4   Wooden Board with the Inscriptions "Academy books are not supposed to leave the academy gate" with explanations.
SOURCE: PHOTO COURTESY OF AUTHOR

Academy's library was thus serving a broader audience of local elites as an important center of knowledge.[35]

The book lending activities of Oksan Academy reveal much about its readers and their interests. The majority of borrowed books were collected writings of scholars connected with the Yŏngnam area and often associated with the Namin (Southerners) political faction: Yi Ŏnjŏk, Kim Ilson, Yi Hwang, Ryu Sŏngnyong 柳成龍 (1542–1607), Chŏng Ku 鄭逑 (1543–1620), Yi Hyŏnil 李玄逸 (1627–1704), Kwŏn Sangil 權相一 (1679–1759), Kim Chongdŏk 金宗德 (1724–1797), etc. The library collection mirrored the ideological profile and orientation of local scholars and played an important role in maintaining the intellectual heritage of Yŏngnam scholars in their competition with other factions and the central government. A large portion of borrowed books also consisted of classics, poetry, historical books, or philosophical or geographical treatises used for private or family education. Very popular were not only classics as such, but also their vernacular editions (ŏnhae 諺解). Books on loan were often used to produce copies and new editions for other scholars or academies, because the Oksan collection possessed many rare old editions or writings of famous scholars, which could be found nowhere else. With the beginning of the 20th century the number of borrowed books started to increase. The rules for borrowing began to be more relaxed and we have records of

---

35   The Sŏch'aek ch'agŏrok is stored in the exhibition hall of Oksan Academy.

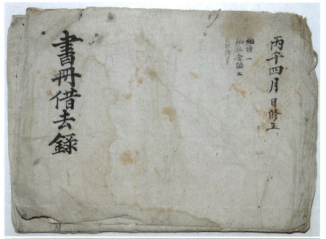

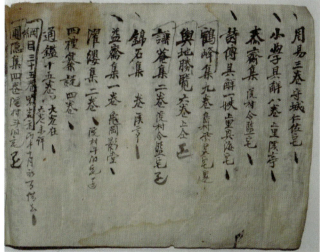

ILLUSTRATION 7.5
Title Page of *Record of Borrowed Books* and page showing individual entries on borrowed books with check markings.
SOURCE: PHOTO COURTESY OF AUTHOR

documenting the borrowing of the most treasured royal book donations or loans to distant destinations beyond the borders of the academy area. Examples of this new trend is the lending of the royal edition of the *Chunqiu* 春秋 (*Spring and Autumn Annals*) in ten volumes (including the book wooden case) to Kwŏn family from Andong or borrowing of seventy-five volumes of the *Koryŏsa* 高麗史 (*History of Koryŏ*) in 1918 on behalf of Chosŏnsa p'yŏnsuhoe 朝鮮史編修會 (Korean History Compilation Committee), an organization created by the Japanese General-Governor of Korea to compile a history of Korea.[36] The difference between traditional times and the modern period does

---

36   See *Sŏch'aek ch'agŏrok* (Record of Borrowed Books), *imin* 壬寅 [1902] 3rd month 1st day — *muo* 戊午 [1918] 9th month 7th day.

not lie in the very fact of borrowings out of the academy itself (such cases happened before), but rather in the style of such requests. Famous scholar Chang Hyŏn'gwang 張顯光 (1554–1637) wrote a letter to the Oksan Academy scholars on behalf of Provincial Governor Ch'oe Kwan 崔瓘 (in office 9th month 1608–2nd month 1609), who compiled a treatise on Korean history and asked for permission to borrow the Oksan Academy copy of the chronicle *Samguk sagi*.[37] Chang Hyŏn'gwang had been the teacher of then-academy director Kwŏn Ŭngsaeng, many other academy scholars were his disciples, and he often lectured in the academy. In spite of his privileged position, Chang Hyŏn'gwang respected the restriction of borrowing out of the academy and formulated his request in a humble way, expressing regret that he is forced to ask for such exception—an attitude very different from the simple order of the almighty Japanese government. This was not the first official request to the academy. In 1599 the royal court asked for the return of 23 volumes of several books formerly donated by the court to the academy back to the Hongmungwan. The academy, untouched by the war with Japan, deferred to the state request and the works survived in the court library, where they were used for new editions of important works.[38] Such requests were however exceptions and from the available records we see that borrowed books were often properly returned. Old editions kept in the academy collection were steadily becoming more and more valuable and together with the number of books enhanced the status of Oksan Academy. Guarding of the collection became more and more complicated especially during the tumultuous 20th century. Kyŏnggak 經閣 (Pavilion of the Classics), the academy's library, survived the Korean War, but its collections were, because of frequent incidents of theft in 1970,[39] moved to a new modern building guarding both books and other treasures of the academy. In 2010, with the help of the Cultural Heritage Administration, a new museum and an archive to preserve the collection in optimal conditions were built.

---

37  See "Yŏ oksan sŏwŏn sarim (Letter to the Scholars of Oksan Academy)," *Yŏhŏn sŏnsaeng sokchip* (Continuation of the Collected Writings of Master Yŏhŏn), Volume 2, Letters, in *Yŏhŏn jip* (Collected Writings of Master Yŏhŏn).
38  See *Yŏrŭp wŏnu sajŏk*, Volume 5, Kyŏngsangdo, Kyŏngju, Oksan Sŏwŏn. [1759].
39  The 1970 robbery of the *Samguk sagi* copy and other books created a big scandal followed by national survey of old books and discussions about the best methods of preservation. In spite of these efforts in 1982 rare prints of the *Koryŏsa*, the *T'oegye chip* and other books were stolen from the academy.

## 6 Oksan Academy Print Culture

### 6.1 Oksan Academy and Chŏnghyesa Temple: Local Centers of Print Culture

Book publication in Chosŏn times can be divided into two categories, official and private production of woodblock prints. Official prints were produced either by agencies in the capital or by local offices. Private prints can be classified according to their origin as Buddhist temple prints, academy prints, or private family prints. The Kyŏngju area used to be, as the former capital of the Silla kingdom, a place of many Buddhist temples and a thriving center of Buddhist print production. During the first period of Chosŏn the main producers of books shifted toward local government officials, who commissioned many books under the flag of Confucian ideology. In later times, academies and local elite families started to be increasingly more active in the field of book printing. Oksan Academy also started to play an important role in the publishing area. Publishing of books was, compared to simple purchase, very expensive. The small academies of the 16th century were not able to carry such a financial burden and for this period only a few cases of such undertakings are attested: Ch'ŏngnyang Academy 清凉書院 in Chunghwa, Ch'ŏngok Academy 川谷書院 in Sŏngju, and Myŏnggok Academy 鳴谷書院 in Sŏch'ŏn. With the development and growth of academies the number of places willing to engage in book publication also increased and printing projects became more frequent. The best source to witness these changes is a list of book matrices compiled in 1796, *Nup'an ko* 鏤板考 (*Survey of Print Matrices*). The survey lists 185 wooden matrices kept in 84 different academies. The first place belonged to Tosan Academy, which owned the wooden matrices to 17 book titles, followed by Oksan Academy and Nogang Academy 魯岡書院 in Wŏnsan, which each owned 7 sets of matrices. In the Kyŏngju area wooden matrices were also kept in Kugang Academy (three sets), Sŏak Academy (two sets), and in Tonggang Academy 東江書院 and Yongsan Academy 龍山書院 (one set each). The publishing of books in Oksan Academy is well verified by various sources; the *Tonggyŏng chapki* (1670), the *Nup'an ko* (1796), or the *Kŭmo sŭngnam* 金鰲勝覽 (*Overall Survey of Kŭmo*) (1936) all mention various works published in the academy.[40] The *Munjip kanyŏk kisa* 文集刊役記事 (*Records of Printing of Collected Writings*), published in 1744 further under "printing place" (*kanso* 刊所) mention Chŏnghyesa temple, belonging to the academy, where the wooden matrices

---

40　See Seoul National University, Kyujanggak han'gukhak yŏn'guwŏn, <http://e-kyujanggak.snu.ac.kr/home/index.do?idx=06&siteCd=KYU&topMenuId=206&targetId=379> (accessed: 01 December 2017).

were stored after printing.[41] The 17th-century *Tonggyŏng chapki* lists 14 sets of matrices for the *Kuinnok* 求仁錄 (*Record of Search for Goodness*), the *Maewŏldang sayurok* 梅月堂四遊錄 (*Records of Four Journeys of Maewŏldang*), the *Pongsŏn chabŭi* 奉先雜儀 (*Miscellaneous Etiquette for Serving Ancestors*), the *Han Ho sosŏ Chŏkpyŏk pu* 韓濩所書赤壁賦 (*Prose-poem on the Red Cliff Handwritten by Han Ho*), the *Hyohaengnok* 孝行錄 (*Records of Acts of Filial Piety*), and other works. Several of these works—*Maewŏldang sayurok*, *Yŏgong p'aesŏl* 櫟翁稗說 (*Lowly Jottings by Old Man "Oak"*), *Chŏkpyŏk pu*, *Ikchae chip* (*Collected Writing of Ikchae*)—were published by the local prefecture, the rest by the printing facility of the academy. Of special attention are books reproducing the handwriting of two of the most famous Korean calligraphers, Namch'ang Kim Hŏnsŏng 南窓 金玄成 (1542–1621) and Sŏkpong Han Ho 石峯 韓濩 (1543–1605). The possession of such works signifies both the prestige and status of the academy as well as considerable printing expertise.

In the Oksan Academy inventory compiled from 1711 to 1793 (35 volumes) we find various kinds of wooden matrices, their total number ranging from 35 sets to 12 sets.[42] This difference is caused by the inclusion or exclusion of the wooden matrices belonging to the nearby Kukang Academy or Kyŏngju prefecture, which were stored in Oksan Academy. If we compare this list with the one to be found in the *Tonggyŏng chapki*, we find several new titles, like the *Jinsilu*, a new edition of *Hoejae's Collected Writing*, the Confucian *Xinjing* or the *Tonggyŏng chi* 東京誌 (*Gazetteer of the Eastern Capital*), but also matrices for several calligraphic works, wooden plaques, and even a portrait of Yi Chehyŏn (*Ikchae hwasang* 益齋畫像). The matrices for the *Hyohaengnok*, the *Xinjing*, the *Ikchae chip*, the *Yŏgong p'aesŏl*, the portrait of Yi Chehyŏn, and the Kyŏngju gazetteer were originally carved in Kyŏngju prefecture, but for the restoration of the woodblocks were temporarily kept in the academy. The *Tonggyŏng chi* was compiled in 1711 by Kyŏngju Prefect Nam Chihun 南至薰 (?–?), who entrusted the printing to the Oksan Academy, which probably kept the woodblocks afterwards. Together with print matrices the academy also stored wooden plaques, which were technically speaking close relatives to the matrices. Oksan Academy thus for example stored the wooden plaque of Haewŏllu 海月樓 (Pavilion of Sea Moon) in Ch'ŏngha county, which was given to the academy probably for the purpose of restoration during the visit of Chŏng Kiyun 鄭岐胤 (?–?), who was the magistrate of Ch'ŏngha from 1692 to 1702. Seven sets of matrices recorded in the *Nup'an ko* in 1796 were probably originally stored in Chŏnghyesa

---

41   *Oksan sŏwŏn chi*, 238–241.
42   See "Ch'aekchil (Order of Book Volumes)," in *Kanso pyŏlbich'aek kajŏn chŏnyŏgi* (Record of Published, Procured, Bought, and Received Books).

Monastery, but after the its reconstruction in 1780 were transferred to the academy. The 1936 *Kŭmo sŭngnam* gives us further details about the relation between monastery and academy. Chŏnghyesa in 1670 possessed 14 sets of matrices including the *Tongsa ch'anyo* 東史纂要 (*Summary of the History of the East*), which was produced in 1609 by the prefecture, but later was transferred to the academy for repairs. The *Kŭmo sŭngnam* also narrates how after the destruction of the monastery by fire in 1836 all woodblocks were transferred to the academy, which kept them in the new storage building.[43]

There were also cases of reversed flow of materials. With the rise of Kugang Academy, dedicated to Yi Chehyŏn, the matrices related to the work of Yi Chehyŏn were transferred there and Oksan Academy further primarily kept the woodblock sets of Yi Ŏnjŏk works, which were systematically updated and republished. Academy scholars used woodblock sets for several reprints and during the later period of the academy this became the main purpose of its publishing activities. During the last survey in 2004–2007 nineteen sets of woodblocks for Yi Ŏnjŏk's works were catalogued numbering 1,121 pages.[44] In spreading Yi Ŏnjŏk's works Oksan Academy frequently cooperated with his descendants, who at the same time played a more and more important role in the management of the academy. Yet the focus on Yi Ŏnjŏk's heritage did not sideline the printing of other books of the Confucian curriculum, which were actively published as well.

### 6.2 *Financing of Academy Printing*

The critical point for the publishing activities of the academy was of course financing. The first prints that can be related to Oksan Academy were the 1574 editions of the *Hoejae sŏnsaeng nyŏnbo* 晦齋先生年譜 (*Chronological Biography of Master Hoejae*), which were published in the academy and the ten volumes of the *Hoejae sŏnsaeng munjip* 晦齋先生文集 (*Collected Writings of Master Hoejae*) published in Kyŏngju Prefecture in 1575. From then until modern times[45] the *Collected Writings of Master Hoejae* have been published ten times, and the history of their editions gives us unique insight into the changing

---

43 See "Chŏnghyesa so changp'an (Printing Blocks Stored in Chŏnghyesa Monastery)," in *Kŭmo sŭngnam* 金鰲勝覽 (Overall Survey of Kŭmo), Volume 4, *Sŏjŏk* (Books).

44 Munhwajae Ch'ŏng, 2004 *nyŏn ilban tongsan munhwajae taryang sojangch'ŏ silt'ae chosa pogosŏ*; and *Kyŏngbuk chiyŏk ŭi mokp'an charyo* (Materials on Printing Blocks in the Kyŏngbuk Region), ed. Han'guk kukhak chinhŭngwŏn kich'o hangmun yuksŏng saŏptan) (Andong: Han'guk kukhak chinhŭngwŏn, 2007).

45 According to Pak Changsŭng the order of publications is as follows: the first edition (1575), revised edition (1600, Kyŏngju Prefecture), third edition (1624, Oksan Academy), fourth edition (1631), fifth edition (1665), sixth edition (1701), seventh edition (1744), eight edition (1794), ninth edition (1864), tenth edition (1926). See Pak Changsŭng, "Kyŏngju sojae

fortune and economy of Oksan Academy and its book publishing operation. The growing intervals between the individual editions mirrors to a certain degree the economic situation of the academy. During the later period of its existence Oksan Academy endured a loss of political prominence and government support which, together with the worsening economic situation, resulted in less and less frequent production of new editions. The weakening of the academy resulted in the decrease of book production, which subsequently weakened the position of the academy. The 18th century in particular witnessed the economic decay of the academy: bad management of the academy, runaway slaves, and dispossession of academy estates located in distant areas curbed the academy's ability to sponsor expensive publication projects. The entry for sixteenth day of the eighth month of 1736 in the academy inventory states that the academy intended to publish the complete collected writings, but due to scarcity of funds was only able to produce partial, less expensive works like the *Kuinnok* or the *Taehak poyu*, for which only the most damaged or worn out woodblocks were replaced. The academy decided to every year put aside twenty *sŏk* of grain in a designated granary and from the interest on this investment accumulate the funds necessary for the printing of the collected writings project.[46] In 1744 the academy administration recorded the academy's history of publishing in the *Munjip kanyŏk kisa*, where we can find a postscript describing an incident of academy scholars discovering that the woodblocks of the 1701 edition were no longer usable. The lack of funds, changes in leadership of the academy, etc., slowed the process of producing a new edition, but finally the academy scholars fulfilled their pledge to publish the *Collected Writings of Master Hoejae*.[47] In 1744 a center for the printing project was established inside Chŏnghyesa Monastery and the academy authorities assembled forty artisans for the carving of 360 woodblocks. The effort lasted three months and in all the expenses climbed up to 500 strings of cash (roughly 5,000 *liang*).[48] The whole project was supported by local officials as well. The provincial governor sent forty *sŏk* of grain and the local prefect donated rice and sent several artisans to

---

sŏwŏnsa-esŏ kanhaeng han chŏnjŏkko (Study of Ancient Books and Records Published by Academies and Shrines in the Kyŏngju Area)," *Silla sahak* 19 (2001): 233–249.

46  See *Tangjung wanŭi* (Inventory of the Institution Property).
47  *Oksan sŏwŏn chi*, 238–239.
48  A certain comparison of financial aspects could be the record of the one-year long reconstruction of the academy lecture hall, which burned down in 1839. The overall expenses reached 1,735 liang 3 chŏn and 7 p'un, i.e. only one-third of the costly book project. See Lee Byoung-hoon, "19 segi ch'o kyŏngju oksan sŏwŏn kangdang chunggŏn kwa wisang pyŏnhwa," 245.

help. We may presume that elite families and scholars connected to the academy contributed as well.

It is necessary to distinguish the costs of woodblock production and costs of printing itself. Printing costs included both material (paper, inks, strings for binding, etc.) as well as labor costs. An inventory of printing costs from 1767 records the response of the academy to a request for two sets of the *Hoejae chip* by scholars from Haman and Angye.[49] The academy printed two sets of the *Collected Writings* edition of 13 volumes in five books. The 184 double-sided matrices required 368 sheets of paper, each worth of 4 *liang*. Expenses for the monk who printed the book were 1 *chŏn* for food, 2 *chŏn* for drinking and other expenses, 2 *chŏn* for beeswax necessary for waxing the book cover and 5 *chŏn* and 7 *p'un* for book binding and other expenses. In the same year the academy ordered revisions and repairs for the new edition of the *Hoejae chip*. The expenses accounted for one woodblock were six *mal* of rice for a carver, carving tools 2 *chŏn* and 5 *p'un*, lacquer for book case 1 *chŏn* and 3 *p'un*, side dishes and tobacco for a carver 1 *chŏn* and 7 *p'un*, etc. Payment to workers included also travel expenses (and often also straw shoes), wages (often paid in kind), a regular supply of alcohol, etc. Book projects were therefore often decided in the assembly of both local and academy literati, and extensive networks of elite families, local offices, or other academies had to be mobilized.

### 6.3  *Distribution of Academy Books*

Once a book was published, a decision on its further destination was made. In 1729 scholars from the town of Kanggye in the remote northern provinces sent a joint letter to the Oksan Academy asking for an edition of the *Hoejae chip* and after a discussion in the academy they received one copy in five volumes. Kanggye was the place of Yi Ŏnjŏk's banishment and local scholars established Kyŏnghyŏn Academy 景賢書院 in his memory. This request for books from the center of Yi Ŏnjŏk veneration, Oksan Academy, was not their last. In 1799 they obtained another of Yi Ŏnjŏk's works, the *Kuinnok* and the *Kugyŏng yŏnŭi*. In the summer of 1848 Kyŏnghyŏn Academy scholars asked for copies of the *T'aegŭk munbyŏn* and the *Taehak changgu poyu*, which were printed and sent to them. The next year ten scholars from Kanggye send a letter of gratitude to Oksan Academy.[50] In 1781 Oksan scholars gifted prints of the *T'aegŭk munbyŏn* and the *Kugyŏng yŏnŭi* to a royal official sent by the court to perform sacrifices in the academy. In 1792 the academy sent copies of the *Pongsŏn chabŭi* to two scholars in Ch'ungch'ŏn province who had sent a request for it.

---

49    See *Kanso pyŏlbich'aek kajŏn chŏnyŏgi, chŏnghae* 丁亥 [1767] 3rd month, 16th day.
50    See *Kanso pyŏlbich'aek kajŏn chŏnyŏgi, kabin* 甲寅 [1734] 2nd month.

In 1767 one copy of *Jinsilu* was printed and sent to a certain licentiate Ch'oe in Sŏnsan. With the exception of the gift to the royal official, all books were sent upon request. There are no records for any payments, but in some cases (Ch'ungch'ŏn and Kanggye scholars) books were returned and probably only lent temporarily for copying.[51] Because of their high value, both economic and symbolic, books were one of the best means to maintain the prestige and the functioning the social networks of the academy. In certain cases we can trace the distribution of academy books and identify their receivers. The *Panjil ki* 頒帙記 (*Record of Book Distribution*), written in 1936, inform us about the distribution of the *Hoejae sŏnsaeng pyŏljip* 晦齋先生別集 (*Separate Writings of Master Hoejae*). In the first round 99 copies were distributed to various destinations and in the second round 30 copies. In the first round altogether 37 copies were distributed to various branches of the Yi family from Yŏngju and 23 to influential families from the area. Other copies were send to allied academies including Tosan Academy, Namgye Academy 藍溪書院 in Hamyang, Tŏkch'ŏn Academy 德川書院 in Chinju, etc. The rest of the books were distributed among various scholars and families from all provinces. A brief look reveals the geographic distribution of academy supporters: the highest number was in Andong (9) and Yŏngch'ŏn (5)—both in the Yŏngnam area—and surprisingly only one in the capital.

## 7   Conclusion

Oksan Academy is one of the few Korean Confucian academies that were able to continuously operate from its founding period until modern times. Dedicated to Yi Ŏnjŏk, who was officially sanctioned by the royal court as one of the luminaries of Korean Learning of the Way, the academy belonged to the upper echelon of Korean academies and during its long existence amassed significant influence. Thanks to its uninterrupted existence and prestige the academy was able to preserve its book collection and now constitutes one of the best examples of the remnants of the traditional book culture of Korean Confucian academies. Modes of book collection, preservation, and production changed significantly during the centuries of the academy's existence. The bulk of the academy library was acquired with the help of Confucian scholars and students, local officials, and, last but not least, royal support through book donations. Changes in the political and economic situation caused the academy to be deprived of the central government's favour for centuries, and it was not

---

51   See *Kanso pyŏlbich'aek kajŏn chŏnyŏgi, kihae* 己亥 [1779] 2nd month, 12th day.

until the end of 19th century that royal support was renewed. These factors to a large degree also influenced the academy library and its inventory. Isolated from state sponsorship, the academy was forced to create its own networks of support, which were structured along local and family allegiances. Solidarity of Yŏngnam area scholars and close connection to Yi Ŏnjŏk's descendants provided much of the needed support for the academy, and Oksan scholars were able to continue the existence of the academy and its library, though with significant changes. The academy's intellectual profile started to be focused predominantly on production and disseminating of Yi Ŏnjŏk's works and the academy became a semi-autonomous local center of the Yŏngnam School of Korean Confucianism. Thanks to the unusual number of documents available in the academy archive we may have a close insight into both the practical operation and the theoretical framework of the academy's book collection. Oksan Academy is a prime example of how Korean academies and their book collections adjusted to the changing environment and new challenges during their long existence. Prohibitions on borrowing books from the academy were occasionally lifted because of pressure from local officials; publishing of Confucian works turned into long projects spanning decades struggling for sufficient funding; woodblock print matrices became one of the most important academy assets, and for the actual process of book printing monks from the adjacent Buddhist monastery were called upon. All these phenomena were nonexistent during the end of the 16th century, when the academy was founded, and emerged only during the long process of the development of a specific Korean Confucian academy culture. The thousand volumes of old documents and books in the Oksan Academy library are monuments to the durability and flexibility of Korean scholars in maintaining and disseminating their own version of the Confucian message.

### References

Chŏng Manjo. "Ch'oegŭn ŭi sŏwŏn yŏn'gu tongyang e kwanhan kŏmt'o 最近의 書院研究 動向에 관한 檢討 (Review of General Research Trends in Recent Academy Studies)." In *Chosŏn sidae sŏwŏn yŏn'gu* 朝鮮時代書院研究 (Studies of Confucian Academies in the Chosŏn period), edited by Chŏng Manjo. Appendix. Seoul: Chimmundang, 1997.

Chŏng Manjo. "Han'guk sŏwŏn ŭi yŏn'gu hyŏnhwang kwa chŏnmang (Present State and Prospects of Korean Academy Studies)." In *Han'guk ŭi sŏwŏn kwa hangmaek yŏn'gu* 韓國의 書院과 學脈 研究 (Studies of School Ties and Academies in Korea), edited by Kyŏnggi taehakkyo sosŏng haksul yŏn'guwŏn, 9–28. Seoul: Kukhak charyowŏn, 2002.

*Hoejae chip* 晦齋集 (Collected Writings of Hoejae). Kyujanggak #奎 1641, Database of Korean Classics. <http://www.db.itkc.or.kr> (accessed 1 December 2017).

Kang Myŏnggwan. "Chosŏn hugi sŏjŏk ŭi suip yut'ong-kwa changsŏga ŭi ch'urhyŏn. 18, 19 segi kyŏnghwa sajok (Import and Circulation of Books in the Late Chosŏn Period and the Rise of the Book Collector)." *Minjok munhaksa yŏn'gu* 9 (1996): 171–194.

*Kanso pyŏlbich'aek kajŏn chŏnyŏgi* 刊所別備冊價錢傳與記 (Record of Published, Procured, Bought, and Received Books). Kyŏngsangdo, Kyŏngju, Oksan Sŏwŏn.

Kim Yunsik. "Chosŏnjo sŏwŏn mun'go e kwanhan ilgoch'al (A Study on Early Chosŏn Academy Libraries)." *Sŏjihak yŏn'gu* 41 (2008): 298–299.

*Kŭmo sŭngnam* 金鰲勝覽 (Overall Survey of Kŭmo), edited and translated by Yi Sŏkhŭm and Yi Sangp'il. Kyŏngju: Kyŏngju munhwawŏn, 2010.

Lee Byoung-Hoon. "19 segi ch'o kyŏngju oksan sŏwŏn kangdang chunggŏn kwa wisang pyŏnhwa (The Reconstruction of the Oksan Academy Lecture Hall in the Early 19th Century and Changes in Status)." *Han'gukhak yŏn'gu* 57 (2016): 267–270.

Lee Byoung-Hoon. "Kyŏngju oksan sŏwŏn ŭi changsŏ sujip mit kwalli silt'ae rŭl t'onghae pon tosŏgwan chŏk kinŭng (Library Functions Seen through the Collection and Management of Books in the Kyŏngju Oksan Academy)." *Han'guk minjok munhwa* 58 (2016): 8–17.

*Sŏch' aek ch'agŏrok* 書冊借去錄 (Record of Borrowed Books). Kyŏngsangdo, Kyŏngju, Oksan Sŏwŏn.

*Sŏch'aek chŏnyŏdorok* 書冊傳與都錄 (Complete Records of Transmitted and Donated Books). Kyŏngsangdo, Kyŏngju, Oksan Sŏwŏn.

*Tonggyŏng chapki* 東京雜記 (Miscellaneous Records of the Eastern Capital). Volume 3, Sŏjŏk 書籍 (Books), Pujang ch'aekp'an 府藏冊板 (Books stored in the Prefectural Seat).

Munhwajae Ch'ŏng (Cultural Heritage Administration). 2004 nyŏn ilban tongsan munhwajae taryang sojangch'ŏ silt'ae chosa pogosŏ (Report on the General Investigation of the State of Registered Cultural Assets in Holding Institutions in 2004). 2004.

Munhwajae Ch'ŏng (Cultural Heritage Administration). *Kyŏngbuk chiyŏk ŭi mokp'an charyo* (Materials on Printing Blocks in the Kyŏngbuk Region), edited by Han'guk kukhak chinhŭngwŏn kich'o hangmun yuksŏng saŏptan. Andong: Han'guk kukhak chinhŭngwŏn, 2007.

Nam Kwŏnhŭi. "Chosŏn sidae kyŏngju kanhaeng ŭi sŏjŏk 朝鮮時代 慶州 刊行의 書籍 (Publication and Books in Kyŏngju during the Chosŏn Period)." *Silla munhwa* 33 (2009): 1–57.

Ok Yŏngjŏng. "Han'guk sŏwŏn ŭi changsŏ wa ch'ulp'an munhwa (Publishing and Librarian Culture of Korean Academies)." In *Han'guk ŭi sŏwŏn munhwa* (Korean academy culture), Munsach'ŏl, (2014): 345–368.

*Oksan sŏwŏn chi* (Records of Oksan Academy). Kyŏngsan: Yŏngnam taehakkyo ch'ulp'anbu, 1993.

Rokutanda, Yutaka. "A Survey of the Variant Versions of the Sŏakchi and their Taxonomy." *The Memoirs of Toyo Bunko* 73 (2005): 111–139.

Son Kyeyŏng. "Ch'ulp'an munhwasa yŏn'gu hyŏnhwang kwa saengwalsa roŭi chŏpkŭn (Current State of Research on the Cultural History of Publishing and a Microhistorical Approach)." *Yŏngnamhak* 13 (2008): 369–397.

*Tangjung wanŭi* 堂中完議 (Inventory of the Institution's Property). Kyŏngsangdo, Kyŏngju, Oksan Sŏwŏn, 1736. <http://kostma.aks.ac.kr/> (accessed: 1 December 2017).

U Chŏngim. "T'oegye Yi Hwang kwa kŭ ŭi mundo tŭrŭi sŏjŏk kanhaeng kwa sŏwŏn ŭi kinŭng (T'oegye Yi Hwang and Book Publishing and Academy Functions under His Disciples)." *Chiyŏk kwa yŏksa* 22 (2008): 215–258.

Yi Haejun. "Sŏwŏn yŏn'gu wa munjung sŏwŏn 書院研究와 門中書院 (Family Lineage Academies and Academy Studies)." In *Chosŏn hugi munjung sŏwŏn yŏn'gu* 朝鮮後期 門中書院研究 (Studies on Later Chosŏn Family Lineage Academies), 1–18. P'aju: Kyŏngin munhwasa, 2008.

Yi Suhwan. *Chosŏn hugi ŭi sŏwŏn. Oksan sŏwŏn ŭl chungsim ŭro* (The Academies of Late Chosŏn. With a Focus on Oksan Academy). Kwach'ŏn: Kuksa p'yŏnch'an wiwŏnhoe, 1992.

Yi Suhwan. "Hoejae Yi Ŏnjŏk kwa Oksan sŏwŏn 晦齋 李彦迪과 玉山書院 (Hoejae Yi Ŏnjŏk and Oksan Academy)." *Kyŏngju sahak* 16 (1997): 391–416.

Yi Suhwan. "Sŏwŏn kirok charyo chŏngni ŭi hyŏnhwang kwa kwaje (Present State and Tasks of the Organization of the Document Sources of the Academy)." *Minjong munhwa nonch'ong* 52 (2012): 423–447.

*Yŏrŭp wŏnu sajŏk* 列邑院宇事蹟 (Academies and Shrines Sites by District). Volume 5. Kyŏngsangdo, Kyŏngju, Oksan Sŏwŏn. [1759].

*Yŏhŏn jip* 旅軒集 (Collected Writings of Master Yŏhŏn). Yonsei University Central Library 811. 98- chang hyŏn'gwang-yŏ-sok, Database of Korean Classics. 1 May 2017. <http://www.db.itkc.or.kr> (accessed: 1 December 2017).

Yun Hŭimyŏn. "Chosŏn sidae sŏwŏn ŭi tosŏgwan kinŭng yŏn'gu (Study on Library Functions of Academies during the Chosŏn Period)." *Yŏksa hakpo* (2005): 1–26.

CHAPTER 8

# Archery Ranges in the Educational Tradition of Confucian Academies in China

*Thomas H.C. Lee*

## 1       Introduction

One of the most prominent features of China's Confucian education is its emphasis on the so-called six arts: rituals, music, archery, charioteering, writing, and mathematics. Of the six, archery and charioteering were clearly closer to what could be called as being physical in nature, distinguished from other arts that are more literary. As time went on, the teaching of music began to decline and although intermittently there were scholars who devoted their time to exploring its theory and knowledge, it received scanty attention throughout history. Archery and charioteering, similarly, were never any significant part of Confucian education (after the Qin unification), despite the occasionally uttered lip-service to their importance as a part of educational content. All in all, it was rituals, writing and, to a slightly lesser degree, mathematics, that had received definitive attention and promotion.

The two physical arts in the meantime evolved to become an integral part of Confucian rituals (and sport, which will be touched on later in this paper), so much so that they could at least continue to claim their worth or importance. For the purpose of this paper, it is useful to say that archery continued to be learned, outside of military circles, by civil scholar-officials, and was occasionally part of ceremonies such as those honoring old people. Such ceremonies were sometimes seriously performed, and others more *pro forma* and casually. Overall, the physical arts were rarely seriously practiced other than as an antiquarian pursuit. Although the idea that "six arts" should make up the core of Confucian education survived mainly as an ideal, there was often an honest desire to return to the original Confucian prescription.

Starting with the Song (960–1279), as academies rose to compete with official government schools, the idea that a complete curriculum of Confucian learning should include the entire "six arts" started to receive renewed attention. Many Confucian scholars in the 11th to 14th centuries were championing the revival of the art of archery and, perhaps, charioteering; of the latter I have found much less information. Archery and the field for practicing it began to appear frequently in government records and local gazetteers. Moreover, in no time, archery ranges also started to become a part of the government school compound.

The earliest record showing that academies (*shuyuan* 書院) also built archery ranges appeared in the mid-11th century; a prominent official, Li Shoupeng 李壽朋 (?–1071) initiated the project of building one in Yuzhang (modern Nanchang of Jiangxi), neighboring a Donghu Academy 東湖書院.[1] This lone evidence does not sufficiently prove that academies in the Song already were commonly equipped with archery ranges. However, government schools, especially the Imperial University, had sporadically built archery ranges since the late Tang, but it was in 1077 that the government officially decreed that the Imperial University should build one, to make archery a part of the teaching curriculum.[2] Since there is no evidence to show that it was abolished subsequently, the range might have been continued through the Mongol rule, and lasted into Ming times (1368–1644), when archery ranges were ordered to be built in all government schools, including local neighborhood (community) schools (*shexue* 社學).[3] It is possible that the Imperial University, the nation's highest educational institution, retained the range. The academies, generally imagined as privately established, maintained their original commitment to independent pursuit of learning (different from the officially sanctioned curriculum and educational purpose) through the Yuan dynasty (1279–1368). By Ming times, most academies had been changed to semi-government schools, steadily becoming little different from the latter: they regularly received government subsidies, conducted teaching on curriculums geared to preparing students to take the imperial examinations and, above all, modeled their architectural styles on government schools. Therefore, it does not surprise us

---

1   Although *Yudi jisheng* 輿地紀勝 (Exhaustive Description of the Empire) says that this "Donghu academy" was built only in 1211, initiated by the then deputy sub-prefect, Feng Youjun 豐有俊, and was built on the site of Li Yin's 李寅 (fl. early 11th century) personal study. Elsewhere in *Yudi guangji*, however, it also refers to the existence of a "Donghu academy" in the same location by which Li Shoupeng built an archery range not long after Li Yin built his study. Thus, it is likely that the range was originally built next to Li Yin's study, which at the time was not an academy. The academy was built, several decades later, perhaps to commemorate the site of Li's study, and presumably included the archery range. Such posthumously built academies to commemorate a renowned scholar were very common, and this may be an example. For relevant sources, see Wang Xiangzhi, *Yudi jisheng* (Exhaustive Description of the Empire), Qing reprint of Song manuscript ed., 26; Wang Anshi, *Wang Jinggong wenzhu* (Commentaries on Wang Jinggong's Writings), Jiayetang congshu edition (1913–1918), 5; Zha Shenxing et al. (ed.), *Xijiang zhi* (Gazetteer of Xijiang), reprinted (Taipei: Chengwen, 1966 reprint of 1720 ed.), ch. 8/22, 10/7.
2   Wang Yinglin, *Yuhai* (Sea of Jade), SKQS ed., ch. 75.
3   For an introduction to Ming community schools, see Sarah Schneewind, *Community Schools and the State in Ming China* (Stanford: Stanford University Press, 2006).

that many, if not all, academies also built archery ranges once the government decreed, in 1370, that all government schools were to build archery ranges.

Through the Ming times, then, academies were often also equipped with archery ranges. The idea that archery should be part of a gentleman's education became widely promoted, and debates arose over whether archery knowledge was a pathway to moral cultivation and a kind of ritualistic performance, or whether it was solely for military training.

Most archery ranges declined with the fall of Ming, and by the Qing times, most records about archery ranges are about them falling into disuse, or desertion. It is possible that such fields were abandoned and only used when the government wished to organize public ceremonies. Open fields available for civic functions especially in the countryside were often used for public proclamation of government edicts or regulations, and, more often than not, for intermittent gatherings for listening to imperial prescriptions. Although the Chinese people are not particularly known for enthusiasm in attending speeches, mobilization of people to attend civil ceremonies was nonetheless a chronic feature of governance. The space or the square in front of the office built specially for such purposes, often called the "public place" (*gongsuo* 公所), was rarely neglected. It is entirely possible that abandoned archery ranges were converted into these buildings. Thus, in a peculiar way, the ranges, especially when attached to the public gathering halls, continued to serve "educational" purposes in the Chinese imagination.

By the early 20th century, a number of old academies were converted into modern middle or high schools; it is possible that their old ranges were transformed into modern sports field. The space continued to be educational, though a new narrative had been reconstructed in a much transformed manner. In what follows I hope to examine the historical changes in the educational significance of the archery education found in Confucian academies.

## 2     Confucius Was a Competent Archer

The role of archery in human history is all too familiar, and it was the same in China. It was in Confucius's time—the 6th to 5th centuries BCE—that it emerged as a part of aristocratic education with ritualistic implications. Confucius reflected on the decline of traditional aristocratic education and proposed that it be revived, and it was he who for the first time spelled out that archery was part of that traditional education. He argued that in archery, one could learn the proper "rite" (*li* 禮) of social and political behavior: "Thus archers were required to meet the requirements of the rituals on entering, leaving, or making turning movements in any direction. When their minds were composed and their posture straight, they grasped the bow and arrow and concentrated. Only when the archer had grasped the bow and arrow and concentrated was it possible to talk of meeting the requirements of the rituals";[4] or, "In archery we have something like the way of the superior man. When the archer misses the center of the target, he turns round and seeks for the cause of his failure in himself";[5] and, even more unerringly, "The superior man has nothing to compete for. But if he must compete, he does it in an archery match, wherein he ascends to his position, bowing in deference. Descending, one drinks the ritual cup."[6] The last quotation clearly suggests that archery contest is the "true" competition, and that it is exactly what ritual performance is all about for Confucius. Indeed, the remark later became widely cited as evidence that Confucius believed that an archery contest was the way to gauge the moral rectitude of archers, and by implication of the educated human.

It is agreed that the art of archery, articulated so seriously and interestingly by Confucius, quickly became accepted as the kind of education Confucius himself received as an aristocrat.[7] Since the late Warring States Periods (483–221 BCE), it had become an established fact that, as an aristocrat, Confucius must have been very familiar with the art of archery. One of the later Confucian classical works, the *Records of Rites* (*Liji* 禮記), claims that he was a competent or even accomplished archer. Since he held a positive attitude towards the art of archery, as seen from the quotations from him above, the art was doubtless part of his education.

The role of archery in Confucius's education was soon given classical importance. Another Confucian classic, *The Rites of Zhou* (*Zhouli* 周禮), which was commonly considered a Han compilation, spelled out that archery was one of the "six arts" that constituted the basic education of "sons of the nation" (*guozi* 國子), that is, the young men of the [extended] family of the ruler.[8]

---

4  *Liji* (Records of Rites), ch. 46: 2, Sheyi (Meaning of Archery).
5  Ibid.
6  *Analects*, 3:7.
7  The earliest serious account that Confucius was born into an aristocratic family can be found in Sima Qian's 司馬遷 (145–85 BCE) *Shiji* 史記 (Record of the Grand Historian) and the *Kongzi jiayü* 孔子家語 (School Sayings of Confucius) compiled by Wang Su 王肅 (195–256). The former suggests that Confucius was born into a "commoner" (non-official) family, while the latter, that Confucius was born an aristocrat, was preferred by most later scholars. The most widely used biography of Confucius, in terms of factual accounts, in modern times is Kuang Yaming, *Kongzi pingzhuan* (A Critical Biography of Confucius) (Nanjing: Nanjing Daxue, 1990).
8  This is from the *Rites of Zhou* (*Zhouli* 周禮), ch. 2 of the late Han commentary, by Zheng Xuan 鄭玄 (127–200). See also various other places in the book for discussions on the "six arts."

Of course, archery was always an essential part of military art and a must for all warriors in possibly all civilizations, and the Chinese was no exception. However, although there is archaeological evidence, the Chinese people did not seem to pay much attention to writing down the technique of making archery weapons. The early notable work *Records of Crafts* (*Kaogong ji* 考工記), believed to have been composed in the fifth or sixth century BCE, does provide details on the methods and materials for making bows and arrows.[9] However, though quite useful, this work was a lone exception. One of the earliest books on military strategy, the so-called *Six Strategies* (*Liutao* 六韜), talks about how to cleverly use archery.[10] However, most ancient writings that touch on archery are primarily on how to accomplish the art of archery, and the mind-body correlation of a good archer was their central concern.[11] In short, by the early Han, the first full-fledged treatise on the meaning of archery appeared and is found in the *Records of Rites*. The essay, entitled "Meaning of Archery" (*Sheyi* 射義) is the most sacrosanct Confucian exposition on the ritualistic significance of archery. Thus, the *Records of Rites*, already considered one of the major Confucian classics, and whose editorship even attributed to Confucius himself, became the orthodox Confucian source of archery's meaning and moral purpose. Meanwhile, educated Chinese people accepted that Confucius must have been brought up studying the art and was a competent archer.

## 3 Archery as Rites and Rituals

The essay "Meaning of Archery" is obviously based on the Confucian ideal of archery: its association with education makes it a basis for judging the moral quality of the people aspiring to office, or for judging whether a noble man has the rectitude to manage his jobs, or a foreign emissary to present his case. Archery contests are held in such occasions as banquets, Village Libation Ceremonies (*xiang yinjiu* 鄉飲酒), and the like. The essay quotes Confucius saying: "How difficult it is to shoot! How difficult it is to listen (to the music)! To shoot

---

9  The work is now included in the *Rites of Zhou* as its sixth part.
10  This book, which is of uncertain authorship, is now available in English translation; see Ralph D. Sawyer, *The Six Secret Teachings on the Way of Strategy* (Boulder, CO: Shambahla, 1997). Please note that *tao* itself means quiver (case) for arrows. Note also that another contemporary but even more famous book on military tactics, the *Sunzi bingfa* 孫子兵法 (The Art of War by Master Sun), attributed to Sun Wu 孫武 (545–470 BCE), says nothing about archery.
11  Notably the *Liezi* 列子 (Master Lie), a Warring States work, even though there are doubts that its modern text is spurious.

exactly in harmony with the note (given) by the music, and to shoot without missing the bull's-eye on the target—it is only the archer of superior virtue who can do this! How shall a man of inferior character be able to hit the mark?"[12]

The stress on the moral significance of "shooting targets" remains the unifying or commanding theme, and of the ceremonies mentioned in the essay, the Village Libation had the most staying power.[13] It was performed throughout Chinese history, if intermittently, and was by the last imperial dynasty, the Qing, still very much alive.[14] Archery was usually, if not always, held during the ceremony. Another ceremony mentioned in the essay, in which archery was also often performed, was the Imperial Banquet Ceremony (*Yanli* 燕禮). This ceremony, in contrast to the Village Libation, obviously was held only in rarer and more esteemed occasions. It was perhaps considered only as a normative ritual and less of common significance. Both made archery almost a central feature, and demonstrated its importance.[15]

The Village Libation Ceremony was first performed in 19 BCE, during Han times, and was accompanied by shooting contests.[16] From the beginning the ceremony was also associated with school education, in both the Imperial University (where the so-called "Great Shooting Ceremony" [*dashe li* 大射禮] was held) and local schools (where Village Libation Ceremonies were held).[17] Although the intention and content of the ceremonies in the Imperial University

---

12  *Liji*, ch. 46: 12, Sheyi.
13  The *Book of Rites* also has a chapter on the meaning of *xiang yinjiu*.
14  Hsiao Kung-chuan, *Rural China: Social Control in Imperial China* (Seattle: University of Washington Press, 1960).
15  I have been able to find only little information about this ceremony was actually performed. The first that I have found was held in 291 CE; see *Tongdian* 通典 (Comprehensive Statutes), SKQS ed., ch. 56; and Han Yu, *Han Changli shiji biannian zhanzhu* (Annotated and Chronologically Arranged Collection of Poetry by Han Changli) (Shanghai: Guji chubanshe, 2002), ch. 7; Han Yu's 韓愈 (768–824) text suggests that this was not commonly held, even though it was theoretically held in connection with the selection of officials. Briefly speaking, the Imperial Banquet Ceremony as such was designed for the nobles or imperial relatives, who had ceased to be of political significance. He further noted that it was no longer held with any frequency. In a broader sense, banquets were held in a variety of formal occasions, and with different variations and significance; although most of them were also called "Imperial Banquets," they were not organized and performed in strict accord with the *Book of Rites* prescription. Shen Yaozhong 沈堯中 of the early 17th century says that the ceremony of Imperial Banquets had been lost by his time. See his *Shenshi xuetao* (Shen's Collected Notes of Learning), Wanli period print copy, ch. 11, in SKQSCM.
16  Xun Yue, *Hanji* (Annals of the Han), SBCK ed., ch. 25 (chengdi, 2).
17  Yuan Hong, *Hou Hanji* (Annals of the Later Han), SBCK ed., ch. 9 (mingdi shang); Chen Shou, *Sanguo zhi* (Records of the Three Kingdoms) (Beijing: Zhonghua shuju, 1959), ch. 59.

and those in local schools were different, the ideas behind them were similar, especially since the two were almost invariably mentioned together in later times.[18] Therefore, it is not surprising that the Village Libation Ceremony was often understood as being combined with an archery performance. It was also generally performed when new officials were selected or inducted into office. Evidence, however, suggests that they were seldom performed from the later Han to the early Song.[19] They were from time to time held *pro forma*, and were apparently not accompanied by archery activity.[20] In other words, the celebration of Village Libation, though related to school activities, did not usually include shooting contests, and I dare say that the Confucian interpretation of the archery activity as a part of gentleman's education was considered less important than rituals as a symbol of good government.[21]

---

18  During the Tang, the "Great Shooting Ceremony" seems to take place even more frequently than the Village Libation Ceremony. However, although often enacted, it lost its elevated status as an imperial ritual during Tang, and was usually performed only as a military ceremony. The Village Libation Ceremony was often also called "Village Shooting" (*xiangshe* 鄉射), "Village Drinking," or "Shooting Festival" (*shejie* 射節), showing that it was not always an occasion for honoring the elders. A few words are in order to explain the meaning of "Village Shooting." It is listed in the *Book of Rites* (*Yili* 儀禮, usually designated as ch. 5) as a separate rite different from the Village Libation Ceremony (discussion of which is found in the *Record of Rites* as an independent chapter, and is thus different from the "Village Shooting" chapter we are concerned with here) at least in theory, but Village Shooting was prescribed, according to this chapter, as a sequel to the Village Libation Ceremony and therefore the two ceremonies were often combined or commingled into one. See Gao Mingshi, "Lun Sui Tang xueli zhong de xiang yinjiu li (On the Village Libation Ceremony of the Sui and Tang School Rites)," in *Xuanzang renwen xuebao*, no. 6 (2006), 33–62.

19  Although the evidences suggest that from the end of the Han to the early Song, Village Libation Ceremonies were occasionally held, during which shooting rarely took place. The ceremony as such was also held primarily in connection with educational affairs.

20  I have thus far only been able to find three or four occasions when the emperors ordered the celebration of village libation, in 270, 277, and 299 CE, and notably held it in the Imperial University (then named Biyong 璧雍). Slightly earlier, in 258 CE, the last ruler of the Wei of the Three Kingdoms also organized a presumably similar ceremony, but the historical source does not specify that it was a Village Libation Ceremony. It was never celebrated from the 4th through the 6th centuries. See Fang Xuanling, *Jinshu* (History of Jin) (Beijing: Zhonghua shuju, 1974), ch. 22. See also p. 109 for a Village Libation Ceremony ordered by the Xianbei ruler Murong Guang 慕容皝 (297–348).

21  It is thus interesting that the Village Libation Ceremony was sometimes held as a ritual for honoring the senior members of noble extended families, communities, or officialdom. See Linghu Defen, *Zhoushu* (History of Zhou) (Beijing: Zhonghua shuju, 1971), ch. 25, for one that was held in 552 to honor the respected and powerful senior official Li Xian 李賢 (504–569).

Throughout Sui and Tang times, archery contest ceremonies and Village Libation Ceremonies continued to have been largely forgotten, even though both Sui and Tang official compendiums on rituals refer to them, and there are occasional records of Village Libation Ceremonies being performed on the occasion of holding civil service examinations.[22] In other words, the ritualist concern with the archery ceremony remained primarily with its use as a part of Chinese concept of a good government. As a contrast, the government did not pay much attention to the art of archery as part of an educational curriculum. It is true that military training including shooting skills must have continued, but even so, the early flourishing of composing archery manuals in the Han did not return in force. In fact, one finds not one single book or treatise on the subject in the bibliographies of the two standard Tang histories. The neglect of the subject matter is quite astonishing, if one imagines Tang as an empire of military prowess. Be that as it may, however, the Tang records did include a couple of memorials by famous officials who recommended encouraging the common people to participate in Village Libation Ceremonies. This may indicate that the ceremonies were still taking place, if perhaps sporadically. It is further significant that these recommendations were for the ruled population to take part, and not just for government officials and aristocratic nobles. These recommendations, nonetheless, do not hide the fact that the ceremony and archery knowledge were deemed unimportant through the 7th to 10th centuries.[23]

---

22  Du You, *Tongdian*, chs. 53, 73; Xiao Song, *DaTang Kaiyuan li* (Ritual Canon of the Kaiyuan Reign of the Great Tang Dynasty), SKQS ed., ch. 127. It is nevertheless useful to note that one can see from these memorials that Tang scholars were aware of the fact that traditional practices included shooting contest at the end of the Ceremony. For records of the occasional Village Libation Ceremonies, see Du You: *Tongdian*, ch. 74. See also next note.

23  The general discussion above on Tang attitudes towards archery is based on checking of the two "Treatises on Books" in the *Jiu Tangshu* (Old Tang History) (Beijing: Zhonghua shuju, 1975), chs. 46–47, and the *Xin Tangshu* (New Tang History) (Beijing: Zhonghua shuju, 1975), chs. 57–60. It is noteworthy that there was indeed a manual on archery, Wang Ju's 王琚 (656–746) *The Classic of Teaching Archery* (*Jiaoshe jing* 教射經, in Ouyang Xiu, *Xin Tangshu*, ch. 59) that is a notable exception. This book is listed as *The Classic of Archery* (*Shejing* 射經), in Tuotuo, *Songshi* (History of the Song) (Beijing: Zhonghua shuju, 1985), ch. 207. Decrees exhorting the commoners to learn archery are found in Du You: *Tongdian*, ch. 74, as mentioned, and Han Yu, *Changli xiansheng wenji* (Collected Writings of Master Changli) (Shanghai: Guji chubanshe, 1994), waiji, ch. 6. Two renowned officials (one of them is Han Yu) recommended in 730 and in the early 9th century respectively that Village Libation Ceremonies should be held not only together with the civil service examinations, but also widely in the countryside. According to Du You, *Tongdian*, ch. 15, Village Libation Ceremonies usually, if not necessarily regularly, included shooting contests or performance.

However, it was around the ninth century that a so-called archery range or shooting terrace appeared for the first time in Chinese history. A memorial submitted by Zhang Yue 張說 (667–730) in 729 concerning the celebration of Emperor Xuanzong's 玄宗 (r. 713–756) birthday, included a reference to a "shooting terrace" (*shepu* 射圃) as a place where commemorative events were held for honoring seniors (ninth day of the ninth month of the lunar calendar).[24]

To recapitulate this section, one sees that besides military training, the skill of archery was also considered as one of the more important rituals held by the court or the local governments from Han through Tang. An archery contest was usually held on the occasion of Village Libation Ceremonies. Since Village Libation Ceremonies were typically held in the campus of nation's highest educational institution, variously named as Imperial University (Taixue 太學), Biyong School 璧雍, or Directorate of National Youth (Guozi jian 國子監), often on occasions of the government admitting new successful examination candidates, or installing new officials, its symbolic meaning related to both good government and education. Thus, archery performance could also be considered as a kind of educational activity, even though it was not spelled out at this time as a part of the teaching curriculum. The Village Libation Ceremony was also from time to time held on the local level to honor senior members of a local community. All in all, however, the ceremonies were held only occasionally (or even haphazardly) and it seems that those held on the local level were not always combined with archery performance. It is not far from the truth that in the eyes of the middle-period Chinese rulers, archery and Village Libation Rites were primarily to symbolize good government, though with an educational connotation.

## 4   Archery and Song Military Thought

The development of Confucian military thinking in the Song is marked by an unprecedented emphasis on Confucian education for military generals, and even better, on generals be civil scholar-officials and thus Confucian by definition. As early as 998, a prominent official, Sun He 孫何 (961–1004), had already dispatched a memorial recommending that the court should consider adopting the Tang practice of appointing only the so-called Confucian generals (*rujiang* 儒將) to command troops, especially those stationed along the border.[25]

---

24   Zhang Yue, *Zhang Yangong ji* (Collected Writings of Duke Zhang of Yan), SKQS ed., ch.15/6.
25   Cao Yanyue: *Jinwo guanjian* (Humble Opinions on Classical Teachings), Yuzhang congshu ed., ch. 4. I have been able to find only very few occurrences in that "Confucian general"

In a lengthy memorial submitted in 1034, Fu Bi 富弼 (1004–1083) argued for the need to establish a military school, and, significantly, recommended that the military personnel were to study military books (that is, to make military books available to them and make sure that they had the literacy to read them), and regularly to participate in archery contests.[26] The continuous appearance of the expression, and hence its ideal, of "Confucian general" is not without significance, because many civil officials were also appointed to lead border troops, fighting the Tangut Xia and the Khitan Liao states. Of them, Fan Zhongyan 范仲淹 (989–1052) and Han Qi 韓琦 (1008–1075) were the most famous. Indeed, beginning with the 11th century the idea that military generals should be also versed in Confucian learning, and be conscious of the moral purposes or implications of war, had become widely acknowledged.[27] The developments discussed above help to explain the rise in archery training in the Song, together with the renewed attention to the Village Libation Ceremonies.

Emperors Taizong 太宗 (r. 976–997) and Zhenzong 真宗 (r. 997–1022) at the turn of the 10th to 11th centuries stand out as the most enthusiastic rulers in terms of archery. There are a number of records showing that both were accomplished archers, and built a couple of archery ranges in Bianjing (modern day Kaifeng), the capital. The most celebrated event was the archery ceremony held in 1009, in which Emperor Zhenzong went to inspect the range (or hall, in this case) his father had built for him, and invited the court officials to join in

---

was used before Song. The *Zhongguo jiben gujiku* database yields a total of as many as eight occurrences in Tang and Five Dynasties works, and not all of them are related to the meaning concerned here. It is true that examples are plentiful to cite that a military general should also be well versed in Confucian values, but the use of the term "*rujiang*" (in the way concerned here) appeared, as far as I can ascertain, for the first time only in the Tang dynasty. See Yao Silian, *Chenshu* (History of Chen) (Beijing: Zhonghua shuju, 1995 punctuated ed.), ch. 11.

26  Fu Bi, "Shang Renzong lun wuju wuxue (Memorial to Emperor Renzong Discussing Military Examination and Learning)," in *Song mingchen zouyi* (Memorials of Famous Ministers of the Song Period), comp. Zhao Ruyü, SKQS ed., ch. 82; a checking of the database (cited in n. 25 above) shows that "Confucian general" appeared as many as 144 times during the Song. Moreover, Li Fang's 李昉 (925–996) encyclopedic *Imperial Perusal of the Taiping [Xingguo] Era* (976–984) (*Taiping yülan* 太平御覽), has a section on "Confucian general." This is unthinkable before the Song.

27  Wu Tingzhi, "Beisong shiren dui 'wenchen tongbing' de helihua lunshu (Literati's Arguments Justifying the Policy, 'Civil Officials Command Troops,' in Northern Song China)," *Qinghua xuebao* 44, no. 4 (2014): 589–628. See also He Guanhuan, "Baijun zhijiang Liu Ping – jianlun Songai de rujiang (The Career of Liu Jianji, a Military Officer of the Northern Song Dynasty)," *Journal of Institute of Chinese Studies, CUHK*, new 8 (1999): 103–135. For information on archery activities of Fan Zhongyan and his son Fan Chunren 范純仁, see Lou Yao, *Fan Wenzheng gong nianpu* (Biography of Lord Fan Wenzheng), ed. Ye Shimei and Ouyang Xi (1517).

composing poems and rhapsodies, while participating in the shooting event. The emperor even ordered opening the shooting range for three days for the commoners to visit.[28] Thus, from almost the beginning Song rulers had been attracted to the ceremonies associated with archery and were building archery terraces, halls, or ranges within the imperial palace. Whereas in previous dynasties, these ceremonies (the Village Libation Ceremony especially) were organized to symbolize good governance, the Song court was unable to prepare reliable manuals on exactly how these ceremonies should be performed. Obviously, Tang people had not been too keen about them.[29] However, as the border wars became frequent and intense, and as more and more civil officials became involved in war strategy decision-making, many of them advocated the policy of giving military men a Confucian education. A number of civil officials were also actually dispatched to command the troops, especially in the northwest. Fu Bi's lengthy memorial, mentioned above, is a product of the changing situations.

In the meantime, Song Qi 宋祁 (998–1061), in a biographical account of a deceased military man, commented that the man was very good in "archery and charioteering" among the "six arts," so much so that Emperor Zhenzong would regularly ask him to perform archery when he received delegations from foreign countries. It is significant because this is almost the first time that we see a military man officially recognized as being competent in the Confucian "six arts" (at least two of them), suggesting that his Confucian education was the foundation for his archery, and other military, expertise. This was in the 1030s to 1040s.[30]

And then in 1077, Emperor Shenzong 神宗 (r. 1068–1085) issued an edict ordering that an archery field be built at the west gate of the Imperial

---

28  See Wang Yinglin, *Yuhai*, chs. 75, 160, 161. It is important to point out that a rite, "The Great Archery Ceremony," mentioned above (see n. 18 above) was revived as again an imperial rite, and would soon be re-connected with schools (Imperial University or Directorate School), as will be demonstrated below, but its distinction with the Village Libation Ceremony became blurred. Additionally, like the Village Libation Ceremony, it was not regularly performed, at least in the first part of the Song period. See Chen Jun, *Song jiuchao biannian beiyao* (Chronologically Arranged Essentials of the Nine Reigns), SKQS ed., ch. 7; Li Tao, *Xu zizhi tongjian changbian* (Long Draft Continuation of the *Comprehensive Mirror for Aid in Governance*) (Taipei: Shijie, 1965, reprint of 1881 Zhejiang shuju ed.), XCB hereafter, ch. 4 (960/3/*xinwei* 辛未) and ch. 48 (1001/3/*yichou* 乙丑).

29  See Zhang Ruyu, *Shantang kaosuo* (Investigative Guide from the Shantang Studio) (Beijing: Zhonghua shuju, 1992), xuji, ch. 26.

30  Song Qi, "Yang Taiwei xingzhuang (Brief Biography of Commandant Yang)," in his *Jingwen ji* (Collected Writing of Jingwen), SKQS ed., ch. 61.

University and ordered students to practice archery there on holidays.[31] This is the first indisputable evidence that archery was officially established by the Song court as a part of the government school curriculum.

Three decades later, the court again issued a set of guidelines for performing the Village Libation Ceremony, and regulations on the procedures of shooting contests were included in these guidelines. Both were to take place when students were admitted to the Directorate of the National Youth School, or to local government schools.[32] From then on, archery became a part of Song government education. The emperor commented at the issuance of the edict that civil officials should also be tested, like their martial counterpart, in their ability in archery skills.

Thus, by the 8th decade of the 11th century, archery had become an integrated part of the University curriculum. The educational significance of the art was now openly acknowledged. Before I round up this section, however, I should also point out that beginning with the Song period, intellectuals began to publish an unprecedented number of books on archery. As mentioned above, very few, if any, treatises on archery skills were published during the Tang dynasty; however, the bibliographical section of the standard *Song History* has as many as 23 works. The contrast is revealing.[33]

The discussion above shows that Confucian thinkers and scholar-officials by the middle of the Northern Song times had become quite interested in the military dimension of Confucian education, and rediscovered, among various things, the important relationship between the art of archery and the Confucian idea of the gentleman. It was now also becoming evident to Song thinkers that the intrinsic relationship was a valuable theme to reemphasize and promote. In fact, by the second half of the Northern Song, government schools were required by the state to incorporate archery training as part of the curriculum. This new direction in thinking picked up its momentum in the early 12th century, especially during the tumultuous days when the Song court moved to South China, under the threat of the invading Jurchen Jin army.

---

31  XCB, ch. 280 (1077) and ch. 335 (1081); this event is also found in several other contemporary and later sources.
32  See note above, see also Wang Yinglin, *Yuhai*, ch. 75; See also Zhang Ruyu, *Qunshu kaosuo* (Investigative Guide to the Numerous Books), SKQS ed., houji, ch. 27; Tuotuo, *Songshi* (History of the Song) (Beijing: Zhonghua shuju, 1977), SS hereafter, ch. 114 (67).
33  See SS, ch. 207 ("zhi" 160).

## 5  Archery Ranges in Song State Schools

The practice of archery continued in the beginning years of the Southern Song. More importantly, in this time of turmoil, the Gaozong 高宗 Emperor (r. 1127–1162) decided that the court should revive the rite of Village Libation (1133), and no sooner than had he instituted it he ordered the ceremony be held regularly upon the admission of successful candidates of the imperial examinations to the court. The ceremony was also often held in prefectures and counties, and was regularly followed by archery contests as well, on occasions similar to those just mentioned above.

There are many records to show that archery contests or training activities were organized on various levels of Song state schools, from the capital to prefectures and counties. Village Libation Ceremonies were also regularly held together with shooting performances or contests when presenting or graduating students for promotion or induction to officialdom.[34] There is no doubt that the ceremony was held much more frequently in the Song than in the Tang.[35]

At about the same time there was also a significant increase in the building of archery ranges, on campuses of government schools, or for general military purposes. Emperor Gaozong was especially keen on promoting archery skills, and was dedicated to polishing himself in it.[36] His concern about the archery skills, his own and his subjects', was not without reason, because the Song were under the threat of the Jurchens. And so, in 1128, he ordered that any man with demonstrable archery competence could be appointed directly to government offices. At the same time, an old garden retreat in Hangzhou, then the imperial capital, was renovated into a shooting hall.[37] In the decades after this, the government began to build a number of shooting terraces. Most of them were

---

34   Here are a few examples: Li Xinchuan, *Jianyan yilai xinian yaolu* (Annual Records of the Most Important Events Since the Jianyan Reign-period), SKQS ed., ch. 160; Zhang Jin et al., *Qiandao Siming tujing* (Maps and Texts of the Siming Area during the Qiandao Reign), ch. 9; SS, chs. 30, 31, 114, 156, 157, Ye Shi, *Shuixin xiansheng wenji* (Collected Writings of Master Shuixin), SKQS ed., qianji, ch. 29; Chen Jian, *Huang Ming tongji jiyao* (Collected Essentials of the Chronicle of the August Ming), ch. 5.

35   The *Jiben gujiku* database shows that the Tang works contain only 50 references to the ceremony, while the Song works contain 1,590 references.

36   Li Xinchuan, *Jianyan yilai xinian yaolu*, 63; *Songshi quanwen* (Complete History of the Song) (Beijing, Zhonghua shuju, 2016), 18B.

37   SS, 25, 158; Li Xinchuan, *Jianyan yilai xinianyaolu*, ch. 18; Zhang Xuan, *Zhida Jinling xinzhi* (New Gazetteer of Jingling in the Zhida Reign), ch. 12A.

expectedly in the lower Yangzi Valley, especially at the proximity of Hangzhou.[38] Even though the Village Libation Ceremonies were not usually mentioned together with shooting training or performance, it is conceivable that the two activities were held simultaneously in most occasions. In addition, schools were usually the site of the archery terraces, and therefore the relationship between the two was quite clear. Whereas Emperor Gaozong's attention to archery skills was motivated primarily by the military, his adopted son and successor, Emperor Xiaozong 孝宗 (r. 1162–1189), was more concerned with the educational implications of archery, and thus ordered in 1174 that Imperial University students be required to learn archery.[39]

The revival of learning archery about 100 years after it was first (i.e. during the Song) introduced into the curriculum of the Imperial University shows that it had lapsed during the last decades of the Northern Song. The lapse was most likely caused by the extended but intense power struggles in the turn of the 11th and 12th centuries, between the reformers and anti-reformers over various policy and institutional matters, including the curriculums of government education and civil service examinations. The wars that were going on in these years also contributed to the negligence; this alarmed the Southern Song rulers, and, as a result, archery reclaimed its military eminence. The second emperor then made sure that archery's education value return to the nation's consciousness.

As noted above, many local schools were also building its archery ranges. Zhu Xi 朱熹 (1130–1200) wrote about one in Tong'an (modern Xiamen, Fujian) that was built in 1155. He was a deputy county magistrate and participated in its construction. The range was for the training of the local militia. Zhu Xi's involvement in the construction of the archery range must have been related to the popularity of archery activities encouraged by the government.[40] In fact, the government continued to encourage archery training. For example, after introducing archery into the curriculum of the Imperial University in 1174, the Emperor Xiaozong further issued a manual on archery and required that new *jinshi* degree holders be invited to participate in shooting performance.[41]

---

38   See note 43 below for an incomplete list of schools equipped with archery ranges in the Song.
39   Xu Song et al. (eds.), *Song huiyao jigao* (Draft of an Institutional History of the Song Dynasty), "Chongru (Venerating Scholars)," 1/40; Li Xinchuan: *Jianyan yilai chaoye zaji*, SKQS ed., jiaji, ch. 3; *Songshi quanwen*, ch. 27A. This record is also found in many local gazetteers and later encyclopedic compendiums, such as Wang Yinglin's *Yuhai*, ch. 75.
40   Zhu Xi, *Hui'an xiansheng Zhu Wengong wenji* (Collected Writings of Zhu Wengong the Master Hui'an), SBCK ed., ch. 77.
41   Wang Yinglin: *Yuhai*, ch. 75. See also Chen Yuanjin, *Yushu leigao* (Classified Drafts of Yushu), SKQS ed., ch. 5.

Among intellectuals, discussions on the significance, as well as skills, of archery also became common. Zhu Xi again is a good example. Besides his many commentaries on Confucian classics in which he expounded on the meaning of "shooting" (usually in reference to the "Meaning of Archery" chapter of *Records of Rites* mentioned above), his discussion on the issue is also found in quite a number of occasions recorded in his conversations with disciples. As expected, archery was considered a part of his *Elementary Learning* (*Xiaoxue* 小學) curriculum. He also repeatedly emphasized, philosophically, that hitting the mark on the target and archers' mental preparedness for achieving it are equally important. This remark on the philosophy of archery and how it was related to the acquisition of true learning (both in terms of breadth and conciseness or succinctness) is found in various places in his collected writings and in his conversation with disciples.

In short, for Zhu Xi, archery was a part of elementary or secondary education, especially in government-funded schools. "Archery ranges" also began to appear in local government schools.[42] In this context, one could almost talk about archery as a parallel to sport in modern education.[43]

Besides Zhu Xi, other leading interpreters of Neo-Confucian thought, such as Lu Jiuyuan 陸九淵 (1139–1192)[44] and his brother, Lu Jiuling 陸九齡 (1132–1180),[45] Chen Liang 陳亮 (1143–1195),[46] and many of Zhu Xi's followers, such as Chen Chun 陳淳 (1159–1223),[47] Zhen Dexiu 真德秀 (1178–

---

42  Zhu Xi, *Zhuzi yulei* (Classified Conversations of Master Zhu), block-print ed. by Chen Wei (1473), chs. 3, 7, 21, *passim*. See also his *Xiaoxue jizhu* (Collected Commentaries on the Elementary Learning), SKQS ed., ch. 2, and his *Hui'an ji* (Collected Work of Hui'an), ch. 40, and ch. 100, for proposed procedures of archery training in elementary instruction. See also note 46 below.

43  Here by sport, I am thinking of Vittorino da Feltre's educational philosophy in which modern physical education saw its inception in elementary school curriculum.

44  A total of 23 occurrences of comments on archery are found in his *Xiangshan ji* (Collected Works of Xiangshan), SBCK ed. Most of them are discussions on the educational or local defense significance of archery, often citing the Classics as authority.

45  Lu Jiuling is famous for his promotion of archery, and known as an accomplished archer. See Lu Jiuyuan's memoir (*xingzhang* 行狀) of him, in his *Lu Jiuyuan ji* (Collected Writings of Lu Jiuyuan) (Beijing: Zhonghua shuju, 1980), ch. 27; see also his biography in SS, ch. 434. His personal fondness for and promotion of archery is similar to that of Wang Yangming (see later), and was often cited as a model scholar-gentleman in Ming works; see Cai Qing, *Sishu mengyin* (Primary Introduction to the Four Books), SKQS ed., ch. 12.

46  Chen Liang, *Chen Liang ji* (Collected Writings of Chen Liang) (Beijing: Zhonghua shuju, 1974), ch. 20. There are 19 occurrences of "shooting" in his *Longchuan ji* (Collected Writings of Longchuan), which is part of the *Chen Liang ji*.

47  See for example, a letter by Chen Chun to Zhu Xi, in his *Beixi daquan ji* (Complete Collection of Beixi), SKQS ed., ch. 37/10, in which he asked about a passage from Mencius on the different merits of archery and charioteering in personal moral cultivation. See

1235),[48] and Wei Liaoweng 魏了翁 (1178–1237)[49] all shared the same narrative that archery was an integral part of a gentleman's education, even if their respective understanding of ancient records of archery activities may vary.

Thus, archery had returned to a central place in Confucian educational imagination by the 12th and 13th centuries. Zhu Xi, for one, was its enthusiastic champion. Since Zhu Xi was also a leading advocate in founding academies, it is expected that he should also have included archery training in the academies, but this turns out not to be the case. An apparent answer to this is that academies were founded primarily to admit more advanced students seeking higher education and therefore archery training had less importance in Zhu's imagination of higher education, in contrast to elementary education or education on the local level.

There is nearly no record to show that Song academies built archery fields on their campus.[50] Be that as it may, the military significance and the ceremonial and educational significance of archery training combined in this critical period of China's intellectual transformation, and left a mark on Ming discourse of education in general. The development in Song ideas of academy education thus incorporated the contemporary Neo-Confucian imagination, and had continued to be an important part of the philosophy of higher education in the later dynasties.

---

      also ch. 17/6 on how Zhu Xi was personally involved in instructing Zhangzhou (modern Zhangzhou, Fujian) local school students on archery. See also ch. 16/6 on a rather detailed discussion of local educational problems.

48    Zhen Dexiu was above all concerned with the classical prescriptions on archery. His *Xishan wenji* (Collected Writings of Xishan), SBCK ed., and *Dushu ji* (Reading Notes), SBCK ed., contained 133 occurrences of "archery."

49    Wei's primary concern with archery is on the classical interests in archery and its educational implications. He mentioned that he was personally present in an archery drill of a local government school. He wrote times again (see e.g. ch. 8) on the procedures of Village Libation Ceremony and the archery performance in it. He even wrote about how to brew the wine used in the ceremony. A total of 106 occurrences are found in his *Chongjiao Heshan xiansheng daquan wenji* (Complete Collected Writings of Master Heshan Recollated), SBCK ed.

50    The interesting single exception is mentioned in n. 1, showing that a Donghu "academy" had an archery range in the early 11th century. Officially, this academy was built in 1211, and although records are plentiful of the building of this academy, none of them mentioned the presumed continuation of the archery field.

## 6 The Heyday of Archery Training as Education

In 1370 the Hongwu 洪武 (r. 1368–1398) emperor of Ming first decreed that all state schools, including the Imperial University, should build archery ranges on the campuses.[51] Because the emperor seemed to be very serious about this matter, and seems to have ordered that the edict be engraved on the so-called horizontal tablet (*hengbei* 橫碑) erected in all school campuses,[52] the practice was dutifully observed throughout the land and through the dynasty. At the same time, the academies, though mostly organized outside of the government's purview, also started to build archery ranges. It is noticeable that the majority of the ranges had a pavilion that was almost routinely named "observing morality" (*guande* 觀德), echoing the original Confucian imagination of the ritualistic significance of archery sport.

I shall not try to provide statistics on the number of archery ranges in the Ming times, but it is useful and necessary to point out that academies, in contrast, had far fewer shooting terraces. The different course the academies took is interesting, and this requires some consideration. However, as mentioned above with regards to Zhu Xi's imagination on the educational purpose of archery, the art was primarily for pupils attending elementary or local schools.

Be that as it may, archery terraces or ranges began to appear in academies not long after the decree on their building in government schools. Since leading advocates of academies were Neo-Confucian thinkers, it is understandable that their views of archery would be primarily educational, in contrast to the Hongwu emperor's military concerns. A reading of related Ming sources bears this out. Most of the records on archery theories are commentaries on the chapters on archery as found in *Records of Rites*, *Book of Rites,* and *Rites of Zhou*, and other occasional remarks on the subject found in other classics (such as *Analects* and *Mencius*). The writings show the predilection on the part of Ming scholars for the educational significance of archery. Wang Yangming 王陽明 (1472–1529) comes first in mind. Wang is known foremost as one who was avidly involved in various educational activities for the commoners, ranging

---

51　Chen Jian, *Huang Ming tongji jiyao*, Ming Chongzhen (1611–1644) ed., ch. 5; see also Zhang Tingyu, *Mingshi* (History of the Ming), ch. 57, parts on "grand archery performance (*dashe zhi li*)."

52　*Jiajing Weixian zhi* (Wei County Gazetteer Compiled in the Jiajing Era), in Tianyi ge cang Mingdai fangzhi xuankan ed. (Shanghai: Guji chubanshe, 1963), ch. 2. This shows that the tablet included the prescription that an archery range should be built in the school compound. I have examined several other tablets, and found that not all of them mentioned this rule. For a discussion on the "horizontal tablets," see my *Education in Traditional China, a History* (Leiden: Brill, 2000), 653–655.

from community compacts (*xiangyue* 鄉約) to local militia (*tuanlian* 團練), to, of course, academies.[53] More important is his being an exemplar of the Confucian ideal of an embodiment of both intellectual and physical accomplishments: he was, in addition to being an influential thinker, also a military commander and avid "sportsman." Although there is no evidence that he was also an adept archer, he did make frequent remarks on the significance of archery for moral cultivation. He regularly built academies with archery ranges.[54] He was also personally and actively involved in archery practice.[55] In other words, he was fully aware of the paradoxical relationship between the two seemingly divergent aspects of archery as an art and as a military skill. He, like Zhu Xi before him, also wrote a famous essay commemorating the building of a "Pavilion for Observing Morality."

It should be noted that Wang Yangming did not consider academies as an important educational institution until he was demoted and exiled to Guizhou. However, even after he became systematically involved in building academies, his primary concern was still with mass education, to which he made many important theoretical and practical contributions.[56] As a result, his disciples did not continue to expand on the idea of archery as a central concern of education. This is quite different from the disciples of Zhu Xi. For Wang Yangming's students, it was public lectures and egalitarian education that made him famous for the next couple of hundred years and more.

At the same time, interest in archery as a military skill seems to have waned somewhat during Ming times. The bibliographic chapters of the official *Ming History*[57] record only 13 works dealing with archery skills. Interestingly, even

---

53  Thomas H.C. Lee, *Education in Traditional China*, 329–337. The Chinese translation of this book includes a few updated references: *Xue yi weiji, Chuantong Zhongguo de jiaoyü* (Hong Kong: The Chinese University of Hong Kong Press, 2015), 307–321. See also Joseph P. McDermott, "Emperor, Elite, and Commoners: The Community Pact Ritual of the Late Ming," in *State and Court Ritual in China*, ed. Joseph P. McDermott (Cambridge: Cambridge University Press, 1999), 299–351; and Zhu Honglin, "Ershi shiji de xiangyue yanjiu (Twentieth Century Studies of Ming-Qing Community Compacts)," *Lishi renleixue xuekan* 2, no. 1 (2004): 175–196.

54  Deng Hongbo, "Wang Yangming de shuyuan shijian yu shuyuan guan (Wang Yangming's realization and view of academies)," *Hunan daxue xuebao* 19/6 (2005): 23–28. One of the most important records about his "archery range academy" is the Lianxi Academy 濂溪書院. See also his article "Like Tea and Rice at Home: Lecture Gatherings and Academies during the Ming Dynasty," in this volume, 159–196.

55  See, for example, the record in Zhang Pu, *Qiluzhai shiwen heji* (Collected Prose and Poetry of Qilu Study), 1636 ed. Guanke section, 1.

56  Besides the items listed above in n. 53, please also consult Zhou Yuwen, *Zhongguo jiaoyu shigang* (A Short History of Chinese Education) (Taipei: Zhengzhong shuju, 2001), *passim*.

57  Zhang Tingyu, *Mingshi*, Yiwen zhi, ch. 133–135.

with so few works on the subject, most of them are works on rituals more than military skills, or the related technics of manufacturing the weapon. The few exceptions include Mao Yuanyi 茅元儀 (1594–1640) and Qi Jiguang 戚繼光 (1528–1588). Mao's *Compendium on Military Readiness* (*Wubei zhi* 武備志) contains much information on the military dimension of archery. Written by a renowned and informed student of military arts, Mao's work has come down to today as a comprehensive manual that serves as an important source book of traditional Chinese weaponry and military strategy. He was critical of the neglect of archery in the state's recruitment examination for civil officials; he complained time and again that the Ming civil service examinations had abandoned testing candidates' skills in archery (and mathematics, law, and horse riding) after it had been tested in the early years of the dynasty.[58] Incidentally, Mao was hailed as a "Confucian general" by his contemporaries, even though, lacking a *jinshi* degree, he did not possess a civil official's status.[59] Qi Jiguang was an accomplished military general, but composed, among several works, the *New Book on Military Efficacy* (*Jixiao xinshu* 紀效新書), which includes one chapter on archery. Qi was also often described as a respectable "Confucian general." The custom of labeling an individual as a "Confucian general," which arose in Song times, continued in Ming times, and Wang Yangming's name immediately comes to mind.[60] A casual check of Ming writings shows that the expression was even more frequently used in Ming than in Song.

Meanwhile, the shift of educational thinking to the ideas and needs of education for the commoners was perhaps inevitable, as the society became wealthier. This was actually a result of the founding emperor's emphasis on the so-called community schools (*shexue* 社學), which were designed to promote imperial ideology.[61] The two trends of thinking, one an educational ideal and another the state's desire to control, coalesced in the 16th and 17th centuries. The much cherished Donglin Academy 東林書院 was representative of this development.

The advance of mass or popular education at the time was of course a reflection of the increasingly wealthy economy and ever more complex society that demanded a higher degree of literacy. This becomes evident when one

---

58 Mao Yuanyi, *Wubei zhi*, Guangxu Li Wentian ed., ch. 5.
59 See Fan Fengyi, "Song Maozongrong zhi dong yue," in his *Fan Xunqing shiwen ji* (Collected Poetry of Fan Xunqing), Chongzhen ed., ch. 15.
60 A Dai Shaowang 戴少望 even compiled a *Jiangjian lunduan* 將鑑論斷 (Discussions and Judgements as the Mirror for Military Generals) in four chapters and classified a few famous military generals as "Confucian generals."
61 Some community schools were also equipped with archery ranges.

sees that Ming rulers moved to devise more and newer methods to propagate official Confucian ideology. In other words, control over speech and thought had become an integrated consideration of statecraft and, in turn, explains the late Ming conflict between southeastern academies and the court in Beijing.

## 7 The Decline of Archery in Academies, in Lieu of Conclusion

The history of Ming academies is above all remembered for the government's repeated attempts to close them down. The increase in the number of academies, and the increasingly important role they played in urbanization in the 17th to 18th centuries, must necessarily have aroused anxiety on the part of the government. At the same time, academies were also an increasingly significant participant in the cultural and intellectual life of the society at large. Many southeastern academies were harbingers of new intellectual ideas. Modern Chinese intellectual history could indeed be said to be that of Chinese academies, particularly in this region. Therefore, if there was an increase in the number of academies that had archery ranges, that could mean, in my opinion, an elevated importance of archery in the mind of Chinese intellectuals. It could also mean that the officialization of academies had reached a new height. There was a significant increase in the records of academies in the Qing times; we also know that in terms of organization, building, management, and curriculum, Qing academies had all but become parts of the state's indoctrination mechanism.

While innovative discourses on archery as an art and a ritual had declined in the Qing times, and while there was a diminished importance in the role of archery skills in wars, the continued building, restoration, or modification of archeries in government schools, especially during the Kangxi 康熙 (r. 1661–1722) reign, reflected the overall peace and the continuation of the notion that archery learning was a symbol of good Confucian governance.[62] The need to provide academies with open space for archery training or ceremonies in urban areas reflected the increasingly visible role the academies served as a buffer or bridge between the ruling class and the ruled populace: the Village Libation Ceremonies, the public lectures, and even social relief activities could all serve as means of indoctrination. And they became only more and more

---

62  A comparison between the records of Ming and Qing academies with archery ranges shows that there were 20 for Ming and 31 for Qing. The records are taken from *Zhongguo jiben guji ku*. The comparison here is offered as only a rough indication, and should not be accepted as definitive.

sophisticated, especially after the Kangxi emperor's reign. Most of these public events were held in the compounds of government offices, but school compounds, especially those with archery ranges, were also frequently used, if local government offices did not have a big-enough covered space to serve the purpose.[63] The need for a broad public space for ritualistic performance or for lectures thus became more and more felt as urbanization caught on after the 16th and 17th centuries. The continued use, expansion, and refurbishing of places like archery ranges thus were constantly called for, as China gradually came of age in terms of its governing technique, while at the same time began to face the outside world.

By the end of the 19th century, academies had declined in its usefulness as a means of Confucian education and indoctrination, of which archery sport was a part. The Chinese state turned to relying more on ideological control than on educational transformation. Obviously, this kind of "public space" is easier to imagine for the Chinese people, and more and more archery ranges became places where most of the activities of indoctrination took place.[64] The public place where ritual performances were held now turned to becoming public squares, with distinct Chinese characteristics. Today, the Tiananmen Square remains the largest public square in the world.

Archery as such is today no longer of much military use, but it has survived in East Asia's imagination of education. It is an art with educational significance, and is nowadays a part of modern physical education. The old archery ranges have been by and large abandoned or converted into sports fields in "modern" schools, with the intention of serving also as squares where national/state ideologies can be propagated. Attempts to revive archery contests occasionally take place in this public space intended for a different purpose.

Before I round out this paper, let me add a few words on the educational purpose of archery and physical education at large as a Chinese narrative.

---

63   Public offices were commonly referred to as "gongsuo 公所," an expression becoming commonplace only in the Ming and Qing times, although the use of it in this sense went back at least to the Han. In pre-Ming times they were more often referred to as "gongxie 公廨." In the Qing times, there were many local government offices that were equipped with special auditoriums, and they were commonly called "Hall of Demonstrating/Illuminating Ethics" (*Minglun tang* 明倫堂); this is in contrast to "Hall of Observing Morality" (*Guande tang*, see above), a name commonly used to name archery fields/halls.

64   By "public space" I mean the image of Areopagus as ancient Athenians, Apostle Paul, John Milton, and even the 1821 Greek Revolutionaries, had given to it, as a place where public policy deliberations were made. This understanding of "public space" is, in my mind, related to Habermas' notion of "public sphere". It is also my contention that the Chinese understanding of a "public space" was rather that for indoctrination; there was no tradition in Chinese history of deliberating public policies in an open space.

I have argued that education in traditional China was above all characterized by the ideal of "learning for one's self" (*xue yi wei ji* 學以爲己). Of course, while this Confucian dictum remained a normative prescription for learning over time, one cannot deny that it took many different forms of realization. One is what we may call the "completion" of a human's life as ideal. There is no doubt that this was found repeatedly in traditional Confucian scholars' writings. But how could "archery" fit in this belief? This calls for a careful articulation. For example, the significance of archery for traditional Chinese education was based on its ritualistic performance. The "fair competition" of contest was considered as important not merely because of "fairness" in competition, but also because of "moral training," that is, orderly and peaceful (and non-aggressive) competition, something that is best expressed by what Confucius elsewhere characterized as "rite," the *li*.

The appearance of archery ranges in Chinese academies contributed not to the significance of academy education as a ground for knowledge transmission, but more as a part of moral indoctrination. As such, shooting ranges from the beginning were always ordered by the state. Therefore, its purpose was more for moral uniformity than the individual's moral self-cultivation. This has been evident from almost the beginning, but it became all but obvious towards the later imperial times. As a physical exercise, archery therefore was less for military training, much less the mere upbringing of a "whole person," but, above all, a mechanism for inculcating ritualistic behavior. Students studied archery, and performed it as a "moral ritual" according to imperially prescribed protocol. In the calculation of the ruling class, archery could help cement ideological uniformity of the masses. Indeed, its perpetuation depended ironically on its function as a ground where members of government schools (which many academies had evolved into) gathered for ritualistic performances and, towards the modern times, to listen to imperial decrees and prescripts; after all, shooting ranges could easily double as open space for public speeches ordered and organized by the state. The existence and continuation of shooting ranges therefore reflected the Chinese government's penchant for moral control and ideological uniformity. Shooting ranges thus could be seen as the beginning of the Chinese "squares," perennially and carefully maintained, and always permeated with "ritualistic" and "spacious" imagery. It was the ironic, if powerful, Chinese answer to the European "public space"—the Areopagus.

# References

Cai Qing 蔡清. *Sishu mengyin* 四書蒙引 (Primary Introduction to the Four Books). SKQS ed.

Cao Yanyue 曹彥約. *Jingwo guanjian* 經幄管見 (Humble Opinions on Classical Teachings). Yuzhang congshu ed. 豫章叢書.

Chen Chun 陳淳. *Beixi daquan ji* 北溪大全集 (Complete Collection of Beixi). SKQS ed.

Chen Jian 陳建. *Huang Ming tongji jiyao* 皇明通紀集要 (Collected Essentials of the Chronicle of the August Ming).

Chen Jun 陳均. *Jiuchao biannian beiyao* 九朝編年備要 (Chronologically Arranged Essentials of the Nine Reigns). SKQS ed.

Chen Liang 陳亮. *Chen Liang ji* 陳亮集 (Collected Writings of Chen Liang). Beijing: Zhonghua shuju, 1974.

Chen Shou 陳壽. *Sanguo zhi* 三國志 (Records of the Three Kingdoms). Beijing: Zhonghua shuju, 1959.

Chen Yuanjin 陳元晉. *Yushu leigao* 漁墅類稿 (Classified Drafts of Yushu). SKQS ed.

Deng Hongbo 邓洪波. "Wang Yangming de shuyuan shijian yu shuyuan guan 王阳明的书院实践与书院观 (Wang Yangming's Realization and View of Academies)." *Hunan daxue xuebao* 19, no. 6 (2005): 23–28.

Du You 杜佑. *Tongdian* 通典 (Comprehensive Statues). SKQS ed., also Beijing: Zhonghua shuju, 1984.

Fan Fengyi 范鳳翼. "Song Maozongrong zhi dong Yue 送茅總戎之東粤 (Seeing Off Commander-in-Chief Mao Dispatched to Eastern Guangdong)." In *Fan Xunqing shiwen ji* 范勛卿詩文集 (Collected Poetry of Fan Xunqing), Chongzhen ed.

Fang Xuanling 房玄齡. *Jinshu* 晋書 (History of Jin). Beijing: Zhonghua shuju, 1974.

Fu Bi 富弼. *Shang Renzong lun wuju wuxue* 上仁宗論武舉武學 (Memorial to Emperor Renzong Discussing Military Training and Examination). In Zhao Ruyu 趙汝愚 (comp.), *Song mingchen zouyi* 宋名臣奏議 (Memorials of Famous Ministers of the Song Period). SKQS ed.

Gao Mingshi. "Lun Sui Tang xueli zhong de xiang yinjiu li 論隋唐學禮中的鄉飲酒禮 (On the Village Libation Ceremony of the Sui and Tang School Rites)." in *Xuanzang renwen xuebao*, no. 6 (2006), 33–62.

Han Yu 韓愈. *Changli xiansheng wenji* 昌黎先生文集 (Collected Writings of Master Changli). Shanghai: Guji chubanshe, 1994.

Han Yu 韓愈. *Han Changli shiji biannian zhanzhu* 韓昌黎詩集編年箋注 (Annotated and Chronologically Arranged Collection of Poetry by Han Changli). Shanghai: Guji chubanshe, 2002.

He Guanhuan 何冠環. "Baijun zhijiang Liu Ping—jianlun Songai de rujiang 敗軍之將劉平 — 兼論宋代的儒將 (The Defeated General Liu Ping—on Song Dynasty Confucian Generals)." *Journal of Institute of Chinese Studies, CUHK*, new 8 (1999): 103–135.

Hsiao, Kung-chuan. *Rural China: Social Control in Imperial China*. Seattle: University of Washington Press, 1960.

*Jiajing Weishi xianzhi* 嘉靖威氏縣志 (Wei County Gazetteer Compiled in the Jiajing Era). In Tianyi ge cang Mingdai fangzhi xuankan 天一閣藏明代方志選刊 ed. Shanghai: Guji chubanshe, 1963.

Kuang Yaming 匡亞明. *Kongzi pingzhuan* 孔子評傳 (A Critical Biography of Confucius). Nanjing: Nanjing Daxue, 1990.

Lee, Thomas H.C. *Education in Traditional China, a History*. Leiden: Brill, 2000.

Lee, Thomas H.C. *Xue yi weij, Chuantong Zhongguo de jiaoyu* 學以爲己, 傳統中國的教育 (Learning for One's Self: Education in Traditional China). Hong Kong: The Chinese University of Hong Kong Press, 2015.

Linghu Defen 令狐德棻. *Zhoushu* 周書 (History of Zhou). Beijing: Zhonghua shuju, 1971.

Li Tao 李燾. *Xu zizhi tongjian changbian* 續資治通鑑長編 (Long Draft Continuation of the *Comprehensive Mirror for Aid in Governance*). Taipei: Shijie, 1965; reprint of the 1881 Zhejiang shuju ed.

Li Xinchuan 李心傳. *Jianyan yilai chaoye zaji* 建炎以來朝野雜記 (Miscellaneous Notes on Politics in and out of the Court Since the Jianyan Reign). *SKQS* ed.

Li Xinchuan 李心傳. *Jianyan yilai xinian yaolu* 建炎以來繫年要錄 (Annual Records of Important Events Since the Jianyan Reign Period). *SKQS* ed.

Liu Xu 劉昫. *Jiu Tangshu* 舊唐書 (*Old Tang History*). Beijing: Zhonghua shuju, 1975.

Lou Yao 樓鑰. *Fan Wenzheng gong nianpu* 范文正公年譜 (Biography of Master Fan Wenzheng). Ye Shimei and Ouyang Xi ed. 葉士美歐陽席刻本 (1517).

Lu Jiuyuan 陸九淵. *Lu Jiuyuan ji* 陸九淵集 (Collected Writings of Lu Jiuyuan). Beijing: Zhonghua, 1980.

Mao Yuanyi 茅元儀. *Wubei zhi* 武備志 (Compendium on Military Readiness). Guangxu Li Wentian 光緒李文田 ed.

McDermott, Joseph P. "Emperor, Elite, and Commoners: The Community Pact Ritual of the Late Ming." In *State and Court Ritual in China,* edited by Joseph P. McDermott, 299–351. Cambridge: Cambridge University Press, 1999.

Ouyang Xiu 歐陽修, and Song Qi 宋祁. *Xin Tangshu* 新唐書 (New Tang History). Beijing: Zhonghua shuju, 1975.

Sawyer, Ralph D. *The Six Secret Teachings on the Way of Strategy*. Boulder, CO: Shambahla, 1997.

Schneewind, Sarah. *Community Schools and the State in Ming China*. Stanford: Stanford University Press, 2006.

Shen Yaozhong 沈堯中. *Shenshi xuetao* 沈氏學弢 (Shen's Collected Notes of Learning). Wanli period print copy. *SKQSCM*.

*Songshi quanwen* 宋史全文 (Complete History of the Song). Beijing: Zhonghua shuju, 2016.

Song Qi 宋祁, "Yang Taiwei xingzhuang 楊太尉行狀 (Brief Biography of Grand Commandant Yang)." In *Jingwen ji* 景文集 (Collected Writing of Jingwen). SKQS ed.

Tuotuo 脫脫. *Songshi* 宋史 (History of the Song). Beijing: Zhonghua, 1985.

Wang Anshi 王安石. *Wang Jinggong wenzhu* 王荊公文注 (Commentaries on Wang Jinggong's Writings). Jiayetang congshu 嘉業堂叢書 edition (1913–1918).

Wang Xiangzhi 王象之. *Yudi jisheng* 輿地記勝 (Exhaustive Description of the Empire). Qing reprint of Song manuscript ed.

Wang Yinglin 王應麟. *Yuhai* 玉海 (Sea of Jade). SKQS ed.

Wei Liaoweng 魏了翁. *Chongjiao Heshan xiansheng daquan wenji* 重校鶴山先生大全文集 (Complete Collected Writings of Master Heshan Recollated). SBCK ed.

Wu Tingzhi 吳挺誌. "Beisong shiren dui 'wenchen tongbing' de helihua lunshu 北宋士人對「文臣統兵」的合理化論述 (Literati's Arguments Justifying the Policy, 'Civil Officials Command Troops,' in Northern Song China)." *Qinghua xuebao* 44, no. 4 (2014): 589–628.

Xiao Song 蕭嵩. *Da Tang Kaiyuan li* 大唐開元禮 (Ritual Canon of the Kaiyuan Reign of the Great Tang Dynasty). SKQS ed.

Xu Song 徐松, et al. (eds.). *Song huiyao jigao* 宋會要輯稿 (Draft of an Institutional History of the Song Dynasty).

Xun Yue 荀悅. *Hanji* 漢紀 (Annals of the Han). SBCK ed.

Yao Silian 姚思廉. *Chenshu* 陳書 (History of Chen). Beijing: Zhonghua shuju, 1995.

Ye Shi 葉適. *Shuixin xiansheng wenji* 水心先生文集 (Collected Writings of Master Shuixin). SKQS ed.

Yuan Hong 袁宏. *Hou Hanji* 後漢紀 (Annals of the Later Han). SBCK ed.

Zha Shenxing 查慎行, et al. (ed.). *Xijiang zhi* 西江志 (Gazetteer of Xijiang). Reprint of 1720 ed. Taipei: Chengwen, 1966.

Zhang Jin 張津, et al (ed.). *Qiandao Siming tujing* 乾道四明圖經 (Maps and Texts of the Siming Area during the Qiandao Reign). Song Yuan difangzhi congshu (Collection of Song-Yuan Local Gazetteers), Volume 8. (reprint).

Zhang Pu 張溥. *Qiluzhai shiwen heji* 七錄齋詩文合集 (Collected Prose and Poetry of Qilu Study). 1636 ed.

Zhang Ruyu 章如愚. *Shantang kaosuo* 山堂考索 (Investigative Guide from the Shantang Studio). Beijing: Zhonghua shuju, 1992.

Zhang Ruyu 章如愚. *Qunshu kaosuo* 群書考索 (Investigative Guide to the Numerous Books). SKQS ed.

Zhang Tingyu 張廷玉. *Mingshi* 明史 (History of the Ming). Beijing: Zhonghua shuju, 1974.

Zhang Xuan 張鉉 (comp.). *Zhida Jinling xinzhi* 至大金陵新志 (New Gazetteer of Jingling in the Zhida Reign).

Zhang Yue 張說. *Zhang Yangong ji* 張燕公集 (Collected Writings of Duke Zhang Yan). SKQS ed.

Zhen Dexiu 真德秀. *Dushu ji* 讀書記 (Reading Notes). SBCK ed.

Zhen Dexiu 真德秀. *Xishan wenji* 西山文集 (Collected Writings of Xishan). SBCK ed.

*Zhongguo jiben guji ku* 基本古籍庫 (Database of Fundamental Old Chinese Books).

Zhou Yuwen 周愚文. *Zhongguo jiaoyu shigang* 中國教育史綱 (Outline History of Chinese Education). Taipei: Zhengzhong shuju, 2001.

Zhu Honglin 朱鴻林. "Ershi shijie de xiangyue yanjiu 二十世紀的鄉約研究 (Twentieth Century Studies of Ming-Qing Community Compacts)." *Lishi renleixue xuekan* 2, no. 1 (2004): 175–196.

Zhu Xi 朱熹. *Hui'an xiansheng Zhu Wengong wenji* 晦庵先生朱文公文集 (Collected Writings of Zhu Wengong the Master Hui'an). SKQS ed.

Zhu Xi 朱熹. *Zhuzi yulei* 朱子語類 (Classified Conversations of Master Zhu). Block-print ed. by Chen Wei 陳煒 (1473).

CHAPTER 9

# Transmissions of the White Deer Grotto Academy Articles of Learning in Korea

*Martin Gehlmann*

## 1   Introduction

In 1179 Zhu Xi 朱熹 (1130–1200), the new prefect of Nankang, went to inspect the former site of the White Deer Grotto Academy (Bailudong shuyuan 白鹿洞書院) at Mount Lu. Widely known as an important place of learning since the Tang dynasty (618–907), the academy had gone through some troubled times and fallen into ruins. The sad sight of the overgrown remnants of this famous institution left Zhu Xi determined to rebuild the academy as a Confucian counterweight to Buddhist monasteries and Daoist shrines in the area.[1] His efforts were successful and under his guidance the academy once again became recognized as one of the important centers of Confucian learning in Southern Song China. After his death, the academy continued to produce a number of famed Confucian scholars and headmasters. While its fortunes again fell and soared, the academy's history and its close association with Zhu Xi ensured that it was well known among all following generations of scholars.

It was this association through which the academy became a model institution for other academies and a symbol representing the rediscovery and revival of Confucian teaching itself. The White Deer Grotto Academy, its reestablishment in a landscape dominated by Buddhist monasteries, and especially the *White Deer Grotto Academy Articles of Learning* (*Bailudong shuyuan jieshi* 白鹿洞書院揭示), formed an image that was transmitted within Zhu Xi's teachings and was received in all countries of the Confucian realm. Therefore, even when looking at the diversity in the development and history of Confucian academies it is possible to find references to the White Deer Grotto Academy in many educational institutions of East Asia, but especially in the academies.[2]

---

[1]   See John W. Chaffee, "Chu Hsi and the Revival of the White Deer Grotto Academy. 1179–1181," *T'oung Pao* 71 (1985): 40.

[2]   See e.g. in this volume alone, Deng Hongbo, "Like Tea and Rice at Home: Lecture Gatherings and Academies during the Ming Dynasty," 187; Chien Iching, "The Transmission and Transformation of Confucian Academy Rituals as Seen in Taiwanese Academies," 446; and Vladimír Glomb, "Shrines, Sceneries, and Granary: The Constitutive Elements of the Confucian Academy in 16th-Century Korea," 349.

Such references in their respective contexts give an idea what academies and their founders aspired to and what their academies were meant to achieve. Yet, Confucian scholars not only gained inspiration and legitimization for the founding of new academies from these transmissions, but also used them to create an individual sense of place for their academies while at the same time positing it among a larger unity of institutions seemingly devoted to the same goal.

For this reason, the transmission of Zhu Xi's *Articles of Learning* and their reception and adaption among state officials and Confucian literati of the Chosŏn kingdom (1392–1897) provide an interesting case for a study of the phenomenon of knowledge re-contextualization. The scholars of Chosŏn quite early followed the established Chinese understanding of the *Articles of Learning* as a general educational guideline that was not exclusively connected to Confucian academies. The *Articles*, however, still transmitted and shaped ideas about the concept of academies on the Korean peninsula.[3] With the rise of the academy system in Korea, the *Articles* were again directly connected to Confucian academies and became, in connection with other accounts of the White Deer Grotto Academy, an expression of the ideal academy. This image met with the individual circumstances of scholars on the Korean peninsula and was reshaped accordingly. To reconstruct this process this paper will look at the textual, institutional, ritual, and aesthetic perceptions of the *Articles of Learning* in Korea. Before this, it is important to briefly reconstruct Zhu Xi's own intentions in establishing the text as this will help to understand the initial usage of the *Articles* in China and Korea.

## 2   The Articles of Learning

When Zhu Xi first drafted the *White Deer Grotto Academy Articles of Learning*[4] in 1180 he surely was not concerned with the transmission of his ideas to

---

3   Basic knowledge about the existence of the White Deer Grotto Academy most probably already came together with the first writings of Zhu Xi during Koryŏ times to Korea. The *Articles of Learning* and the *Bailudong fu* 白鹿洞賦 (White Deer Grotto Rhapsody) prose-poem were included in the *Great Compendium on Human Nature and Principle* (*Xingli daquan* 性理大全) that was available to Chosŏn literati from beginning of the 15th century. The Ming dynasty version of the *Complete Writings of Zhu Xi* (*Zhuzi daquan* 朱子大全), which included many of Zhu Xi's texts on the academy, first circulated in the 16th century on the Korean peninsula.

4   The conventional translation of Zhu Xi's *Bailudong shuyuan jieshi* 白鹿洞書院揭示, which this article will follow, is *White Deer Grotto Academy Articles of Learning*. However, in the literature we find many other names, e.g. *Bailudong xuetiao* 白鹿洞學條, from which the translation as "Articles of Learning" probably derives. Also *White Deer Grotto Academy*

faraway places, but was quite focused on what he determined to be the problems of his time. This can be vividly seen in his comments on the creation and purpose of the *Articles*. Dissatisfied with the educational focus on examination preparation in many schools, Zhu Xi proposed a return to the methods of instruction used by the sages and worthies of antiquity. According to him, all that was needed to cultivate oneself and then spread virtue among the people could be found in the *Classics*. Therefore, he created the *Articles* not as regulations for the academy, but as a constant reminder of these virtues that was to be hung in the lecture hall.[5]

A further clue on Zhu Xi's intentions for composing the *Articles* might be gained by placing them in their timeframe within his life and intellectual production.[6] Before he first arrived in Nankang, Zhu Xi had spent quite some time

---

*Study Regulations* (*Bailudong shuyuan xuegui* 白鹿洞書院學規) and many reductions of this form (*Ludonggui* 鹿洞規, *Donggui* 洞規, etc.). Sometimes also direct references to Zhu Xi as the author of the *Articles* can be found as they are called *Study Regulations of Master Zhu* (*Zhuzi xuegui* 朱子學規). For more on Buddhist influences on the *Articles* see Thomas H.C. Lee, "Chu Hsi, Academies and the Tradition of Private Chiang-hsüeh," *Hanxue Yanjiu* 2, no. 1 (1984): 313–321; Huang Xirong, "Chanmen qinggui dui 'Bailudong shuyuan jieshi' de yingxiang (The Influence of Chan School Monastic Rules on the *White Deer Grotto Academy Articles of Learning*)," *Jiangxi jiaoyu xueyuan xuebao* 34, no. 2 (2014): 183–185.

5 A full translation of his comment to the *Articles* can be found in Yi Hwang, *To Become a Sage: The Ten Diagrams on Sage Learning by Yi T'oegye*, trans. Michael C. Kalton (New York: Columbia University Press, 1988), 104–105. Other English translations can be found in Wm. Theodore de Bary, *The Liberal Tradition in China* (New York: Columbia University Press, 1983), 89; and also partly in Hoyt Cleveland Tillman, *Confucian Discourse and Chu Hsi's Ascendancy* (Honolulu: University of Hawai'i Press, 1992), 111. For detailed discussions of Zhu Xi's understanding of education, its aims, and his methods of instruction see Zhu Xi, *Learning to be a Sage: Selections from the Conversations with Master Chu, Arranged Topically*, trans. Daniel K. Gardner (Berkeley: University of California Press, 1990); and Wm. Theodore de Bary, "Chu Hsi's Aims as an Educator," in *Neo-Confucian Education: The Formative Stage*, ed. Wm. Theodore de Bary and John W. Chaffee (Berkeley: University of California Press, 1989), 186–218.

6 Discussing the inspiration for the *Articles* Wing-Tsit Chan rejected the idea that Zhu Xi was guided by the regulations of Buddhist institutions. The impulse for this rejection may have come from the original designation of the *Articles* as *jieshi* 揭示, translated as "public announcement" or "posted notice" by Chan, which is quite close to the term *kaishi* 開示 (revelation), which frequently features in Buddhist texts. In Chan's opinion it was the Community Compact (*xiangyue* 鄉約) of Lü Dajun 呂大鈞 (1029–1080) that had influenced Zhu Xi's *Articles*. (See Wing-Tsit Chan, *Chu Hsi. His Life and Thought* (Hongkong: The Chinese University Press, 1987), 57–62, 177.) Cheng Nensheng posits that moral education was the main aim of Confucian academies and that this was reflected in all their functions, beginning with the *Articles*. (See Cheng Nensheng, *Zhongguo shuyuan wenxue jiaoyu yanjiu* (Research on Literature Education in China's Academies) (Beijing: Zhongguo shehui kexue chubanshe, 2014), 16–19.) Lü Zuqian 呂祖謙 (1137–1181) and the rules he drew up for his Lize Academy 麗澤書院 in 1167 are mentioned by Hoyt Tillman as a possible influence on the *Articles*. (See Hoyt Cleveland Tillman, *Confucian Discourse and Chu Hsi's Ascendancy*,

without serving in an official post, but already had produced an extensive scholarly output.[7] Just four years earlier he had, together with Lü Zuqian, edited the *Jinsilu* 近思錄 (*Reflections on Things at Hand*), a compilation of the most important passages from the works of Zhou Dunyi 周敦頤 (1017–1073), Cheng Hao 程顥 (1032–1086), Cheng Yi 程頤 (1033–1107), and Zhang Zai 張載 (1020–1077). In the years prior to the compilation of the *Jinsilu*, Zhu Xi had worked on his elucidations of the *Analects* and the *Mencius*, as well as written a commentary on Zhou Dunyi's *Tongshu* 通書 (*Penetrating the Book of Changes*).[8] The *Articles of Learning* were also drafted before the *Xiaoxue* 小學 (*Elementary Learning*), which was published by Zhu Xi in 1187 and also included the five cardinal relationships (*wulun* 五倫) at its beginning as the aim of all learning.[9]

In the following the full text of the *White Deer Grotto Articles for Learning* will be discussed with some added explanations and commentary:

> Between Father and Son there should be affection.
> Between Ruler and Minister there should be righteousness.
> Between Husband and Wife there should be proper distinction.
> Between Elder and Younger there should be proper order.
> Between Friends there should be faithfulness.
> To the right [above] are the items of the Five Instructions.
> Yao and Shun appointed Xie as Minister of Instruction to reverently set forth the Five Instructions, that is, these [Five Relationships]; Learning is a matter of learning these and that is all.[10]

---

112–113.) Wang Bin states that the Lü's regulations only influenced Zhu Xi in so far that he viewed them as superficial. Therefore, contrary to such detailed regulations he himself in his *Articles* tried not to rely on restrictions and prohibitions, but rather to give more encouraging guidelines for study. (Wang Bin, "Cong 'Bailudong shuyuan jieshi' kan Zhu Xi de xuegui linian (looking at Zhu Xi's Concept of Study Regulations from the *Bailudong Academy Articles of Learning*)," *Zibo shizhuan xuebao* 35, no. 1 (2014): 62).

7  For biographies of Zhu Xi see Wing-Tsit Chan, *Chu Hsi: His Life and Thought*; Julia Ching, *The Religious Thought of Chu Hsi* (Oxford: Oxford University Press, 2000); and Tillman, *Confucian Discourse and Chu Hsi's Ascendancy*.

8  See Zhu Xi and Lü Zuqian, *Reflections on Things at Hand*, trans. Wing-Tsit Chan (New York: Columbia University Press, 1967), 323.

9  See Theresa M. Kelleher, "Back to Basics: Chu Hsi's Elementary Learning (Hsiao-hsüeh)," in *Neo-Confucian Education: The Formative Stage*, ed. Wm. Theodore de Bary and John W. Chaffee (Berkeley: University of California Press, 1989), 219.

10  Translation (which slight changes) by Michael Kalton in Yi Hwang, *To Become a Sage*, 102. The original text of the regulations can be found in the different *Records of the Bailudong Academy* republished in the ZGLDSYZ 1: 359, 1: 574, 1: 905, 2: 94–95.

The five relationships are taken from the *Mencius* 3A:4, which also refers to a Minister Xie 契 instructing the people of them.[11] In his *Collected Commentary on the Mencius* (*Mengzi jizhu* 孟子集注) Zhu Xi, after some glosses on pronunciation and meaning, remarks on this particular passage:

> As man has a moral nature, [Mencius is] saying that all have such normal behavior in their nature. Yet if not educated, they will indulge in pleasure seeking and idleness and then will lose it. Therefore, the sages have installed ministers and taught the relationships to the people, just to retain this moral nature they naturally possess and nothing more.[12]

In a comment on an earlier passage (*Mencius* 3A:3) in the same chapter, Zhu Xi talks more concretely about *renlun*:

> *Xiang* 庠 (hamlet schools in antiquity) took the nurturing of elders as what is right, *Xiao* 校 (schools) took the education of the people as what is right, *Xu* 序 (local districts schools) took the exercise of archery as what is right, all of them were local schools. *Xue* 學 was the highest school of the country, through the whole time [of the three dynasties] it never had a different name. The relationships (*lun* 倫) are in sequence. Between father and son there should be affection, between ruler and minister there should be righteousness, between husband and wife there should be proper distinction, between elder and younger there should be proper order, between friends there should be faithfulness, these are the great relationships of man. *Xiang, Xu, Xue,* and *Xiao,* all clarified these and nothing more.[13]

As these schools of antiquity all engaged in the clarification of the cardinal relationships, it was just a natural choice for Zhu Xi to also put them at the center of his own academy. He combined the relationships with a short reference to their supposed origin during the reigns of the legendary Emperors Yao and Shun. Rather than a mere recapitulation of the classical importance put on the relationships, Zhu Xi's decision to put them at the beginning of his *Articles* shows how much, on one hand, he valued educational institutions as a

---

11  Mencius elaborated on this part originally found in the Canon of Shun (*Shundian* 舜典) in the *Book of Documents* (*Shangshu* 尚書); see Kŭm Changt'ae, *Sŏnghak sip'to wa t'oegye ch'ŏrhak ŭi kujo* (The Ten Diagrams of Sage Learning and the Structure of T'oegye's Philosophy) (Seoul: Sŏul taehakkyo ch'ulp'anbu, 2001), 114.
12  Zhu Xi, *Zhuzi quanshu* (Complete Writings of Master Zhu), Volume 6 (Shanghai: Shanghai guji chubanshe, 2002), 316.
13  Ibid., 311.

tool to regain the order of antiquity. On the other hand this shows how he thought the schools of his time had lost this focus and needed to return to it.

The following passages of the *Articles* reflect that the main influence in their drafting was Zhu Xi's composition of the *Jinsilu* and his continuous work on what would later become the *Collected Commentaries on the Four Books in Phrases and Paragraphs* (*Sishu zhangju jizhu* 四書章句集注).

> There are likewise five steps in the process of learning which are set forth to the left [below]. Broadly Study – Accurately Inquire – Carefully Think – Clearly Discriminate – Earnestly Practice.
> The four methods of study, inquiry, thinking, and discriminating are the essentials of investigating the principle.[14]

The first part of the quote is taken from the *Zhongyong* (*Doctrine of the Mean*); however, it also appears as a quotation by Cheng Yi in the second chapter on "The Essentials of Learning" in the *Jinsilu*: "Study extensively, inquire accurately, think carefully, sift clearly, and practice earnestly. Learning which neglects one of these is not learning."[15] Most of the following parts of the *Articles* can as well be found in the *Jinsilu*:

> The essentials of earnest practice at each stage are cultivating one's person, dealing with affairs, and treating others, these are arranged to the left [below].
> Integrity and trustworthiness in speech, earnestness and mindfulness in deed.[16]
> Restrain anger, block desires,[17] refer good to others, correct transgressions.[18]
> These are the essentials of cultivating one's person.
> Be correct according to what is right, and do not consider profit.
> Think only of seeking the Way, and do not calculate accomplishments.[19]
> These are the essentials of dealing with affairs.
> What you do not wish done to yourself, do not do to others.

---

14   Translation by Michael Kalton in Yi Hwang, *To Become a Sage*, 102.
15   Translation by Wing-Tsit Chan in Zhu Xi and Lü Zuqian, *Reflections on Things at Hand*, 69; A quotation expounding the meaning of the passage from Zhu Xi's *Zhongyong Huowen* 中庸或問 (*Several Questions on the Doctrine of the Mean*) can be found Ibid.
16   See Ibid., 58; *Jinsilu* 2.43; quote attributed to Cheng Hao, original in *Lunyu* 15.6.
17   See Ibid., 160; *Jinsilu* 5.9; quote attribute to Cheng Yi, original in *Yijing* 易經 (Book of Changes).
18   See Ibid., 154, *Jinsilu* 5.1; quote attributed to Zhou Dunyi.
19   See Ibid., 57, 294, *Jinsilu* 2.40 and 14.7, both attributed to Dong Zhongshu, original in *Hanshu* 漢書 (History of Han) in the biography of Dong.

When your activities do not succeed, reflect and seek the reason within yourself.[20]

These are the essentials of how to treat others.[21]

It becomes clear that the compilation work on the *Jinsilu* must have been a major inspiration for Zhu Xi's draft of the *White Deer Grotto Articles of Learning*. This also explains why among quotes from the *Classics*, he included a passage from the Biography of Dong Zhongshu 董仲舒 (179–104 BCE), found in the *Hanshu* 漢書 (*History of Han*). Even though Dong Zhongshu played an important part in the transmission of Confucian teachings during the Former Han dynasty (206 BCE–9 CE), he was never considered as part of the orthodox transmission of the Way by Zhu Xi. It therefore seems highly plausible that Zhu Xi, after finding it in the works of the Cheng brothers and including it in the *Jinsilu*, valued the brevity of the passage as it reflected his own convictions. While he obviously was aware of the locus classicus of all the quotes arranged in the *Articles*, the high frequency of passages also appearing in the *Jinsilu* suggests that Zhu Xi compiled the *Articles of Learning* as an even more condensed version of the ideas presented in the *Jinsilu*. While the *Jinsilu* was aimed at the "young man in the isolated village"[22] the *White Deer Grotto Academy Articles of Learning* were targeted at aspiring students who had already found their way into an educational institution. Posted on the wall in the lecture hall, they would serve as a reconfirmation of the purpose and process of learning during study and lecture sessions. Zhu Xi also used the *Articles* in this format in his Wuyi 武夷 and Zhulin 竹林 Study Halls (*jingshe* 精舍), as well as in the local schools when he served as official in Zhangzhou, Tanzhou, and Hunan.[23] It is therefore plausible that Zhu intended the *Articles* for all students, not just for those in his academy, just as the *Jinsilu* was to be used by everyone willing to study, and the *Articles* were not viewed as exclusively connected to academy education.

The *White Deer Grotto Articles* quickly found endorsement by the state. In 1241, shortly after Zhu Xi's own lifetime, Emperor Lizong 理宗 (r. 1224–1264) wrote the *White Deer Grotto Academy Articles of Learning* in his own hand for the Imperial College and demanded that they would be obeyed in every school

---

20 These two quotes are not included in the *Jinsilu*. The first passage is the very well-known golden rule as it appears in the *Lunyu* 12.2; and the second passage is from the *Mencius* 4A.4.
21 Translation by Michael Kalton in Yi Hwang, *To Become a Sage*, 102.
22 Translation by Wing-Tsit Chan in Zhu Xi, Lü Zuqian, *Reflections on Things at Hand*, 2.
23 See Li Bangguo, "Zhu Xi 'Bailudong shuyuan jieshi' de jiaoyu shijian he zhexue jichu (The Philosophical Basis and Educational Realization of Zhu Xi's *White Deer Grotto Academy Articles of Learning*)," *Hubei shifan xueyuan xuebao* 14, no. 1 (1994): 77.

of the empire.[24] Already before, the *Articles* had been adopted by other academies, e.g. in 1194 by the Yuelu Academy 岳麓書院 in Changsha, but as Zhu Xi himself at this time served as military commissioner (*anfushi* 安撫使) in Hunan this was probably done at his behest. Interestingly, the academy later changed the name of the *Articles* to *Master Zhu's Academy Articles of Instruction* (*Zhuzi shuyuan jiaotiao* 朱子書院教條) under which they can still be found hanging in the academy today.[25]

A more significant change, or addition, to the *Articles* was made by later headmaster of the White Deer Grotto Academy, Hu Juren 胡居仁 (1434–1484) in the early Ming dynasty. After becoming director of the academy for the first time in 1467, Hu drafted his own new regulations, which he called *Supplement to the White Deer Grotto Study Regulations* (*Xu Bailudong Xuegui* 續白鹿洞學規) consisting of the following six points:

> Set a true direction and establish the will.
> Foremost is the sincerity and reverence abiding in the mind.
> Broadly investigate events and principle to extend knowledge thoroughly.
> Examine subtleties as essential to consider one's response to events.
> Govern one's efforts as the way to bring oneself to completion.
> Put oneself in the place of things as the accomplishment to broaden the completion of things.[26]

As John Meskill points out, while Hu Juren's regulations in a sense mirror Zhu Xi's *Articles*, they also include changes that hint at the future developments of Confucian thought during the Ming period.[27] Wing-Tsit Chan called the focus on seriousness or sincerity in Hu Juren's oeuvre a "radical modification of Zhu

---

24  See Zhang Pinduan and Kim Hongsu, "Chu Hŭi sŏwŏn kyoyuk sasang e taehan Yi Hwang ŭi kyesŭng kwa paljŏn. Paengnoktong sŏwŏn kesi rŭl chungsim ŭro (Lee Hwang' Successions and Developments of Zhu Xi's thoughts in Seowon Education)," *Andonghak* 11 (2012): 220.

25  See Zhu Hanmin and Deng Hongbo, *Yuelu shuyuan shi* (History of the Yuelu Academy) (Changsha: Hunan jiaoyu chubanshe, 2013), 139–140.

26  Translation, with slight changes, by John Meskill, *Academies in Ming China: A Historical Essay* (Tucson: University of Arizona Press, 1982), 56.

27  Ibid. For other detailed studies of Hu Juren, his regulations and his general understanding of Confucian academies see Feng Huiming, "Hu Juren de 'Xu Bailudong xuegui' jiqi jiaoyu sixiang (Hu Juren's *Supplement to the 'White Deer Grotto Study Regulations'* and His Educational Thought)," *Jiangxi jiaoyu xueyuan xuebao* 31, no. 2 (2010): 112–115. Feng discusses the individual points of the regulations and Hu Juren's added quotes from the Classics. He argues that Hu's regulations are essentially a reprint of Zhu Xi's *Articles*; see also Zhang Jinsong, "Ming chu lixue jia Hu Juren de shuyuan jiaoyu shijian yu shuyuanguan lüelun (Short Discussion of Early Ming Lixue Scholar Hu Juren's Educational Academy Practice

Xi's order for learning and cultivation" as it gives a subordinated position to the extension of knowledge or investigation of principle that was so valued by the Song dynasty scholars.[28] This is certainly reflected in Hu's continuation of the *Articles of Learning* by his placing sincerity and reverence as a step between the establishment of a direction and the steps of learning. Besides these modifications, Hu Juren's supplement shows that Zhu Xi's *Articles*, originally called *jieshi*, by the early Ming were already widely understood and known as universal study regulations (*xuegui* 學規) applicable in all educational settings.

## 3  Textual Perception of the Articles in Chosŏn

The first documented official mention of the *Articles of Learning* in Korea can be found in the *Veritable Records of the Chosŏn Dynasty* (*Chosŏn Wangjo Sillok* 朝鮮王朝實錄) during the reign of King Sejong 世宗 (r. 1418–1450). In 1439 an official from Sŏnggyun'gwan 成均館, the royal academy in Seoul, by the name of Song Ŭlgae 宋乙開 (?–?),[29] requested the king to determine study rules for the official schools. The king relegated the request to be discussed among officials of the Ministry of Rites (Yejo 禮曹) and the Sŏnggyun'gwan, who proposed:

> To respectfully follow Master Zhu, who during the Chunxi period (1174–1189) in Nankang requested the court to [re]build the White Deer Grotto Academy and made rules [for it]. They are roughly like this: "Between father and son there should be affection, between ruler and minister there should be righteousness, between husband and wife there should be proper distinction, between elder and younger there should be proper order, between friends there should be faithfulness. To the right are the items of the Five Instructions. Yao and Shun appointed Xie as Minister of Instruction to reverently set forth the Five Instructions, that is these; learning is a matter of learning these and that is all." These words are only the main points. In the later edited *Elementary Learning*, not only by

---

and Understanding of the Academies)," *Jiangxi jiaoyu xueyuan xuebao* 31, no. 5 (2010): 101–105.

28  Wing-Tsit Chan, "The Ch'eng-Chu School of Early Ming," in *Self and Society in Ming Thought*, ed. Wm. Theodore de Bary (New York: Columbia University Press, 1970), 41–42.

29  There is little information about Song Ŭlgae. He passed the civil service examination in 1405 in fourth spot and worked as a Censor (*chŏngŏn* 正言) in the office of the censor-general. In 1439, he is identified as holding the concurrent post of "chubu" 注簿 of the Sŏnggyun'gwan, which could indicate his role was being in charge of procurement and management of the Sŏnggyun'gwans resources.

clarifying the relationships, but through establishing instruction as first and through making one's person mindful as last, there is nothing that is not furnished for the great method of cultivating one's character. Therefore, Xu Luzhai [Xu Heng 許衡 (1209–1281)] when he assembled his students spoke to them: "Today you will hear the first step of learning, if you are certain you wish to follow this, discard all verses and habits learned before this day and follow the *Elementary Learning*. Otherwise, look for another teacher." The students wholly said: "Yea." The gentlemen also day and night incessantly chants the Classics, is steadfast in his purpose and diligent in action, is personally the first and even in the severe cold or sweltering heat does not quit. Relying on precedents by the esteemed Master Zhu and Xu Luqi, the Sŏnggyun'gwan, the four study halls and to the local schools all should use the *Elementary Learning* as study rules.[30]

After the State Council (Ŭijŏngbu 議政府) had agreed with this assessment, it was enacted. There are several interesting parts in this record. Foremost, the *Articles of Learning* are mentioned only with regards to its containing the five relationships; it is instead the *Elementary Learning* that is suggested for implementation as study regulations for all state operated schools. The significance of the *Articles* is therefore in how the five relationships are articulated as expression of an ideal society and ultimate goal of learning, which as mentioned before also appears in the *Elementary Learning*. The sequence of study presented in the *Articles* is not discussed as a possible guideline for learning.

Moreover, how the five relationships are mentioned in this statement is also of interest. A modern day visitor to the Myŏngnyundang 明倫堂 (Hall of Clarifying Relationships), the lecture hall of the Sŏnggyun'gwan, in Seoul can still find the wooden board[31] inscribed with the *White Deer Grotto Articles of Learning* hanging on the beams of the hall.

The board with the *Articles* is on the right side of the hall facing west. Next to it is a separate board containing Zhu Xi's commentary on the *Articles*. Both are in the calligraphy of Song Chun'gil 宋浚吉 (1606–1672), who also composed most of the other boards containing regulations or admonitions hanging in the lecture hall.[32] There is no clear indication of when the boards

---

30   *Sejong Sillok* 21/9/29#5.
31   These inscribed wooden boards are called *hyŏnp'an* 懸板, or sometimes *p'yŏnaek* 扁額, in Korean. For a general study of extant boards in Korea see Im Nojik, "P'yŏnaek e taehan ihae (Understanding Wooden Plates)," in *Ttŭsi tamgin hyŏnp'an p'yŏnaek* (Wooden Plates Filled with Meaning), ed. Kim Pyŏngil (Andong: Han'guk kukhak chinhŭngwŏn, 2009), 238–251.
32   See Choi Da-eun, "Sŏnggyun'gwan hyŏnp'an yŏn'gu. Taesŏngjŏn gwa Myŏngnyundang p'yŏnaek ŭl chungsim ŭro (A Study on the Hanging Boards in Seonggyungwan. Focused

ILLUSTRATION 9.1    Wooden hanging board containing the "White Deer Grotto Regulations" in the Myŏngnyundang of the Sŏnggyun'gwan in Seoul.
SOURCE: PHOTO COURTESY OF AUTHOR

were created or hung. In 1658, Song Chun'gil had compiled important texts of Song dynasty Confucian scholars and presented them to the Crown Prince.[33] It is possible that these writings were the basis of the inscriptions on the boards. At first glance, the board seems to show the *White Deer Grotto Articles* similarly to how they can be found in the *Complete Writings of Zhu Xi* (*Zhuzi daquan* 朱子大全). However, on further comparison it becomes apparent that the reference to the minister Xie and the sage kings Yao and Shun has been left out of this particular display of the *Articles*. While the five relationships are listed and also marked as the five items (or goals) of instruction, the inscription afterwards immediately jumps to the statement that "learning is a matter of learning these and that is all." Little information on the history of the wooden board

---

on the Signboards of Daeseongjeon and Myeongnyundang)," *Sŏyehak yŏn'gu* 29 (2016): 147.

33   See Lee Bong-kyoo, "The Neo-Confucian Thought of Song Chun-gil and Its Meaning in the History of Philosophy," *Seoul Journal of Korean Studies* 11 (1998): 165. One of his students, Hwang Sejŏng 黃世楨 (?–?), mentions that Song transcribed the *Articles for Learning* and hung them in his own lecture hall, together with Yulgok Yi I's 栗谷 李珥 (1536–1584) *Rules for the Ŭnbyŏng Study Hall* and the *Rules for the Munhŏn Academy*, for the students to contemplate in the morning. See Hwang Sejŏng, "Yusa (Memorabilia)," in *Tongch'undang sŏnsaeng pyŏljip* (Separate Collected Works of Master Tongch'undang), Volume 9.

is available, making it difficult to explain this omission. Whether the passage was dropped due to concerns of space, aesthetics, or as a didactical measure to further emphasize the five relationships, therefore remains speculation. The existence of this omission and the reduction of the original text, however, show that Zhu Xi's *White Deer Grotto Articles of Learning* were not considered to be an untouchable text.

A third minor point of interest in the above statement from the *Vertiable Records of the Chosŏn Dynasty* is the inclusion of the story about Xu Heng lecturing his new students about the *Elementary Learning*.[34] First, it is presented slightly differently than in the original account where Xu mentions the *Elementary Learning* and the *Four Books* (*Sishu* 四書) as basis of all learning.[35] Second, it points towards a transmission of Zhu Xi's writings to Korea through the Mongol court in Beijing, where Xu Heng lectured.

The first Korean scholar who concentrated his scholarly efforts on Zhu Xi's *Articles of Learning* was Pak Yŏng 朴英 (1471–1540). Pak came from an important family and already at the age of seventeen, in 1487, went to China for the first time. He served in various military posts, including Second Minister in the Ministry of War (*Pyŏngjo ch'amp'an* 兵曹參判), and towards the end of his life as Military Commander of Left Yŏngnam (*Yŏngnam chwa chŏldosa* 嶺南左節度使). He went to Beijing again in the summer of 1519 and returned the next year, avoiding the literati purge at the court in Seoul. Already earlier he had lamented the poor education of many military men and sought to take up the study of Confucian texts himself. In a statement conferring a posthumous title to Pak, Kim Chaero 金在魯 (1682–1759) relates the following anecdote: "In the *kabin* year [1494], Pak entered the palace one night after he could not sleep and spoke while sobbing: 'Riding a horse and wielding a sword is a matter of bravery, nothing more. Men that do not study, how can they become gentlemen (*kunja* 君子)?' And thereupon he made up his mind up to return home."[36] After returning to his home in Miryang, Pak built a study close to the Nakdong River and sought out Chŏng Pung 鄭鵬 (1467–1540) as teacher. "Sindang [Chŏng Pung] knew he [Pak] had the quality to receive learning and invited

---

34   The anecdote is contained in the *Yuanwenlei* 元文類 (Categorized Literature from the Yuan) compiled by Su Tianjue 蘇天爵 (1294–1352) in 1334. It is part of a spirit path stele (inscription) *Shendao bei* 神道碑 in the *Mu'anji* 牧庵集 (Collected Works of Mu'an) of Yao Sui 姚燧 (1238–1313), a student of Xu Heng.

35   See Yao Sui, "Zhong shu zuo cheng Yao Wenxian gong shendaobei (Memorial stelae written by Assistant Director of the Left in the Secretariat Yao Wenxian)," in *Mu'anji*, SKQS ed. This version reads: 謂其徒曰: '曩所授受皆非. 今始聞進學之序. 若必欲相從, 當盡棄前習, 以從事于《小學四書》爲進德基. 不然, 當求他師.' 衆皆曰: '惟.'

36   Kim Chaero, "Sijang (Conferring the Posthumous Title)," in *Songdang sŏnsaeng munjip* (Collected Works of Songdang), 4:1b. All biographical information of Pak Yŏng is also found there.

him in. He bluntly asked: 'You are a military man, why do you want to study?' Pak replied: 'I regret, but I have lost my way like a flood coming down the mountain, I seek to study to know a direction, nothing more.' Sindang took the *Great Learning* and said: 'The Way of studying is in the investigation of things to extend knowledge. You ought to intensively read this book.' Pak returned to his study and without break read and re-read it."[37] The study of the *Great Learning* must have left an impression on Pak Yŏng as he returned to it often. He composed a diagram to clarify its meaning and wrote a text called *Method of Reading the Great Learning* (*Tok Taehak Pŏp* 讀大學法). During his time as Magistrate (*pusa* 府使) of the northern frontier town Kanggye from 1516 to 1518, he also composed a text called *Explanations of the White Deer Grotto Regulations* (*Paengnoktong kyu hae* 白鹿洞規解). Kim Chaero describes the *Explanations* in the following way: "[Pak] followed Master Zhu and supplemented it with several Confucian sayings. At the end he himself wrote a postscript again explaining [it] clearly, to teach the scholars of Kanggye and for them to transform the people there."[38] The *Explanations* comprise the separate passages of the *Articles of Learning* with added quotes from the Classics, the *Mencius*, the *Lunyu*, the Cheng brothers, and other foundational Neo-Confucian texts—in a sense, reengineering the classical sources used for the original *Articles*. However, Pak Yŏng added two quotations from the *Lunyu* at the end of the regulations: "The Master said, 'Shen, my doctrine is that of an all-pervading unity.' The disciple Zeng replied, 'Yes'" (*Lunyu* 4.15), and "Yan Yuan asked how the government of a country should be administered. The Master said, 'Follow the seasons of Xia. Ride in the state carriage of Yin. Wear the ceremonial cap of Zhou. Let the music be the Shao with its pantomimes. Banish the songs of Zheng, and keep far from specious talkers. The songs of Zheng are licentious; specious talkers are dangerous'" (*Lunyu* 15.11).[39] Pak himself explains: "The two quotations to the right [above], I have obtained from the *Lunyu* and written them at the end of the regulations to demonstrate to students that these regulations undoubtedly can be put into action and to show their constant exquisiteness reaching [up to] the Way of governing a country."[40] Here Pak's background as a seasoned government and military official stands out, connecting the *Articles of Learning* not to individual learning, but to the rightful governance of the state.

---

37   *Songdang sŏnsaeng munjip*, 4:2a.
38   *Songdang sŏnsaeng munjip*, 4:5a.
39   Both translations from the *Lunyu* are by James Legge.
40   Pak Yŏng, "Paengnoktong kyu hae (Explanations of the White Deer Grotto Regulations)," in *Songdang sŏnsaeng munjip*, 1:19a.

> Among the several articles of the regulations, all take sincerity and reverence as the foremost. If one does not take reverence as the foremost, then there is definitely no place to start one's efforts. In momentary self-reflection, reverence naturally occurs. If one is capable of reverence, one can comfortably hold on to it. There is no other method of preserving and nourishing it. By clearly holding on to reverence, one is closest to it.[41]

Pak Yŏng continues with several references to the *Great Learning* and its ultimate goal of renewing the people, which he also connects to rightful governance and law. This topic is also put forward in a postscript to the *Explanations*, the author of which remains unknown.[42]

> The explanations to the right [above] are all obtained from the minds of the gentlemen of the past, making it not easy for someone to understand them. Generally, all things under heaven emerge from one and all obtain one principle. Therefore, one can say that the principle is never opposed to itself. How much more so with humanness? There is no distinction between past and present, between far and near, between sage and fool. All are of the same mind and principle. Shun was a man from the Eastern Barbarians. King Wen was a man from [near to] the Western Barbarians. They were separated in time more than a thousand years and they were apart in space more than a thousand miles, yet their success in imposing their will on the Middle Kingdom was like two parts of a tally that fit together perfectly.[43] It can be clearly seen that this is the confirmation that principle cannot be two. Following these words how can the people of Kanggye [Ch'ŏngwŏn 清源] be different from the people of the south? Those who possess official rank in riding and shooting do not have time for learning. Therefore, the direction of the [five] cardinal relationships is not yet known [to them]. These people who do not turn their aim towards study are certainly wrong and the [text] above has nothing to teach them. Now, the rulers respect and study Confucius and Mencius and

---

41 Ibid.
42 Kim Chaero's above statement seems to suggest Pak wrote the postscript himself. Kŭm Changt'ae follows this view; see Kŭm Changt'ae, *Sŏnghak sip'to wa t'oegye ch'ŏrhak ŭi kujo*, 117. Chang Yunsu marks the author as unknown; see Chang Yunsu, "Songdang Pak Yŏng ŭi tohakchŏk hakp'ung kwa sŏngnihak chŏk sayu (Song Dang Pak Yŏng's Academic Tradition and Speculation on Metaphysics)," *Han'gukhak Nonjip* 66 (2017): 360. The postscript mentioned by Kim could also refer to the short statement by Pak after the two added quotations from the *Lunyu* at the end of the *Explanations*.
43 From *Mencius* 4B.29.

govern in the manner of the three dynasties. Those who have official rank in reading and study, but cannot easily advance to the territory of the sage, use the *White Deer Grotto Regulations* of Master Zhu, which were declared (揭示) to the four directions. They are the northern star of gradual advancement to thorough understanding. And now the gentlemen has added explanations, giving them even more strength. How could this not deepen their esteemed meaning? In a later age the people of a remote area can know the ways of piety to parents, respect to older brothers, loyalty to the monarch and faith towards one's friends, so that scholars respecting rulers and family come forward and can make a name for themselves in the capital for the time to come. If not for these explanations, who then could? 18th day of the sixth month of *muin* [1518], written in the Ŏch'ŏn lodge/posthouse.[44]

Again the *Articles* are understood as a text that could help to produce loyal subjects if taught to the common people. Especially the people of the border regions, like Kanggye, who were mostly trained to become soldiers and not scholars, are viewed as the perfect audience of the *Articles* as they concisely provide the right direction and the tools for study.[45] Remarkably, there are no references or discussions of Confucian academies in the *Explanations* or in any other extant work of Pak Yŏng. It seems that for him, the *Articles of Learning* had no specific relation to Confucian academies. This further reflects Pak's own background as during his life no academies existed on the Korean peninsula,[46] but also shows that the *Articles* in general were understood as more universal regulations on teaching and study.

The *Explanations of the White Deer Grotto Regulations* by Pak Yŏng also bear a curious resemblance to Hu Juren's supplement of Zhu Xi's *Articles*, in that both authors relied on quotations from the Classics and later scholars to expound the meaning of the individual articles in a quite similar way. Additionally, both stress the notions of sincerity (Chin. *cheng*, Kor. *sŏng* 誠) and reverence (Chin. *jing*, Kor. *kyŏng* 敬) as most important, which is something that in this combination cannot be found in the original *Articles*.[47] It is,

---

44  "Paengnoktong kyu hae pal (Postscript to the Explanations of the White Deer Grotto Regulations)," in *Songdang sŏnsaeng munjip*, 3:5b–6a. There is also a text by Hwang Hyohŏn 黃孝獻 (1491–1532) that is rather short and just mentions that the explanations by Pak Yŏng are not to be ignored by scholars. See *Songdang sŏnsaeng munjip*, 3:6a–6b.

45  See Chung Soon-woo, "The Nature and Educational Activities of Sungyang Academy in Kaesŏng," in this volume, 69–71, for a discussion of the cultural bias towards the northern Korean regions.

46  Pak Yŏng himself was later venerated, among others, in Kŭmo Academy 金烏書院 in Kyŏngsang province and Songgye Academy 松溪書院 in Ch'ungch'ŏng province.

47  Hu Juren writes; 主誠敬以其心, Park Yŏng writes: 皆以誠敬爲主.

however, difficult to construe any connection between the two texts and while Pak quotes some Chinese scholars of the Yuan dynasty, like Hu Bingwen 胡炳文 (1250–1333), in his other writings, no Ming scholars nor their works are mentioned.

It was none other than T'oegye Yi Hwang 退溪 李滉 (1501–1570), who later criticized Pak Yŏng's interpretation of the *Articles* for his overt emphasis on sincerity and reverence.

> As for his saying that reverence is foremost, it does not yet amount to a grave mistake, despite some pressing mistakes and faulty reasoning. In saying that sincerity is foremost, there are many more errors. Teaching has to be done in the proper sequence. Words have to be valued and chosen at the right time. Now, hastily discussing the integral substance and great function of the Way and extending it to sincerity expresses no beginning, but a fault.[48]

In a letter to Hwang Chullyang 黃俊良 (1517–1563) T'oegye discusses several other errors in the *Explanations* and also takes issue with the two quotes from the *Lunyu* that Pak had added.[49] He also connects Pak's interpretation of Zhu Xi's *Articles* to his background as a military official and even though praising him as a great man, T'oegye views his explanation as insufficient. Yet, he also does not connect the *Articles* to Confucian academies in his criticism.

> This person [Pak Yŏng], to lift himself out of the common customs, threw away his weaponry to study and had continued to think about the Way while being a military man. And although he encountered humiliation in this, he was not discouraged, but even took the words of former worthies on teaching and added commentary so the world could understand them. Indeed one can resolutely say that he is a great man [*taejangbu* 大丈夫]. Regrettably, his views are rather scattered and insufficient.[50]

Of course, T'oegye Yi Hwang in 1568 himself produced the probably most important interpretation, both in image and text, of the *White Deer Grotto Articles of Learning* in Korea. The inclusion of the *Articles* in his *Sŏnghak Sipto* 聖學十

---

48  TGCS 19:215b.
49  See Kŭm Changt'ae, *Sŏnghak sip'to wa t'oegye ch'ŏrhak ŭi kujo*, 117; and Chang Yunsu, "Songdang Pak Yŏng ŭi tohakchŏk hakp'ung kwa sŏngnihak chŏk sayu," 360–363. A full English translation of this letter can be found in Yi Hwang, *A Korean Confucian Way of Life and Thought. The Chasŏngnok by Yi Hwang,* trans. Edward Y.J. Chung (Honolulu: University of Hawai'i Press, 2016), 107–113.
50  TGCS 19:217a.

圖 (*Ten Diagrams of Sage Learning*) as the fifth diagram surely made the *Articles*, and with them the White Deer Grotto Academy, even more well known in Korea. The *Sŏnghak Sipto* was intended as a teaching aide for the young King Sŏnjo 宣祖 (r. 1567–1608) and for this T'oegye had arranged the texts he viewed as most important to acquire the proper method of learning.[51] Following the *Great Learning* as well as the *Elementary Learning*, the *Diagram of the White Deer Grotto Regulations* (*Paengnoktong kyu to* 白鹿洞規圖) forms a conclusion to these three diagrams setting up the correct sequence of instruction.[52]

The creation of diagrams to educate the royal house on matters of scholarship or the Confucian Way was nothing novel by the time T'oegye created the *Sŏnghak Sipto*. Usage of the diagrammatical format was popularized by early Song Confucians, like Zhou Dunyi, and provided a certain prestige to the creator, resulting in quite a few Korean scholars trying their hand at the composition of such diagrams. Their succinct format was considered perfect for introductory texts to arouse interest in the students and guide them through their basic meaning. Students were not expected to immediately gain thorough understanding of the meaning behind the diagram, but to continuously study and meditate on it as their scholarship proceeded. Consequently, the diagrams were supposed to be always visible to validate gained knowledge and to reaffirm correct progression.[53]

In his comments to the diagram, T'oegye focuses on the five relationships as the main point of the *Articles*, stating that their realization is the purpose of all learning and self-cultivation.[54] His arrangement of the *Articles* also seems to emphasize a dichotomy, rather than a hierarchy, between study and practice. The inclusion of the *Articles* in the *Sŏnghak Sipto* must have surely spurred their perception among the literati and especially among scholars that considered themselves as *sarim* 士林, the same faction that actively espoused the academy system opposite the supposedly corrupt state-school system. Therefore, the role of the T'oegye's diagram cannot be underestimated, especially since T'oegye himself played an important part in the spread of Confucian academies in Chosŏn Korea.[55]

---

51  See Yi Hwang, *To Become a Sage*, 24–28.
52  Ibid., 101.
53  See Vladimír Glomb, "Circulating Pictures: Confucian Diagrams, Ch'ŏnmyŏng to and Intellectual Debate in 16th Century Korea," in *Bochumer Jahrbuch zur Ostasienforschung* 39/2016 (München: Iudicium, 2017), 52–54.
54  See Yi Hwang, *To Become a Sage*, 105–106.
55  Among the large number of later Korean texts concerned with the *Articles of Learning*, two more examples should briefly be mentioned here. The first one is Yun Hyu's 尹鑴 (1617–1680) short *Explanation of the Meaning of the White Deer Grotto Regulations* (*Paengnoktong kyu sŏgŭi* 白鹿洞規釋義), which connects the *Articles* with the Ming scholar

# THE WHITE DEER GROTTO ACADEMY ARTICLES IN KOREA

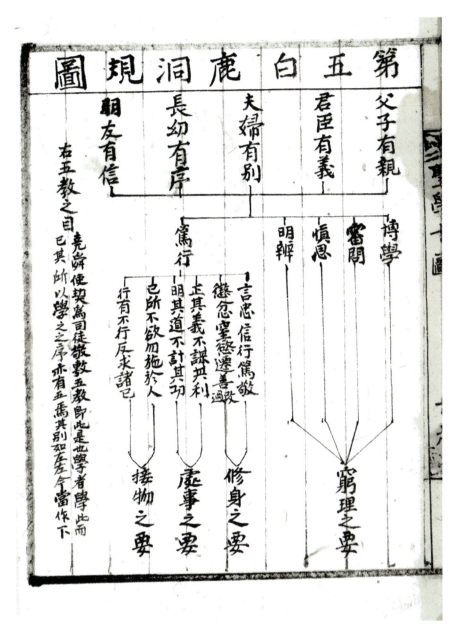

ILLUSTRATION 9.2   Handwritten version of the *Diagram of the White Deer Grotto Regulations* as included in the *Ten Diagrams of Sage Learning* by Yi Hwang, produced in the 18th or 19th century.
SOURCE: PRIVATE COLLECTION BERLIN

## 4   Institutional Perceptions of the *Articles* in Chosŏn

While his discussion of the *Articles* in the *Ten Diagrams of Sage Learning* mentions their origins in the White Deer Grotto Academy and shortly expands on the history of the academy, T'oegye does not further connect the *Articles of Learning* explicitly to Confucian academies, which at this point in time had already appeared on the Korean Peninsula.

The first academy in Chosŏn was the White Cloud Grotto Academy (Paegundong sŏwŏn 白雲洞書院), founded in P'unggi county by Magistrate Chu Sebung 周世鵬 (1495–1554) in 1543, which a few years later was royally chartered as Sosu Academy 紹修書院.[56] Not only in name, but also in the circumstances of its establishment, Chu Sebung openly connected his academy to Zhu Xi and his revival of the White Deer Grotto Academy. Answering critical voices complaining that the building of an academy was excessive in a time of drought, he justified his actions, as is documented in the *Chukkyeji* 竹溪誌 (*Records of Bamboo Stream*):

> When we observe Zhu Xi at Nankang, during the period of one year he ordered the reparation of the White Deer Grotto Academy; established a shrine to Confucius; set up a shrine to the five teachers and one to the three masters; and built an imposing pavilion to Garrison Officer Liu [Ningzhi]. This was the time when the Jin were plundering and attacking China. The world was at war. [...] Now at the "old home" of An Hyang, if one wishes to spread cultivation, one must begin with An Hyang. I am nobody, and this is a time of peace. However, I am in charge of an area. In this one county seat, I must assume responsibility and exert myself to the utmost. I have dared to set up this shrine and construct this academy; to supply it with paddy fields and to collect books for it; all in accord with the example of the White Deer Grotto Academy.[57]

---

Fang Xiaoru's 方孝孺 (1357–1402) *Four Admonitions of Family Models* (*Jiafan sizhen* 家範四箴) into a poem for easier memorization. Second is the *Extended Meaning of the White Deer Grotto Regulations* (*Paengnoktong kyu yŏnŭi* 白鹿洞規衍義) by Kang P'irhyo 姜必孝 (1764–1848) in which Kang tried to synthesize the teachings of T'oegye and Yulgok. He also modeled his own study after Zhu Xi's academy and wrote a supplement to the *Jinsilu*.

56    The circumstances around the establishment and chartering of this academy are described by Milan Hejtmanek in "The Elusive Path to Sagehood: Origins of the Confucian Academy System in Korea Chosŏn Korea," *Seoul Journal of Korean Studies* 26, no. 2 (December 2013): 233–268.

57    Chu Sebung, "Chukkyeji sŏ (Introduction to the Records of Bamboo Stream)," in *Chukkyeji* (Records of Bamboo Stream), 1a–6a. Translation, with minor changes, by Milan Hejtmanek in "The Elusive Path to Sagehood," 251–252.

As Milan Hejtmanek has shown, Chu's motivations for the foundation of the academy were linked to his relationship with the locally influential An family, whose ancestor An Hyang 安珦 (1243–1306) was worshipped in the shrine of the academy and therefore carried a slight flavor of opportunism.[58] Through evoking Zhu Xi's revival of the White Deer Grotto Academy, Chu not only sought to silence critics and find legitimization for his project, but also connected himself, the academy, and the area of P'unggi to this story of Zhu Xi's academy. A look at the last two verses of the *Todonggok* 道東曲 (*Song of the Way in the East*), a tune written by Chu Sebung that was to be performed in front of the spirit tablet of An Hyang in the shrine of the academy, reveals the extent of this connection:

> Human greed was endless like vast waves flooding the earth until after 1,500 years Huiweng 晦翁 [Zhu Xi] came forward and made reverence the fundament of the dam and continued the magnificent way of Zhongni 仲尼 [Confucius].
> After thousands of years in Korea a real Confucian descended and Mt. Sobaek was like Mt. Lu and the Chukkye was like the waters of Lian,[59] in reviving learning, defending the Way and respecting rituals he was to some extent like Hui'an [Zhu Xi][60] and his achievements were great. Once our Way came to the east, where else could a similar scenery be found?[61]

---

58   Hejtmanek, "The Elusive Path to Sagehood," 258–259. An Hyang was usually viewed as an important figure in the transmission of Zhu Xi's teachings to Korea during Koryŏ times, see Martina Deuchler, *The Confucian Transformation of Korea: A Study of Society and Ideology* (Cambridge, MA: Harvard University Press, 1995), 14–24.

59   Mt. Sobaek (Sobaeksan 小白山) is a mountain next to the Sosu Academy, Mt. Lu (Lushan 廬山) is the mountain the White Deer Grotto Academy is located below. Chukkye 竹溪 (Bamboo stream) is the stream next to Sosu Academy and springs from Mt. Sobaek, Lianxi 濂溪 (Lian stream) springs from Mt. Lu (but is also the posthumous name of Zhou Dunyi, as he had built a study at the same stream in 1062).

60   While not explicitly mentioned the last part refers to An Hyang as bringing the Way of Zhu Xi to the East (Korea). Zhu Xi's style name was Huiam 晦庵 (Kor. Hoeam), following this An Hyang choose Hoehŏn 晦軒 (Chin. Huixuan) as his style. For more on the song see Kim Mun'gi, "Sŏwŏn kyoyuk kwa Sinjae Chu Sebung (Academy Education and Sinjae Chu Sebung)," *Kugŏ kyoyuk yŏn'gu* 38 (2005): 18–19.

61   Chu Sebung, "Todonggok kujang (Song of the Way in the East in Nine Verses)," in *Chukkyeji*, 1b:8a–9a; The song is composed in the then popular style of *kyŏnggich'e ga* 景幾體歌, praising the local area. Especially An Ch'uk 安軸 (1282–1348), a member of the An family who from 1544 was also venerated in the White Cloud Grotto Academy, was famous for poems and songs in this style. See Ch'oe Yongsu, "Kyŏnggich'e ga e taehan Chu Sebung ŭi insik t'aedo (Chu Sebung's Attitude towards *Kyŏnggich'e ga*)," *Hanminjok ŏmunhak* 38 (2001): 256.

It becomes evident that Chu understood, or at least sought to portray, the whole area of P'unggi as a reincarnation of Nankang during the Southern Song dynasty. By equating the local surroundings to this faraway place, both in time and space, An Hyang came to embody Zhu Xi's role and also figured in the transfer of the narrative of the White Deer Grotto Academy to Korea. In his official biography in the *Myŏngjong Sillok*, Chu was later criticized for using similar hyperbole in his biography of Yi Haeng 李荇 (1478–1534), comparing him to figures like Zhuge Liang 諸葛亮, Kong Rong 孔融, and Liu Xiang 劉向.[62]

Chu's focus on the rites for An Hyang is also reflected in his academy regulations (*wŏn'gyu* 院規) that are mostly concerned with the veneration of worthies, the correct execution of the rites, and financial matters, rather than the goal of learning, matters of curriculum or lecture proceedings. The *Articles* seemed to have played a minor role for Chu Sebung's perception of Zhu Xi's academy. They are included among many other texts connected to the White Deer Grotto Academy and Zhu Xi in volume five of the *Chukkyeji*, titled Miscellaneous Records (*chamnok* 雜錄).[63] Chu was criticized by both T'oegye and Hwang Chullyang for this, especially for mixing matters of the academy and Zhu Xi's writings on education with the records of the An family in the *Chukkyeji* and by this giving the work a confusing character.[64]

Despite all his criticism, T'oegye later championed the chartering of the White Cloud Grotto Academy.[65] Since he personally hoped to see the spread of Confucian academies, he actively supported other academies as well. He (re)connected the somewhat renowned *Articles of Learning* to the concept of the Confucian academy and expanded the admiration given to Zhu Xi's academy to all Confucian academies, thereby legitimizing their spread in Chosŏn. The regulations he drafted for Isan Academy 伊山書院 were later adopted by

---

62  See Hejtmanek, "The Elusive Path to Sagehood," 248–250, original in *Myŏngjong Sillok* 9/7/2#3: 嘗作李荇行狀, 極其稱譽, 至以忠比劉向, 節比孔融, 勇比諸葛亮. 以此識者鄙之.

63  For the publication history of the *Chukkyeji* see Ok Yŏngjŏng, "Chukkyeji ŭi p'yŏnch'an kwa p'anbon e kwanhan sŏjijŏk yŏn'gu (A Bibliographical Study of Compilation and Edition of the *Chukkyeji*)," *Sŏjihak yŏn'gu* 31 (2005): 297–321.

64  See TGCS 12:25b; *Chukkyeji* 1b:14a–17a; and also Chu Sebung's reply in *Chukkyeji* 1b:17b–19b.

65  See Hejtmanek, "The Elusive Path to Sagehood," 259–261. Interestingly, Deng Hongbo and Li Bangguo both propose that the royal chartering system of academies in Korea was modeled after accounts of the White Deer Grotto Academy being bestowed books and land by the emperor. See Deng Hongbo, "Zhu Xi yu Chaoxian shuyuan (Zhu Xi and Korean Academies)," *Guizhou jiaoyu xueyuan xuebao* 1 (1989): 46; Li Bangguo, "Zhu Xi yu Bailudong shuyuan zai Chaoxian Riben de yingxiang (The Influence of Zhu Xi and the White Deer Grotto Academy in Korea and Japan)," *Hubei shifan xueyuan xuebao* 15, no. 1 (1995): 99.

other academies in the area and included the *White Deer Grotto Articles of Learning* in their fifth point:

> In the Myŏngnyun Hall of the Sŏnggyun'gwan the *Four Admonitions* (*Siwuzhen* 四勿箴) of Master Yi Chuan [Cheng Yi],[66] Master Huiam's *White Deer Grotto Regulations* and his *Ten Instructions* (*Zhuzi shixun* 朱子十訓),[67] and Chen Maojing's [Chen Bo 陳栢, ?–1565] *Admonitions to Rise Early and Retire Late* (*Suxingyemei zhen* 夙興夜寐箴)[68] are written and hung and their meaning is good. These should also be posted on the walls of the academy to advise and admonish each other.[69]

The *Articles* were grouped together with other regulations or admonitions that were to be hung in the lecture hall of the academies, following the example of the Sŏnggyun'gwan in the capital. Oksan Academy 玉山書院 and Sŏak Academy 西岳書院, both in the Kyŏngju area, followed these regulations as can be seen from their records.[70] Inside Sŏak Academy and in Yongsan Academy 龍山書院, also located close to Kyŏngju, the wooden boards inscribed with the *Articles* and other admonitions and regulations are still hanging today. However, the *Articles* were not only hung in the Sŏnggyun'gwan and the academies, but can sometimes also be found in local or village schools (*hyanggyo* 鄉校). The regulations of the Pokch'ŏn hyanggyo 福川鄉校 in Chŏlla province for example state: "The *White Deer Grotto Regulations* of Master Zhu [here as 朱文公] are always to be written and hung in the lecture hall and the dormitories, for the students to advise and admonish each other."[71] These regulations were written in 1585 by Kim Puyun 金富倫 (1531–1598), a student of T'oegye Yi Hwang, and were designed to provide the local schools with comparable regulations to the schools in the capital.[72] The same regulations were used in the

---

66   Also known as *sizhen* 四箴, a text by Cheng Yi based on *Lunyu* 12.1.
67   Also known as *Master Zhu's Instruction of the Ten Regrets* (*Zhuzi shi hui xun* 朱子十悔訓). A text mentioning improper behavior that one will regret later on.
68   The *Admonitions to Rise Early and Retire Late* most likely have their origin in Shangcai Academy 上蔡書院 in Taizhou (in Zhejiang province) and are also included in the *Ten Diagrams of Sage Learning*.
69   TGCS 41:647. See also Pak Chŏngbae, "Chosŏn sidae ŭi hangnyŏng mit hakkyu (Rules and Regulations in Confucian Academies of Chosŏn Period)," *Han'guk kyoyuk sahak* 28, no. 2 (2006): 226–228.
70   *Oksan sŏwŏn chi* (Records of Oksan Academy) (Kyŏngsan: Yŏngnam taehakkyo ch'ulp'anbu, 1993), 36–37 (the *Articles* are also still hanging in the lecture hall of Oksan Academy); and *Sŏak chi* (Records of Sŏak), 62b–63a.
71   See Pak, "Chosŏn sidae ŭi hangnyŏng mit hakkyu," 218.
72   Ibid., 217–218.

Kyŏngju hyanggyo 慶州鄉校, where the *Articles* are also still hanging in the lecture hall.[73] The wooden board of the Kyŏngju local school, containing the *Articles* and the *Admonitions to Rise Early and Retire Late*, is quite similar to the board hanging in Sŏak Academy, just a few miles away.

The specific use of the *Articles* in this context suggests a close relation to a certain area, i.e. Kyŏngju, or a certain school, i.e. the institutions associated with the disciples of T'oegye. However, the *Articles* could also be found hanging in other places. An example describing how they were physically present in an academy, far away from Kyŏngju, can be found in the writings of Sim Cho 沈潮 (1694–1756). His diary records a visit to Tobong Mountain close to Seoul in September 1754, in which he describes the layout of the lecture hall of Tobong Academy 道峰書院 in detail.

> I came down the mountain and galloped to the entrance of the Tobong hollow. After getting off the horse I sat for a good while, until my fellow travelers arrived on foot and we entered the academy. After paying respects at the shrine, I sat in the lecture hall. The lecture hall is named the Hall of Continuous Enlightenment (Kyegaedan 繼開堂). Hoisted on its northern wall are the four characters "Tobong Academy" on the royally bestowed wooden plate. On the first eave of the northern wall the records of the academy, as written by Master Yulgok, are hoisted towards the east. In the west the poems of Master U [Song Siyŏl] are hoisted. It was Master Hansujae [Kwŏn Sangha] who wrote them. Underneath the hanging wooden plate with the name of the hall, to the east are attached the lecture rules of Hanch'ŏn, to the west the study rules of Ŭnbyŏng. On the east wall the *Admonitions for a Mindfulness Studio* are hoisted; on the west wall the *White Deer Grotto Regulations* are attached. The shrine is built in the north; the lecture hall in the south, and between them is a wide courtyard.[74]

Besides showing the presence of the *Articles* in the lecture hall of the academy, certainly to be used during lecture and study sessions, this short passage also reveals another function of the public display of the *Articles*. Sim Cho's description of the wooden plates hanging in the lecture hall of Tobong Academy infuse it with a certain identity. Tobong Academy was founded in 1573 to

---

73   See Yŏngnam Taehakkyo. Minjok Munhwa Yŏn'guso (ed.), *Kyŏngbuk hyanggyo charyo chipsŏng* (Collection of Kyŏngbuk Local School Materials) (Kyŏngsan: Yŏngnam taehakkyo ch'ulp'anbu, 1992), 26–27.

74   Sim Cho, "Tobong-haeng Ilgi (Diary of the Travel to Tobong)," in *Chŏng Chwawa sŏnsaeng Chip* (Collected Writings of Master Chŏng Chwawa), 12:311a–312b.

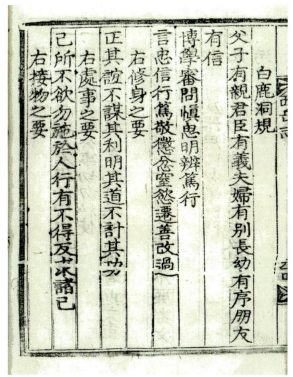

ILLUSTRATION 9.3
Academy rules from the *Records of Sŏak*, 64b.
SOURCE: PRIVATE COLLECTION BERLIN

venerate the Confucian literatus Cho Kwangjo 趙光祖 (1482–1519). In 1696, Song Siyŏl 宋時烈 (1607–1689) was added to the shrine of the academy. Presentation of his writings, together with the writings of his student Kwŏn Sangha 權尚夏 (1641–1721), as well as those of Yulgok Yi I 栗谷李珥 (1536–1584),[75] place the academy in a specific Korean academic tradition, much as the presence of the certain boards in the academies and schools in the Kyŏngju area identify another scholarly tradition.[76] In this setting the wooden boards inscribed with the *Articles,* which could be found among most major academies and some local schools, irrespective of any factional connections, established

---

[75] See Vladimír Glomb's contribution on Yulgok's views on academy education, "Shrines, Sceneries, and Granary: The Constitutive Elements of the Confucian Academy in 16th Century Korea," in this volume, 321–325.

[76] Yulgok Yi I, Song Siyŏl and Kwŏn Sangha are often considered to be part of the so-called Kiho faction. The Kyŏngju area is usually associated with T'oegye Yi Hwang and the so-called Yŏngnam faction.

and communicated a general connection to the Zhu Xi, the *Daoxue* tradition, and the White Deer Grotto Academy.[77]

## 5  Ritual and Aesthetic Perceptions of the Articles in Chosŏn

Looking for descriptions of the practical use of the *Articles* in academies or other institutions, there is ample evidence that the regulations were ritually recited by the students on multiple occasions. One example can be found in Yulgok Yi I's *Hakkyo mobŏm* 學校模範 (*Model for Schools*), a text designed to introduce young students to the correct method of studying the Confucian way.[78] Article three of the text bears a close resemblance to the *Articles*. "Once the student has completed gaining control of his demeanor in a Confucian way, then he must through reading and study illuminate the principle; only then will he advance in learning and will not lose direction. Receiving instruction from a teacher, his study will be broad, his inquiry will be accurate, his thinking will be cautious, and his discrimination will be clear."[79] This is of course a rephrasing of the passage from the *Zhongyong*, or the central sequence of study in the *Articles*. Yulgok's direct mention of the *Articles* in the last point of the *Hakkyo mobŏm* underlines not only his knowledge of the rules, but also his regard for them and the importance they must have had in his eyes toward educational procedure.

> Article 16. Reading Methods
> On the day of new moon of every month, all students gather together in the study hall. With their hands folded they bow to the ground paying their respects to the shrine, and keep sitting until the ritual is concluded. If the school master is present, he sits to the north wall and the students gather on three sides around him. The supervisor (or if he is absent an official or a person well-versed in reading can replace him) reads out the *White Deer Grotto Articles of Learning* and the *Model for Schools* once in a reverberating voice. Thereafter, there is discussion amongst each other

---

77  A claim that Tobong Academy was similar to the White Deer Grotto Academy was used in 1733 in order to gain a tax exemption for the fields of the academy. *Yŏngjo Sillok* 9/6/16#1, Original: 我朝道峰書院與朱文公白鹿洞書院相類. 道峰山明水麗, 八路罕比, 而先正臣趙光祖, 宋時烈所享之院也. 昔有賜給田結, 今入於出稅之中, 請依前還給.

78  See Vladimír Glomb, "Reading the Classics till Death: Yulgok Yi I and the Curriculum of Chosŏn Literati," *Studia Orientalia Slovaca* 11 2 (2012): 321.

79  YGCS 15:35a.

and encouragement for practical study; if the school master is present he raises questions.[80]

Here the *Articles*, together with Yulgok's own *Model for Schools,* are the texts ritually read during lecture gatherings. This undoubtedly served as a form of mutual affirmation, not only of the schools or academies' shared identity, but also to remind the students of the actual purpose of studying inside the institution. The reading, or rather chanting, of the *Articles* in a ritualized manner was also meant to instill ideas through regular reiteration.

A similar usage of the *Articles* can be found in the lecture regulations (*kanggyu* 講規) of Soksil Academy 石室書院.

> After the lecture the assistant on duty reads the *White Deer Grotto Regulations* and the *Model for Schools*. The *Model for Schools* is divided into three parts. [...] At every gathering they are read in this order. (In the months of the sacrifices, the inscriptions on the steles must also be read in order to increase remembrance and admiration [for the enshrined worthy]). Even though there can be no more lecture that day, if time is left questions and doubts can be discussed and solved, but heterodox and unrelated books are not allowed to be read.[81]

The lecture regulations of Soksil Academy were written in the middle of the 18th century by Kim Wŏnhaeng 金元行 (1702–1772).[82] Again such inclusions of the *Articles* in the fixed schedule of the institution are to be found not only in Confucian academies, but in village or town schools as well. The Yŏnggwang hyanggyo 靈光鄉校 in Southern Chŏlla required its students to read the *Articles* aloud at the monthly lectures and daily classes to honor Zhu Xi.[83]

A more personal approach to the *Articles*, nevertheless connected to an academy, can be found in the writings of Kim Inhu 金麟厚 (1510–1560), who had studied together with T'oegye at the Sŏnggyun'gwan and later served in the Office of Special Councilors (Hongmun'gwan 弘文館). His works includes a poem titled *Reading the White Deer Grotto Regulations* (*Tok paengnoktonggyu* 讀白鹿洞規).

---

80  YGCS 15:39a–b.
81  Kim Wŏnhaeng, "Sŏksil sŏwŏn kanggyu (Lecture Regulations of Soksil Academy)," in *Miho chip* (Collected Writings of Miho), 14:21b.
82  See Pak, "Chosŏn sidae ŭi hangnyŏng mit hakkyu," 232.
83  See "Yŏnggwang hyanggyo chi (Records of Yŏnggwang Local School)," in SWCCS 8: 124.

The ancients were already gone, the Classics faded away and teaching was also in ruins;
the Song established peaceful administration and accordingly true Confucians came forward.
From Lian[84] and Luo[85] came the key, then Huiweng cast his regulations.
Looking at the White Deer Grotto, in old times it had a state school as foundation,
lying in waste long without repair, the teaching without teacher and students,
its structures built upon these ruins, to raise flowers on the banks of a river.[86]
Heaven ordered the five relationships and released them upon the people,
Yao and Shun ruled vast and wide; this has surely not been surpassed?
Study, inquiry, thinking, discrimination, and earnest practice are first to be known.
Cultivate one's person, then carry it out and accept all that is proper.
These are the essentials of learning, upon which the Confucian should tirelessly focus.
Raise these clear admonishments among the eaves; the path of the sage has no crossroads.
Why are there scholars in the world who ignore and do not do this, quarrelling to dazzle with flowery words, pursuing wealth and rank?
Repeat Master Zhu's regulations three times, and through the ages be awed.[87]

Kim Inhu's poem is interesting for a few of reasons. Not only does it provide another example of a contemporary understanding of the *Articles* usage as a tool for education and self-cultivation, but it also gives insight into the emotional response they stirred in their audience. It is important to know that Kim Inhu's poem about the White Deer Grotto Regulations is an obvious reference to Zhu Xi's own poem *Bailudongfu* 白鹿洞賦 (*White Deer Grotto Rhapsody*). The *Bailudongfu* was one of the more famous poems by Zhu Xi and played an important role for the literary genre of *Shuyuanfu* 書院賦 (Academy

---

84   Zhou Dunyi's honorific name is Lianxi 濂溪.
85   Cheng Hao and Cheng Yi were born in Luoyang 洛陽.
86   This passage is direct reference to Zhu Xi's *Bailudongfu* and is usually understood as taking delight in the teaching of talented students.
87   Kim Inhu, "Tok paengnoktonggyu (Reading the White Deer Grotto Regulations)," in *Hasŏ sŏnsaeng chŏnjip* (Complete Collection of Master Hasŏ), 2:1a.

rhapsodies).[88] In his poem on the White Deer Grotto Academy, Zhu Xi recounts the history of the academy at Mt. Lu, while describing with melancholy the ruin of the academy and more generally of Confucian teachings across the ages. The poem, however, ends quite jubilant as now the reconstruction of the academy enables the instruction of pupils and transmission of the teachings into the future.[89] Because Kim Inhu's poem follows similar patterns and partly employs direct references, it is certain that he himself knew and was inspired by the *Bailudongfu*.[90] This demonstrates that Kim's embrace of the image of the White Deer Grotto Academy was not exclusively formed by his reading of the *Articles*, but also by an emotional reaction to his readings of Zhu Xi's poem. The *Articles* simply became the main manifestation for this feeling and the narrative behind it.

In 1590, P'iram Academy 筆嚴書院 in Southern Chŏlla province was founded to honor Kim Inhu. He was born in the area and often returned to it in order to avoid the political struggles in the capital. Following his own poem, a wooden board was raised in the lecture hall of the academy. It depicts the *White Deer Grotto Articles*, Zhu Xi's commentary, and also features Kim's poem *Reading the White Deer Grotto Regulations*.

The board is dated to 1710, yet it has no markings indicating authorship. The arrangement of the *Articles* uses blank spaces and different character sizes to organize and indicate the various items and texts inscribed on the board. All three texts are arranged in descending hierarchy. The poem by Kim Inhu is depicted smallest and is set lower and smaller than both other texts. The combination of the *Articles*, Zhu Xi's commentary, and the related poem of a local scholar in the display illustrates the individual connection this academy formed with the narrative of Confucian academies and their place and usage. The wooden board therefore represents both, the continuation and the adaptation of the academy model found in the writings of Zhu Xi by Korean scholars. While the reading of the board is not stipulated in the regulations of P'iram

---

88  See Zhang Siqi, "Cong 'Bailudongfu' kan Zhuxi de shiyi qi ju (Zhu Xi's Poetic Habitation in White Deer Cave)," *Xihua daxue xuebao* 27, no. 6 (2008): 11–17. Also on Song dynasty *Shuyuanfu* more in general see Qin Wei, "Lun songdai de shuyuan he shuyuan fu (Academies and Academy *Fu* in Song Dynasty)," *Liaodong xueyuan xuebao* 18, no. 1 (2016): 14–18.

89  For a more thorough discussion see Wu Zhanggeng and Kim Hongsu, "Paengnoktong sŏwŏn ŭi puhŭng e kkich'in chu hŭi ŭi ironchŏk kohŏn (Zhu Xi's Theoretical Contributions to the Renaissance of Bailudong Seowon)," *Andonghak* 11 (2012): 158–160.

90  Kim Inhu was quite famous for his rhapsody writings skills and he is said to have written an excellent poem while taking the civil service examinations.

ILLUSTRATION 9.4  Wooden hanging board in P'iram Academy containing the *White Deer Grotto Regulations*, *Zhu Xi's Commentary*, and Kim Inhu's poem *Reading the White Deer Grotto Regulations*.
SOURCE: PHOTO COURTESY OF AUTHOR

Academy, the *Articles* were, and still are, read after the sacrificial rites in the shrine and before every Confucian event conducted in the academy.[91]

## 6  Conclusion

Tracing the reception of the *White Deer Grotto Articles of Learning* in Korea reveals two layers of significance. First, it becomes clear that from an early point onwards the *Articles* were not explicitly associated with Confucian academies, but became an educational guideline in their own right. The most significant expression of this development is that the *Articles* were widely known and referred to as regulations soon after its composition. This change already occurred during the Song dynasty and the *Articles* were subsequently transmitted to Korea in this form. Most textual discussions of the *Articles* in Korea are

---

[91]  See Kim Kyŏngsŏn et al., *Sŏwŏn hyangsa. Musŏng sŏwŏn, P'iram sŏwŏn* (Academy Rites: Musŏng Academy: P'iram Academy) (Taejŏn: Kungnim munhwajae yŏn'guso, 2013), 266.

not concerned with their connection to Confucian academies, but with their value and usage as an introductory text to Confucian learning in general. Their treatment within institutional settings also confirms this. The *Articles* were one among many regulations or guidelines visibly hung, not so different from a diagram, in the educational institution to accompany the student through his scholarly progress as a constant reminder and a source of encouragement. This is remarkable in so far, as usually the academies are understood to reflect the trends set by social, academic, and cultural developments, not as shaping them. The emergence of an understanding of the *Articles* as general pedagogical treatise out of the history of the White Deer Grotto Academy however, can be viewed as such an instance.

Second, the White Deer Grotto Academy and its revival by Zhu Xi became an influential narrative within the general history of *Daoxue* Confucianism and accordingly was transmitted to the Korean peninsula as well. The academy at the foot of Mt. Lu became a metaphor for the intellectual bloom and rightful recapture of an area in the face of opposition (from Buddhists, local elites, the court, etc.) brought on by the refinement and steadfastness of one man. In her study of Southern Song academies Linda Walton describes how Zhu Xi and other scholars involved with the academy movement attempted to create sacred spaces through and around their academies. The surrounding landscapes were perceived as physical representations of the eruditeness of former teachers who had taught or studied there. The shrines and rites at the academies would conserve this spirit and transmit it to the next generation of scholars, ultimately connecting the landscape to the transmission of the Way itself.[92] Accordingly, the White Deer Grotto Academy also became a place of pilgrimage.[93] Such notions were also transmitted to the Korean scholars, who, being well versed in Chinese literature and culture could grasp them, but were nonetheless physically barred from visiting these sacred places. Andreas Müller-Lee and Christian Han, in their respective research, both have shown how and why such images, discourses, or narratives were transferred and contextualized in Korea.[94] In invoking the White Deer Grotto Academy as a model for his own academy, Chu Sebung sought to bestow and transfer the spirit of Nankang,

---

92   See Linda Walton, *Academies and Society in Southern Sung China* (Honolulu: University of Hawai'i Press, 1999), 103–112.

93   See Susan Naquin, Chün-fan Yü, "Introduction," in *Pilgrims and Sacred Sites in China*, ed. Susan Naquin, Chün-fan Yü (Berkeley: University of California Press, 1992), 18.

94   See Andreas Müller-Lee, "The Sleeping Dragon in Korea: On the Transmission of the Images of Zhuge Liang in Korea," *Seoul Journal of Korean Studies* 20 (2007): 45–70; and Christina Hee-Yeon Han, "Territory of the Sages: Neo-Confucian Discourse of Wuyi Nine Bends Jingjie" (Ph.D. diss., University of Toronto, 2011).

which he found in the texts, onto P'unggi. Accordingly, for him the *Articles* represented just one text among many others in the writings of Zhu Xi that taught him about academies and their role in Southern Song China.

While both layers of significance moved in different trajectories, they remained intrinsically entangled. Without their connection to the authority of Zhu Xi and the White Deer Grotto Academy the *Articles* would not have found such the wide circulation and adaption in Korea. Simultaneously, they carried the narrative of the revival of the White Deer Grotto Academy and Confucian academies in general and introduced this concept to every new generation of scholars. With the appearance of Confucian academies on the Korean peninsula this connection came to the forefront and was used to legitimize the spread of this new institution by building on the already accepted value of the *Articles*. The poem *Reading the White Deer Grotto Regulations* by Kim Inhu quite strikingly embodies this entanglement. By putting the *Articles* at the center, Kim reflects on the history of the White Deer Grotto Academy, while ultimately connecting himself and his surroundings to that narrative. He reveals to the reader not only his knowledge of the institution, but also his understanding of its role and place, which he or his disciples sought to transfer to their own surroundings by hanging the wooden plate inside their own academy. However, it is also important to mention that all along, the *Articles* maintained their reception as a general educational guideline and were accordingly not used just in Confucian academies.

The transmission of ideas is never a one-way process, as diachronic and/or spatial transfers of knowledge always produces change in the knowledge itself. This change can be reflected in the content or can be found in the modes of its representation, yet for knowledge to be valid in its respective time and space, it needs to be adapted. This process of re-contextualization can be achieved through obvious methods of rewriting, addition, censure, or can happen in much subtler ways, like changes to the structure of a document or its usage within a different setting, that neither have to be discussed or emphasized. While ascription to tradition and its proven value is often what provides knowledge with legitimacy in the first place, change is essential to the subsistence and validity of ideas in new surroundings. With this in mind, it is important to emphasize that the perceptions of the White Deer Grotto Academy and its regulations were not pure transmissions of knowledge from one place to another. On the contrary, each of the above-mentioned examples illustrates how, and sometimes also why, the *Articles* in their new context were reduced, adapted, changed, and infused with new meaning, or simply ignored. This, with a view to Confucian academies in general, demonstrates how even the basic institutional model, for most academies after the Song dynasty, was understood, interpreted, and realized in quite different ways.

## References

Chaffee, John W. "Chu Hsi and the Revival of the White Deer Grotto Academy. 1179–1181." *T'oung Pao* 71 (1985): 40–62.

Chan, Wing-Tsit. "The Ch'eng-Chu School of Early Ming." In *Self and Society in Ming Thought*, edited by Wm. Theodore de Bary, 29–51. New York: Columbia University Press, 1970.

Chan, Wing-Tsit. *Chu Hsi: His Life and Thought*. Hongkong: The Chinese University Press, 1987.

Chang Yunsu. "Songdang Pak Yŏng ŭi tohakchŏk hakp'ung kwa sŏngnihak chŏk sayu (Song Dang Pak Yŏng's Academic Tradition and Speculation on Metaphysics)." *Han'gukhak Nonjip* 66 (2017): 339–377.

Cheng Nensheng 程嫩生. *Zhongguo shuyuan wenxue jiaoyu yanjiu* 中国书院文学教育研究 (Research on Literature Education in China's Academies). Beijing: Zhongguo shehui kexue chubanshe, 2014.

Ching, Julia. *The Religious Thought of Chu Hsi*. Oxford: Oxford University Press, 2000.

Ch'oe Yongsu. "Kyŏnggich'e ga e taehan Chu Sebung ŭi insik t'aedo (Chu Sebung's Attitude towards Kyŏnggich'e ga)." *Hanminjok ŏmunhak* 38 (2001): 247–267.

Choi Da-eun. "Sŏnggyun'gwan hyŏnp'an yŏn'gu. Taesŏngjŏn gwa Myŏngnyundang p'yŏnaek ŭl chungsim ŭro (A Study on the Hanging Boards in Seonggyungwan. Focused on the Signboards of Daeseongjeon and Myeongnyundang)." *Sŏyehak yŏn'gu* 29 (2016): 141–173.

*Chŏng Chwawa sŏnsaeng Chip* 靜坐窩先生集 (Collected Writings of Master Chŏng Chwawa). After 1756. Kyujanggak #古 3428–800. Database of Korean Classics. <http://www.db.itkc.or.kr> (accessed: 1 March 2018).

*Chukkyeji* 竹溪誌 (Records of Bamboo Stream). 1544. Korea University Library 晚松 貴重書228. Database of Korean Classics. <http://www.db.itkc.or.kr> (accessed: 1 March 2018).

de Bary, Wm. Theodore. *The Liberal Tradition in China*. New York: Columbia University Press, 1983.

de Bary, Wm. Theodore. "Chu Hsi's Aims as an Educator." In *Neo-Confucian Education. The Formative Stage,* edited by Wm. Theodore de Bary and John W. Chaffee, 186–218. Berkeley: University of California Press, 1989.

Deng Hongbo 邓洪波. "Zhu Xi yu Chaoxian shuyuan 朱熹与朝鲜书院 (Zhu Xi and Korean academies)." *Guizhou jiaoyu xueyuan xuebao* 1 (1989): 43–46.

Deuchler, Martina. *The Confucian Transformation of Korea: A Study of Society and Ideology*. Cambridge, MA: Harvard University Press, 1995.

Feng Huiming 冯会明. "Hu Juren de 'Xu Bailudong xuegui' jiqi jiaoyu sixiang 胡居仁的'续白鹿洞学规'及其教育思想 (Hu Juren's Supplement to the White Deer Grotto Study Regulations and His Educational Thought)." *Jiangxi jiaoyu xueyuan xuebao* 31, no. 2 (2010): 112–115.

Glomb, Vladimír. "Reading the Classics till Death: Yulgok Yi I and the Curriculum of Chosŏn Literati." *Studia Orientalia Slovaca* II 2 (2012): 315–329.

Glomb, Vladimír. "Circulating Pictures: Confucian Diagrams, Ch'ŏnmyŏng to and Intellectual Debate in 16th Century Korea." In *Bochumer Jahrbuch zur Ostasienforschung* 39/2016: 39–61. München: Iudicium, 2017.

Han, Christina Hee-Yeon. "Territory of the Sages: Neo-Confucian Discourse of Wuyi Nine Bends Jingjie." Ph.D. diss., University of Toronto, 2011.

*Hasŏ sŏnsaeng chŏnjip* 河西先生全集 (Complete Collection of Master Hasŏ). 1802. Kyujanggak 가람古 819. 52 G42h–v.1–8. Database of Korean Classics. <http://www.db.itkc.or.kr> (accessed: 1 May 2017).

Hejtmanek, Milan. "The Elusive Path to Sagehood. Origins of the Confucian Academy System in Korea Chosŏn Korea." *Seoul Journal of Korean Studies* 26, no. 2 (December 2013): 233–268.

Huang Xirong 黄熙蓉. "Chanmen qinggui dui 'Bailudong shuyuan jieshi' de yingxiang 禅门清规对'白鹿洞书院揭示'的影响 (The Influence of Chan School Monastic Rules on the *White Deer Grotto Academy Articles of Learning*)." *Jiangxi jiaoyu xueyuan xuebao* 34, no. 2 (2014): 183–185.

Im Nojik. "P'yŏnaek e taehan ihae (Understanding Wooden Plates)." In *Ttŭsi tamgin Hyŏnp'an P'yŏnaek* (Wooden Plates Filled with Meaning), edited by Kim Pyŏngil, 238–251. Andong: Han'guk kukhak chinhŭngwŏn, 2009.

Kelleher, Theresa M. "Back to Basics: Chu Hsi's Elementary Learning (Hsiao-hsüeh)." In *Neo-Confucian Education. The Formative Stage*, edited by Wm. Theodore de Bary and John W. Chaffee, 219–251. Berkeley: University of California Press, 1989.

Meskill, John. *Academies in Ming China: A Historical Essay*. Tucson: University of Arizona Press, 1982.

*Miho chip* 渼湖集 (Collected Writings of Miho). 1799. Kyujanggak #奎 7028. Database of Korean Classics. <http://www.db.itkc.or.kr> (accessed: 1 March 2018).

Müller-Lee, Andreas. "The Sleeping Dragon in Korea: On the Transmission of the Images of Zhuge Liang in Korea." *Seoul Journal of Korean Studies* 20 (2007): 45–70.

Naquin, Susan, and Chün-fan Yü. "Introduction." In *Pilgrims and Sacred Sites in China*, edited by Susan Naquin and Chün-fan Yü, 1–38. Berkeley: University of California Press, 1992.

Kim Kyŏngsŏn, Kim Hŭit'ae, Yi Haejun, Ch'oe Sun'gwŏn, Yi Myŏngjin, and An Kyŏnghŭi. *Sŏwŏn hyangsa. Musŏng sŏwŏn, P'iram sŏwŏn* (Academy Rites. Musŏng Academy, P'iram Academy). Taejŏn: Kungnim munhwajae yŏn'guso, 2013.

Kim Mun'gi. "Sŏwŏn kyoyuk kwa Sinjae Chu Sebung (Academy Education and Sinjae Chu Sebung)." *Kugŏ kyoyuk yŏn'gu* 38 (2005): 1–26.

Kŭm Changt'ae. *Sŏnghak sip'to wa t'oegye ch'ŏrhak ŭi kujo* (The Ten Diagrams of Sage Learning and the Structure of T'oegye's Philosophy). Seoul: Sŏul taehakkyo ch'ulp'anbu, 2001.

Lee, Bong-kyoo. "The Neo-Confucian Thought of Song Chun-gil and its Meaning in the History of Philosophy." *Seoul Journal of Korean Studies* 11 (1998): 153–188.

Lee, Thomas H.C. "Chu Hsi, Academies and the Tradition of Private Chiang-hsüeh." *Hanxue Yanjiu* 2, no. 1 (1984): 301–329.

Li Bangguo 李邦国. "Zhu Xi 'Bailudong shuyuan jieshi' de jiaoyu shijian he zhexue jichu 朱熹'白鹿洞书院揭示'的教育实践和哲学基础 (The Philosophical Basis and Educational Realization of Zhu Xi's *White Deer Grotto Academy Articles of Learning*)." *Hubei shifan xueyuan xuebao* 14, no. 1 (1994): 76–82.

Li Bangguo 李邦国. "Zhu Xi yu bailudong shuyuan zai Chaoxian Riben de yingxiang 朱熹与白鹿洞书院在朝鲜日本的影响 (The Influence of Zhu Xi and the White Deer Grotto Academy in Korea and Japan)." *Hubei shifan xueyuan xuebao* 15, no. 1 (1995): 99–101.

Ok Yŏngjŏng. "Chukkyeji ŭi p'yŏnch'an kwa p'anbon e kwanhan sŏjijŏk yŏn'gu (A Bibliographical Study of Compilation and Edition of the *Chukkyeji*)." *Sŏjihak yŏn'gu* 31 (2005): 297–321.

*Oksan sŏwŏn chi* 玉山書院志 (Records of Oksan Academy). Kyŏngsan: Yŏngnam taehakkyo ch'ulp'anbu, 1993.

Pak Chŏngbae. "Chosŏn sidae ŭi hangnyŏng mit hakkyu (Rules and Regulations in Confucian Academies of Chosŏn Period)." *Han'guk kyoyuk sahak* 28, no. 2 (2006): 213–237.

Qin Wei 秦玮. "Lun songdai de shuyuan he shuyuan fu 论宋代的书院和书院赋 (Discussing Academy and Academy Fu in Song Dynasty)." *Liaodong xueyuan xuebao* 18, no. 1 (2016): 14–18.

*Songdang sŏnsaeng munjip* 松堂先生文集 (Collected Works of Songdang). 1905. Kyujanggak #古 3428–231. Database of Korean Classics. <http://www.db.itkc.or.kr> (accessed: 1 March 2018).

Tillman, Hoyt Cleveland. *Confucian Discourse and Chu Hsi's Ascendancy*. Honolulu: University of Hawai'i Press, 1992.

*Tongch'undang sŏnsaeng pyŏljip* 同春堂先生別集 (Separate Collected Works of Master Tongch'undang). 1702. Kyujanggak 奎 4876. Database of Korean Classics. <http://www.db.itkc.or.kr> (accessed: 01 March 2018).

Walton, Linda. *Academies and Society in Southern Sung China*. Honolulu: University of Hawai'i Press, 1999.

Wang Bin 王彬. "Cong 'Bailudong shuyuan jieshi' kan Zhu Xi de xuegui linian 从'白鹿洞书院揭示'看朱熹的学规理念 (Looking at Zhu Xi's Concept of Study Regulations from the *Bailudong Academy Articles of Learning*)." *Zibo shizhuan xuebao* 35, no. 1 (2014): 59–62.

Wu Zhanggeng, and Kim Hongsu. "Paengnoktong sŏwŏn ŭi puhŭng e kkich'in chu hŭi ŭi ironchŏk kohŏn (Chu Hsi's Theoretical Contributions to the Renaissance of Bailudong Seowon)." *Andonghak* 11 (2012): 149–178.

Yao Sui 姚燧. "Zhong shu zuo cheng Yao Wenxian gong shendaobei 中書左丞姚文獻公神道碑 (Spirit Path Stele Written by Assistant Director of the Left in the Secretariat Yao Wenxian)." In *Mu'anji* 牧庵集 (Collected Works of Mu'an). SKQS ed.

Yi, Hwang (comp.). *To Become a Sage: The Ten Diagrams on Sage Learning by Yi T'oegye*. Translated by Michael C. Kalton. New York: Columbia University Press, 1988.

Yi Hwang (comp.). *A Korean Confucian Way of Life and Thought. The Chasŏngnok by Yi Hwang*. Translated by Edward Y.J. Chung. Honolulu: University of Hawai'i Press, 2016.

Yŏngnam Taehakkyo. Minjok Munhwa Yŏn'guso 嶺南大學校 民族文化硏究所 (ed.). *Kyŏngbuk hyanggyo charyo chipsŏng* 慶北鄉校資料集成 (Collection of Kyŏngbuk Local School Materials). Kyŏngsan: Yŏngnam taehakkyo ch'ulp'anbu, 1992.

Zhang Jinsong 张劲松. "Ming chu lixue jia Hu Juren de shuyuan jiaoyu shijian yu shuyuanguan lüelun 明初理学家胡居仁的书院教育实践与书院观略论 (Short Discussion of Early Ming *Lixue* Scholar Hu Juren's Educational Academy Practice and Understanding of the Academies)." *Jiangxi jiaoyu xueyuan xuebao* 31, no. 5 (2010): 101–105.

Zhang Pinduan, and Kim Hongsu. "Chu Hŭi sŏwŏn kyoyuk sasang e taehan Yi Hwang ŭi kyesŭng kwa paljŏn. Paengnoktong sŏwŏn kesi rŭl chungsim ŭro (Lee Hwang' Successions and Developments of Chu Hsi's Thought in Seowon Education)." *Andonghak* 11 (2012): 215–236.

Zhang Siqi 张思齐. "Cong 'Bailudongfu' kan Zhuxi de shiyi qiju 从'白鹿洞赋'看朱熹的诗意栖居 (Zhu Xi's Poetic Habitation in White Deer Cave)." *Xihua daxue xuebao* 27, no. 6 (2008): 11–17.

Zhu Hanmin 朱汉民, and Deng Hongbo 邓洪波. *Yuelu Shuyuan shi* 岳麓书院史 (History of the Yuelu Academy). Changsha: Hunan jiaoyu chubanshe, 2013.

Zhu, Xi. *Learning to be a Sage. Selections from the Conversations with Master Chu, Arranged Topically*. Translated by Daniel K. Gardner. Berkeley: University of California Press, 1990.

Zhu Xi. *Zhuzi quanshu* 朱子全書 (Complete Writings of Master Zhu). Shanghai: Shanghai guji chubanshe, 2002.

Zhu, Xi, and Lü, Zuqian. *Reflections on Things at Hand*. Translated by Wing-Tsit Chan. New York: Columbia University Press, 1967.

PART 3

*Social Role and Environment of Confucian Academies*

∴

CHAPTER 10

# Confucian Academies and Their Urban Environments in Qing China

*Steven B. Miles*

## 1        Introduction

Previous scholarship has taught us a great deal about the intellectual, institutional, and pedagogical history of Confucian academies in China from the Song through Qing dynasties. Because a central question has concerned the influence of particular academies on intellectual trends and political movements, scholarship has understandably tended to focus on the most renowned academies, whether Bailudong Academy 白鹿洞書院 in the Song, Donglin Academy 東林書院 in the Ming, or Yuelu Academy 岳麓書院 in the Qing.[1] Nevertheless, the various roles that academies played in local society can only be fully appreciated when we turn our attention from the small number of renowned, often unique, academies to the vast majority of mainstream academies, and when we attempt to situate all academies in their local environments. In contrast to earlier dynasties, when academies were often associated with sacred sites in suburban or rural areas, during the Qing era most academies were located in decidedly urban environments.[2] This was particularly the case,

---

1    For examples of English-language scholarship, on Bailudong see John W. Chaffee, "Chu Hsi and the Revival of the White Deer Grotto Academy, 1179–1181 AD," *T'oung Pao* 71 (1985): 40–62, and Martin Gehlmann, "Transmissions of the White Deer Grotto Academy Articles of Learning in Korea," in this volume, 252–286; on Donglin see John Meskill, *Academies in Ming China: A Historical Essay* (Tucson: The University of Arizona Press, 1982), 73–75, 151–155; on Yuelu during the Qing see Daniel McMahon, "The Yuelu Academy and Hunan's Nineteenth-Century Turn Toward Statecraft," *Late Imperial China* 26, no. 1 (June 2005): 72–109. A representative Chinese-language survey highlighting the most influential academies is Deng Hongbo, *Zhongguo shuyuan shi* (History of Academies in China), revised edition (Wuhan: Wuhan daxue chubanshe, 2013).
2    On Song-era academies and sacred landscapes, see Linda Walton, *Academies and Society in Southern Sung China* (Honolulu: University of Hawai'i Press, 1999), 91–113; and her chapter "Songyang Academy in Time and Place: From Confucian Academy to Cultural Heritage," in this volume, 397–436.

as Tilemann Grimm shows in his study of Confucian academies in Guangdong, for the larger and more influential academies.³

Examining the relationship between Confucian academies and their urban environments raises some fundamental questions that have not received a great deal of attention. For example, how much access did local residents have to academies? With what kinds of urban festivals and other activities did academy-based rituals have to compete for the attention of city residents? For the inner circle of officials and literati who did have easy access to academies, how did academies fit into their daily and annual routines? In answering these kinds of questions, it is important to expand research on academies to include not only famous institutions but also, and perhaps more importantly, run-of-the-mill academies that specialized in preparing students for civil service examinations. In doing so, we find that the definition of an "influential" Confucian academy changes when we consider the impact of a particular academy upon the daily, seasonal, or annual rhythms of urban life. That is, for the vast majority of urban residents, mainstream academies most closely associated with the civil service examinations had a much larger presence than did the elite, alternative academies that have received the most attention from scholars.

This chapter explores the relationship between academies and their urban environments in Qing China through a case study of 19th-century Guangzhou and its nine most prominent urban academies (see Table 10.1).⁴

The first five academies in this list may be considered mainstream academies in that they largely specialized in preparing students for civil service examinations. Yuexiu shuyuan 粵秀書院 (Yue, or Guangdong, Excellence Academy) and Yuehua shuyuan 越華書院 (Yue, or Guangdong, Florescence Academy) were purportedly open to students from anywhere in Guangdong, whereas Yangcheng shuyuan 羊城書院 (City of Rams, or Guangzhou, Academy) served residents of Guangzhou Prefecture and Xihu shuyuan 西湖書院 (West Lake Academy) and Yushan shuyuan 禺山書院 (Yu Hill Academy) served residents of Nanhai and Panyu, the two counties that shared jurisdiction of the city of Guangzhou. Founded as charitable schools in the 18th century, Xihu and Yushan were converted into county-level academies in 1803. Most students at Yuexiu, Yuehua, Yangcheng, Xihu, and Yushan were either apprentice students (*tongsheng* 童生) seeking to pass the lowest level of the civil service

---

3   Tilemann Grimm, "Academies and Urban Systems in Kwangtung," in *The City in Late Imperial China*, ed. G. William Skinner (Stanford: Stanford University Press, 1977), 486–487.
4   Liu Boji, *Guangdong shuyuan zhidu* (The Institution of Academies in Guangdong) (Taipei: Zhonghua congshu weiyuanhui, 1958), 44–68; Steven B. Miles, *The Sea of Learning: Mobility and Identity in Nineteenth-Century Guangzhou* (Cambridge, MA: Harvard University Asia Center, 2006), 74–80, 195–196.

TABLE 10.1  Prominent academies of 19th-century Guangzhou

| Academy | Location | Constituency/ orientation | Date founded/ converted |
| --- | --- | --- | --- |
| Yuexiu Academy | Old City | provincial | 1710 |
| Yuehua Academy | Old City | provincial | 1755 |
| Yangcheng Academy | Old City | prefectural | 1820–1821 |
| Xihu Academy | Old City | Nanhai County | 1723/1803 |
| Yushan Academy | Old City | Panyu County | 1730/1803 |
| Xuehaitang | Yuexiu Hill | alternative | 1821, 1825 |
| Jupo Retreat | Yuexiu Hill | alternative | 1867 |
| Yingyuan Academy | Yuexiu Hill | *juren* | 1869 |
| Guangya Academy | Northwestern suburb | bi-provincial/ alternative | 1887 |

SOURCE: LIU BOJI, *GUANGDONG SHUYUAN ZHIDU*

examinations, held at county and prefectural seats, or licentiates (*shengyuan* 生員) seeking to earn the *juren* 舉人 degree in the provincial examinations. All five of these academies were located in the center of Guangzhou's walled urban core, the Old City; this placed the academies in close proximity to the yamen of the city's numerous officials. These five academies were all functioning by the early 1820s. Newer academies were established on Yuexiu Hill, still within the city wall that ran along the top of the hill, but at some remove from the urban core. Yingyuan 應元書院 (Placing First Academy) also specialized in preparation for civil service examinations, but specifically for *juren*, or provincial-degree holders, seeking to pass the metropolitan examinations. In contrast, the Xuehaitang 學海堂 (Sea of Learning Hall), Jupo jingshe 菊坡精舍 (Chrysanthemum Slope Retreat), named after Cui Yuzhi 崔與之 (1158–1239), and Guangya shuyuan 廣雅書院 (Broad Refinement Academy) were alternative academies in the sense that their founders designed broader curricula that they claimed transcended a narrow focus on civil service examinations.

In expanding research on academies to include the interaction between academies and their urban environments, it is necessary to move beyond the celebratory writings of academy promoters, who tended to exaggerate the

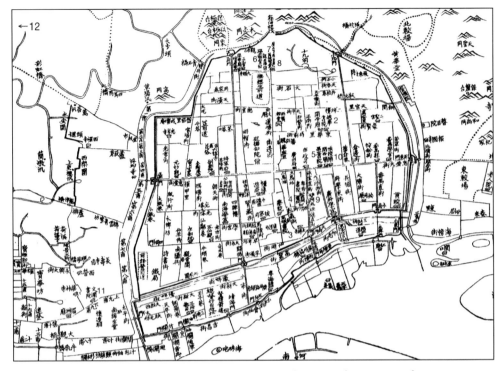

ILLUSTRATION 10.1   Map of Guangzhou, showing the locations of: 1. Yuexiu Academy, 2. Yuehua Academy, 3. Yangcheng Academy, 4. Xihu Academy, 5. Yushan Academy, 6. Xuehaitang, 7. Jupo Retreat, 8. Yingyuan Academy, 9. Shuangmendi, 10. City God Temple, 11. Wenlan Academy, 12. Guangya Academy.
SOURCE: ADAPTED FROM THE 1879 *GUANGZHOU FU ZHI*

intellectual and social impact of their institutions, and shift attention to a broader range of sources. These sources might include central government and county archives; the Ba county archives, for example, would surely allow for a fruitful study of academies in Chongqing. In this chapter, I draw examples from my past research on the Xuehaitang and my current research on the seasonality of urban life in 19th-century Guangzhou, largely relying on diaries written by urban literati and, for the late 19th-century, the newspapers *Shenbao* 申報 (*Shanghai News*) and *Xunhuan ribao* (*Tsun Wan Yat Po*) 循環日報 (*Universal Circulating Herald*). I examine three levels of interaction between academies and the urban population, asking how academies fit into the lives of the city's academic elite, academy directors, and supervisors; how aspiring elites, academy students, utilized academies; and how academies competed with other urban phenomena for space and influence over the city's residents.

## 2   Scholar-Officials: Academic Elites and the City's Officialdom

Much attention has been focused on the impact that Confucian academies had on changing trends in classical exegesis, on literary styles, and on the formation of local elites and the articulation of local identities. Such studies tend to highlight the roles of a very small number of relatively prestigious academies.[5] But when one shifts focus from the writings (in academy gazetteers and collected writings [*wenji* 文集]) that celebrate the influence of prestigious academies, one finds that less famous but more mainstream academies often had a more prominent place in the daily lives of a given city's academic elites. For Guangzhou, in the routines of the city's elite, the more mainstream academies (Yuexiu, Yuehua, Yangcheng, and to a lesser extent Xihu and Yushan) located in Guangzhou's urban core (Old City) and specializing in preparation for civil service examinations had the greatest presence. Excerpts from two separate years in the diary of Xie Lansheng 謝蘭生 (1760–1831), a holder of the highest civil service examination degree, convey the important place that academies held in the life of an eminent literatus. In 1823 (DG3) Xie was director (*yuanzhang* 院長 / *zhangjiao* 掌教) of the new Yangcheng Academy, and diary entries give a sense of the rhythm of academy activities.[6] Entries for the first twenty days of the first lunar month are missing, but in subsequent entries one can see the beginning of the academy's annual cycle:

DG3.1.21[7]   short visit to the academy
DG3.1.28   results for Yangcheng Academy entrance examination posted (*zhenbie fabang* 甄別發榜)

---

5   A few examples are Benjamin A. Elman, *From Philosophy to Philology: Intellectual and Social Aspects of Change in Late Imperial China* (Cambridge, MA: Council on East Asian Studies, 1984); Barry C. Keenan, *Imperial China's Last Classical Academies: Social Change in the Lower Yangzi, 1864–1911* (Berkeley: University of California Press, 1994); Liu Yucai, *Qingdai shuyuan yu xueshu bianqian yanjiu* (Research on Qing Dynasty Academies and Changes in Scholarship) (Beijing: Beijing daxue chubanshe, 2008); Cheng Nensheng, *Zhongguo shuyuan wenxue jiaoyu yanjiu* (Research on Literature Education in China's Academies) (Beijing: Zhongguo shehui kexue chubanshe, 2014); and my *Sea of Learning*. For a review of recent Chinese-language works on academies, see my "The Nature and Impact of Late Imperial Chinese Academies: A Review of Some Recent Publications in China," *Frontiers of Education in China* 10, no. 4 (December 2015): 634–656.
6   Xie Lansheng, *Changxingxingzhai riji* (Diary from the Studio of Constant Awareness), manuscript, 1819–1829, held at National Library of China.
7   Dates use the lunar calendar and Chinese reign names. DG3.3.1 indicates the first day of the third month of the third year of the Daoguang reign. Other reigns used in this chapter are JQ (Jiaqing), XF (Xianfeng), TZ (Tongzhi), and GX (Guangxu).

DG3.2.1 [academy] officially opened for the year (*qiguan* 啓館); in early morning went to academy to perform rituals to gods; in mid-morning Prefect Zhong[8] arrived to conduct rituals; Supervisor (*jianyuan* 監院) Huang[9] invited me for breakfast

Annual entrance examinations (*zhenbie* 甄別) administered in the first or second lunar month determined who would fill the student rolls for each of the mainstream academies. Diary entries for the third month show the routine of regular examinations. I have excerpted from the diary entries all activities related to the academy:

DG3.3.1 read ... examination papers (*yue* 閱 ⋯ *kejuan* 課卷)
five students visited (*zhusheng ye zhe wu ren* 諸生謁者五人)
DG3.3.2 read ... examination papers
governor-general's examination topic: ...
DG3.3.3 read ... examination papers
five students visited
DG3.3.4 finished reading students' examination papers
DG3.3.5 four students visited
DG3.3.6 six students visited
DG3.3.7
DG3.3.8 one student [came for] audience
DG3.3.9 [examination] topic
two students visited
DG3.3.10 two students visited
DG3.3.11 three students visited
Academy Supervisor Huang came
DG3.3.12 four students visited
DG3.3.13 read ... examination papers
two students visited
DG3.3.14 read ... examination papers
six students visited
DG3.3.15 read ... examination papers
three students visited
DG3.3.16 read ... examination papers
examination set for today was moved to the seventeenth

---

8 Zhong Ying, *Guangzhou fu zhi* (Guangzhou Prefecture Gazetteer), 1879, 23:14.
9 Huang Yunxun. See entry for DG2.8.13.

| | |
|---|---|
| DG3.3.17 | prefect's examination topic: ... |
| | read ... examination papers |
| DG3.3.18 | read ... examination papers the whole day, finishing in the evening |
| DG3.3.19 | one student visited |
| DG3.3.20 | |
| DG3.3.21 | |
| DG3.3.22 | two students visited |
| DG3.3.23 | |
| DG3.3.24 | [examination] topic: ... |
| | one student visited |
| DG3.3.25 | three students visited |
| DG3.3.26 | lectured on "Explanation of the Diagram of the Supreme Ultimate" |
| | two students visited |
| DG3.3.27 | |
| DG3.3.28 | lectured on the "Western Inscription" |
| DG3.3.29 | read ... examinations papers |
| | four students visited |
| DG3.3.30 | read ... examinations papers |

Examinations alternated between those with topics set by the city's officials (2nd and 16th days) and those set by the director, Xie Lansheng (9th and 24th days). Because Yangcheng was a prefectural academy, the examination topic for the sixteenth day of each month was set by the Guangzhou prefect. The official examination administered on the second day of the spring months rotated among the city's higher officials. On most days, Xie either read examination papers or received visits from students, presumably Yangcheng students. The surprising thing about Xie's schedule during the spring of 1823 is that, rather than residing at Yangcheng Academy as might be expected, Xie stayed at his home in the New City, a more recently walled and more highly commercialized portion of Guangzhou that lay between the Old City and the Pearl River.[10]

In addition to administering examinations, reading examination papers, receiving visits from students, and lecturing, Xie Lansheng's role as the director of a major academy obliged him to interact with officials, other academy leaders, and members of the commercial and religious elites. Close interaction with officialdom is a feature of academic life in Qing China that stands in stark contrast to earlier periods in China and to the situation in Korea, where, as

---

10  E.g. entries for DG3.3.5, DG3.3.8, DG3.3.9, DG3.3.29.

Vladimír Glomb describes in this volume, academies were places where scholars could survive outside government. In the third month, for example, on the twelfth day Guangzhou's three major academies' directors—Xie, Yuexiu director He Nanyu 何南鈺 (1756–1831), and Yuehua director Liu Binhua 劉彬華 (1770–1828)—together attended a banquet hosted by the salt controller, Zhai Jinguan 翟錦觀 (?–?).[11] Two days after the banquet, the salt controller paid a return visit to Xie, and on the same day Xie visited the Guangzhou prefect to offer birthday wishes. On the twenty-sixth day, the three academy directors attended a banquet hosted by Maritime Customs Superintendent Dasan 達三 (1762–?). Earlier in the month, Yuexiu supervisor He Qijie 何其杰 (?–?) visited Xie.[12] On separate occasions in the fourth month, Xie received a visit from the Guangdong governor (DG3.4.5), visited Yuexiu and Yuehua directors He and Liu (DG3.4.6), attended a banquet hosted by the maritime merchant Wu Bingjian 伍秉鑑 (Howqua, 1769–1843) (DG3.4.7), and offered birthday wishes to the Nanhai County magistrate (DG3.4.13).

These relationships were oiled by gift exchanges. In the days preceding the Dragon Boat Festival in 1823, Xie received festival gifts (*jie li* 節禮) from the Guangdong governor, provincial judge, education commissioner, salt controller, grain intendant, customs superintendent, and the county magistrates of Nanhai and Panyu. Four of the city's major Buddhist monasteries also sent gifts. Some gifts that Xie received could be considered as part of his income as Yangcheng director, if not the gifts that Yangcheng supervisor Huang sent, then at least the festival gifts and teaching salary (*xiujin* 脩金) sent by the Guangzhou prefect and the "remunerative gifts" (*zhi wu* 贄物) of various sorts offered by his students (DG3.5.1–5.4).

Diary entries from 1819–1820 (JQ24), when Xie Lansheng was not serving as an academy director, show that as a high-ranking member of the city's literati elite he still had access to academies, and these academies were important destinations on his business and social itineraries. Xie seems to have been a private teacher at this time, but he had achieved the highest civil service examination degree and he had previously served as director of Yuexiu Academy. He visited academies on the following days (entries for the first two months are incomplete):

JQ24.3.29    Yuehua
JQ24.4.22    Yuexiu

---

11   Qian Shifu, *Qingdai zhiguan nianbiao* (Chronological Tables of Qing Dynasty Officials) (Beijing: Zhonghua shuju, 1980), vol. 3, 2131. vol. 4, 3254.
12   Xie, *Riji*, DG3.3.9, 3.12, 3.14, 3.26.

JQ24.7.8     Xihu
JQ24.8.7     Yuehua
JQ24.8.22    Yuehua
JQ24.8.28    Yuehua
JQ24.9.3     Yuehua
JQ24.9.12    Yuehua
JQ24.9.19    Yuehua
JQ24.9.22    Yushan, Yuehua
JQ24.9.29    Yuehua
JQ24.10.2    Yuehua
JQ24.10.3    Yuehua
JQ24.10.5    Yuehua
JQ24.10.6    Yuehua
JQ24.10.7    Yuexiu, Yuehua
JQ24.10.9    Yuehua
JQ24.10.10   Yuehua
JQ24.10.16   Yuehua
JQ24.11.5    Yuexiu
JQ24.11.11   Yuexiu
JQ24.12.7    Yuehua
JQ24.12.10   Yuexiu, Yuehua

Some of Xie's many visits to Yuehua, located in the Old City urban core, in this year were related to his participation on the editorial board of the Guangdong provincial gazetteer, then in the process of its compilation and eventually published in 1822.[13] For example, members of the gazetteer bureau attended a banquet at Yuehua on 8.22. Several events at Yuehua in the autumn were related to celebrations of the Jiaqing 嘉慶 (r. 1795–1820) Emperor's birthday, on 10.6. Thus, on 9.3 Xie met at Yuehua with the city's commercial and academic elites to make preparations for celebrating the imperial birthday. On 10.3, operas were staged at Yuehua and attended by "high civil and military officials"; operas continued for several days. On the emperor's birthday, Xie went to Yuehua in formal cap and gown to perform the ceremonial kowtow. Aside from these special occasions, as a member of Guangzhou's academic elite, even though not currently serving as an academy director, Xie placed academies on his social itinerary, whether picking up academy director Liu Binhua at Yuehua on 9.19 to visit the Nanhai and Panyu county magistrates, or visiting Yuexiu on 11.5

---

13   *Guangdong tongzhi* (Guangdong Provincial Gazetteer), 1822, prefatory material.

to offer birthday wishes to director Chen Changqi 陳昌齊 (1743–1820) and again on 11.11 to call on supervisor Wu Lanxiu 吳蘭修 (?–1839).[14]

The ways in which academy directors were involved in social exchanges with officials can be seen in news about Guangzhou reported in the Hong Kong-based newspaper *Xunhuan ribao* in the early 1880s. The section containing news from Guangzhou (*Yangcheng xinwen* 羊城新聞) usually begins with reports of comings and goings of the Guangdong-Guangxi governor-general and the Guangdong governor (*Du-fu xian yuan bao* 督撫憲轅報). In some reports, academy directors appear among various officials with whom the governor-general and governor interact on a regular basis. In 1880, for example, on 2.20 Yingyuan director Li Wentian 李文田 (1834–1895) and Yuehua director Pan Yantong 潘衍桐 (1841–1899) joined a banquet hosted by one of the provincial officials, and on 5.17 they called on the governor-general.[15] On 6.8, visitors included the director of Yushan, a county-level academy, and a high-ranking official, the customs superintendent.[16] On 6.12, the governor-general received birthday wishes from the Guangzhou garrison general and lieutenant-general, the governor, the naval commander-in-chief, the customs superintendent, and the Yingyuan, Yuexiu, Jupo, and Yushan academy directors. Directors of Yuehua and Yangcheng are listed among those who dispatched subordinates to offer congratulations, and they paid personal visits four days later.[17] On 8.18, Governor-general Zhang Shusheng 張樹聲 (1824–1884) called on the directors of Yuehua, Yuexiu, and Yangcheng academies.[18] These interactions continued under Zhang Shusheng's successor, Zhang Zhidong 張之洞 (1837–1909). In reporting on the new governor-general receiving the seals of office in July, 1884, *Xunhuan ribao* lists the directors of Yuehua, Yingyuan, Yangcheng, Yuexiu, and Jupo academies together with the civil and military officials who either personally expressed congratulations or sent representatives to do so.[19]

One interesting point about these interactions recorded in *Xunhuan ribao* between 1880 and 1886 is the absence of Xuehaitang co-directors. Although the Xuehaitang is normally seen as the most prestigious academy in Guangzhou from its founding in the 1820s until the 1880s, the eight co-directors do not seem to have the same official status enjoyed by directors of the city's other

---

14 Chen Changqi, appointed academy director in JQ24, died in the following year. *Yuexiu shuyuan zhi* (Yuexiu Academy Gazetteer), ed. by Liang Tingnan, 1847, reprint, ZGLDSYZ 3: 9.25b.
15 *Xunhuan ribao*, GX6.1.24, 2, GX6.5.22, 2.
16 *Xunhuan ribao*, GX6.6.13, 2.
17 *Xunhuan ribao*, GX6.6.16, 2, GX6.8.20, 2.
18 *Xunhuan ribao*, GX6.8.23, 2.
19 *Xunhuan ribao*, GX10.R5.24, 2.

academies, and hence they do not appear on the governor-general's or governor's itineraries. In contrast, the director of Yushan, a county-level academy in Guangzhou, does occasionally appear.[20] In the eyes of editors and readers, then, directors of Guangzhou's academies were part of the city's officialdom. Much of this is not surprising, but it should lead us to rethink the impact of famous academies such as the Xuehaitang. Although the Xuehaitang may have transformed Cantonese elite culture in many ways,[21] it does not have a prominent place in sources that show us the quotidian interactions of the city's bureaucratic and academic elites.

*Xunhuan ribao* also reported on academies' opening ceremonies (*kaiguan* 開館) when they were attended by officials as part of their ritual cycle. For each year from 1882 to 1885, *Xunhuan ribao* reported that the governor, and in some years also the governor-general, on 3.1 offered incense (*xing xiang* 行香) at three state temples—Wenmiao 文廟, Wumiao 武廟, and Wenchangmiao 文昌廟—before going to Yuehua and Yuexiu for opening ceremonies. In one year, the governor did the same for Yangcheng on 3.2.[22] Here again it is clear which academies were most important in the view of editors and their presumed audience: Yuexiu, Yuehua, and to a lesser extent Yangcheng, Yingyuan, and Xihu. Likewise, in his diary for 1866, the Guangdong governor Guo Songtao 郭嵩濤 (1818–1891), who was also an important patron of the Xuehaitang, recorded in his diary that he and the governor-general (Ruilin 瑞麟, ?–1874) presided over opening ceremonies at Yuexiu and Yuehua on 3.2.[23] In the annual rhythm of official participation in academy rituals, the Xuehaitang examinations seem much less important. Academies generally taken as the most influential ones only received attention through the intervention of particularly activist officials. In 1889, *Shenbao* reported that the entrance examination of Guangya Academy was held on 2.22, that results were soon thereafter announced, and that Zhang Zhidong, Guangya's founder, personally arrived at the academy for opening ceremonies on 3.2.[24] From sources such as diaries and newspapers, which allow readers to perceive the seasonal rhythms and daily interactions of Qing officials and academy directors, one gains the impression that, in Guangzhou, bureaucrats and teachers were closely associated with one another. Thus, directors, and, to a certain extent, supervisors, of Guangzhou's mainstream academies were "scholar-officials" in the sense that they were an ad-

20  E.g. *Xunhuan ribao*, GX9.9.8, 2.
21  Miles, *Sea of Learning*, 119–124.
22  *Xunhuan ribao*, GX8.3.5, 2, GX9.3.5, 2, GX10.2.27, 2, GX10.3.5, 2, GX11.3.6, 2.
23  Guo Songtao, *Guo Songtao riji* (Guo Songtao Diary) (Changsha: Hunan renmin chubanshe, 1981), 360.
24  *Shenbao*, GX15.3.20, no. 5745, 2.

ministrative and ritual extension of the city's officialdom. Although academy directors were not formal officials in the way that, say, county school directors (*jiaoyu* 教諭) and assistant directors (*xundao* 訓導) were, in the pages of late 19th-century newspapers, academy directors take on the appearance of informal officials.[25] The fact that many academy directors at one point or another served as county or prefecture school officials further suggests an overlap between official and academic roles.

## 3    Academy Consumers and the Urban Economy of Examinations

Diaries and newspapers also reveal how academies fit into the daily lives of aspiring elites, the students who were consumers of Guangzhou's various academies. In addition to reporting on social interactions between academy directors and officials, newspapers in the 1880s often announced important events in the annual cycle of academy activities. None was more important than the annual entrance examination. It is clear from newspaper reports that the examinations at different academies were often held on different days, thereby allowing students to sit for entrance examinations for multiple academies. The following sample, with months and days in the lunar calendar, is compiled from reports in *Xunhuan ribao*:[26]

|      |      |
| ---- | ---- |
| 1882 |      |
| 2.3  | Yuehua and Yuexiu |
| 2.5  | Yangcheng |
| 2.28 | Sanhu 三湖 (an academy in the Nanhai County countryside) |
|      |      |
| 1883 |      |
| 2.2  | Yuehua and Yuexiu |
| 2.5  | Xihu |
| 2.8  | Sanhu |
| 2.9  | Jupo |
|      |      |
| 1885 |      |
| 2.2  | Yuexiu |

---

25  For the independence of academies from official control and the distinction between directors and officials, see Mary Backus Rankin, *Elite Activism and Political Transformation in China: Zhejiang Province, 1865–1911* (Stanford: Stanford University Press, 1986), 53–54, 97; Keenan, *Last Classical Academies*, 2.

26  *Xunhuan ribao*, GX8.1.19, 2, GX9.1.20, 2, GX11.1.30, 2.

| 2.4 | Yuehua |
| 2.7 | Jupo |

In general, entrance examinations for academies, especially those at different levels—provincial, prefectural, and county—were held on different days. Policy regarding when to hold examinations for the two provincial academies, Yuexiu and Yuehua, whether on the same day or on different days, seems to have fluctuated. They were held on different days (Yuexiu on 2.3, Yuehua on 2.6) in 1861 but on the same day in 1864, 1865, and 1866.[27] In 1885, Governor-general Zhang Zhidong adopted a policy of allowing candidates to sit for both Yuexiu and Yuehua entrance examinations.[28] The resulting schedule is seen in reports from 1888:[29]

| 2.2 | Yuexiu |
| 2.4 | Yuehua |
| 2.9 | Yangcheng |
| 2.15 | Yingyuan |

This policy whereby officials staggered the days on which entrance examinations were scheduled only makes sense in a context in which many students sat for multiple examinations in any given year. This practice becomes clear in the diary of one avid consumer of academy services, the Cantonese literatus Liang Qi 梁起 (?–?), covering the years 1861–1862. Liang's family was at one point involved in the salt trade, but in recent generations had gained gentry status; his father was a *shengyuan*, and an uncle was a *juren*.[30]

During the period in his diary when Liang sat for entrance and regular academy examinations, he resided either at the Liang home in Guangzhou's western suburb, Xiguan 西關, or at the home where he was hired as a tutor. When the diary begins at the New Year festival in 1861 (XF11), Liang was recovering from an illness, but he was soon busy taking examinations. Between 1.20 and 1.25, Liang and other members of his family composed rhapsodies (*fu* 賦) and poems (*shi* 詩) that had been announced as topics for the Xuehaitang's winter examination (*dongke ti* 冬課題) of the previous year. Their writings were delivered to the Xuehaitang on 1.25. Liang took entrance examinations for Yuexiu

---

27  Liang Qi, *Yusheng riji* (Liang Qi Diary), in *Qingdai gaochao ben*, vol. 1 (Guangzhou: Guangdong renmin chubanshe, 2007), 345; Guo, *Riji*, 151, 215, 352. I read "Yuefeng" 越峰 in TZ3 as a mistake for "Yuehua."
28  *Shenbao*, GX11.2.9, no. 4288, 2.
29  *Shenbao*, GX14.2.21, no, 5348, 2, GX14.2.21, no. 5369, 2.
30  *Nanhai xian zhi* (Nanhai County Gazetteer), 1911, 15:23b–24a.

on 2.1 and Yangcheng on 2.10. On 2.29 he worked on a parallel prose essay (*pianti xu* 駢體序), noting that it was a topic for the Xuehaitang spring examination. On 3.22, having only been named an affiliated, or appended, (*fuke* 附課) student at Yangcheng, Liang took a supplementary examination (*bukao* 補考). He did the same for Yuexiu on 4.3. On 4.14 Liang was disappointed to learn that even after the supplementary examination he was still only designated an affiliated student at Yangcheng, but was consoled by having one of the poems for the Xuehaitang winter examination ranked in the second grade (*ciqu* 次取), for which he would receive a financial award. On 4.26 he wrote a poem for the Xuehaitang summer examinations, one that would eventually be included in a published collection of model student essays and poems.[31]

By the sixth and seventh months, Liang settled into a routine, if hectic, examination schedule, often noting that he returned home from taking examinations late at night:[32]

| 6.3 | Yuexiu |
| 6.5 | Xuehaitang (submitted an essay) |
| 6.9 | Yangcheng |
| 6.13 | Yuexiu |
| 6.16 | Yangcheng |
| 6.23 | Yuexiu |
| 6.24 | Yangcheng[33] |
| 7.2 | Yangcheng |
| 7.3 | Yuexiu |
| 7.13 | Yuexiu |
| 7.16 | Yangcheng |
| 7.23 | Yuexiu |
| 7.24 | Yangcheng |

Liang seems to have missed some examinations, for example presumably Yangcheng's on 7.9; however, he sat for or submitted examination essays or poems on thirteen separate occasions during this two-month period. As a consumer, Liang here used three academies: Xuehaitang, Yangcheng, and Yuexiu. Surprisingly, Liang's only close interaction with academy directors appears to

---

31    Liang, *Riji*, 327–334; *Xuehaitang siji* (Fourth Series of Xuehaitang Collected Writings), 1886, reprint, ZGLDSYZ 14: 25.7a–b.
32    Liang, *Riji*, 337–342.
33    Liang notes in his diary that he was unable to complete the Yangcheng examination on this day because he was in a poor state of mind (*yi xinxu bu jia, gousi weijiu* 以心緒不佳 搆思未就).

be on 5.27, when he entered the Old City to visit Yuexiu director Shi Cheng 史澄 (1814–?). In the following year, Liang would take entrance examinations at Yuexiu, Yuehua, and Yangcheng.[34]

One motivation for Liang Qi to take so many academy examinations was in order to hone his skills in the hopes of increasing his chances of passing civil service examinations. But some of his diary entries also suggest that stipends earned from performing well on academy examinations were an important source of supplemental income. On two occasions Liang emphasized the importance of stipends from Xuehaitang examinations, in one case justifying his continuing to take examinations, while in mourning for his father, in order financially to support his mother.[35] In this sense, Liang Qi was like many other urban literati in the late Qing who supplemented their income by working as what amounted to professional examination-takers. Sharpening their skills by regularly taking academy examinations, people like Liang Qi increased their earning potential both as stipend- and award-winning examinees and as tutors for younger aspiring examinees.

*Shenbao* editors deemed it newsworthy to print in the fifth month of 1885 that, because Governor-general Zhang Zhidong was preoccupied with official business (this was during the Sino-French War), he had not yet rated papers for the governor-general's examinations for Yuehua and Yuexiu administered earlier in the year. As a result, results had still not been announced and stipends not yet awarded, leaving "hundreds of impoverished scholars desperate for news."[36] Similarly, an 1893 article reported on the county academy for Panyu, Yushan Academy. When the director distributed awards (*jiangyin* 獎銀) at the end of the last month of the previous lunar year, many students had returned to their homes for the new year festivities or were otherwise preoccupied and thus had not gone to the academy to retrieve the awards. When students arrived back at the academy at the beginning of the current year, the director claimed that the time for distribution was long past and that the funds had been returned to officials. In fact, the newspaper explains, the director had embezzled the money. Students refused to accept the director's explanations and were on the verge of assaulting him.[37] Such reports suggest the importance

---

34   Liang, *Riji*, 336, 345.
35   Liang, *Riji*, 334, 356. It is unclear whether or not Xuehaitang regulations prohibited students from taking examinations during a mourning period. Regulations published in the academy gazetteer do not address this issue. See *Xuehaitang zhi* (Xuehaitang Gazetteer), 1838, reprint (Taipei: Guangwen shuju, 1971).
36   *Shenbao*, GX11.5.6, no. 4373, 3. For a similar example, see *Shenbao*, GX15.3.20, no. 5745, 2.
37   *Shenbao*, GX19.7.24, no. 7318, 2–3.

of stipends and awards as important sources of supplemental income for students of Guangzhou's urban academies.

One clue to the relative importance of mainstream academies, such as Yuexiu and Yuehua, vis-à-vis supposedly more influential academies, such as the Xuehaitang and Guangya Academy, lies in the large numbers, throughout the 19th century, of aspiring students who sat for entrance examinations at the mainstream academies. For Yangcheng entrance examinations, Xie Lansheng recorded numbers ranging from over 1,400 in 1828 to precisely 2,124 in 1829.[38] *Shenbao* reported similarly high numbers in the 1880s: as many as 4,000 students sitting for Yuexiu and Yuehua entrance examinations in 1887, and over 1,000 examinees in 1888 and again in 1893 for entrance examinations for the county-level Xihu Academy.[39]

As Liang Qi's diary suggests, one incentive to gain a place on the student rolls of Guangzhou's academies was to earn a stipend. In addition, students who performed well on regular examinations, responding to questions prepared alternately by the city's officials and academy directors, would earn financial awards for outstanding compositions. This may explain the high turnout of over 1,200 examinees in the third month of 1889, when Zhang Zhidong jointly administered the governor-general's examination for Yuexiu and Yuehua students. Because of unexpectedly large numbers, Zhang abandoned his plans to fête the examinees with tea and snacks and instead distributed one hundred copper coins to each examinee.[40]

Another incentive is that affiliation with some academies provided a shortcut to participation in the triennial provincial civil service examinations. In 1888, *Shenbao* attributed the high turnout of over 3,000 students for entrance examinations at Yuexiu and Yuehua to the fact that provincial examinations were scheduled for later in the year.[41] In the month prior to a provincial examination, selected Yuexiu, Yuehua, and Yangcheng students could sit for a special examination (*luyi* 錄遺) administered by a provincial official that would qualify successful examinees for the provincial examinations, and these

---

38    Xie, *Riji*, DG8.1.18, DG9.1.21.
39    *Shenbao*, GX13.2.16, no. 4989, 2, GX14.2.7, no. 5355, 3, GX19.2.9, no. 7156, 2. Competition for entrance into Xihu must have been intense, as *Shenbao* reported in 1890 that the Nanhai county magistrate raised the quota of *shengyuan* and *jiansheng* admitted into the academy from 15 to 30. This quota presumably did not include apprentice students. *Shenbao*, GX16.2.10, no. 6053, 2. Quotas at the larger, provincial academies could be much higher. For example, by 1809, Yuexiu Academy had a quota of one hundred formal students (*zhengkesheng* 正課生) and fifty outer students (*waikesheng* 外課生). *Yuexiu shuyuan zhi*, 2:20b.
40    *Shenbao*, GX15.4.13, no. 5768, 2.
41    *Shenbao*, GX14.2.21, no. 5369, 2.

special examinations offered a higher chance of qualifying than did regular qualifying examinations through registration in government county and prefectural schools.[42] Participation in Xuehaitang or Jupo examinations did not provide this shortcut to the provincial examinations. In this sense, Yuexiu, Yuehua, and Yangcheng were much more fully integrated into the pulse of urban elite life.

The mainstream academies were thus vital components of an examination economy driven by the routine of both academy examinations and civil service examinations. This examination economy was an urban phenomenon, centered both on civil service examinations administered by the Qing state and on entrance examinations and routine examinations administered by the city's Confucian academies. The examinations provided important sources of income for academy directors, administrators, and students, all of whom stood to gain financially. Guangzhou's academies were financially supported by endowments, often in the form of rent-producing shops and agricultural land or of interest-earning deposits with pawnshops; such endowments usually originated in grants provided by Qing officials assigned to Guangzhou. Academy students were expected to offer annual gifts, at Yuehua ranging from 2.1 to 2.8 taels, to their teachers. Nevertheless, for students these costs were more than offset by income in the form of monthly stipends, at Yuehua in 1828 amounting to between 9 and 18 taels per year. In addition, students who excelled in routine examinations might win awards, at Yuehua ranging from 0.3 taels to 1 tael.[43] Aside from providing primary or supplemental income for academy staff and students, the examination economy also increased business for nearby book shops, restaurants, and other commercial enterprises.

A biting critique of academy practices, written by Feng Minchang 馮敏昌 (1747–1806), offers a glimpse into how this examination economy supported a broad range of urban residents, from students and teachers to government and academy staffs. Feng served as director of Yuexiu in 1801, later directed Yuehua, and then returned to Yuexiu, where he died in 1806. Feng was a native of the relatively remote and rural southwestern Guangdong, and this background seems to have compounded his revulsion toward urban life in the cosmopolitan city of Guangzhou.[44] In a set of policy proposals that he wrote upon

---

42  *Shenbao*, GX11.8.6, no. 4461, 3, also GX14.7.26, no, 5522, 3. On these special examinations and their relationship to Guangzhou's academies, see Shen Baiyan, *Qingmo Guangdong xianji keju qushi jishi* (A factual account of county-level civil examinations in late-Qing Guangdong), 1930, unpaginated; Miles, *Sea of Learning*, 79–80.
43  Liu, *Guangdong shuyuan zhidu*, 268, 286, 290.
44  Feng, *Xiao Luofu caotang wenji* (Collected Prose from the Small Luofu Thatched Hall), 1846, reprint, *Qingdai shiwen ji huibian*, vol. 418 (Shanghai: Shanghai guji chubanshe, 2010), 9:18a–b, 29a.

assuming the Yuexiu directorship for the second time, Feng identified a series of problems that he saw as stemming from the practice at "Guangdong's so-called three major academies"—Duanxi 端溪 in Zhaoqing and Yuexiu and Yuehua in Guangzhou—of holding entrance examinations annually instead of triennially.[45] Feng also observed that students were attracted to Yuexiu primarily as a means of being admitted for the special qualifying examinations, for entrance into the provincial examinations, described above. Hence, Feng noted, the numbers of students sitting for academy entrance examinations (in early spring) skyrocketed in years when provincial examinations (in autumn) were scheduled, and everyone profited from the spike in customary fees and gifts.[46] Accordingly, Feng argued for scaling back entrance examinations to once every three years.

Feng Minchang noted other ways in which academies, and Yuexiu in particular, fit into the broader economy of academy and civil service examinations. As the provincial capital, Guangzhou was the center of Guangdong's examination economy. Hence, a steady stream of students and scholars from surrounding areas sought long-term residence in the city. A number of institutions met this demand. It was common for men from the countryside to reside in one of Guangzhou's temples or monasteries while pursuing their studies in the city.[47] In years in which civil service examinations were held, students might stay in a hostel (*shiguan* 試館) designed for such purposes.[48] Academies were another option. In the early 19th century, residence at Yuexiu Academy seems to have been especially popular among students and scholars from Jiaying Department in northeast Guangdong. Students from Jiaying, part of an area that has been dubbed the Hakka homeland, would have spoken a dialect distinct from the Cantonese dialect.[49] Writing in the first decade, Feng Minchang observed that most students at the academy were from Guangzhou prefecture, and most of the rest from Jiaying department.[50] After one entrance examination, Feng counted a total of 149 formal (*zheng* 正) and affiliated (*fu* 附) students, 127 of whom were from Guangzhou prefecture, 11 from Jiaying,

---

45  Feng, *Wenji*, 9:31a. An abridged version of Feng's proposals is in *Yuexiu shuyuan zhi*, 15:38a–44a.
46  Feng, *Wenji*, 9:40b, 51a.
47  E.g. Ye Jinguang, *Ye Yunbao nianpu* (Chronological biography of Ye Yunbao), 1883, 4a–5a; Zhu Ciqi *Zhu Jiujiang xiansheng ji* (Collected writings of Zhu Ciqi), *Jindai Zhongguo shiliao congkan*, vol. 127 (Taipei: Wenhai chubanshe, 1967), *nianpu*, 6b.
48  Xie, *Riji*, JQ24.8.7; *Shenbao*, GX11.7.19, no. 4444, 2.
49  Sow-Theng Leong, *Migration and Ethnicity in Chinese History: Hakkas, Pengmin, and Their Neighbors* (Stanford: Stanford University Press, 1997), 75–76.
50  Feng, *Wenji*, 9:39b.

and 11 from other places (including the Guangzhou banner garrison).⁵¹ The author of a Yuexiu Academy gazetteer compiled in 1847 observed that many poor scholars from Jiaying came to Guangzhou to study, and since they could not afford to rent a place to live, they viewed Yuexiu as a "public place for study" (*dushu gongdi* 讀書公地) and "invited one another in" (*ze xiang shuai er ru* 則相率而入); some resided at the academy for several years. This critique reminds us that academies were exclusive institutions catering to male literati; academy grounds were not designed to serve as public spaces open to the urban populace. Even though Feng Minchang was shocked by this practice, the author notes, Feng could do nothing about it. In the four decades after Feng's directorship, despite some temporarily successful official efforts to remove interloping Jiaying natives, the practice continued. It is possible that the Jiaying connection was facilitated by the fact that Yuexiu's two co-supervisors in the 1820s were Jiaying scholars. The gazetteer author also notes that in some cases Jiaying scholars residing at the academy would put up visiting relatives.⁵²

In listing what he saw as yet another problem with annual, as opposed to triennial, entrance examinations, Feng Minchang noted that many students moved out of the academy after the ceremonial end of the academic year on 12.2.⁵³ But a significant number of students continued to reside in the academy, and, since it was by no means certain that they would pass entrance examinations after the lunar new year, they had little incentive to help maintain the academy buildings and grounds. This was especially the case for students from Jiaying, according to Feng. Commenting that "it is difficult to guard against a thief from within the family," Feng noted that such students would rip off window lattices and door leaves to use as fuel for cooking, ignoring the supervisor's efforts to stop them.⁵⁴

Feng once complained of an instance in which it was discovered that one of the Jiaying natives residing at the academy had taken a county/prefectural examination in place of an aspiring *shengyuan*. When the cheating was discovered, the student fled and thereby escaped punishment, but the Yuexiu supervisor was removed from his position. The academy's reputation was

---

51  Feng, *Wenji*, 9:37b–38a.
52  *Yuexiu shuyuan zhi*, 5:20a–b, 16:34a–b. Another example of an academy in which unaffiliated people resided is Wencheng shuyuan, in the eastern suburb of Guangzhou. In the summer of 1881 a poor husband and wife came to Guangzhou from a nearby county, Dongguan, in search of work. Perhaps because the watchman at the academy was also from Dongguan, the couple was able to rent a room in the academy. *Xingke tiben*, 4065-016/GX8.5.29; *Panyu xian xu zhi* (Continuation of Panyu County Gazetteer), 1931, 2:3a.
53  *Yuexiu shuyuan zhi*, 2:31a–b; *Xunhuan ribao*, GX10.12.6, 2.
54  Feng, *Wenji*, 9:35b–37a.

stained when provincial officials posted a notice on the academy's gate reading "sheltering evil and accepting filth" (*cang gou na wu* 藏垢納污).[55] Feng also recalled that, during his first tenure at Yuexiu (1801), students tutored neighborhood children in their academy dormitories. The commotion caused by a dozen children frolicking on academy grounds disrupted the serious air of the academy, and the grain intendent was forced to issue a proclamation prohibiting this practice.[56] Feng advocated enforcing academy regulations keeping the gate shut except for two times a day to allow students to purchase daily provisions, as this would prevent academy students from taking civil service examinations on behalf of others and from making money as pettifoggers. Feng met a great deal of protest from students for enforcing this policy.[57] This outcry of course suggests that it was common practice for students resident at academies to involve themselves in the broader urban economy, not only driving the examination culture but also branching out into litigation.

Many of the ways in which resident students made use of Yuexiu Academy show how this institution was deeply embedded in the larger economy of examinations. For scholars from remote Jiaying, residence in Yuexiu offered a place in Guangdong's capital city, where provincial examinations took place. Resident students who tutored neighborhood children were further linked to this economy, both profiting from it and training a new generation of examinees. Finally, whether one resided in the academy or outside it, affiliation with Yuexiu and other mainstream academies offered both the necessary training to succeed in civil service examinations at all levels and the possibility of increasing one's chances of qualifying for the provincial examinations in particular. In this sense, mainstream academies had a much greater impact on the routines of the urban elite than did alternative academies such as the Xuehaitang.

## 4     Academies, Urban Spectacles, and City Residents

In addressing the influence that Confucian academies had on society beyond the narrow circle of teachers and students affiliated with academies, Xiao Yongming suggests that the spectacle of academy rituals may have had an impact on local commoners, potentially imbuing them with an appreciation for the values that academy rituals espoused and thereby serving as a means of

---

55    Feng, *Wenji*, 9:38a–b.
56    Feng, *Wenji*, 9:39a.
57    Feng, *Wenji*, 9:29a–b, 38b; *Yuexiu shuyuan zhi*, 7:43a–b, 15:37a.

social control.[58] Xiao's work opens up an important new line of inquiry in the study of Confucian academies in China, their impact on local populations beyond academy teachers and students; however, his assertion raises the question of what kind of competition academies faced in garnering the attention of urban populations. For 19th-century Guangzhou, records of Yuexiu Academy's relations with its neighbors and accounts of the ways in which founders of alternative academies sought to distance their new institutions from the urban core while maintaining a necessary link to the city shed some light on the issue of the relationship between academies and urban commoners in Qing China.

### 4.1 Yuexiu Academy and Its Noisy Neighbors

Guangzhou's big three academies, Yuexiu, Yuehua, and Yangcheng, were all located in the walled Old City, near numerous yamen, but also in close proximity to a number of institutions whose spectacles must often have overwhelmed academy activities. The opening ceremonies described above were perhaps one occasion in which the academy commanded the attention of its neighbors, at least when high provincial officials arrived or departed. Likewise, neighbors must have mingled with crowds of academy hopefuls who watched the posting of the results of the annual entrance examinations outside Yuexiu's main gate.[59] Based on its location, and as an important component of the examination economy, activity in and around Yuexiu fluctuated with the examination cycle. South of the academy was Shuangmendi 雙門底, a street filled with shops that sold books, stationery, and other examination paraphernalia. In the summer and autumn of years in which provincial examinations were held, hostels for examinees were filled to capacity and the book shops became especially crowded, even holding night markets in order to meet demand.[60] But perhaps nothing had a greater impact on the neighborhood surrounding Yuexiu than construction projects. This was especially the case when shops and residences that had encroached on academy grounds were demolished during the course of a reconstruction project, as at Yuexiu in 1792.[61]

In these ways, the presence of Yuexiu was surely felt by commoners who resided nearby. Nevertheless, one wonders what kind of competition Yuexiu faced in garnering the attention of city residents. One strategy for approaching this question is to read the frank complaints made by Yuexiu's early

---

58  Xiao Yongming, *Ruxue, shuyuan, shehui: shehui wenhua shi shiye zhong de shuyuan* (Confucianism, academies, and society: a sociocultural historical perspective on academies) (Beijing: Shangwu yinshuguan, 2012), 363–368.
59  *Yuexiu shuyuan zhi*, 1:2b–3a; Feng, *Wenji*, 9:35a; Guo, *Riji*, 360.
60  *Shenbao*, GX11.7.19, no. 4444, 1–2, GX11.8.6, no. 4461, 3; *Yuexiu shuyuan zhi*, 总图.
61  *Yuexiu shuyuan zhi*, 5:12a–b.

19th-century director, the cantankerous Feng Minchang. Upon assuming the directorship for a second time, Feng bemoaned the urban bustle encroaching upon the academy from all sides. A towering commercial building on the eastern edge of the academy geomantically disrupted the academy's main hall, the roof of a granary south of the academy had the same effect on the main gate and spirit wall, and the rear building of another shop pressed against the supervisor's residence. Most disturbing for Feng was the fate of a library building at the rear of the campus that housed books bestowed upon the academy by the emperor. Recently, Feng complained, a large restaurant had opened just behind this library. The restaurant's kitchen abutted student dormitories on one side of the academy and was not far from the studio where Feng was expected as academy director to grade examination papers. Yet from the break of dawn through the evening, Feng and his students were assaulted by the sounds of animals being slaughtered in the kitchen and of the restaurant's inebriated patrons playing drinking games and brawling. Feng explains that he had the supervisor report this to the lieutenant-governor, who in turn ordered the Nanhai and Panyu county magistrates to prohibit the opening of restaurants in the vicinity of the academy and the consequent disruption of academy activities. Feng explains that in response to official actions the restaurant owner simply dismantled the second floor of the restaurant's rear hall, which was closest to the academy. Soon, the restaurant was open for business again, with a makeshift structure replacing the disassembled portion of the restaurant, and with revelers as noisy as before.[62]

Aside from the persistent din of the entertainment industry and other aspects of commercial life in surrounding neighborhoods, popular seasonal festivals surely provided much greater spectacles than did academy rituals such as official opening ceremonies or the posting of names of people who passed the entrance examinations. Two such festivals overtook Shuangmendi during the autumn in successive years, 1880 and 1881, when, perhaps not coincidentally, no provincial examinations were scheduled. In 1880, *Xunhuan ribao* reported that officials had ordered organizers of a popular religious festival (*jiao* 醮) to dismantle one story of a temporary structure erected at Shuangmendi.[63] In the following year, the same newspaper described a theft that occurred

---

62  Feng, *Wenji*, 9:52b–53b; *Yuexiu shuyuan zhi*, 7:43b–44a.
63  On the characteristics of *jiao*-festivals as Daoist communal sacrifices, see Kenneth Dean, *Taoist Ritual and Popular Cults of Southeast China* (Princeton: Princeton University Press, 1993), 45–53; on *jiao*-festivals in the Pearl River delta, see David Faure, *Emperor and Ancestor: State and Lineage in South China* (Stanford: Stanford University Press, 2007), 96.

when dense crowds gathered at Shuangmendi to watch a parade associated with a temple festival.[64]

In addition to contending for urban space, on the pages of newspapers in the 1880s news of academy activities competed for readers' attention with reports about the less refined but surely much more popular pursuits of urban life. For example, in one 1883 issue, immediately following an announcement that the Yuexiu entrance examination was scheduled for the second day of the second month, one finds news of an only marginally effective pronouncement by the Nanhai and Panyu county magistrates prohibiting parades of lion and dragon dancers that often occurred at night during the Lantern Festival.[65] Liang Qi's diary reveals that over two decades earlier this frequent academy examinee also patronized the parades of dancing lions and dragons near his home in Xiguan during the Lantern Festival. In the days surrounding this festival in the middle of the first month, before regular academy examinations commenced, Liang alternated his time between joining the festivities and composing prose and poetry for Xuehaitang examinations, at times performing the latter task while still tipsy from drinking during the festivities.[66]

Institutions and events just north of Yuexiu Academy also drew the attention of both officials and commoners. Perhaps the greatest attraction in this neighborhood was the City God Temple (Chenghuangmiao 城隍廟), a short walk from Yuexiu and neighboring Yushan Academy. Provincial officials performed rituals here annually in the seventh month and they prayed for rain during droughts or for sunshine during floods.[67] A British clergyman and his wife who visited the temple on several occasions in the mid-1870s described its courtyards on normal days as being "crowded with the stalls of fortune tellers, doctors, dentists, chiropodists, tobacconists, and pastrycooks. Around these stalls, from morning until evening are assembled men, who are in all ranks, and conditions of life."[68] During the annual festival in the seventh month, the British couple estimated crowds as large as 24,000 people, ranging from officials conducting ceremonies, to the sick seeking to be healed, to female devotees, whom they estimated constituted more than half of the crowd.[69] It is difficult

---

64　*Xunhuan ribao*, GX6.8.27, 2, GX7.8.4, 2. For similar crowds at an 1884 festival at a temple near Yuehua Academy, see *Xunhuan ribao*, GX10.4.1, 2.
65　*Xunhuan ribao*, GX9.1.16, 2.
66　Liang, *Riji*, 327–328.
67　E.g. *Xunhuan ribao*, GX7.7.29, 2. On the spectacle of officials' rainmaking rituals, see Jeffrey Snyder-Reinke, *Dry Spells: State Rainmaking and Local Governance in Late Imperial China* (Cambridge, MA: Harvard University Asia Center, 2009), 95–101.
68　John Henry Gray, *Walks in the City of Canton* (Hongkong: De Souza, 1875), 415–416.
69　Mrs. (John Henry) Gray, *Fourteen Months in Canton* (London: Macmillan and Co., 1880), 188–193.

to imagine that activities associated with Yuexiu Academy could have held the attention of its neighbors for very long in the face of such bustling daily activities, let alone the boisterous crowds that gathered for festivals at Shuangmendi or the City God Temple. Rather than Yuexiu ceremonies transforming customs in the Old City, it seems more likely that such attractions as the gambling house that *Shenbao* reported on nearby Xihu Street or the pornographic materials for sale at religious supply stores there would have transformed Yuexiu students' morals.[70]

### 4.2 Siting Alternative Academies: Xuehaitang and Guangya Shuyuan

Yuexiu Academy was inextricably embedded in its urban environment. Even though his academy's location in the Old City placed it outside the most commercialized sectors of Guangzhou, such as the New City or Xiguan, in the first decade of the 19th century Director Feng Minchang felt the bedlam of urban life seeping in from all sides. Throughout the rest of the century, any director who might have dreamed of Yuexiu transforming local customs must have been pessimistic, with far more spectacular spectacles and everyday temptations competing for the attention both of the academy's students and of its neighboring residents. Founders of new academies that were meant to remain aloof from the urban examination and entertainment economies sought to situate their new academies at some remove from the urban life that surrounded Yuexiu. But if they established their academies too far from the city, they risked making them irrelevant to the city's population of aspiring literati, who were hardly inclined to separate themselves from the city-centered examination economy. Moreover, even though the curricula of alternative academies incorporated many elements not emphasized in civil service examinations, for academy consumers such as Liang Qi, examinations held by alternative academies were readily integrated into the broader examination economy in which mainstream academies such as Yuexiu played a central role. The tension between the urge to separate alternative academies from the urban core and the need to remain part of city life is seen in descriptions of the processes by which two 19th-century governors-general selected sites for their new, alternative academies.

The 1838 Xuehaitang gazetteer describes the long process by which this academy's founder, Ruan Yuan 阮元 (1764–1849), selected a site for his new academy in the mid-1820s, listing the reasons why Ruan rejected his initial options. First he considered a site known as the Southern Garden because it was associated with eminent Cantonese poets during the Ming; however, he

---

70    *Shenbao*, GX11.5.13, no. 4380, 2, GX13.R4.3, no. 5065, 2.

decided against this site in the New City because it was "too damp and narrow." Another option was to utilize the campus of an existing academy, Wenlan Academy (Wenlan shuyuan 文瀾書院), a multifunctional institution that held literary competitions and largely served literati from wealthy merchant families based in Xiguan, including Liang Qi's family. But Ruan was deterred from this site because it "did not have much scenery," perhaps referring to the stores, pawnshop towers, and warehouses that filled this suburb or to the results of a devastating fire in Xiguan that just two years earlier had destroyed thousands of homes and shops. Ruan's third option was the neighborhood around Sea Banner Monastery (Haichuang si 海幢寺), a popular tourist site in Henan 河南, a suburb to the south across the Pearl River. Yet Ruan "disliked its proximity to the market." Among other things, "the market" might have referred to the salt junks or flower boats that lined the shore of Henan, or perhaps the mansion of the maritime merchant Wu Bingjian. In any case, each of these potential sites was located in one of the three most commercialized sectors of the city, New City, Xiguan, and Henan. It is interesting that, in this account, Ruan did not even consider a location in the core of the Old City, near the mainstream academies. After Ruan finally identified his ideal site, at the foot of Yuexiu Hill north of the city center but still within the city walls, the new academy's regulations allowed the "short-sleeved and bare-footed" masses only to peer into the academy grounds from outside the gate. No one with "vulgar language or vile airs" was welcome.[71]

Six decades later, in a letter that he sent to his new academy's first director, founder Zhang Zhidong portrayed in very similar terms his process of selecting a site for Guangya Academy. Zhang explained that he wanted a place somewhat removed from the city but not too remote. Perhaps due to sixty years of urban sprawl, Zhang was forced to look further into the city's suburbs than had Ruan Yuan. Zhang ruled out two potential sites in Xiguan and two others in Henan for a variety of reasons: high real estate prices, lack of space, and close proximity to maritime firms and commercial tax offices with their cacophonous chatter. After ruling out sites at the east gate and outside the north gate, Zhang finally found an appropriate location in what was then a relatively remote northwestern suburb.[72] *Shenbao* reported that, as the academy was near-

---

[71] *Xuehaitang zhi*, 6b, 44a. On Wenlan Academy and the Liang family's association with it, see *Nanhai xian zhi* (Nanhai County Gazetteer), 1835, 11:50b–51a; *Wenlan zhongshen lu* (Record of Wenlan Academy Gentry), 1892, reprint, *Guangzhou dadian*, vol. 188 (Guangzhou: Guangzhou chubanshe, 2015), 374–375.

[72] "Guangya shuyuan chuangban liushi nian, Guangya zhongxue chengli saqi nian jinian tekan (Special publication to commemorate the sixtieth anniversary of the creation of Guangya Academy and the thirty-seventh anniversary of the establishment of Guangya

ing completion, Zhang Zhidong decided to allow "literati and commoners" (*shimin* 士民) to visit the campus before the academic year's opening ceremonies. Every day, the article relates, as many as "several thousand" people toured the grounds, so much so that business at local tea houses, a hallmark of the urban entertainment economy, tripled.[73] If this report is accurate, it suggests that the new academy was not so far removed from urban crowds after all, if not neighboring residents then at least curious local tourists.

## 5 Conclusion

This chapter represents an initial exploration of the place of academies in the rhythms of urban life in 19th-century Guangzhou. I hope that it suggests some ways in which research on Confucian academies might be expanded. If one wishes to understand the impact of academies on local society, from scholarly elites to commoners, it is necessary to situate academies in their local environments. For Guangzhou prefecture in the 19th century, and more broadly in Qing China, this means that the history of academies must to a large extent also be urban history. In this respect, at least, the history of Confucian academies in Qing China stands in contrast to earlier periods in Chinese history, as seen in studies of Song-era academies by Linda Walton and Hoyt Tillman in this volume, and to the situation in Chosŏn Korea, where Confucian academies were almost by definition rural, rather than urban, institutions.[74]

Moreover, if we wish to gain a greater understanding of how academies fit into the annual, monthly, or daily routines of academic elites, students, and the broader urban population, it is important to shift attention from "influential" academies, such as the Xuehaitang, to more mundane ones, such as Yuexiu Academy. In both English-language and Chinese-language scholarship, unique institutions such as the Xuehaitang have received far greater scholarly attention than have mainstream academies. Yet, as we have seen, in many ways the more mainstream academies had a much greater presence in the rhythm of urban life for most city residents, from the academy directors who hobnobbed with high officials to non-academic commoners who witnessed

---

Middle School)," (Guangzhou: Guangdong sheng li Guangya zhongxue, 1948), 2–3. This passage is also quoted in Zhou Hanguang, *Zhang Zhidong yu Guangya shuyuan* (Zhang Zhidong and Guangya Academy) (Taipei: Zhongguo wenhua daxue, 1983), 309. Also see *Shenbao*, GX13.R4.13, no. 5075, 10.

73  *Shenbao*, GX14.5.10, no. 5447, 9.
74  Martina Deuchler made this important point during the Confucian Academies in East Asia workshop.

academy rituals. By the 19th century, China's mainstream, urban Confucian academies were important components, along with private tutors and government schools, and extending to book stores, hostels, and tea houses, of a thriving examination economy.

In shifting attention from alternative academies to mainstream academies, one is immediately faced with the problem of sources, since famous academies such as the Xuehaitang tend to be the most well-documented ones. At the same time, an emphasis on situating academies within their urban environments provides an opportunity to utilize different kinds of sources in the study of Confucian academies. Archival sources are a promising option; one can find in central government archives occasional references to academies in such cities as Guangzhou, but county archives surely contain a much greater wealth of information on academies in such places as Chongqing. For the late 19th century, newspapers can reveal a great deal about both the annual cycle of examination activities and the relationships among academy teachers, academy students, and other urban residents. Diaries, especially those authored by less eminent figures such as Liang Qi, can show how consumers drove the examination economy.

Finally, in seeking to situate academies in their urban environments, old sources may be read in new ways. It is quite common to find in such sources as academy gazetteers and academy regulations, or in the collected writings of academy teachers, exhortations not to abandon moral cultivation in a single-minded pursuit of the skills needed to pass civil service examinations. A good example of this is found in the academy regulations of the early 16th-century Guangdong academy director Zhan Ruoshui 湛若水 (1466–1560). As we have seen, three centuries later another Guangdong academy director, Feng Minchang, admonished his students in a similar fashion. It is important to keep in mind that sources such as academy regulations are prescriptive texts designed to encourage, or force, students to behave in a certain way. In Feng's writings, however, one also finds detailed descriptions of bad behavior, at least in Feng's eyes. By paying more attention to the types of behavior that a particularly activist academy director like Feng Minchang discouraged, we might arrive at a more accurate picture of the ways in which academies were inextricably linked to their urban environments, including the city-based examination economy, in Qing China.

## References

Chaffee, John W. "Chu Hsi and the Revival of the White Deer Grotto Academy, 1179–1181 AD" *T'oung Pao* 71 (1985): 40–62.

Chan, Wing-Tsit. *A Source Book in Chinese Philosophy*. Princeton: Princeton University Press, 1963.

Cheng Nensheng 程嫩生. *Zhongguo shuyuan wenxue jiaoyu yanjiu* 中国书院文学教育研究 (Research on Literature Education in China's Academies). Beijing: Zhongguo shehui kexue chubanshe, 2014.

Dean, Kenneth. *Taoist Ritual and Popular Cults of Southeast China*. Princeton: Princeton University Press, 1993.

Deng Hongbo 邓洪波. *Zhongguo shuyuan shi* 中国书院史 (History of Academies in China). Revised edition. Wuhan: Wuhan daxue chubanshe, 2013.

Elman, Benjamin A. *From Philosophy to Philology: Intellectual and Social Aspects of Change in Late Imperial China*. Cambridge, MA: Council on East Asian Studies, 1984.

Faure, David. *Emperor and Ancestor: State and Lineage in South China*. Stanford: Stanford University Press, 2007.

Feng Minchang 馮敏昌. *Xiao Luofu caotang wenji* 小羅浮草堂文集 (Collected Prose from the Small Luofu Thatched Hall). 1846. Reprint. *Qingdai shiwen ji huibian*, vol. 418. Shanghai: Shanghai guji chubanshe, 2010.

Gray, John Henry. *Walks in the City of Canton*. Hongkong: De Souza, 1875.

Gray, Mrs. (John Henry). *Fourteen Months in Canton*. London: Macmillan and Co., 1880.

Grimm, Tilemann. "Academies and Urban Systems in Kwangtung." In *The City in Late Imperial China*, edited by G. William Skinner, 475–498. Stanford: Stanford University Press, 1977,

*Guangdong tongzhi* 廣東通志 (Guangdong Provincial Gazetteer). 1822.

"Guangya shuyuan chuangban liushi nian, Guangya zhongxue chengli saqi nian jinian tekan 廣雅書院創辦六十年, 廣雅中學成立卅七年紀念特刊 (Special Publication to Commemorate the Sixtieth Anniversary of the Creation of Guangya Academy and the Thirty-seventh Anniversary of the Establishment of Guangya Middle School)." Guangzhou: Guangdong sheng li Guangya zhongxue, 1948.

*Guangzhou fu zhi* 廣州府志 (Guangzhou Prefectural Gazetteer). 1879.

Guo Songtao 郭嵩濤. *Guo Songtao riji* 郭嵩濤日記 (Guo Songtao Diary). Changsha: Hunan renmin chubanshe, 1981.

Keenan, Barry C. *Imperial China's Last Classical Academies: Social Change in the Lower Yangzi, 1864–1911*. Berkeley: University of California Press, 1994.

Leong, Sow-Theng. *Migration and Ethnicity in Chinese History: Hakkas, Pengmin, and Their Neighbors*. Stanford: Stanford University Press, 1997.

Liang Qi 梁起. *Yusheng riji* 庚生日記 (Liang Qi diary). *Qingdai gaochao ben*, vol. 1. Guangzhou: Guangdong renmin chubanshe, 2007.

Liu Boji 劉伯驥. *Guangdong shuyuan zhidu* 廣東書院制度 (The Institution of Academies in Guangdong). Taipei: Zhonghua congshu weiyuanhui, 1958.

Liu Yucai 刘玉才. *Qingdai shuyuan yu xueshu bianqian yanjiu* 清代书院与学术变迁研究 (Research on Qing Dynasty Academies and Changes in Scholarship). Beijing: Beijing daxue chubanshe, 2008.

McMahon, Daniel. "The Yuelu Academy and Hunan's Nineteenth-Century Turn Toward Statecraft." *Late Imperial China* 26, no. 1 (June 2005): 72–109.

Meskill, John. *Academies in Ming China: A Historical Essay*. Tucson: The University of Arizona Press, 1982.

Miles, Steven B. "The Nature and Impact of Late Imperial Chinese Academies: A Review of Some Recent Publications in China." *Frontiers of Education in China* 10, no. 4 (December 2015): 634–656.

Miles, Steven B. *The Sea of Learning: Mobility and Identity in Nineteenth-Century Guangzhou*. Cambridge, MA: Harvard University Asia Center, 2006.

*Nanhai xian zhi* 南海縣志 (Nanhai County Gazetteer). 1835.

*Nanhai xian zhi* 南海縣志 (Nanhai County Gazetteer). 1911.

*Panyu xian xu zhi* 番禺縣續志 (Continuation of Panyu County Gazetteer). 1931.

Qian Shifu 錢實甫. *Qingdai zhiguan nianbiao* 清代職官年表 (Chronological Tables of Qing Dynasty Officials). Beijing: Zhonghua shuju, 1980.

Rankin, Mary Backus. *Elite Activism and Political Transformation in China: Zhejiang Province, 1865–1911*. Stanford: Stanford University Press, 1986.

Shen Baiyan 沈拜言. *Qingmo Guangdong xianji keju qushi jishi* 清末廣東縣級科舉取士紀實 (A Factual Account of County-level Civil Examinations in Late-Qing Guangdong). 1930.

*Shenbao* 申報. Digital archive. Green Apple Data Center. <http://shunpao.egreenapple.com/WEB/INDEX.html> (accessed: 01 September 2017).

Snyder-Reinke, Jeffrey. *Dry Spells: State Rainmaking and Local Governance in Late Imperial China*. Cambridge, MA: Harvard University Asia Center, 2009.

Walton, Linda. *Academies and Society in Southern Sung China*. Honolulu: University of Hawai'i Press, 1999.

*Wenlan zhongshen lu* 文瀾衆紳錄 (Record of Wenlan Academy Gentry). 1892. Reprint. *Guangzhou dadian*, vol. 188. Guangzhou: Guangzhou chubanshe, 2015.

Xiao Yongming 肖永明. *Ruxue, shuyuan, shehui: shehui wenhua shi shiye zhong de shuyuan* 儒学, 书院, 社会: 社会文化史视野中的书院 (Confucianism, Academies, and Society: A Sociocultural Historical Perspective on Academies). Beijing: Shangwu yinshuguan, 2012.

Xie Lansheng 謝蘭生. *Changxingxingzhai riji* 常惺惺齋日記 (Diary from the Studio of Constant Awareness). Manuscript, 1819–1829. Held at National Library of China.

*Xingke tiben* 刑科題本 (Board of Punishments Routine Memorials). Held at Zhongguo diyi lishi dang'anguan 中国第一历史档案馆 (The First Historical Archives of China), Beijing.

*Xuehaitang siji* 學海堂四集 (Fourth Series of Xuehaitang Collected Writings). 1886. Reprint. ZGLDSYZ Volume 14.

*Xuehaitang zhi* 學海堂志 (Xuehaitang Gazetteer). 1838. Reprint. Taipei: Guangwen shuju, 1971.

*Xunhuan ribao (Tsun Wan Yat Po)* 循環日報. *Old HK Newspapers.* Multimedia Information System. Hong Kong Public Libraries. <https://mmis.hkpl.gov.hk/old-hk-collection> (accessed: 01 September 2017).

Ye Jinguang 葉覲光. *Ye Yunbao nianpu* 葉云葆年譜 (Chronological Biography of Ye Jinguang). 1883.

*Yuexiu shuyuan zhi* 粵秀書院志 (Yuexiu Academy Gazetteer), edited by Liang Tingnan 梁廷楠. 1847. Reprint. ZGLDSYZ, Volume 3.

Zhou Hanguang 周漢光. *Zhang Zhidong yu Guangya shuyuan* 張之洞與廣雅書院 (Zhang Zhidong and Guangya Academy). Taipei: Zhongguo wenhua daxue, 1983.

Zhu Ciqi 朱次琦. *Zhu Jiujiang xiansheng ji* 朱九江先生集 (Collected Writings of Zhu Ciqi). Reprint. *Jindai Zhongguo shiliao congkan*, vol. 127. Taipei: Wenhai chubanshe, 1967.

CHAPTER 11

# Shrines, Sceneries, and Granary: The Constitutive Elements of the Confucian Academy in 16th-Century Korea

*Vladimír Glomb*

## 1      Introduction[1]

What was the view of Korean scholars on Confucian academies in the 16th century? The implementation, proliferation, and subsequent decline of Confucian academies in Korea is often understood as part of the political and intellectual development of the Chosŏn dynasty, i.e. copying the simple model of founding-flourishment-stagnation-decline. This approach, focusing on institutional history, has largely determined our understanding of the intimate relation between the academies and force behind them, the Korean literati, who lived and vanished together with these institutions.

The splendour of the Confucian academies and their buildings, as well as the magnitude of their diffusion on the Korean Peninsula should not hide the fact that these institutions were only one of the many forms of educational and social organization of Confucian elites. The academies were not situated at the apex of society, but rather at multiple intersections of various interests coming from the Korean state, competitive schools, and individual scholars. An understanding of Confucian academies as institutional, economical, and social units—which in recent decades has shed light on many important data—should be combined with a microhistorical approach analyzing the discursive strategies surrounding these institutions. Such an approach can enable us to describe in a more precise manner their role in the history of Korean Confucianism in particular, and the history of ideas and mentalities in general. The individual opinions of Korean scholars about the first Confucian academies have been rarely studied systematically, except the case of T'oegye Yi Hwang 退溪 李滉 (1501–1570), who played an active role in the first decades of the academies' existence in Korea.[2] However, there were other significant

---

1  I would like to thank Isabelle Sancho for her stimulating comments.
2  See Chŏng Sunmok, "T'oegye ŭi sŏwŏn kyoyukkwan (T'oegye's Views on Education in Confucian Academies)," in *Han'guk sŏwŏn kyoyuk chedo yŏn'gu* (Studies on Education System

thinkers who exercised great influence on the formation of the Korean model, or models, of Confucian academies. The most important of them is Yulgok Yi I 栗谷 李珥 (1536–1584).[3] Considering that his school of thought largely represented the dominant interpretation of the Learning of the Way in Chosŏn intellectual space for the three centuries following his death, one can argue that Yulgok's opinion on the Confucian academies weighed heavily. Yulgok composed a significant number of texts about Confucian academies, among which the most notable are his *Munhŏn sŏwŏn hakkyu* 文憲書院學規 (*Rules for the Munhŏn Academy*) and *Ŭnbyŏng chŏngsa hakkyu* 隱屏精舍學規 (*Rules for the Ŭnbyŏng Study Hall*).[4] During his lifetime he personally participated in the management of the academies[5] and debated at court on the system of the

in Korean Confucian Academies) (Taegu: Yŏngnam taehakkyo ch'ulp'anbu 1989, 3rd edition), 59–78; Chŏng Manjo, "T'oegye Yi Hwang ŭi sŏwŏnno—kŭ ŭi kyohwaron kwa kwallyŏnhayŏ (T'oegye Yi Hwang's Arguments on Confucian Academies: In Relation to His Views on Transformation by Education)," in *Chosŏn sidae sŏwŏn yŏn'gu* (Studies on Confucian Academies of Chosŏn Period) (Seoul: Chimmundang 1997), 49–84. Several studies focus on the first founder of Confucian academy in Korea, Chu Sebung 周世鵬 (1495–1554), although he was generally not considered by later generations as an influential scholar. For studies on him see Chung Soon-woo, *Sŏwŏn ŭi sahoesa* (Social History of Korean Confucian Academies) (Seoul: T'aehaksa, 2013), 19–64 and Milan Hejtmanek, "The Elusive Path to Sagehood: Origins of the Confucian Academy System in Chosŏn Korea," *Seoul Journal of Korean Studies* 26, no. 2 (2013): 233–268.

3  Chŏng Sunmok, "Yulgok ŭi sŏwŏn kyoyukkwan (Yulgok's Views on Education in Confucian Academies)," in *Han'guk sŏwŏn kyoyuk chedo yŏn'gu* (Taegu: Yŏngnam taehakkyo ch'ulp'anbu, 1989, 3rd edition), 79–95.

4  Yulgok's rules give one of few extant examples of the regulations applied to academies in the 16th century, others being the *Paegundong Sosu sŏwŏn ipkyu* 白雲洞紹修書院立規 (Admission Regulations for Paegundong Sosu Academy) by Chu Sebung, *Isan wŏngyu* 伊山院規 (Yisan Academy Regulations) by T'oegye and *Yongsan sŏwŏn chaehŏn* 龍山書院齋憲 (Dormitory Regulations of Yongsan Academy) by Pak Kwangjŏn 朴光前 (1526–1597). See Pak Chŏngbae, "Chosŏn sidae ŭi hangnyŏng mit hakkyu (Rules and Regulations in Confucian Academies of the Chosŏn Period)," *Han'guk kyoyuk sahak* 28, no. 2. (2006): 213–237.

5  Research on Yulgok's relation to the academies is, on a material basis, seriously hampered by two factors. Many documents perished during the Imjin War (1592–1598), when his Ŭnbyŏng Study Hall was destroyed. Only fragments remain from his extensive correspondence on the Ŭnbyŏng Study Hall and the nearby Munhŏn Academy. In addition, both of the academies associated most intimately with Yulgok, the Munhŏn Academy (preserved until 1945) and the Sohyŏn Academy 紹賢書院, are located in North Korea and the archives are not available. Given the fact that Sohyŏn Academy documents were not rescued to the South, we may presume that those materials which were not destroyed still remain somewhere in the DPRK. During the process of nationalisation, libraries and archives of Confucian academies were confiscated and judging from extant information, at least some materials related to Sohyŏn Academy are held in the state archives. The catalogue of rare books of Kim Il-sung University published in 1958 shows, for example, an entry on a book called *Sohyŏn sŏwŏn sŏngnon piha kich'aek* 紹賢書院聖論陴下記冊. See *Tosŏ mongnok* I–III (*Hansŏ pullyu mongnok*) (Book

academies. After his death he was enshrined in no fewer than 21 academies.[6] His stance towards Confucian academies—their purpose, students, shrines, and economic management—shows that there were shifting patterns in the Korean model of the Confucian academy at his time, which enables us to compare his ideas, which were both traditional and innovative, with the latter destiny of these Confucian institutions.

Yulgok's case could serve also as an illustration of the broader trends between both classical and contemporary China and Chosŏn Korea. What were reasons to revive and implement a centuries-old Song-times institution in Korean environment? What were reactions of the Korean scholar on the sudden boom of Confucian academies? What were his reasons to personally participate in academies' activities?

## 2    Life and Academies

Born only a few years before the founding of the oldest Korean *sŏwŏn*, the Paegundong Academy 白雲洞書院, in 1543, Yulgok belonged to the first generation of Chosŏn literati who witnessed the spread of the new model of Confucian education in praxis. It is a certain paradox that despite his later influence on the academy system, Yulgok himself never studied in an academy. The academy system was, in the 1550s, still limited to a few counties and served only a rather small circle of enthusiastic *sarim* 士林 scholars. After finishing his studies under the guidance of various relatives and masters, Yulgok soon came into contact with several scholars connected to the academies. The first important figure was without doubt his own father-in-law, No Kyŏngnin 盧慶麟 (1516–1568), who gave him his daughter in marriage in 1557, and provided him with solid economic support and important family ties. When he was the magistrate of Sŏngju county in Kyŏngsan province, No Kyŏngnin supervised the establishment of the Ch'ŏn'gok Academy 川谷書院 (initially called Yŏngbong Academy 迎鳳書院). No Kyŏngnin and the Ch'ŏn'gok Academy had also close ties with a leading figure of the academy movement, T'oegye.[7] Yulgok met the famous scholar during his visit to his relatives in Kangnŭng, when he stopped in Yean to visit T'oegye in his Tosan Study Hall 陶山書堂 (later Tosan

---

Catalogue I–III: Books in Classical Chinese Catalogue by Categories) (Kim Ilsŏng chonghap taehak tosŏgwan 1958), 45. For recent changes see the Postscript in this volume, 489–490.

6    According to the *Record of Academy Sacrifices* (*Wŏnhyangnok* 院享錄) in his collected writings, see YGCS 34: 58b–62a.

7    See three of T'oegye letters to No Kyŏngnin (TGCS 22:3a–9a) and his *Yŏngbong sŏwŏn ki* 迎鳳書院記 (Account of Yŏngbong Academy), TGCS 42:31b–35a.

Academy). This meeting was the beginning of a profound connection between the elderly master and the young talented scholar, and it is likely that during their conversations, T'oegye shared with Yulgok some of his ideas about the Confucian academies. These formative events occurred during the first stage of Yulgok's illustrious official career during which Yulgok placed first in the state examinations no fewer than nine times. In 1564, he was named to his first official function, assistant section chief of the Ministry of Taxation (Sr. rank 6). The trajectory of Yulgok's bureaucratic career, which ended shortly before his death with a last appointment to the position of Minister of Personnel (Sr. rank 2), had an essential influence on his relation to the academies. Yulgok, for most of his life, served in high positions at court and was only occasionally assigned to provincial posts. Moreover, he retired or was relieved from these posts on rare occasions and only for short periods. As a busy official in central offices located in the capital, his ability to engage actively with the local academies was limited. Most of his activities concerning Confucian academies, when he could spend time in study halls, supervising community compacts or teaching disciples, were reserved to the short breaks between various postings.

As a high official, Yulgok had broad access to court politics and certain functions of the official education system occasionally fell under his responsibility. This provided him with a good overview of both the flaws and needs of the public schools, which explains his positive attitude toward public school reform. In Yulgok's writings (contrary to T'oegye's) there is no dichotomy expressed between the purportedly corrupted state schools and the idealistic and pure Confucian academies. There is also no intention to preserve academies as much as possible from state interventions. Many of his educational texts (such as the *Hakkyo mobŏm* 學校模範 [*Model for Schools*], or *Hakkyo samok* 學校事目 [*Articles of Service in School*], written in 1582) were composed by royal command or submitted directly to the king (as, for example, *Sŏnghak chibyo* 聖學輯要 [*Collected Essentials of Learning to Be a Sage*], written in 1575). Despite his occasional disillusionment with the political situation, Yulgok was above all a loyal official who strived for reform within the system of the government, not wishing to harbour dissent in an isolated academy.

In reading T'oegye's plea from 1549 concerning government support of the Paegundong Academy addressed to the provincial governor Sim T'ŏngwŏn 沈通源 (1499–1572), a desperate note can be discerned in some of T'oegye statements. For example, he writes: "There is no way to remedy the extremity of the corruption of the local schools [*hyanggyo* 鄉校], which is indeed disheartening. The only means available is the cultivation of the *sŏwŏn*."[8] A similar

---

8 TGCS 9:4a–8b. The translation follows Smith ("The Rise of the Sŏwŏn," 95–97) quoted in Hejtmanek, "The Elusive Path to Sagehood," 260.

tone is never to be found in the works of Yulgok. From the vantage point of his official position, Yulgok saw the academies as an integral part of an ideal educational system and worked toward their better functioning for the sake of the community of literati and the state. His general ideas on the relation of academies and the state were introduced in a reform proposal for King Sŏnjo 宣祖 (r. 1567–1608), the fictive dialogue *Tongho mundap* 東湖問答 (*Questions and Answers at the Eastern Lake*) composed in 1569.

> The plan for the current situation is that we must order [the officials] in the Eight Provinces and the Five Districts of the capital to select, on one occasion every year, a few candidates from among the classics licentiates (*saengwŏn*), the literary licentiates (*chinsa*) and the ordinary students; [they should select candidates] who have the intention to devote themselves to their studies and who are not morally inferior people. The criteria for selection does not have to be too demanding; it is merely enough that those who know that there should be given to the Learning of the Way the highest priority will be included. Their names should be recorded, and they should be all moved to the Ministry of Personnel and the Ministry of Rites. The Ministry of Personnel and the Ministry of Rites will assemble them in one place, control the list [of candidates] and once again further discuss these matters. They will admit two hundred people to be students in government institutions and lodge them at the National Academy, dividing them into five groups of forty students each. Even students from the countryside must arrive at the scheduled day. Two hundred young students without any degree should be selected as well. Divide the students among the Four Schools, so each school would receive fifty students which will then be further divided into five groups so that each group has ten students. They will be called the "selected scholars." Separately, make a choice of Confucian scholars whose learning is well completed and who are respectable in their behaviour, and make them officials in the National Academy and Four Schools; engage them to teach all students. [...] If there are among the students in the countryside certain individuals who should be included in this selection, then place them in local schools or Confucian academies according to their number and consider their division into smaller groups as well. The local officials should provide them with equipment and have them receive instruction from appointed teachers.[9]

---

9   YGCS 15:28b–29b.

Yulgok was well aware of the deficiencies of the extant educational system and knew that the National Academy (Sŏnggyun'gwan 成均館) and the network of local schools were not sufficient to bring about the requisite massive change of mores and spirit in the young literati;[10] nonetheless, he proposed to distribute the resources of the state evenly between the reform of the official schools and the creation of an additional network of academies.[11] The belief in the possibility of reform and the trust placed in the notion that the government would heed the advice of Confucian scholars was typical of Yulgok, and contrasts greatly with the ethos of an older generation of Korean scholars who had personal experience with the bloody purges of the literati in the first half of the 16th century, subsequently often shunning close contact with the government and turbulent court policy. During Yulgok's era, a new generation of devoted proponents of the Learning of the Way gained the upper hand over conservative circles of the court and began to demand radical reform and official support for their ideas with a new confidence. No more telling example of this generational change in attitude can be found than the comparison of these two events: T'oegye, who lost his brother during the purges, penning a polite request in 1549 to the mighty Sim T'ŏngwŏn[12] to kindly grant his support for the Paegundong Academy; and Yulgok, who in 1576 submitted to the throne his memorial discussing the crimes and misdeeds of the very same Sim T'ŏngwŏn.[13] Yulgok was extremely fortunate to have conducted an official career during the golden age of Confucian literati, falling as it did between the end of the purges of the literati and the beginning of the factional fights, which shadowed only the last years of his life. He thus had not much reason to perceive academies as the last resort of persecuted idealistic scholars—as was the frequent motive of the older *sarim* generation—; neither did he seek to establish his own power basis via academies, as was the dominant strategy after the factional splits of Korean literati.

The most important biographical factor in the story of Yulgok's relation to the Confucian academies was his untimely death. Involvement with academies was often the privilege of elderly and retired scholars, who had the authority, erudition, and time to engage with teaching young students in a

---

10   YGCS 6:25a.
11   Ibid.
12   For the description of Sim T'ŏngwŏn and his role see Hejtmanek, "The Elusive Path to Sagehood," 259–268.
13   YGCS 3:18b–20a. This incident also reveals the complicated networks of Korean elites since Sim T'ongwŏn intervened (probably due to his friendship with Yulgok's father) on Yulgok's behalf when he was harassed by fellow students in the National Academy; see Han Yŏngu, *Yulgok p'yŏngjŏn* (Biography of Yulgok) (Seoul: Minŭmsa, 2016), 29.

pleasant environment. It is no accident that most of Yulgok's activities connected to various academies occurred in the last years of his life when he was trying to extricate himself from court obligations and had time to visit local academies, present lectures, or compose texts on the topic. There are clear indices that he envisioned academies as being an integral part of his later years: his desire to spend his retirement in an academy is visible in his memorandum excusing himself from a royal summons, in which Yulgok states his willingness to be of use as the head of the local academy.[14] The most explicit statement of his intention to become a permanent member of the local academy is expressed in his reform proposal for an academy system, in which he offers his services for this purpose:

> [Your Majesty], do not trouble yourself with your summons and let me take up a place according to my status. If I will, in Haeju Academy, take responsibility for the function of headmaster, teach uneducated youth, and correct their reading marks, your Sage Court does not cast away anything, and your ignorant subject will not receive a stipend for nothing.[15]

Would this really have been the focus of Yulgok's activities in his later years, if he had lived longer? His wish was fully in accord with his general proposal, raised in the same text, to employ retired officials as teachers in academies, in order to make use of their talent and experience. Would the fate of Yulgok, in his later years, have been similar to that of T'oegye, who was still lecturing in Yŏktong Academy 易東書院 on Zhen Dexiu's 真德秀 (1178–1235) *Xinjing* 心經 (*Classic of the Mind*) at the age of seventy, shortly before his death?[16] From Yulgok's correspondence,[17] we know that he considered taking a position in the Munhŏn Academy, where he also occasionally lectured, but this plan never materialized.

## 3   Court Debates

An important component of Yulgok's official career was the formulation of reactions or policy concerning existing academies, already a topic of complex debate in his lifetime. The spread of Confucian academies in the first decades

---

14   YGCS 6:26b.
15   YGCS 6:25b. See also the entry in *Sŏnjo sillok* 11/5/1#1.
16   TGCS *T'oegye sŏnsaeng nyŏnbo* 2:21b.
17   YGCS 12:15a–b.

after 1543 was a speedy and enthusiastic process: T'oegye, who petitioned in 1549 for the creation of a royal plaque to commemorate the first academy, would, only a few years later, amuse himself by composing a poem about no fewer than nine academies to which he was personally connected.[18] The growing number of academies inevitably led to the practical problems which accompanied their existence; in some cases, these issues were encoded in the very concept of the Korean model of the Confucian academy. The alliance between local elites, who were eager to enhance their status by founding an academy, and the Confucian literati, who perceived academies as the instrument for the propagation of the Learning of the Way was rather tenuous in many cases. Many problems stemmed from the practical consideration as to who was to be in charge of the academy and responsible for the education of students. The original concept of Zhu Xi, along with the academy model of the Song era, was based on the conviction that the nucleus of the academy is formed by the teacher who provides moral guidance and a scholarly example to students, often with the assistance of invited scholars, who usually lectured in the academy during their visits. Finding a headmaster who could fulfill these criteria or creating an ideal management structure for the academy were delicate tasks that determined the success and failure of the institution in question. A vivid illustration of this dilemma is to be found in T'oegye's attempt to solve the tension between the administrator and the students of the Sosu Academy 紹修書院, a conflict which had emerged as early as 1553.[19] The picture of the conflict which can be reconstructed today indicates that administrator Kim Chungmun 金仲文 (?–?)—who behaved in an allegedly arrogant manner toward the students and lacked substantial scholarship—was named to his position thanks to the contributions he made for the founding of the academy as well as the support of the local elites. Those village circles, for their part, perceived the value of the academy largely in its housing a shrine dedicated to their ancestor, An Hyang 安珦 (1243–1306). In any event, Kim Chungmun was obviously not the ideal scholar to impart to young students the illumination of the Learning of the Way. Issues concerning the practical guidance of students in the academies soon reached the official level and became the subject of court debates, in which Yulgok was also involved. His memorandum to the throne from the fifth month of 1578 is an important contribution in

---

18   See T'oegye's poem, *Ten Songs on Academies* (*Sŏwŏn sip yŏng* 書院十詠) in TGCS 4:1b–3a.
19   For T'oegye's writings concerning this affair see TGCS 12:30a–34b, 34b–39b, see also Chŏng Manjo, *Chosŏn sidae sŏwŏn yŏn'gu* (Studies on Confucian Academies of the Chosŏn Period) (Seoul: Chimmundang, 1997), 79–80.

the debate concerning the presence and future of Confucian academies in the lifetime of King Sŏnjo:

> The establishments of academies in recent times could imbue scholars with a proper intention to study and their benefits are not shallow. The only problem is that there are no [good] masters of academies: therefore, the students gather together and follow their impulses, indulging themselves in excesses. They have no one to revere and imitate, and one does not see the result of acquiring wisdom and cultivation. Surely, this lay behind the original intention of the state to establish academies. This is the reason why there are some people who, in discussions concerning academies, slander these institutions and believe that they should be abolished. This is not a correct opinion and it stems from hate and resentment. Now your subject foolishly wishes to request that the academies in important locations install appointees in the functions of director and headmaster along the lines of the Chinese system, and, similar to the case of teachers of children [in the local schools], provide them with some salary. Select those whose scholarship and conduct may become exemplary, together with those retired officials and scholars living in seclusion and have them occupy these positions. If you entrust them with the proper guidance of students, there surely will be visible results of this education, and in the future, the state will obtain educated talents.[20]

The introductory comment acknowledging problems in the newly established academies is a very rare reference to the critique of the academy system, still in the early stages of its existence. Although it is clear that there existed substantial opposition to academies as an alien intervention in the established social hierarchy, as well as being a potential threat to the standing order, academy archives, official records, and collected writings were produced mostly by Confucian literati sympathetic to the idea of the academies, and therefore voices of dissent against the new academy movement were not given expression in their writings. The structure and motivation of the group of those who did dissent is often difficult to identify: Yulgok himself writes to his friend Ugye Sŏng Hon 牛溪 成渾 (1535–1598) that in Haeju there was a certain ranking official "deeply jealous of academy students,"[21] but Yulgok does not attribute any particular reason for this attitude. There is no shortage of a critique of academies from

---

20  YGCS 6:26b.
21  YGCS 11:9a.

the 17th century onwards[22]—as they grew more influential, both as socioeconomic and political factors in Korean society—but entries in the *Chosŏn Dynasty Annals* for the early decades of the academy system do not bear witness to any critical voices, and portray state involvement with academies as exclusively positive. Yet there clearly were individuals who could, for various reasons, foresee problems which might be engendered by a system of independent academies beyond the reach of state control. One such voice came from a person whose critique led Yulgok to present his reaction to the court. This was the high official Im Ki 林芑 (?–?), who submitted to the throne, four days before Yulgok's proposal, his memorial criticizing Confucian academies (among other important political topics). Im Ki's memorial has not been preserved but its arguments, as presented in *Veritable Records* and Yulgok's diary,[23] while no doubt not a very objective picture of the original text, can still serve as a basis for reconstructing the two main arguments of Im Ki concerning the haughty manners of academy members as well as the considerable disadvantage to the local population caused by the academies' presence. The sudden appearance of exclusive groups of young academy students beyond the reach of state control was, for some officials, a blatant challenge to the established order. Im Ki was, thanks to his complaint and other political activities, portrayed as a villain trying to impede the entirety of the Learning of the Way, but given Yulgok's own acknowledgement that academy students often lacked proper guidance, the question of the students' proper supervision was probably quite well known. Yulgok's proposal in the court debate would likely have solved both problems: the granting of state salaries to academy headmasters would attract experienced scholars and officials who could maintain discipline among the students, and state support for academies would lessen at the same time the economic burden on local communities. The idea of greater state involvement in the management of academies was developed under the pretext of following the so-called Chinese model; it was implemented neither in Yulgok's lifetime nor subsequently, but it was also not completely forgotten. A few years later, another scholar close to Yulgok, Cho Hŏn 趙憲 (1544–1592), again raised the topic of academy headmasters and the structural problems of these insti-

---

22   Basic motives of this critique were described well already by Yi Man'gyu, *Chosŏn kyoyuksa I* (History of Korean Education) (Seoul: Ŭryu munhwasa, 1947), 260–263. See also Ch'oe Yŏng-ho, "The Private Academies (Sŏwŏn) and Neo-Confucianism in Late Chosŏn Korea," *Seoul Journal of Korean Studies* 21, no. 21 (2008): 139–191.

23   YGCS 29:98b–100b. Im Ki's memorial and subsequent debate is recorded, at considerable length, in *Sŏnjo sillok*; see entries 9/7/20#1, 9/7/20#2, 9/7/21#1, 9/7/22#2, 9/7/22#5, 9/7/23#1, 9/7/26#1, 9/7/27#1, 9/7/28#1, 9/8/1#5,6, 9/8/4#1, 9/8/6#1, 9/8/8#1, 9/8/11#1, 9/8/13#1, 9/8/26#2. It also appears in *Sŏnjo sujŏng sillok* 9/7/1#2.

tutions. Cho Hŏn, later a hero of the resistance against the Japanese invasion, remarked that "each Chinese academy has a headmaster to teach students," and named some examples of academies such as the Myŏnggok Study Hall 鳴谷精舍 in Sŏch'ŏn, where there "was no special master responsible for the study hall," and students were, therefore, "making no progress in their studies," despite their talents.[24] The critical tone assumed even by devoted Confucian scholars suggests that one generation after the establishment of the first academies in Korea, there were already some obvious flaws in the system and the situation called for reforms or adjustments. The crucial problems of the academy system—maintaining discipline among the students and recruiting dedicated teaching personnel—were similar to those existing in the official school system. Yulgok's treatise on the educational curriculum and the discipline of students, *Hakkyo mobŏm*, as well as his compilation of articles about the problem of teaching staff recruitment, *Hakkyo samok*, display striking similarities to his proposal for the reform of academies, including the employment of retired officials or the use of a recommendation system for students. Although there are clear differences between Yulgok's writings on the reform of state schools, such as the above-mentioned treatises, and his private works targeted either to students in general, as in the case of *Kyŏngmong yogyŏl* 擊蒙要訣 (*Important Methods of Eliminating Youthful Ignorance*), or to academy students, such as the formulation of rules for the Haeju academy, all these texts share many commonalities and borrow heavily from each other. One typical example is Yulgok's reading curriculum for students that is described in the *Kyŏngmong yogyŏl*[25] but was intended for students from both state schools and academies. As a universally valid guide, it was also used in the education of the royal family.[26] The same could be said in regards to the detailed passages concerning the personal conduct of students contained in *Kyŏngmong yogyŏl, The Regulations of Munhŏn Academy,* or his *Ŭnbyŏng Study Hall Pledge* (*Ŭnbyŏng chŏngsa yaksok* 隱屛精舍約束), which are in many cases identical in their formulations of regulations for state schools, academies, and individual students. In order to detect the specific features of his writings on the academy system and the place that he ascribed to these institutions within the structure of Confucian education, we must turn our attention to his practical proposals

---

24  *Sŏnjo sujŏng sillok* 19/10/1#4.
25  See Vladimír Glomb, "Reading the Classics Till Death: Yulgok Yi I and the Curriculum of Chosŏn Literati," *Studia Orientalia Slovaca* 2, no. 2 (2012): 315–329.
26  JaeHyun Kim Haboush, "The Education of the Yi Crown Prince: A Study in Confucian Pedagogy," in *The Rise of Neo-Confucianism in Korea,* ed. Wm. Theodore de Bary and Ja-Hyun Kim Haboush (New York: Columbia University Press, 1985), 192–196.

ILLUSTRATION 11.1   Current state of Ŭnbyŏng Study Hall

and experiences with the Munhŏn Academy in Haeju, the capital of Hwanghae province, where many of his ideas were implemented.

## 4     Rules

The possibility of putting some of his ideas concerning Confucian academies into practice materialized for Yulgok during his later years, when he had decided to settle in the vicinity of Haeju: this was the location where he had spent most of his time in between Seoul government assignments and where, in addition, his extended family owned substantial estates. The target of manifold plans and reforms he conducted in the area was the Munhŏn Academy, which subsequently was formed according to Yulgok's ideals. The academy belonged to the very first wave of Korean academies and shared many points in common with the first of them, Paegundong Academy. It had been founded by Chu Sebung 周世鵬 (1495–1554) during his official assignment in the area and it shared the same organizational structure as Paegundong Academy. The academy was originally called Suyang Academy 首陽書院 after the nearby Suyang Mountain. In 1555 it was given a royal plaque and renamed Munhŏn Academy. The new name was an allusion to the posthumous title of the famous Koryŏ scholar enshrined in the academy shrine, Ch'oe Ch'ung

崔沖 (984–1068), himself a native of Haeju, whose descendants were the driving force behind the founding of the academy. Yulgok was in frequent contact with the academy through his various local connections. In addition to the regulations that he composed for this institution, he ascribed a crucial role to the Munhŏn Academy in several of his other projects in the area, most notably the implementation of his community compact scheme and the related project of the creation of a community granary. In Yulgok's conception, the academy played a twofold role: it was both a school and shrine, serving as a gathering point for local scholars and students, but it was also meant to serve as a center for the entire community, reorganized for further projects. At the same time that he composed his rules for Munhŏn Academy in 1578, Yulgok initiated several other projects in the locality of Haeju, including the establishment of a scholarly retreat and a place for his disciples to gather, the Ŭnbyŏng Study Hall. A comparison between these two institutions is crucial for understanding Yulgok's thought about Confucian academies. Despite their temporal affinity and their common location in the area around Haeju, the purposes and meanings of these institutions differed radically. Dissimilar to the case of Ŭnbyŏng Study Hall, which Yulgok designed primarily for his own disciples and according to his own personal inclinations in a secluded beautiful natural setting, the Munhŏn Academy was the established centre of the local community, located in a suburban area that had been settled two decades earlier. The regulations for the Munhŏn Academy thus provide a vivid picture of existing academy culture and how its amelioration was envisioned, unlike the *Ŭnbyŏng Study Hall Regulations* or the *Ŭnbyŏng Study Hall Pledge*, both of which were designed to fulfill Yulgok's vision of the ideal scholarly institution. The most interesting part of comparison between these two Confucian centers of education are Yulgok's solutions for various neuralgic points of the academy system, in particular the question of discipline among the students, academy management and above all, student admissions. As has been suggested, the Munhŏn Academy served the needs of the local Confucian elites and as such, it was inevitably entangled in the existing structures of the rather small confines of the socioeconomic realities of Haeju. The opening paragraph of Yulgok's proposed Rules, dealing with the issue of school admissions, provides insight into some of the vices he wished to reform:

> The rule for admitting scholars should not be based on their age. Those who have the intention to engage in study and whose name and behaviour are without blemish should be admitted. The scholars of the academy should discuss together the question of whether to allow the adepts to enter. If the meeting does not fill the quota at least of ten academy

members, then a decision should not be taken. (If there are at least three graduates of the first round of state examinations participating in the meeting, then admission may be allowed.) Licentiates or advanced scholars are directly allowed to enter without discussion. Any student who tries to gain admission via prominence or attempts to force his cause by contacting the provincial governor or local officials will not be allowed to enter the academy.[27]

The most obvious and predictable problem was corruption on a personal level, when students sought admission via nepotism in relation to both local and provincial officials. This, however, was only the case for the students who were not graduates of basic levels of state examinations; the graduates were admitted automatically. Another striking feature is the process of admissions based on a collective decision-making combined with privileges for graduates of state examinations. All these features are difficult to locate in the *Rules for Ŭnbyŏng Study Hall*, in which other values are emphasized:

> Concerning the rules for admission to the academy rooms, discussion as to whether a person is of a literati family, or belongs to any category of the common people, is prohibited. All those harboring the intention to study are admitted. Those who were admitted to the institution earlier may scrutinize and discuss whether a candidate should be admitted. Only after that may a candidate be admitted. If there are candidates who would wish to enter, but have, in their past, acted contrary to propriety, or have been recalcitrant, let them first change their errors and improve by themselves. When we have completely observed [the candidate's] behaviour and have definitively determined that he has improved his behaviour, only after such a point will the candidate be allowed to enter. If someone with an unknown past wishes to be admitted, tentatively place him in the close village (or in the Dormitory of Fostering Correct Behaviour) or in a mountain monastery. Visit him and inquire after his studies; observe his aspirations and interests or habits and identify whether he is an acceptable person. Only after that will he be allowed to enter.[28]

In expressing his own ideas concerning the study hall, Yulgok gave free rein to his deepest convictions as to what an ideal Confucian education should look like. The students he sought were by no means the sons of local prominent

---

27  YGCS 15:49a.
28  YGCS 15:43b.

families, and therefore we do not see a warning against the dangers of nepotism as in the case of the Munhŏn Academy; instead, there is an explicit statement prohibiting any social discrimination against students of a non-elite background. There is no doubt that Yulgok wanted his own study hall to be free of discrimination, since we know from his personal example that he was a staunch opponent of bias against secondary sons or low-born students.[29] Yulgok was well aware of the sensitivity of local elites concerning their elevated status, and in the case of the Munhŏn Academy we can see that he was willing to make certain concessions, such as in the case of the community compact gatherings in the academy, where he reserved a separate place for "youngsters and secondary sons."[30] However no such provisions are made in his own study hall. His egalitarian attitude is also extremely visible in his disregard for official titles in the admissions process: in the Study Hall, there were no privileges for graduates of state examinations. A decision concerning new members was based on the will of the whole study hall collective, and not on a specific quorum as in the case of the academy. A truly remarkable point is the minute personal screening of candidates, a process which could take a long time and in which, obviously, social background or academic credentials played no role.

An important component in the building of the community of scholars, both in the academy and study hall, was the continual stress on organization (seat arrangements, the order of precedence at ceremonies, and so on) of the members according to one single criterion, age. The physical placement of scholars according to their ages—and not their status—was one of the principles created by Confucian scholars for public projects such as the community compacts, and it met with strong opposition from the local elites;[31] it was however a crucial strategy in bolstering the inner cohesion of the community of Confucian literati. In both sets of regulations, stress is placed on how "during meals, both older and younger sit according to their age,"[32] and although it may seem trivial from today's perspective, it was a topic that was a subject of heated contemporary debate. Yulgok's authoritative statement on the topic was considered important enough to be quoted in his *Biography* (*Yŏnbo* 年譜):

---

29    It is a well-known fact that Yulgok named his secondary son as his heir, a rather unusual event in his times and circles. For a discussion about the social status and admission to academies see Ch'oe, "The Private Academies (Sŏwŏn)," 149–153.
30    YGCS 16:28a. The text explicitly mentions several times specific prescriptions for secondary sons and "others who are not of literati status."
31    See T'oegye's case described in Cho Hwisang, "The Community of Letters: The T'oegye School and the Political Culture of Choson Korea, 1545–1800" (Ph.D. diss., Columbia University, 2010), 75–76.
32    YGCS 15:44b, 15:50a.

At that time, the students of Sŏnggyun'gwan were seated according to their age, but many people insisted on the prevailing custom, and considered this to be wrong. Someone claimed: "In the list of successful examinations candidates, the first graduate is honoured and respected, so how is it possible that somebody would be seated above him?" Master [Yulgok] said: "Honouring the first graduate is possible during the gathering of candidates, but the National Academy is the place of illumination of moral relations, and thus the order between older and younger may not by confused. Even in ancient times, when a royal prince entered school, he deferred his place according to the principle of age, so in the case of the first graduates there is nothing to discuss."[33]

The privileging of age above status and worldly fame formed part of the idea that the new communities of scholars gathered in the academies should be devoted purely to Confucian ideals and not to the reigning customs of Korean society. The academic debates and the pursuit of Sage Learning were considered to be the highest values; graduates of state examinations had no special study hall privileges and were treated like any other community member. The common problem of both institutions was the topic previously mentioned in contemporary discussions: the maintenance of discipline. It is necessary to note that the regulations of the Munhŏn Academy and the Ŭnbyŏng Study Hall are extremely detailed about students' prescribed behaviours and activities. These regulations discuss at considerable length the question of what to do when these rules are disobeyed. The academy's rules are in this sense very strict and apply two different levels of punishment: firstly, a temporary level for lighter offenses, which included expulsion from the seat (i.e. the prohibition to participate in lectures and sessions); and secondly, a permanent level for serious misdeeds (expulsion from the academy and removal from the academy register). Students were to be expelled from their seats for disrespecting academy rules, laziness or lack of manners, taking books out of the academy, or not participating in the spring and autumn offerings without a proper excuse. More serious or repeated offenses were punished after a joint discussion by expulsion from the academy. Both the joint discussions and collective decision-making of academy members about punishments and discipline were a specific feature of Yulgok's regulations: compare, for example, T'oegye's solution for the Isan Academy 伊山書院, where academy officials were the only people involved in making concrete disciplinary decisions.[34] Similar measures

---
33   YGCS 33:46a.
34   TGCS 41:52a.

for guaranteeing discipline among students were taken in the Ŭnbyŏng Study Hall, but with several important modifications. The rules for the study hall placed much more stress on the possible reform of students' behaviours, and the formulation of the rules was far less repressive when compared to those of the academy:

> If someone has no excuse, or only pretends to have a reason not to participate [in prescribed activities], or has been absent on two occasions, he should be expelled from his seat for one month. (To be expelled from the seat means that he is excluded and is not allowed to take his seat in the row of scholars. This is customarily termed "dismiss student.") When he can sit again together with the others, he must acknowledge his guilt and apologize for his mistakes before both lines of scholars. In the case of a student's misdeeds or mistakes, the director, secretaries, and assistants should discuss it together in the study hall, and according to the gravity [of the student's actions], expel the student or make him acknowledge his behaviour as a warning. If somebody is, within the space of a year, expelled twice from his seat and does not reform, he will be expelled from the study hall altogether.[35]

In comparison to the academy, the study hall offered a much broader space for repentance and discreet solutions, as the ultimate authority was not a set of rules but the master who presided over the study hall (i.e. Yulgok himself), as well as the community. Given the fact that study hall students were carefully selected disciples or even friends, a certain benevolence in dealing with offenders may be noted:

> If somebody violates the regulations, the secretaries must thoroughly report it to the dean and supervisor, who then must jointly press for the rules to be honoured. If the culprit does not repent, he will be reported to the master. If he does repent and improve, the record [of his misdeeds] is annulled, and nothing is reported to the master.[36]

The mention of "records" is probably the most specific feature of Yulgok's regulations: this was a systematic register of the good and bad deeds of students. The idea of recording the behaviours of students was well known during the earlier times of the dynasty, but in both concept and practice had been neither

---

35  YGCS 15:47b.
36  YGCS 15:46a.

prominent nor systematic.[37] Yulgok was probably the first scholar who strived to establish a consistent administrative framework for the evaluation of the students' progress and erudition, as well as of their faults and misdeeds. The idea of record keeping was known in the environment of the state schools, but was certainly unusual in the circles of Confucian academies. There are no previous mentions of disciplinary records in the regulations of earlier academies; the reasons probably had to do with a less developed awareness of potential problems in students' behaviour among the idealistic founders of the first generation of academies, and the rather strict and uncomplicated quality of supervision in these institutions. As both factors were probably involved, the hierarchical structure of academies allowed the headmaster or his deputies to determine disciplinary cases on the basis of their own judgements, and there was probably not too much need to establish any written documentation of their decisions. Another aspect was the rather local nature of the first academies, where students and teachers knew each other very well. This phenomenon is visible in the absence of disciplinary records for the Munhŏn Academy, where Yulgok required only that a general roster of students be maintained. On the other hand, for Ŭnbyŏng Study Hall, Yulgok devised a systematic plan to create a concise and clear register of the students' deeds, both good and bad:

> The assistants must manage to keep records of both the good and bad deeds of students, and inspect all the activities of the students, whether in school or at home. Whether the students' speech or behaviour concurs with school principles, or is in violation of school regulations, it must be all recorded. At the new moon, these records will be submitted to the master and elders.[38]

There were several reasons for the instigation of this procedure, and many of them were motivated by the specific nature of the study hall as opposed to the academy. Unlike the Munhŏn Academy, designed primarily for local youth, the Ŭnbyŏng Study Hall attracted students from far away who came to study specifically under the guidance of Yulgok. Students hailing from an unknown background were a potential risk for the scholarly community and Yulgok proscribed a detailed screening process in his admission regulations in order to assure that only persons of lofty ideals and strong will to study would be admitted.

---

[37] Pak Hyŏnjun, "Chosŏn sidae sŏnakjŏk yŏn'gu (Study on Registers of Good and Bad Deeds in the Chosŏn Period)," *Kyoyuk sahak yŏn'gu* 22, no. 1 (2012): 37–60.
[38] YGCS 15:46a.

The registration of good and bad deeds helped to evaluate students during their stay and allowed the study hall community to take appropriate collective decisions during joint sessions. Written records were also necessary because of another specific feature of the study hall: the frequent absence of the master, in this case Yulgok himself. Unlike in the academy, where the headmaster was meant to reside permanently, or at least make regular visits, the study hall master was typically a renowned scholar who was frequently on leave because of his official duties. In other words, Yulgok, who could visit his study retreat and students only occasionally, was in need of a systematic overview of students' activities during his absence in order to evaluate their progress. As an experienced administrator, Yulgok was very much in favour of written documentation as a means of managing Confucian institutions. He also took a similar approach in dealing with the economic matters of the study hall. In order to have effective control over the functioning of the study hall, Yulgok stipulated: "All goods must be recorded, and when it is time for the change of shift of the secretaries, the records and registers must be handed over to the new secretary."[39] A similar rule was applied for the most valuable source concerning our understanding of the life and education of the academies—the records of lectures. Yulgok stipulated: "Everything that is said during the lectures, including discussions by teachers, disciples, or friends of the literati [must be recorded]; the secretaries are in charge of these records which will later serve as a basis for material for the next round of examinations."[40] Unfortunately, no such records for the Ŭnbyŏng Study Hall are extant as in all likelihood they were destroyed during the Japanese invasion. However, the study hall's successor, the Sohyŏn Academy, did leave to us a few late examples of this genre that were preserved in the writings of private scholars in such texts as *Sohyŏn sŏwŏn Taehak kangsŏl mundap* 紹覽書院大學講說答問 (*Questions and Answers during the Lecture on the "Great Learning" in Sohyŏn Academy*) or *Sohyŏn sŏwŏn Nonŏ kangsŏl mundap* 紹覽書院論語講說答問 (*Questions and Answers during the Lecture on the "Analects" in Sohyŏn Academy*).[41] Yulgok's concept of sys-

---

39  YGCS 15:44a.
40  Ibid.
41  *Pyŏnggye sŏnsaeng chip* 屏溪先生集 (Collected Writings of Master Pyŏnggye), 41:25a–27a, 27a–36b. For general rules concerning academies lectures see Pak Chŏngbae, "Hakkyu rŭl t'onghaesŏ pon Chosŏn sidae ŭi sŏwŏn kanghoe (Lectures in Confucian Academies of the Chosŏn Period Seen through Academy Rules)," *Han'guk kyoyuk sahak* 19, no. 2 (2009): 59–83. In spite of all orders to keep track of all academy activities, few records of lectures are extant, mostly dating from the late Chosŏn period. For examples see Ch'oe Kwangman, "19 segi sŏwŏn kanghak hwaltong sarye yŏn'gu: Hogye kangnok ŭl chungsimŭro (Case-study of Lecture Activities in 19th Century Confucian Academies: Focusing on *Hogye kangnok*)," *Kyoyuk sahak yŏn'gu* 22, no. 1 (2012): 109–145; Pak Chongbae,

tematic records of students' activities was not reserved to his personal projects; the same idea, devised for Ŭnbyŏng Study Hall, was put forth later by him in his reform plan for state schools, the *Hakkyo mobŏm*. Here once again, he recommends the creation of a systematic registry of students' good and bad deeds, including the introduction of these records into state examination protocol in order to guarantee an accurate profile of the candidates.[42] Written records were later a standard part of the school system, and some of the extant documents show us the tribulations, but also the joys, of teachers as they comment upon their students.[43] Yulgok's administrative approach to his students was certainly innovative in the context of the Confucian academies but it should be mentioned that it had a direct precedent in other areas of the Confucian project to civilize Korean society: the local institution of community compacts.

## 5  Compact and Granary

In order to fully understand Yulgok's writings and plans for the economic and social development of the Haeju academy, it is necessary to mention several characteristics of his official profile as a scholar. As an outstanding literary talent and experienced bureaucrat, Yulgok had a natural tendency to compose his proposals or ideas in a very precise manner with a profound understanding of the prevailing social and economic conditions. As a man who was capable of dealing with military logistical matters and impressing Chinese envoys with his erudition, he was well able to balance his classical scholarship with a detailed knowledge of the problems of Korean society. The reform of the Munhŏn Academy formed only one part of his activities in the Haeju area to improve both the Confucian ethos and the living conditions of local population. Yulgok's family lived in the area; his relatives owned substantial properties there, and his standing among the local elite was extremely high, not only because of his scholarship and his position in the court, but because he used to

---

"Pyŏngsan sŏwŏn kyoyuk kwangye charyo kŏmt'o (Examination of Documents on Education in Pyŏngsan Academy)," *Kyoyuk sahak yŏn'gu* 18, no. 2 (2008): 31–59; and Han Yewŏn, "Honam chiyŏk sŏwŏn ŭi kyoyuk hwaltong: Chuksu sŏwŏn chi rŭl t'onghae pon yugyo kyoyang ŭi suyong (Educational Activities of Confucian Academies in Honam Area: Acceptance of Confucian Education Seen Through *Chuksu sŏwŏn chi*)," *Yugyo yŏn'gu* 22 (2010): 45–71.

42  YGCS 15:39a–43b.

43  Almost none of these records survived; for some examples from the 19th-century local schools see Pak Hyŏnjun, "Chosŏn sidae sŏnakchŏk yŏn'gu," 37–60.

serve as governor (*kwanch'alsa* 觀察使) of Hwanghae province. All these components gave Yulgok the possibility to create reform proposals on various community administrative levels, as well as the sufficient authority and material conditions to put them into praxis. The regulations of the Munhŏn Academy, various sections of the Haeju Community Compact, or Yulgok's vernacular regulations for his own household, *Tonggŏ kyesă* 同居戒辭 (*Admonitions for Living Together*), were interconnected undertakings—composed in the same environment, in the same time period, and for the same population—and so in many aspects these regulations were part of one overall endeavor.[44] The community compacts were also the direct inspiration for Yulgok's implementation of the registry of good and bad deeds; Yulgok had used the idea of recording and discussing the behaviour of community compact members already in 1570 in his community compact for Sŏwŏn County (*Sŏwŏn hyangyak* 西原鄉約). There he recommended the implementation of written evaluations in order to create materials for further discussion concerning the reward or punishment of individual compact members. The registry of good deeds and wrongful conduct was also integral to the Haeju Community Compact, where it played a similar role.

Community compact and the local academy were, in Yulgok's formulation, interconnected and mutually beneficial institutions. The academy accompanied the compact from the very beginning, and the very founding of the community compact was enacted in the academy, where the founding members of the compact should "meet to discuss and adopt the charter and then select the director, the associate director, the officer of the month, and the treasurer." Moreover, the treasurer "shall be a scholar enrolled in the academy."[45] The subsequent articles prescribe that the compact shall grant certain further functions to the academy. The academy was envisioned as a meeting place for the entire community, organized within the framework of the community compact as stipulated in the Fourth Article: "The inaugural meeting shall be held at the academy, where paper tablets for the sages and the notables are set up; all shall join in burning incense and bow twice to them." Collective gatherings formed part of the broader aspects of the community compact; in addition to their economic function, they were also meant to educate members of the community in Confucian virtues, along with the original plan of Zhu Xi as outlined in his version of the Revised Lü Family Community Compact (which was

---

44  This idea was understood very well by the editors of Yulgok's collected writings, who compiled his texts concerning the Munhŏn Academy and the Haeju Community Compact in two subsequent volumes.
45  YGCS 16:7a–b.

also the part of the Haeju Community Compact). The ritual and educational role of the academy is described in the section devoted to the management of gatherings, sacrifices, and lectures on community rules in the academy. Community gatherings were to be held in the academy on a monthly basis, and Yulgok took great effort to plan them down to the last detail, including specifications as to whether the academy should provide dishes for the participants' meals, and how appropriate clothing for the participants should look like. The most extensive description was devoted to ritual matters and the proper order of all participants: literally every step and movement taking place during the meeting was carefully choreographed in advance. The first phase of the meeting was composed of offerings to Confucius and ancient scholars (Yanzi, Zengzi, Zi Si, and Mencius) followed by the Song masters (Zhou Dunyi, the Cheng brothers, and Zhu Xi). Special attention was devoted as well to Ch'oe Ch'ung, the local patron of the academy. His shrine was opened, cleaned, and prepared for the burning of incense. While the ceremony was taking place, the directors "ascend to the shrine of Venerable Munhŏn, where the people who have followed them divide on the eastern and western sides and perform the burning of incense." After numerous arrangements according to seniority and status and prescribed rituals, all participants proceeded to the more profane point of the meeting dealing directly with community compact matters. The first and most important step was to remind members of the compact of their duties: "The officers of the month read the text of community compact in a loud voice, and the deputy directors explain its meaning in detail. Those who do not understand are allowed to ask questions." The public reading of the community compact was followed by a discussion on the behaviour of community members, which, after inspection, was recorded in the relevant registries. Unlike good deeds, which were later read aloud, the records of individual misconduct were circulated among the audience "where everyone looked at them in silence." After lunch and a period of rest, discussions and lectures about "community matters and classics" continued. With the coming of nighttime, all finally dispersed.

The importance of the academy for the community compact gatherings is very visible in the comparison of the Haeju Community Compact and the version composed for Sŏwŏn county. Although the earlier compact includes similar rules for the organization of public meetings, there were significant differences on the level of ritual propriety and the structural organization of participants. Both compacts strived equally to convey their message to a broad audience: the Sŏwŏn county version even speaks explicitly about illiterate community members, to whom "[the compact] should also be explained."[46] The most significant difference is, in the Sŏwŏn county version, the complete absence of Confucian rituals and offerings for sages and worthy individuals. The Munhŏn Academy and the adjacent shrine to Ch'oe Ch'ung played a crucial role in the Haeju Community Compact. The presence of the shrine and the academy provided an impressive spiritual framework for the entire gathering, and the veneration of spirits sanctioned the transformation of the community according to Confucian ideals. Yulgok described the influence of the academy shrine on students in his *Account of the Tobong Academy* (*Tobong sŏwŏn ki* 道峰書院記):

> If you do not aim your intentions seriously, continue under the evil influence of your old habits, frolic only with literary fripperies, focus only on success via state examinations, and amuse yourselves by eating and drinking and throwing away any single moment with no regret, then your offense to our Teacher [Cho Kwangjo] is indeed great. How could you, with such a face, be able to enter the gate of a shrine?[47]

The transformative effect of the presence of the sages in the academy shrine had an impact not only on the students, but affected the whole village community, including the members of the community compact. The local nature of the academy played an important role as well; in addition to the lofty and distant figures of the Confucian pantheon, the shrine to the local notable, Ch'oe Ch'ung, was intended to render the sense of awe and respect for moral values promulgated in the academy even more impressive. The presence of Ch'oe Ch'ung's spirit, firmly bound to his hometown, was reinforced as well by the connection with his descendants, still residing in the area and a major force in the academy and the enforcement of the community compact. The mystery of shrine doors opened, the bowing scholars, and the fragrance of burning incenses were also a highly effective means of inspiring respect for Confucian values among the peasants and slaves gathered at the shrine, instructed, as they were, to be present at the ceremonies together with their landlords and masters. The many personal ties between the academy and the community—scholars from the academy were officials of the compact, and

---

46  YGCS 16:6b. In the case of the Haeju community granary rules, the same approach was used and the text of the granary rules was also turned into a vernacular version, see YGCS 16:47a.
47  YGCS 13:38a.

members of the compact studied in the academy—were further enhanced by the economic role ascribed to the Munhŏn Academy by Yulgok.

The community compact was, in addition to its disciplinary nature, above all an economic entity, and the same was also valid for the academy. The new community members were obliged to "submit one bolt of cloth and one peck of rice to be stored at the academy under the supervision of the treasurer." The basic economic duties of members were further to "pay dues of one peck of rice at every meeting of the eleventh month"; these dues were then employed for the expenses of the compact. In the case of surplus, it was to be "loaned to the people at 20 percent interest, as in the village granary system."[48] The basic framework of dues and expenses for the various needs of the community compact outlined its founding text was further described in detail in a separate regulatory text of the community granary *Sach'anggye* 社倉契 (Community Granary Contract). This regulation stipulated rules for the distribution of grain to the destitute, the rights of non-members to granary support, the duties of new members, interest on loans (two-tenths of a peck when interest is repaid, and three-tenths of a peck "if the stored grain has not yet reached the stage of accruing interest"), and of course punishments for failing to repay debt, or repaying it with lesser quality rice. Both the communal granaries and the community compact existed in Korea long before his lifetime,[49] but the way in which Yulgok defined the relation between the academy, the community compact and the communal granary was undoubtedly new. The entire system was described in his biography, and it was, later on, considered important enough to be quoted as a model for rectifying community matters in a chapter of the official encyclopaedia *Chŭngbo Munhŏn pigo* 增補文獻備考 (*Augmented Reference Compilation of Documents*):

> When Yi I was in Haeju together with the people of the village, he had discussed with people having intentions and brought into practice the

---

48  YGCS 16:9a.
49  For the development of the community compact system in Korea (including Yulgok's role) see Sakai Tadao, "Yi Yulgok and the Community Compact," in *The Rise of Neo-Confucianism in Korea*, ed. Wm. Theodore de Bary and JaHyun Kim Haboush (New York: Columbia University Press, 1985), 323–348, and the chapter "The Community Compact System (*Hyangyak*)" in James B. Palais, *Confucian Statecraft and Korean Institutions: Yu Hyŏngwŏn and the Late Chosŏn Dynasty* (Seattle: University of Washington Press, 1996), 705–743. The most comprehensive analysis of the phenomena is offered in Martina Deuchler, "The Practice of Confucianism: Ritual and Order in Chosŏn Dynasty Korea," in *Rethinking Confucianism: Past and Present in China, Japan, Korea, and Vietnam*, ed. Benjamin A. Elman, John B. Duncan, and Herman Ooms (Los Angeles: UCLA Asian Pacific Monograph Series, 2002), 292–334.

community compact in order to rectify bad mores. He took the old rules of the Lü family, and again deliberating about it in the light of current conditions, adjusted its articles so the essentials would be appropriate to current customs; and yet he did not violate ancient arrangements. He also fixed meetings for the reading of the compact regulations; once each month, [there was] the reading and teaching of the compact in the academy. In the lecture hall, he displayed the tablets, which had been established there before, of the Master, the Four Sages: Master Zhou, the two brothers Cheng, and Master Zhu. Those who came all prostrated twice, and then prostrated in the Munhŏn shrine. After performing the rites, all assembled, in the proper order, in the hall, [to hear] the reading of the compact text; they discussed it and finished. In Yadu Village, Yulgok also approximately imitated ideas left by Master Zhu and established a community granary. In spring and autumn, the granary distributed and collected grain with two-tenths interest in order to assist both literati and [ordinary] people who were in need of food. Consequently, he created a granary pledge. Its articles were more detailed than in case of a community compact, in order to make it more convenient for the common people.[50]

All of Yulgok's interventions are presented here as the fulfilment of various parts of Zhu Xi's legacy; this interpretation is no doubt correct. In the same manner in which he enlarged and amended Zhu Xi's original version of community compact, Yulgok took as a model for his community granary the original version, developed by Zhu Xi in the late 1160s and early 1170s.[51] Levying a charge of interest 20 percent was inspired by Zhu Xi as well.[52] The novelty of Yulgok's system lay in the interconnection of all parts of the community compact and academy on economical, disciplinary, ritual, and moral grounds. This is a feature which we do not observe in the earlier academies and community compacts, where even one mention of the long-neglected idea of a community granary fails to appear.

---

50  CBMHPG 84:7b–8a.
51  See Hoyt Tillman, "Intellectuals and Officials in Action: Academies and Granaries in Sung China." *Asia Major*, Third series, Volume IV, Part II (1991): 1–14; and Richard von Glahn, "Community and Welfare: Zhu Xi's Community Granary in Theory and Practice," in *Ordering the World: Approaches to State and Society in Sung Dynasty China*, ed. Robert P. Hymes and Conrad Schirokauer (Berkeley: University of California Press, 1993), 221–254.
52  For discussion on levying interest charge of 20 percent see Richard von Glahn, "Community and Welfare," 236. For an implementation of the 20 percent interest policy in communal granaries for the Korean environment see James B. Palais, *Confucian Statecraft and Korean Institutions*.

## 6 Study Hall

Putting Zhu Xi's social and economic reforms into practice in the Korean environment was only one part of Yulgok's activities. There was another legacy—less visible and more private, but more important, that Yulgok took as well from the Song master. Zhu Xi served as a model for Korean literati not only on a doctrinal level, but above all as a paragon of a sage to be emulated in one's personal life. Zhu Xi's biography, poetry, and personal relations formed an endless inspiration for Yulgok as well, and in many of his activities he strove to follow the path of life as demonstrated by the Song thinker. Yulgok was well aware that in addition to Zhu Xi's involvement with the academies, there had been an even more important sphere of his activity connected to three study halls, which Zhu Xi used: the Hanquan Study Hall 寒泉精舍 (1170), the Wuyi Study Hall 武夷精舍 (1183), and the Zhulin Study Hall 竹林精舍 (1194).[53] In particular, the Wuyi Study Hall captured the imagination of Korean scholars: it became the imagined ideal of a scholar's paradise where the master sage speaks freely with his disciples, enjoys the beauty of nature, and devotes his time to moral cultivation and poetry. Unlike academies, which were public institutions, study halls were—following the example of Zhu Xi—understood as places where a Confucian scholar could give himself over entirely to the pursuit of self-cultivation and study. The private nature of the study hall was not in a strict sense opposed to the public nature of academies. They shared many similarities, but almost an equal number of differences as well. As in the case of academies, the study halls of Korean scholars also accepted disciples, often housed a shrine, and were dedicated to the pursuit of the Learning of the Way. It is no accident that in many cases these study halls were transformed at a later date into academies without too many serious hindrances. On the other hand, study halls were established by individuals, and not by local scholars and communities, so their relation to the state was minimal. Scholars resided there during their leisure time, students were selected individually by the master, and they were dedicated to more advanced studies, as well as to discussion between master and disciple, much more so than in the academies. Yulgok's concept of the study hall displays many interesting features of a conscious emulation of Zhu Xi's legacy in both in his private and public life, and demonstrates a broad variety of alternative methodologies of Confucian education in praxis.

---

53  Wing-tsit Chan describes the role of study halls (*jingshe*) for Zhu Xi in the chapter "*Ching-she* and Pupils" in his *Chu Hsi: New Studies* (Honolulu: University of Hawai'i Press, 1989), 336–355.

The story of Ŭnbyŏng Study Hall began in the fifth month of 1571, when Yulgok, then aged 36, was roaming in the vicinity of Kosan Brook close to his home in Sŏktam Village near Haeju. Amazed by natural beauty of the scenery of the meandering stream and its ponds, Yulgok gave a name for each of the nine bends of the stream, composed an account of the landscape and the notable sights, and resolved to settle in the area.[54] The reasons for his decision were well described later in his biographical entry for year 1577, when he finally materialized his plan.

> Between those two mountains there is a stream which flows forty *li*, bends nine times and then enters the sea. In every bend, there is a pond deep enough to operate a ship. By chance, it looks exactly like the Nine Bends of Mount Wuyi. [...] Master built there a study hall. He took the meaning of the Screen of Great Recluse of Mount Wuyi and named the building with a plaque that says: The Screen of Recluse. His idea was to live there in order to venerate Kaoting [Zhu Xi]. At the eastern side of the study, there was the Hall of Listening to the Stream. Master composed the Song of the Nine Bends of Kosan; it imitated the Boat Song of Wuyi. After this point, even more students came from near and afar.[55]

Yulgok's decision to settle in the fifth bend of the Kosan Brook was a conscious emulation of Zhu Xi's residence in the Wuyi Study Hall. Names for the local sceneries derived from Chinese toponyms and building the study hall and composing a song were proclamations of Yulgok's intention to follow the way of Master Zhu not only in his public activities but in his private life as well. The place of the study hall was not selected at random: already during his first visit Yulgok confirmed with joy that there were exactly nine bends in the brook so as to fit the imagined recreation of Zhu Xi's world.[56] The purpose of this undertaking was not only aesthetic: the recreated landscape was supposed to inspire a better understanding of Zhu Xi's work as explicitly stated in the poetic manifesto Yulgok composed for this undertaking. The first verses speak clearly about the planned activities in the scenery of Kosan:

> People do not know the nine bends and ponds of Kosan:
> Cutting grass, I dwell here, all friends arrive—

---

54  YGCS 33:32b–33a.
55  YGCS 34:7a–b.
56  YGCS 13:47a.

Ah! I imagine Mount Wuyi, going to learn from Master Zhu...[57]

The decision to find a study hall and establish a base for himself and his disciples paid off handsomely in the later years of Yulgok's life when he decided to withdraw from a court life that was increasingly plagued by factional strife. As late as 1579, his close disciples assembled in Ŭnbyŏng Study Hall and "students from the whole province and local scholars from all directions, who heard the news gathered there in such numbers that the school was not able to accommodate them."[58] The original lodge quickly developed into large complex of buildings[59] able to accommodate disciples, visitors and provide all other necessities. Yulgok's correspondence mentions a study hall servant or slave (*chaebok* 齋僕) who delivered correspondence between Yulgok, when on leave, and his students in Kosan. The study hall probably employed many more assistants than just one sole servant or slave, as in his letter to Pak Yŏryong 朴汝龍 (1541–1611), Yulgok writes about his wish to published his diary of royal lectures there.[60] Yulgok clearly presumed that the existence of his study hall would continue after his death, and in addition would be able to complete the complex task of publishing his work, a role typically reserved for academies. Nonetheless, the Ŭnbyŏng Study Hall played a crucial role for Yulgok's circle of disciples, and it attracted many new students who were seeking his guidance. A glimpse of the study hall atmosphere is visible in many entries of his *Ŏrok* 語錄 (*Recorded Conversations*), which document the discussions among Yulgok and his disciples. These reports show the study hall as a place of rigorous study, but also as a meeting place of good friends. The painterly environment contributed to the easeful atmosphere in which Yulgok often roamed about with his students, enjoying the beautiful natural setting. These features were even described in the study hall regulations, in which Yulgok even recommended students to spend some more time in relaxation, but still maintaining caution about their studies: "After meal they may on occasion wade or swim in the pond, but they should at the same time carefully observe nature, investigate its principles, and discuss jointly the meaning of things."[61] In fact, the at-

---

57   This vernacular version of *Kosan kugok ka* is recorded in Changsŏgak Archive manuscript *Pŏngwa chŏnsŏ, Akhak sŭmnyŏng* 瓶窩全書 樂學拾零. (Complete Writings of Pŏngwa, Titbits of the Study of Music), 15b.
58   YGCS 38:10a.
59   For an architectural description of the study hall and the later academy complex see Kang Sŏngwŏn, "Sohyŏn sŏwŏn e panyŏngtoen Yulgok ŭi kŏnch'uk mihak e kwangan yŏn'gu (Study on Yulgok's Architectural Aesthetics as Mirrored in Sohyŏn Academy)" (MA Thesis, Myŏngji taehakkyo, 2003).
60   YGCS 38:24b. Yulgok's collected writings were there published in 1611.
61   YGCS 15:45a

mosphere of the study hall was on occasion much closer to the leisure time pavilions of the literati (often also called *chŏngsa*) than to a strict educational institution. Several dialogues in the *Ŏrok* begin with a description of a visitor arriving, jugs of wine in tow, to engage in intellectual discussion. These meetings were understood as an integral part of study hall function. The aesthetic, academic, and alcohol-infused nature of such meetings is quite visible in the introductory section of one such conversation.

> Several friends each took a jug of wine and gathered in the study hall. They joined Master in the enjoyment of the flowers, and when the wine was half-consumed, Master said: "When people of old lagged behind in their capabilities, they certainly were asked whether their effort had been great or little. Gentlemen, what have you been seriously studying as of late?"[62]

As regards the Ŭnbyŏng Study Hall, most of the students were experienced adult scholars who were resolved in their pursuits, and there was no real need to restrain them from alcohol. Drinking, even accompanied by scholarly debate, was not a recommended activity in the academies, and already T'oegye had named, as one of the most important restrictions, the production of alcohol in the academy.[63] On the other hand, the beauty of the natural setting coupled with the pleasant companionship attracted visitors to the academies, and an attitude of scholarly seriousness was often blended with a decidedly relaxed atmosphere. A good illustration of this can be observed in a travel account to the Tobong Academy, composed by Yi Chŏnggyi 李廷龜 (1564–1635). It is the very same academy where Yulgok urged students to "with each passing day, spend [it] dwelling in calm, and pursuing [cultivation] deeper, so that you may be called the one able to repay Teacher's [Cho Kwangjo] generosity."[64] Yi Chŏnggyi, during his visit, followed the prescribed ritual: immediately after reaching the academy he and his companion "paid obeisance to the shrine" but spent the rest of his stay in the academy in a rather relaxed mood:

> Tired and weary, we returned and sat down in the Hall of Flowing Pillows in the Eastern Pavilion. For a long time, there had been no pavilion; it has been added recently. It is neatly constructed and adorable. We lodged for the night in the Hall of Flowing Pillows. Waves of sound touched the

---

62  YGCS 31:46b–47a.
63  TGCS 41:52a.
64  YGCS 13:38a.

pillars of the pavilion and the mountain moon entered through the doors. About third watch I awoke from sleep, and it was like in a dream, as when Li Bai went to the Three Chasms. Old Paeksa nudged me with his leg and said: "Where would you be able to find such splendid scenery?" Then he filled several cups of wine and ordered Myŏnghan to sing. Then he walked to the front steps to pavilion and recited Suzhan's *Poem of the Red Cliff*. I felt relaxed, imagining that I was riding the wind and had become an immortal.[65]

Both the academies and the study halls were constructed in order to meet the demand not only of a place for academic debate and the instructions of young students, but to create hidden sanctuaries of rest and quiet contemplation. They were as well occasionally used for the pleasure of partaking of the beauty of the surrounding mountains and countryside.

Ŭnbyŏng Study Hall was certainly different from the Munhŏn Academy, and both played a different role in Yulgok's life, and yet they were also strongly connected. Both institutions were only few miles distant from each other, and the study hall residents were the same members of the local community as the academy students. The study hall members also participated in the rites, ceremonies, and events taking place in the academy; they also took their share of responsibility in matters of community compact. Yulgok's letter to the study hall students in which he expresses his anxiety about community granary matters and delivers his ideas on grain crops and payments demonstrates that the study hall students were Yulgok's deputies in many local matters. On the other hand, the academy was the undisputable official centre, backed both by royal legitimation and the presence of the shrine, where all the local literati (including those in Ŭnbyŏng Study Hall) were expected to pay their respects. The original idea of *jingshe*—a merely pleasant place for meeting up with friends—was replaced, among the *sarim* literati, by the concept of a study hall remarkably similar to the academy; it was either the direct successor of the study hall or created in symbiosis with it, as in Yulgok's case. The study hall belonged to the same network as that of the academies. In later times, they were considered to be an integral part of literati community in the area. Andong, the stronghold of the T'oeye school, hosted three academies and 23 study halls, all forming a part of the network of local literati.[66] The famous study halls of the older generation of Korean literati, such as T'oegye's Tosan Sodang

---

65   *Wŏlsa sŏnsaeng chip* 月沙先生集 (Collected Writings of Master Wŏlsa), 38:25a–b.
66   Martina Deuchler, *Under the Ancestors' Eyes: Kinship, Status, and Locality in Premodern Korea* (Cambridge, MA: Harvard University Press, 2015), 310.

or the study hall of Nammyŏng Cho Sik 南冥 曹植 (1501–1572), Sanch'ŏnjae 山天齋, occurred in parallel with the birth of the academy system, but their concept was more or less spontaneous (and lacked written regulations). In Yulgok's lifetime, we see already the need and the volition for a more systematic approach. Yulgok knew that his study hall would ideally maintain a similar spirit to the local academy, and that it would probably evolve in a similar direction (as it indeed did occur), similar to Tosan Study Hall and the other retreats of famous scholars.[67] Several versions of the written regulations for Ŭnbyŏng Study Hall were certainly new in terms of the development of a study hall concept modelled after the academy, but certain similar cases may be observed. One of them can be seen in the study hall of Yulgok's lifelong friend, Ugye, who established his Ugye Study Room (Ugye sŏsil 牛溪書室, also known as Ugye chŏngsa) around 1570 in P'aju.[68] The students of this study hall followed a specific set of regulations termed "Etiquette of Ugye Study Room" (*Ugye sŏsirŭi* 牛溪書室儀). The 22 articles of regulations that Ugye composed for his students are similar in many points to Yulgok's, including seating arrangements, recommendations for walks after study, or reporting misbehaviour. The regulations for the Ugye and the Ŭnbyŏng study halls were very similar, if not in many respects identical to those of the academy: this point is further demonstrated by the fact that in later times they often were employed as standardized academy regulations. Yun Sŏn'gŏ 尹宣擧 (1610–1669) mentions the use of Ugye's rules in the P'asan Academy;[69] Kang P'irhyo 姜必孝 (1764–1848) recommended, as school regulations, "Master Zhu's *Regulations for the White Deer Grotto Academy*, venerable T'oegye's Yisan *Academy Rules*, and *Study Room Etiquette of P'asan*."[70] In academies that adhered to Yulgok's school of thought, the use of his regulations was supposed to be automatic, and Toam Yi Chae 陶菴 李縡 (1680–1746), in his regulations for the Simgok Academy 深谷書院, emphasizes that in addition to Zhu Xi's *Regulations for the White Deer Grotto Academy*, there are no better regulations than the Ŭnbyŏng Study Hall Regulations and Pledge.[71]

---

67  As Thomas Lee already observed for the Chinese case, "it actually was the *ching-she* (literally, house of essence) which embodied the ideal, and that the academies were the institutional and thus permanent extension of the more informal ching-she educational conception." Thomas H.C. Lee, "Chu Hsi, Academies and the Tradition of Private Chianghsüeh," *Hanxue yanjiu* 2, no. 1 (1984): 302. We may conclude that this phenomenon was also valid in 16th-century Korea.

68  See Pak Kyunbyŏn, "Ugye sŏsirŭi yŏn'gu (Study on *Ugye sŏsirŭi*)," *Han'guk kyoyuk sahak* 20 (1998): 165–197.

69  *Nosŏ sŏnsaeng yugo* 魯西先生遺稿 (Literary Remains of Master Nosŏ), 16:9b.

70  *Haeŭn sŏnsaeng yugo* 海隱先生遺稿 (Literary Remains of Master Haeŭn) 11:2b.

71  *Toam sŏnsaeng chip* 陶菴先生集 (Collected Writings of Master Toam), 25:20a.

ILLUSTRATION 11.2   Wooden nameplate of Ŭnbyŏng Study Hall in Sohyŏn Academy

## 7        Shrines

Yulgok's activities connected to the Munhŏn Academy form an important testimony for a discussion concerning the ritual significance of local academies vis-à-vis literati communities. The ritual role of academies had been deemed crucial ever since the founding of the first such institutions in Korea. Chu Sebung, in connection with the Paegundong Academy, emphasized: "Cultivation must begin with the veneration of worthy individuals. This is the reason for setting up shrines to honour such worthies. This is the reason to honour virtue, and for establishing academies to esteem learning."[72] Similarly T'oegye, in his proposal for chartering the same academy, stated that academies should be established in "places in which there are remains of the exploits of former worthy individuals."[73] The selection of these worthy individuals for the academy shrine was a complicated process, as the demands of the local elites and Confucian literati ideals were often in conflict with each other. The two letters written in 1577 by Yulgok to Ch'oe Hwang 崔滉 (1529–1603) show the delicate nature of maintaining a balance between the requirement for a worthy indi-

---

72   *Myŏngjong sillok* 1554/07/02, for the translation see Hejtmanek, "The Elusive Path to Sagehood," 252.
73   TGCS 9:7b; for the translation see Hejtmanek, "The Elusive Path to Sagehood," 260.

vidual to be enshrined and the need to keep up good connections with the local community. Village families often championed their own candidates—i.e. the more renowned members of their clans—for enshrinement, and they understood the act of building an academy shrine as a tool for enhancing their own elite status. Confucian literati, on the other hand, demanded that the enshrined person to be a scholar of significant moral credit and outstanding scholarship according to the requirements of the Learning of the Way. Probably the most renowned case of such a conflict—which entered into Korean folklore—is the story of the enshrinement of the Silla general Kim Yusin 金庾信 (595–673) in the Sŏak Academy 西岳書院 in Kyŏngju. When a Confucian scholar objected to the enshrinement in the academy of a military figure lacking scholarly accomplishment, the infuriated ghost of the Silla general approached the startled Confucian and reproached him for his misbehaviour.[74]

The conflicts between local elites and zealous young Confucian students were present as well in the Haeju academy. Many literati were not satisfied with the enshrinement of Ch'oe Ch'ung, who was an important local personality but—being a scholar of the Koryŏ era—his commitment to the Learning of the Way and scholarship were in doubt.[75] According to Yulgok's statement "all literati believe that Munhŏn's teaching concerned only state examinations, and moreover, that he composed stelae texts for Buddhist monasteries." The consequence of this attitude was that the students of the academy often did not participate in offerings for such a figure and that some of them, when before the shrine, "do not [even] bow, but only raise their clasped hands."[76] The conscientious Confucian students did not consider Ch'oe Ch'ung to be worthy of their respect, but at the same time, the removal of an important local personality from an academy shrine could lead to potential conflict with the village community who could always be counted on to come to the defence of their ancestors. Yulgok himself was a distant relative of the Ch'oe family and stressed this fact as a sign of his impartiality when attempting to reconcile both parties. His resolution to this conflict was to move Ch'oe Ch'ung to an adjacent shrine and reserve the main position in the shrine for Confucius: this would honour both the Sage and Ch'oe Ch'ung, who would be enshrined as a

---

[74] See various editions of *Tonggyŏng chapki* 東京雜記 (Miscellaneous Records of the Eastern Capital) or *Ch'ŏnyerok* 天倪錄 (Record of Equal Workings of Heaven).
[75] For a general information of the development of Ch'oe Ch'ung's cult see Yi Sŏngho, "Ch'oe Ch'unge taehan yŏktae insik pyŏnhwa wa Munmyo chongsa onŭi ŭi ihae (Changes of Historical Perception of Ch'oe Ch'ung and Understanding of Argument during the Process of Application for his Introduction into Confucius Shrine)," *Yŏksawa kyŏnggye* 3 (2012): 95–135.
[76] YGCS 12:14a.

local worthy individual (*hyanghyŏn* 鄉賢). This solution finally prevailed and is reflected in the regulations of the academy which speaks of two shrines, which peacefully co-existed. Witness to discussions surrounding the topic is borne out by Yulgok's second letter in which he offers an overview of the whole issue in significant details. In the time period between the writing of the two letters, the conflict had escalated and Yulgok was obliged to employ both threats and arguments now to bring the two sides to reconciliation. The academy students were reluctant to venerate Ch'oe Ch'ung as the main patron of the academy, and Ch'oe Ch'ung's family and their local allies were horrified by the possible demotion or removal of their ancestor from the shrine. The most extreme solution would be the establishment of two separate academies, one venerating Confucius and one Ch'oe Ch'ung, but this could create, according to Yulgok, even more animosities and jealousy. Yulgok further argued that two separate academies for one single community would not at all be economically feasible, and he threatened both parties that under such circumstances he would cease all involvement with the academy. Yulgok continued to maintain that a solution of compromise—namely, to devote the main location in the shrine to Confucius and to move Ch'oe Ch'ung to an adjacent location—by no means offended anybody, since the highest respect belonged to Confucius, and in "there is no shame at all in sacrificing to Munhŏn as to a local worthy."[77] Yulgok's argumentation was not based solely on his personal views, but relied heavily on precedents from previous traditions, both Chinese and Korean, as to the necessary qualifications for a person to be enshrined in an academy. Local elites or families of scholars often pushed for the enshrinement of their candidate, but Yulgok warned that matters of such importance "must be entrusted to public debate and not disputed according to the selfish emotions of the ancestors' descendants." The enshrinement of important local figures could attract the economic support of local families to a new academy, but the venerated individual needed to have the sufficient moral prestige and record of scholarship in order to gain the respect of the Confucian literati. The Korean literati preaching the radical interpretation of the Learning of the Way generally had little respect for scholars or officials outside of *sarim* circles and tradition: in their eyes, the main qualifications which called for enshrinement were flawless scholarship and an utmost devotion to Confucian ideals. Prominent local personalities were often officials from the Koryŏ or early Chosŏn eras who were interested in securing an elite status for their families; hence, Yulgok and other *sarim* literati did not consider them as part of their own tradition. For Yulgok, genuine Confucianism, i.e. the Learning of Principle (*ihak* 理學)

---

[77]   YGCS 12:16a.

began in Korea only with Cho Kwangjo 趙光祖 (1482–1519), and he had a rather sceptical view concerning the credentials of older generation scholars. In his treatise composed for King Sŏnjo, Yulgok even flatly denied the existence of authentic Confucianism in Korea during previous times, stating: "At the end of the Koryŏ period, Chŏng Mongju 鄭夢周 (1337–1392) had the slight spirit and appearance of a Confucian scholar, but he was not able to accomplish his learning, and if we trace his deeds, he was nothing more than a loyal subject."[78] The dilemma Yulgok faced was not the first case of tension between local elites and Confucian literati, and he made the remark that "there are indeed many unsuitable people who are enshrined in academies."[79] The solution Yulgok proposed in the case of Ch'oe Ch'ung was based on the subtle difference between enshrinement as a local worthy individual in an adjacent shrine, or as the main shrine figure (*chŏngwi* 正位). This strategy was derived from the earlier case of a similar problem with which Yulgok was quite familiar, and he quoted it as a precedent. In order to persuade Ch'oe Hwang to agree with the proposed adjustment of the academy shrine, he introduced the example of his own father-in-law, who had discussed in 1560 with T'oyegye a similar problem about the enshrinement of Yi Chonyŏn 李兆年 (1269–1343) in the Sŏngju Academy.[80] Several scholars have noted that Yi Chonyŏn's portrait bears features of Buddhist iconography, leading to the supposition that he was an adherent of Buddhism. T'oegye defended Yi Chonyŏn and considered his enshrinement as legitimate,[81] but as a compromise solution, removed him to an adjacent position so that "to Yi Chonyŏn were offered sacrifices as to local worthy, and the brothers Cheng and Master Zhu were installed in the central position of the shrine."[82] T'oegye was even more sceptical of the qualities of Koryŏ era scholars than Yulgok,[83] but both thinkers understood very well that the

78   YGCS 19:9a.
79   YGCS 12:16b.
80   There was probably close exchanges between T'oegye and Yulgok on both cases of Sŏngju Academy and Munhŏn Academy. Note that in the same way Yulgok knew the first precedent, T'oegye was well informed about the process of enshrinement in Haeju and observed it with a full approval; see Hejtmanek, "The Elusive Path to Sagehood," 267.
81   TGCS 21:35b.
82   YGCS 12:16b.
83   For T'oegye's opinion on the Genealogy of the Way in Korea see Chung Soon-woo, "T'oegye tot'ongnon ŭi yŏksa ŭimi (Historical Meaning of T'oegye's Version of The Genealogy of the Way)," *T'oegye hakpo* 111 (2002): 1–42. There are numerous indices that T'oegye supported the enshrinement of certain scholars for rather pragmatic motivations and privately openly doubted their Confucian qualities. When in 1567 two Chinese envoys asked about the state of scholarship in Korea, T'oegye indicated several famous Korean scholars (see Martina Deuchler, "Reject the False and Uphold the Straight: Attitudes Toward Heterodox Thought in Early Yi Korea," in *The Rise of Neo-Confucianism in Korea*, ed. Wm. Theodore

support of local elites was crucial for the success of the academy and were willing to somewhat relax their strict standards. Local figures could therefore be enshrined in academies, but the central place in the shrine was reserved for a venerable scholar or sage of undisputed scholarly renown, such as Zhu Xi, the brothers Cheng, or Confucius, by himself or together with the Song masters as was the case in the Munhŏn Academy. Yulgok's opinion concerning local worthies is best illustrated by his own choice, when he had the opportunity to decide such a question on his own. In the course of the year 1578, he started to plan a shrine dedicated to Zhu Xi[84] as a part of the Ŭnbyŏng Study Hall. It was completed only after his death, but the dedication of a shrine to Zhu Xi in the study hall that Yulgok himself planned and built shows that it was intended to serve Confucian ideals alone and that he felt no particular need or desire to find any strategy accommodating local powerful families via the enshrinement of their prominent illustrious ancestors. Both Yulgok and T'oegye exhibited strong scepticism concerning local figures who were selected for enshrinement in academy shrines, yet they accepted this custom as a practical method of securing the support of the local elites for the academies.[85]

    de Bary, JaHyun Kim Haboush [New York: Columbia University Press, 1985], 385–386). In the following personal letter, he distanced himself from his official reply by expressing his doubts about the selected scholars. The special target of his critique was An Hyang (whom he supported in the case of Paegundong Academy): "People like Ch'oe [Chiwŏn], Sŏl [Ch'ong], Ch'oe [Ch'ung], An [Hyang] were at the beginning praised as good Confucians by ministry officials who have selected this kind of people. I did not want to reject entirely their candidates and use just my personal decision, so I kept them in the text of the reply but explained critically that literati and Confucians of these two periods were not representatives of the Learning of the Mind." TGCS 17:43a.

84    Zhu Xi's enshrinement in Korean academies was studied by Deng Hongbo, "Zhu Xi yu Chaoxian shuyuan (Zhu Xi and Korean Academies)," *Guizhou jiaoyu xueyuan xuebao* 1 (1989): 43–46, and Chŏng Hyŏnjŏng, "Chosŏn chunggi Chuja chehyang sŏwŏnŭi sahoesajŏk sŏnggyŏk (Socio-historical Character of Zhu Xi' s Enshrinements in Confucian Academies in Middle Chosŏn Period)," *Han'guk sŏwŏn hakpo* 1 (2011): 87–124. Chŏng Hyŏnjŏng's data show interesting phenomena concerning the selection of Zhu Xi as the main figure for academy shrines: with 25 academies Zhu Xi was the third most frequently revered worthy in Korean academies' shrines (after Song Siyŏl 宋時烈 [1607–1689] with 44 academies, and T'oegye with 29). However, the peak of Zhu Xi's enshrinement trend came during the reign of King Sŏnjo (enshrined in eight academies) and most of the academies devoted to Zhu Xi were located in Hwanghae province. This indicates that, at least in certain cases, there was a tendency to enshrine Zhu Xi rather than local Korean worthies in the early stages of academies' dissemination.

85    For later critique of enshrinement abuses see Ch'oe Yŏng-ho, "The Private Academies (Sŏwŏn) and Neo-Confucianism in Late Chosŏn Korea." However, my argument is that both T'oegye and Yulgok considered enshrinement of local figures as problematic from the very beginning of their engagement with academies. T'oegye even privately argued

## 8  Conclusion

The spread of Confucian academies in the second half of the 16th century in Korea was accompanied by several structural problems which began to form the subject of public debate from 1560 onwards. Discussions focused on the topics of how to provide students in academies with proper guidance and how to maintain discipline among them. Yulgok's solution to these dilemmas is reflected in his court proposal calling for a greater involvement of the state, which, as he wrote, should provide salaries to the masters of the academies and employ retired officials as well. Concerning the problem of discipline among the students, Yulgok, in his sets of regulations for academies, introduced the need for a more systematic overview of students' behaviour via written registries of their conduct and established a precise set of rules for the management of academies. Dissimilarly to the rather abstract and moral accent of the older regulations for the Paegundong or Isan academies, Yulgok introduced consistent rules for the admission of students (stressing broad access to academy education), created fixed patterns for academy decision-making (often based on collective decisions), and stipulated a detailed system of punitive measures intended to maintain discipline among the students. Compared to the regulations of other contemporary Korean academies, Yulgok's regulations were all-encompassing and focused in detail on all features of academy management, including pragmatic social and economic aspects which were often not included in the rather abstract texts of other Korean examples of this genre. Putting his principles into action at the Haeju Munhŏn Academy, Yulgok strived to connect the role of local academy with two other components of Zhu Xi's heritage, the community compact and the community granary. Yulgok ascribed a central place to the local academy in managing community affairs, connecting the responsibility of academy officials with both the community compact and the collective granary. In addition, he determined the local academy to be the spiritual and ritualistic centre of the community, where meetings of community members, lectures, and discussions were to be held. Combining of all three Zhu Xi's concepts (academy, compact, granary) into a single model was a significant innovation without precedents in the Korean (and perhaps also Chinese) environment. Local academy activities were, in Yulgok's case, accompanied by his endeavours concerning his Ŭnbyŏng Study Hall. The purpose and the organizational structure of Yulgok's study hall shows striking similarities to that of the nearby Haeju academy,

that shrines do not have to be part of academies as in the Chinese case; see Chŏng Manjo, *Chosŏn sidae sŏwŏn yŏn'gu*, 67–68.

with, however, some significant differences. As opposed to the Munhŏn Academy, where Yulgok was forced to seek a modus vivendi with the local elites, in his study hall he was able to create a model academy according to his own wishes. This pattern was embodied in the regulations he composed for his own study hall, his selection of worthy individuals for the study hall shrine, and his relation to his disciples in the study hall. The vision of a study hall Yulgok created at the bank of Kosan Brook was, in many aspects, an alternative version of the established academy model, and yet proved to be very compatible with the latter, as is well demonstrated by the smooth transformation of Ŭnbyŏng Study Hall into Sohyŏn Academy, as well as by the validity of Yulgok's regulations for Ŭnbyŏng Study Hall that served many Korean academies for centuries to come.

### References

Chan, Wing-tsit. *Chu Hsi: New Studies.* Honolulu: University of Hawai'i Press, 1989.

Cho, Hwisang. "The Community of Letters: The T'oegye School and the Political Culture of Choson Korea, 1545–1800." Ph.D. diss., Columbia University, 2010.

Chŏng Hyŏnjŏng. "Chosŏn chunggi Chuja chehyang sŏwŏn ŭi sahoesajŏk sŏnggyŏk (Socio-historical Character of Zhu Xi' s Enshrinements in Confucian Academies in Middle Chosŏn Period)." *Han'guk sŏwŏn hakpo* 1 (2011): 87–124.

Chŏng Manjo. "T'oegye Yi Hwang ŭi sŏwŏnnon—kŭ ŭi kyohwaron kwa kwallyŏnhayŏ (T'oegye Yi Hwang's Arguments on Confucian Academies: In Relation to His Views on Transformation by Education)." in *Chosŏn sidae sŏwŏn yŏn'gu* (Studies on Confucian Academies of Chosŏn Period), edited by Chŏng Manjo, 49–84. Seoul: Chimmundang, 1997.

Chŏng Sunmok. "T'oegye ŭi sŏwŏn kyoyukkwan (T'oegye's Views on Education in Confucian Academies)." In *Han'guk sŏwŏn kyoyuk chedo yŏn'gu* 韓國書院教育制度研究 (Studies on Education System in Korean Confucian Academies), edited by Chŏng Sunmok, 59–78. 3rd edition. Taegu: Yŏngnam taehakkyo ch'ulp'anbu, 1989.

Chŏng Sunmok. "Yulgok ŭi sŏwŏn kyoyukkwan (Yulgok's Views on Education in Confucian Academies)." In *Han'guk sŏwŏn kyoyuk chedon yŏn'gu* 韓國書院教育制度研究 (Studies on Education System in Korean Confucian Academies), edited by Chŏng Sunmok, 79–95. 3rd edition. Taegu: Yŏngnam taehakkyo ch'ulp'anbu, 1989.

Ch'oe Kwangman. "19 segi sŏwŏn kanghak hwaltong sarye yŏn'gu: Hogye kangnok ŭl chungsimŭro (Case-study of Lecture Activities in 19th Century Confucian Academies: Focusing on *Hogye kangnok*)." *Kyoyuk sahak yŏn'gu* 22, no. 1 (2012): 109–145.

Ch'oe Yŏng-ho. "The Private Academies (Sŏwŏn) and Neo-Confucianism in Late Chosŏn Korea." *Seoul Journal of Korean Studies* 21, no. 21 (2008): 139–191.

Chung Soon-woo. *Sŏwŏn ŭi sahoesa* (Social History of Korean Confucian Academies). Seoul: T'aehaksa, 2013.

Chung Soon-woo. "T'oegye tot'ongnon ŭi yŏksa ŭimi. (Historical Meaning of T'oegye's Version of The Genealogy of the Way)." *T'oegye hakpo* 111 (2002): 1–42.

Deng Hongbo 邓洪波. "Zhu Xi yu Chaoxian shuyuan 朱熹与朝鲜书院 (Zhu Xi and Korean Academies)." *Guizhou jiaoyu xueyuan xuebao* 1 (1989): 43–46.

Deuchler, Martina. "The Practice of Confucianism: Ritual and Order in Chosŏn Dynasty Korea." In *Rethinking Confucianism: Past and Present in China, Japan, Korea, and Vietnam*, edited by Benjamin A. Elman, John B. Duncan, and Herman Ooms, 292–334. Los Angeles: UCLA Asian Pacific Monograph Series, 2002.

Deuchler, Martina. "Reject the False and Uphold the Straight: Attitudes Toward Heterodox Thought in Early Yi Korea." In *The Rise of Neo-Confucianism in Korea*, edited by Wm. Theodore de Bary, JaHyun Kim Haboush, 375–410. New York: Columbia University Press, 1985.

Deuchler, Martina. *Under the Ancestors' Eyes: Kinship, Status, and Locality in Premodern Korea*. Cambridge, MA: Harvard University Press, 2015.

Glomb, Vladimír. "Reading the Classics Till Death: Yulgok Yi I and the Curriculum of Chosŏn Literati." *Studia Orientalia Slovaca* 2, no.2 (2012): 315–329.

*Haeŭn sŏnsaeng yugo* 海隱先生遺稿 (Literary Remains of Master Haeŭn). 1895. Yonsei University Library #811.98/Kang P'ilyo/Hae. Database of Korean Classics. <http://db.itkc.or.kr> (accessed 1 May 2017).

Han Yewŏn. "Honam chiyŏk sŏwŏn ŭi kyoyuk hwaltong: Chuksu sŏwŏn chi rŭl t'onghae pon yugyo kyoyang ŭi suyong (Educational Activities of Confucian Academies in Honam Area: Acceptance of Confucian Education Seen Through *Chuksu sŏwŏn chi*)." *Yugyo yŏn'gu* 22 (2010): 45–71.

Han Yŏngu. *Yulgok p'yŏngjŏn* (Biography of Yulgok). Seoul: Minŭmsa 2016.

Hejtmanek, Milan. "The Elusive Path to Sagehood: Origins of the Confucian Academy System in Chosŏn Korea." *Seoul Journal of Korean Studies* 26, no. 2 (2013): 233–268.

Kang Sŏngwŏn. "Sohyŏn sŏwŏn e panyŏngto en Yulgok ŭi kŏnch'uk mihak e kwangan yŏn'gu (Study on Yulgok's Architectural Aesthetics as Mirrored in Sohyŏn Academy)." MA Thesis, Myŏngji taehakkyo, 2003.

Kim Haboush, JaHyun. "The Education of the Yi Crown Prince: A Study in Confucian Pedagogy." In *The Rise of Neo-Confucianism in Korea,* edited by Wm. Theodore de Bary, JaHyun Kim Haboush, 192–196. New York: Columbia University Press, 1985.

Lee, Thomas H.C. "Chu Hsi, Academies and the Tradition of Private Chiang-hsüeh." *Hanxue yanjiu* 2, no. 1 (1984): 301–329.

*Nosŏ sŏnsaeng yugo* 魯西先生遺稿 (Literary Remains of Master Nosŏ). 1712. Kyujanggak #奎 5324. Database of Korean Classics. <http://db.itkc.or.kr> (accessed 1 May 2017).

Pak Chŏngbae. "Chosŏn sidae ŭi hangnyŏng mit hakkyu (Rules and Regulations in Confucian Academies of Chosŏn Period)." *Han'guk kyoyuk sahak* 28, no. 2. (2006): 213–237.

Pak Chŏngbae. "Hakkyu rŭl t'onghaesŏ pon Chosŏn sidae ŭi sŏwŏn kanghoe (Lectures in Confucian Academies of Chosŏn Period Seen through Academy Rules)." *Han'guk kyoyuk sahak* 19, no. 2 (2009): 59–83.

Pak Chŏngbae. Pyŏngsan sŏwŏn kyoyuk kwangye charyo kŏmt'o (Examination of Documents on Education in Pyŏngsan Academy)." *Kyoyuk sahak yŏn'gu* 18, no. 2 (2008): 31–59.

Pak Hyŏnjun. "Chosŏn sidae sŏnakchŏk yŏn'gu (Study on Registers of Good and Bad Deeds in Chosŏn Period)." *Kyoyuk sahak yŏn'gu* 22, no. 1 (2012): 37–60.

Pak Kyunbyŏn. "Ugye Sŏsirŭi yŏn'gu (Study on Ugye *Sŏsirŭi*)." *Han'guk kyoyuk sahak* 20 (1998): 165–197.

Palais, James B. *Confucian statecraft and Korean Institutions: Yu Hyŏngwŏn and the late Chosŏn Dynasty*. Seattle: University of Washington Press, 1996.

*Pyŏnggye sŏnsaeng chip* 屏溪先生集 (Collected Writings of Master Pyŏnggye). 1802. Kyujanggak Archive #奎 6663. Database of Korean Classics. <http://db.itkc.or.kr> (accessed 1 May 2017).

Sakai Tadao. "Yi Yulgok and the Community Compact." In *The Rise of Neo-Confucianism in Korea*, edited by Wm. Theodore de Bary and JaHyun Kim Haboush, 323–348. New York: Columbia University Press, 1985.

Tillman, Hoyt. "Intellectuals and Officials in Action: Academies and Granaries in Sung China." *Asia Major*, Third series, Volume IV, Part II (1991): 1–14.

*Toam sŏnsaeng chip* 陶菴先生集 (Collected Writings of Master Toam). 1803. Kyujanggak #古 3428-27. Database of Korean Classics. <http://db.itkc.or.kr> (accessed 1 May 2017).

*Tosŏ mongnok* I–III. (*Hansŏ pullyu mongnok*) (Book Catalogue I–III: Books in Classical Chinese Catalogue by Categories). Kim Ilsŏng chonghap taehak tosŏgwan, 1958.

von Glahn, Richard. "Community and Welfare: Zhu Xi's Community Granary in Theory and Practice." In *Ordering the World: Approaches to State and Society in Sung Dynasty China*, edited by Robert P. Hymes, Conrad Schirokauer, 221–254. Berkeley: University of California Press, 1993.

*Wŏlsa sŏnsaeng chip* 月沙先生集 (Collected Writings of Master Wŏlsa). 1688. Kyujanggak #古3428-30. Database of Korean Classics. <http://db.itkc.or.kr> (accessed 1 May 2017).

Yi Man'gyu. *Chosŏn kyoyuksa I* (History of Korean Education I). Seoul: Ŭryu munhwasa, 1947.

Yi Sŏngho. Ch'oe Ch'unge taehan yŏktae insik pyŏnhwa wa Munmyo chongsa nonŭi ŭi ihae (Changes of Historical Perception of Ch'oe Ch'ung and Understanding of Argument during the Process of Application for His Introduction into Confucius Shrine)." *Yŏksawa kyŏnggye* 3 (2012): 95–135.

CHAPTER 12

# Disputes between Confucian Academies and Buddhist Monasteries from a Sociocultural View: The Case of the Wufeng Academy Litigation

*Lan Jun*

## 1        Introduction

Since Buddhism first entered China in the 1st century CE, Confucianism and Buddhism gradually engaged in a rather complex relationship of mutual assimilation, fusion, outright contradiction, and struggle. Since the Tang (618–907) and Song (960–1279) dynasties Confucian scholars had, in order to meet their own cultural and educational needs, developed Confucian academies as an educational institution combining official and private learning as well as the strengths of Buddhist and Daoist education.[1] As their educational institutions, Confucian academies and Buddhist monasteries, inherited the dichotomous relation of Confucianism and Buddhism, Confucian scholars and Buddhist monks of the Song and Ming (1368–1644) periods often came into contact, not only on an intellectual level, but also in their daily lives. It is widely known that Zhu Xi 朱熹 (1130–1200), during his years in Shaoxing when he received an education from his teacher Li Tong 李侗 (1093–1163), was a resident in Xilin Temple 西林寺院.[2] Another well-known example of a Confucian scholar visiting and staying in a Buddhist monastery is the cartographer Luo Hongxian 羅洪先 (1504–1564). In his *Winter Travelogue* (*Dongyouji* 冬遊記) he records his travel from Zhenjiang to Nanjing in the 12th month of the 18th year

---

1   See Thomas H.C. Lee, *Education in Traditional China: A History* (Leiden: Brill, 2000), 84–85; and Peter K. Bol, *"This Culture of Ours": Intellectual Transitions in T'ang and Sung China* (Stanford; Stanford University Press, 1992), 18–22.

2   *Yanping fu zhi* (Yanping Prefecture Gazetteer), Volume 13 (Qianlong), in *Zhongguo fangzhi congshu huazhong difang* (Series of Chinese Local Records, Central China) (Taipei: Chengwen chubanshe, 1985), No. 99 states: "Xilin [Temple] is located in the southeast of the county seat and was built in the state Later Liang (907–923) of the Five Dynasty period (907–960). Master Zhu sought audience with Li Yanping [Li Tung] to receive his education, and stayed here." For a discussion on Zhu Xi and Buddhism see Julia Ching, *The Religious Thought of Chu Hsi* (Oxford: Oxford University Press, 2000), 171–189; and Charles Wei-hsun Fu, "Chu Hsi on Buddhism," in *Chu Hsi and Neo-Confucianism*, ed. Wing-tsit Chan (Honolulu: University of Hawai'i Press, 1986), 377–408.

of the Jiajing 嘉靖 reign (1539) to pay a visit to Wang Ji 王畿 (1498–1583) and chronicles his meetings and activities during the trip. On his journey he relied mainly on Buddhist or Daoist temples for accommodation, and not only did monks provide vegetarian foods, but also local scholars often came carrying meats and wine to visit him and to hold banquets in the temples. This surely illustrates how close and harmonious the relations between Buddhist monks and Confucian scholars could be. In the Tang and Song dynasties many Confucian academies or private studios (*jingshe* 精舍) were attached to Buddhist monasteries or built close by. Even Yuelu Academy 岳麓書院, which was well known as one of the four great Chinese academies and had its origins at the end of the Five Dynasties period had received land and books from the monk Zhixuan 智璿 (?–?)[3] for its construction and operation, letting the local scholars "obtain a place to stay, obtain books to study."[4]

Investigating the conflicts between Confucianism and Buddhism, many cases of struggle for cultural hegemony in their environments between Confucian academies and Buddhist monasteries can be found, often outwardly appearing as mere disputes over land and estates. Taking such disputes as the starting point for an inquiry into which regional forces supported Confucian academies, examining their characteristics and their reaction to opposition, can help to build a more multifaceted picture of Confucian academies within their environments. Efforts to reconstruct the academies' specific historical situations through a sociocultural view and the investigation of its relationship with local communities are important aspects of current research on Confucian academies. Xiao Yongming, in his book *Ruxue, shuyuan, shehui* (*Confucianism, Academies, and Society*), gives an overview of the respective motivations and aims of historical rulers, all levels of officials, local family member, scholars, merchants, etc., for supporting the development of academies. By this he laid the foundations for the academic community to further investigate the interactions between Confucian academies and the various social strata in local societies.[5] Chen Shilong's study of Tianzhen Academy 天真書院 analyzes a confrontation between the central government and local officials, gentry,

---

3 See Zhu Hanmin and Deng Hongbo, *Yuelu shuyuan shi* (History of the Yuelu Academy) (Changsha: Hunan jiaoyu chubanshe, 2013), 10; For an English discussion of the History of Yuelu Academy see Daniel McMahon, "The Yuelu Academy and Hunan's Nineteenth-Century Turn Toward Statecraft," *Late Imperial China* 26, no. 1 (June 2005): 72–109.
4 *Xunzhai wenji* (Collected Works of Xunzhai), Volume 7, in SKQS Wenyuan ed., Collections, Book 122 (Shanghai: Shanghai guji chubanshe, 1987).
5 Xiao Yongming, *Ruxue, shuyuan, shehui: shehui wenhua shi shiye zhong de shuyuan* (Confucianism, Academies, and Society: A Sociocultural Historical Perspective on Academies) (Beijing: Shangwu yinshuguan, 2012).

monks, and other groups, revealing the two-way interaction between the state and local society in the middle and late Ming dynasty.[6] Ding Gang and Liu Qi have demonstrated the strenuous relationship between Confucian academies and Buddhist or Daoist temples since the Tang dynasty by looking at the two aspects of institution location and their economic estates.[7] Following in the course of these previous studies, the present paper focuses on the relationship between Wufeng Academy 五峰書院 and the society of Youxian township in Yongkang through analyzing the lawsuit between the Confucian scholars of Wufeng and the monks of Shoushan Monastery 壽山寺 and their supporters of the Hu family during the Jiajing reign (r. 1521–1567).[8] The lawsuit documents the relations between the academy, the court, local authorities, scholars, family members, and monks and shows its position within the local society.

## 2  Confucian-Buddhist Relations in Wufeng before the Lawsuit

When observing a cultural conflict, like the one between Confucianism and Buddhism, a long term view should be maintained. Academies and monasteries usually did not have intensely antagonistic relations to begin with. Often a change in the subjective or objective circumstances resulted in a gradual deterioration of the relations between both. Looking at records of the Wufeng area in Yongkang, Zhejiang province, no obvious conflict between the Confucian scholars and the monks of the monastery before the foundation of the academy can be found. The beginning of the conflict can be traced to the expansion of the Confucian community in Wufeng, caused by the popularity of a then relatively new school of thought, founded by Wang Yangming 王陽明 (1472–1529), among the scholars of the community. This new community of scholars changed the ideological balance of power in the area. Confucian scholars were starting to be more active in propagating their teachings vis-à-vis Buddhism and urged by their own needs, took practical steps to secure their control over the area. In search for more lecture space they decided to demolish the local

---

6  Chen Shilong, "Lun Tianzhen Shuyuan de jinhui yu chongjian (On the Destruction and Reconstruction of Tianzhen Academy)," *Mingshi yanjiu luncong* 4 (2013): 115–124.

7  Ding Gang and Liu Qi, *Shuyuan yu zhongguo wenhua* (Academies and Chinese Culture) (Shanghai: Shanghai jiaoyu chubanshe, 1992).

8  For a study on the establishment of Wufeng Academy see Lee Junghwan, "Wang Yangming Thought as Cultural Capital. The Case of Yongkang County," *Late Imperial China* 28, no. 2 (December 2007): 41–80, while Lee draws some different conclusions regarding the local power structures in Yongkang in the 16th century, his study traces the backgrounds of the families involved in the Academy and provides maps on their property.

Arhat Hall (Luohan tang 羅漢堂) and constructed Wufeng Academy in its place, which led to the later lawsuit.

### 2.1   Shuoshan Monastery

Before Confucian scholars institutionalized their presence in Wufeng, the area was a predominantly Buddhist region with Shoushan Monastery at its core. Shoushan Monastery, its old name being Taoyan Monastery 桃巖寺, was built in 520.[9] Although having a very long history, its fortunes remained quite varying and even though being located inside a famous mountain range it did not produce any eminent monks. Therefore historical data are scarce. Interestingly the records of Wufeng Academy and the local chronicles contain most of the available information on the monastery. The *Wufeng Academy Records* (*Wufeng shuyuan zhi* 五峰書院志), printed during the Qianlong 乾隆 period (r. 1735–1796) in the Qing dynasty, in their introduction state: "The academy was founded in the Ming, before the Jiajing era this place was dedicated to Shakyamuni, so the songs recited there praised the Buddha, but even though it used to splendid, it was not recorded."[10] The *Yongkang County Gazetteer* (*Yongkang xian zhi* 永康縣志) of the Kangxi period 康熙 (r. 1661–1722) refers to it as a shrine for local worthies, explaining that "originally Shoushan Monastery had a statue of Hu Ze 胡則 (963–1039), that was damaged already a long time ago. In the twenty-second year of the Kangxi reign [1683] his descendant Hu Weisheng 胡惟聖 (?–?) reconstructed a shrine to him, and changed it to the current name."[11] Hu Ze was the ancestor of the Kuchuan Hu family in Wufeng, who in 989 gained his *jinshi* 進士 (licentiate degree) and later held the positions of Undersecretary of Military Personnel (Bingbu shilang 兵部侍郎), as a scholar in the Academy of Scholarly Worthies (Jixianyuan 集賢院), and died in 1039.[12] During the Song dynasty reign of Emperor Lizong 理宗 (r. 1224–1264) he was conferred the honorary posthumous title Zhenghui Gong 正惠公 (Lord of Righteous Compassion). During his career as official, Hu Ze once proposed the exemption of western Zhejiang and Jinhua[13] from tax and levies, so after his death the local populace started to worship him in the local shrines and it

---

9    *Yongkang xian zhi* (Yongkang County Gazetteer), Volume 14 (Kangxi edition 1675), in *Zhongguo fangzhi congshu huazhong difang* (Series of Chinese Local Records, Central China), No. 528 (Taipei: Chengwen chubanshe youxian gongsi 1985).

10   Cheng Shangfei (comp.), *Wufeng shuyuan zhi* (Records of Wufeng Academy), Volume 1, in ZGLDSYZ 9: 160.

11   *Yongkang xian zhi*, Volume 8 (Kangxi edition 1675), in *Zhongguo fangzhi congshu huazhong difang*, 469.

12   See Tuotuo, *Songshi* (History of the Song), Volume 299 (Beijing: Zhonghua Shuju, 1974), 9941–9942.

13   Jinhua was the nearest major city, located around 50 miles to the west of the Wufeng area.

gradually turned him into a deity of local folk belief. When he was young, he lived and studied in Guangci Monastery 廣慈寺 in Fangyan,[14] and after his death his spirit is said to have stayed there so his descendants built a temple to worship him at the place of his study.[15] During the Shaoxing 紹興 period (1131–1163) the court granted the temple the name Heling 赫靈 (Gloriously Efficacious).[16] Besides Heling Temple in Fangyan other temples to Hu Ze could be found all over the county, in close to one hundred districts.[17] The Kuchuan Hu family settled close to Wufeng and erected a statue of Hu Ze in the later Shoushan Monastery, making it convenient for family members to worship close by. Their family history states that "the great forefather is worshipped twice a year, now the worship is done. On the eleventh day of the ninth month there will be sacrifice again at the shrine in the Shoushan cavern, to settle our minds."[18] The Kuchuan Hu family had a longstanding connection to Shoushan Monastery and became an important party involved with the lawsuit.

Since the compiler of the *Wufeng Academy Records,* Cheng Shangfei 程尚斐 (1730–1803) himself was involved in a dispute with the Hu family it is possible he still held some enmity towards Shoushan Monastery and intentionally concealed documents concerning it. However, in his description of the scenic features of the Wufeng area he divulges some information about the monastery. "Outside the grotto is the old monastery of Mt. Shou, today known as the ancestral shrine of Venerable Hu (Hu Gong miao 胡公廟). In the front of the hollow there are three terraces which are quite wide, but during the Wanli era it started to be demolished. Today only its foundations remain. Above the platform are the three red characters saying *Doushuaitai* 兜率台, which are said to written by Zhu Xi."[19] The Wufeng region mostly belonged to Shoushan

---

14　See "Bie Fangyan (Leaving Fangyan)," in *Yongkang xian zhi*, Volume 8 (Kangxi edition 1675), in *Zhongguo fangzhi congshu huazhong difang*, 1017. Fangyan is the district in which the Wufeng mountain range is located.

15　See "Fangyan dushu tang ji (Records of the Fangyan Study Hall)," in *Kuchuan Hu shi zongpu* (Genealogy of the Kuchuan Hu Family), in *Jinhua zongpu wenxuan jicheng*, Book 14, 335.

16　See "Hu shilan miao beiyin ji (Record on the Memorial Stele in the Shrine to Vice Minister Hu)," in *Jinhua zongpu wenxuan jicheng*, Volume 14, 335.

17　For English discussions of Hu Ze, also known as Hu Gong, and his legacy see Gene Cooper, *The Market and Temple Fairs of Rural China: Red Fire* (New York: Routledge, 2013), 155–160, 171–176.

18　"Fangyan dadi ji qianjin bai ting qizhe yuanyou (Arriving at the Main Hall of the Fangyan Buddhist Temple to Worship)," in *Jinhua zongpu wenxuan jicheng*, Book 14, 342.

19　*Wufeng shuyuan zhi*, Volume 1, in zgldsyz 9: 163. We have no proof that Zhu Xi was involved and it is rather doubtful as the three characters carry a distinctive Buddhist meaning. *Doushuaitian* 兜率天 is the Chinese transliteration of the Sanskrit word Tusita, which marks the realm of contentment in Buddhist mythology. The three characters here

ILLUSTRATION 12.1–2  Map of the Wufeng area, adapted from *Wufeng shuyuan zhi* showing locations of: 1. Guhou Peak, 2. Arhat Hall/Wufeng Academy, 3. Lize Shrine, 4. Doushuaitai writing, 5. Shoushan Monastery.

SOURCE: CHENG SHANGFEI [COMP.], *WUFENG SHUYUAN ZHI*, IN *ZGLDSYZ*, VOL. 9, 162

Monastery, but by the reign of the Wanli Emperor 萬曆 (r. 1572–1620) the monastery was either abandoned or destroyed. The Yongkang county annals produced during the Zhengde 正德 (r. 1505–1521) and Jiajing reigns simply convey the temple's former name and its construction period. Annals produced in the Guangxu 光緒 reign (r. 1875–1908) during the Qing dynasty have the following short description under the entry for Mt. Shou:

> Beneath Gouhou [peak] is a large stone cavity opening wide and spacious, which could hold a thousand people. Inside there used to be a Buddhist temple called Shoushan Monastery, which in the front had a tall pavilion building with a platform on top, surrounded by a railing, all perfectly held up against the rock by wood. The platform was not covered by any beams or roof tiles since rain, snow, or frost, none could naturally reach it [because it is hidden under the rock]. It offers extraordinary scenery. Above the grotto are the three red characters *Doushuaitai* which are said to have been written by Zhu Xi. The monastery is now in ruins and the embankment is destroyed as well. In the western direction there is a stone cavity near a waterfall where in old times Arhat Hall was located.[20]

From the map we can see that Shoushan Monastery was located in a large opening within the rock of the mountain beneath Guhou peak (in Illustration 12.1–2 above, at the place of the *Doushuaitai* writing). The Arhat Hall (which later became Wufeng Academy) was located within a smaller cavern above Guhou peak and was built belonging to the monastery. The relationship between these two places can still be discerned in the map included in the *Wufeng Academy Records*.

### 2.2 The *Daoxue* Movement of Southern Song Dynasty Confucians

The *Daoxue* movement entered the Wufeng area with the influx of Song dynasty scholars Lü Zuqian 呂祖謙 (1137–1181), Chen Liang 陳亮 (1143–1195), and Zhu Xi. During the Southern Song (1127–1279) the center of the Confucian movement in Liangzhe province (roughly modern Zhejiang province) was Jinhua, which produced a number of prominent Confucian scholars. Being made

---

could therefore be translated as "Platform of contentment." For a discussion of Zhu Xi's involvement and alleged involvement with Jinhua prefecture academies see Sukhee Lee, "Zhu Xi was Here. Family, Academy, and Local Memory in Later Imperial Dongyang," in *Journal of Song-Yuan Studies*, No. 41 (2011): 267–293.

20  *Yongkang xian zhi* 永康县志 (Yongkang County Gazetteer), Volume 1 (Guangxu), in *Zhongguo fangzhi congshu huazhong difang* (Series of Chinese Local Records, Central China), No. 68 (Taipei: Chengwen chubanshe, 1985), 75.

famous by Lü Zuqian as the representative of Wu school (Wuxue 婺學)[21] and Chen Liang as the head of the Yongkang School, the area was also visited by Zhu Xi, Ye Shi 葉適 (1150–1223), and other great scholars. Their activities initiated a local rise in gatherings and lectures (usually subsumed under the term *jiangxue* 講學 or *jianghui* 講會), which were usually held in academies or places that would later turn into academies.[22]

During the Qiandao 乾道 (1165–1173) and Chunxi 淳熙 (1174–1189) periods Chen Liang, Lü Zuqian, his younger brother Lü Zujian 呂祖儉 (?–1198), and Ye Shi stood in frequent contact and held lectures discussing ideas in and around Jinhua. Wufeng, just located at the foot of Mt. Shou in Fangyan about twenty miles to the east of Jinhua and surrounded by four green mountains, became a favorite lecture and gathering place for many Confucian scholars as it was the most scenic place in the area. This was later also attested by Wang Yangming, who described Mt. Shou, in the northwest of Yongkang county, in the following way: "Its cliffs have many bizarrely shaped rocks, open caverns, and clear plateaus. In all directions green mountains surround it and the five peaks are looming over."[23] The *Wufeng Academy Records* offer a more detailed description of the natural and cultural landscape of the area:

> The Mountain has five peaks, all of which are [steep] cliffs that rise sharply out of the level terrain and surround it like a city wall. They are called Guhou, Pubu, Fufu, Taohua, and Jiming. Below Guhou [peak] there is large cavern about sixty feet high and more than fifty feet wide; therefore a temple was built inside, which was later abandoned. […] There is also a smaller cavern in which is the Arhat Hall; next to it is the one of the springs of the waterfall branches, that from [Gu]Hou peak arrives at Fufu peak and flows into the main current. […] Before Pubu is the waterfall pond. The water comes from Taohua peak and gushes out between the rocks, spraying like mist. It is possible to see, but impossible to get close. It is indeed an excellent view.[24]

The earliest instances of disciples receiving lectures and attending debates at the grounds of Mt. Shou was by Lü Hao 呂皓 (?–?) of the local Taiping Lü

---

21  Wu 婺 generally describes the area around Jinhua.
22  For explanations of the concept of *jiangxue* or *jianghui* see Deng Hongbo, "Like Tea and Rice at Home: Lecture Gatherings and Academies during the Ming Dynasty," in this volume, 159–196.
23  *Wang Yangming quanji* (Complete Works of Wang Yangming), Volume 36 (Shanghai, Shanghai guji chubanshe, 2014), 1474.
24  *Wufeng shuyuan zhi*, Volume 1, in ZGLDSYZ 9: 164.

family. His descendant Lü Yuan 呂瑗 (?–?) recollects on this in the *Records of the Reconstruction of Wufeng Academy* (*Chongjian wufeng shuyuan ji* 重建五峰書院記): "Wufeng Academy in the Song was where esteemed Yunxi [Lü Hao], received the knowledge of Master Zhu. He invited the gentlemen Ye Shuixin [Ye Shi], Chen Longchuan [Chen Liang] and Lü Donglai [Lü Zuqian] to lecture there. Based on the fact that he donated fields in Shiguliao and commanded resources for the lecturing, how could he not have been in charge of this place?"[25] Lü Hao was close friends with Chen Liang and Lü Zuqian, often inviting them to come and discuss their studies. According to Cheng Shangfei's textual studies in the Qing, Lü Hao, Lü Zuqian, and others already at this point sought to construct a residence to lecture at Mt. Shou and moreover had set aside fields to fund their activities.[26] With Lü Zuqian, Chen Liang, Ye Shi, and other scholars coming to give lectures and the external conditions created by Lü Hao the fame of Wufeng to grew rapidly and students started flocking there. The records of the academy tell us of these activities: "When Chen Tongfu [Chen Liang] and Ye Zhengze [Ye Shi] came there on their travels, the local people joined their activities in admiration. Lü Zuqian and his brother Lü Zujian constantly came there with disciples of Master Chen and Master Lü."[27]

In 1182, when Zhu Xi served as tea and salt supervisor in the Eastern Liangzhe circuit, he arrived in Yongkang and Chen Liang invited him to give a talk at the cavern within Mt. Shou. They engaged in intense discussions on the issue of "Wang ba yi li" 王霸義利 (Morality and profit under kings and hegemons) and other topics in front of a large audience for more than a month. For Lü Zuqian, Mt. Shou was a recreational place where he wanted to log wood to build a residence for lecturing. Zhu Xi later wanted to build a private studio (*jingshe*) there in order to complete the untimely deceased Lü's last wish.[28] Two years later, in 1184, Zhu Xi visited Chen Liang again in Yongkang and in 1198 he returned to the caverns of Mt. Shou to escape persecution and revise his *Daxue zhangju* 大學章句 (*Commentary on the "Great Learning" in Phrases and Paragraphs*). Because Zhu Xi stayed in Wufeng on multiple occasions engaging in teaching as well as writing, after the deaths of Chen Liang and Lü Zuqian their students turned to him for scholarship, and through He Ji 何基 (1188–1268), Wang Bai 王柏 (1197–1274), Jin Lüxiang 金履祥 (1232–1303), and Xu Qian 許謙 (1270–1337), who inherited and promoted his thought, formed a distinctive Zhu Xi School cluster in Jinhua.

---

25   *Wufeng shuyuan zhi. Zengding ben* (Records of Wufeng Academy. Revised and enlarged edition) (Beijing: Zhongguo wenshi chubanshe, 2010), 15.
26   *Wufeng shuyuan zhi*, Volume 6, in ZGLDSYZ 9: 242–243.
27   *Wufeng shuyuan zhi*, Volume 1, in ZGLDSYZ 9: 164.
28   Ibid.

## 2.3 The Establishment of Lize Shrine

Continuing the Southern Song *jiangxue* movement of Lü Zuqian, Chen Liang, and Zhu Xi in the early 16th century, Ying Dian 應典 (1480–1547), a representative of the Yangming School from Yongkang again established a presence in Wufeng. He set up Lize Shrine 麗澤祠 (Beautiful Ponds Shrine)[29] as a place for worship and lecturing.

At the end of the Zhengde and beginning of the Jiajing reign, Ying Dian represented a group of younger scholars from Yongkang that had inherited the Jinhua Zhu Xi School, but also went to Shaoxing to learn from the disciples of Wang Yangming. During the early Ming period, Zhang Mao 章懋 (1437–1522) from Lanxi is considered to be the main representative of the Zhu Xi school in Jinhua. In 1466 he achieved the first place in the imperial examinations and was chosen to serve as Bachelor (*Shujishi* 庶吉士) in the Hanlin Imperial Academy (Hanlin yuan 翰林院) till 1478. After returning home he kept on lecturing for about twenty years and became well known as Teacher Fengshan 楓山. In 1522 he was appointed as the Minister of Rituals (*Libu shangshu* 禮部尚書) and after his death was enshrined in the Jinhua Shrine of Orthodox Learning (Zhengxue ci 正學祠),[30] being honored as "eminent minister of Learning of Principle" and "this generation's great Confucian."[31] He was worshipped along with the four great gentlemen of Jinhua: He Ji, Wang Bo, Jin Lüxiang and Xu Qian. Huang Zongxi 黃宗羲 (1610–1695) in the *Records of Ming Scholars* (*Ming ruxue an* 明儒學案) later commented: "His study guarded the Confucianism of the Song, whose foundations he obtained himself without receiving transmission. […] At first his learning did not seem profound, but after reexamining it again and again, there was nothing incorrect. In Jinhua after He [Ji], Wang [Bo], Jin [Lüxiang], Xu [Qian] he received and transmitted their teachings."[32] Zhang Mao held great influence on the scholars of Jinhua in the middle and late Ming dynasty and Zhu Xi's teaching were followed relatively unchanged, adding only light explanations to its practice. "There was no need to comment

---

29   See Linda Walton's explanation of the name Lize in her chapter, "Songyang Academy in Time and Place: From Confucian Academy to Cultural Heritage," in this volume, 423n76. The name was surely also chosen as a connection to the name of the shrine dedicated to Lü Zuqian in Jinhua; see Lee, "Wang Yangming thought as Cultural Capital," 48–49.

30   On such local shrines see Ellen G. Neskar, "The Cult of Worthies: A Study of Shrines Honoring Local Confucian Worthies in the Sung Dynasty" (PhD diss., Columbia University, 1993).

31   *Jinhua fu zhi* (Jinhua Prefecture Gazetteer), Volume 23, in *Zhongguo fangzhi congshu*, Huazhong difang No. 489 (Taibei: Chengwen chubanshe, 1983), 1703.

32   *Mingru xue'an* (The Records of Ming Scholars), Volume 45 (Beijing: Zhonghua shuju, 2008), 1074.

on the classics after Cheng and Zhu, only to honor what one heard and put this knowledge into action, and to weed out the wild plants among the quotations of their disciples if permissible."[33] Because of the increasing rigidness of the Cheng-Zhu School of Principle (*lixue* 理學), the local scholars started to be attracted to Wang Yangming's teachings and thanks to its representatives in the area—Ying Dian, Cheng Wende 程文德 (1497–1559), Cheng Zi 程梓 (1498–1585), and Lu Kejiu 盧克久 (1503–1579)—it was growing quickly. Under the guidance of Ying Dian, large numbers of scholars from Yongkang traveled to Shaoxing to receive Wang Yangming's teaching of innate knowledge (*liangzhi* 良知). The genealogy of the Yangming School in Jinhua is documented in the *Wufeng Academy Records*: "With regard to his [Wang Yangming] words and teachings being transmitted to Yongkang, from his time in Nanjing as an official, Zhou Shifeng was the first disciple, thereafter Li Dongxi [Li Hong], Ying Shimen [Ying Dian], Cheng Songxi [Cheng Wende], Lu Yisong [Lu Kejiu], Cheng Fangfeng [Cheng Zi], and several other gentlemen and students listened and responded to it."[34] In order to gather scholars for lectures and promote the teachings of Wang Yangming in Yongkang, the creation of a fixed place for the lectures became an urgent task for Ying Dian and the others. Because of its scenery and its historical connection to the Southern Song masters Chen Liang, Lü Zuqian, and Zhu Xi and also because of its proximity to leading scholars' homes, Wufeng became the preferred location to build a place for their lectures.

In 1522, Ying Dian, Cheng Zi, and other scholars established Lize Shrine in the small cavern beneath Guhou peak as a place for their lectures. Early in the Zhengde reign, Cheng Wende, Cheng Zi, and Zhou Deji 週德基 (?–?) already held occasional lectures in the caverns of Mt. Shou, but the establishment of Lize Shrine laid the foundation for fixed a place. After Cheng Wende failed the imperial examinations in 1520 he returned home and gathered scholars in the caverns of Mt. Shou for joint discussions. This is described in his biography: "Just several *li* from the residence [of Cheng Wende] is Mount Shou, in which is Wufeng Academy, where Zhu Huiweng [Zhu Xi], Lü Donglai [Lü Zuqian], Chen Longchuan [Chen Liang], and other gentleman have lectured. The gentleman [Cheng Wende] gathered students and friends to engage in study there."[35] The *Records of Wufeng Academy* relate his attitude towards the establishment of the lectures in the area to us:

---

33   Ibid., 1075.
34   *Wufeng shuyuan zhi*, Volume 2, in ZGLDSYZ 9: 169.
35   *Songxi Cheng xiansheng nianpu/Cheng Wende ji* (Chronological Biography of Master Songxi Cheng/Collected Writings of Cheng Wende), Appendix II (Shanghai: Shanghai guji chubanshe, 2012), 588.

Once, paying respects to Zhang Fengshan [Zhang Mao], he said: "The younger generation needed to gain a foothold and just be as fond of being an upright person as the worthies that at the time here built this foothold [...] This is who Fengshan would be today, and if you examine everywhere throughout the country, could you find a person that reaches Fengshan? And Fengshang's status, how could it be possible to reach it?"[36]

We can see that at this point Cheng Wende had not yet left the ideas of the Jinhua School behind. Cheng Zi and Zhou Deji also often returned to the caverns of Wufeng to hone their skills. Although traces of the great Confucians of the Southern Song were still there, time had passed on and there were no rooms to study in next to the cavern. It became difficult to house the scholars attending the lectures, often leaving them to reside outdoors in the stone caverns. To alleviate this problem, in 1522 Ying Dian, Cheng Zi, Zhou Deji, and Li Gong 李珙 (?–?) donated money to build the Lize Shrine inside the small cavity beneath Guhou peak. "Divining the cavern as the roof of the hall, dozens of pillars were built. Its southwest corner was for sacrifice to the three gentlemen and in front of it was a porch for housing scholars from all directions. Its name was Lize Shrine and the scholars could increase their diligence and flourish there on a daily basis."[37]

When Ying Dian and the other scholars built Lize Shrine, it was initially just a fixed place for their lectures. Although it was close to the Arhat Hall, Confucians and Buddhists still desired to maintain good relations in Wufeng. The scholars of Lize Shrine began to worship Zhu Xi, Zhang Shi 張栻 (1133–1181), Lü Zuqian, and Lu Jiuyuan 陸九淵 (1139–1192), the four masters of Southern Song Confucianism, intending to continue their past tradition of lectures and forming new young talents. Worshipping the four masters of Song Confucianism also shows the willingness of the scholars to embrace Zhu Xi's and Lu Jiuyuan's teachings at the same time. An explanation by Ying Dian is found in Cheng Wende's biography: "Master Ying spoke: Ziyang [Zhu Xi] went to teach others, Donglai [Lü Zuqian] taught by example and Nanxuan [Zhang Shi] and Xiangshan [Liu Jiuyuan] by kindness. Becoming firm they combined human feeling, keeping it for long settled. Reaching the same goal by different roads, one hundred thoughts become one; how can the Way of the sage be two?"[38] The selection of worshipped individuals shows that Ying Dian and the other Ming-era

---

36   *Wufeng shuyuan zhi. Zengding ben*, 586.
37   *Cheng Zhengyi ji* (Collected Writings of Cheng Zhengyi), Volume 5 (Shanghai: Shanghai guji chubanshe, 2012), 153.
38   *Songxi Cheng xiansheng nianpu/Cheng Wende ji*, Appendix II, 189.

scholars adopted a rather safe strategy for their activities. In the Jinhua area, with its strong tradition of Zhu Xi learning, they were not too eager to openly present themselves as followers of Wang Yangming during the initial establishment of their scholarly community, but rather to extend their range to attract even more of the local scholars. Also, at this point they had no interest, or rather any power, to stir up controversy with the Buddhists of Wufeng.

### 2.4 The Destruction of Arhat Hall and Construction of the Wufeng Academy

From 1533 to 1535 the scholars of Wufeng, with support from local officials and their families, demolished Arhat Hall and in its stead erected Wufeng Academy. This step led to a serious deterioration of the relationship between the Confucians and the Buddhists of the area. In 1533, the prefect of Jinhua, Yao Wenzhao 姚文炤 (?–?), and the Yongkang county magistrate, Hong Yuan 洪垣 (?–?), visited Ying Dian in Wufeng and witnessed the problems of accommodation for the scholars visiting Lize Shrine. Prefect Yao followed up on this by "ordering County Magistrate His Lordship Hong Yuan to clear away the portrait of Arhat and to erect Wufeng Academy in the middle of the cavern as a place for the arriving scholars."[39] Yao Wenzhao (personal name Zaiming 在明) from Putian became prefect of Jinhua in 1530. During his term he repaired Lize Shrine and the Sixian Academy 四賢書院, and built multiple shrines for Zhang Mao and Lu Heshan 陸鶴山 (?–?). After he left his post it is reported in the local gazetteer that young and old shed tears and sought to set up a shrine for him while he was still alive, and there were several songs praising his benevolent rule that spread around all counties and prefectures.[40] Hong Yuan (personal name Junzhi 峻之) from Guanyuan in Jiangxi, who gained his licentiate degree in 1532, received teaching from Zhan Ruoshui 湛若水 (1466–1560) and was an enthusiastic supporter of the *jianghui* movement in the Ming dynasty.[41] Magistrate Hong gave the concrete responsibility of the construction of Wufeng Academy into the hands of Lü Yuan, from the Taiping Lü family: "then decreeing that Master Lü Yuan was to purchase materials and start construction, therefore making under these rocks several buildings to let numerous scholars come."[42] The Lü family contributed a large amount of money and construction began in the middle of the cavern in Mt. Shou. After Hong Yuan was

---

39  *Wufeng shuyuan zhi*, Volume 1, in ZGLDSYZ 9: 164.
40  See *Jinhua fu zhi* (Jinhua Prefecture Gazetteer), Volume 14, in *Zhongguo fangzhi congshu*, 971.
41  *Mingshi* (History of the Ming), Volume 208 (Beijing: Zhonghua shuju, 1974), 5509.
42  *Taoyan Lize jingshe ji, Wufeng shuyuan zhi* (Records of Taoyan Lize Studio, Records of Wufeng Academy), Volume 4, in ZGLDSYZ 9: 189.

promoted to imperial censor (*Yushi* 御史) his successor Gan Xiangpeng 甘翔鵬 (?–?) continued to support the construction of Wufeng Academy. The academy was completed in 1536. At first it was named Peach Cliff Lize Studio (Taoyan lize jingshe 桃岩麗澤精舍), but later Prefect Chen Jing 陳京 (?–?) bestowed the name Wufeng Academy. After the construction was finished Ying Dian put the emphasis of study for the scholars in Wufeng on seeking the Way within oneself, and by this expounded and propagated Yangming thought. His *Lectures on the Meaning of the Phrase "Making One's Intentions Sincere"* (*chengyi zhang jiang yi* 誠意章講義)[43] record:

> In the thousands of words of the sages, there is nothing that deters us from seeking the cause within oneself. [...] Therefore the foremost point in bringing out sincerity lies within the three characters of not deceiving oneself (*wu zi qi* 毋自欺). [...] Some know the study of body and mind only imitates imagination, if one is not ready to practice labor, then there is no need for action, no observing and learning from practice, and in the end one cannot escape the wrongdoing of deceiving oneself. Today our students also have this failing, hoping to overcome this by exerting themselves at today's meeting.[44]

Hong Yuan, writing the memorial for the construction of the academy, also wished that the teaching continued with lectures for noblemen and friends at the Lize Shrine, promoting the Yangming School.[45] It becomes evident that the local officials played a key role in the destruction of Arhat Hall and the construction of Wufeng Academy.

In the time from the establishment of Lize Shrine to the construction of Wufeng Academy, the community of scholars led by Ying Dian through its inclusive lectures and the support of the local government attracted a large number of students. They arrived from various counties and cities in western Zhejiang (Qu 衢), Jinhua (Wu 婺), and Lishui (Kuocang 括蒼). The biography of Cheng Wende states that "culture was once again thriving in Wuzhou (Jinhua), and the pulse of the innate knowledge was flourishing in Wufeng; other counties just dared to imitate."[46] Although Yangming thought at this point was widely disseminated by his disciples, it had not yet received recognition by the imperial court and was even deliberately suppressed. The Wufeng scholars,

---

[43] This phrase can be found in the *Great Learning* (*Daxue* 大學).
[44] *Wufeng shuyuan zhi*, Volume 1, in ZGLDSYZ 9: 226.
[45] *Songxi Cheng xiansheng nianpu/Cheng Wende ji*, Appendix II, 190.
[46] *Songxi Cheng xiansheng nianpu/Cheng Wende ji*, Appendix II, 195.

however, with the support of the local government and their families, had already formed a powerful community and with the opening of the academy in 1536 now openly worshipped their former master in the academy shrine and taught his teachings in its hall. Under the leadership of Cheng Wende the scholars also made substantial adjustments to the original sacrificial figures of Lize Shrine: Zhang Shi and Lu Jiuyuan, who had never taught at Wufeng, were taken out of the sacrifices, which were offered only to Zhu Xi, Lü Zuqian, and Chen Liang.[47] This adjustment shows that the scholars of the academy no longer needed the name of Lu Jiuyuan and its connection to the Yangming School to attract a wide range of scholars, but that they were eager to emphasize the Southern Song lecture tradition at Wufeng before Wang Yangming, which also marked their adoption of a localized orthodoxy. The demolition of the Arhat Hall and the building of Wufeng Academy further can be regarded as a turning point for the local Confucian scholars from restraint to expansion. This is reflected by the support of their families and the local government, suppressing local Buddhist forces in order to expand their own practice and unwittingly laying the grounds for a grander confrontation between the two groups in Wufeng.

## 3    The Wufeng Buddhist-Confucian Litigation Case

The litigation case between the monks and scholars of Wufeng was the result of the contradictions raised by demolition of Arhat Hall and the construction of Wufeng Academy. The case occurred in 1541 when Lu Kejiu raised an appeal after being beaten up by the members of the Hu family and then, under the pressure of a countersuit brought forward by the monks, Wufeng Academy had to close. After a row of appeals by the Confucian scholars the whole affair was resolved in 1544. Involved in the lawsuit were the local scholars, monks, court and local officials, and many local families and other forces, revealing a complicated landscape of political and social interests. At the core of the conflict, however, stood the families backing both institutions—the Confucian academy and the Buddhist monastery.

---

47    See "Shoushan Lizeci wu xiansheng gaowen (Announcement of Five Gentleman of Mt. Shou Beautiful Ponds Shrine)," in *Cheng Wende ji* (Collected Writings of Cheng Wende), Volume 17 (Shanghai: Shanghai guji chubanshe, 2012), 253. For more on this reconfiguration of the shrine also see Lee, "Wang Yangming Thought as Cultural Capital," 54–61.

## 3.1 Beginning of the Lawsuit

Up to 1540 many of the local officials who had supported the construction of Wufeng Academy retired or had left their posts, while the conflicts between the academy scholars and the monks had steadily increased and eventually led to the Wufeng lawsuit in 1541. One of the reasons for the outbreak of the conflict was the rising number of scholars participating in the lecturing activities. As it became increasingly difficult to accommodate them in the academy, the leader of the scholars Lu Kejiu began teaching disciples at the Doushuaitai platform close to Shoushan Monastery. Lu Kejiu (personal name Deqing 德卿, style Yisong 一松) was a local scholar from Yongkang. Lu together with Cheng Zi had received their education from Wang Yangming and had studied with Qian Dehong 錢德洪 (1496–1574), Wang Ji, Zou Shouyi 鄒守益 (1491–1562), and other famous disciples of Wang. After Wang Yangming passed away, Lu Kejiu and other disciples settled in Quzhou and together with Ying Dian, Zhou Ying 周瑩 (?–?), Li Gong, Zhou Tong 周桐 (?–?), and Cheng Zi formed the Wufeng Academy community. Compared to the other followers of Wang in Yongkang, Lu Kejiu was quite young but surpassed many in his academic attainments in the School of Mind (*xinxue* 心學), being considered to be exceptionally profound.[48] The already tense relationship between the scholars of Wufeng Academy and the monks of the monastery intensified when, during one of Lu Kejiu's lectures, it came to a physical altercation with the monks and members of the Hu family. Cheng Zi later recounted the attack:

> In these parts there are the 58 members of the Hu family, behaving so badly that people don't dare to speak. On the fourth day of the fourth month this clique came to the mountain excessively drinking, tearing apart the windows of the academy, being violent and harassing [people]. Of the students who were at mountain at this time, those old in age and aware of the situation did not enter into the dispute, and those few of young age could not beat them back, randomly clashing and resisting, then being surrounded and beaten by the rogues, their reputation being dishonored. Because of this the elders presented to the local [administration], intending a slight disciplinary action; how could this turn into a major calamity? Seizing the opportunity and getting hirelings from Yiwu county's Xuefeng and Chanming Temples and Yongkang county's Jingming Temple, the cunning former monk Hu Yongzhang, farfetchedly and groundlessly colluded with them to falsely accuse the academy of being

---

48  *Mingshi* (History of the Ming), Volume 384, in *Xuxiu* SKQS (Addendum to the SKQS), Book 331 (Shanghai, Shanghai guji chubanshe, 2002), 108.

privately built, fabricating words that it holds the monks' fields and raising other false charges.⁴⁹

According to Cheng Zi's account, it was members of the Hu family who took the initiative and provoked the dispute, with Lu Kejiu and his students being beaten. Afterwards the Lu family petitioned to the county yamen requesting punishment for 58 members of the Hu family. Yet the incident of mutual assault has to be viewed as a result of the active expansion of the Confucian scholars in the region after the establishment of Wufeng Academy and the intensification of the conflict with Shoushan Monastery. It is also noteworthy that after the incident, a group of scholars rose to attack the monks of Shoushan monastery petitioning the county government. However in the struggle between the academy and the monastery, the monks also never remained completely passive and seemed to take the initiative to counterattack once a favorable opportunity arose.

Hu Yongzhang 胡永章 (?–?) and the members of the Hu family sought to use the imperial policy of outlawing academies and appealed to the Regional Inspector (*xunan yushi* 巡按御史) of Zhejiang, leading to a ban of Wufeng Academy, and its scholars' losing their ranks and degrees. From 1537 to 1538 Censor You Jujing 遊居敬 (1509–1571) and Xu Zan 許贊 (1473–1548), the Minister of Personnel (*libu shangshu* 吏部尚書), had continuously petitioned for the banning of academies, citing it as the will of the people:

> In the fourth month of the seventh year of Emperor Shizong Jiajing [1528], Minister of Personnel Xu Zan petitioned for the abolishment of the Confucian academies. This was continued [...] till in the second month of the sixteenth year of the emperor [1537], Imperial Censor You Jujing accused Minister of the Ministry of Personnel Zhan Ruoshui in a memorial, citing his heterodox teachings spreading hooliganism and him privately creating an academy, imploring to warn and instructing the minds of the upright people. The emperor urged Zhan to stay, but decreed to demolish all his academies. At this point, Xu Zan reiterated his points, for the government to build more academies, where scholars could congregate, provide levies, taxes and corvee labor and for [other academies] to be urgently demolished. This shall be proclaimed.⁵⁰

---

49   "Pu song ci (Words on the Litigation)," in *Wufeng shuyuan zhi*, Volume 6, in ZGLDSYZ 9: 231.
50   *Xu Wenxian tongkao* (Addendum to the Comprehensive Investigations Based on Literary and Documentary Sources), Volume 50 (Hangzhou: Zhejiang guji chubanshe, 1988), 3246.

Following this, the court ordered a ban on heterodox academies: "Academies that are not deferring to imperial command and are privately built, must be administered, corrected, or destroyed. From this day on, privately founded [academies], have to report to the Regional Inspector (*xunan yushi canzou* 巡按御史參奏). In recent years they have on the surface imitated the Learning of the Way, but secretly harbored wicked practices, still having to be strictly constrained and should not be allowed to carry on as before, which would lead to the ruin of scholarly behavior."[51] The prohibition of the academies during the Jiajing reign came about as opposing factions at the court used the defense of the Cheng-Zhu School of Principle as a pretext to attack the Wang Yangming School and Zhan Ruoshui, accusing their ideas as false or heterodox learning and referring to them as an evil faction or scoundrels. Wanting to quickly get rid of their opponents, they first prosecuted scholars and then their academies as places of their teachings, gradually leading to the first of three prohibitions for Confucian academies during the Ming dynasty.[52] Within this context, Hu Yongzhang and the members of the Hu family in 1541 accused Cheng Zi, Lu Kejiu, and their students to the imperial censor in Zhejiang of erecting heterodox shrines, spreading false learning, and disorienting the minds of the scholars.[53] That scholars of Yongkang understood Wufeng Academy as a place of studying Wang Yangming's teachings was surely one of the causes for the court to ban the academy. However it was the accusations of the monks that led to the prohibition as well as Cheng Zi, Lu Kejiu, Ying Qing 應清 (?–?), Chen Gong 陳恭 (?–?) and Lü Chengzhang 呂成章 (?–?) losing their *shengyuan* licenses (*shengyuan gongming* 生員功名). So this originally rather common dispute between Buddhist monks and Confucian scholars developed amidst a turbulent power struggle around the banning of the academies.

After the ban of the academy, Cheng Zi and the other four scholars who had lost their degrees were interrogated by the authorities. Cheng Zi drafted the "Pusong ci" 普訟詞 (Words on the Litigation), a document defending their position. Cheng Zi (personal name Yangzhi 養之) lived in Yongkang and had received training by the School of Principle scholars of Jinhua. After receiving his *shengyuan* degree, he went to Yuyao to study Yangming thought, together with Wang Ji. Therefore Lu Kejiu put Cheng Zi's signature at the top in the

---

51  See Chen Gujia and Deng Hongbo, *Zhongguo shuyuanshi ziliao* (Sources of the History of Chinese Academies) (Hangzhou: Zhejiang jiaoyu chubanshe, 1998), 811.
52  See Deng Hongbo, *Zhongguo Shuyuanshi* (History of Chinese Academies) (Wuhan: Wuhan daxue chubanshe, 2012), 369.
53  *Wufeng shuyuan zhi*, Volume 1, in ZGLDSYZ 9: 153. "Thereupon, local rogues proceeded to the office of the imperial censor to accuse Deqing [Lu Kejiu] of erecting licentious shrines, spreading false learning and disorienting the minds of the scholars."

document presented to the authorities accusing the 58 members of the Hu family, making Cheng Zi to be the first questioned after the lawsuit broke out and defending the scholars one by one to all accusations in the "Pusong ci."

In response to the first point of the monks accusing the academy of being established privately, Cheng elaborated in detail on the tradition of lecturing in Wufeng since the Southern Song and the process of establishment of the Lize Shrine and Wufeng Academy in order to prove that the establishment of the academy really had been an official act by the government:

> Twenty miles east of the county municipal seat is the Taoyan cavern, being very close to Shoushan Monastery. During the Chunxi era of the Song, Ziyang Master Zhu and Donglai Master Lü, visiting Longchuan Master Chen, met each other as friends and lectured [there]. Although the worthies of the past are gone, their manuscripts still remain. Therefore the local gentleman Shimen Master Ying [Dian] in pursuing the ancients erected a shrine, respecting and honoring their will. Continuing to carry out [their will], the promoted Prefects Liangshan Minister Zhang, and Xugu Minister Yao, and the County Magistrate Jueshan Minister Hong, all contributed from their official salaries to the expansion, collecting books and carving a stone stele, called "Lize Shrine," firstly used to worship the former worthies, and secondly to advise and encourage later students. Undoubtedly, it was government property, open to the public, and given to later generations."[54]

Cheng Zi believed that, as during the Southern Song Wufeng was a place of lecture of the former worthies Lü Zuqian, Chen Liang, and Zhu Xi, and because Ying Dian and the others were following the teachings of these worthies by building a shrine in the area, this was an embodiment of the court honoring Confucianism and reaffirming its teachings (and therefore was ethically and morally reasonable). Subsequently, Cheng emphasized the close relationship between Lize Shrine, Wufeng Academy, and the local officials. After the completion of Lize Shrine, Prefect of Jinhua Zhang Yue 張鉞 (?–?) personally created the calligraphy for the shrine and the later Prefect Yao Wenzhao composed the writings on the Lize Shrine stone stele (*Lizeci beiji* 麗澤祠碑記). Also after the construction of Wufeng Academy the former County Magistrate Hong Yuan wrote the *Records of Taoyan Lize studio* (*Taoyan Lizi jingshe ji* 桃岩麗澤精舍記), and former Prefect Chen Ling wrote the wooden name board for the academy. "So Lize Shrine was built by officials, initiated during the Zhengde

---

54   *Cheng Zhengyi ji*, Volume 5, 231.

reign, and the later prefects and magistrates followed this by completing it in the tenth year of Jiajing [1531] and registered it in the *Yellow Book* (*Huang ce* 黃冊)."[55] Cheng Zi repeatedly emphasized that both buildings were officially sponsored and listed in the registration books, his purpose being to show that the academy and its estate were recognized as state property and various initiatives of former local officials to support the academy should be regarded as recognitions of its legitimacy.

Secondly, Cheng investigated the personal living conditions of Hu Yongzhang and the situation of land tenancy of Shoushan Monastery, denying the allegations that the academy was "expelling monks and occupying their fields."[56] He pointed out that even though Hu left his family and was a monk at Shoushan Monastery from a young age, in 1512 he was convicted for a crime and banished. Soon after he was "roaming around two counties, harming and abandoning many temples, selling and destroying temple property, or making it his private property, now buying 46 of the town's peasant fields and embracing his nephew as his successor."[57] And at the time of the occurrence of the lawsuit he had "left Shoushan Monastery for more than thirty years, however now falsely accuses Cheng Zi and the others of beating him in the fifteenth year of the Jiajing reign [1536], a complaint that cannot stand close scrutiny."[58] Cheng Zi also made a detailed explanation of the estates and tenancy belonging to Shoushan Monastery to prove the academy had not taken a share of these lands. "The estates of the monastery are rented and administered by monks Cai Yongshao 蔡永邵, Hu Fuhao 胡福浩 Ying Decang 應德滄, they are separately offered for lease to the local people, owning all the land and overseeing the tenant farmers with one hundred eyes together bearing witness of this. So is it unclear who owns them?"[59] While Cheng Zi confidently demonstrated the ownership of the fields by the monastery, he deliberately avoided some other more sensitive issues. For example, while the construction of Wufeng Academy was ordered by the government, the demolition of Arhat Hall which belonged to the monastery surely could be seen as an attack on the local Buddhist community.

### 3.2   *The Scholars' Road to Rehabilitation*

Besides Cheng Zi and Lu Kejiu, of the other academy leaders, Ying Dian had retired from his government post and Cheng Wende was serving as an official at the court. Because of their experiences as government officials, Ying and

---

55   Ibid.
56   Ibid.
57   Ibid.
58   Ibid
59   Ibid.

Cheng had close contacts with other officials who followed Wang Yangming's teachings and therefore played a major role in the settlement of the lawsuit.

Ying Dian (personal name Tianyi 天彝, style Shimen 石门) was from Zhiying in Yongkang and received his *jinshi* degree in 1514, holding posts from secretary in the Bureau of Operations in the Ministry of War (*zhifangsi zhushi* 職方司主事) up to aide in the Office of Seals (*shangbaosi cheng* 尚寶司丞). Ying kept close relationships with Director of the Board of Rites (*Libu shangshu* 禮部尚書) Huang Wan 黃綰 (1480–1554) of Nanjing, and Ying Liang 應良 (1480–1549), who worked in the Provincial Administration Commission (*Buzhengshi* 布政使) for Guangxi. After he asked for a leave of office, he visited the two in Taizhou and debated with them:

> Following the worthy Nanzhou Duke Ying Liang of Xianju, staying in the mountain ranges to pay respects to Nanzhou, [Ying Dian] also followed Nanzhou to Huangyan, visiting Jiuan Duke Huang Wan. The two Masters had traveled to Lord Wang Yangming and Lord Zhan Ganquan [Zhan Ruoshui], being elucidated in the lost knowledge of the Song Confucians Zhou [Dunyi] and [the] Cheng [brothers], and Ying Dian therefore obtained their views, returning and practicing these principles, verifying their nature, focusing on their actions, trying to commit to the study of morality all his life.[60]

Before the establishment of Lize Shrine, Ying Dian had invited Huang Wan for a tour of the Wufeng area. The *Record of Traveling the Lands of Yongkang* (*You yongkang shanshui ji* 遊永康山水記) written by Huang during his time there portray Ying Dian as the center of the initial gatherings of the academic community in Yongkang:

> Sitting among the travel companions Lin Dianqing 林典卿, Zhou Fengming 周鳳鳴 (1489–1550), Ying Yizhi 應抑之, Zhou Dechun 周德純, and after Zhou Jinming 周晉明 and Zhou Zhongqi 周仲器 arrived, we discussed amongst each other in a joyous atmosphere. Master Shimen then desired the construction of this Lize Shrine. At sundown, they retired at the [Buddhist] monastery [...] The biting cold. Tree leaves completely red. Friends leaving one by one. Ying Tianlan 應天監, Zhao Mengli 趙孟

---

60  "Shimen xiansheng zhuan (Biography of Master Shimen)," and "Yingzhi Yingshi zongpu (Genealogy of the Yingzhi Ying Family)," in *Jinhua zongpu wenxuan jicheng* (Literature Collection of Jinhua Genealogies), ed. Huang Lingeng and Tao Chenghua, Book 15 (Shanghai: Shanghai guji chubanshe, 2013), 394.

立 and Xu Zishi 徐子實 returned one after the other, with each debate having learned something. The young scholars among the mountains Cheng Zi, Zhou Ling 周玲, and Sun Tong 孫桐 all exerted themselves for this goal.[61]

The significance of Huang Wan's trip to Wufeng was that even before the scholars of Yongkang had formally established an academy, they already had acquired the protection and support of distinguished scholars. After the outbreak of the lawsuit, Ying Dian wrote a letter to Huang Wan and sought assistance from Ying Liang. Both jointly pleaded with the Capital Censorate (Duchayuan 都察院) on his behalf. Under their pressure the ban of the academy was lifted and Cheng Zi and the others *shengyuan* titles were restored (and the crisis ended). The records of the academy document the following: "Therefore, the surrounding scholars pled their cause, and the officials and gentlemen like the great Minister Lord Huang Wan and great Administrator Lord Ying Liang corrected this wrong for the public good, bringing this injustice in front of the Censorate (Yushitai 御史台) and its supervisors. Justice was therefore restored for the scholars. The shrine was renewed and the sacrifices to the three gentlemen continued as of old."[62]

In 1542 Cheng Wende, in his position as Director of Equipment and Communications in the Ministry of War (*bingbu chejiasi langzhong* 兵部車駕司郎中), after hearing of the Wufeng incident, immediately wrote a letter to Cheng Zi, comforting and encouraging him, but also actively seeking ways to help:

> The matter was made known to me yesterday. Once I read it, I could not overcome my shock that it has come so far to this unexpected disaster. This is akin to old times when Gongye [Chang] was in chains.[63] The friendship of us scholars—how could we stay indifferent? I expect at this time brother Shimen certainly has already spent some time to deal with it, and right or wrong are already clear. Otherwise I will write a letter to the new great inspector to ask for assistance.[64]

---

61   "You Yongkang shanshui ji (Record of traveling the lands of Yongkang)," in *Huang Wan ji* (Collected Writings of Huang Wan), ed. Zhang Hongmin, Volume 14 (Shanghai: Shanghai guji chubanshe, 2014), 261.
62   *Wufeng shuyuan zhi*, Volume 1, in ZGLDSYZ 9: 153.
63   Gongye Chang was a disciple of Confucius who is said to have been falsely imprisoned. See *Analects* 5.1.
64   "Shang Shu Song Xiweng shu (Letter to High Official Song Xiweng)," in *Cheng shi zong pu* (Genealogy of the Cheng Family), in *Jinhua zongpu wenxuan jicheng*, 581.

Whether the "new great inspector" whom Cheng Wende refers to in this letter for help was the Vice Provincial Education Commissioner in Zhejiang Kong Tianyi 孔天胤 (1505–1581), who had the final word in the litigation case, cannot be established as there is no conclusive evidence. However, Cheng and Kong were good friends. Letter exchanges between the two Chengs mention a joyous outing of in the vicinity of Hangzhou.[65] Kong was apt in the study of *lixue* and practiced it diligently, and besides Cheng Wende also held contact with Huang Wan and Qian Dehong.[66] In 1544 Kong Tianyin traveled to Yongkang wanting to revitalize Wufeng Academy. Xu Wentong in a letter to gentleman Lu Kejiu suggested assisting Kong in the restoration of the Wufeng lectures. "I also heard that Kong Wengu came to the mountains, and sincerely has the intention to revive [the academy]. This is the same as what Yisong is seeking, he is naturally sympathetic. It is by not having power that we arrived at this."[67] When the scholars of the academy seized this opportunity to request that Vice Commissioner Kong punish the culprits who had accused the academy, Kong replied: "After an investigation to gather the facts, I angrily punished the Hu family for their falsehoods. The matter is therefore cleared."[68] The ultimate success of the academy scholars in the lawsuit also swept away all obstructions to the expansion of their power in the area of Mt. Shou. The loss of the lawsuit led to the gradual decline of Shoushan Monastery and after it was destroyed during the Wanli reign it disappeared from the pages of history.

## 4   The Lawsuit and Its Background of Disputes of Local Rights

The lawsuit between the scholars of Wufeng Academy and the monks of Shoushan Monastery was a typical battle between Confucian academies and Buddhist monasteries. Such disputes were a common occurrence in the history of the academies, reflecting one aspect of the contemporary conflicts between Confucianism and Buddhism. I want to emphasize that in observing such conflicts, it is especially important to have a multidimensional perspective on the

---

65  See "Yu Kong Wengu duxue shu (Letter to Education Commissioner Kong Wengu)," in *Cheng Wende ji* (Collection of Cheng Wende), Volume 15 (Shanghai, Shanghai guji chubanshe, 2012), 217.

66  "Yu Cheng Songxi xiansheng (To Gentlemen Cheng Songxi)," and "Yu Qian Xushan nian zhang (To Elder Qian Xushan)," and "Yu Huang Jiu'an xiansheng (To Gentlemen Huang Jiu'an)," in *Kong Wengu ji* (Collected Writings of Kong Wengu), Volume 15, in SKQSCM, Book 95 (Jinan: Jilu sushe, 1997), 208–209.

67  "Yu Yisong xiansheng shu (Letter to Gentlemen Yisong)," in *Lu shi zong pu* (Genealogy of the Lu Family), in *Jinhua zongpu wenxuan jicheng*, 638.

68  *Wufeng shuyuan zhi. Zengding ben*, 20.

conflicts of interest among the various social forces that are behind the cultural divide.

### 4.1   The Family Interests behind the Lawsuit

The main guarantee for the continued existence of Wufeng Academy was that it was located in the homeland of the Zhiying Ying family, the Yanxia Cheng family, the Taiping Lü family, and the Yongkang Chen family. Looking at the participants involved in the lectures that spread Yangming thought through the area, it becomes clear that the sons of these families built the backbone of the academy. Taking the Zhiying Ying family for example, after the formation of the Wufeng scholar community, members of the family took active positions organizing the lecturing activities and handed these responsibilities down among their family members. After Ying Dian, his nephew Ying Jian 應兼 (1492–1577) continued to take charge of the lectures. Ying Jian at an early age was taught by his uncle Ying Dian and later together with Cheng Zi and Zhou Tong went to learn from the Wang Yangming disciples in Shaoxing, and there formed a close relation with the high disciples of the Wang School Ying Liang and Huang Wan.[69] The local gazetteer describes him as having "further continued being in charge of the bond at Wufeng studio [academy], and together with his fellows Lu Kejiu and Cheng Zi debated at Lize [Shrine], attendees coming from all directions in unison following him, for more than thirty years. This scholar is Gentlemen Gulu [Ying Jian]."[70] Ying Jian's younger brother Ying Tingyu 應廷育 (1497–1578), after retiring from his government post, also devoted himself to teaching in Wufeng. Ying Tingyu, who received his *jinshi* degree in 1523, served as Assistant Surveillance Commissioner (*ancha siqian shi* 按察司僉事) of Fujian province[71] and after returning home headed the lectures at Wufeng together with Cheng Wende and Zhou Tong, especially emphasizing exhortations against fear and the skill of learning, questioning, thinking, and distinguishing. Besides the Zhiying Ying family, Cheng Wende and Cheng Zi as representatives of the Yanxia Cheng family are another local force that contributed to the development of Wufeng Academy. After Cheng Wende and Cheng Zi, Cheng Zhengyi received his *jinshi* in 1571 and during the Wanli reign served as Metropolitan Governor (*jing zhaoyin* 京兆尹). After he retired he returned home and spent his remaining years teaching in Wufeng.

---

69   See "Ying Gulu gong zhuan (Biography of Lord Ying Gulu)," in *Cheng Zhengyi ji*, 143–144.
70   *Yongkang xian zhi*, Volume 7 (Guangxu), in *Zhongguo fangzhi congshu huazhong difang*, 389.
71   See "Ji'an xiansheng zhuan (Biography of Master Ji'an)," in *Zhiying yingshi zong pu* (Genealogy of the Zhiying Ying Family), in *Jinhua zongpu wenxuan jicheng*, Volume 15, 409.

Furthermore, the academy and the various families formed a close and shared relationship. The families already viewed Wufeng Academy as their personal business. From its construction, maintenance of its buildings, administration of the fields, and its financial organization were all taken care of by members of a few families. As mentioned before, the construction of Wufeng Academy was specifically led by the Taiping Lü family. At the launch of the lecturing activities in Wufeng, Ying Dian, Cheng Zi, and Lu Kejiu invested in the purchase of fields and every year used the interest to fund the lectures. Later, the Xiangzhu Wang family, the Taiping Lü family, and the Yongkang Chen family joined the ranks in the financing of the academy. The *Academy Records* convey: "Originally, the three families Ying, Cheng and Lu, provided fields for the gatherings, to finance it. Recently, the Chen, Cheng, Wang, and Lü families also contributed so that the funds are not insufficient. The descendants of the Ying, Cheng, and Lu till today have not stopped [contributing]."[72] The land owned by the various families became the basis for continued existence of the Wufeng academic activities.

As the Wufeng lawsuit occurred in this context, it cannot only be viewed as a cultural conflict between Confucian Academies and Buddhist monasteries, but must also be understood as entangled in the conflict of interests between local families. Hu Yongzhang, who was involved in the lawsuit, was a monk in Shoushan Monastery and led the members of the Hu family that assaulted Lu Kejiu and his disciples. Looking at the intertwined history of the monastery and the shrine to Hu Ze, the ancestor of the Hu family, it becomes clear that this conflict also occurred between the families in the area.

During the Wanli period, Shoushan Monastery decayed and disappeared from the Wufeng area. However the Kuchuan Hu family was still seeking an opportunity to retaliate against the scholars of Wufeng Academy. After the destruction of Shoushan Monastery, even though its site was close to the academy, it could not be occupied by the Confucian scholars. According to *The Wufeng Academy Records* it was eventually changed into an ancestral temple honoring Hu Ze, showing that the Kuchuan Hu family moved to the fore again, replacing Shoushan Monastery and continuing the confrontation with the scholars of Wufeng. As mentioned above, Wufeng Academy had the combined support of the Zhiying Ying family, the Yanxia Cheng family, the Shima Lu family, and the Taiping Lü family, all bound by mutual interest as well as through their friendships and master-disciple relationships. The families also got further interlinked by intermarrying and gradually formed a local community of

---

72   *Wufeng shuyuan zhi*, Volume 9, in ZGLDSYZ 9: 164.

shared interest.[73] After unseating Shoushan Monastery the families jointly launched a reconstruction effort for the academy in 1780 and used this opportunity to expand the fields belonging to the academy with representatives of all the families involved.

During the Qianlong period, the families contributed lands in Yongkang county in close proximity to the academy. The fields of this area had already been involved in the first lawsuit during the Ming dynasty and were moreover intertwined with the lands of the Kuchuan Hu family as all were irrigated from the mountains, making this a sensitive issue. Hu Jingyu 胡景輿 (?–?), the representative of the descendants of the Hu family, used this as a cause to incite a second lawsuit against the families of the Wufeng scholarly community. Cheng Shangfei in *The Genealogy of the Cheng Family* recounts: "My forefathers Lord Songxi [Cheng Wende] and Lord Fangfeng [Cheng Zi], who had lectured at Wufeng Academy in Mt. Shou, were once falsely accused by the Hu family, as one can see in the 'Words on litigation' that I know by heart. Recently their descendants Jingli and Hongtu renovated the academy and the members [of the Hu family] again bring forth this old grudge for accusations."[74] Triggering the Cheng-Hu family dispute was a tenth of an acre of mountain land that the Cheng family donated to the academy. The genealogy of the Cheng family contains a *Written Agreement on the Shoushan Legal Case* (*Shoushan yue ju gongan* 壽山約據公案) that gives a detailed record of the land dispute:

> Written Agreement on the Shoushan Legal Case
> 
> Establishing an agreement between the parties of the Hu Gong family and the three houses of the scholars Ying, Cheng, and Lu. Because their lands in Mt. Shou have bordered each other in two places for a long time already, the boundaries have been blurred. Today both parties convene to examine this and make it clear. From the gates of the monastery down the path until a little less than 300 feet to the rock where one saddles his horse, this shall be the boundary. The embankment below this rock has already been agreed on as boundary. Before this the foot of Taohua peak forms a parallel boundary. Below the embankment is the land of the scholars, and above the embankment is the land of the Hu family. From now on both families understand this boundary of the land and must not infringe on it. Agreement of Qianlong, 4th year [1739], first month, [Signed:] Lu Youmei, Ying Yousheng, Cheng Zilin, Erheng, Shixian,

---

73　For more information on the intermarriage practices of these families in Youxian see Lee, "Wang Yangming Thought as Cultural Capital," 61–67.

74　*Wufeng shuyuan zhi*, Volume 15, in ZGLDSYZ 9: 429.

Jinghua, Fuwu, Hu Guoquan, Shengxiang, Shengjiu, Shunyu, Suzhang, Hanzhang, Yunzhang, Scribe Cheng Jianwu.

Words on the Lawsuit

Investigating Cheng Shangfei's and Hu Jingyu's counter lawsuits about the fields in the mountain, category number 1296, in sum there is a little more than a half-acre of field, the Cheng family put forward a fifth part of it and the Hu family put forward four fifths. Both parties accused each other of cutting trees to contest the boundary. Investigation of the site shows that the boundary established in the agreement made in the fourth year of Qianlong [1739] is not clear, with the result that both sides were fighting over it. The county magistrate personally inspected the site and clarified this, including a map in this volume. Following the present investigation, it is decreed that the footway from the monastery down to the flat terrain serves as the boundary, to the left belongs to the shrine of Lord Hu and the right belongs to the gathering of the scholars. Each shall administer their own land. Also for the chopped trees, neither party has to pay compensation. Put up engraved stones to mark the boundary, and to hinder later disputes refer to this case file.[75]

We can see that Hu Jingyu, as the representative of the Kuchuan Hu family, was, after the destruction of Shoushan Monastery, in control of the shrine to Hu Ze. During the first lawsuit the representative of Shoushan Monastery was Hu Yongzhang. Considering that the first lawsuit by the monks brought serious harm to the academy, during the Qianlong period, the descendants of the Ying, Cheng, and Lu families this time solved the struggle over lands within the framework of the local government. Under the auspices of the county magistrate, representatives of the Ying, Cheng, and Lu families settled the dispute over the expansion of their lands through setting up a "public case file" (*gongan* 公案) with the Kuchuan Hu family. By defining and recording the borders of the fields of both parties, the further growth of the academy was ensured. The renovation of the academy and the settling of the lawsuit in the Qianlong years show that the Ying, Cheng, and Lu families still played pivotal roles in guaranteeing the smooth development of Wufeng Academy.

### 4.2  *Confucian-Buddhist Struggles for Official Power*

Since the Tang and Song dynasties, academies and official schools (prefectual, county, etc.) were part of the Confucian educational system. The latter, under

---

75  *Cheng Wende ji*, Volume 5, 429–430.

the control of the court, enjoyed strong governmental protection and even though there are plenty of cases of disputes between academies and Buddhist monasteries, only few incidents of lawsuits involving official schools can be found. In the struggle for space and estates between academies and monasteries, the attitudes of local officials often played the decisive role. Ding Gang and Liu Qi in their analysis of contestations of academy and temple sites concluded that "monasteries often changed into academies, as this was mostly initiated with the support of local officials who gave the order to enforce such change. In doing so, they firstly expelled Buddhist thought and influence and secondly at the same time also solved difficulties of financing and maintaining the expenditure and the sites of academies. Looking for academies turning into monasteries, often the monks only acquired a tacit acceptance from local officials to transform abandoned academies into monasteries, and only rarely is active involvement from the official side visible."[76]

Although the Wufeng lawsuit involved several groups and interests contesting for control, the decisive role was held by officials. The rapid expansion of the Wufeng Academy before the lawsuit cannot be viewed separately from wide support that local officials provided at this time. However, Ying Dian and Cheng Wende's scholarly accomplishments and experiences at the court, making friends with regional officials, built a significant foundation. In 1514 Ying Dian first obtained the *jinshi* rank and held the position as secretary in the Bureau of Operations in the Ministry of War and in 1523 Ying Tingyu received his *jinshi* rank. Following his father Cheng Ji, who participated in the imperial examinations in 1499, Cheng Wende in 1529 took second place in the examinations. Their accomplishments from 1499 to 1529 in the examinations made the Wufeng academic community quite prominent. The establishment of Lize Shrine happened not long after the Jiajing emperor's ascension to the throne and the court's selection of worthies for duty, in which Ying Dian was recommended for the position as aide in the Office of Seals. Because it was Ying Dian's wish to teach in his hometown he did not leave to take up the post; however, this call still had a huge influence on the local officials. Zhang Yue, the magistrate of Jinhua at the time, personally made the inscription for the foundation of Lize Shrine and his successor Yao Wenzhao wrote the Lize Shrine tablet inscription. Cheng Wende during his term as official more actively befriended the parent officials of his county or other officials involved with Jinhua in the capital, and so accumulated a wealth of political resources for the Wufeng community. In 1530 when Yao Wenzhao was appointed as prefect for Jinhua, Cheng Wende invited all officials in Bejing originally from Jinhua to

---

76  Ding Gang and Liu Qi, *Shuyuan yu zhongguo wenhua*, 29.

celebrate and feast in the Lingji Temple (Lingji gong 靈濟宮), "as the right person for all was chosen."[77] During the feast Yao took the initiative to ask Cheng Wende and the others for advice: "When I am in office, how can I be of benefit to all these gentlemen?"[78] All present officials one after the other gave advice that can be found in the "Memorial for Sending Yao off to be the Magistrate of Jinhua." After Yao Wenzhao arrived in Jinhua he immediately gave his support to the Wufeng scholars. Cheng Wende also stood in contact with Yongkang Magistrate Hong Yuan. When Hong started to take up his position in Yongkang, Cheng led about ten fellow countrymen officials to the east gate of Beijing and wrote another memorial. In it, Cheng expressed his elation over the court's pick for the magistrate of his native place and expected that Hong would revitalize the culture and education in the area. "Master Hong wishes have for a long time been in [promoting] the Way, tirelessly and distinguishedly, in his heart and in his outward conduct. [...] Jueshan's [Hong Yuan] behavior, how could you increase his sincerity? How could he be more dutiful? And foremost is how could he be one of more scholarly airs?"[79] In 1550 Cheng Wende and twenty others Beijing officials from Jinhua established the "collective voice of Wu group" (*Wu ji tongsheng hui* 婺集同聲會) in the capital, which would meet once a month, to help people and receive reports from their area:

> It was in the *gengxu* year of Jiajing, the twenty-ninth year of his ascension [1550]. At this time officials of Jinhua and their fellows, about twenty people—some were second class officials, some were chosen as first in the examinations, some were part of the royal palace, some attended the censorate, some were in different ministries, some were observing politics; not only were they a lot full of gowns and hats, but they truly enjoyed sharing the teaching of the way and righteousness—all sought to exert themselves, saying: "To assist these people is akin to honoring Jinhua. All the more, how can we serve our homeland? The landscape is as of old, the customs have not been broken off; hearing about the worthies of old, how can we be bear the ruin of the younger? One hundred years in an instant, how brief is human life! If we don't exert and inform [ourselves], then we might as well just be drunk for a lifetime and dream till we are dead. Let alone, that what is right has already been established, but even so, how can we assist it? To finish cultivation is to bide one's time, the root is to

---

77  "Zeng Yao Xigu shou Jinhua xu (Writing for Seeing Magistrate of Jinhua Yao Xugu Off)," in *Cheng wende ji*, Volume 5, 59.

78  "Zeng Yao Xigu shou jinhua xu," in *Cheng Wende ji*, Volume 5, 59.

79  "Zeng Jueshan Hong dafu zai wu yi xu (Memorial for Great Minister Jueshan Hong Leaving for Our Home County)," in *Cheng wende ji*, Volume 6, 70.

reach the simple and to reach the change, to harbor sincerity and be proper in solitude, then one can follow the sages and follow Heaven. If the officials will honor the ruler and protect the people, then the relationships will be true and customs correct.[80]

With Cheng Wende as the center, the Wu collective voice group formed a strong association of scholar-officials from the same area and at the same time a strong force whom the Wufeng scholars could rely on in the capital. As mentioned before, the Wufeng scholars' victory despite their difficult situation was due mainly to close interactions of Ying Dian, Cheng Wende with high level officials like Huang Wan, Ying Liang, and Kong Tianyin using their influence to intervene in the lawsuit.

The monks of Shoushan Monastery involved in the lawsuit and the Kuchuan Hu family also used the power of the court and local officials to launch their attack on the academy. Faced with the active expansion of the scholars at Wufeng already before the 1540s, the monks did not counteract this because at this point, the local officials all had close relations with Ying Dian or Cheng Wende and were fully supportive of the further development of the academy. However after the officials devoted to spreading the School of Mind had left their posts, and the government prohibited academies teaching Wang Yangming and Zhan Ruoshui thought, the monks of Shoushan Monastery quickly cooperated with the Kuchuan Hu family and entered into open dispute with the Wufeng scholars. When Lu Kejiu and others appealed to the prefectural office, the monks on the other hand tried to avoid interaction with the local government and sought support of the regional investigation inspectors. According to the local records from 1541 to 1543, this post was held by Dang Chengci 黨承賜 (?–?).[81] In the "Pusong ci" Cheng Zi mentions this particular inspector's prejudice against Wang Yangming and his teachings. "The censor therefore harbors ill will against Lord Bo'an [Wang Yangming] and is certainly displeased with the School of Principle too, saying to the gentlemen it is false learning, removing the teachers' honor and discarding their shrines."[82] Cheng Zi expressed his strong dissatisfaction with the inspector's trust in the one-sided argument of the monks and his hasty verdict without any detailed investigation of the case. "And thus now without any investigation making a decision, implicating righteous people in serious crimes and dragging the area

---

80  *Cheng Wende ji*, Volume 9, 111–112.
81  Ma Rulong and Yang Xi, *Hangzhou fu zhi* (Hangzhou Prefecture Gazetteer), Kangxi ed. (1686), Volume 18 (Beijing: Zhonghua shuju, 2008), Volume 12. Unpaginated.
82  *Wufeng shuyuanzhi*, Volume 15, in ZGLDSYZ 9: 53.

into darkness and disorder, leaving no opportunity to excuse, is this the logic of pacifying the realm?"[83]

Comparing both sides the Wufeng scholars won the lawsuit as they, through Ying Dian and Cheng Wende, had close contacts and personal connections to a network of officials in the government providing them with official resources. In contrast, the monks of Shoushan Monastery had no opportunity to enter into official careers and although they were connected to the local family of the Kuchuan Hu, from the Yuan and Ming dynasties their sway with official forces declined and left them with limited political resources.

## 5   Summary

The construction, prohibition, and rehabilitation of the Wufeng Academy during the Jiajing reign reflects to some extent the growth and decline of Confucian and Buddhist forces in the area. At first, the scholar community of Yongkang built Lize Shrine at the site of the Buddhist Arhat Hall. This did not immediately demonstrate any intent of Confucians to contend against the Buddhists of the area. However with the backing of the local government and families involved in the academy, Arhat Hall was ultimately destroyed and Wufeng Academy built in its place. In the lawsuit the scholars of Wufeng Academy and the monks of Shoushan Monastery mutually engaged in a complex struggle against each other, involving powerful families, monks, scholars, and officials at all levels, letting us quite directly observe the emerging contrast in power between Confucian academies and Buddhist monasteries. Wufeng Academy had to rely on Huang Wan, Ying Liang and other senior officials sympathetic to the Yangming School to successfully lift the ban of the academy by the imperial investigators.

From the Confucian-Buddhist lawsuit in Wufeng, it can be seen how academies as local cultural educational organizations had to deal with challenges from local families, Buddhist monasteries, and Daoist temples, challenges that were an important dynamic for the long term survival of the institution. For this goal, besides taking root in the local community, academies needed leaders who were integrated into larger networks of academic communities and could activate power resources. The families, leading scholars, and local officials all played different roles in the development of the academy, all were are inextricably linked through the academy, blood relations, master-disciple

---

83    Ibid.

relationships, and geographical affiliation, revealing to us a locality with a vivid political and social scenery.

**References**

Bol, Peter K. *"This Culture of Ours": Intellectual Transitions in T'ang and Sung China*. Stanford: Stanford University Press, 1992.

Chen Gujia 陈谷嘉, and Deng Hongbo 邓洪波. *Zhongguo shuyuanshi ziliao* 中国书院史资料 (Sources of the History of Chinese Academies). Hangzhou: Zhejiang jiaoyu chubanshe, 1998.

Chen Shilong 陈时龙. "Lun Tianzhen Shuyuan de jinhui yu chongjian 论天真书院的禁毁与重建 (On the Destruction and Reconstruction of Tianzhen Academy)." *Mingshi yanjiu luncong* 4 (2013): 115–124.

Cheng Shangfei 程尚斐 (comp.). *Wufeng shuyuan zhi* 五峰書院志 (Records of Wufeng Academy). In ZGLDSYZ, Volume 9.

Cheng Wende 程文德. *Cheng Wende ji* 程文德集 (Collected Writings of Cheng Wende). Shanghai: Shanghai guji chubanshe, 2012.

Cheng Zhengyi 程正誼. *Cheng Zhengyi ji* 程正誼集 (Collected Writings of Cheng Zhengyi). Shanghai: Shanghai guji chubanshe, 2012.

Cheng Zhuchang 程朱昌 and Cheng Yuquan 程育全. *Wufeng shuyuanzhi zengding ben* 五峰书院志 增订本 (Records of Wufeng Academy, Revised and Enlarged Edition). Beijing: Zhongguo wenshi chubanshe, 2010.

Ching, Julia. *The Religious Thought of Chu Hsi*. Oxford: Oxford University Press, 2000.

Cooper, Gene. *The Market and Temple Fairs of Rural China: Red Fire*. New York: Routledge, 2013.

Deng Hongbo 邓洪波. *Zhongguo shuyuan shi* 中国书院史 (History of Chinese Academies). Wuhan: Wuhan daxue chubanshe, 2012.

Ding Gang 丁钢, and Liu Qi 刘琪. *Shuyuan yu zhongguo wenhua* 书院与中国文化 (Academies and Chinese Culture). Shanghai: Shanghai jiaoyu chubanshe, 1992.

Fu, Charles Wei-hsun. "Chu Hsi on Buddhism." In *Chu Hsi and Neo-Confucianism*, edited by Wing-tsit Chan, 377–408. Honolulu: University of Hawai'i Press, 1986.

Hong Yuan 洪垣. *Taoyan Lize jingshe ji, Wufeng shuyuan zhi* 桃岩麗澤精舍記, 五峰書院志 (Records of Taoyan Lizhe Private Study, Records of Wufeng Academy). In ZGLDSYZ, Volume 9.

Huang Lingeng 黃霖庚, and Tao Chenghua 陶誠華 (ed.). *Jinhua zongpu wenxuan jicheng* 金華宗譜文獻集成 (Literature Collection of Jinhua Genealogies). Shanghai: Shanghai guji chubanshe, 2013.

Huang Wan 黃綰. *Huang Wan ji* 黃綰集 (Collected Writings of Huang Wan), edited by Zhang Hongmin 張宏敏. Shanghai: Shanghai guji chubanshe, 2014.

Huang Zongxi 黃宗羲. *Mingru xue'an* 明儒學案 (The Records of Ming Scholars). Beijing: Zhonghua shuju, 2008.

Jiang Bao 姜寶. *Songxi Cheng xiansheng nianpu/Cheng Wende ji* 松溪程先生年譜 / 程文德集 (Chronological Biography of Master Cheng Songxi/Collected Works of Cheng Wende). Shanghai: Shanghai guji chubanshe, 2012.

*Jinhua fu zhi* 金華府志 (Jinhua Prefecture Gazetteer). Volume 14, Wanli ed. In *Zhongguo fangzhi congshu* 中國方志叢書華中地方 (Collection of Chinese Local Records, Central China), no. 489. Taipei: Chengwen chubanshe, 1985.

Kong Tianyin 孔天胤. *Kong Wengu ji* 孔文谷集 (Collected Writings of Kong Wengu). Volume 15, in SKQSCM, Ji bu 集部, Book 95. Jinan: Jilu sushe, 1997.

Lee, Junghwan. "Wang Yangming Thought as Cultural Capital: The Case of Yongkang County." *Late Imperial China* 28, no. 2 (December 2007): 41–80.

Lee, Sukhee. "Zhu Xi was Here. Family, Academy, and Local Memory in Later Imperial Dongyang." *Journal of Song-Yuan Studies*, no. 41 (2011): 267–293.

Lee, Thomas H.C. *Education in Traditional China: A History*. Leiden: Brill, 2000.

Ma Rulong, and Yang Xi (eds.). *Hangzhou fu zhi* 杭州府志 (Hangzhou Prefecture Gazetteer). Kangxi edition (1686), Volume 18. Beijing: Zhonghua shuju, 2008.

McMahon, Daniel. "The Yuelu Academy and Hunan's Nineteenth-Century Turn Toward Statecraft." *Late Imperial China* 26. no. 1 (June 2005): 72–109.

Neskar, Ellen G. "The Cult of Worthies: A Study of Shrines Honoring Local Confucian Worthies in the Sung Dynasty." PhD diss., Columbia University, 1993.

Ouyang Shoudao 欧阳守道. *Xunzhai wenji* 巽斋文集 (Collected Writings of Xunzhai). Volume 7, in SKQS, Collections 集部, Book 122. Shanghai: Shanghai guji chubanshe, 1987.

Toqtoγa/Tuotuo 脫脫. *Songshi* 宋史 (History of the Song). Beijing: Zhonghua shuju, 1974.

Wan Sitong 萬斯同. *Mingshi* 明史 (History of Ming). In Xuxiu Siku quanshu 續修四庫全書 (Addendum to the SKQS). Shanghai: Shanghai guji chubanshe, 2002.

Wang Shouren 王守仁. *Wang Yangming quanji* 王阳明全集 (Complete Works of Wang Yangming). Shanghai: Shanghai guji chubanshe, 2014.

Xiao Yongming 肖永明. *Ruxue, shuyuan, shehui: shehui wenhua shi shiye zhong de shuyuan* 儒学, 书院, 社会: 社会文化史视野中的书院 (Confucianism, academies, and society: a sociocultural historical perspective on academies). Beijing: Shangwu yinshuguan, 2012.

*Xu Wenxian tongkao* 續文獻通考 (Addendum to the *Comprehensive Investigations Based on Literary and Documentary Sources*). Volume 50. Hangzhou: Zhejiang guji chubanshe, 1988.

*Yanping fu zhi* 延平府志 (Yanping Prefecture Gazetteer). Qianlong edition, reprint in *Zhongguo fangzhi congshu huazhong difang* 中國方志叢書華中地方 (Series of Chinese Local Records, Central China), No. 99. Taipei: Chengwen chubanshe, 1985.

*Yongkang xian zhi* 永康縣志 (Yongkang County Gazetteer). Volume 1, Guangxu edition, in *Zhongguo fangzhi congshu huazhong difang* 中國方志叢書華中地方 (Series of Chinese Local Records, Central China), No. 68. Taipei: Chengwen chubanshe, 1985.

*Yongkang xian zhi* 永康縣志 (Yongkang County Gazetteer). Volume 8, Kangxi edition 1675, in *Zhongguo fangzhi congshu huazhong difang* 中國方志叢書華中地方 (Series of Chinese local Records, Central China), No. 528. Taipei: Chengwen chubanshe youxian gongsi, 1985.

Zhang Tingyu 張廷玉. *Mingshi* 明史 (History of the Ming). Beijing: Zhonghua shuju, 1974.

Zhu Hanmin 朱汉民, and Deng Hongbo 邓洪波. *Yuelu shuyuan shi* 岳麓书院史 (History of the Yuelu Academy). Changsha: Hunan jiaoyu chubanshe, 2013.

# PART 4

## *From Religious Landscape to Cultural Heritage*

∴

CHAPTER 13

# Songyang Academy in Time and Place: From Confucian Academy to Cultural Heritage

*Linda Walton*

## 1    Introduction

Tracing the history of Songyang Academy 嵩陽書院 from its beginnings in the 10th century and fame as one of the "Four Great Academies" of the Northern Song[1] through its revival in the late 20th and early 21st centuries, this chapter seeks to show how the meaning of this site was transformed over time under the influence of religious, intellectual, political, and social forces. What role did Songyang Academy play in Northern Song Neo-Confucianism? To what extent did the Qing revival of the academy continue the Cheng-Zhu tradition associated with its Song origins? What can the history of this institution tell us about the landscape it inhabits, and how did the changing historical environment reshape the institution? How does the contemporary transformation of Songyang Academy into a site of cultural heritage tourism inform our understanding of modern Chinese attitudes toward the past and modern Chinese cultural identity?

## 2    Setting: The Religious Landscape of Mount Song

Mount Song 嵩山 is a range of peaks in present-day Dengfeng 登封 county, about 80 kilometers southwest of Zhengzhou, the provincial capital of Henan. The major peaks of the Mount Song range are Mount Shaoshi 少室 (1,512 meters above sea level) and Mount Taishi 太室 (1,140 meters). Songyang 嵩陽 ("the southern side of [Mount] Song") lies in the foothills below Mount Taishi. As one of the Five Sacred Peaks (*wuyue* 五嶽),[2] Mount Song was a potential site

---

[1]  Although there are slightly differing versions of the "Four Great Academies," a typical description is that by Lü Zuqian (1137–1181), which includes Songyang, Yuelu 嶽麓, Suiyang 睢陽, and White Deer Grotto 白鹿洞 (see Linda Walton, *Academies and Society in Southern Sung China* [Honolulu: University of Hawai'i Press, 1999], 25–26).

[2]  For the origins and development of the Five Sacred Peaks and its cosmographical significance, see James Robson, *Power of Place: The Religious Landscape of the Southern Sacred Peak (Nanyue*

ILLUSTRATION 13.1 View of Mount Song from Songyang Academy today.
SOURCE: PHOTO COURTESY OF AUTHOR

for the imperial *feng* 封 and *shan* 禪 sacrifices.[3] The name of the modern county where Mount Song is located, Dengfeng 登封 ("ascending to offer"), in fact, alludes to these imperial sacrifices. Although Mount Tai was the usual site for the performance of these rites, emperors at times visited other Sacred Peaks such as Mount Song on imperial peregrinations to assert their sovereignty. A notable feature of Songyang Academy today is the two huge cypress trees that dominate the main courtyard and are said to have been granted military titles by Emperor Wu of Han 漢武帝 (r. 140 BCE–87 BCE) on his imperial tour here in 110 BCE.[4] Tang Gaozong 唐高宗 (r. 649–683) planned to offer the *feng* and *shan* sacrifices here, but died before he could do it. Empress Wu 武則天 (r. 690–705) did perform them in 696 in the name of her new dynasty, Zhou; but after 705 and the return of the mandate to the Tang imperial house, Xuanzong 唐玄宗 (r. 712–756) carried them out at Taishan 泰山, the main site for the performance of these rites.[5]

Along with Mount Song's importance as one of the Five Sacred Peaks of imperial cosmography, it gained a reputation as a numinous site animated by

---

南嶽) *in Medieval China* (Cambridge and London: Harvard University Asia Center, 2009), 25–52. Mount Song is the central peak.

3   For background on the *feng* and *shan* sacrifices, see Howard J. Wechsler, *Offerings of Jade and Silk: Ritual and Symbol in the Legitimation of the Tang Dynasty* (New Haven and London: Yale University Press, 1985), Ch. 9.

4   Zhang Hui, "Songyang shuyuan luyou ziyuan kaifa yanjiu (Study on the Development of Tourism Resources at Songyang Academy)," *Sanmenxia zhiye jishu xueyuan xuebao* 11.2 (June 2012): 24.

5   Wechsler, *Offerings of Jade and Silk*, 188–189, 192.

a rich array of gods and spirits. The mountain's dramatic landscape attracted Daoists and Buddhists, luring Daoists as early as the Han. Practitioners of both Daoism and Buddhism established themselves on Mount Song beginning in the Six Dynasties (220–589).[6] Songyang Temple 嵩陽寺, founded by a Chan priest, was built in 484 during the reign of Northern Wei (386–535) emperor Xiao Wendi 孝文帝 (r. 471–499) on the site that would later become Songyang Academy.[7] An inscription on an Eastern Wei (534–550) stele erected in 535, and preserved at Songyang Academy today, commemorates this Chan temple and its founder.[8] During the Sui and Tang, the temple was transformed into a Daoist abbey, Songyang guan 嵩陽觀.[9] In 683 Tang Gaozong and his empress stayed there during their imperial tour of Mount Song, and established Offering to Heaven Palace (*fengtian gong* 奉天宮) nearby.[10] Songyang Abbey was where the Daoist master Sun Taichong 孫太沖 (?–?) prepared cinnabar longevity elixirs for Tang emperor Xuanzong, inspiring the famous Great Tang Stele of 744, titled *Da Tang Songyang guan ji shengde ganying song bei* 大唐嵩陽觀紀聖德感應頌碑 (Great Tang Songyang Abbey Stele Record in Praise of the Spiritual Resonance of Imperial Virtue), professing Xuanzong's belief in Daoism.[11] Daoist masters continued to frequent Songyang Abbey throughout the Tang and into the Five Dynasties era (907–960). Mount Song became a retreat for eminent Daoist masters of the Maoshan 茅山 (Shangqing 上清) School, as well as Confucian literati who sought refuge there in increasingly

---

6     For a discussion of Mount Song's importance as a sacred site, see Bernard Faure, "Relics and Flesh Bodies: The Creation of Ch'an Pilgrimage Sites," in *Pilgrims and Sacred Sites in China*, ed. by Susan Naquin and Yü Chün-fang (Berkeley, Los Angeles, Oxford: University of California Press, 1992), 153–165.
7     Gong Songtao, *Songyang shuyuan* (Songyang Academy) (Changsha: Hunan daxue chubanshe, 2014), 4. I have relied extensively on this recent secondary source on the academy's history, supplemented where possible with primary sources. The author does not disclose his sources, many of which must be held by the academy (such as steles with inscriptions that have not been printed) but are otherwise inaccessible. An earlier edition of this book (2001) contains much more detail on steles in particular. All references here are to the 2014 edition.
8     See Gong, *Songyang shuyuan*, 4, for excerpts from the inscription text.
9     According to the Kangxi era (1696) Dengfeng county gazetteer, Tianfeng guan 天封觀 was built on the old foundation of Songyang Academy, formerly Northern Wei Songyang Temple, then Tang Songyang Abbey; later it was named Tianfeng Abbey, and during the Song it became Tianfeng Palace (*gong* 宮). This must be at a somewhat different location because we know that it was Songyang Academy in the Song. Zhang Shenggao et al. (comps.), "Dengfeng xian zhi (Records of Dengfeng County)," in SKQSCM ed. [1696], 8.3a; Gong, *Songyang shuyuan*, 5.
10    Ouyang Xiu, Song Zhi (comps.), *Xin Tang shu* (New Tang History), 14.351 (accessed at <http://hanchi.ihp.sinica.edu.tw/>).
11    Gong, *Songyang shuyuan*, 5; 134–144.

chaotic political conditions from the late Tang on. With the rise to prominence of Northern Chan Buddhism, Mount Song also attracted monks from all over China, and eventually by the Song, from Japan (and Korea?) as well.[12]

As China began to be reunified in the tenth century, Mount Song, the site of Songyang Temple and later Songyang Abbey, was appropriated by rulers who sought to absorb territory here in the service of the state. By no means, however, did they eradicate—or even try to eradicate—Buddhist and Daoist sites on the mountain. Shaolin Monastery 少林寺 is only the most famous Buddhist site on Mount Song, and the mountain landscape continued to be dotted with stupas and steles, as well as with Daoist abbeys and shrines to Daoist masters and deities along with local gods and spirits. Scattered references to 10th-century scholars studying or seeking retreat at Songyang testify to its reputation as a place of withdrawal from the official world to study Daoist as well as other texts. Shu Yuan 舒元 (923–977), for example, studied with the Daoist master Yang Na 楊訥 (?–?) at Songyang, but Shu Yuan himself was known for his learning in the three traditions of the *Zuozhuan*.[13] Although Shu Yuan's son Shu Zhibai 舒知白 (942–1022) was recommended for office, he eventually returned to the retreat at Songyang and devoted himself to Daoist study, granted the "purple crown and robe" and taking the Daoist title Chongxuan da shi 崇玄大師 (Grand Master of the Exalted Mystery).[14] By contrast, however, Shi Xizai 石熙載 (928–984) spent time studying with Daoists at Songyang, but he ended up disdaining Daoist beliefs and adhering to Confucian ones, a harbinger, perhaps, of things to come.[15]

## 3  Songyang Academy in the Northern Song

The immediate precursor of Songyang Academy was founded in 955 when the Latter Zhou (951–960) ruler transformed Songyang Abbey into Taiyi 太乙 Academy, reportedly because of the beauty of the surrounding landscape. He set up a library and dormitories, and recruited scholars and students to gather

---

12   Faure, "Relics and Flesh Bodies," 155–157.
13   Tuo Tuo et al., *Songshi* (History of the Song) (Beijing: Zhonghua shuju ed.), 478.13864 [hereafter SS]. See also Wang Deyi et al. (eds.), *Songren zhuanji ziliao suoyin* (Index to Song Biographical Materials) (Taipei: Dingwen shuju, 1974–1976), IV.3054 [hereafter cited as *Songren*].
14   SS 478.13865. His son, however, held office and took a *jinshi* degree (SS 478.13865).
15   SS 263.9103; *Songren* I.433–434.

there for study and teaching.[16] In Song and later sources, it is called Taishi 太室 Academy because of its location on the southern slopes of Mount Taishi.[17] According to a modern account, like other academies in the early Northern Song, it was granted a bequest of the Nine Classics and other works from the imperial government in 997, and reportedly again in 1010.[18] In 1035, a name tablet was bestowed by the court renaming it Songyang Academy.[19] The powerful court official Wang Zeng 王曾 (978–1038) memorialized for the appointment of a headmaster and for the provision of one *qing* 頃 (= 100 *mu* 畝) of land to support the academy.[20] A further 10 *qing* were granted, providing a substantial allocation for the academy's support.[21] In 1059 the Dengfeng county magistrate appointed teachers and recruited students, and the stage was thus set for the heyday of Songyang Academy as one of the "Four Great Academies of the Northern Song."[22]

16 Gong, *Songyang shuyuan*, 6; Geng Jie (comp.), Li Yuan (ed. and annot.), *Songyang shuyuan zhi (Records of Songyang Academy)*, 2 [hereafter cited as SYSYZ], in *Songyue wenxian congkan*, v. 2, ed. Zhengzhou shi tushuguan wenxian bianji weiyuanhui (Zhengzhou: Zhongzhou guji chubanshe, 2003), 1.

17 See the references in Sun Yanmin, *Songdai shuyuan zhiduzhi yanjiu* (Study of the Song Dynasty Academy System) (Taipei: Guoli zhengzhi daxue, 1963), 68, all of which refer only to Taishi Academy, including in the Latter Zhou.

18 Gong, *Songyang shuyuan*, 7. Gong appears to be basing these dates primarily on Zhang, *Dengfeng xianzhi*, 4.8b. But Song sources differ from this 17th-century account. For example, *Song huiyao jigao* (Draft Compendium of Song Documents) (Taipei: Xin wenfeng, 1976), v. 3, 2193 [54.*chongru* 2.41a] gives the year 996 for the bequest of the name plaque "Songyang Academy," and goes on to state that neither Songyang nor Maoshan 茅山 Academy were subsequently known, and they were not considered among the "Four Great Academies." Not surprisingly, it is impossible to reconcile these dates and the inconsistency of names, but fortunately neither is it crucial to the basic story line of Songyang Academy's history. However, I cannot find the 1010 bequest mentioned elsewhere (either in the Qing gazetteer account or in Song sources), and Gong provides no reference.

19 Zhang, *Dengfeng xian zhi*, 4.8b.; Li Tao, *Xu zizhi tongjian changbian* (Continued Long Edition of the *Comprehensive Mirror for Aid in Government*) (Taipei: Shijie shuju, 1964), 119.11b, has this occurring in 1036, but the annotation points out that the cyclical terms for the years of Renzong's reign (r. 1022–1063) in this chapter are actually for the Huangyou 皇祐, not the Jingyou 景祐 eras, and so a scribal error that introduces doubt for this source. The 1030s were noted for the Song court's promotion of education, which included academies as well as prefectural schools, so it is safe to say that attention to Songyang Academy in the mid-1030s was entirely consistent with broader educational policy.

20 Zhang, *Dengfeng xian zhi*, 4.8b. For Wang Zeng, see Herbert Franke (ed.), *Song Biographies* (Wiesbaden: Franz Steiner Verlag, 1976), vol. 3, 1159–1161 (Tonami Mamoru).

21 Gong, *Songyang shuyuan*, 7. Again, this information is according to Gong, but Li Tao, *Xu zizhi tongjian changbian*, 122.2a, has the 10 *qing* bequest only and nothing for the earlier bequest of land. The following historical account for the Song is based on Gong.

22 Gong, *Songyang shuyuan*, 7.

During the reign of Emperor Shenzong 神宗 (r. 1068–1085), Cheng Hao 程顥 (1032–1085) and Cheng Yi 程頤 (1033–1107) were said to have lectured at Songyang Academy, where they drew multitudes of students, including Zhang Zai 張載 (1020–1077), Fan Chunren 范純仁 (1027–1101), Yang Shi 楊時 (1053–1135), Shao Bowen 邵伯溫 (1057–1134), Yin Dun 尹焞 (1071–1142), Lü Dalin 呂大臨 (1044–1091), and others.[23] Songyang Academy had a close relationship with Extending Prosperity Palace (Chongfu gong 崇福宮), which lay not far to the east of it just beneath Ten Thousand Year Peak (Wansui feng 萬歲峰). This was originally Ten Thousand Year Palace (Wansui gong 萬歲宮), established by Han emperor Wu when he toured Mount Song, and it was named for the congratulatory calls of "Ten Thousand Years!" that supposedly echoed from the mountains during his visit.[24] During the Tang, it became Grand Unity Abbey (Taiyi guan 太乙觀), named for the astral deity Taiyi.[25] In the Song this was renamed Extending Prosperity Palace, where Emperor Zhenzong 真宗 (r. 998–1022) prayed for good fortune on behalf of the empire.[26] Officials were deputed from the court to manage it, and during the reforms of Wang Anshi 王安石 (1021–1086) his opponents sought refuge from political persecution by holding sinecures here. Among these were Sima Guang 司馬光 (1019–1086), Cheng Xiang 程珦 (1006–1090, father of the Cheng brothers), the Cheng brothers themselves, Yang Shi, and others. When Sima Guang opposed Wang Anshi's reforms, for example, he left Kaifeng for Luoyang and eventually for Extending Prosperity Palace. Once there, Cheng Hao invited him to lecture at Songyang Academy. Chapters 9 through 21 of the *Zizhi tongjian* 資治通鑒 (*Comprehensive Mirror for Aid in Government*) were said to have been written while Sima Guang was in exile at Extending Prosperity Palace and Songyang Academy.[27] By the early 1090s, however, the academy was in ruins, so the Dengfeng county magistrate petitioned to restore it.[28] There are no extant records from that

---

23 Gong, *Songyang shuyuan*, 8.
24 Ban Gu (comp.), *Hanshu* (Han History), 6.190 (accessed at <http://hanchi.ihp.sinica.edu.tw>); see also Faure, "Relics and Flesh Bodies," 153–154.
25 Judith Boltz describes a series of Grand Unity Palaces (*gong* 宮) established in 10th- and 11th-century Kaifeng dedicated to this astral deity, the propitiation of which was to ensure abundant crops along with prosperity and longevity for all. See her *A Survey of Taoist Literature: Tenth to Seventeenth Centuries* (Berkeley: University of California Institute of East Asian Studies, Center for Chinese Studies, 1987), 121–122. The name Taiyi likely has some connection to the early Northern Song name given to what later became Songyang Academy.
26 Zhang, *Dengfeng xian zhi*, 8.3a.
27 Gong, *Songyang shuyuan*, 8.
28 Gong, *Songyang shuyuan*, 7. Again, I have been unable to locate any corroborating primary source evidence for this.

time to indicate whether or not restoration took place, but we do know that a stone tablet of the *Zhenwu jing* 真武經 was carved in 1099 and placed in the west wall of Songyang Academy's Lecture Hall.[29] The carving of this Daoist text, the *Perfected Warrior Canon*, is a reflection of the developing tradition in the 11th century of the Perfected Warrior,[30] but it also resonates with the Daoist history of this site and eventual Daoist renaming of Songyang Academy as Songyang Palace.

## 4  Southern Song, Jin-Yuan, and Ming: From Ruins to Recovery

After the Jurchen conquest of the north, during the reign of Jin Emperor Shizong 金世宗 (r. 1161–1189), the academy was renamed and repurposed by Daoists, who called it Receiving Heaven Palace (Chengtian gong 承天宮).[31] The Jin poet Yuan Haowen 元好問 (1190–1257) was said to have visited the site during his years in Henan, as did other Jin poets.[32] Yuan Haowen's later poems are poignant expressions of the death and disorder that accompanied the collapse of the Jin state and the Mongol conquest, here as elsewhere.[33] One rare essay from this period that relates to Songyang as a place, though not the academy, is a preface written for a painting entitled "Returning to Retreat at Songyang." The author, Li Ting 李庭 (1194–1277), writes about his friend Zhao Peng 趙朋

---

29  For a brief description of this text see Ren Jiyu (ed.), *Daozang tiyao* (Summaries of the Daoist Canon) (Beijing: Zhongguo shehui kexue chubanshe, 1991), 26. For background on this scripture and its religious context, see Chao Shin-yi, *Daoist Ritual, State Religion, and Popular Practice: Zhenwu Worship from Song to Ming (960–1644)* (London and New York: Routledge, 2011), 4. As Chao points out, in the Ming edition of the Daoist Canon, the full title is *Yuanshi tianzun shuo beifang zhenwu miaojing* 元始天尊說北方真武妙經 (Marvelous Scripture of the Perfected Warrior of the North Spoken by the Primordial Celestial Worthy), adding the character *miao* to the original inscription (123–124, n. 10). See Gong, *Songyang shuyuan*, 193. According to Gong, in 1987 it was re-embedded in the west stele gallery of the academy. See also Lu Ji'e, Hong Liangji (comps.), *Dengfeng xian zhi* (Dengfeng County Records) (1787 printed edition), 30.48b. Available at: <http//ctext.org>.
30  Evolving from Xuanwu 玄武, the "Dark Lord," the original entwined tortoise and snake symbol was anthropomorphized into the "Perfected Warrior" to became one of the most important deities in the Daoist pantheon. Symbolic of defence against threats from the north, this deity was patronized by the imperial house, which viewed it as a protector deity of the state. For a comprehensive study of this, see Chao, *Daoist Ritual, State Religion, and Popular Practice*.
31  Gong, *Songyang shuyuan*, 9.
32  Gong, *Songyang shuyuan*, 233–234.
33  See, for example, Stephen H. West, "Chilly Seas and East-Flowing Rivers: Yüan Hao-wen's Poems of Death and Disorder, 1233–1235," in *China under Jurchen Rule*, ed. Hoyt Cleveland Tillman and Stephen H. West (Albany: State University of New York Press, 1995), 281–304.

(?–?), who "took up the Confucian profession" (*juye Ru* 舉業儒) but "withdrew to [practice] medicine" at Songyang.³⁴ According to Li Ting, Zhao Peng's forebears were from Zezhou 澤州, just north of the Yellow River, forced to cross the river and take up residence in Luoyang's Dengfeng county because of endemic warfare. Li Ting describes Songyang as a place where many retreated from war and disorder, while longing for home. Like Zhao Peng, the Yuan acupuncturist Hua Shou 滑壽 (1304–1389) from nearby Xuzhou 許州 was also reported to have come here during the course of his medical studies, and following sojourns in his youth at academies in Jiangnan.³⁵

During the last reign of the Mongol Yuan dynasty (1341–1368), Receiving Heaven Palace was again renamed Songyang Palace, a name it retained until after the mid-Ming.³⁶ The Mongol author Nasen 迺賢 (1309–1368), whose home was in nearby Nanyang 南陽 (Jia county 郟縣), visited it during his travels to ancient sites in the north. After relating the name changes over time, he described the two large cypresses, the Great Tang Stele, and a stone pillar to the east of the main hall, carved with the names of Han Yu 韓愈 (768–824) as well as those of Buddhist priests and Daoist masters, dated 809.³⁷ Apparently, there was not much else to see by the mid-14th century, and for the 15th century there are not even the fleeting textual glimpses that we find in Nasen. By mid-Ming, things had begun to change, undoubtedly influenced by the increase in the founding and restoration of academies during the 16th century.³⁸

In 1526 Hou Tai 侯泰 (?–?), a *juren* from Jiading 嘉定, took up office as Dengfeng county magistrate and restored Songyang Academy.³⁹ He did away with

---

34 Li Xiusheng et al. (eds.), *Quan Yuanwen* 全元文 (Complete Prose of the Yuan Dynasty) (Nanjing: Fenghuang chubanshe, 2004), 53.122–123. For Li Ting, see Wang Deyi et al. (eds.), *Yuanren zhuanji ziliao suoyin* (Index to Yuan Biographical Materials) (Beijing: Zhonghua shuju ed., 1987), I.477 [hereafter cited as *Yuanren*]; as for Zhao Peng, he may or may not be the person referenced in *Songren*, IV.3327.
35 Gong, *Songyang shuyuan*, 256. *Yuanren* III.1571.
36 Gong, *Songyang shuyuan*, 9.
37 Nasen, *Heshuo fanggu ji* (A Record of Visiting Ancient Sites in Heshuo [literally "north of the Yellow River"]), *Shike shiliao xinbian*, coll. 3 (Taipei: Xin wenfeng, 1979), v. 25, 181.
38 John Meskill, *Academies in Ming China* (Tucson: University of Arizona Press, 1982), 66.
39 Hou Tai was one of the editors of the [*Jiajing*] *Dengfeng xin zhi* (Jiajing Era New Record of Dengfeng) printed in 1529; see Nanjing tushuguan guben shanben congkan (ed.), editor's preface, 12, for Hou Tai's status and place of origin. The Hou Tai listed in *Mingren zhuanji ziliao suoyin* (Index to Ming Biographical Materials), ed. Guoli zhongyang tushuguan (Taipei: Guoli zhongyang tushuguan, 1978) [hereafter cited as *Mingren*], 374, cannot be the same person; nor can either of the Ming era men with the same name listed in the China Biographical Database be the individual referenced here. See Harvard University, Academia Sinica, and Peking University, China Biographical Database (January 1, 2018) <https://projects.iq.harvard.edu/cbdb> [hereafter cited CBDB], Person ID 0352943;

Songyang Palace and restored the school buildings at the old academy site, including the Cheng Brothers Shrine (Er Cheng ci 二程祠).[40] Three years later (1529), Wang Shangjiong 王尚絅 (1478–1531, 1502 *jinshi*), a local scholar, wrote a brief commemorative inscription for the restoration of Songyang Academy by Hou Tai.[41] The academy drew teachers and students and became an officially managed academy, evidently producing illustrious students.[42] However, in his poem "Three Generals Cypresses at Songyang Palace (Songyang Gong San Jiangjun Bai 嵩陽宮三將軍柏)," Ming painter and poet Huang Kehui 黃克晦 (1524–?) described the ruined atmosphere of the place, so the revival could not have lasted beyond the late 1500s.[43]

In the absence of more formal historical documentation, along with poetry, travelers' accounts provide some glimpses of what had become of Songyang Academy in the late Ming. In 1623 the Ming traveler Xu Xiake 徐霞客 (1586–1641) went to Mount Song, following a route that took him to several scenic and sacred mountains. He reached the ruins of Songyang Palace on March 22, and described it in his travel diary:

> …the only intact remains of the place are the Three Generals Cypresses that stand dark and flourishing like the crown of a hill. These ancient trees were decorated during the Han Dynasty. The largest needs seven men with outstretched arms to girdle it, the middle-sized one requires five men, and the small one, three. To the north of the cypresses is a shrine of three rooms, sacred to the two great Cheng scholars. West of it is a single stone pillar, half sunk in the ground, bearing the signature of

0253718. The entry on Songyang Academy in this Ming gazetteer, unfortunately, is cursory (1.14b).

40  Zhang, *Dengfeng xian zhi*, 4.8b; 6.4a.

41  For Wang Shangjiong, see *Mingren*, 39. His biography by Xue Yingqi (1500–1575, 1535 *jinshi*) reveals nothing about local involvement in Songyang Academy, and the inscription itself is very short and formulaic, telling little beyond the conventional reference to the Four Great Academies and praise for Hou Tai. For the biography, see Xue Yingqi, *Fangshan Xue xiansheng quanji* (Complete Writings of Master Fangshan Xue) 26.1a–3b, in *Xuxiu Siku quanshu*, v. 1343 (Shanghai: Shanghai guji chubanshe, 1995). The inscription is not included in Geng Jie's *Songyang shuyuan zhi*, but a rubbing is found in *Beijing tushuguan zang Zhongguo lidai shike taben huibian* (Beijing Library Collection of Chinese Historical Stone Rubbings), eds. Beijing tushuguan zubian (Zhengzhou: Zhongzhou guji chubanshe, 1997), v. 54, 176.

42  Gong, *Songyang shuyuan*, 10. Cui Yingke (?–?, 1595 *jinshi*) from Dengfeng was reportedly one of these. See Person ID 0349929.

43  For Huang, see *Mingren*, 652. The poem reads: 人間柏大此全稀, 老幹寧論四十圍. 蓋偃曾傾天子葆, 露寒應覆侍臣衣. 猶看連影容千騎, 那識何枝系六飛. 惆悵茂陵無限樹, 荒丘殘隴草菲菲.

many Song names but the only ones discernible now are those of Zu Wuze 祖無擇 of Fanyang 范陽, Kou Wuzhong 寇武仲 of Shanggu 上谷, and Su Caiweng 蘇才翁. A lofty stone tablet, most exquisitely carved with dragons, stands in majesty southeast of the trees. On its right is a Tang stone tablet with inscriptions, the essay being the work of Pei Jiong 裴迥 and the calligraphy, in the *bafen* 八分 style, being by Xu Hao 徐浩 (703–782).[44]

Two *li* farther east are the ruins of Chongfu Temple [*gong*], also known as Wanshou gong 萬壽宮 (Ten-thousand Year Temple). It was the place where important Song officials sometimes held sinecures.[45]

According to Xu's account, there was no functioning academy at the site—only what he calls Songyang Palace—by the 1620s. At the end of the Ming, even the remaining buildings that Xu saw were destroyed, and one of the three iconic cypress trees was burned to the ground.[46]

## 5  Qing: Revival and Restoration

Within a generation after the Manchu conquest, however, Songyang Academy was revived and restored as a Confucian institution. In 1674 Dengfeng County Magistrate Ye Feng 葉封 (1623–1687; 1658 *jinshi*) added buildings, a kitchen, baths, and a wall to enclose the surviving two cypresses within the academy courtyard.[47] One of the most important buildings was the Various Worthies Shrine (Zhuxian ci 諸賢祠), which venerated a series of individuals beginning with the scion of a powerful Northern Song political family and prefect of Kaifeng, Han Wei 韓維 (1017–1098), and including altogether 14 men.[48] In 1677 local scholar Geng Jie 耿介 (1623–1693; 1652 *jinshi*) returned home from office because of mourning for his mother and began to contribute to the restoration

---

44  Other sources credit Xuanzong's powerful chief minister Li Linfu (683–752) with composing the inscription, Pei Jiong (as a regional official) with commissioning and erecting it, and the famous calligrapher Xu Hao with the writing of it. See below.

45  Li Chi (trans.), *The Travel Diaries of Hsü Hsia-k'o* (Hong Kong: The Chinese University of Hong Kong, 1974), 138. I have followed this translation with a few minor changes, in addition to transliterations in *pinyin*. See Xu Xiake, *You Songshan riji* (Diary of a Journey to Songshan), <http://www.open-lit.com> (accessed 24 March 2017). The *bafen* style of calligraphy is a form of clerical script (*lishu*) with clear brushstrokes.

46  Gong, *Songyang shuyuan*, 10.

47  Gong, *Songyang shuyuan*, 10. For Ye Feng, see CBDB Person ID 00073061.

48  Zhang, *Dengfeng xian zhi*, 4.8b. For Han Wei, see *Songren*, V.4150–1.

of Songyang Academy.[49] He continued the building projects started by Ye Feng, and also erected a series of pavilions in the surrounding area near Layered Stone Creek (Dieshi xi 疊石溪).[50] In 1678 Zhang Xun 張壎 (?–1694) became magistrate of Dengfeng county and invited Geng Jie to become a teacher at the academy, where he instructed the students in Cheng-Zhu learning.[51] Both Zhang Xun and a succeeding Dengfeng county magistrate, Wang Youdan 王又旦 (1635–1685; *jinshi* 1658), built dormitories at the academy, while provincial education commissioner Wu Ziyun 吳子雲 (1634–?) allotted 100 *mu* of school land.[52] Zhang Mu 張沐 (1630–1712; 1658 *jinshi*) learned of Zhang Xun's revival of the academy and joined Geng Jie in lecturing there.[53] In 1679 Ran Jinzu 冉覲祖 (1637–1718; *jinshi* 1691) was invited by Geng Jie to teach at the academy, where he lectured on Mencius.[54] In 1682 Wang Ji 汪楫 (1636–1689), as prefect of Henan *fu*, established school land for the academy and appointed Geng Jie to hold the lecture seat.[55] Two years later (1684), Provincial Governor Wang Rizao 王日藻 (1623–1700; 1655 *jinshi*) supported the establishment of a library, and the provincial education commissioner Lin Yaoying 林堯英 (?–?, 1661 *jinshi*) provided resources to build a lecture hall.[56] In 1686 Dou Keqin 竇克勤 (1653–1708; *jinshi* 1688), who studied with Geng Jie at Songyang Academy, contributed funds to build the Exemplary Person Pavilion (Junzi ting 君子亭) above Layered Stone Creek, and this became a retreat for the academy.[57] In 1689 the Henan Provincial Governor Yan Xingbang 閻興邦 (1635–1698) allotted funds to establish the Unified Way Shrine (Daotong ci 道統祠).[58] All these men contributed inscriptions commemorating the restoration of Songyang Academy to the academy record compiled and edited by Geng Jie.[59] By far the most

---

49  Zhao Ersun et al. (comps.), *Qingshi gao* (Draft History of the Qing), 480.13102 (accessed at <http://hanchi.ihp.sinica.ed.tw>).
50  Zhang, *Dengfeng xian zhi*, 4.8b.
51  Zhao, *Qingshi gao*, 476.12974; for Zhang Xun, see CBDB Person ID 0080031.
52  Gong, *Songyang shuyuan*, 11. For Wang Youdan, see CBDB Person ID 0069041; for Wu Ziyun, see CBDB Person ID 0078230.
53  Zhao, *Qingshi gao*, 476.12973; CBDB Person ID 0079965.
54  Zhao, *Qingshi gao*, 480.13137; CBDB Person ID 0073285.
55  Zhao, *Qingshi gao*, 484.13351; CBDB Person ID 100065752.
56  Zhang, *Dengfeng xianzhi*, 4.8b. For Wang Rizao, see CBDB Person ID 0059944; for Lin Yaoying, see CBDB Person ID 0364079.
57  Gong, *Songyang shuyuan*, 11. For Dou Keqin, see Zhao, *Qingshi gao*, 480.13137-8; CBDB Person ID 0090904.
58  Zhang, *Dengfeng xianzhi*, 4.8b. For Yan Xingbang, see CBDB Person ID 0089040.
59  See SYSYZ, *juan* 2; see also facsimile reprint Zhongguo wenxian zhenben congshu edition of *Songyang shuyuan zhi* in *Zhongguo shuyuan zhi* (Chinese Academy Records), vol. 9, eds. Jiang Yasha et al. (Beijing: Quanguo tushuguan wenxian shuwei fuzhi zhongxin, 2005), *juan* 2.

ILLUSTRATION 13.2  Songyang Academy in its Dengfeng county setting.
SOURCE: GENG JIE ET AL. (EDS.), SONGYANG SHUYUAN ZHI [1701?], 1.24–25

prominent inscription author, however, was Tang Bin 湯斌 (1627–1687), like Geng Jie a 1652 *jinshi* and one of the principal scholars associated with the revival of Cheng-Zhu learning in the early Qing.[60] The late 17th-century restoration and expansion of Songyang Academy was part of this revival (see ills. 13.2 and 13.3).[61]

Cheng-Zhu learning was court-sanctioned from as early as 1645, when the interpretations of Cheng Yi and Zhu Xi were declared to be orthodoxy for the

---

60  For Tang Bin, see Arthur W. Hummel (ed.), *Eminent Chinese of the Ch'ing Period* (Taipei: Chengwen, 1970) [hereafter ECCP], 709–710 (Fang Chao-ying).

61  See Willard J. Peterson, "Chapter 13: Dominating Learning from Above During the K'anghsi Period," in *Cambridge History of China*, Volume 9, Part 2, ed. Willard J. Peterson (Cambridge: Cambridge University Press, 2016), 571–605; On-cho Ng, *Cheng-Zhu Confucianism in the Early Qing: Li Guangdi (1642–1718) and Qing Learning* (Albany: State University of New York Press, 2001); Kai-wing Chow, "The Development of Sung Learning in Ch'ing Thought," *Hanxue yanjiu* 13.2 (1995): 47–76. For a specific focus on Songyang Academy's role in this intellectual development, see Wang Shengjun, "Songyang shuyuan yu Qingchu Luoxue fuxing (Songyang Academy and the Revival of Luo Learning at the Beginning of the Qing Dynasty)," *Jiaoyu pinglun* 4 (2013): 129–131.

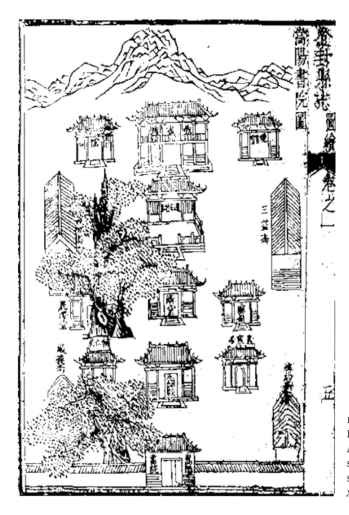

ILLUSTRATION 13.3
Drawing of Songyang Academy.
SOURCE: ZHANG SHENGGAO, *DENGFENG XIAN ZHI* [1696 ED.]

civil service examination curriculum.[62] During the reign of Kangxi, the court promoted Cheng-Zhu learning and patronized scholars who followed it, such as Tang Bin. Tang was a northerner from Henan who passed the examinations and held office under the Manchus before retiring to care for his father in 1659. Following the period of mourning, he studied with Sun Qifeng 孫奇逢 (1585–1675), who moved to northernmost Henan (Huixian 輝縣) after the Manchu conquest and became a renowned teacher and scholar.[63] The same year that Tang Bin became his disciple (1666), Sun published his *Lixue zongzhuan* 理學宗傳 (*Ancestral Traditions of Lixue*), a biographical collection of Confucian

---

62  Ng, *Cheng-Zhu Confucianism,* 6.
63  ECCP, 671–672 (Fang Chao-ying).

scholars since the Song period, which was an inspiration to Tang Bin's own *Luoxue bian* 洛學編 (*Compilation of Luo Learning*) on the northern Henan school.[64] Following the Manchu conquest, initial anti-Manchu sentiment led to attacks on the Wang Yangming School of late Ming, blaming that school's focus on inner self-cultivation for neglect of the realm of politics and consequent fall of the Ming. But anti-Manchu feeling quickly gave way to attempts to reconcile Cheng-Zhu emphasis on moral nature with that of Wang Yangming thought on heart/mind through textual studies of the Classics that would lead to moral cultivation of self and society.[65] Although Sun Qifeng compiled his *Lixue zongzhuan* to establish the correct transmission to Wang Yangming from the Northern Song masters, throughout his scholarly and official career, Tang Bin tried to reconcile the Wang Yangming and Zhu Xi traditions.[66]

Teaching at Songyang Academy during the late 17th century likewise mirrored the trend toward reconciling Cheng-Zhu and Wang Yangming thought, but inclined toward the Cheng-Zhu part of the equation. In his 1683 preface to the *Songyang shuyuan zhi*, Dou Keqin reflects this perspective:

> Learning lies in the human heart/mind, penetrating through from the past to the present. From the Son of Heaven to the people, all have the duty [to seek] ultimate knowledge through the investigation of things, sincerity of intention, rectification of the heart/mind, cultivation of the self, managing the family, ordering the state, and pacifying all under Heaven.[67]

The 1682 preface by Guo Wenhua 郭文華 (1652 *jinshi*), similarly states: "My colleague [*nianyou* 年友] Geng Yi'an 逸庵 [Jie] proclaims and clarifies the Learning of the Way [*daoxue* 道學] [...so that scholars] can obtain and grasp the human heart/mind and customs of hundreds and thousands of years."[68] The third preface (also 1682) by Jiao Qinchong 焦欽寵 (?–?) relates the educational mission of Songyang Academy to the compilation of its record: "Those who

---

64   ECCP, 672.
65   Chow, "The Development of Sung Learning in Ch'ing Thought," 61; Ng, *Cheng-Zhu Confucianism*, 6–8.
66   Willard J. Peterson, "Chapter 11: Arguments over Learning Based on Intuitive Knowing in Early Ch'ing," in *Cambridge History of China*, Vol.9, Part 2, ed. Willard J. Peterson (2016), 472–474; Peterson, "Chapter 13: Dominating Learning from Above," 594.
67   SYSYZ, first preface, 1.
68   SYSYZ, second preface, 2. I cannot identify Guo Wenhua other than by his own statement that he was a degree holder (also *niandi* 年弟) in the same year as Geng Jie.

read this record in the future will be enlightened as to the source of the human heart/mind."[69]

Much of the discussion in Tang Bin's inscription concerns the textual roots of Cheng-Zhu learning in the Great Learning and the Doctrine of the Mean; and he praises Geng Jie as one who "can be said to have obtained the orthodox purpose of Cheng and Zhu."[70] An inscription by Lin Yaoying on lecturing at the academy describes the revival under Ye Feng in 1651, explicitly noting the shift from sacrificing to the fourteen Song era intendants of Extending Prosperity Palace to the current (in Lin's own time) rebuilding of the hall for sacrifices only to the Cheng brothers and Zhu Xi:

> In 1651 my friend Ye Feng built a three-column hall to sacrifice to the fourteen Song intendants of Extending Prosperity Palace. Today we have rebuilt this hall specially to sacrifice to the Two Cheng [brothers] and Zhu Xi, and along the sides have built school buildings, where scholars of purpose gather, to train there, and carry on discussions. This was the creation of Master Geng Yi'an [Jie].[71]

Lin goes on to describe Geng Jie's connection with Tang Bin and with Zhang Mu, identifying the intellectual relationship among these three with the flourishing of scholars in the Henan heartland. Zhang Xun's inscription on the academy similarly refers to the relationship between Tang Bin and Zhang Mu, but focuses as a matter of course on Geng Jie's successful promotion of Cheng-Zhu learning:

> [Geng Jie] established the *Furen huiyue* 輔仁會約 [Assembly Covenant for Assisting Virtue], gathering the students for classes the first three days of the month, holding a lecture discussion on the eighteenth day, in cold or heat, wind or rain, they did not cease, truly [it is] today's Goose Lake [Temple] or White Deer Grotto. [...] Reading his compilation *Lixue yaozhi* 理學要旨 (*Essential Principles of* Lixue), it is incisive and clear, entirely descended from the Masters Cheng [brothers] and Zhu. [...] [He] examines the distinctions between Heavenly Principle and human desire, such that scholars from the four directions clearly know the Song Confucians [*ru* 儒]. [...] Standing in the snow at their [Cheng brothers'] gate, following

---

69   SYSYZ, third preface, 2. Jiao was also an editor of the 1696 *Dengfeng xian zhi*, but I cannot identify him further.
70   SYSYZ, 2.85–86.
71   SYSYZ, 2.90–91. Geng Jie himself wrote an inscription on the dedicated sacrifices to the Cheng brothers and Zhu Xi (SYSYZ, 2.95–97).

this the true Confucians [*ru* 儒] emerge, and the unity of Guan-Min-Lianluo 關閩濂洛[72] is transmitted to the present.[73]

In his own inscription on the academy library, Geng Jie foregrounds the concept of heart/mind, relating it in turn to the *Changes, Odes, Documents, Rites, Music,* and *Spring and Autumn Annals*. For example, "The basis of knowing [how to] govern lies in the Way; the Way is rooted in heart/mind, and thus 'my heart/mind' has the *Documents*."[74] Finally, in his inscription on the Unified Way Shrine (Daotong ci 道統祠), Geng Jie again devotes substantial attention to heart/mind in relation to the Way:

> Now the manifold sages transmit a single Way, and the manifold sages transmit a single heart/mind. The heart/mind of Yao, Yu, and the Duke of Zhou, is just the heart/mind of Shun, Tang, Wen, and Wu. The heart/mind of Shun, Tang, Wen, and Wu is just the heart/mind of Confucius. The heart/mind of Confucius is just the heart/mind of Yan, Zeng, Si, Meng, Zhou, Cheng, Zhang, and Zhu. What is heart/mind? It is reverence [*jing* 敬] and that is all.[75]

In his inscription on a visit to Songyang Academy at the invitation of Geng Jie, Ran Jinzu focuses less on intellectual tradition and more on the physical setting of the academy, including the buildings as well as the landscape (see ills. 13.3 and 13.4), beginning with the pair of giant cypresses:

> Without looking around carefully, I hastened to visit the Hall of Great Completion (Dacheng dian 大成殿) to kneel in front of the sages. Turning to the left, I reverently bowed at the shrine to the Two Cheng [brothers] and Zhu Xi, and passed the Lecture Hall to reach the Library. I took a rest and looked around, quietly observing the porticos and corridors; at

---

72  That is, the geographical identifiers for the intellectual traditions associated with Zhou Dunyi (Lian[xi]), Zhang Zai (Guan[zhong]), the Cheng brothers (Luo[yang]), and Zhu Xi (Min[zhong]).
73  SYSYZ, 2.93–94. For the *Furen huiyue*, see SYSYZ, 2.142–143; see also Deng Hongbo (ed.), *Zhongguo shuyuan xuegui jicheng* (Collected Regulations of Chinese Academies) (Shanghai: Zhongxi shuju, 2011), 894–895; for related documents, see 895–898. The phrase *furen* is from the *Analects*, referring to the association with friends as a way of cultivating humaneness: "曾子曰： '君子以文會友，以友輔仁.'" There are also other documents concerning the academic mission, school regulations and schedule in SYSYZ and in Geng Jie's collected works.
74  SYSYZ, 2.101.
75  SYSYZ, 2.109.

the side of the Library, there were two dormitories, facing east and west, called Three Benefits and Four Prohibitions. To the west of the Lecture Hall, side by side with the Lecture Hall but facing south, was the Various Worthies Shrine. At the side of the Hall of Great Completion, to the left and facing south was the Assisting with Humaneness Residence (Furen ju 輔仁居), and to the right and facing south was the Beautiful Pools Hall (Lize tang 麗澤堂).[76] Within the gate facing east and west were two dormitories, called Reverent Intention and Erudition/Essentialism. Beautiful Pools Hall stood between the two cypresses; in front was the smaller one and behind was the larger one. [...] There was a crape myrtle at the gate as high as a person's shoulder with a circumference of at least two feet.[77]

Ran Jinzu's account provides a lively visual and interactive record of the reconstructed academy in the late 17th century.

Accomplishing the intellectual and educational mission of the academy, of course, depended on obtaining the necessary resources to support teachers and students as well as to erect buildings and maintain them. Beginning with the land allotted by Wu Ziyun, a series of prefects, regional officials (such as provincial education commissioners), and local scholars either officially allocated land or privately donated it to support teachers, students, and rites performed at the academy. According to the 1787 *Dengfeng xian zhi,* allocations of land during the Kangxi reign totaled more than 1420 *mu,* reflecting a not insubstantial amount of support for the academy.[78] However, the *Songyang shuyuan zhi* notes that resources were inadequate and so the academy's expenses were subsidized by Geng Jie, who donated two *qing* 頃 (200 *mu*) for school land.[79] During this time, many illustrious scholars came to Songyang Academy, and

---

76   This name refers to one of the eight trigrams, explained as referring to the mutual discussions and learning among friends practiced by "exemplary persons" (*junzi* 君子) and associated with symmetrical pools of water. See Luo Zhufeng (ed.), *Hanyu dacidian* (Shanghai: Hanyu dacidian chubanshe, 1995), v. 12, p. 1299.
77   SYSYZ, 2.107–108.
78   Lu and Hong, *Dengfeng xian zhi,* 17.11b–12a.
79   Gong, *Songyang shuyuan,* 11–12. According to SYSYZ, 1.27, in 1661 Geng Jie established (置) two *qing* 頃 of school land. Geng is described here as "local gentry" 邑紳 (yishen), so the inference is that he donated this land to support the academy as a personal contribution because he was not acting in an official capacity. The amounts listed in this source through Kangxi 40 (1701) total 1,170 *mu,* considerably less than the amount totaled from the allocations listed in the 1787 *Dengfeng xian zhi.* Since Geng Jie is the compiler of the SYSYZ, we cannot discount an element of self-promotion in his making the point about the inadequacy of resources and therefore enhancing the importance of his donation.

many successful men came from the ranks of those who studied there; in 1711, for example, the Kaifeng *juren* included five from Songyang.[80]

By the early Qianlong period, however, neglect had taken its toll on academy buildings, and in 1739 the Dengfeng county magistrate allotted a further 123 *mu* to support their repair and to provide income for annual maintenance.[81] With this official support, a member of the local gentry took responsibility for the rebuilding of the Unified Way Shrine, Library, Lecture Hall, Various Worthies Shrine, and the Main Gate.[82] Copies of the Qing government's newly issued *Five Classics*, the *Kangxi Dictionary* (*Kangxi zidian* 康熙字典), the *Complete Writings of Zhu Xi* (*Zhuzi Daquan* 朱子大全), and other works of Cheng-Zhu thought were added to the Library.[83] Songyang Academy was thus restored to the flourishing state of its heyday in the Northern Song.[84]

Like the restoration of Songyang Academy, recovering and rebuilding on foundations from the past, the custom of seeking antiquities had been a preoccupation of scholars since the Northern Song. For example, a late 17th-century epigraphical collection recounts the 1607–1612 Dengfeng county magistrate and *juren* Fu Mei 傅梅's (?–1645) description of his experiences searching for the past on Mount Song: "I frequently traversed the foothills of Mount Song, and in the midst of the overgrown tiles and stones, I saw pieces of stone tablets left by men in the past. When they were rubbed clean, it was possible to understand the text."[85] By the mid-18th century, searching for steles was a leisure pursuit of painters that often related to the subject matter of their paintings. Late in his career, the Qing painter Huang Yi 黃易 (1744–1802), painted an album entitled *Investigating Steles in Mount Song and Luoyang* (*Song Luo fangbei tu* 嵩洛訪碑圖), evoking his scholarly activity searching for steles.[86] In the

---

80  Gong, *Songyang shuyuan*, 12.
81  Lu and Hong, *Dengfeng xian zhi*, 17.12a.
82  Gong, *Songyang shuyuan*, 12.
83  Lu and Hong, *Dengfeng xian zhi*, 17.12a.
84  Gong, *Songyang shuyuan*, 12.
85  Ye Feng (ed.), "Songyang shike jiji (Collection of Stone Inscriptions from Songyang)," in SKQSCM ed., v. 684, *xia*, 39a. For Fu Mei, see *Mingren*, 680; *Dengfeng xian zhi*, 6.5b.
86  Yang Chia-Ling, "Power, Identity and Antiquarian Approaches in Modern Chinese Art," *Journal of Art Historiography* 10 (June 2014), 9. Nearly a century later, in 1891, Wu Dacheng (1835–1902), a leading official at the late Qing court and amateur literatus artist and collector of rubbings and antiquities, viewed and copied the original set of 24 paintings that made up Huang Yi's album (Yang, op. cit., 15). Wu Dacheng had earlier made his own painting of the subject, *Investigating Steles at Mount Song*, ca. 1866–1872 (Yang, op. cit., 12). See also Lillian Lan-Ying Tseng, "Retrieving the Past, Inventing the Memorable: Huang Yi's Visit to the Song-Luo Monuments," in *Monuments and Memory, Made and Unmade*, ed. Robert S. Nelson and Margaret Olin (Chicago and London: University of Chicago Press, 2003), 37–58.

travel diary where he recorded his journeys in search of steles, he gives a physical description of Songyang Academy at the time:

> Thirteenth day [of the third month, 1796], windy. I decided to climb in the bamboo sedan chair and go five *li* out from the city wall to Songyang Academy, wanting to see the Tang Tianbao [era] stele outside the gate there. It was as tall as a residence wall, and the carving on it was clear and skilled. Xu Jihai [Hao] had written it strongly and clearly in [eight]-piece [*fen*] style. I preserved [made a rubbing of] the original small stone tablet title, and ordered the workmen to add [by making a rubbing of] the entire tablet side, to make clear the list of men carved on the backside. [...] Entering the academy, I saw the Great General Cypress with a girth so large that seven men could surround it. The leaves were lush and full, and on the south side the wood was pure white. I wrote my name in a single line on it in order to record this delightful visit. The Assistant General Cypress was large enough for three men to surround it, and it was also luxuriant. Visible at the heart of the enclosure was a crape myrtle tree that was elegantly refined. Along the gallery were three stone [tablets] of Wenlu gong 文潞公 [Wen Yanbo 文彥博, 1006–1097; 1027 *jinshi*], Zhang Gao 張杲, and Wang Zhi 王邳.[87] Along the east wall was the 1099 Song version of the Zhenwu Scripture 真武經 written in small character script, with extreme skill. Formerly there was a stone pillar under the cypress with the names of Song men inscribed on it, but it is no longer there.
>
> Going three or four *li* farther I arrived at Chongfu gong 崇福宮. At the rear of the hall are images of the Three Purities [Daoist divinities], along with images of Heavenly Master Wang 王天君 and Zhao Yuantan 趙元坦, which are extremely awesome. These were made during the Song and Jin periods.[88]

The foreword to Huang Yi's *Song Luo fangbei tu* fills in some additional details about what Huang saw and described. Qing epigraphical records from the late

---

87   An eminent political figure and associate of of Sima Guang in Luoyang, it is not surprising that there was a tablet for Wen Yanbo at this site (see *Songren* 1.43–4). In fact, he seemed to be particularly revered here (see also below). But both Zhang Gao and Wang Zhi are difficult to identify with any certainty, even to the extent of dating them in the Tang, Song, Ming, or Qing dynasties.

88   Huang Yi, "Song Luo fangbei riji (Diary of Investigating Steles at Mount Song and Luoyang)," in *Shike shiliao xinbian*, coll. 3, v. 29, 598 (4a–b); see also Weng Fanggang, "Ti Song Luo fangbei tu (On the Album Investigating Steles in Mount Song and Luoyang)," in *Shike shiliao xinbian*, coll. 3, v. 29, 591 (2b).

18th century (though before Huang's visit here) describe details of Northern Song names inscribed on an eight-sided stone pillar at Songyang Academy (called here Songyang Palace), and state that, while there used to be several pillars, only one still existed.[89] This same source corroborates to a degree Huang Yi's description of the Zhenwu Scripture, though it states that it is inscribed on the west wall of the Lecture Hall at the academy—evidently that is confused with the east wall of the gallery by our observer.[90]

After Huang Yi's visit, it was not until 1830 that the Dengfeng county magistrate even tried to restore Songyang Academy, without success. However, it was finally restored in 1878–1881, and an 1881 inscription commemorating this restoration identifies the local gentry Geng Jianhou 耿健侯 (?–?, a descendant of Geng Jie?) as one of the managers of this effort.[91] In 1894 the Dengfeng county magistrate, along with Supervisor of Labor (?) 監工 Geng Baoqin 耿葆欽 (?–?, also a descendant of Geng Jie?) used donated funds (1,500 方文) to further rebuild the academy.[92]

## 6   Songyang Academy: Reform, Revolution, Restoration

Efforts to create a modern school system in the early 20th century brought about a different kind of renewal for Songyang Academy: in 1905 it was transformed into Songyang High School and Elementary School, with three teachers and 39 students, and an annual income of 1,037 *liang* of silver. A teacher training program was also set up here.[93] But knowledge of, and interest in, this historic site remained. In 1918 the Japanese archaeologist and architectural historian Sekino Tadashi 關野貞 (1868–1935) visited Mount Song and the site of Songyang Academy in the course of his tour of cultural and historical relics in the expanding Japanese empire. On June 18, he recorded this in his diary:

> In the morning, I went to greet the [Dengfeng] county magistrate. In the afternoon, with a minor clerk as a guide and accompanied by two soldiers, I visited Songyang Abbey to the northeast of the city wall. Situated in the southern foothills of Mount Song, from the Song on it developed as

---

89   Lu and Hong, *Dengfeng xian zhi*, 30.46b–47a.
90   Lu and Hong, *Dengfeng xian zhi*, 30.48a–b.
91   Gong, *Songyang shuyuan*, 12. The inscription is found on a stele in the collection held by Songyang Academy.
92   Gong, *Songyang shuyuan*, 12. I have been unable to find biographical information about either of these individuals surnamed Geng.
93   Gong, *Songyang shuyuan*, 12–13.

an academy. Now it has become a high school and elementary school. In the courtyard there are the Three Generals Cypresses enfeoffed in the Han. The largest is 40 *chi* 尺 [about 40 feet] around, and it is about the height of a 10-*jian* 間 house, a giant cypress unlike any I have ever seen before. The other two cypresses are comparatively small. There is still a stone stele in front of Songyang Abbey, about the same size as the Tianbao era "*Xuanzong yuzhu xiaojing bei* 玄宗禦注孝經碑 (Stele of Xuanzong's Imperial Annotations on the Classic of Filial Piety)," a product of the early Tang.[94]

Sekino's observations were brief, as his interests lay much more in Buddhist sites and monuments, of which there were many at Mount Song; but his description of Songyang Abbey at this critical time provides a record of what remained despite its transformation into a modern school.[95]

In 1936, on the eve of the Japanese invasion of China, the Belgian botanist Joseph Hers (1884–1965) published an article based on his visit to Mount Song, where he also observed Songyang Abbey's conversion into a school and noted a "fine specimen" of silver bark pine in the courtyard along with the Three Generals cypress trees. He describes many stone tablets and images surrounding the trees and celebrating their antiquity and merits, but expresses doubts about the authenticity of two of them: "One of these trees is apparently genuine. It has a circumference of thirty-eight feet at the base. The other two are much smaller, and are substitutes which were planted at a later date to take the place of two dead ones."[96] Another visitor to Songyang in 1936 was Generalissimo Chiang Kai-shek, who celebrated his 50th birthday in Luoyang and decided to visit Mount Song to see the cultural sites. When he saw the former

---

94 Sekino Tadashi kenkyūkai (ed.), *Sekino Tadashi nikki* (The Diary of Sekino Tadashi) (Tokyo: Chūō koron bijutsu shuppan, 2009), "Yusai nikki" (Diary of a Journey West), 323. Sekino refers to three cypresses, as do later visitors, but we know that there were only two remaining at the end of the Ming so another cypress must have been planted during the Qing. Later commentators also mention that two of the three seem younger than the other (see Hers's comments below), or, in the case of Liu Dunzhen (see below), he mentions only the large one. Today there are two.

95 The value of Sekino's visit was enhanced for his Chinese hosts when, in 2011, a collaboration between the Luoyang Longmen International Travel Company and Tokyo University's East Asian Research Center Director Haneda Tadashi and professors there brought about the gift of four photos taken by Sekino to Songyang Academy. These photos provided important evidence to track the history of the academy's relics that were later destroyed. See Gong, *Songyang shuyuan*, 273–275.

96 Joseph Hers, "The Sacred Mountains of China: Sung Shan the Deserted (Honan)," *The China Journal/Zhongguo kexue meishu zazhi* 24 (1936): 81.

academy site, he wanted to place a troop training facility here. Because that would require a source of water sufficient for a thousand men, he ordered the Henan authorities to build a well. In 1937 men came to do this, but the planned occupation by Nationalist soldiers evidently never took place.[97]

Not only foreigners engaged in documenting the monuments and environment of Mount Song in the early 20th century. In 1937 the Chinese architectural historian Liu Dunzhen 劉敦楨 (1897–1968), who received his professional education as an architect and engineer in Japan (1913–1922), published a report on his investigation of ancient architecture in the northern part of Henan.[98] This report included a brief description of what he refers to as "Songyang Academy":

> Songyang Academy is five *li* to the northwest [?] of the county wall. The original name was Songyang Temple [寺]. It was built in the eighth year of the Northern Wei Taihe era [484]. During Sui Daye era [605–618], it was changed to a Daoist hall. The Tang named it Songyang Abbey [觀]. During Gaozong Yongchun era [682–683], Fengtian Palace 奉天宮 was built nearby. During the Latter Zhou of the Five Dynasties era, the Daoists began to be expelled, and it again became a "place of chanting and singing" [Confucian school]. During the Northern Song, it was first called Taishi 太室 Academy, and then changed to what it is today. At that time, together with White Deer, Suiyang, and Yuelu, they were called the "Four Great Academies." During the Jin and Yuan, the area was devastated. During the Ming, it was somewhat restored, but again subjected to war and chaos and destroyed. During the Qing Kangxi era (1662–1722) it was rebuilt by Lu Xu 陸續 [?]. At the end of the Qing, it was turned into a school. After the founding of the Republic, the Nationalist Army was based here, fought a series of campaigns, and the buildings were completely destroyed. Inside is the Great General Cypress enfeoffed by Han Wudi. Five trunks are wound together, and the size is several arm spans. It is certainly not a recent thing! On the south side of the cypress is an octagonal stone pillar, with many names of Song men inscribed on it.[99]

---

97 Gong, *Songyang shuyuan*, 154.
98 For background on Liu Dunzhen and his contributions to the development of architectural history in China, see Tian Yang, "The Making of an Architectural Historian: Liu Dunzhen and the Knowledge of Traditional Chinese Architecture, 1917–1937" (MA Thesis, Department of Architecture, National University of Singapore, 2003).
99 Liu Dunzhen, "Henan sheng beibu gu jianzhu diaocha ji (Report on an Investigation of Ancient Architecture in Northern Henan Province)," *Zhongguo yingzao xueshe huikan* 6.4 (June, 1937): 94.

Liu goes on to describe the Great Tang Stele to the southwest of the academy, and in the next section, he relates the history of Extending Prosperity Palace. Photographs accompany the text, including one of the Great Tang Stele and the former foundation of Extending Prosperity Palace, but nothing of the former academy site.

By the 1940s, as the Japanese invasion was underway, the site of Songyang Academy became a middle school, and during the Civil War and early post-1949 period it was used as a cadre training site and meeting center. In 1958–1962 it became the Kaifeng Teacher Training Institute, and temporarily during this period (1958–1959), it was the Kaifeng Party School. The prominent Marxist philosopher Ai Siqi 艾思奇 (1910–1966) lectured and convened Marxist study sessions there.[100]

During the Cultural Revolution, some of the buildings became housing for local people, while some were used as a dining hall for the local production brigade, as well as a meeting place for the PLA. In the 1970s the academy site was used for local teacher training, and finally, under the influence of the Cultural Revolution, as a worker-peasant-soldier school. In 1980, a branch of the Kaifeng Teacher Training Institute was established here; and in 1983, when the school was moved, the east part of the site came under the administration of the Kaifeng Cultural Relics Preservation Office. By the mid-1990s (1996–1998), management of the entire academy site was transferred to this office.[101]

Attempts to conserve Songyang Academy as a historic site, however, began as early as 1960, when Songyang Academy was declared a "conservation domain" (*baohu fanwei* 保護範圍) by the Dengfeng People's Committee. This meant that boundaries were established that restricted farming to zones that did not encroach on academy property. These boundaries were expanded in 1965. But it was in the 1980s that conservation efforts really began in earnest. Provincial authorities allocated 360,000 *yuan* to the Dengfeng County Cultural Relics Preservation Office and the Mount Song Scenic Landscape Management Agency for a five-year plan to relocate the Dengfeng teacher training school and move people's residences away from the front of the academy, as well as to restore academy buildings. In 1984 the National Cultural Relics Bureau allotted over 30,000 *yuan* for the Henan Provincial Ancient Architecture Conservation Research Office and the county Cultural Relics Conservation Office to jointly restore the Great Tang stele. Their work on this project earned them third prize

---

100  Gong, *Songyang shuyuan*, 239. For Ai's earlier influence on Marxist philosophy and relationship with the thought of Mao Zedong, see Nick Knight, "The Role of Philosopher to the Chinese Communist Movement: Ai Siqi, Mao Zedong and Marxist Philosophy," *Asian Studies Review* 26, no. 4 (Dec. 2002): 419–445.
101  Gong, *Songyang shuyuan*, 13–15.

in the Henan Provincial Cultural Office 1987–1988 Science and Technology Advancement competition. During the Cultural Revolution, this remarkable and very valuable stele came very close to being destroyed by the Red Guards. Gong Xi 宮熙 (1928–2001, perhaps related to the current director, Gong Songtao 宮嵩濤?) had worked for the Dengfeng Cultural Relics Bureau and found out that the Great Tang Stele was to be blown up. He begged the Red Guards not to do this, citing its historical, artistic, and scientific value, but to no avail. Only when he pleaded with a local unit of the PLA to prevent it was it possible to stop the Red Guards from destroying it.[102] In 1988 the Henan Provincial Cultural Relics Bureau allotted a further 120,000 *yuan* for the same prize-winning team to restore the Library, the Guanshan Hall, and the Esteeming Confucians Shrine, as well as to carry out a painting project. In the same year, the Dengfeng County Songyang Academy Cultural Relics Management Office was set up and attached to the County Cultural Relics Bureau. By the end of 1989, Songyang Academy had been named a "Cultural Conservation Unit and Domain" at both the national and provincial levels.[103]

The provincial, and especially national, level of recognition garnered Songyang Academy attention from Greater China when Hong Kong entrepreneur He Yaoguang 何耀光 (1907–2006) came to Songyang in 1991 and donated 210,000 *yuan* to repair the pond bridge. Over the next decade, the Dengfeng Municipal Cultural Relics Bureau invested substantial amounts of money in rebuilding projects at the academy, including structures commemorating the Qianlong 乾隆 emperor's (r. 1735–1796) visit (the temporary residence and the stele pavilion). At this point, the preservation project was essentially completed, preserving the Qing era academy, both buildings and the surrounding environment. In 1999, Songyang Academy was named a provincial-level "Patriotic Education Site." A decade later, in 2009, a "Dengfeng Songyang Academy Conservation Plan" was approved by the Henan Provincial Cultural Relics Management Bureau that provided for collaboration with Qinghua University's Architectural Design Research Institute and the Beijing-Qinghua Urban Planning Design Research Institute. The Dengfeng Municipal Cultural Relics Management Bureau had collected for display at Songyang Academy steles from the Northern Dynasties, Tang, Song, and later, numbering nearly 100, along with 200 other historical items such as maps, photos, etc., thus making this an important tourist attraction. In order to continue the academy tradition of "gathering and lecturing" (*huijiang* 會講), the Dengfeng Municipal Government, Qinghua University, Shaolin Temple, the Henan Tourism Bureau, Shandong Satellite TV, Henan's

---

102  Gong, *Songyang shuyuan*, 279–280.
103  Gong, *Songyang shuyuan*, 18.

*Dahe bao* 大河报 newspaper, the Zhengzhou branch of the Bank of China, and other agencies, have invited famous writers, scholars, and journalists, as well as professors from Renmin University, musicians, martial arts experts, Buddhists, Daoists, and so on. Groups of students regularly visit to participate in cultural activities at the academy, and in 2006, the academy was named a fourth-level national youth education site. As of 2014, Songyang Academy annually hosts domestic and foreign visitors in the number of 360,000, and takes in a total of 3,500,000 *yuan* in income from tourism.[104]

Two other developments in the history of Songyang Academy in the 21st century merit notice: the partnership between the academy and Zhengzhou University that was inaugurated in 1999 and became increasingly important over the next decade; and the assignment of UNESCO World Heritage Site status to Songyang Academy in 2010 as part of the "Historic Monuments of Dengfeng in the Centre of Heaven and Earth" (see illustration 13.4). The allocation of funds in 2007 by Zhengzhou University, a major university in the provincial capital, to support rebuilding at Songyang Academy marked the adoption of the academy as a Confucian classroom for the university's new National Studies curriculum.[105] Collaboration between the university and the academy was proudly displayed in the posting of both names together (written in the calligraphy of the provincial Party Secretary Xu Guangchun 徐光春, much as rulers in the past had done to demonstrate their approval) on the main entrance gate to the university: Songyang Academy–Zhengzhou University.[106] This partnership promoted recognition of both institutions at the provincial, regional, and conceivably even national levels—national because of Zhengzhou University's having been designated as one of the "211 ("100 for the 21st century") universities, an elite tier of higher education institutions.[107] Global recognition came in 2010 with Songyang Academy's incorporation into the sites associated with the Chinese government's successful application to UNESCO for inscription of the Mount Song complex of historic sites on to the World Heritage Site list.

---

104   Gong, *Songyang shuyuan*, 20.
105   See my "The 'Spirit' of Confucian Education in Contemporary China: Songyang Academy and Zhengzhou University," *Modern China* 44.3 (2018): 313–342.
106   *Zhengzhou wanbao*, 3 September 2009. <http://news.sina.com.cn/c/2009-09-03/082316 233745s.shtml>.
107   The continuing importance of Songyang Academy for Zhengzhou University is reflected in a recent article on the planning process. See Li Weiying, "Zhengzhou daxue Songyang shuyuan zongti guihua sheji fenxi (Analysis of the Overall Design Plan of Zhengzhou University's Songyang Academy)," *Zhengzhou daxue xuebao (gongxue ban)* 36, no. 2 (March 2015): 71–74.

422　LINDA WALTON

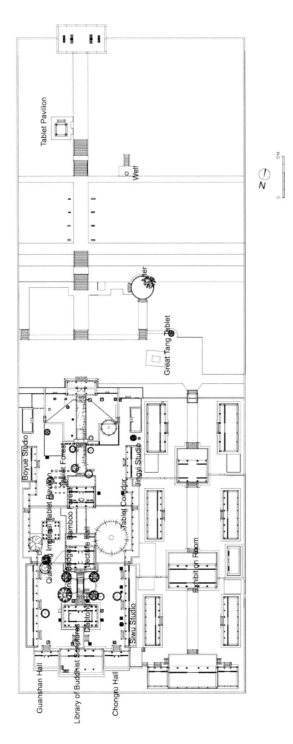

ILLUSTRATION 13.4 Diagram of Songyang Academy from UNESCO submission.
SOURCE: P. 349 AT <HTTP://WHC.UNESCO.ORG/EN/LIST/1395/DOCUMENTS/>.

## 7   Transformations of Songyang Academy: Perspectives from Sources and on Meaning

In considering how our sources convey the history of Songyang Academy from its origins to the present, we might begin with the most recent, and Chinese official, source: the documents submitted to UNESCO as part of the Chinese government's application for the "Historic Monuments of Mount Songshan."[108] Referred to in these documents as "Songyang Academy of Classical Learning," it is one of eight designated cultural heritage sites that include three Buddhist temples and complexes along with a Yuan-era observatory and Han-era stone watchtowers. The most important cultural relic associated with Songyang Academy is the Great Tang Stele, along with the historic steles embedded in the gallery walls of the academy. Because the most ancient of the academy buildings are relatively recent, from the Qing, they do not stand out as important cultural relics. However, the General and Assistant General Cypresses are regarded as one of the most important treasures of the academy—not human-made, but certainly cultivated, preserved, and appreciated by people. The extensive documentation required by UNESCO and submitted on behalf of the (ultimately) successful application naturally highlights the cultural and historical significance of this cluster of sites as both a uniquely Chinese contribution to world heritage and a world-class set of monuments that share features with other sites around the globe. The English-language presentation of the required documentation by its very nature is aimed at a particular audience with a very specific purpose.

A far more detailed and recent account of the history of Songyang Academy alone is found in two editions of *Songyang shuyuan* (2001 and 2014) by Gong Songtao, Deputy Director of the Dengfeng Municipal Administration of Cultural Heritage (the English translation of 登封縣文物局 used for the UNESCO report, where he is listed as one of the authors responsible for the documentation). The two editions, not surprisingly, have much in common, and are distinguished primarily by the addition of information in the 2014 edition surrounding the successful application and inscription of the academy, along with the other "Historic Monuments of Mount Songshan" in 2010. The 2001 edition is shorter (166 pages) than that of 2014 (268 pages), which obviously goes into greater detail in many regards and is organized both chronologically

---

108   For documentation submitted and other information, see <http://whc.unesco.org/en/list/1305>.

and topically.[109] As might be expected, the 2014 edition has a far more self-conscious framework of cultural heritage preservation ideology, paying explicit attention to this because of the 2010 World Heritage Site inscription.

These two recent histories of Songyang Academy can be viewed as modern versions of the Qing era *Record of Songyang Academy* 嵩陽書院志, one of the extant academy records that share features with local gazetteers (*difang zhi* 地方誌) as well as with "mountain records" (*shanzhi* 山志).[110] As noted in the modern preface, this academy record is heavily Qing in content, with little about either the foundational period of the Northern Song or the brief period of reconstruction during the Ming. The editor/annotator also notes that the collected works of Geng Jie, the author of the academy record, contain items that relate to the academy that are not in the academy record; and we know that the text of the *Songyang shuyuan zhi* that has come down to us is not the original text because it contains material on events that occurred after Geng Jie's lifetime.[111] There are three original prefaces, two dated 1682, and one, 1683.[112] In the "General Principles" (*fanlie* 凡列) that follow the prefaces and precede the two *juan* record, Geng Jie explicitly identifies the model for this work as the *White Deer Academy Record* (*Bailu shuyuan zhi* 白鹿書院志).[113] But he also laments the scarcity of sources:

> The academy was founded in the Song, as a place where the two Cheng masters were active. How could it lack "records on metal and stone" that can be selected and compiled as sources? But the eras are distant and the years have disappeared, the stone tablets are broken and completely overgrown. Alas! [Because] those in the future who look at today will also use today to look at the past, [we must] carefully select those poems and

---

109   Although, as noted above (n. 7), the 2001 edition of this history of the academy does incorporate far more detail about the steles as historical source materials.
110   SYSYZ, cited above.
111   SYSYZ, editor's preface, 3. For collected works of Geng Jie, see Liang Yuwei et al. (eds.), *Jingshu tang wenji* (Collected Documents from the Hall of Reverence and Tolerance), Gudu Zhengzhou wenhua congshu bian wei hui (Zhengzhou: Zhongzhou guji chubanshe, 2005).
112   Concerning the dating of this text, in recent unpublished work, Zhao Wei 赵伟, a doctoral student of Professor Deng Hongbo 邓洪波, has investigated the textual history of the *Songyang shuyuan zhi* and offers convincing evidence for dating its completion to 1690 and revision to 1701.
113   For a modern edition of this, see Jiang Yasha et al. (eds.), *Zhongguo shuyuan zhi*, vol. 9.

literature that will benefit the preservation of upright learning, to enable those in the future to investigate it.[114]

Following the standard illustrations, landscape, historical changes, rites, library collection, and landholding sections, the remainder (close to two-thirds) of the first *juan* is poetry.[115]

The narrative that positions Songyang Academy as one of the Four Great Academies of the Northern Song relies first of all on its association with the Cheng brothers, who were said to have taught there.[116] However, no extant Song sources specifically identify Songyang Academy as the place where they taught.[117] The *locus classicus* for the well-known classical quote (*diangu* 典故) "standing in the snow at the gate of the Cheng" 程門立雪 (*Chengmen lixue*), frequently cited in reference to Songyang Academy,[118] is the dynastic history biography of Yang Shi.[119] This tells the story of Yang Shi and You Zuo 遊酢 (1053–1123) going to learn from Cheng Yi, who was meditating, and the two disciples waited outside for him so long that the snow piled up around them a meter high. Thus the phrase "standing in the snow at the gate of the Cheng" has

---

114 SYSYZ, 1.
115 Zhao Wei's unpublished research, cited above, also addresses the issue of the unusual (for an academy gazetteer) prominence of literary content, especially poetry, with regard to both the context of early Qing Neo-Confucian thought and the model of the White Deer Academy Record (*Bailu shuyuan zhi* 白鹿書院志). He suggests that, unlike the disregard for literature characteristic of its model, the *Songyang shuyuan zhi* elevated the position of poetry as a legitimate Neo-Confucian approach to apprehending the Way (Dao 道).
116 Virtually all references to Songyang Academy cite the presence of the Cheng brothers at the academy as the primary reason for the role of the academy in the spread of their teachings. See, for example, Gong, *Songyang* shuyuan, 7.
117 The biographies of Cheng Yi and Cheng Hao in Franke, *Song Biographies* (169–174 [Cheng Hao] and 174–170 [Cheng Yi]), both by Wing-tsit Chan, make no reference to Songyang Academy, nor does the biography of Yang Shi (pp. 1226–1230) by Julia Ching in the same work, although she does reference the famous snow incident (p. 1227) and dates it to around 1093, which accords with Yang Shi's *Songshi* biography, placing this incident around the time Yang Shi was 40 (1093). Wing-tsit Chan dates the incident to around 1082. The important point for our purposes here, however, is that there is no mention in any of these sources of Songyang Academy (this includes the *nianpu* of both Cheng Hao and Cheng Yi [Chi Shengchun, Zhu Xingshao (eds.), *Er Chengzi nianpu* (Chronological Biography of the Two Masters Cheng), in *Songren nianpu congkan*, vol. 4 (Chengdu: Sichuan daxue chubanshe, 2003), 2415–2702]). Nor is there any reference to Songyang Academy in the *Er Cheng yishu* compiled by Zhu Xi, or in either the *Er Cheng quanshu* or the *Er Cheng wenji* (<http://ctext.org>).
118 See for example, Gong, *Songyang shuyuan*, 96.
119 SS 428.12738–12743.

come to mean great respect for a teacher and his teachings.[120] However, the fact remains that there is no specific reference in Song sources to Songyang Academy as the place where the Cheng brothers taught, nor where the "Chengmen lixue" incident took place. While not absolutely definitive, more telling, perhaps, is the lack of a reference to Songyang Academy in the name index (under miscellaneous terms) to the *Song-Yuan xue'an* 宋元學案 (*Annals of Song and Yuan Schools of Thought*).[121] Many other academies are listed, but nowhere does Songyang Academy appear, and this raises the question—given the primary focus of this text on Neo-Confucian thought—of just how important a role Songyang Academy played as a setting for the Cheng brothers' teaching.

Extending Prosperity Palace (see above) has a far more conspicuous presence in the sources as a place where Northern Song officials out of favor—especially during the reform era of Wang Anshi—held sinecures as intendants or supervisors of that Daoist temple. Even before the time of Wang Anshi, Fan Zhongyan's 范仲淹 (989–1052; *jinshi* 1015) name was added to the roster of those said to have lectured at Songyang Academy.[122] It is plausible that Fan did in fact visit Songyang Academy when he was commissioned to bring a portrait of the emperor to be venerated at nearby Extending Prosperity Palace; but there is no reference to either event in Fan's major biographical sources.[123]

Many scholars during the Song joined the ranks of those appointed to sinecures as intendant of Extending Prosperity Palace. When it was first established during the reign of Zhenzong, it was regarded as an honorable appointment to represent the emperor because of the imperial association with it as the place where Zhenzong offered prayers for the good fortune of his reign and the empire. But after Zhenzong's reign, it became a place of retreat and withdrawal for political figures who were at odds with those in power at court. Probably the most famous of these was Sima Guang, who was appointed to the post of intendant of Extending Prosperity Palace in 1073 after he had refused to support

---

120  See Hangzhou daxue Zhongwen xi (ed.), *Gushu diangu cidian* (Nanchang: Jiangxi jiaoyu chubanshe, 1989), 462.
121  Kinugawa Tsuyoshi (ed.), *Sō-Gen gakuan – Sōgen gakuan hō-i: Jinmei jikō betsumei sakuin* (Index to Persons in the *Song Yuan xue'an and its Supplement*) (Kyoto: Kyoto daigaku jimbun kagaku kenkyūjo, 1974).
122  Gong, *Songyang shuyuan*, 47.
123  *Songren*, 11.1648–1652. See Lou Yao (comp.), *Fan Wenzheng gong nianpu* (Chronological Biography of Master Fan Wenzheng), in Siming Congshu ed., series 3, vol. 2. Even sources specific to Mount Song, the *Songshu* (6.8a) and *Shuo Song* (17.7b), both relate only the official visit to Extending Prosperity Palace and the fact that Fan, together with Ouyang Xiu and the poet Mei Yaochen 梅堯臣 (1002–1060), wrote poems about Mount Song.

the reforms of Wang Anshi and withdrawn from the capital to Luoyang.[124] This was the same time that he began to build his famous garden in Luoyang, the Garden of Solitary Pleasure 獨樂園 (Dule yuan). Sima Guang served in this post through 1085, until he returned to the court in Kaifeng after the death of Shenzong. Modern accounts of Songyang Academy claim that Sima Guang wrote a number of chapters of his *Great Mirror for Aid in History* there.[125] The location of Extending Prosperity Palace is close to Songyang Academy, although proximity alone is not sufficient evidence. However, a site at Songyang Academy today is regarded as the location of a retreat used by Sima Guang; it is identified by a barely legible phrase describing its association with Sima Guang by Jing Rizhen 景日昣 (1661–1733; 1691 *jinshi*) carved in stone there.[126]

Among other Northern Song prominent figures associated both with Sima Guang and with Songyang Academy, Wen Yanbo has left a legacy far larger than his actual connection with the academy would suggest.[127] Wen Yanbo served two emperors—Yingzong and Shenzong—as a senior military official, and eventually replaced his friend and colleague Sima Guang (after Sima Guang's death) as chief councillor. Throughout his career, he sided with Sima Guang and the anti-reformers, and in his later years resided in Luoyang, where he belonged to the group associated with Sima Guang known as the "Old Heroes Society" (*Qiying hui* 耆英會). In 1922 a stele was erected with an inscription to commemorate a visit Wen Yanbo made to Mount Song in 1060, when he inscribed his name at Songyang Academy and also wrote poems about Shaolin Temple and other sites on the mountain.[128] Like many other travelers to Mount Song, Wen Yanbo visited Songyang Academy and left his mark, but his association with it does not go beyond this. Unlike Sima Guang, Wen Yanbo never held a sinecure at Extending Prosperity Palace, nor did he spend extended periods at Mount Song because his official career was centered at the court in Kaifeng.

In the transition between Northern and Southern Song, Li Gang 李綱 (1083–1140; 1112 *jinshi*), an ardent irredentist who served as chief councillor under Huizong and Qinzong, was appointed intendant at Extending Prosperity Palace in 1132 and said to have lectured for over eight years at Songyang Academy until his death in 1140.[129] The famous disciple of the Cheng brothers, Yang Shi

---

124 Ma Luan, and Gu Donggao (eds.), *Sima Guang nianpu* (Chronological Biography of Sima Guang) (Beijing: Zhonghua shuju, 1990), 171–172. A search of *Sima Guang wenji* at <http://ctext.org> also turns up no references to either Songyang Academy or even Songyang.
125 For example, Gong, *Songyang shuyuan*, 8.
126 Gong, *Songyang shuyuan*, 126–127.
127 See n. 87 above.
128 Gong, *Songyang shuyuan*, 178–179.
129 For basic biography, see *Songren* 11.901–903; Gong, *Songyang shuyuan*, 231.

(see above), failed in his official capacity to defend against the invading Jurchen in 1124, and asked to retire, taking a sinecure as intendant of Extending Prosperity Palace.[130] In 1125–1126, he left Kaifeng for Mount Song, where he prayed at Extending Prosperity Palace and reportedly lectured at Songyang Academy nearby.[131] He was also said to have influenced resistance to the Jurchen among the local people, but as this also failed, he fled southward toward his Fujian home in 1127, already 74 years old. Yang Shi's departure marked not only the end of the Northern Song but also the decline of lecturing activities at Songyang Academy.

During the Southern Song, the biographies of a number of officials record their sinecures as intendants of Extending Prosperity Palace. Zhu Xi, of course, as befits the ambivalence with which he regarded official appointments, served as intendant of Expending Prosperity Palace, among other sinecures, all of which afforded him time to work on his writing and teaching.[132] But there is no mention of any association with Songyang Academy in the sources, as obvious a connection as this would have been to the teachings of the Cheng brothers. More puzzling—unless the sinecure at Extending Prosperity Temple was simply a title with no reality, which it well may have been—is the fact that, after the Jurchen conquest (which included the Mount Song area), appointments to a sinecure at Extending Prosperity Palace, such as that of Zhu Xi, continued to be made (or at least recorded). The *Song shi* biography of Ni Si 倪思 (1147–1220; 1166 *jinshi*), for example, states that he was named to this post.[133] A modern account claims that he also taught at Songyang Academy, although I can find no direct evidence of this.[134] Because there are no other records of the academy for this time, all we have are the fragmentary accounts of these appointments, which remain a mystery if they are—as they seem—Southern Song posts and not Jin, which controlled the Mount Song area. Less perplexing and, in fact, to be expected, are accounts of scholars during this era living in retreat at Mount Song where they studied and taught. Gao Zhongzhen 高仲振 (?–?) and his disciples Zhang Qian 張潛 (?–?) and Wang Rumei 王汝梅 (?–?) all lived, studied, and taught in retreat on Mount Song, and were said to have

---

130 SS 428.12742.
131 Gong, *Songyang shuyuan*, 232.
132 SS 429.12758. See also the still valuable study by Conrad Schirokauer, "Chu Hsi's Political Career: A Study in Ambivalence," in *Confucian Personalities*, ed. Arthur F. Wright and Denis Twitchett (Stanford, CA: Stanford University Press, 1962), 162–188.
133 For basic biography, see *Songren*, III.1981–1983; see also SS 398.12116; Franke, *Sung Biographies*, 797–800.
134 Gong, *Songyang shuyuan*, 232.

lectured at Songyang Academy.[135] Gao and Zhang at least were northerners, so likely adapted to Jin rule. Xue Juzhong 薛居中 (?–?), a 1201–1208 *jinshi*, was a Jin appointee to the post of Dengfeng county magistrate in 1218 and he recognized the value of Songyang Academy, teaching there himself and recruiting teachers and students.[136] Beyond this, and the poetic records of Yuan Haowen as well as other Jin and Yuan poets, we have no other records from the Jin or the Yuan. The early Qing county gazetteer and similar sources simply state tersely, "In the Jin and Yuan it disappeared."[137]

Apart from the brief inscription in the Ming (1529) by Wang Shangjiong celebrating the restoration of Songyang Academy, the records of Songyang Academy during this period are limited to travel diaries, such as that of Xu Xiake, and poetry written by visitors to Mount Song who happened to go to the academy site. The Ming author and Dengfeng county magistrate Fu Mei compiled the *Song shu* 嵩書 (author preface 1612) as a gazetteer of Mount Song, beginning with chapters listing natural features, administrative areas, buildings (including academies), imperial connections (the deputing of officials from the court to offer prayers at the mountain, for example), officials, eremites, Daoists, Buddhists, as well as flora, fauna, rocks, etc., numinous events, poetry, and documents.[138] A similar collection from about a century later, the *Shuo Song* 說嵩 (author preface 1716) by Jing Rizhen contains primarily entries on scenic

---

135   Gong, *Songyang shuyuan*, 233. The only information on these three individuals is found in Yuan Haowen's *Zhongzhou ji*. For specific references to this source (though no dates), see Gao Zhongzhen entry in Umehara Kaoru and Kinugawa Tsuyosh (eds.), *Ryō-Kin-Gen jin denki sakuin* (Kyōto: Kyōto daigaku jinbun kagaku kenkyūjo, 1972) [hereafter cited as Umehara], no. 1559, 108–109; for Zhang Qian, see Umehara, no. 1782, 122–123; for Wang Rumei, see Umehara, no. 175, 12–13.

136   Gong, *Songyang shuyuan*, 233. I have not been able to find any corroborating biographical information in any of the standard sources, apart from a brief entry in Zhang, *Dengfeng xian zhi*, 6.1b, which notes his service as county magistrate.

137   Zhang, *Dengfeng xian zhi*, 4.8b.

138   For basic bibliographical information, see Wang Chongmin, *Zhongguo shanben shu tiyao* (Summary of Rare Chinese Books) (Shanghai: Shanghai guji chubanshe, 1986 [1983]), 208. Meir Shahar, *The Shaolin Monastery: History, Religion, and the Chinese Martial Arts* (Honolulu: University of Hawai'i Press, 2008), describes this work as a "history of the [Shaolin] temple" and refers to "Fu's book on the Shaolin Monastery" (11), but also mentions in a note that it "covers all the mountain's sacred sites (Buddhist and Daoist)," 206n8. However, it obviously covers much more than Shaolin-related material, so it is inaccurate to call it a history of Shaolin. See also Timothy Brook, *Geographical Sources of Ming-Qing History* (Ann Arbor: University of Michigan Center for Chinese Studies, Monograph #58), 130, where the title is simply translated as the "The book on the Song Mountains." Shahar also uses a similar translation in the bibliographical entry, where he notes that chapters relevant to Shaolin have been extracted and reprinted in a separate collection (252–253), thus confirming that the entire book is not dedicated solely to Shaolin Temple.

sites on Mount Song.[139] Jing Rizhen studied at Songyang Academy from 1673 to 1686 with the prominent official Tang Bin and Geng Jie.[140] Jing was also the author of *Songyang xuefan* 嵩陽學凡 (Guide to Learning at Songyang), a treatise on the principles of Cheng-Zhu learning, and was further known for his work in gynecology that was transmitted to Japan. All that is left of his retreat today are some characters inscribed on rock, but his legacy otherwise lives on in the tradition of Songyang Academy.

Both the *Songyang shuyuan zhi*, the account of Songyang Academy, and the earliest edition of the *Dengfeng xian zhi*, the local county gazetteer, date to the early 1680s (although there is later material included and publication of both took place at the end of the 17th century). These are the main sources dedicated to the academy itself and its local setting, although there are, of course, the collections of writings on Mount Song collected in the Ming *Song shu* and the Qing *Shuo Song*. There is only a brief mention of Songyang Academy in the *Song shu* (3.31a–b), and the biographical entries for famous Northern Song officials (*juan* 6) who were associated with Mount Song do not specifically refer to the academy. As one of the Five Sacred Peaks, Mount Song was also rich in Buddhist and Daoist sites and lore, and Songyang Academy itself became part of this religious landscape throughout much of its history as it was renamed Songyang Abbey or Songyang Palace (but not, evidently, restored to its original name as Songyang Temple).[141] As a Confucian institution, it struggled to claim a foothold in this mountain setting of one of the Five Sacred Peaks.

If we accept the received tradition of Songyang Academy as one of the Four Great Academies (although recognizing that there are variations as to exactly which four are included and that in some versions Songyang is omitted), we can acknowledge that its proximity to Luoyang, the home of the Cheng brothers and frequently a place of political retreat and refuge for others, such as Sima Guang, made Songyang Academy an attractive place for scholars to study and teach. But actual records of activities at and connections with the academy are sparse indeed. Many poems by famous scholars evoke the misty peaks and valleys of Mount Song, but little or nothing of an institution of Confucian learning there. Despite efforts to restore the site in the Ming, little remains to tell us more than that such restoration took place temporarily. It is only in the Qing that there is a substantial renewal of Songyang Academy, and those

---

139   Brook, *Geographical Sources of Ming-Qing History*, 131.
140   Gong, *Songyang shuyuan*, 127–128; see also Zhou Shude, "Jing Rizhen yu *Shuo Song* (Jing Rizhen and the *Shuo Song*)," *Henan tushuguan xuekan* 21, no. 4 (2001): 78–79.
141   For academies in the religious landscape of the Song and Yuan, see Linda Walton, "Academies in the Changing Religious Landscape," in *Modern Chinese Religion, 1: Song-Liao-Jin-Yuan* (960–1368), ed. John Lagerwey and Pierre Marsone (Leiden: Brill, 2015), 1235–1269.

associated with its restoration in the late 17th century were dedicated to Cheng-Zhu Confucianism. The last major renewal before the end of the 19th century was recorded was in 1739, and we know that the Qianlong emperor paid a visit in 1750, but we don't know how active a place Songyang Academy may have been by that time.[142] When Huang Yi visited at the end of the 18th century, his description was that of a tourist visiting a historic site, which is exactly what he was doing in his quest for steles and other ruins in the Mount Song landscape. And when Songyang Academy was restored again finally in the late 19th century, there was little time before it was swept up in the modernizing reforms of the early 20th century.

The next, and final, restoration of Songyang Academy came with a renewal of interest in and claims to the past, gradually and tentatively in the 1960s, but more steadily and earnestly in the post–Cultural Revolution era. Songyang Academy became a representation of the cultural heritage of the nation, both Chinese and Confucian.[143] In its collaboration with Zhengzhou University's National Studies program, Songyang Academy symbolizes both a national heritage and a regional one, drawing on the notion of the Central Plain as the heartland of Chinese civilization and a birthplace of Chinese culture.[144] The regional and national cultural heritage exemplified by Songyang Academy has now expanded to a global audience through its inclusion in the 2010 inscription of the "Historic Monuments of Mount Song" as a UNESCO World Heritage Site.

While there is much more to be learned about the historical character and function of the academy, especially in the early Qing intellectual world, we can adopt an interpretive framework highlighting a narrative tradition that begins with Songyang Academy as one of the Four Great Academies of the Northern Song and ends (for the moment at least) with the academy belonging to a cultural heritage that is regionally, nationally, *and* globally produced. Given what we can reconstruct from historical records, the academy's role in

---

142  Gong, *Songyang shuyuan*, 152–154. A pavilion at the academy commemorating the visit was restored in 1999–2000 (153).
143  The theoretical and practical literature on cultural heritage is voluminous. For a recent study of Confucian academies as cultural heritage (including Songyang), see my "Confucian Academies and the Materialisation of Cultural Heritage," in *The Heritage Turn in China: (Re)invention, Dissemination, and Consumption of Heritage*, ed. Carol Ludwig, Linda Walton, and Yiwen Wang (Amsterdam: Amsterdam University Press, forthcoming 2020).
144  See, for example, Walton, "The 'Spirit' of Confucian Education," for analysis of a collection of writings documenting the reception of Songyang Academy by faculty and students at Zhengzhou University and for a discussion of the academy's role in the National Studies curriculum adopted by Zhengzhou University.

the formation of Neo-Confucianism appears to be more a creation of received traditions about personalities and associations with place than of documented historical events and circumstances. The site of the academy was a place densely inhabited by Buddhists and Daoists, and therefore not the most fertile ground for nurturing Confucian ideas. This is not to deny the presence at Songyang of Northern Song luminaries from Fan Zhongyan and Sima Guang to the Cheng brothers, but to question the actual role of the academy in fostering Neo-Confucian intellectual culture. While demands for "authentic" antiquity determined by global organizations such as UNESCO drive contemporary international competition for cultural heritage value—a status successfully achieved when Songyang Academy was inscribed as a World Heritage Site in 2010—the assertion of Songyang Academy's place in the narrative of Neo-Confucianism's beginnings can be seen as a product of the need to substantiate a connection between place (particularly a place situated in the heartland of Chinese civilization) and the Confucian past in the service of the locality (Dengfeng county), the region, and, ultimately, the nation.

## References

Ban Gu 班固 (comp.). *Han shu* 漢書 (Han History). <http://hanchi.ihp.sinica.edu.tw> (accessed: 01 November 2017).

Beijing tushuguan zubian 北京图书馆组编 (eds.). *Beijing tushuguan zang Zhongguo lidai shike taben huibian* 北京圖書館藏中國歷代石刻拓本彙編 (Beijing Library Collection of Chinese Historical Stone Rubbings). Zhengzhou: Zhongzhou guji chubanshe, 1997.

Boltz, Judith. *A Survey of Taoist Literature: Tenth to Seventeenth Centuries*. Berkeley: University of California Institute of East Asian Studies, Center for Chinese Studies, 1987.

Brook, Timothy. *Geographical Sources of Ming-Qing History*. Ann Arbor: University of Michigan Center for Chinese Studies, Monograph #58, 1988.

Chao, Shin-yi. *Daoist Ritual, State Religion, and Popular Practice: Zhenwu Worship from Song to Ming (960–1644)*. London and New York: Routledge, 2011.

Cheng Hao 程顥, and Cheng Yi 程頤. *Er Cheng wenji* 二程文集 (Writings of the Two Chengs). <http://ctext.org> (accessed: 01 November 2017).

Chi Shengchun 池生春, and Zhu Xingshao 諸星杓 (eds.). *Er Chengzi nianpu* 二程子年譜 (Chronological Biography of the Two Masters Cheng). In *Songren nianpu congkan* 宋人年譜叢刊, vol. 4. Chengdu: Sichuan daxue chubanshe, 2003.

Chow, Kai-wing. "The Development of Sung Learning in Ch'ing Thought." *Hanxue yanjiu* 13.2 (1995): 47–76.

Deng Hongbo 邓洪波 (ed.). *Zhongguo shuyuan xuegui jicheng* 中国书院学规集成 (Collected Regulations of Chinese Academies). Shanghai: Zhongxi shuju, 2011.

Faure, Bernard. "Relics and Flesh Bodies: The Creation of Ch'an Pilgrimage Sites." In *Pilgrims and Sacred Sites in China*, edited by Susan Naquin and Yü Chün-fang, 150–189. Berkeley, Los Angeles, Oxford: University of California Press, 1992.

Franke, Herbert (ed.). *Song Biographies*. Wiesbaden: Franz Steiner Verlag, 1976.

Geng Jie 耿介, et al. (comps.). Li Yuan 李遠 (ed. and annot.). *Songyang shuyuan zhi* 嵩陽書院志 (Record of Songyang Academy) [1701?]. In *Songyue wenxian congkan* 嵩岳文獻叢刊, v. 2, edited by Zhengzhou shi tushuguan wenxian bianji weiyuanhui, Zhengzhou: Zhongzhou guji chubanshe, 2003.

Geng Jie 耿介, et al. (comps.). *Songyang shuyuan zhi* 嵩陽書院志 (*Record of Songyang Academy*). [1701?]. In *Zhongguo shuyuan zhi* 中國書院志 (Records of Chinese Academies), vol. 9, edited by Jiang Yasha 姜亞沙 et al. Beijing: Quanguo tushuguan wenxian suowei fuzhi zhongxin, 2005.

Gong Songtao 宮嵩濤. *Songyang shuyuan* 嵩陽書院 (Songyang Academy). Changsha: Hunan daxue chubanshe, 2014.

Gong Songtao 宮嵩濤. *Songyang shuyuan* 嵩陽書院 (Songyang Academy). Beijing: Dangdai shijie, 2001.

Guoli zhongyang tushuguan 國立中央圖書館 (eds.). *Mingren zhuanji ziliao suoyin* 明人傳記資料索引 (Index to Ming Biographical Materials). Taipei: Guoli zhongyang tushuguan, 1978.

Hangzhou daxue Zhongwen xi 杭州大学中文系 (eds.). *Gushu diangu cidian* 古書典故辭典 (Dictionary of Ancient Literature). Nanchang: Jiangxi jiaoyu chubanshe, 1989.

Harvard University, Academia Sinica and Peking University, China Biographical Database (January 1, 2018). <https://projects.iq.harvard.edu/cbdb> (accessed: 01 November 2017).

Hers, Joseph. "The Sacred Mountains of China: Sung Shan the Deserted (Honan)." *The China Journal/Zhongguo kexue meishu zazhi* 24 (1936): 76–82.

"Historic Monuments of Mount Song." <http://whc.unesco.org/en/lists/1305/> (accessed: 01 November 2017).

Hou Tai 侯泰, and Wang Yuxuan 王玉鉉 (eds.). [*Jiajing*] *Dengfeng xin zhi* 嘉靖登封新志 (Jiajing Era New Record of Dengfeng). (1529). Beijing: Xianzhuang shuju, 2003.

Huang Yi 黃易. "Song Luo fangbei riji 嵩洛訪碑日記 (Diary of Investigating Steles at Mount Song and Luoyang)." In *Shike shiliao xinbian* 石刻史料新編, coll. 3, v. 29. Taipei: Xin wenfeng, 1979.

Hummel, Arthur W. (ed.). *Eminent Chinese of the Ch'ing Period*. Taipei: Chengwen, 1970.

Kinugawa Tsuyoshi 衣川強 (ed.). *Sō-Gen gakuan – Sōgen gakuan hō-i: Jinmei jikō betsumei sakuin* 宋元學案－宋元學案補遺: 人名字號別名索引 (Index to Persons in the *Song Yuan xue'an and its Supplement*). Kyoto: Kyoto daigaku jimbun kagaku kenkyūjō, 1974.

Knight, Nick. "The Role of Philosopher to the Chinese Communist Movement: Ai Siqi, Mao Zedong and Marxist Philosophy." *Asian Studies Review* 26.4 (Dec., 2002): 419–445.

Li, Chi (trans.). *The Travel Diaries of Hsü Hsia-k'o*. Hong Kong: The Chinese University of Hong Kong, 1974.

Li Tao 李燾. *Xu zizhi tongjian changbian* 續資治通鑒長編 (Continued Long Edition of the *Comprehensive Mirror for Aid in Government*). Taipei: Shijie shuju, 1964.

Li Weiying 李蔚英. "Zhengzhou daxue Songyang shuyuan zongti guihua sheji fenxi 鄭州大學嵩陽書院總體規劃設計分析 (Analysis of the Overall Design Plan of Zhengzhou University's Songyang Academy)." *Zhengzhou daxue xuebao* (*gongxue ban*) 36, no. 2 (March 2015): 71–74.

Li Xiusheng 李修生, et al. (eds.). *Quan Yuanwen* 全元文 (Complete Prose of the Yuan Dynasty). Nanjing: Fenghuang chubanshe, 2004.

Liang Yuwei 梁玉瑋, et al. (eds.). *Jingshu tang wenji* 敬恕堂文集 (Collected Documents from the Hall of Reverence and Tolerance). Gudu Zhengzhou wenhua congshu bian wei hui. Zhengzhou: Zhongzhou guji chubanshe, 2005.

Liu Dunzhen 劉敦楨. "Henan sheng beibu gu jianzhu diaocha ji 河南省北部古建築調查記 (Report on an Investigation of Ancient Architecture in Northern Henan Province)." *Zhongguo yingzao xueshe huikan* 6.4 (June, 1937): 30–150.

Lu Ji'e 陸繼萼, and Hong Liangji 洪亮吉 (comps.). *Dengfeng xian zhi* 登封縣志 (Records of Dengfeng County). 1787 printed edition. <http://ctext.org> (accessed: 01 November 2017).

Luo Zhufeng 羅竹風 (ed.). *Hanyu dacidian* 漢語大詞典 (Comprehensive Chinese Dictionary). Shanghai: Hanyu dacidian chubanshe, 1995.

Ma Luan 馬巒, and Gu Donggao 顧棟高 (eds.). *Sima Guang nianpu* 司馬光年譜 (Chronological Biography of Sima Guang). Beijing: Zhonghua shuju, 1990.

Meskill, John. *Academies in Ming China*. Tucson: University of Arizona Press, 1982.

Nasen 迺賢. *Heshuo fanggu ji* 河朔訪古記 (A Record of Visiting Ancient Sites in Heshuo [literally "north of the Yellow River"]). *Shike shiliao xinbian* 石刻史料新編 ed., coll. 3, vol. 29. Taipei: Xin wenfeng, 1979.

Ng, On-cho. *Cheng-Zhu Confucianism in the Early Qing: Li Guangdi (1642–1718) and Qing Learning*. Albany: State University of New York Press, 2001.

Ouyang Xiu 歐陽修, and Song Zhi 宋祁 (comps.). *Xin Tang shu* 新唐書 (New Tang History). <http://hanchi.ihp.sinica.edu.tw> (accessed: 01 November 2017).

Peterson, Willard J. "Chapter 11: Arguments over Learning Based on Intuitive Knowing in Early Ch'ing." In *Cambridge History of China*, Volume 9, Part 2, edited by Willard J. Peterson, 458–512. Cambridge: Cambridge University Press, 2016.

Peterson, Willard J. "Chapter 13: Dominating Learning from Above During the K'ang-hsi Period." In *Cambridge History of China*, Volume 9, Part 2, edited by Willard J. Peterson, 571–605. Cambridge: Cambridge University Press, 2016.

Ren Jiyu 任繼愈 (ed.). *Daozang tiyao* 道藏提要 (Summaries of the Daoist Canon). Beijing: Zhongguo shehui kexue chubanshe, 1991.

Robson, James. *Power of Place: The Religious Landscape of the Southern Sacred Peak (Nanyue 南嶽) in Medieval China*. Cambridge and London: Harvard University Asia Center, 2009.

Schirokauer, Conrad. "Chu Hsi's Political Career: A Study in Ambivalence." In *Confucian Personalities*, edited Arthur F. Wright and Denis Twitchett, 162–188. Stanford, CA: Stanford University Press, 1962.

Sekino Tadashi 關野真 kenkyūkai (eds.). *Sekino Tadashi nikki* 關野真日記 (The Diary of Sekino Tadashi). Tokyo: Chūō koron bijutsu shuppan, 2009.

Shahar, Meir. *The Shaolin Monastery: History, Religion, and the Chinese Martial Arts*. Honolulu: University of Hawai'i Press, 2008.

*Song huiyao jigao* 宋會要輯稿 (Draft Compendium of Song Documents). Taipei: Xin wenfeng, 1976.

Sun Yanmin 孫彥民. *Songdai shuyuan zhiduzhi yanjiu* 宋代書院制度之研究 (Study of the Song Dynasty Academy System). Taipei: Guoli zhengzhi daxue, 1963.

Tian, Yang. "The Making of an Architectural Historian: Liu Dunzhen and the Knowledge of Traditional Chinese Architecture, 1917–1937." M.A. Thesis, Department of Architecture, National University of Singapore, 2003.

Tseng, Lillian Lan-Ying. "Retrieving the Past, Inventing the Memorable: Huang Yi's Visit to the Song-Luo Monuments." In *Monuments and Memory, Made and Unmade*, edited by Robert S. Nelson and Margaret Olin, 37–58. Chicago and London: University of Chicago Press, 2003.

Tuo Tuo 脫脫, et al. *Song shi* 宋史 (History of the Song). Beijing: Zhonghua shuju, 1974.

Umehara Kaoru 梅原郁, and Kinugawa Tsuyoshi 衣川強 (eds.). *Ryō-Kin-Gen jin denki sakuin* 遼金元人傳記索引 (Index to the Biographies of Liao, Jin, and Yuan). Kyoto: Kyoto daigaku jimbun kagaku kenkyū jo, 1972.

Walton, Linda A. *Academies and Society in Southern Sung China*. Honolulu: University of Hawai'i Press, 1999.

Walton, Linda A. "Academies in the Changing Religious Landscape." In *Modern Chinese Religion, 1: Song-Liao-Jin-Yuan (960–1368)*, edited by John Lagerwey and Pierre Marsone, 1235–1269. Leiden: Brill, 2015.

Walton, Linda A. "The 'Spirit' of Confucian Education in Contemporary China: Songyang Academy and Zhengzhou University." *Modern China* 44.3 (2018): 313–342.

Walton, Linda A. "Confucian Academies and the Materialisation of Cultural Heritage." In *The Heritage Turn in China: (Re)invention, Dissemination, and Consumption of Heritage*, edited by Carol Ludwig, Linda Walton, and Yiwen Wang. Amsterdam: Amsterdam University Press, forthcoming 2020.

Wang Chongmin 王重民. *Zhongguo shanben shu tiyao* 中國善本書提要 (Summary of Rare Chinese Books). Shanghai: Shanghai guji chubanshe, 1986 [1983].

Wang Deyi 王德毅, et al. (eds.). *Songren zhuanji ziliao suoyin* 宋人傳記資料索引 (Index to Song Biographical Materials). Taipei: Dingwen shuju, 1974–1976.

Wang Deyi 王德毅, et al. (eds.). *Yuanren zhuanji ziliao suoyin* 元人傳記資料索引 (Index to Yuan Biographical Materials). Beijing: Zhonghua shuju, 1987.

Wang Shengjun 王勝軍. "Songyang shuyuan yu Qingchu Luoxue fuxing 嵩陽書院與清初洛學復興 (Songyang Academy and the Revival of Luo Learning at the Beginning of the Qing Dynasty)." *Jiaoyu pinglun* 4 (2013): 129–131.

Wechsler, Howard J. *Offerings of Jade and Silk: Ritual and Symbol in the Legitimation of the Tang Dynasty.* New Haven and London: Yale University Press, 1985.

Weng Fanggang 翁方綱. *Ti Song Luo fangbei tu* 題嵩洛訪碑圖 (On the Album Investigating Steles in Mount Song and Luoyang). In *Shike shiliao xinbian* 石刻史料新編, coll. 3, v. 29. Taipei: Xin wenfeng, 1979.

West, Stephen H. "Chilly Seas and East-Flowing Rivers: Yüan Hao-wen's Poems of Death and Disorder, 1233–1235." In *China under Jurchen Rule*, edited by Hoyt Cleveland Tillman and Stephen H. West, 281–304. Albany: State University of New York Press, 1995.

Xue Yingqi 薛應旂. *Fangshan Xue xiansheng quanji* 方山薛先生全集 (Complete Writings of Master Fangshan Xue). Xuxiu Siku quanshu ed., v.1343.

Yan Yuyi 閻禹錫, comp. *Er Cheng quanshu* 二程全書 (Complete Writings of the Two Chengs). <http://ctext.org> (accessed: 01 November 2017).

Yang, Chia-Ling. "Power, Identity and Antiquarian Approaches in Modern Chinese Art." *Journal of Art Historiography* 10 (June 2014): 1–33.

Ye Feng 葉封 (ed.). *Songyang shike jiji* 嵩陽石刻集記 (Collection of Stone Inscriptions from Songyang). SKQS ed.

Zhang Hui 張慧. "Songyang shuyuan luyou ziyuan kaifa yanjiu 嵩陽書院旅遊資源開發研究 (Study on the Development of Tourism Resources at Songyang Academy)." *Sanmenxia zhiye jishu xueyuan xuebao* 11.2 (June 2012): 23–25.

Zhang Shenggao 張聖誥, et al. (comps.). *Dengfeng xian zhi* 登封縣誌 (Records of Dengfeng County). [1696]. SKQSCM ed.

Zhao Ersun 趙爾巽, et al. (comps.) *Qingshi gao* 清史稿 (Draft History of the Qing). <http://hanchi.ihp.sinica.ed.tw> (accessed: 01 November 2017).

*Zhengzhou wanbao*. 3 September 2009. <http://news.sina.com.cn/c/2009-09-03/082316 233745s.shtml> (accessed: 01 November 2017).

Zhou Shude 周樹德. "Jing Rizhen yu *Shuo Song* 景日昣與說嵩 (Jing Rizhen and the *Shuo Song*)." *Henan tushuguan xuekan* 21.4 (2001): 78–79.

Zhu Xi 朱熹 (comp.). *Er Cheng yishu* 二程遺書 (Remnant Books of the Two Chengs). <http://ctext.org> (accessed: 01 November 2017).

CHAPTER 14

# The Transmission and Transformation of Confucian Academy Rituals as Seen in Taiwanese Academies

*Chien Iching*

## 1   Introduction

The history of the establishment of Confucian academies in Taiwan began with the establishment of the Xidingfang Academy 西定坊書院 in Taiwan prefecture (present-day Tainan) in 1683 and culminated in the establishment of the Chongji Academy 崇基書院 (Jilong subprefecture; present-day Keelung) in 1893. During this time, academies spread from southern Taiwan to the north and eventually could be found throughout Taiwan, including the islands of Penghu and Jinmen.

During the reign of the Yongzheng emperor 雍正 (r. 1723–1735), there were a total of six academies in Taiwan, four of which were Academies for Correct Pronunciation (*zhengyin shuyuan* 正音書院), the aim of which was to disseminate the Mandarin dialect of Beijing. The other two—Nanshe Academy 南社書院 and Zhongshe Academy 中社書院—followed a rather different model. At this time, neither of these two institutions was called "academy," and they were renamed as Confucian academies only in later times. During the Yongzheng reign, Nanshe Academy was the site of the Pavilion for Revering Sages (Jingshenglou 敬聖樓), which had been built on the former site of a study for candidates for the civil service examinations and was dedicated to Imperial Lord Wenchang (Wenchang dijun 文昌帝君).[1] Zhongshe Academy had originally been the Kuixing Hall (Kuixingtang 魁星堂), dedicated to Kuixing 魁星 (lit. Chief Star),[2] and according to the *Chongxiu Kuixing tang beiji* 重修魁星堂碑記 (*Inscription on the Renovation of Kuixing Hall*) was built in 1726 by Wu Changzuo 吳昌祚 (?–?), Intendant of the General Surveillance Circuit (*xundao*

---

1   Imperial Lord Wenchang is a Chinese god said to preside over the civil service examinations. On the Wenchang cult, see Gao Wu, *Wenchang xinyang xisu yanjiu* (Chengdu: Bashu shushe, 2008); Nikaidō Yoshihiro, "Bunshō shinkō to shoin—Taiwan ni okeru Bunshō teikun byō wo rei ni (Wenchang Dijun Worship in the Academy. The Wencgang Dijun Shrine in Taiwan)," *Higashi ajia bunka kōshō kenkyū* 4 (2011).
2   In Daoism, Kuixing is a star god presiding over high official positions and riches. See Ma Shutian, *Zhongguo minjian zhushen* (Chinese Folk Deities) (Beijing: Tuanjie chubanshe, 1997).

巡道). According to this inscription, which dates from 1774 when the Kuixing Hall was repaired, previously a statue of Kuixing had been enshrined in the Kuixing Hall. While students in Taiwan understood Kuixing to exercise miraculous powers related to the civil service examinations, the Kuixing cult remained to be considered as heterodox belief and had not yet found its way into Taiwanese academies.[3] However, that the Pavilion for Revering Sages, dedicated to Imperial Lord Wenchang, and the Kuixing Hall, dedicated to Kuixing, were respectively renamed as Nanshe Academy and Zhongshe Academy, while the statues of the gods Wenchang and Kuixing remained, clearly shows the emerging tendency of identifying academies in Taiwan with pavilions (*lou* 樓) in which Wenchang was enshrined or halls (*tang* 堂) in which Kuixing was enshrined. Academies, which were associated with Confucianism, and Wenchang and Kuixing, who were associated with Daoism, became inseparably connected in Taiwan.

If we take the example of the Penghu Academy 蓬壺書院, the only academy on Taiwan proper today that preserves an academy entrance hall (*menting* 門廳), a Wenchang Pavilion (Wenchangge 文昌閣), and a statue of Kuixing, we see that the Wenchang Pavilion stands in the southeastern corner (southeast being regarded as an auspicious direction in geomancy) and next to it is a temple dedicated to the God of the Sea (or Dragon King, Longwang 龍王). A Confucian academy and a Daoist temple stand on the same grounds, and while Confucian scholars are enshrined in the Five Masters Shrine (Wuzici 五子祠), there is also Wenchang Pavilion, placed after geomantic considerations, with statue of Kuixing inside. The architectural style of the Penghu Academy gives concrete expression to an intermingling of Confucianism, Daoism, and folk beliefs and forms a composite ritual space.

This ritual space of the Penghu Academy is a typical example of syncretism, and to outsiders it may seem like a chaotic space in which various religions and beliefs coexist. However, for the local people who visited the site and performed religious rites, it was a harmonious sacred space, or cosmos, that had been planned in accordance with the teachings of geomancy and in which spirits and gods were deployed in an orderly manner. Furthermore, the situation at the Penghu Academy was no exception and represented a standard style, common also for other Taiwanese academies.

Within Confucian academies the orthodox objects of veneration in the rites were Confucius, his direct disciples, and later Confucian scholars considered

---

3 *Chongxiu Kuixing tang beiji* (Inscription on the Renovation of Kuixing Hall), in *Taiwan nanbu beiwen jicheng* (Collection of Stele Inscriptions in Southern Taiwan) (Taipei: Taiwan yinhang jingji yanjiushi, 1966).

to have succeeded to the academic tradition of Confucius. This can be regarded to be in general conformity with official Confucius temples (Kongzi miao 孔子廟). Imperial Lord Wenchang and the god Kuixing, on the other hand, originated in star cults and local folk beliefs and had been incorporated into the doctrines of Daoism and were venerated in Daoist institutions. The two main factors contributing to the combination of these two traditions of disparate origins were geomantic thought and the civil service examinations. The installation of a Wenchang Pavilion was believed to improve the geomantic conditions of the academy, while Imperial Lord Wenchang and the god Kuixing had a firm following among examination candidates as gods who presided over success in the literary arts.[4] The Wenchang cult and Wenchang Pavilions could also be found in academies in mainland China,[5] and their position in academies gradually rose, but because of the constraints of Confucian orthodoxy they never gained a level of veneration on a par with that of Confucian rites.[6] However, in Taiwan the situation was different.

Those who availed themselves of the academies of Taiwan were chiefly immigrants from the mainland, but their level of education was generally lower than the people on the mainland and they had little knowledge of standard features of Confucian academies. Government officials who were appointed to Taiwan from the mainland considered Taiwan not only to be geographically situated on China's periphery, but also to lie on its cultural periphery. They therefore attempted to transplant the cosmos and ethos of mainland Confucian academy culture onto Taiwan. They first introduced Neo-Confucian modes of academy rites in an attempt to mould the morals of Taiwanese scholars and the population. Later, in a process of trial and error, they brought in, one by one, Wenchang Pavilions and beliefs in Wenchang and Kuixing, associated with material benefits, as well as geomantic ideas for sanctifying physical spaces. The final result was rather a blend of orthodox ideas and local influences. Interestingly, however unusual the mainland scholars perceived

---

4  See Liang Gengyao, "Shiren zai chengshi: Nansong xuexiao yu keju wenhua jiazhi de zhanxian (Scholars in the City: Southern Song Schools and the Value of the Examinations)," in *Jingjishi, dushi wenhua yu wuzhi wenhua* (Economic History, Urban Culture and Material Culture) (Taipei: Zhongyang yanjiuyuan lishi yuyan yanjiusuo, 2002).

5  For example, from 1817 the Yuelu Academy instituted religious rites dedicated to Imperial Lord Wenchang in line with state sacrificial rites. For details, see Chien Iching, "Shilun shuyuan jisi yu minjian xinyang—yi Wenchang ge yu Wenchang xinyang wei zhongxin (Discussion of Sacrificial Rites in the Academies and Folk Beliefs. With a Focus on Wenchang Pavilions and Wenchang Belief)," *Zhongguo shuyuan* 8 (2013): 650–669.

6  On academy rites in mainland China, see Xiao Yongming 肖永明 and Zheng Mingxing 郑明星, "Lisu ronghui de shuyuan wenhua kongjian (Integration of Sacrificial Customs in the Academy Cultural Space)," *Minsu yanjiu* (2015): 21–29.

this blend as being, the view of the Taiwanese population was just the opposite. Acceptance of the elements that were brought in one by one from the mainland resulted in the creation of a unique perception of Confucian academies as a syncretic ritual space.

In this paper, I consider questions concerning the transmission and transformation of academy rites through an analysis of academy rites in Taiwan. I first examine the differences between standard academy rites in mainland China and academy rites in Taiwan. Next, I undertake an analysis of Wenshi Academy 文石書院 and consider the changes that occurred in Taiwanese academy rites from the middle of the Qianlong 乾隆 reign (1735–1796) until the Guangxu 光緒 reign (1875–1908). By examining various aspects of the development of academy rites in an immigrant society, I consider the characteristics of Taiwanese academy rites and questions concerning their transmission and transformation.

## 2     Academy Rituals

Academies have their origins in the Tang period, but no specific Confucian rites were performed at academies during the Tang. During the Northern Song, the imperial court conferred on academies a "ritual function" in order to make up for the inadequacies of government schools and turned them into schools that, like government schools, were involved in both lecturing and performing religious rites.[7] Initially, the religious rites performed at academies followed those of government schools and were dedicated to Confucius and his disciples. Yuelu Academy 嶽麓書院 and the White Deer Grotto Academy (Bailudong shuyuan 白鹿洞書院), the two leading academies of the Song period, during the Northern Song (960–1126) both had clay statues of Confucius and his ten leading disciples,[8] and the religious rites were directed at these statues. However, during the Southern Song (1127–1279) the White Deer Grotto Academy had only a statue of Confucius, and statues of the ten leading disciples were

---

7   For details, see Chien Iching, "Ryōsō ni okeru shoin saishi no henka—saishi kūkan to saishi taishō wo chūshin ni (A Study on Changes of the Academy Sacrifice between the Northern and Southern Song Dynasties: Focusing on Ritual Areas and Objects of Worship)," *Chūgoku tetsugaku ronshū* 39 (2013): 65–85.
8   Confucius's ten leading disciples were Yanzi 顏子, Min Ziqian 閔子騫, Ran Boniu 冉伯牛, Zhong Gong 仲弓, Zai Wo 宰我, Zigong 子貢, Ran You 冉有, Jilu 季路, Ziyou 子游, and Zixia 子夏.

substituted with paintings.[9] Another feature that differed from the Northern Song was that, in line with Zhu Xi's 朱熹 (1130–1200) thinking, rites dedicated to Mencius were also introduced.

In 1194, after having returned to Fujian, Zhu Xi built the Bamboo Grove Hermitage (Zhulin jingshe 竹林精舍), where he perfected and performed what he considered to be the ideal rites for an academy. Once the hermitage was completed, he performed the food offering rite (*shicai* 釋菜) in the lecture hall. On this occasion, Confucius was the main object of veneration, while Yanzi 顏子 (521?–481 BCE), Zengzi 曾子 (505–435 BCE), Zisi 子思 (481?–402 BCE), and Mencius were worshipped alongside him. In addition Zhou Dunyi 周敦頤 (1017–1073), Cheng Hao 程顥 (1032–1085), Cheng Yi 程頤 (1033–1107), Shao Yong 邵雍 (1011–1077), Sima Guang 司馬光 (1019–1086), Zhang Zai 張載 (1020–1077), and Li Tong 李侗 (1093–1163) were also included among the objects of veneration, but only "paper tablets" (*shi paizi* 紙牌子) were installed, with no clay statues being used. The method employed at this academy by Zhu Xi, worshipping Yanzi, Zengzi, Zisi, and Mencius alongside Confucius, was subsequently adopted at government schools, while the inclusion of his teacher (Li Tong) was adopted by other academies too and became one of the characteristics of academy rites.

The objects of veneration at academy rites were no longer confined to Confucius and his disciples, and leading figures in each school of thought and the teachers of the founders of academies also became objects of veneration. The objects of veneration at academies gradually diversified and included also people who had made notable contributions to local education or to academies. During this process, even Daoist deities such as Wenchang and Kuixing, who were believed to exercise miraculous powers related to the civil service examinations, became objects of veneration.

Rites dedicated to Imperial Lord Wenchang, also known as Imperial Lord Zitong (Zitong dijun 梓潼帝君), were especially popular at Taiwanese academies. Rites for the star Wenchang can be traced back to an ancient fire ritual

---

9  According to the *Yuelu shuyuan ji* 嶽麓書院記 (Records of the Yuelu Academy) by Zhang Shi 張栻 of the Southern Song (included in *Huguang tongzhi* 湖廣通志; Wenyuange edition of SKQS, fasc. 106), a statue of Confucius was installed in the Yuelu Academy and images of his disciples were painted on the walls. Further, according to the *Bailudong zhi* 白鹿洞志 (Records of White Deer Grotto Academy) (Jiajing edition, fasc. 2), the plans of Zhu Xi of the Southern Song to rebuild the White Deer Grotto Academy included a clay statue of Confucius and paintings of his ten leading disciples. See also Julia K. Murray, "Heirloom and Exemplar: Family and School Portraits in the Song and Yuan Periods," *Journal of Song-Yuan Studies* 41 (2011): 227–266; and Deborah Sommer, "Destroying Confucius: Iconoclasm in the Confucian Temple," in *On Sacred Grounds. Culture, Society, Politics and the formation of the Cult of Confucius*, ed. Thomas A. Wilson (Cambridge, MA: Harvard University Press, 2002): 95–133.

called *youliao* 櫵燎. Wenchang is the name of a six-star constellation, and among the six stars great importance was attached to the two stars Siming 司命 and Silu 司祿, both in popular beliefs and in official rites.[10] Among the common folk, Siming was also known as Wenquxing 文曲星 or Wenxing 文星 and was said to preside over success in the literary arts. While there is textual evidence for the performance of rites dedicated to the constellation Wenchang, among the general population Wenchang merged with Zitong, a local god of Sichuan. As a result of forced interpretations and various convolutions Wenchang became a god who embodied a constellation, a deity, and a person. Later, as the civil service examinations grew in importance and because of the great importance attached to assessments at Qing-period academies,[11] the importance attached to the cult naturally grew as well. In addition to the Wenchang cult, Kuixing too was worshipped at Taiwanese academies and the combination of both cults let to worship of the so-called, Five Wenchang.[12]

It is not known when rites for the Five Wenchang began at academies in Taiwan. The *Fengshan xianzhi* 鳳山縣志 (*Gazetteer of Fengshan County*), published in 1720, includes a section titled "Five Wenchang," according to which:

> The Immortals Hall (Xiantang 仙堂) is in the Ashe 阿社 in front of Changzhi Village. He Kan 何侃 (?–?), a local, gathered people together and built it. They enshrined the Five Wenchang and performed spirit writing (*fuji* 扶乩). A bamboo grove and flowering and fruiting trees were planted around it, and it was a most lovely sight. Later, a thatched cottage was built, and it served as a resting place for travelers. In recent years, King Lord of the East (Dong Wanggong 東王公) and Queen Mother of the West (Xi Wangmu 西王母) have been enshrined together there.[13]

There is, however, no explanation of the Five Wenchang. But in the *Chongxiu Fengshan xianzhi* 重修鳳山縣志 (*Revised Gazetteer of Fengshan County*), published in 1764, we read:

---

10  For details on the Wenchang cult, see Gao, *Wenchang xinyang xisu yanjiu*.
11  See Steven Miles, "Confucian Academies and Their Urban Environments in Qing China," in this volume, 289–318.
12  The Five Wenchang generally refer to Imperial Lord Wenchang (Imperial Lord Zitong), Imperial Lord Sage Guan (Guan sheng dijun 關聖帝君; Han Marquis of Shouting [Han Shouting hou 漢壽亭侯], i.e. Guan Yu 關羽), Divine Lord Zhuyi (Zhuyi shenjun 朱衣神君), Astral Lord Kuidou (Kuidou xingjun 魁斗星君; Kuixing, Imperial Lord Lüyi [Lüyi dijun 綠衣帝君]), and Imperial Lord Fuyou (Fuyou dijun 孚佑帝君; Ancestor Lü [Lüzu 呂祖], i.e. Lü Dongbin 呂洞賓).
13  Chen Wenda, *Fengshan xianzhi* (Gazetteer of Fengshan County) (Taipei: Taiwan yinhang jingji yanjiushi, 1961), 162.

> The Immortals Hall is in the Ashe in front of Changzhi Village. The Five Wenchang—Zitong, Han Marquis of Shouting, Kuixing, Zhuyi, and Ancestor Lü—are enshrined there, and later King Lord of the East and Queen Mother of the West were enshrined. During the Kangxi reign, the villager He Kan enlisted people to build it. A bamboo grove was planted around it, and it was a most lovely sight.[14]

This shows that at the Immortals Hall in Fengshan county in Taiwan Zitong, Han Marquis of Shouting, Kuixing, Zhuyi, and Ancestor Lü were enshrined as the Five Wenchang. This is the oldest reference to worship of the Five Wenchang that has been found to date. Taiwan is a society of immigrants, the majority of whom came from the three regions of Zhangzhou, Quanzhou, and Yue. There was a custom of worshipping the Five Wenchang at village schools in Quanzhou,[15] and it is to be supposed that this was one factor that had an influence on academy rites in Taiwan. Academies where the Five Wenchang are enshrined include the Zhenwen 振文書院, Xingxian 興賢書院, and Huangxi 磺溪書院 Academies.[16]

However, these types of academies were not very large and probably did not exercise much influence on an institutional level either. In the early Qianlong reign, the most famous academy in Taiwan were the Haidong 海東書院, Chongwen 崇文書院, and Baisha 白沙書院 Academies. Taiwanese academies of this period were mainly concerned with training talented men to sit for the civil service examinations. Not only did they receive the support of officials appointed to Taiwan, but they also gained support from the imperial court in respect to both funding and teaching staff and had similarities with academies of the early Northern Song. Furthermore, their use of architectural geomancy, as can be seen by the Kuixing Pavilion, also resembled the practices of government schools, which went back to the Song period.[17] These points all show that at this time Taiwanese academies were largely following established

---

14   Wang Yingzeng, *Chongxiu Fengshan xianzhi* (Revised Gazetteer of Fengshan County) (Taipei: Taiwan yinhang jingji yanjiushi, 1962), 268.
15   In the section on establishing schools (Kaixue 開學) in Wang Gu, *Quanzhou fengsu suotan* (Discussion of the Customs of Quanzhou) (printed by Quanzhou Meishu Yinshuasuo, 1936), we read: "In the end, it was the Five Wenchang Masters who were the most worshipped at village schools. Therefore, when establishing a school, a sheet of red paper was affixed to a wall and the spirit tablets of the Five Wenchang Masters were drawn on it."
16   See Wang Zhenhua, *Shuyuan jiaoyu yu jianzhu* (Academy Education and Architecture) (Taipei: Guxiang chubanshe, 1986), 79, 83.
17   For details, see Chien Iching, "Shoin no saishi to fūsui ni tsuite: Taiwan no Sūbun shoin to Kaitō shoin wo chūshin ni shite (A Study on the Ritual and Fengshui of Shuyuan: Focusing

mainland models and with regard to religious rites there were no local innovations as most academies were merely inheriting trends from the Fujian region. Academy rites in Taiwan began to change only in the middle of the Qianlong reign, and it can be seen in their objects of veneration that Taiwanese academies took on their own distinctive qualities and manifested special phenomena different from orthodox Confucian rites. In the next two sections, I first analyze the types of Taiwanese academies and then, taking the Wenshi Academy as an example, consider the transmission and transformation of academy rites in Taiwan on the basis of their objects of veneration.

## 3   Taiwanese Academies

During 210 years in the Qing period, from 1683 to 1893, more than sixty academies were built in Taiwan. Academies entered Taiwan during the Ming-Qing transition, but there are few source materials on early Taiwanese academies, making it difficult to gain an overall picture. Not only is the character of these academies unclear, but it is not even known whether they possessed the functions of lecturing, libraries, and religious rites. A total of nine academies can be found in local gazetteers, all of which were built in present-day Tainan, with many of them being named after the localities where they were situated. Judging from statements in local gazetteers such as "The prefect Jiang Yuying 蔣毓英 (?–?) built it (*or* It was built for the prefect Jiang Yuying); an image is enshrined there" and "The censorate director Wang Zhaosheng 王兆陞 (?–?) built it (*or* It was built for the Censorate Director Wang Zhaosheng); an image is enshrined there," these nine academies were probably academies that served as temples of local government officials during their lifetime (*shengci shuyuan* 生祠書院). At such academies predominantly religious rites were performed, and they did not possess the functions of ordinary academies.

During the Kangxi 康熙 reign (1661–1722), Chongwen and Haidong Academies existed, but because the political situation was still unstable they had to be relocated numerous times. Their operations lacked stability and continuity, and the contents of their instruction are not known, as well as rituals performed at these two academies. During the Yongzheng reign that followed, no further academies were built in Taiwan apart from Academies for Correct Pronunciation, which were being actively expanded by the Yongzheng emperor.

---

on Chongwen Shuyuan and Haidong Shuyuan in Taiwan), *Chūgoku tetsugaku ronshū* 41 (2015): 47–64.

At the beginning of the Qianlong reign, officials who had been appointed to Taiwan actively involved themselves in the construction of academies, as a result of which the Chongwen and Haidong Academies profited. School regulations were laid down and school fields were established for the academies, and the Chongwen and Haidong Academies were turned into schools that were institutionally sound and were fully capable of continuing their operations far into the future. With increasing political stability, the types of Taiwanese academies began to diversify. In Korea, and some of the more famous academies of mainland China tended to be built in locations of scenic beauty that had a rich natural environment and were at some distance from towns and cities. However in Taiwan academies were usually built inside the city walls beside a government office. This was, first, because it was convenient for their management and, secondly, for reasons of safety. For example, the Haidong and Baisha Academies were built in close proximity to a Confucius temple, to which they were affiliated. They had no ritual functions and were like preparatory schools for the civil service examinations.

Probably the only academy among Taiwanese academies that was built with any definite consideration for the beauty of its surroundings was Nanhu Academy 南湖書院. At the start of an inscription composed by Jiang Yunxun 蔣允焄 (?-?) it is explained, with reference to Sun Fu 孫復 (992-1057) and Li Bo 李渤 (773-831), that the environment too is quite important when engaging in scholarship,[18] but Taiwan's Chongwen Academy was located in a noisy and coarse environment, and so Jiang Yunxun built a new school beside a lake, with the lecture hall next to the temple Fahuasi 法華寺, and called it South Lake (Nanhu) Academy.

Basically, Taiwanese academies can be broadly divided into two types. The first type is academies that were supervised by government officials, were comparatively large in size, had school regulations, fields, and were fully provided with the necessary buildings. The Chongwen, Haidong, Baisha, and Wenshi Academies can all be included in this type. The Mingzhi 明志書院 and Xuehai 學海書院 Academies had no school regulations, but they did have school fields, and the spirit tablet of Zhu Xi was enshrined in the Mingzhi Academy, with rites being performed in spring and autumn. Also, a local diary explains that "the Xuehai Academy has a great wealth of books, and it no doubt also possesses school books published by successive dynasties."[19] It is evident also

---

18   Jiang Yunxun, *Xinjian Nanhu shuyuan beiji* (Memorial Stele of New Construction of Nanhu Academy), in Xie Jinluan, *Xuxiu Taiwan xianzhi* (Gazetteer of Counties in Taiwan, Continued), Volume 7 (Taipei: Taiwan yinhang jingji yanjiushi, 1962), 504.
19   Jiang Shiche, *Taiyou riji* (Taiyou Diary) (Taipei: Taiwan yinhang jingji yanjiushi, 1957), 94–95.

from the diagrams of the Mingzhi and Xuehai Academies included in the *Danshui tingzhi* 淡水廳志 (*Gazetteer of Danshui Subprefecture*) that these academies were comparatively large.[20] Further, the Wenkai 文開書院 and Fengyi 鳳儀書院 Academies were not only large in size, but also had school fields and were unusual regarding their objects of veneration.

The second type are academies that had been founded by officials, scholars, or influential locals, were comparatively small, and in character close to charity schools (*yixue* 義學). The Yufeng 玉峰書院, Luoqing 螺青書院, Yinxin 引心書院, Cuiwen 萃文書院, Xingxian, Dengyun 登雲書院, Shuren 樹人書院, and Yingcai 英才書院 Academies were all academies of this type. This type of academy was often established in regions where school education had not yet spread, made use of a Daoist shrine or temple, and the object of veneration in their rites was usually Imperial Lord Wenchang or the Five Wenchang.

## 4  Rites of Wenshi Academy

Chongwen Academy was the first academy to possess the function of rites in Taiwan.[21] Academy rites in Taiwan began to show signs of change and take on a distinctive character from 1766, when the Wenshi Academy, founded by the assistant prefect Hu Jianwei 胡建偉 (1718–1796), enshrined Kuixing and Wenchang in addition to Confucian scholars. A detailed account of the arrangement of the buildings of the Wenshi Academy and the objects of veneration at its rites can be found in the *Penghu jilüe* 澎湖紀略 (*Brief Account of Penghu*).

> The Wenshi Academy is an academy that was established with the assistance of 100 taels donated by the assistant prefect Hu Jianwei from his salary, and a place of scenic beauty in Wen'ao was chosen. The construction of the academy began in the tenth month of Qianlong 31 (1766), and it was completed in the fourth month of Qianlong 32 (1767). The main building is the lecture hall, which is 3 bays in size, and the name plaque reads "*Ludong xinchuan* 鹿洞薪傳 (Keeping On the Fire of Learning at Ludong)." In the center of the lecture hall there are enshrined Zhu Xi, Cheng Yi, Cheng Hao, Zhou Dunyi, and Zhang Zai. In front of the lecture hall stands the main gate, 3 bays in size, and in the center of the main gate a pavilion has been erected, which is used for rites dedicated to Kuixing.

---

20  Chen Peigui, *Danshui tingzhi* (Gazetteer of Danshui Subprefecture) (Taipei: Taiwan Yinhang Jingji Yanjiushi, 1963), 1.
21  For details, see Chien Iching, "Shoin no saishi to fūsui ni tsuite."

Behind the lecture hall stands a rear hall, 3 bays in size, and in the center of the rear hall Wenchang is enshrined; the space of 2 bays on either side serves as the residence of the head of the school. On the east and west sides of the lecture hall is a study, each of 10 bays, where students read books. Collectively, the buildings are called the Wenshi Academy.[22]

It is evident from this account that Wenshi Academy was completed in 1767 and its objects of veneration were the Confucian scholars Zhu Xi, Cheng Yi, Cheng Hao, Zhou Dunyi, and Zhang Zai as well as the Daoist deities Kuixing and Wenchang, who were believed to provide miraculous help to those sitting the civil service examinations. This is the first mention of rites for the gods Kuixing and Wenchang at a Taiwanese academy. In contrast, whereas there was a building called the Kuixing Pavilion at the Chongwen Academy, there is no record of Kuixing having been worshipped there.

The rites at the Wenshi Academy clearly show that academy rites in Taiwan had begun to take on their own distinctive characteristics. The first of these characteristics was that it was not only Zhu Xi who was worshipped here, but Zhu Xi, Cheng Yi, Cheng Hao, Zhou Dunyi, and Zhang Zai were all worshipped together. One of the sources of Confucian learning in Taiwan was the scholarship of Fujian (*Minxue* 閩學) and its lineage had been passed down from Zhou Dunyi to the Cheng brothers, Zhang Zai, and then Zhu Xi. At the time, the Aofeng Academy 鰲峰書院, the largest academy in Fujian, had, in addition to rites dedicated to Wenchang, a Five Masters Shrine, which according to the *Aofeng shuyuan zhi* 鰲峰書院志 (*Records of Aofeng Academy*) was dedicated to "Yuangong Zhouzi 元公周子, Zhenggong Chengzi 正公程子, Chungong Chengzi 純公程子, Wengong Zhuzi 文公朱子, and Minggong Zhangzi 明公張子,"[23] i.e. Zhou Dunyi, the Cheng brothers, Zhang Zai, and Zhu Xi. The Wenshi Academy differed from the Aofeng Academy in that Zhu Xi was ranked first, probably because of the influence of the Chongwen Academy. However, the aim of enshrining these five masters at the Wenshi Academy in Taiwan was naturally to rectify the lineage of the orthodox Confucian teachings. This was the same as in the case of the Aofeng Academy, where "there is a rite at the academy in which the *shicai* ritual is performed. The masters Zhou Dunyi, the

---

22  Hu Jianwei, *Penghu jilüe* (Brief Account of Penghu) (Taipei: Taiwan yinhang jingji yanjiushi, 1961). Hu Jianwei hailed from Sanshui 三水 in Guangdong and was called Master Mianting 勉亭.
23  You Guangyi et al., *Aofeng shuyuan zhi* (Records of Aofeng Academy), Volume 2, in ZGLDSYZ 10: 291.

Cheng brothers, Zhang Zai, and Zhu Xi have truly made the study of the Way flourish, and therefore the Five Masters are enshrined there."[24]

The second distinctive characteristic is that, as is stated in the *Penghu jilüe* by Hu Jianwei, in addition to Confucian scholars the Daoist deities Kuixing and Wenchang were also enshrined at the academy. In 1801 the Jiaqing emperor 嘉慶 (r. 1796–1820) issued an edict to the Ministry of Rites, as a result of which rites dedicated to Imperial Lord Wenchang were formally incorporated into official rites, but during the Qianlong reign, in which the academy was founded, Imperial Lord Wenchang had not yet been incorporated into official rites. In the section on the Wenchang Pavilion in *Aofeng shuyuan zhi* it is stated that "the pavilion's first name was Kuiguang 奎光, and it was founded in the seventeenth year of the Qianlong reign (1752), but these were private rites performed by officials and examination candidates."[25] Further, although "the fourth and third stars of Wenchang are called Sizhong 司中 and Siming in canonical works and Silu in historical works, and therefore Wenchang is worshipped,"[26] it is clearly indicated that Wenchang was not officially worshipped at the Aofeng Academy. In contrast, the Wenshi Academy was quite open about this and did not keep it secret, and this is a distinctive feature of Taiwanese academy rites.

The third distinctive characteristic is that for religious rites, Wenshi Academy simultaneously adopted and amalgamated features of the Chongwen and Haidong Academies. The rites at the Chongwen Academy were mainly dedicated to Zhu Xi, and while no rites were performed at the Haidong Academy, it had been influenced by the geomantic designs advocated by Yang Eryou 楊二酉 (1705–1780).[27] Yang Eryou renovated the Haidong Academy, installing a statue of Imperial Lord Wenchang in the Smaller South Gate and a statue of Kuixing in the Larger South Gate and erecting a new Xiufeng Pagoda (Xiufengta 秀峰塔), and from 1739–1741 he composed a series of geomantic plans that included the Haidong Academy. He regarded Haidong Academy, the Confucius Temple, and the Hall for Clarifying Proprieties (Mingluntang 明倫堂), which all lay within the same precinct, as a single large learning center. In order to stimulate its geomantic qualities he first created statues of Imperial Lord Wenchang and Kuixing, both gods of the civil service examinations, and then erected a new Xiufeng Pagoda to strengthen the geomantic qualities of the southeast, all with the aim of enabling students at the Haidong Academy to pass the civil

---

24  Ibid.
25  Ibid.
26  Ibid.
27  Yang Eryou hailed from Taiyuan in Shanxi. He became a *jinshi* 進士 in 1733 and was appointed to Taiwan in 1739. On his geomantic plans, see Chien, "Shoin no saishi to fūsui ni tsuite."

service examinations with ease. Yang Eryou's advocacy of geomancy and belief in Wenchang and Kuixing could be said to have been fully reflected in the Wenshi Academy, which can be understood when one considers the importance that was attached especially to the geomantic qualities of its Kuixing Pavilion.

In the *Xuxiu Wenshi shuyuan ji* 續修文石書院記 (*Account of the Wenshi Academy, Continued*) in connection with the Wenshi Academy it is stated: "In the fourth year of Jiaqing [1799] the Kuixing Pavilion was rebuilt at the rear. Further, in the fourth month of the ninth year of Daoguang 道光 [1829] the Kuixing Pavilion was rebuilt so that it faced southeast and was made a symbol of the flourishing state of education, being completed in the eleventh month of the tenth year of Daoguang [1830]."[28] This alteration to the direction in which the Kuixing Pavilion faced corresponds to Yang Eryou's advocacy of erecting the Xiufeng Pagoda in order to strengthen the geomantic qualities of the southeast. According to the *Wenshi shuyuan Dengying lou luocheng ji* 文石書院登瀛樓落成記 (*Account of the Completion of the Dengying Pavilion at the Wenshi Academy*),

> To the east of the Academy there is a pavilion that is more than 10 *wu*[29] wide and is surrounded by curved railing; Master Dakui 大魁 is enshrined on top of the pavilion. The pavilion is more than 2 *zhang* 丈 high, shines brightly, is brand-new, is higher than the mountains of the thirty-six islands, and can hear the sound of huge waves advancing from 30,000 *li* 里 away. It is a grand sight in the western seas and well deserves to be regarded as a symbol of scholars' success in the civil service examinations.[30]

Judging from this passage, from 1765 through to 1875 the god Kuixing continued to be worshipped at the Wenshi Academy.

## 5      Concluding Remarks

In the *Xuxiu Taiwan xianzhi* 續修臺灣縣志 (*Gazetteer of Counties in Taiwan, Continued*) by Xie Jinluan 謝金鑾 (1757–1820) there is a section on the

---

28   *Xuxiu Wenshi shuyuan ji* (Revised Records of Wenshi Academy), in *Taiwan jiaoyu beiji* (Memorial Inscription of Taiwan Education) (Taipei: Taiwan yinhang jingji yanjiushi, 1959), 39–40.
29   A *wu* 武 (approx. 0.9 m) is a unit of length, equivalent to 3 *chi* 尺.
30   *Wenshi shuyuan Dengying lou luocheng ji* (Account of the Completion of the Dengying Pavilion at the Wenshi Academy), in *Taiwan jiaoyu beiji*.

Kuiguang Pavilion (Kuiguangge 奎光閣; also known as Wenchang Pavilion), which reads as follows:

> In the old gazetteer it says that Imperial Lord Zitong's family name was Zhang 張 and his personal name was Yazi 亞子. He lived on Mount Qiqu (Qiqushan 七曲山) in Shu 蜀, served the Jin dynasty, and died in battle. His temple is in Zitong county in Baoning prefecture, and during the Tang and Song his title was progressively raised until he became King of Heroic Prominence (*Yingxian wang* 英顯王). Daoists say that the Celestial Thearch ordered Zitong to take charge of matters concerning Wenchang and of life registers in the human realm, and therefore the Yuan dynasty further conferred the title of "Imperial Lord," as a result of which schools throughout the realm worshipped him. During the Jingtai 景泰 era of the Ming, his former temple in the capital was rebuilt, and every year on his birthday on the third day of the second month an imperial envoy was sent and a religious service was held. In the first year of the Hongzhi 弘治 era, Zhou Hongmo 周洪謨, minister of rites, and others suggested that, since Zitong had performed miracles in Shu, it would be a good idea to erect a temple there to worship him, and they petitioned the emperor to order schools throughout the realm to abolish shrines dedicated to him. But many schools continued to worship him. It was said that the six stars of Wenchang in the Enclosure of Purple Tenuity (Ziweiyuan 紫微垣) lie to the south of Doukui 斗魁 and are all offices for the promotion of education, and therefore they are worshipped together with Kuixing. In the sixth year of the Jiaqing reign of the Qing, he was incorporated by imperial command into the ceremonial statutes, and religious services for him were performed in spring and autumn, as in the case of Martial Temples (Wumiao 武廟).[31]

Since the academy rites had essentially Confucian nature, there are no divine images and predominantly spirit tablets are used. That Taiwanese academies of the Qing period attached importance to assessment and study was in many cases for the purpose of sitting the civil service examinations, and gods associated with the examinations, such as Wenchang and Kuixing, were naturally held in high esteem by students. It is evident from the above passage that Wenchang and Kuixing were often worshipped together at schools. However, whereas the rites for Wenchang were incorporated into the ceremonial statutes and regulations by prescribing the days on which the rites were to be

---

31   Xie Jinluan, *Xuxiu Taiwan xianzhi*.

performed and the sacrificial utensils and offerings, this was not the case with the rites for Kuixing.

In the *Chongxiu Kuixing tang beiji* dating from 1774, it is clearly stated that the Kuixing Hall was renovated for no other reason than that Taiwanese students pinned high hopes on Kuixing.[32] Likewise, the *Chongxiu Kuixing ge beiji* 重修魁星閣碑記 (*Inscription on the Renovation of Kuixing Pavilion*) of 1816 describes the origins and activities of Kuixing as a tutelary god of literary success in the following terms:

> Among the twenty-eight lunar mansions, the god Kuixing comes under wood and is foremost among the seven lunar mansions in the west. His light illuminates the Northern Dipper, and he is able to drive off armies with the power of the pen. He silently holds the list of successful examination candidates and discloses the main points of successful answers. Kuixing shines on scholars endowed with virtue and learning and helps them succeed. This is why everyone throughout the realm performs rites for Kuixing.[33]

Kuixing was, like Wenchang, a favourite among students, but rites dedicated to him remained at the level of folk belief and, unlike the rites for Wenchang, were not incorporated into state ceremonial statutes. This became the greatest difference between the two.

Deng Chuan'an 鄧傳安 (1764–?) writes as follows in the *Xiujian Luoqing shuyuan beiji* 修建螺青書院碑記 (*Inscription on the Rebuilding of the Luoqing Academy*):

> Today's prefectural and county schools (*xuegong* 學宮) correspond to the local schools (*xiangxue* 鄉學) of former times. That cities and rural districts have built their own academy is a survival of the ancient custom of local schools called *shuxu* 術序 and *dangxiang* 黨庠. In the *Zhouli* 周禮, it is stated that there is a ceremony in which the school official (*dangzheng* 黨正) performs a sacrifice in autumn. In the chapter "Methods of Sacrifice" in the *Liji* 禮記, it says that *youyong* 幽禜 is a sacrifice to the stars. In the heavens, Wenchang corresponds to the six stars of Sizhong and Siming. Since ancient times, books about virtuous conduct and the arts of the Way have invariably regarded filiality as foremost. Were one to

---

32  *Chongxiu Kuixing tang beiji*, in *Taiwan nanbu beiwen jicheng*.
33  *Chongxiu Kuixing ge beiji* (Inscription on the Renovation of Kuixing Pavilion), in *Taiwan nanbu beiwen jicheng*.

ascertain the identity of the god Wenchang, who in later times has changed his appearance in accordance with the period, one could say that his beginnings lie in Zhang Zhong 張仲, who is praised for his virtues of filiality and fraternity in a poem in the Minor Odes of the *Shijing*. That being so, the worship of Wenchang at academies is a fine thing.[34]

Judging from the passages quoted above, it could be said that the inner attitude of scholars towards Wenchang and Kuixing was quite different. Not only was Imperial Lord Wenchang a god of the civil service examinations, but he also came to be regarded as a god endowed with the Confucian virtues of filiality and fraternity, whereas this was not the case for the god Kuixing. For this reason academy rites for Wenchang were deemed to be fine, but rites for Kuixing were regarded as a superstition. At the Wenshi Academy in Taiwan, the worship of the Five Masters of Guanzhong and Fujian represented the tradition of the orthodox lineage of Confucianism, while the worship of Wenchang and Kuixing was for passing the civil service examinations. At the Wenshi Academy, rites for Imperial Lord Wenchang began to be performed prior to their incorporation into state rites, but there was still a perception that they ran counter to the system of rites. The rites for Kuixing remained to an even greater degree a subject of debate among Taiwanese scholars, but his rites were never suspended at the Wenshi Academy, and they became one of the characteristics of academy rites in Taiwan.

In the academy rites of the mainland, a hierarchy existed ranking Confucianism, Daoism, and folk beliefs in this order with Confucianism being ranked highest. However, in Taiwan they were considered to be of equal rank, and people were gratified that everything that ought to be there was present and felt a sense of security. This was partly due to Taiwan being located in a frontier region and its people considering the customs of more developed regions as standard. However, when the frontier adopts a system that has gradually evolved over time in a more developed region, there is generally a tendency for the historical background of the system's constituent elements to be ignored and for them to be regarded as a single ready-made package and accepted uncritically. Especially in the case of religious beliefs, concerned with questions of miraculous effects on mind and body and of protection and salvation, people are unable to remain dispassionate if they feel that even a single element is missing.

---

34   Deng Chuan'an, *Xiujian Luoqing shuyuan beiji* (Inscription on the Rebuilding of the Luoqing Academy), in *Taiwan zhongbu beiwen jicheng* (Collection of Stele Inscriptions in Central Taiwan) (Taipei: Taiwan Yinhang Jingji Yanjiushi, 1962), 27.

Chaos and cosmos can be readily reversed depending on the standpoint of the person concerned. The yardstick for determining whether to view the ritual space of Taiwanese academies in which Confucianism and Daoism are intermingled in equal measure as chaos or cosmos is the importance one attaches to Confucianism. In the view of mainland scholars, it was only Confucian rites that were indispensable constituent elements of a cosmos, and while Daoist rites and rites based on folk beliefs were tolerated to a certain extent, an excess of these was considered to destroy the cosmos and lead to chaos. In Taiwan, on the other hand, a state in which Confucian rites coexisted with the rites of Daoism and folk beliefs that was regarded as a cosmos, and this was also confirmed by scholar-officials who arrived from the mainland. Considering the flourishing state of Taiwanese academies today and the continuity of their rites, such perceptions espoused by Taiwanese academies were not necessarily wrong. Moreover, even at the Yuelu Academy, a leading mainland academy, the Wenchang cult flourished from the Jiaqing reign of the Qing period onwards, and represented a state of coexistence between Confucianism and Daoism.[35] If that was so, then the receptive capacity of academy rites on the mainland was underestimated, and it is clear that Daoist rites and rites based on folk beliefs, here typified by the Wenchang cult, did not vitiate the essence of the academy rites. The essence of the academy rites does not have its origins solely in Confucianism, it also resides in Daoism and folk beliefs.

In this paper, I have analyzed academy rites in Taiwan and considered questions pertaining to their transmission and transformation, chiefly with reference to the Wenshi Academy. It has been confirmed that the rites performed at Taiwanese academies are by no means heterodox and that they are in fact a rich topic of research that could lead to the elucidation of the essence of academy rites. Unlike in mainland China, many Taiwanese academies still enjoy an uninterrupted existence and various rites are still being actively performed by them, which could be the object of future research.

### References

Chen Peigui 陳培桂. *Danshui tingzhi* 淡水廳志 (Gazetteer of Danshui Subprefecture). Taipei: Taiwan yinhang jingji yanjiushi, 1963. <http://tcss.ith.sinica.edu.tw> (accessed: 01 December 2017).

---

35   See Xiao and Zheng, "Lisu ronghui de shuyuan wenhua kongjian," 27–28.

Chen Wenda 陳文達. *Fengshan xianzhi* 鳳山縣志 (Gazetteer of Fengshan County). Taipei: Taiwan yinhang jingji yanjiushi, 1961. <http://tcss.ith.sinica.edu.tw> (accessed: 01 December 2017).

Chien Iching 簡亦精. "Ryōsō ni okeru shoin saishi no henka—saishi kūkan to saishi taishō wo chūshin ni 両宋における書院祭祀の変化―祭祀空間と祭祀対象を中心に (A Study on changes of the Academy Sacrifice between the Northern and Southern Song Dynasties: Focusing on Ritual Areas and Objects of Worship)." *Chūgoku tetsugaku ronshū* 39 (2013): 65–85.

Chien Iching 簡亦精. "Shilun shuyuan jisi yu minjian xinyang—yi Wenchang ge yu Wenchang xinyang wei zhongxin 试论书院祭祀与民间信仰―以文昌阁与文昌信仰为中心 (Discussion of Sacrificial Rites in the Academies and Folk Beliefs. With a Focus on Wenchang Pavilions and Wenchang Belief)." *Zhongguo shuyuan* 8 (2013): 650–669.

Chien Iching 簡亦精. "Shoin no saishi to fūsui ni tsuite: Taiwan no Sūbun shoin to Kaitō shoin wo chūshin ni shite 書院の祭祀と風水について: 台湾の崇文書院と海東書院を中心にして (A Study on the Ritual and Fengshui of Shuyuan: Focusing on Chongwen Shuyuan and Haidong Shuyuan in Taiwan)." *Chūgoku tetsugaku ronshū* 41 (2015): 47–64.

Deng Chuan'an 鄧傳安. *Xiujian Luoqing shuyuan beiji* 修建螺青書院碑記 (Inscription on the Rebuilding of the Luoqing Academy). In *Taiwan zhongbu beiwen jicheng* 臺灣中部碑文集成 (Collection of Stele Inscriptions in Central Taiwan). Taipei: Taiwan yinhang jingji yanjiushi, 1962. <http://tcss.ith.sinica.edu.tw> (accessed: 01 December 2017).

Gao Wu 高梧. *Wenchang xinyang xisu yanjiu* 文昌信仰習俗研究 (Study of Beliefs and Customs of Imperial Lord Wenchang). Chengdu: Bashu shushe, 2008.

Hu Jianwei 胡建偉. *Penghu jilüe* 澎湖紀略 (Brief Account of Penghu). Taipei: Taiwan yinhang jingji yanjiushi, 1961. <http://tcss.ith.sinica.edu.tw> (accessed: 01 December 2017).

Jiang Shiche 蔣師轍. *Taiyou riji* 臺游日記 (Taiyou Diary). Taipei: Taiwan yinhang jingji yanjiushi, 1957. <http://tcss.ith.sinica.edu.tw> (accessed: 01 December 2017).

Jiang Yunxun 蔣允焄. *Xinjian Nanhu shuyuan beiji* 新建南湖書院碑記 (Memorial Stele of New Construction of Nanhu Academy). In *Xuxiu Taiwan xianzhi* 續修臺灣縣志 (Gazetteer of Counties in Taiwan, Continued), edited by Xie Jinluan 謝金鑾. Volume 7. Taipei: Taiwan yinhang jingji yanjiushi, 1962. <http://tcss.ith.sinica.edu.tw> (accessed: 01 December 2017).

Liang Gengyao 梁庚堯. "Shiren zai chengshi: Nansong xuexiao yu keju wenhua jiazhi de zhanxian 士人在城市: 南宋學校與科舉文化價值的展現 (Scholars in the City: Southern Song Schools and the Value of the Examinations)." In *Jingjishi, dushi wenhua yu wuzhi wenhua* 經濟史, 都市文化與物質文化 (Economic History, Urban Culture and Material Culture). 265–326. Taipei: Zhongyang yanjiuyuan lishi yuyan yanjiusuo, 2002.

Ma Shutian 马书田. *Zhongguo minjian zhushen* 中国民间诸神 (Chinese Folk Deities). Beijing: Tuanjie chubanshe, 1997.

Murray, Julia K. "Heirloom and Exemplar. Family and School Portraits in the Song and Yuan Periods." *Journal of Song-Yuan Studies* 41 (2011): 227–266.

Nikaidō Yoshihiro 二階堂善弘. "Bunshō teikun shinkō to shoin—Taiwan ni okeru Bunshō teikun byō wo rei ni 文昌帝君信仰と書院—台湾における文昌帝君廟を例に (Wenchang Dijun Worship in the Academy: The Wenchang Dijun Shrine in Taiwan)." *Higashi ajia bunka kōshō kenkyū* 4 (2011): 11–19.

Sommer, Deborah. "Destroying Confucius. Iconoclasm in the Confucian Temple." In *On Sacred Grounds: Culture, Society, Politics and the formation of the Cult of Confucius*, edited by Thomas A. Wilson. 95–133. Cambridge, MA: Harvard University Press, 2002.

*Taiwan jiaoyu beiji* 臺灣教育碑記 (Memorial Inscription of Taiwan Education). Taipei: Taiwan yinhang jingji yanjiushi, 1959. <http://tcss.ith.sinica.edu.tw> (accessed: 01 December 2017).

*Taiwan nanbu beiwen jicheng* 臺灣南部碑文集成 (Collection of Stele Inscriptions in Southern Taiwan). Taipei: Taiwan yinhang jingji yanjiushi, 1966. <http://tcss.ith.sinica.edu.tw> (accessed: 01 December 2017).

Wang Gu 王嘏. *Quanzhou fengsu suotan* 泉州風俗瑣談 (Discussion of the Customs of Quanzhou). Printed by Quanzhou Meishu Yinshuasuo 泉州美術印刷所, 1936.

Wang Yingzeng 王瑛曾. *Chongxiu Fengshan xianzhi* 重修鳳山縣志 (Revised Gazetteer of Fengshan County). Taipei: Taiwan yinhang jingji yanjiushi, 1962. <http://tcss.ith.sinica.edu.tw> (accessed: 01 December 2017).

Wang Zhenhua 王鎮華. *Shuyuan jiaoyu yu jianzhu* 書院教育與建築 (Academy Education and Architecture). Taipei: Guxiang chubanshe, 1986.

Xiao Yongming 肖永明 and Zheng Mingxing 郑明星. "Lisu ronghui de shuyuan wenhua kongjian 礼俗融会的书院文化空间 (Integration of Sacrificial Customs in the Academy Cultural Space)." *Minsu yanjiu* (2015): 21–29.

You Guangyi 游光繹, et al. *Aofeng shuyuan zhi* 鰲峰書院志 (Records of Aofeng Academy). Volume 2, in ZGLDSYZ, Volume 10.

CHAPTER 15

# Between Ruins and Relics: North Korean Discourse on Confucian Academies

*Vladimír Glomb and Eun-Jeung Lee*

## 1 Introduction[1]

Confucian academies were for centuries part of both the Korean cultural landscape and the intellectual heritage of the Chosŏn 朝鮮 dynasty (1392–1910). Many of them survived into modern times and after the division of the Korean peninsula, their destinies further continued under two sharply different rival states whose treatment of Confucian academies significantly differed. The regime of the Republic of Korea, often appealing to Confucian values, has stressed a positive approach toward the academies' legacy and actively supported their preservation. The fate of academies in the Northern part of the peninsula has been much more complicated. Confucian academies were seen as a part of the oppressive feudal regime of the past centuries; Marxist-Leninist ideology and its later variations had little inclination to "find in the *sŏwŏn* a potent legacy of the past."[2] The Czech scholar Jaroslav Bařinka, who during the 1950s and 1960s travelled extensively in North Korea, described the state of the Confucian academies in melancholy tones:

> Nowadays, almost one century later [after the Taewŏn'gun reforms] there remain only a few, mostly dilapidated, Confucian academies, sparsely scattered over [North] Korea; they are the mere ruins of a formerly suggestive environment. [...] The entire world of the *sŏwŏn* and the cultural traditions related to them attracts only minimal attention today. Confucian academies, formerly witnesses of the difficult past of the traditional

---

[1] This chapter is an expanded and revised version of our article "Dens of Feudalism: North Korean Discourse on Confucian Academies," *Journal of Korean Religions* 8, no. 2 (October 2017): 147–180. Authors would like to thank the *Journal of Korean Religions* for permission to reuse the material from that article here.

[2] Milan Hejtmanek, "The Elusive Path to Sagehood: Origins of the Confucian Academy System in Chosŏn Korea," *Seoul Journal of Korean Studies* 26, no. 2 (2013): 235.

Korean countryside are now, as the representatives of the strictest conservatism, subject of the scorn of the majority of modern Koreans.[3]

The South-North division can be clearly seen as well in academic activity regarding the role and legacy of the academies; in comparison to hundreds of articles or academic theses and dozens of monographs concerning Confucian academies in South Korea, there are only a few academic works hailing from the DPRK.[4] Yet this numerical disproportion does not mean that the North Korean perspectives on Confucian academies are less complex or interesting than their South Korean counterparts. It is evident that the position of the academies underwent several changes in North Korea: in recent years, they have become an object of growing attention (at least judging by the number of academic articles or scholarly contacts on the topic).[5] They also play a significant role as a part of the cultural heritage.

To be able to evaluate both the current and possibly future developments concerning the general view in the DPRK on Korean history, as well as a specific understanding of the role of Confucian academies, we first must undertake an analysis of the formative stage of Confucian academies discourse

---

3 Jaroslav Bařinka, "Staré konfuciánské ústavy v Koreji," *Nový Orient* 23 (1968): 266.
4 Even more rare, until recently, were attempts to describe features and specific nature of the academies located in the northern provinces of the peninsula. Almost all South Korean works unfortunately focus on academies located in the Republic of Korea and none of the general works on academies takes into consideration (from the academies' point of view the very recent) division of the peninsula. A short overview of academies located in the present day DPRK is offered by Cho Sangsun, *Pukhanŭi sŏwŏn kwa sau* (North Korean Confucian Academies and Confucian Shrines) (2012). A detailed list of all northern academies with brief descriptions is to be found in Sŏwŏn yŏnhap hoe, *Hanguk sŏwŏn ch'ongnam* II (General Survey of Korean Confucian Academies II) (2011): 1115–1219. The pioneering South Korean works on North Korean academies are Chung Soon-woo's contribution in this volume analyzing the Sungyang Academy in Kaesŏng (the same academy is treated also in the work of Ruth Scheidhauer, "A Historiography of Cultural Heritage Interpretation and Policy in Kaesŏng, DPR Korea and Their Possible Impact on Inter-Korean Rapprochement" [Ph.D. diss., University College London, 2011], 276–278.) describing North Korean cultural heritage policy with a focus on the Kaesŏng area) and a historical overview of Pyongyang schools and academies by Pak Chongbae, Shigeyo Hasuike, "Ŭpchi rŭl t'onghaesŏ pon Chosŏn sidae P'yŏngyang ŭi hakkyo wa kŭ unyŏng (Pyongyang Schools and their Management during the Chosŏn Period Seen Through Local Gazetteers)," *Kyoyuk sahak yŏn'gu* 27, no. 1 (2017): 71–101.
5 During the last decade, a high number (measured by North Korean standards) of academic studies related to Confucian academies has been published; see the three studies by Ch'oe Yŏnju. Recently there even has been a study dealing with Chinese academies, see Ri Suil, "Chungse Chunggug esŏŭi sŏwŏn kyoyuk e taehan myŏtkaji koch'al (Some Observations on Education in Medieval Chinese Confucian Academies)," *Ryŏksa kwahak* 205, no. 1 (2008): 55–57.

occurring in the decisive decades of the 1950s and 1960s, as this established the basic patterns of North Korean notions of cultural heritage, historiography, and education. The research of these topics enables us to understand better the place of the academies within North Korean academic debate as well as the topic of Confucian culture and legacy surrounding the issue. The present study thus focuses on the formative stage of North Korean discourse on Confucian academies during the early decades of the regime, and attempts to encompass the contours North Korean stances concerning the multifaceted phenomena known as Confucian academies.

## 2      Cultural Relics

In dealing with the debates on the Confucian academies in the DPRK we cannot avoid the material aspect of these debates, i.e. the physical existence of the *sŏwŏn* and their preservation, destruction, neglect or conversion under the people's democratic regime. The northern Korean provinces, after the 1945 liberation forming the territory of the DPRK, were traditionally conceived as less civilised, i.e. Confucian, than their central or southern counterparts,[6] but they had traditionally hosted a significant number of academies, which were maintained with no less vigour than in the southern Confucian strongholds of Kyŏngsan or Kyŏnggi province. A statistical approach could do battle with a precise definition of academies (with their mixed nature of both academy and shrine) and various other factors (their decline or abolition during past centuries, and so on) but the rough statistical analysis presented by Yun Hŭimyŏn shows that the three Northern provinces hosted, in various periods, a total of 58 Confucian academies (out of a total of 680) and 135 shrines (*sau* 祀宇) of Confucian scholars or other heroes out of a total of 1,041.[7] Their distribution reflected the traditional prejudices of the elites of the Korean capital toward the northern population of the peninsula: they were viewed as martial, barbarian, and uneducated, i.e. as sharing many characteristics with the neighbouring ethnic groups of the Manchurian area. Backward and remote Hamgyŏng province hosted only 15 Confucian academies; P'yŏngan province, with 25 academies, compares only slightly better, and the even more southern Hwanghae province with 25 academies (the nowadays-divided Kangwŏn province

---

6   See Jang Yoo-seung, "Regional Identities of Northern Literati: A Comparative Study of P'yongan and Hamgyong Provinces," in *The Northern Region of Korea: History, Identity, and Culture*, ed. Kim Sun Joo (Seattle: University of Washington Press, 2010), 62–92.

7   Yun Hŭimyŏn, *Chosŏn sidae sŏwŏngwa yangban* (Academies and Yangban of the Chosŏn Period) (Seoul: Chimmudang, 2004), 84.

had 23 institutions) could not compete with major Confucian centers like Kyŏngsan province, with an imposing 370 academies.[8]

This South-North ratio remained unchanged even during the most turbulent event of the history of Korean Confucian academies, the destruction of the *sŏwŏn* system during Taewŏngun's 大院君 rule in 1868–1871. Out of 47 academies and shrines (including a total of 16 academies proper) spared by Taewŏngun, only a few were located in the northern provinces. These were the academies devoted to the scholars venerated in the Seoul Confucius shrine: the Munhoe Academy 文會書院, which venerated Yulgok Yi I 栗谷 李珥 (1536–1584) in Paech'ŏn, and the Pongyang Academy 鳳陽書院 dedicated to Pak Sech'ae 朴世采 (1631–1695) in Changyŏn (both in Hwanghae province). Other northern shrines in the list demonstrate further proof of bias against the uncultivated North. The interesting choice of enshrined persons focuses on military figures, various loyal subjects or martyrs, but not on Confucian scholars. In P'yŏngan province were located Ch'ungminsa 忠愍祠, venerating Nam Yihŭng 南以興 (1576–1627) and other defenders against the Manchu invasion of 1627; P'yochŏlsa 表節祠, dedicated to a local magistrate who died during the Hong Kyŏngnae 洪景來 rebellion of 1812, Such'ungsa 酬忠祠 venerating monk-general Hyujŏng 休靜 (1520–1604), Samch'ungsa 三忠祠 (or Waryongsa 臥龍祠) for Chinese military genius Zhuge Liang 諸葛亮 and Pyongyang Muyŏlsa 武烈祠, a place of offerings to the Ming Minister of War Shi Xing 石星 (?–1599), who helped to save Korea during the Hideyoshi invasion. Hwanghae province hosted two shrines: Ch'ŏngsŏngsa 清聖廟 dedicated to Bo Yi 伯夷 and Shu Qi 叔齊 and T'aesasa 太師祠 for Koryŏ founding merit subjects. Hamgyŏng province retained only one academy in Pukch'ŏng, the place of the scholar Yi Hangbok's 李恒福 (1556–1618) death in banishment, dedicated to him.[9]

---

8  The precise figures could differ according to the method or source employed: Chung Soon-woo bases his numbers on a traditional source, *Yŏllyŏsil kisul* 燃藜室記述 (Narrative of Yŏllyŏsil) and indicates twenty academies for Hwanghae, the same number for P'yŏngan, and ten academies for Hamgyŏng. The *Chŭngbo munhŏn pigo* 增補文獻備考 (Augmented Reference Compilation of Documents) compiled in 1908 gives twenty academies for Hwanghae, sixteenth for P'yŏngan, and eleven academies for Hamgyŏng (CBMHPG 213: 28a–40a). All sources demonstrate a disproportion of academy numbers along the North-South axis; this disproportion is certainly to be attributed to government policy and bias of capital elites against northerners (well described by Chung Soon-woo), but economic and demographic factors probably played a significant role as well. In particular, Hamgyŏng province was simply less populated and lacking resources to build numerous academies. The same phenomenon is present in the southern provinces too: periphery islands including Cheju were also almost without any academy.

9  Yun Hŭimyŏn, *Chosŏn sidae sŏwŏngwa yangban*, 163–165.

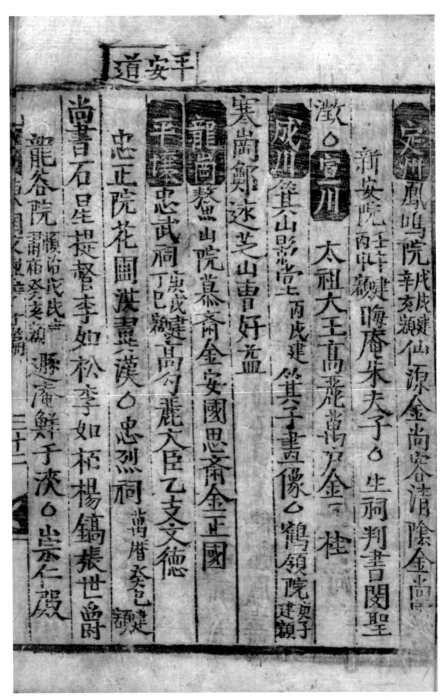

ILLUSTRATION 15.1 List of academies and shrines in P'yongan province located in Pyongyang out of *Tongguk munhŏnnok*

ILLUSTRATION 15.2  Japanese colonial postcard of Sungyang Academy with the tourist stamp

The short list of the few academies left by the Taewŏngun reforms presents us with a difficult riddle as it does not name many of the North Korean academies, including the most famous ones, the Sohyŏn Academy 紹賢書院 near Haeju or the Ryonggok Academy 龍谷書院 in the vicinity of Pyongyang, which have survived until the present day. This question requires individual research on specific academies to determine whether they escaped abolition during Taewŏngun rule, or were reopened at a later date, but it is possible to state that as in the southern provinces, many academies did avoid abolition and survived, or were allowed to reopen at a later date. Their destiny in the turbulent years at the end of Korean independence and Japanese occupation during 1910–1945 often varied, but many academies were maintained and respected as a significant part of the Korean cultural landscape. This did not, in certain aspects, change immediately after the liberation in 1945.

The new North Korean regime was hostile to the Confucian message of the academies and brutally liquidated en masse the *yangban* class who supported the *sŏwŏn* system; at the same time, however, it considered them as new state property and to certain degree as well a part of the cultural heritage of the Korean masses. The process of expropriation and nationalisation of academies took various forms, but the result effectively ended the existence of Confucian academies. The academies' archives were confiscated and the abandoned buildings were employed for various other purposes. The losses endured during this process of expropriation and abandonment were further accelerated by the damages and turmoil caused by the Korean War, although their secluded location saved many academies from destruction. In spite of all these difficulties, the post-war DPRK was still home to many academies or related relics. The existence of many of them in our period of 1950–1960 can be verified only by oral testimony, as most of the official documentation is not available for international research. A few official publications dealing with the cultural heritage and property in DPRK offer, however, a basic overview of academies, which nonetheless gained state recognition and protection.

The state approach to Confucian academies as a cultural heritage has a certain precedent in the Japanese recognition of Sosu Academy 紹修書院 as a historical relic, and such status was attributed at least to some academies during the establishment of the preservation of cultural heritage by the new regime. The survey *Chungyo yujŏkmyŏngsŭng chʻŏnyŏn kinyŏmmul illam* (*An Overview of Important Historical Relics, Cultural and Natural Monuments*), created in 1956 by the Committee for Preservation of Material Culture Relics (*Muljil munhwa yumul pojon wiwŏnhoe*) offers an interesting list of the most important and cultural and natural monuments, including Sohyŏn Academy and Sungyang Academy 崧陽書院 in Kaesŏng; it also includes valid legislation on the topic. Government decisions (all signed by the *Susang* [Prime Minister] Kim Ilsŏng) from 1946 to 1955 provide a basic framework for the "protection, preservation and rational management" of both cultural and natural monuments,[10] and threatens those who "destroy, damage, seize of use them without authorisation"[11] with punishment according to the law.

The question of how many academies were preserved in the DPRK, and what status they enjoyed, is partially answered by a later overview of cultural and historical heritage, *Myŏngsŭng, kojŏk, chʻŏnyŏn kinyŏmmul pʻyŏllam* (*Guide to Famous Places, Historical Relics and Natural Monuments*), published in 1966. It gives a detailed description of only one institution, Sohyŏn Academy, but it offers a detailed maps of historical relics, where, in addition to many village schools (*hyanggyo* 鄕校), some of the extant academies are also indicated: Sohyŏn Academy, Sungyang Academy, Munhoe Academy 文會書院 in Paechʻŏn, Kyŏnghyŏn Academy 景賢書院 in Chaeryŏng, Hamgyŏng Academy (?)[12] in Unhŭng, or locations where *sŏwŏn* had stood are indicated, as, for example, in the case of Ryongjin Academy 龍津書院 and Munpʻo Academy 汶浦書院 in Munchʻŏn, or Hanchʻŏn Academy (?) in Kaechʻŏn, commemorative stelae

---

10  Muljil munhwa yumul pojon wiwŏnhoe, *Chungyo yujŏkmyŏngsŭng chʻŏnyŏn kinyŏmmul illam* (An Overview of Important Historical Relics, Cultural and Natural Monuments) (Pyongyang: Muljil munhwa yumul pojon wiwŏnhoe, 1956), 151.
11  Ibid., 152.
12  In 1957 it was commonly known as "Unhŭng sŏwŏn" among the local population.

ILLUSTRATION 15.3  North Korean postcard of Sungyang Academy. English caption: "Soong-yang Suwon (a school in the feudal age) in Kaesong." Folk song "Kaesong Nambong Ka (Kaesong Gay Fellow)."

ILLUSTRATION 15.4
Sungnyŏl Academy commemorative stela, *Sungnyŏl sŏwŏn yuhŏ pi* in Ch'ŏngjin

(*yuhŏbi* 遺墟碑) of Sungnyŏl Academy 崇烈書院 in Ch'ŏngjin, etc. Both surveys are far from complete[13] but show a solid position of (at least some) of the Confucian academies within the framework of cultural preservation in the DPRK.

Unlike village schools *hyangyo*, which were in some cases still in use in the 1950s, the academies were largely deserted, and although protected, they had no further use, apart from certain exceptions such as the Ryonggok Academy, attached as a recreational site to the Academy of Sciences. It is difficult to assess the relative position of academies within the ideological framework of the cultural preservation programme in the DPRK, but it seems clear they were not prioritized. Surveys from the 1950s and 1960s speak about Confucian academies in relatively neutral language, but they were, in general, understood to be the remnants of reactionary feudal forces of property, and given the economic

---

13   An example of an omitted academy could be Tumundong Academy 杜門洞書院 near Kaesŏng dedicated to Koryŏ loyalists. It was still active during the Japanese occupation (in 1937 it republished the academy chronicle).

restrains of the postwar period, they were not particularly explored or emphasized. North Korean archeology and history of art research were focused on prehistoric sites or famous art objects, and the relatively simple academy buildings were—also because of their relatively recent origin—not of particular interest.[14]

It is rather significant that the leading journal of art history from the period, *Munhwa yusan* (*Culture Heritage*), describes only one *hyanggyo*,[15] and the prestigious archeological *Kogo hakpo* (*Journal of Archeology*), or the similar *Kogo minsok* (*Archeology and Ethnology*) does not mention any academy at all. Once deprived of their spiritual charm, academies were nothing much more than solid buildings from the second half of the Yi dynasty, possibly located in a romantic backdrop. The combination of these factors and ideological biases is very visible in a short entry on *sŏwŏn* architecture in *Chosŏn munhwasa* (*The History of Korean Culture*):

> The most important *sŏwŏn* buildings constructed in the second half of the 16th century are the Oksan Academy (1572), the Sohyŏn Academy (1578), the Tosan Academy (1574) and others. The Confucian academies were in many cases established in the countryside residences or houses of the person thus commemorated. *Sŏwŏn* architectural features thus reflect the housing style of the *yangban* class of that time. This kind of religious institutional architecture was connected to the feudal ruling class's pursuit of class overlordship and in its use for Confucian offerings and as

---

14  Another factor for this attitude could be also the lasting influence of Japanese colonial groundworks of cultural heritage based on a different approach to the values of historical heritage. Japanese registers of cultural monuments showed a significant focus on Buddhist relics and monuments (see Munhwajae kwalli kuk, *Chosŏn ch'ongdokpu mit mungyobu parhaeng munhwajae kwan'gye charyojip* [1992], 67–156) and this did not change when they were taken over by both DPRK and South Korea (Scheidhauer, "A Historiography of Cultural Heritage Interpretation and Policy in Kaesŏng," 106). The common policy of both Japanese and North Korean researchers was well described by Ruth Scheidhauer: "The North is less interested in larger architectural structures, but more in unearthing artifacts, which might potentially become national treasures: and for this they should not be older than the Koryŏ period" (Scheidhauer, "A Historiography of Cultural Heritage Interpretation and Policy in Kaesŏng," 205). This explains a certain paradox in the North Korean heritage policy where on the other hand Buddhism was labeled as the more backward ideology, compared to Confucianism (Chŏng Chaehun, *Chosŏn siadaeŭi hakp'a wa sasang* [Schools and Thought of the Chosŏn Period] [Seoul: Sin'gu munhwasa, 2008], 261), but the cultural protection was concentrated on Buddhist monasteries and much less on Confucian academies.

15  Pak Hwangsik, "Chongsŏng hayanggyo ŭi kŏnch'uk yangsik (Architectural Form of Chongsŏng Local School)," *Munhwa yusan* 4 (1956): 42–44.

a tool of propaganda for feudal Confucian ideas, it was extremely formalised and standardised. It does not truly reflect the superior architectural art of [the Korean] people.[16]

*Chosŏn kŏnch'uksa* 1 (*History of Korean Architecture* 1) published in 1989 also speaks in similar fashion about formalised architecture of academies, which forced their builders to follow established Confucian patterns.[17] It is nonetheless important to stress there was no articulated bias against the Confucian nature of the academies, as many other prized heritage structures in the DPRK were in fact of Confucian origin, for example, the National Academy Sŏnggyungwan 成均館 in Kaesŏng, built during the Koryŏ dynasty (918–1392).

Decisions of the new regime were however often made *ad hoc* and it combined hostility toward feudal relics with the ideas of cultural preservation. A good example could be relics connected to the patron of Pyongyang, the legendary Kija/Jizi 箕子. North Korean authorities on the one hand approved reconstruction of his shrine, Sunginjŏn 崇仁殿, damaged by the war,[18] but at the same time ordered destruction of his grave and also razed an altar dedicated to him (Kujudan 九疇壇) and the adjacent pavilion Kijagung 箕子宮 (also called Kija chaegung 箕子齋宮) to the ground.[19]

Another factor contributing toward a tolerance of the Confucian academies was the reunification issue, already hinted at in the quotation above. Although many surveys of Korean cultural heritage published in North Korea focussed only on artefacts in the DPRK,[20] the notion of connection with the southern part of the peninsula was never completely lost; in the case of the Confucian academies, the authorities in the DPRK were well aware of the preservation

---

16 Ch'oe T'aeksŏn, Hŏ Haesuk, *Chosŏn munhwasa* (The History of Korean Culture) (Pyongyang: Kwahak, paekkwasajŏn ch'ulp'ansa, 1977), 444.
17 Ri Hwasŏn, *Chosŏn kŏnch'uksa* I (History of Korean Architecture I) (Pyongyang: Kwahak, paekkwasajŏn ch'ulp'ansa, 1989), 427.
18 See the detailed report on the building and its reconstruction Pak Hwangsik, "P'yŏngyang ŭi Sunginjŏn ponjŏn kŏnch'uk ŭi yangsik kwa nyŏndae e taehayŏ (On Dating and the Original Architectural Form of Sunginjŏn in Pyongyang)," *Kŏnch'uk kwa kŏnsŏl* 2 (1957): 38–44.
19 Kija Palace was in 1957 still recorded as one of the important historical relics of the city, see P'ŏngyang t'osa p'yŏnjip wiwŏnhoe, *P'ŏngyang chi* (Pyongyang Gazette) (P'ŏngyang: Kungnip ch'ulp'ansa, 1957), fig. 70. According to oral testimonies (Vladimír Glomb interviews with the staff of Kim Il Sung University, October 2012) there was a big debate among archeology specialists as to which monuments are to be preserved and which should be liquidated. The second choice was the more frequent.
20 This fact was commonly understood but not very emphasized. For example: *Chungyo yujŏkmyŏngsŭng ch'ŏnyŏn kinyŏmmul illam* bears only one tiny note in the imprint. "[valid] for the northern part of the Republic."

efforts devoted to famous complexes like the Sosu Academy and the Tosan Academy 陶山書院 in South Korea, and understood academies located in the DPRK as a representative of a larger Korean whole. *Myŏngsŭng p'yŏllam* therefore speaks about the Sohyŏn Academy as a well-known important historical relic, which "together with Yulgok's birth house Ŏjukhŏn in Kangnŭng, Kangwŏn province; with T'oegye Yi Hwang's Tosan Academy in Yean, Northern Kyŏngsang; Kaesŏng Sungyang Academy (Chŏng Mongju's former residence) and others, represent the old *sŏwŏn* of our country."[21] With the publication of more representative overviews of the cultural relics in later and recent decades of the regime, we can usually find a description of the three main North Korean academies, Ryonggok, Sungyang and Sohyŏn, rendered at times in considerable detail (architectural plan, history, and so on.).

A very peculiar and typically North Korean feature of academies' portrayal in the DPRK—which does not appear in the early decades of the regime—is the infusion of the cult of personality in connection with the Confucian academies, i.e. the visits and related remarks of the beloved leaders to the *sŏwŏn*. *Uri nara ryŏksa yujŏk* (*Our Country's Historical Relics*) in 1983 introduces the entry on Ryonggok Academy with following note:

> Our beloved leader comrade *Kim Ilsŏng* instructed us to preserve the Ryonggok Academy in its original state and keep it as a historic monument in order to show it to the people.[22]

In the case of the Ryonggok Academy, the precise date of Kim Ilsŏng's visit (March 10, 1963) is indicated, as well as two visits (in September 1960 and November 1974) to the Sohyŏn Academy, where the great leader commented upon the natural landscape and recommended that the location be turned into a place of cultural recreation (*munhwa hyusikt'ŏ*).[23] The same was valid in later

---

21  Ch'oe Kyuhwan (ed.), *Myŏngsŭng, kojŏk, ch'ŏnyŏn kinyŏmmul p'yŏllam* (Guide to Famous Places, Historical Relics and Natural Monuments) (Pyongyang: Kunjung munhwa ch'ulp'ansa, 1966), 64.
22  Munhwa pojon yŏn'guso, *Uri nara ryŏksa yujŏk* (Our Country's Historical Relics) (Pyongyang: Kwahak, paekkwasajŏn ch'ulp'ansa, 1983), 39.
23  See Chosŏn ŭi onŭl (Chosŏn Today), "Kyegok mada chŏlssŭng – sŏhae myŏngsŭng sŏktam kugok," (available at: <http://www.dprktoday.com/index.php?type=2&no=6872>.) A detailed description of this visit is offered in Chu Sŏngch'ŏl, Rim Hosŏng, Kim Sŭngil, *Changgunnim gwa ryŏksahak* (General and History Science) (Pyongyang: Sahoe kwahak ch'ulp'ansa, 2014), 176–186. The description of the academy visit contains several positive evaluations of the academy's role like "seeing buildings of the academy, we may perceive how great attention devoted our ancestor to fostering of educational environment," etc.

ILLUSTRATION 15.5  Ryonggok Academy in 1959. The two buildings in the lower left corner of the picture are no longer extant and a stone wall around the compound was added later.
SOURCE: PHOTO COURTESY OF JAROSLAV BAŘINKA

times for Kim Chŏngil, who visited Ryonggok and Sohyŏn Academies "several times."[24]

We may state that the Confucian academies were, from the start of the new regime, included in the category of objects of cultural heritage, and that in the known cases—or more precisely, in the case of the well-known academies—they enjoyed state protection. It is also important to note that the three officially protected and preserved academies, Sungyang, Sohyŏn, and Ryonggok, are parts of larger protected areas. Sungyang Academy has been protected as a part of Kaesŏng city, Sohyŏn Academy has been understood as a part of the Nine River Bends of Sŏktam,[25] and Ryonggok Academy was traditionally

---

24   Ri Ch'ŏl, Ri Kiung et al., *Munhwa yusan aehogadŭrŭi pŏt* (Friend of Cultural Heritage Lovers) (Pyongyang: Chosŏn munhwa pojŏnsa, 2005), 98–99.
25   The Sŏktam Bends were acknowledged as a natural monument and ranked along other DPRK scenic spots like Diamond and Myohyang Mountains, Moranbong, etc. See the

part of the Mount Ryongak culture heritage area; their high visibility shielded them from the destiny of lesser known academies. Since they were deprived of their inhabitants, libraries, archives, and ritual characteristics, however, they remained hollow shells, their buildings empty, serving only as an occasional curiosity for tourists.

## 3 North Korean Historiography and Confucian Academies

Confucian academies were generally considered as an important institution of Korean history, and the description of their role and legacy was a standard part of works both on the general history of Korea, as well as the history of the Chosŏn period. The length of entries on Confucian academies differed according to the form of the publication, from brief mentions to several pages, but the topic was never fully omitted; even the very concise *Chosŏnsa nyŏnp'yo* (*The Chronology of Korean History*) lists the year 1543 as significant in the relation to the founding of the first *sŏwŏn*, the Paegundong Academy 白雲洞書院.[26]

The descriptions and evaluations of the Confucian academies published in the 1950s form part of the first wave of historiographical works produced under the auspices of the new regime: these later become the authoritative models for historical research in the DPRK in the subsequent decades. In many cases, these books established definite narrative and structural patterns which can be traced through successive versions of these published works up to the present day.[27] Among the works dealing with the Confucian academies, *Chosŏn t'ongsa I* (*The General History of Korea*) and *Chosŏn chungsesa II* (*The Medieval History of Korea II*), both published in 1956 and both authored by Pak Sihyŏng 朴時亨 (1910–2001), are prototypical.

---

      entry in O Chongik, *Chosŏn ŭi myŏngsŭng* (Famous places of Korea) (Pyongyang: Kunjung munhwasa, 1960), 91–94.

26  *Kwahagwŏn ryŏksa yŏn'guso, Chosŏnsa nyŏnp'yo* (Chronology of Korean History) (Pyongyang: Chosŏn minjujuŭi inmin kwahagwŏn, 1957), 282. *Chosŏn chŏnsa: nyŏnp'yo 1* (Complete History of Korea: Chronology 1) published in 1983 omits any mention of Confucian academies for the year 1543 but mentions as an important historical event the award of royal plaque and name to Sosu Academy in 1550. In the same manner the founder of Paegundong Academy, Chu Sebung 周世鵬 (1495–1554), was recognized and later listed as an important person, in *Yet saram irŭm p'yŏllam* (Handbook of Names of Historical Personalities), see O Hŭibok, *Yet saram irŭm p'yŏllam* (Handbook of Names of Historical Personalities) (Pyongyang: Kim Ilsŏng chonghap taehak, 1980), 124.

27  For an overview of older North Korean historiography see Kang In'gu, Yi Sŏngmi (ed.), *Pukhan ŭi hangukhak yŏn'gu sŏnggwa punsŏk: yŏksa, ch'ŏrhak* (Nature and Analysis of the North Korean Studies on Korea: History, Philosophy) (Sŏngnam: Hanguk chŏngsin munhwa yŏn'guwŏn, 1991).

*Chosŏn t'ongsa* was compiled under the auspices of the History Institute (*Ryŏksa yŏn'guso*) of the Academy of Sciences; it can be considered as the first production of North Korean academic historiography, later to be followed by many other similarly formulated works such as *Chosŏn t'ongsa I*, published in 1962, and *Chosŏn t'ongsa*, in 1977. This lineage was later expanded upon by the multi-volume *Chosŏn chŏnsa* (*The Complete History of Korea*), published in 1980, and more recently, by the even larger project entitled *Chosŏn tandaesa* (*A History of Korea in Historical Periods*). The high profile of the publication is demonstrated by the participation of Pak Sihyŏng, the director of the institute and a prominent historian.

The role of the Confucian academies is in both cases analysed within the framework of Marxist-Leninist historiography, based on the idea that "the history of all hitherto existing societies is the history of class struggle." In the case of the Confucian Academies, this means that the main focus of analysis is not their role as part of the intellectual history of Korean Confucianism, but as an "institution for the repressive exploitation of the people grounded in the collective power of the local *yangban* landowners,"[28] where scholars of *yangban* origin stand in opposition to the oppressed masses, i.e. Korean peasants emphatically called *inmin* 人民. The academies were thus discussed within the broader context of class antagonisms in traditional Korean society, and it is no surprise that their role was judged as being similar to that of the feudal *yangban* scholars—the creators and users of academies. The relatively brief treatment of the Confucian academies in the volume *Chosŏn t'ongsa I* presents the academies as "an institution, the stated purpose of which is that it pursues study, and performs sacrifices to famous scholars, politicians, generals, etc."[29] Nonetheless, the overall evaluation of academies was based on their social and economic role in relation to the oppressed masses.

> The collective power instruments of the *yangban* landowners such as Confucian academies (*sŏwŏn*), community compacts (*hyangyak*), and local schools (*hyanggyo*), became in every region outrageous institutions in the service of expanding the iron chain of feudal rule, plundering the masses and suppressing their resistance.[30]

---

28 Kwahagwŏn ryŏksa yŏn'guso, *Chosŏn t'ongsa* I (The General History of Korea I) (Chosŏn minjujuŭi inmin konghwaguk kwahagwŏn, 1956), 371.
29 Ibid.
30 Ibid.

Despite the colourful rhetoric, the entry identifies the basic problems of the perspective on *sŏwŏn* and their role within Korean history in relation to two crucial players—the peasant masses and the state. In the first case, we see the description of the development of the academies, originally few in number, into mighty institutions perceived as a crucial instrument of the oppression of the people and their exploitation. The second, but no less important aspect of the development of academies was their role in undermining state power via economic (the accumulation of wealth unaccompanied by taxation and the evasion of military conscription) as well as political means, i.e. the usurping of state authority, which is another recurring topic of studies on Confucian academies in the DPRK.

Both these motives were further elaborated in the more detailed history of traditional Korea, *Chosŏn chungsesa*, which devotes a chapter to the subject entitled "The growth of *sarim* and the emergence of the Confucian academies." As with every other introductory description of the academies, this institution was defined in terms of their founders, the *sarim* 士林 literati. These were characterised as small and medium landowners, who after a series of bloody purges retreated to the countryside where they pursued Confucian studies and prepared for future conflicts with the central government meritocracy—the rich and powerful families, the so-called *hun'gup'a* 勳舊派—who had monopolised power ever since the foundation of the dynasty. The foundation of the Paegundong Academy is seen as the beginning of the rapid growth of academies, an institution which proved to be so crucial for the literati class in the following centuries. As for the reasons for the enormous success of the Confucian academies and their rapid expansion, the decline of the government school system is invoked: it was allegedly not able to compete with the academies with their concentrations of dedicated Confucian scholars and the ability of academies to concentrate significant economic wealth as well.

The economic wealth of academies was, according to Pak Sihyŏng, based on their ability to expand their initial property holdings (originally granted by either the king or local *yangbans*) via tax evasion, i.e. using the privilege of tax exemption for chartered academies and extending it as much as possible. This attracted many small landowners to seek tax shelter with the academies and entrust their property to academies, thus avoiding the government tax authorities (and military service as well). The third source of the growing wealth of the academies was the forcible expropriation of peasant smallholders. This economic power led to a large degree of autonomy on the part of the academies vis-à-vis local government, and Pak Sihyŏng could, with some justification, speak of academies as "small kingdoms,"[31] easily able to resist local officials. The greed of *yangban* literati, together with competition for wealth and power, contributed as well to the emergence of factional struggles plaguing Korea from the 16th century onward, during which academies served as the bases for various factions.

All these aspects of the Confucian academies reveal them to be institutions abandoning their original pedagogical intent and transforming into pure instruments of the struggle for power. The complete loss of original Confucian ideals is well described in the following passage:

> Instead of memorising Confucius and Mencius, talking about brothers Cheng and Master Zhu, discussing lectures and preparing for their future political role, the majority of *yangban* enrolled in academies ignored these "far-reaching" ideas and turned their attention rather to questions of mundane profit which were close at hand. Their immediately used their collective power to oppress the people and exploit them.[32]

In order to find a clear-cut definition of the role of the Confucian academies, it is necessary to turn our attention from the relative high profile publications of the Academy of Sciences to a more simple and concise source: history textbooks. The 1950s saw a wide range of publications aimed at various levels of the education process, from universities to high schools and other educational institutions of the new North Korean regime. In addition to university history textbooks, high school textbooks are worthy of special attention, as they offer a very simple and understandable definitions of the role of academies and their evaluation intended for Korean youth.

The paperback textbooks represented the first steps in attempting to explain to young students the complex relations of the former feudal society, and this was (despite the frequent use of illustrations and simplified language) not an easy task. The situation was complicated by the fact that education policy was at the time creating a system of dissemination for the new ideology, seeking to distance itself from previous traditions of nationalist or colonial education. There were virtually no precedents available as to how the new Marxist-Leninist educational system—adjusted to the specific conditions of Korean history—should function, and the regime was forced to educate not only the students but above all the pedagogues themselves.

---

31   Pak Sihyŏng, *Chosŏn chungsesa* II (The Medieval History of Korea II) (Pyongyang: Kungnip ch'ulp'ansa, 1956), 177.
32   Ibid., 175.

The dearth of secondary literature in history education called for some provisional solutions. Since the first historical dictionary was published only much later,[33] in 1956 the manual *Chosŏn ryŏksa kyogwasŏ yongŏ haesŏl* (*An Explanation of Terminology for Korean History Textbooks*) was published for provisional use: it contains a short but authoritative entry describing the history and meaning of the Confucian academies. Educational institutions struggled to supply teachers with as many materials for the demands of the new curriculum as possible. The real gem among these materials is the *Chosŏn ryŏksa kyosu ch'amgosŏ* (*Reference Materials for Teachers of Korean History*), published in 1956 and intended for teachers of history courses in the first year of middle school (*ch'ogŭp chunghakkyo*). Authored by the historian O Changwan, it was intended as a manual to accompany textbooks of Korean history issued by the publishers Kyoyuk tosŏ ch'ulp'ansa (Education Books Publishing House) in 1955.

This book offers step-by-step instructions as to how to present Korean history, including the Confucian academies and related phenomena. A fascinating witness of its era, the text shows the first attempts to teach Korean history in the spirit of the new ideology:

Chapter 10
16th-Century domestic development and 1592–1598 Patriotic War (12 hours)
Lecture 1.
1) Title of lecture: Inner division of *yangbans* and the weakening of the central feudal authority
2) Basic content of the lecture: From the 16th century onward, *yangbans* involved in the central government began to acquire even more land. As a consequence of the frequent conversion of public land for private use, the state was not able to give appointed officials their property stipend. Among the *yangbans* in central government, a violent struggle for land property thus ensued. Additionally, small and medium landowners, *sarim*, started to pillage land property by employing the establishment of the *sŏwŏn*. They also organised community compacts and strengthened the oppression of the people.
3) Goal of teachers' education: Through the exposition of the contradictions of society in the 16th century in terms of the structure of land property, together with an analysis of power struggles within the ruling class,

---

33   This was the *Ryŏksa sajŏn* I–II (Historical Dictionary I–II) (Pyongyang: Sahoe kwhagwŏn ch'ulp'ansa, 1971).

students should be made to understand the domestic economical-political situation prior to the 1592–1598 Patriotic War.
4) Teacher's preparation: It is necessary to prepare pictures of Confucian academies, organisation charts of community compacts, etc.
5) Lecture itinerary
The *sarim* literati were small and medium land-owners holding power mainly in Kyŏngsan, Ch'ungch'ŏn and Chŏlla Provinces; they denounced the corruption of the big landowners of the central government. Through the establishment of the *sŏwŏn*, they strived to consolidate their power and subsequently launched a scramble for political authority. This must be stated and the origin and nature of the *sŏwŏn* should be closely examined. The *sŏwŏn* were at first founded by the *sarim* who sought to establish, in the countryside, an economic base for their rivalry with the big land-owners of the central government. Outwardly it appeared that the *sŏwŏn* were intended to support the cultivation of the local population, foster talents, and perform sacrifices to famous scholars, but under this guise the *sŏwŏn* were in fact exploitative institutions taking advantage of and oppressing local populations, concentrating on amassing of landed property in order to increase their own power.
6) Lesson review questions
What were the *sŏwŏn* and community compacts?[34]

The sole purpose of the educational lesson was to present the Confucian academies as institutions involved in power struggles within the *yangban* elite, and tools of the oppression of the people. Any claims to a positive cultural or pedagogical role of academies was summarily dismissed as a mere camouflage of their essentially exploitive nature. The task for historians was to document the precise functioning of this oppression and exploitation, and make it comprehensible to the younger generation.

## 4    Academies and History of Education

The focus on the sociopolitical and economic role of academies overshadowed their significance as educational institutions, but this aspect was not completely ignored. Several North Korean publications on the history of education analysed the role of the Confucian academies within this context, and the

---

[34]  O Changhwan, *Chosŏn ryŏksa kyosu ch'amgosŏ* (Reference Materials for Teachers of Korean History) (Pyongyang: Kyoyuk tosŏ ch'ulp'ansa, 1956), 296–300.

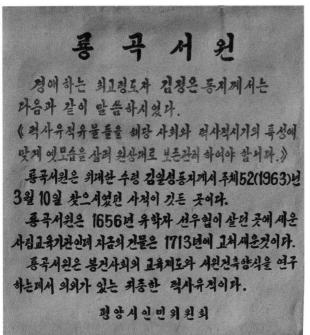

ILLUSTRATION 15.6
Cultural heritage information tablet in front of Ryonggok Academy installed by the People's Committee of Pyongyang City. The first part of the inscription quotes, in honorific red-lettering, a statement by the current North Korean leader Kim Chŏngŭn on the necessity of cultural heritage protection. It is followed by a commemoration of Kim Ilsŏng's visit in 1963 and a description of the academy in plain black letters.

series of three works bearing the same title of *Chosŏn kyoyuksa* (*The History of Korean Education*), published in respectively 1947, 1961, and 2012, provide us with opinions in this field from the early, middle, and contemporary eras.

In searching for the first history of Korean education, we have to go back to the times of the Japanese occupation and the days of the "stick and carrot" policy toward Korean intellectuals in 1930s. The first phase of the story begins at the moment in 1910 when a young medical school graduate, Yi Man'gyu 李萬珪 (1882–1978),[35] began to be more attracted to the calling of teacher and educator rather than that of medical doctor. His combination of patriotism and the fervour to educate the Korean people led the young Yi Man'gyu to combine the teaching career with support for the Korean cause, and eventually lead to his participation in several pro-independence organisations involved in clashes with the Japanese occupation authorities, as well as to several arrests by those authorities. During one such episode in 1938, Yi Man'gyu lost his position at the school then known as Paiwha Girls' High School (*Paehwa yŏja kodŭng hakkyo* 培花女子高等學校), earning him a 31-month forced holiday, during which he explored old documents: subsequently, he decided to write a history of Korean education.

---

35  In North Korean publications spelled as Ri Man'gyu.

The fruits of his work were published only after liberation in 1947, and 1949 when the volume entitled *Chosŏn kyoyuksa* 朝鮮教育史 I–II (*History of Korean Education*) was issued in Seoul by the Ŭryu munhwasa publishing company. Yi Man'gyu's book was, in his own words "the first history of Korean education written by the hand of a Korean" and not a "worthless book written by the Japanese [as previously]."[36] His joy after the publication was not to be long-lasting. His position in the Working People's Party (*Kŭllo inmindang*), the assassination of his companion Yŏ Unhyŏng 呂運亨 (1886–1947), and the worsening political situation for the leftist intellectuals in the South all contributed to his decision, in 1948, to remain in Pyongyang, where he became a prominent academic and public figure. This step sealed the destiny of his book in South Korea, where it was re-published only in 1988. Yi Man'gyu's book represents the view of Korean history (including the Confucian academies) shared by many left-leaning intellectuals of the Japanese occupation period who later were formative in the creation of academic institutions in the DPRK; despite its pre-liberation origin, it can be considered as a foundational work in the North Korean history of education.

*Chosŏn kyoyuksa* was a product of the author's leisure time, but its structure and content shows excellent work with the sources, as well as the author's erudition as a historian. The relatively short but precise description of the rise and fall of the Confucian academies uses extensive quotations from the *Chosŏn Dynasty Annals* and other sources, such as the works of the famous scholars T'oegye Yi Hwang 退溪 李滉 (1501–1570), or Tasan Chŏng Yagyong 茶山 丁若鏞 (1762–1836), and indicates why Yi Man'gyu was, because of his skills, later invited to participate in North Korean translation projects of the *Koryŏsa* 高麗史 (*History of Koryŏ*) and the above-mentioned *Chosŏn Dynasty Annals*.

Yi Man'gyu's views on Confucian academies combine both a patriotic tendency to discover glorious moments in the Korean past and his stance of reform scholar, attempting to emancipate the Korean people from the bonds of this selfsame reactionary past. The presented evaluation of the *sŏwŏn* acknowledges the positive ideal which accompanied academies' beginnings, and stressed that for the pursuit of genuine study and fostering talents for the state service, Confucian academies were much more suitable than the extant (and often corrupted) governmental school system. But his critical conviction led him to immediately note that we should not forget "however perfect a system you may create within feudal society, due to the abuse of power and privileges

---

36  Yi Man'gyu, *Chosŏn kyoyuksa* I (History of Korean Education) (Seoul: Ŭryu munhwasa, 1947), 2.

it will [inevitably] lead to many evils."[37] The Confucian ideals of the founding period of the academies had to be compared with their later development of the academies, demanding a resolute critique. Ever the good instructor, Yi Man'gyu presented the main flaws of the *sŏwŏn* system systematically point by point. The evils of the Confucian academies were as follows:

1) Because of the transfer of the village school (*hyanggyo*) students into Confucian academies (*sŏwŏn*), academies were one of the causes of the decline of village schools.
2) Because of the lack of responsible headmasters, academies were often place of entertainment and feasting.
3) Confucian academies were a shelter for those who sought to evade military service.
4) In many cases, they become the nurseries of villains who reigned over the impoverished local population through exploitation and abuse.
5) The land owned by the academies evaded taxation, and its earnings were wasted on feeding Confucian students.
6) During factional fights for power, academy students became antagonised, further exacerbating these conflicts.[38]

Yi Man'gyu's critique basically reiterates the traditional points raised in many memoirs recorded in the *Dynasty Annals*, and we can state that such opinions were almost unanimously shared by all modern Korean scholars of his era. Even the conservative intellectual and historian Ch'oe Namsŏn 崔南善 (1890–1957), who stood on the completely opposite side of the political spectrum, referred to Confucian academies in his works as "dens of rotten Confucians" (腐儒의 巢窟).[39] But the tone employed in *Chosŏn kyoyuksa*, although critical, is nonetheless reminiscent of the bygone, gentleman-like manner of colonial bourgeois times. Even as Yi Man'gyu criticises feudal ideology, (i.e. Confucianism) he formulates his statements in a genteel, polite manner. His typical tone is seen in his call to "re-evaluate the question as to whether the veneration of the worthies who were proponents of the feudal thought is admissible in the educational system of today."[40] In post-liberation North Korea this question was already irrelevant, and the new regime answered it in a very articulated way. The fact that Yi Man'gyu's book was seen as belonging more to

---

37  Ibid., 260–261.
38  Ibid., 263.
39  Ch'oe Namsŏn, *Yuktang Ch'oe Namsŏn chŏnjip 3* (Complete Works of Yuktang Ch'oe Namsŏn) (Chosŏn sangsik mundap, Chosŏn sangsik) (Seoul: Hyŏnamsa, 1973), 349.
40  Yi Man'gyu, *Chosŏn kyoyuksa 1*, 264.

the past than the present, and that the regime of the DPRK required a much stricter view of the history of education, is attested by other sources as well. In 1958, the journal *Inmin kyoyuk* (*People's Education*) published several comments on the series of materials concerning the history of education in Korea which had been published in the journal and 1956 and 1957. In addition to numerous proposals as to how this topic should be properly treated (for example, calling for a stricter critique of the traditional state examination system and Zhu Xi's philosophy), the author stresses the necessity of publishing original historical materials on the topic of education because "until now there has been no systematic work completed on the history of education in our country."[41]

Yi Man'gyu could well be a loyal supporter of the DPRK, but the new regime required a critique of the past of much heavier calibre than academic work from 1938 completed in one's spare time. Yi Man'gyu continued his research on the history of education and in 1957 published a manual for teachers, *Chosŏn kyoyuksa yŏn'gu mit charyo I* (*Studies and Materials on History of Korean Education I*) including a short overview of history of Confucian academies. This work was understood as a preparatory step for the "compilation of a regular history of Korean education."[42]

The new authoritative *History of Korean Education* was finally published by a collective of authors in 1961.[43] Based on Marxist-Leninist methodology, it was announced as an important step in "completing our country's revolution and promoting the building of socialism."[44] This work also introduces some new phenomena which were still recent in 1960: the book, for example, opens with an extensive quotation from Kim Ilsŏng on the meaning of the study of history.[45] The story of the Confucian academies described in the book is largely based on the concept of the originally small *sarim* literati institutions which later degenerated into the powerfully oppressive system of the academies.

In comparison with other North Korean sources, there was a greater focus on the spiritual and educational role of the Confucian academies, although this was in the context of an overall negative evaluation: "Confucian academies

---

41 Ri Namsan, "*Chosŏn kyoyuksa ch'amgo charyo rŭl ilkko* (Reading Reference Documents of History of Korean Education)," *Inmin kyoyuk 8* (1958): 26.

42 Yi Man'gyu, *Chosŏn kyoyuksa yŏn'gu mit charyo I* (Studies and materials on history of Korean education I) (Pyongyang: Kyoyuk tosŏ ch'ulp'ansa, 1957), 11.

43 The book was originally published in Pyongyang by Kyoyuk tosŏ ch'ulp'ansa. In 1963 it was reprinted by the publishing house of the General Association of Korean Residents in Japan (*Ch'ongnyŏn*) Hagu sŏbang.

44 *Chosŏn kyoyuksa* (History of Education in Korea) (Tokyo: Hagu sŏbang, 1963), 5.

45 Ibid., 5.

played often a negative role [in the social and economic area], but at the same time they did play certain role in the development of students' education and the theoretical development of the Zhu Xi school of thought (*Chujahak*)."⁴⁶ The Confucian values taught in academies might have played a positive role at some point, but seen from the larger perspective of a North Korean scholar, these were still only the values of the ruling class, intrinsically devoid of anything positive. The vices, described in detail, of the Confucian curriculum were as follows:

> The ruling class educated their future generations wholly by the ideas of Confucian moral obligations and the morals of the Three Bonds and Five Relationships (*samgang oryun*). This was vexing to the life of the younger generation. In particular, by forcing them to follow all formalistic rites and customs, such as those used during capping, marriage, mourning, and making offerings to ancestors, the *sŏwŏn* suppressed any social development. Through the dogmatism of Master Zhu's teaching, the academies inhibited freedom of scholarship and paralysed the students' creativity and capacity for critical thought. The ruling classes had exclusive control of the educational process and for the subjugated classes it only lead them into coerced blind obedience and ignorance.⁴⁷

Among the further evils of the Confucian academies, we may also include teaching students "contempt for physical labour."⁴⁸

It is clear that this evaluation in 1961 of Confucian academies from the point of history of education was almost exclusively negative. Such stereotypes were methodologically based on drawing parallels between the socioeconomic development of the academies and their intellectual and spiritual significance. In both cases the example of the decadence of the originally progressive academies was employed—institutions originally developed to defend the aims of literati degenerating into power-hungry institutions privatised by mighty families and ruining the state. In this sense, both works—the volume referred to above by Yi Man'gyu and the *Chosŏn kyoyuksa*, published in 1961—share the same narrative of how academies "pretending to be the guardian of the so-called beautiful customs and rites" developed under this pretext into institutions "oppressing and exploiting the people."⁴⁹

---

46   Ibid., 58.
47   Ibid., 86.
48   Ibid., 87.
49   Ibid., 58.

## 5 Land and Money

In spite of the rather negative attitude, the Confucian academies were an integral part of Korean history and a serious academic object of attention in North Korea. We can state that although not the most prominent target of research during the hectic formulation of the North Korean perspective on feudal society, they still posed an important and interesting challenge. Probably the best (and almost the only) representative of scholarly debate on Korean Confucian academies in the 1950s is O Changhwan's analysis of the Confucian academies in *Sŏwŏn e taehan yakkan ŭi koch'al* (*Some Examinations Concerning Confucian Academies*), published in 1956 in the main journal of historical research, *Ryŏksa kwahak* (*History Science*).

O Changhwan's study remains, even today, the most precise historical work on the Confucian academies within the DPRK and offers in-depth insight into the questions of North Korean scholars concerning the *sŏwŏn* and their role in traditional Korean society. The author's name was already mentioned above in connection with early teaching materials for Korean history. O Changhwan was in fact a prolific historian, and the Confucian academies were among his favourite topics. He was also one of the first North Korean scholars[50] who called for research into possible analogies between the role of monasteries in the decline of Koryŏ and the role of Confucian academies in the decline of the Chosŏn dynasty, publishing studies on both topics.[51] His study of the academies is composed of three parts presenting some rather obvious, but also some rather unusual themes, namely the origin and development of the academies, their role as large scale property holders, and the role of the academies as money-lending institutions.

The first task in the analysis of the rise and fall of Confucian academies was to determine the historical conditions which gave rise to these phenomena. The well-known fact that certain forms of *sŏwŏn*[52] existed even before the 1543 founding of the Paegundong Academy simply demonstrates that the idea of the academies had been present for a long time and its rapid development dur-

---

50   A few years later Kim Sŏkhyŏng briefly compared both types of institutions in his study on the *yangban* class. See Kim Sŏkhyŏng, "Ryangballon (Discussion on *yangban*)," *Ryŏksa nonmunjip* 3 (1959): 80–88.

51   See O Changhwan, "Rijo ponggŏn sigi sawŏn kyŏngjeŭi myŏtkaji koch'al (Several Observations on Buddhist Temples during the Feudal Period of the Yi Dynasty)," *Ryŏksa kwahak* (1955): 44–58.

52   The study quotes the famous order of King Sejong from 1418 to praise and reward "those who privately established *sŏwŏn* and teach their students." *Sejong sillok* 1/11/3#12, 其有儒士私置書院, 教誨生徒者. A concrete example of founders of a *sŏwŏn* are, in 1420, named as Chŏng Kon 鄭坤 (?–?) and Ch'oe Pomin 崔保民 (?–?). See *Sejong sillok* 2/1/21#3.

ing the second half of the 16th century was caused by the fruition of social and economic conditions for such a process. But what were the reasons which triggered such a rapid growth of this institution which had remained dormant since the founding of the dynasty?

The primary reason for the establishment of the Confucian academies was the need of the *sarim* literati to secure an economic and power base in the countryside. The huge success and rapid development were enabled and accelerated by several factors. The first was the growth of agricultural land and the significant shattering of the property structure after the Imjin War. The second was the intensive fractional strife which caused various literati groups to organise their own economic destinies independent of state salary structures. The third was the general decline of government-run schools occasioned by corruption and nepotism, leading many literati to seek educational alternatives. The fourth and the most interesting reason was the growing tendency of the free peasants to entrust themselves to academies and thus evade "growing feudal exploitation."

This process was enhanced by the decline of local schools and Buddhist monasteries which had provided shelter for their clients in previous times, as well as by the positive approach of the *sŏwŏn* landowners who sought a labour force for their new estates. The process of growth of the Confucian academies is well supported by the statistical evidence based on the available data from old documents used by the author, such as the *Chodurok* 俎豆錄 (*The Record of Offerings*) and so on, which *cum grano salis* demonstrate the trajectory of academies' development.

The curve of founded academies peaked during the reign of King Sukchong; this leads to the question as to the reasons for the decreasing number of new academies after the mid-18th century. The crucial factor was the transformation of the forces that supported the academies: the literati, who were, at the beginning of the story of academies, small and medium landowners.

In contrast to the first period of the academies system, when these literati were busy founding academies and attracting impoverished peasants, during the later era they were not able to compete with the big landowners and they themselves had become "fallen *yangbans*." The major landowners had no further need to establish new academies, since their existing property was already secured and they were even able, with state assistance, to impose limits on the founding of new academies.

The situation changed as well for the lowest stratum of the *sŏwŏn* community: the peasants. Because of demographic changes and "intensification of feudal oppression," academies ceased to be attractive as an economic haven. Instead of entering academies, peasants were leaving them and trying their

TABLE 15.1  Founding of academies by royal reign

| Royal reign | Founded sŏwŏn | Chartered sŏwŏn |
| --- | --- | --- |
| Chungjong 中宗 (1506–1544) | 4 | 4 |
| Myŏngjong 明宗 (1545–1567) | 16 | 4 |
| Sŏnjo 宣祖 (1567–1608) | 82 | 24 |
| Kwanghaegun 光海君 (1608–1623) | 39 | 15 |
| Injo 仁祖 (1623–1649) | 49 | 7 |
| Hyojong 孝宗 (1649–1659) | 35 | 9 |
| Hyŏnjong 顯宗 (1659–1674) | 67 | 42 |
| Sukchong 肅宗 (1674–1720) | 300 | 129 |
| Kyŏngjong 景宗 (1720–1724) | 10 | 7 |
| Yŏngjo 英祖 (1724–1776) | 32 | 10 |
| Chŏngjo 正祖 (1776–1800) | 14 | 19 |
| Sunjo 純祖 (1800–1834) | 3 | 2 |
| Hŏnjong 憲宗 (1834–1849) | 2 | 1 |
| Ch'ŏljong 哲宗 (1849–1863) | 1 | 1 |
| Unknown | 34 | 1 |
| *Total* | 688 | 275 |

SOURCE: O, CHANGHWAN. "SŎWŎNE TAEHAN YAKKANŬI KOCH'AL (SHORT STUDY ON CONFUCIAN ACADEMIES)." RYŎKSA KWAHAK NO. 6 (1956): 73

fortunes in the new environments of the emerging cities, mining, or various alternative occupations (as peddlers, and so on). The same new economic factors influenced the strategies of the big landowners, who turned more frequently to the possibilities offered by the emergence of the money economy and new industries and instead of founding new academies focused on cultivation of the existing resources. The last—but not least—factor was the strong political pressure of the kings Yŏngjo and Chŏngjo, who tried to reduce number of academies as a part of their anti-factional policy.

The connection between political factions and the academies further contributed to the degeneration of their original ideals, and as many traditional authors remarked, led in many cases to the veneration of the ancestors of *sŏwŏn* owners, as well as persons who were far from being ideal scholars. In the case of Confucian scholars, factionalism caused them to place emphasis on the illustrious individuals of their own factions based upon both political affiliation and geographical location. Kyŏnggi province thus hosted no shrines to Yi Hwang, and three dedicated to Yi I, but Kyŏngsang had sixteen shrines dedicated to Yi Hwang, and only one to Yi I; Chungch'ŏng province was a stronghold of the veneration of Song Siyŏl; Hwanghae preferred Yi I, and so on.

O Changwan provided valuable charts trying to detect the geographical distribution of venerated persons in relation to the ratio of chartered and unchartered academies: this effectively demonstrates the political influences inherent in the system. Kyŏnggi province hosted only 62 academies, but 51 of them (82%) were chartered, unlike in the dissident Kyŏngsang province, where there were 248 academies, but only 68 (27%) of them were chartered. Very interesting as well is his chart showing the most frequently venerated scholars, which somehow differ from what one might expect when compared for example with the authoritative list of Korean worthies enshrined in the Seoul Confucius Shrine (munmyo 文廟).

The neuralgic point of such a statistical overview of the rise and decline of Confucian academies was the problematic relation between numbers and the true state of affairs. O Changhwan was well aware that "although the numbers of academies were decreasing, their reactionary functions were in fact increasing and ever more empowered."[53] In order to understand the operation of the academies within Korean society, he looked for economic analysis supported by hard data. That was not an easy task, since the existing material was plagued by the typical problems of Korean historical sources.

The seemingly natural approach based on prescriptive texts was hardly possible, since legal mentions in relation to academies were of relatively late origin; *Soktaejŏn* 續大典 (*Supplements to the Great Code*), dating from 1744, was the first systematic attempt to regulate these institutions. We can therefore state that during the first centuries of their existence, based on the analogies with other schools and similar institutions (including the school fields system, *hakchŏn* 學田) and amended by *ad hoc* royal edicts regulating number of students, tax exemptions, and so on, the *sŏwŏn* were operating within a very loose legal framework. The situation was further complicated by the fact that legal

---

53   O Changhwan, "Sŏwŏn e taehan yakkan ŭi koch'al (Short Study on Confucian Academies)," *Ryŏksa kwahak* no. 6 (1956): 75.

TABLE 15.2  The most frequently enshrined scholars

| Name of scholar | Number of academies dedicated |
| --- | --- |
| Song Siyŏl 宋時烈 (1607–1689) | 36 |
| Yi Hwang 李滉 (1501–1570) | 30 |
| Yi I 李珥 (1536–1584) | 20 |
| Cho Kwangjo 趙光祖 (1482–1519) | 17 |
| Yi Ŏnjŏk 李彦迪 (1491–1553) | 16 |
| Chŏng Ku 鄭逑 (1543–1620) | 15 |

SOURCE: O, CHANGHWAN. "SŎWŎNE TAEHAN YAKKANŬI KOCH'AL (SHORT STUDY ON CONFUCIAN ACADEMIES)." RYŎKSA KWAHAK NO. 6 (1956): 75

restrictions and prescriptions often did not correspond to the actual state of the Confucian academies, especially in the case of the two vital components of the system: land property and the employed labour force. North Korean scholars were well aware that a proper analysis of the land property structure was essential for the understanding of traditional society and so they invested much energy in decoding the extremely complicated process of land distribution during the Chosŏn period.

O Changhwan's attempt to provide data for the Confucian academies property structure was part of a larger effort of the DPRK scholars to provide a comprehensive analysis of the land property transformation processes: this was crowned in 1961 with the issuing of the essential publication on this topic, *Chosŏn t'oji chedosa 2* (*A History of the Korean Land System*), devoting large passages of the text also to the problem of the academies' land property. The questions of the North Korean researcher are in many cases yet to be answered both in general, and in relation to the Confucian academies: How did *yangban* appropriation of state land function exactly; are the official data of the household registers reliable; what was the real nature of the slave *nobi* 奴婢 system, and so on.

The starting point of the precise nature of the *sŏwŏn* property, institutional scale, and people (students, slaves, dependent peasants, and so forth) inevitably starts with the legal stipulation regulating the academies. A 1710 regulation determined the number of students to be 30 for academies dedicated to a person enshrined in the Confucius Shrine, 20 students for a chartered academy, and 15 for an unchartered academy. This should be compared with the old school system prescribing, for example, 200 students for the National Academy Sŏnggyungwan 成均館; the Four Schools (*Sahak* 四學), each with 100 students; the provincial level local schools with 90; the county (*kun* 君) schools with 50; and finally, the district (*hyŏn* 縣) schools with 30 students. The corresponding figures are the land allotments ascribed to these institutions: Sŏnggyungwan with 200 *kyŏl*, each of the Four Schools with 100 *kyŏl*, the provincial level schools each allotted 10 *kyŏl*, the prefecture schools with 7 and the district level *hyanggyo* with 5 *kyŏl*.

It is clear that the officially allowed number of 3 *kyŏl* tax-exempted fields for the chartered academy would not play an important role in the overall context of the Korean economy and the accumulation of much significant wealth by the academies was probably far bigger. But how can the precise numbers be determined? O Changwan took as a sample 6 academies (2 chartered and 4 unchartered) in Ŭiju 義州 prefecture at the beginning of the 19th century. Based on the local gazetteer *Ryongmanji* 龍灣誌,[54] first published in 1768, he provided interesting data. When all land units are converted and counted it is revealed that the average land property of an individual academy was 32 *kyŏl*. In other words, even just a few selected academies in the insignificant northern provincial prefectures had, together, the same amount of land as the official National Academy. We may also presume that these were rather low numbers compared with the southern provincial academies, the land ownings of which amounted to hundreds of *kyŏl*.

The land property itself does not encompass the real socioeconomic power of the academies, which was to a large degree constituted by vassal relations and the labour force an academy owned or commanded. The human resources factor was clearly visible already in the founding process of the academies when the village elders and various scholars often made contributions not only of land grants but also of labour force ordered to assist in construction and suchlike. This form of support was often obtained from local magistrates and officials as well: they were not able to contribute land (state property) but were nonetheless able to mobilise the local population to provide valuable resources (timber and so on), as well as manpower. Academy slaves (*wŏnno* 院奴) were often given to the *sŏwŏn* together with land grants and counted as part of the academies' property. During Hyojong's reign (1649–1659), their number was limited to 7 slaves for a chartered academy and 5 for an unchartered academy.

---

54   Relatively unknown (in South Korea), *Ryongmanji* is in DPRK treated as an important historical source. See its description in Munhŏn yŏn'gusil, *Chosŏn kojŏn haeje* 1 (Bibliographical Notes on Classical Korean Literature) (Pyongyang: Sahoe kwahagwŏn ch'ulp'ansa, 1965), and the recent study by Kim Ch'ŏlsu, "Ryongmanjie taehan yŏn'gu (Study of *Ryongmanji*)," in *Minjok kojŏn yŏn'gu nonmunjip* 28 (Pyongyang: Sahoe kwahak ch'ulp'ansa, 2011), 5–97.

The very fact of the need for decree and regulations on this topic demonstrates that the numbers were, in reality, probably much higher (also because of the hereditary nature of the system); slaves, however, were not an essential part of the production system and they were used mainly for various tasks within the academy. The backbone of the *sŏwŏn* economy were the vassal peasants, often called *moibin* 募入人, who provided a workforce for the growing estates. The nature of their relation to the academy as "regardless of various designations, not different from that of agriculture slaves."[55] is observed in various records: the main motivation of peasants to enter into a relation of dependence with the *sŏwŏn* was to obtain the tax and military shelters which the academy could offer. This led many peasants to entrust themselves, together with their land, to academies, further enlarging the academies' wealth. The final result of this process was the creation of entire villages consisting of peasants dependent and under the direct control of the central academy, the so-called academy villages, *sŏwŏnch'on* 書院村.

The third factor influencing the power of Confucian academies was money. In their analysis of traditional Korean society, the scholars of the DPRK invested much energy in the topic of the emergence and development of the monetary economy (*hwap'ye kyŏngje*). This phenomenon was considered by both nationalist and leftist scholars as one of the indicators of advanced national development, demonstrating that Korea was not economically backward in relation to China and Japan; within the Marxist-Leninist discourse, however, it signified another important issue as well.

The monetary economy was understood to be one of the indicators of the capitalist system of production: its existence in traditional Korean society served as an indicator of the first stages of capital accumulation, to be followed by the transition from a feudal to a bourgeois society with all the attendant political consequences (emergence of the proletariat, and so on). The discovery of the domestic proto-capitalism tradition meant the discovery of a nascent proletarian revolutionary movement in feudal Korea. But what was the role of the academies within this process, if any?

Money played a hugely important role in the economy of the academy, and from the 16th century onward we find a large number of materials documenting this fact. The Confucian academies were one of the few local institutions which were able to operate outside the limits of the traditional village exchange economy, and so very early on, they become monetary economic institutions in the proper sense. O Changhwan's study focused on one of the most interesting aspect of the economic existence of the *sŏwŏn*: loan-sharking. The

---

55   O Changhwan, "Sŏwŏn e taehan yakkan ŭi koch'al," 82.

very fact that academies were studied as "usher institutions" (*koridae kigwan*) facilitating the advent of capitalism was not accidental: this was one of the darkest moments in the history of the complex relations between the academies and peasants.

The economic role of academies was based on several facts: they were wealthy institutions in their own right, and since their founding, they were strongly connected through the community compacts (*hyangyak* 鄉約) to the local village economy. Already in the *Haeju Community Compact* or *Pledges for the Village Grannary* (*Sach'anggye* 社倉契), composed by Yulgok Yi I, we find instructions concerning loans made from the community compact surplus to the local population at an interest rate of 20 percent, and discussion of punishment for debtors. The combination of the social ties provided by the connections between the community compact, the local granaries, and the academy created ideal conditions for the emergence of the *sŏwŏn* as quasi-banking institutions able to charge exorbitant interest rates. The power of the academy was in many cases either supported by local officials, or even a source of concern for them, as their unlimited power enabled them to become loan-sharking institutions undisturbed by the authorities. The symbol of this power were the so-called black tallies (or warrants) (*hŭkp'ae* 黑牌),[56] issued by the academies for governing the population and the extortion of debts, which were "feared more than the orders of the local governors."[57]

But the suffering of peasants plagued by academies' usury (seen from the Marxist-Leninist perspective, but probably from the peasants' perpective as well) was overshadowed by another point: the failure of academies to accelerate the wheel of history. The most important failure of the *sŏwŏn* described by the North Korean scholar was the fact that although they theoretically had the opportunity, they "played no role in the creation of capitalist production relations."[58] Would not be the course of Korean history have been different if the academies had assumed the role of the primary centres of capital accumulation?

> As was already mentioned, Confucian academies did not convert usury profits or agricultural surplus into the process of monetary accumulation or handicraft production, but mainly used it to maintain their luxurious lifestyle, academy expenses or the purchase of land. [...] They focused

---

[56] In the South Korean literature the more frequently used term is *mokp'ae* 墨牌 ("ink tally"), both terms referring to a black academy seal.
[57] O Changhwan, "Sŏwŏn e taehan yakkan ŭi koch'al," *Ryŏksa kwahak* no. 6 (1956), 89.
[58] Ibid., 90.

solely on the maintenance of the feudal order and the continuation of the existence of academies. They were incapable of thinking about anything else beyond their own corrupted daily existence.[59]

## 6  Conclusion

The overall picture of Confucian academies offered by the early North Korean sources show us a strikingly negative, yet very interesting description of these "institutions [created] for the exploitation of the people."[60] The intention of this a priori bias against these remnants of the old feudal order was to deprive Confucian academies of their intellectual splendour; on the other hand, it still highlighted them, albeit in the light of a certain negative publicity.

The early decades of the regime of the DPRK were still much in the spirit of "the liquidation of and struggle with the remaining old ways of thinking"[61] and both scholars and teachers systematically avoided any positive remarks concerning the old ideologies and more specifically, Confucianism. Yet in order to understand the nature of the class struggle of the Korean people in the past centuries, it was necessary to re-evaluate history—including Confucian academies—according the needs of the new regime. Most, if not all, of the studies thus focused on the role of the academies within the socioeconomic relations of traditional society, ignoring their intellectual and religious dimensions.

Especially remarkable is the complete silence concerning the most striking "feudal superstitions": rituals, cults, and the offerings performed by the academies. Indeed, from the point of religious studies, the most interesting aspect of the DPRK studies of Confucian academies is that they deliberately ignore their religious nature. Nonetheless, the demonization of the academies as one of the cornerstones of the oppressive former feudal regime called for their detailed research, and gave them a small yet stable and important position within North Korean interpretations of traditional society and its life.

---

59   Ibid., 89.
60   Ibid., 70.
61   Chŏng Chinsŏk, Chŏng Sŏngch'ŏl, Kim Ch'angwŏn, *Chosŏn ch'ŏrhaksa* 1, 2nd edition (History of Korean Philosophy) (Pyongyang: Kwahagwŏn ch'ulp'ansa, 1962), 1960 foreword.

## Postscript

Many of the questions raised in this chapter have been a concern for the research team of the FU Berlin in recent years and were the topics of several rounds of cooperation with North Korean experts in the field. The main tasks, to document the destinies of Confucian academies after the liberation of the Korean peninsula and the current state of such historical monuments in the DPRK are still to be further explored but the cooperation with Kim Il-sung University and other institutions already yielded some positive results that should be mentioned here briefly.

During a research trip in November 2019 Eun-Jeung Lee, Vladimir Glomb, and Martin Gehlmann had the chance to see several documents concerning North Korean academies kept in the archives of the university. Of special interest were the *Kaesŏng Tumundong sŏwŏn che sŏnsaeng an* 開城杜門洞書院諸先生案 (*Roster of Several Masters in Kaesŏng Tumundong Academy*), a collection of inscription rubbings from Sungyang Academy in Kaesŏng, and two short documents of Sohyŏn Academy: one is a brief description of academies related to Yulgok Yi I (*Yulgok sŏwŏn chŏlmok* 栗谷書院節目) and the other a list of donators for the construction of stelae. Further sources included the chronicles of several Confucian shrines including Ch'ungnyŏl sa 忠烈祠 in Ryongch'ŏn County of Pyŏngan Province, Hakpongsa 鶴峰祠 in Ŭiju, and Hyŏnch'ungsa 顯忠祠 in Pyŏngan Province.

Another institution holding a major collection of sources is the Grand People's Study House (*Inmin taehak sŭptang*) located in central Pyongyang, which in the last decades has played the role of both national library and state archive. Its collection stores fundamental documents related to the major academies located in North Korea as well as many other related sources. A special place among them is occupied by the three volumes of the records of Sohyŏn Academy (*Sohyŏn sŏwŏn sajŏk mongnok* 紹賢書院事蹟目錄) and the *Roster of Sohyŏn Academy Masters* (*Sohyŏn sŏwŏn sŏnsaeng an* 紹賢書院先生案). These well-preserved manuscripts are the only extant copies of core documents handed down within the most famous academy of the northern provinces. Other manuscripts like the *Kyŏnghyŏn sŏwŏn kuji* 景賢書院舊誌 (*Old Chronicle of Kyŏnghyŏn Academy*), the *Munjŏng sŏwŏn huhak nok* 文井書院後學錄 (*Record of Munjŏng Academy Students*), or another version of the *Tumundong Academy Records* (*Tumundong sŏwŏn pyŏlji* 杜門洞書院別誌) present invaluable testimony about the story of the northern academies. Apart of the documents related to the academies in the northern provinces, the collection also contains several sources related to academies in the rest of the country as well as general works commenting on these Confucian institutions like the

*Haedong sŏwŏn nok* 海東書院錄 (*Record of Academies in the East of the Sea*) or the *P'allo kak sŏwŏn myŏnghyŏn nok* 八路各書院明賢錄 (*Record of Illustrious Worthies from Every Academy in the Eight Provinces*). These and many other documents will certainly play a crucial role for future research on Korean academies. We would like to thank all our North Korean colleagues for their assistance.

## References

Bařinka, Jaroslav. "Staré konfuciánské ústavy v Koreji" (Old Confucian Academies in Korea)." *Nový Orient* 23 (1968): 261–266.

Cho Pyŏngman (ed.). *Chosŏn ryŏksa kyogwasŏ yongŏ haesŏl* (Explanation of Terms Used in Textbooks of Korean History). Pyongyang: Kyoyuk tosŏ ch'ulp'ansa, 1956.

Cho Sangsun. "*Pukhanŭi sŏwŏn kwa sau* (North Korean Confucian Academies and Confucian Shrines)." Web pages of the Sŏwŏn yŏnhap hoe 書院聯合會, 2012. <http://www.seowonstay.com/bbs/board.php?bo_table=koreanseowon&wr_id=48> (accessed: 01 March 2017).

*Chosŏn kyoyuksa*. (History of Education in Korea). Tokyo: Hagu sŏbang, 1963.

Chŏng Chaehun. *Chosŏn siadaeŭi hakp'a wa sasang* (Schools and Thought of Chosŏn Period). Seoul: Sin'gu munhwasa, 2008.

Chŏng Chinsŏk, Chŏng Sŏngch'ŏl, and Kim Ch'angwŏn. *Chosŏn ch'ŏrhaksa* 1 (History of Korean Philosophy). 2nd edition. Pyongyang: Kwahagwŏn ch'ulp'ansa, 1962.

Ch'oe Kyuhwan (ed.). *Myŏngsŭng, kojŏk, ch'ŏnyŏn kinyŏmmul p'yŏllam*. (Guide to Famous Places, Historical Relics and Natural Monuments). Pyongyang: Kunjung munhwa ch'ulp'ansa, 1966.

Ch'oe Namsŏn. *Yuktang Ch'oe Namsŏn chŏnjip* 六堂崔南善全集 *3* (Complete Works of *Yuktang* Ch'oe Namsŏn). (*Chosŏn sangsik mundap* 朝鮮常識問答, *Chosŏn sangsik* 朝鮮常識). Seoul: Hyŏnamsa, 1973.

Ch'oe T'aeksŏn, and Hŏ Haesuk (eds.). *Chŏsŏn munhwasa* (The History of Korean Culture). Pyongyang: Kwahak, paekkwasajŏn ch'ulp'ansa, 1977.

Ch'oe Yŏnju. "Chosŏn ponggŏn wangjo sigi sŏwŏn sŏlch'iwa kŭ chach'i sŏnggyŏk (Founding of Confucian Academies and the Character of their Autonomy during the Time of Chosŏn Feudal Kingdom)." *Ryŏksa kwahak* 230, no. 2 (2014): 61–64.

Ch'oe Yŏnju. "Chosŏn ponggŏn wangjo sigi sŏwŏn sŏngwŏndŭrŭi immyŏng kwa sinbun kwan'gyerŭl t'onghayŏ pon sŏwŏn ŭi paninminjŏk sŏnggyŏk (Antipeople Character of Confucian Academies during the Time of Chosŏn Feudal Kingdom Seen Through their Academy Members and Personnel Social Status)." *Kim Ilsŏng chonghap taehakpo* (ryoksa, pŏphak) 60, no. 1 (2014): 50–53.

Ch'oe Yŏnju. "Rijosigi sŏwŏn ŭi pyŏch'ŏn kwajŏng e taehan koch'al (Study of Confucian Academies Transformation Process During the Time of Yi Dynasty)." *Ryŏksa kwahak* 214, no.2 (2010): 30–33.

Chu Sŏngch'ŏl, Rim Hosŏng, and Kim Sŭngil. *Changgunnim kwa ryŏksahak* (General and History Science). Pyongyang: Sahoe kwahak ch'ulp'ansa, 2014.

Hejtmanek, Milan. "The Elusive Path to Sagehood: Origins of the Confucian Academy System in Chosŏn Korea." *Seoul Journal of Korean Studies* 26, no. 2 (2013): 233–268.

Jang, Yoo-seung. "Regional Identities of Northern Literati: A Comparative Study of P'yongan and Hamgyong Provinces." In *The Northern Region of Korea: History, Identity, and Culture*, edited by Kim Sun Joo, 62–92. Seattle: University of Washington Press, 2010.

Kang In'gu, and Yi Sŏngmi (eds.). *Pukhan ŭi hangukhak yŏn'gu sŏnggwa punsŏk: yŏksa, ch'ŏrhak* (Nature and Analysis of the North Korean Studies on Korea: History, Philosophy). Sŏngnam: Hanguk chŏngsin munhwa yŏn'guwŏn, 1991.

Kim Ch'ŏlsu. "Ryongmanjie taehan yŏn'gu (Study of *Ryongmanji*)." in *Minjok kojŏn yŏn'gu nonmunjip* 28, 5–97. Pyongyang: Sahoe kwahak ch'ulp'ansa, 2011.

Kim Sŏkhyŏng. "Ryangballon (Discussion on *yangban*)." *Ryŏksa nonmunjip* 3 (1959): 3–129.

*Kwahagwŏn ryŏksa yŏn'guso. Chosŏnsa nyŏnp'yo* (Chronology of Korean History). Pyongyang: Chosŏn minjujuŭi inmin kwahagwŏn, 1957.

*Kwahagwŏn ryŏksa yŏn'guso. Chosŏn t'ongsa* 1 (The General History of Korea 1). Chosŏn minjujuŭi inmin konghwaguk kwahagwŏn, 1956.

Muljil munhwa yumul pojon wiwŏnhoe. *Chungyo yujŏkmyŏngsŭng ch'ŏnyŏn kinyŏmmul illam* (An Overview of Important Historical Relics, Cultural and Natural Monuments). Pyongyang: Muljil munhwa yumul pojon wiwŏnhoe, 1956.

Munhŏn yŏn'gusil. *Chosŏn kojŏn haeje* 1 (Bibliographical Notes on Classical Korean Literature 1). Pyongyang: Sahoe kwahagwŏn ch'ulp'ansa, 1965.

Munhwa pojon yŏn'guso. *Uri nara ryŏksa yujŏk* (Our Country's Historical Relics). Pyongyang: Kwahak, paekkwasajŏn ch'ulp'ansa, 1983.

O Changhwan. *Chosŏn ryŏksa kyosu ch'amgosŏ* (Reference Materials for Teachers of Korean History). Pyongyang: Kyoyuk tosŏ ch'ulp'ansa, 1956.

O Changhwan. "Rijo ponggŏn sigi sawŏn kyŏngje ŭi myŏtkaji koch'al (Several Observations on Buddhist Temples during the Feudal Periopd of Yi Dynasty)." *Ryŏksa kwahak* (1955): 44–58.

O Changhwan. "Sŏwŏn e taehan yakkan ŭi koch'al (Short Study on Confucian Academies)." *Ryŏksa kwahak* no.6 (1956): 70–90.

O Chongik. *Chosŏn ŭi myŏngsŭng* (Famous places of Korea). (Pyongyang: Kunjung munhwasa, 1960).

O Hŭibok. *Yet saram irŭm p'yŏllam* (Handbook of Historical Personalities' Names). Pyongyang: Kim Ilsŏng chonghap taehak, 1980.

Pak Chongbae, and Shigeyo Hasuike. "Ŭpchi rŭl t'onghaesŏ pon Chosŏn sidae P'yŏngyang ŭi hakkyo wa kŭ unyŏng (Pyongyang Schools and their Management during the Chosŏn Period Seen Through Local Gazetteers)." *Kyoyuk sahak yŏn'gu* 27, no. 1 (2017): 71–101.

Pak Hwangsik. "Chongsŏng hayanggyo ŭi kŏnch'uk yangsik (Architectural Form of Chongsŏng Local School)." *Munhwa yusan* 4 (1956): 42–44.

Pak Hwangsik. "P'yŏngyang ŭi Sunginjŏn ponjŏn kŏnch'uk ŭi yangsik kwa nyŏndae e taehayŏ (On Dating and the Original Architectural Form of Sunginjŏn in Pyongyang)." *Kŏnch'uk kwa kŏnsŏl* 2 (1957): 38–44.

Pak Sihyŏng. *Chosŏn chungsesa* II (The Medieval History of Korea II). Pyongyang: Kungnip ch'ulp'ansa, 1956.

Pak Sihyŏng. *Chosŏn t'oji chedosa* II (A History of the Korean Land System II). Pyongyang: Kwahagwŏn ch'ulp'ansa, 1961.

P'yŏngyang t'osa p'yŏnjip wiwŏnhoe. *P'yŏngyang chi* (Pyongyang Gazetteer). Pyongyang: Kungnip ch'ulp'ansa, 1957.

Ri Ch'ŏl, Ri Kiung, and Kim Myŏngch'al. *Munhwa yusan aehogadŭrŭi pŏt* (Friend of Cultural Heritage Lovers). Pyongyang: Chosŏn munhwa pojŏnsa, 2005.

Ri Hwasŏn. *Chosŏn kŏnch'uksa* I (History of Korean Architecture I). Pyongyang: Kwahak, paekkwasajŏn ch'ulp'ansa, 1989.

Ri Namsan. "Chosŏn kyoyuksa ch'amgo charyo rŭl ilkko (Reading Reference Documents of History of Korean Education)." *Inmin kyoyuk* 8 (1958): 26–30.

Ri Suil. "Chungse Chunggug esŏ ŭi sŏwŏn kyoyuk e taehan myŏtkaji koch'al (Some Observations on Education in Medieval Chinese Confucian Academies)." *Ryŏksa kwahak* 205, no. 1 (2008): 55–57.

*Sahoe kwahagwŏn ryŏksa yŏn'guso. Chosŏn chŏnsa: nyŏnp'yo 1* (Complete History of Korea: Chronology 1). Pyongyang: Kwahak, paekkwasajŏn ch'ulp'ansa, 2004.

*Sahoe kwahagwŏn ryŏksa yŏn'guso. Ryŏksa sajŏn I–II* (Historical Dictionary I–II). Pyongyang: Sahoe kwahagwŏn ch'ulp'ansa, 1971.

Scheidhauer, Ruth. "A Historiography of Cultural Heritage Interpretation and Policy in Kaesŏng, DPR Korea and Their Possible Impact on Inter-Korean Rapprochement." Ph.D. diss., University College London, 2011.

Sŏwŏn yŏnhap hoe 書院聯合會. *Hanguk sŏwŏn ch'ongnam* I–II 韓國書院總覽 I–II (General Survey of Korean Confucian Academies I–II), 2011. <http://www.seowonstay.com/ebook01/EBook.htm> (accessed: 01 March 2017).

Yi Man'gyu. *Chosŏn kyoyuksa* I 朝鮮教育史 (History of Korean Education). Seoul: Ŭryu munhwasa, 1947.

Yi Man'gyu. *Chosŏn kyoyuksa* (History of Korean Education). Seoul: Kŏrŭm, 1988.

Yi Man'gyu. *Chosŏn kyoyuksa yŏn'gu mit charyo* I (Studies and Materials on History of Korean education I). Pyongyang: Kyoyuk tosŏ ch'ulp'ansa, 1957.

Yun Hŭimyŏn. *Chosŏn sidae sŏwŏn kwa yangban* (Academies and Yangban of the Chosŏn period). Seoul: Chimmudang, 2004.

# Index

abolishment of academies   9–10
   in Korea   10, 197–198, 327
   in China   376
   in Japan   133
Academies for Correct Pronunciation (*zhengyin shuyuan*)   437
academy chronicles. *See* academy records
academy estates. *See* study fields
academy gazetteers. *See* academy records
academy networks   6–7, 202–206, 221–222, 276–277
academy records   8, 14, 245, 245n62, 489–490
   of Bailuzhou Academy   169
   of Donglin Academy   175
   of Fuzhen Academy   190
   of Gongxue Academy   178–179
   of Guanzhong Academy   174
   of Oksan Academy   200, 209, 216, 273
   of Sŏak Academy   205, 205n19, 273, 275
   of Soksil Academy   83
   of Songyang Academy   425n115, 428–430
   of Sosu Academy   270–272
   of Tumundong Academy   464n13
   of Wenshi Academy   449
   of White Deer Grotto Academy   255n10
   of Wufeng Academy   167, 362–368, 370, 381, 384
   of Xuegu Academy   172–174
   of Xuehaitang   303n35, 312
   of Yuelu Academy   161, 177, 441n9
   of Yuexiu Academy   307
academy regulations   9, 40–41
   *Articles of Learning. See* White Deer Grotto Academy
   of Hongdao Academy   162, 181, 186
   in Japan   145–147
   in Korea   83, 197, 272–273, 277, 320n4, 349
   in Ming China   169, 172, 188–189
   of Oksan Academy   201, 211–213
   in Qing China   303n35, 308, 313, 315, 445
   in Vietnam   101, 110–112, 113–115
   by Yulgok   329–331, 334–339, 355–356, *See also* Yulgok
academy rules. *See* academy regulations
academy slaves (*wŏnno*)   199, 220, 341, 484–486

academy villages (*sŏwŏnch'on*)   486
administrator   94, 213, 326
admission of students   300–308, 304n39, 331–332
affiliated student (*fuke*)   302
Ai Siqi   419
Akademia   1, 65
alcohol   221, 347–349
*Analects. See* Lunyu
An Hyang   38–39, 270–272, 326, 353n83
Aofeng Academy   447–448
apprentice students (*tongsheng*)   290, 304n39
archery ranges   227–228, 238–240, 242–247
Areopagus   246–247
Ashikaga Gakkō   128
assistant directors (*xundao*)   300
   in Vietnam   113
awards (*jiangyin*)   303, *See also* stipends

Bailudong shuyuan. *See* White Deer Grotto Academy
Baisha Academy   443, 445
Bamboo Grove Hermitage. *See* Zhulin jingshe
banishment. *See* exile
Bařinka, Jaroslav   3, 456
Biyong   234, *See also* Imperial University, Directorate of Education
black tallies (*hŭkp'ae*)   487
book lending   213–215
Border Defense Command   70
*boshi*   89–90, 176
*Book of Rites. See* Liji
Bo Yi   72, 459
Buddhist monastery   8, 252, 363, 400, 480
   conflicts with   375–379
   dependent monasteries   199–200, 217–223
   and cultural protection   423, 465n14
   stay in monasteries   306, 332, 359–360
Buddhist monks   95, 374–379, 339–340
   and academy lectures   170, 176n8, 187–188
   assisting academies   221–223
Bùi Dương Lịch   118

Cangzhou jingshe  29, *See also* Zhulin jingshe
Chagye Academy  205
Chan Buddhism  61, 400
Chang'an  54, 56–60
Chang Hyŏn'gwang  216
Chan, Wing-tsit  2–3, 21–22, 254n6, 259
charity schools  290, 446
chartering  72, 272n65, 471, 482–483, *See also* plaque
  in Korea  73, 197–198, 201, 206
  of Oksan Academy  207
  of Sosu Academy  270, 272, 350
  of Sungyang Academy  74, 79
Che Daren  187
Chen Baisha  36, 187
Chen Baogu  169
Chen Changqi  298
Chen Chun  240
Chen Gang  109
Chen Gong  377
Chen Jing  373
Chen Liang  240, 366–370, 374, 378
Chen Ning  174
Chen Qi'en  167–168
Chen Shifang  168
Cheng brothers  22, 29, 258, 264, 402, 425, 425n116, 426–428
  enshrinement in academies  36, 340, 405, 411–412, 446–448
Cheng'en Hall  61
Chengjiang Academy  177
Cheng Hao  28, 255, 257n16, 278, 402, 441, 446–448
Cheng Shangfei  363, 368, 385–386
Cheng Wende  189, 370–371, 373–374, 379, 381–385, 387–390
Cheng Xiang  402
Cheng Yi  28, 255, 257–258, 273, 278, 402, 408, 411–412, 425
Cheng-Zhu School  370, 377, 397, 407–411, 414, 430–431
Cheng Zi  370–371, 375–379, 381–385, 389
Chiang Kai-shek  417
Chinese edition (*t'angp'anbon*)  209
Ch'oe Ch'ung  75–76, 330–331, 340–341, 351–353
Ch'oe Hwang  350, 353

Ch'oe Kwan  216
Ch'oe Sŏkhang  205
Cho Hoik  73, 76–77
Cho Hŏn  77–78, 328–329
Cho Ik  78
Cho Kwangjo  72–78, 80, 275, 341, 347, 353, 484
Chŏng Kiyun  218
Chŏng Ku  73, 77, 214, 484
Chŏng Mongju  72–76, 78–81, 82, 85, 353, 467
Chŏng Pung  263
Chŏng Yagyong  476
Chŏng Yŏch'ang  73, 78, 80
Ch'ŏngok Academy  217
Chŏnghyesa Monastery  199–200, 220
Ch'ŏngnyang Academy  217
Chongji Academy  437
Chŏngjo  70, 208, 213, 482
Ch'ŏn'gok Academy  321
Chongwen Academy (in Hangzhou)  182, 184
Chongwen Academy (in Taiwan)  445, 446–448
Chongzheng Academy  169
Cho Sik  349
Cho Yusŏn  82
*Chukkyeji (Records of Bamboo Stream)*  270–272
*Chŭngbo Munhŏn pigo (Augmented Reference Compilation of Documents)*  342, 459n8
*Chunggyŏng chi (Gazetteer of the Middle Capital)*  85
Ch'unghyŏn Academy  74, 79
*Chunqiu (Spring and Autumn Annals)*  202, 215, 412
  and curriculum  138, 148, 184
Chunyang Terrace Academy  37
Chu Sebung  39–40, 270–272, 281, 319n2, 330, 350, 469n26
Chu Wuliang  53–54, 56, 64
*Classic of Filial Piety. See* Xiaojing
classics licentiate  291, 301, 304n39, 307, 323, 377, 381
Citadel of Purple Tenuity (Ziweicheng)  47
civil service examinations. *See* state examinations, examinations in academies
commoners  95–96, 129–130, 139, 229n7, 233n23, 244, 308–309, 314

INDEX 495

communal granary   331, 338–343, 348, 355, 487
community compact   163, 188, 243, 254n6, 322, 331, 333, 338–343, 348, 355, 470, 473–474, 487
community school. See local school
competition   13, 24, 214, 229, 247, 304n39, 309, 472
*Complete Writings of Zhu Xi (Zhuzi daquan)*   207, 253n3, 262, 414
Confucian generals (*rujiang*)   234, 244n60
Confucius   228–230, 265, 271, 412
    as teacher   177
    offerings to   9, 28–29, 340, 441, 441n9
    shrine to   39–40, 270, 351–352, 438–439
    statue of   440
Confucius temple   71, 130, 299, 439, 445, 448, 459, 483
    enshrinement in   37, 71, 79, 81, 198–199, 207, 351n75, 483–484
copyists   58–59
correspondence. See letters
cultural heritage   10–12, 15, 69, 142, 423–424, 431–432, 457–458, 461–462, 465n14, 466, 468–469, 475, See also UNESCO
Cui Yuzhi   291
Cultural Revolution   3, 11, 21, 419–420
curriculum   128–149, 226–227, 233–234, 239–240
    in academies   14–15, 83, 181, 184–185
    reading requirements   201, 329
    of state examinations   96, 409

*Đại Việt sử kí toàn thư (The Complete Annals of the Great Việt)*   98–99, 115–116
Daigakuryō (State Academy)   127
Daming Palace (Daminggong)   56, 57–58
Daodong Academy   190
Daoism   24, 61, 188, 399, 400, 403n30, 415, 421, 429, 438–439
    relation with Confucianism   92, 95, 359, 447–448, 452–453
Daoist structures   8, 13, 32, 252, 360, 361, 390, 399–404, 418, 426, 430, 438, 439, 446
*daotong* (Genealogy of the Way)   72, 79, 81–82, 87, 353n83, 407, 412, 447, 452
Dasan   296

*Daxue (Great Learning)*   264–265, 268, 373, 411
    commentary on   136, 203, 204, 208, 220, 221, 264, 368
    and curriculum   84, 138, 148, 184, 209
    lectures on   172, 337
Dayan calendar   46, 61–62, 64
Deng Chuan'an   451
*Diagram of the White Deer Grotto Regulations (Paengnoktong kyu to)*   268–269
Directorate of Education   25, 93, 95–96, 100, 113, 127, 234, 237
director of academy   8, 34, 39, 83, 92, 106, 109–110, 169, 179, 187, 216, 259, 293, 315, 335, 337, 340, 401, 477
    selection of   295–300, 325–329, 339
    salary   23, 39, 96, 296, 327–328
discipline of students   34–35, 40, 138–140, 181, 307, 328–335
divination   60, 371
*Doctrine of the Mean.* See Zhongyong
domain schools (*hankō*)   93, 129–130, 132–133, 136
donations
    of books   202, 204, 206, 208, 310, 401
    of land   74, 413, 485
    of money   37, 118, 175–176, 371–372
    of slaves   199, 203
Donghu Academy   227, 227n1
Donglin Academy   9, 165–166, 172, 175, 244, 289
Dongshan Academy   181
Dong Zhongshu   258
dormitories   35, 73, 192, 197, 273, 308, 310, 332, 400, 407, 413
Dou Keqin   407, 410
Du Weixi   168
Duanxi Academy   306
Duan Youxian   174

economy of academies   200, 485–487
    and donations   74, 201–208, 368, 371, 385, 413n79, 4123–416, 446
    and examination economy   300–308
edict attendant   63–64, 100
educator   96, 112, See also assistant directors
Ehu Academy   172, 190, 411

*Elementary Learning (Xiaoxue)* 240, 255, 260–261, 268
   commentary on 199, 240n42
   and curriculum 84, 138, 148, 201, 209
   lectures on 209, 138, 263
Enclosure of Purple Tenuity (Ziweiyuan) 47, 450
enshrinement. *See* shrine
envoys 6n13, 102–107, 110–111, 117, 208
examinations in academies 34–35, 144, 182–184, 294–295
   training for 26
exile 73, 86–87, 221, 243, 379, 402, 459

*Family Rituals. See* Jiali
Fan Chunren 402
Fan Zhongyan 235, 426, 432
female education. *See* women education
Feng Congwu 172, 174
Feng Minchang 305–307, 310, 312, 315
Fengshan Academy 181
fields. *See* study fields
five agents (*wuxing*) 51, 60
five cardinal relationships (*wulun*, or *renlun*) 255–256, 261, 262, 263, 265, 268, 278, 479
*Five Classics* 199, 201, 206–207, 414
   and curriculum 115–116, 131, 134, 145, 147
   publication of 101
   lectures on 138, 182–183
Five Celestial Thearchs 51–52
Five Masters Shrine (Wuzici) 438, 447–448, 452
Five Worthies of Chosŏn (Chosŏn ohyŏn) 81
folk beliefs. *See* popular religions
food offering rite (*shicai*) 441, 447
*Four Books* 41, 199, 207, 263
   commentary on 30, 41, 117, 240n45, 257
   and curriculum 131, 145, 147, 201
   lectures on 83, 134, 138, 182–186
   publication of 117
Four Schools (Sahak) 323, 484–485
Fu Bi 235–236
Fugu Academy 169, 189–190, 191
Fujiwara Seika 129
Fuli Academy 173
Fu Mei 414, 429
Fu Xi 29
Fuzhen Academy 190–191

Gan Xiangpeng 373
Gao Panlong 175
Gao Zhongzhen 428–429
Gaozong (Tang) 53, 398–399, 418
Gaozong (Song) 238–239
gazetteers 68, 227, 239n39, 424, 444, *See also* academy records
Geng Jie 406–408, 410n68, 411–416, 424, 430
geomancy 310, 438–439, 443, 448–449
granary 220, 310
Granet, Marcel 48–50
*Great Learning. See* Daxue
God of the Sea (Longwang) 8, 438
Gongxue Academy 178–179, 182
Guande Pavilion/Hall 242, 246n63
Guangshun Gate (Guangshunmen) 54, 56–58
Guangtai Hall (Guangtaidian) 61–62, 64
Guangxu 366, 440
Guangya Academy 291–292, 299, 304, 312–314
Guanzhong Academy 172, 174–175
guests. *See* visitors
Guo Songtao 299
Guo Wenhua 410
Guozijian. *See* Directorate of Education
Gu Xiancheng 175

Haidong Academy 443, 444–445, 448–449
*Hakkyo mobŏm (Model for Schools)* 83, 276–277, 322, 329, 338
*Han Feizi* 148
Hangnyŏ Academy 73
Han Ho 218
Hanlin Imperial Academy 58, 59, 100, 369
Han Qi 235
Hanquan jingshe 344
*Hanshu (Book of Han)* 148, 205, 258
Han Wei 406
Han Yu 104, 231n15, 233n23, 404
Hao Jing 36
Hayashi Kakuryō 144, 150
Hayashi Razan 129
Hayashi Ryōsai 136, 139
headmaster. *See* director of academy
He Ji 368–369
He Kan 442–443
He Nanyu 296
He Qijie 296

hermitage   58, 60, 168, *See also* jingshe
hermitry   31, 188, 399, 400–404, 426–428, 430, 471
Hers, Joseph   417
heterodoxy   83, 130, 277, 376–377, 438, 453
Hideyoshi Invasions   198, 216, 320n5, 329, 337, 459, 473–474, 481
Hirose Tansō   131
*Hoejae chip* (*Collected Writings of Hoejae*)   203–204, 219, 221–222, *See also* Yi Ŏnjŏk
Hongdao Academy   162, 181, 184–185
Hongmun'gwan (Office of Special Councilors)   204, 216, 277
Hong Ponghan   69
Hong Samik   205
Hongwu   242
Hong Yuan   372–373, 378, 388
Hou Tai   404–405
Hŏ Yŏp   82
Hua Shou   404
Huaqing Palace (Huaqinggong)   60
Huang Kehui   405
Huang Wan   380–383, 389, 390
Huang Yi   414–416, 431
Huang Zongxi   369
Huangu Academy   181
Hu Bingwen   267
Hu Guang   115, 116
Hu Hong   26
*Hui'an xiansheng Zhu Wengong wenji*. *See* Complete Writings of Zhu Xi
*huijiang* (gatherings for lectures)   162–164, 178, 420
Hu Jianwei   446–448, 447n22
Hu Jingyu   385–386
Hu Juren   37–38, 187, 259–260, 266
human nature   26, 84, 174, 190, 256, 410
Hu Shi   10n20
Hu Weisheng   362
Hu Yongzhang   375–377, 379, 384, 386
Hu Ze   362–363, 384
Hwagok Academy   76, 82
Hwang Chullyang   267, 272
Hyojong   482, 485
Hyujŏng   459

Ikeda Sōan   134, 135–140
Imgo Academy   79, 208
Imjin War. *See* Hideyoshi Invasions
Im Ki   328
Im Kyuyŏng   85
Imperial Lord Wenchang. *See* Wenchang
Imperial University (Taixue)   68, 227, 231, 234, 236n28, 239, 242, *See also* Directorate of Education
Inhyŏn Academy   72–73, 77
inscriptions   21, 27, 32, 36, 79, 104–105, 107, 168, 206, 261, 363, 387, 399, 405, 405n11, 411–412, 415–416, 427, 429, 437–438, 445, 451, 475, *See also* wooden boards, stelae
Isan Academy   272, 334, 349
Itō Hirobumi   144

Jesuits   1, 7
Jiajing   109, 160, 167, 203, 360, 376, 387
*Jiali* (*Family Rituals*)
  and curriculum   185, 201, 209
*jianghui*   37, 83, 160–166, 161n6, 367, 372, *See also* lectures
*jiangxue. See* lectures
Jiang Yu   176
Jiang Yunxun   445
Jiang Yuying   444
Jiao Qinchong   410
Jiaqing   297, 448, 450
Jiayi Academy   169
Jie Lu (Zhong You)   178
Jing Rizhen   427, 429–430
jingshe   180, 291, 344–350
  and Zhu Xi   344n53, 345–346, 368, 372
  and academy regulations   258, 331–337
Jin Lüxiang   368–369
*Jinsilu* (*Reflections on Things at Hand*)   205, 209, 218, 222, 255, 257–258, 270n56
  and curriculum   138, 149, 185–186, 20
*Jiu Tangshu* (*Old Book of the Tang*)   49, 52, 53, 57, 60, 61, 176n48, 233n23
Jixian Shuyuan   45–46, 53–60, 62–65, 90
Jizi. *See* Kija
Jupo jingshe   291
*juren* graduates   180, 182, 291, 301, 404, 414

Kan Chazan (Sazan)   131
Kanezawa Bunko   128
Kangaku juku   6, 130–135, 141–145, 150–153

Kangien   131
Kang Kamch'an   74
Kang P'irhyo   268n55, 349
Kangxi   30, 245, 246, 362, 409, 413, 418, 443–444
Kano Jigorō   149
Kasuga Sen'an   135, 136
Ki Chahŏn   205
Ki Chun   73, 78, 205
Kija   72, 77, 466
Kim Chaero   263–264
Kim Ch'anghyŏp   84
Kim Changsaeng   72, 75–76
Kim Chongdŏk   214
Kim Chungmun   326
Kim Hŏnsŏng   218
Kim Ilson   205, 214
Kim Il-Sung   11, 462, 467, 475, 478
Kim Inhu   277–280, 282
Kim Koengp'il   72, 75–76, 80
Kim Puyun   273
Kim Sanghŏn   74, 76, 78, 84
Kim Sit'ak   82
Kim T'aegyŏng   81, 85
Kim Wŏnhaeng   82–84, 277
Kim Yuk   76, 78
Ki Taesŭng   205
Kŏ Ch'ŏllo   79
Kojong   85
Kondō Tokuzan   136
Kong Rong   272
Kong Tianyi   382, 389
*Koryŏsa* (*History of Koryŏ*)   215, 476
Kugang Academy   199, 213, 217, 219
*Kuinnok* (*Record of Search for Goodness*)   218, 220, 221
Kuixing   437–439, 441–443, 446–449, 450–452
*Kŭmo sŭngnam* (*Overall Survey of Kŭmo*)   217, 219
Kwŏn Sangha   274–275
Kwŏn Sangil   214
Kwŏn Ŭnghwa   204
Kyŏnghyŏn Academy (Kanggye)   73, 77, 221
Kyŏnghyŏn Academy (Chaeryŏng)   75, 462, 489
Kyŏngju hyanggyo (Kyŏngju local school)   274

*Kyŏngmong yogyŏl* (*Important Methods of Eliminating Youthful Ignorance*)   329
Kyosŏgwan   200

Lạn Kha Academy   92–94, 120
lectures   32–34, 41, 82–85, 134, 138, 151, 176–179, 182–185, 246, 295, 337, 370–373, 407, 472
    lecture hall   27, 30, 41, 180, 220n48, 254, 258, 261, 273–274, 279, 343, 407, 412–416, 445–447
    lecture register   34, 188, 189, 209, 426
    lecture gatherings   37, 161–165, 182–183, 367
    lecture regulations   83, 187–188, 277, 337
    records of lectures   337, 337n41
*Lesser Learning*. See Elementary Learning
letters   207, 216, 221, 267, 313, 320–321, 325, 346, 348, 350–352, 353n83 381–382
    of Zhu Xi   27, 176n50, 208, 240n47
Lianshan Academy   190
Liang Lingzan   62, 63–64
Liang Qi   301, 303–304, 311–313, 315
library   25, 60, 65, 89–91, 310, 489
    in academies   7, 15, 25, 56–65, 186, 192, 200–216, 310, 400, 407, 414
Li Bo   445
Li Gang   427
Li Gong   371, 375
*Liji* (*Record of Rites*)   48, 209, 229–230, 240, 242, 399–400, 451
    commentary on   63
    and curriculum   149, 184
Li Linfu   63, 406n44
Lin Yaoying   407, 411
Linde calendar   61
Li Maoming   169
Lí Nhân Tông   95
Li Shoupeng   227
literary licentiate   89–90, 96, 112, 239, 244, 323, 362, 380, 383, 387
Lí Thánh Tông   95
Li Tianlin   174
Li Ting   403–404
Li Tong   359, 441
Liu Bangcai   189
Liu Binhua   296, 297
Liu Chuquan   169

INDEX 499

Liu Dunzhen  418
Liu Gong  109
Liu Wenmin  189
Liu Xiang  272
Liu Xiao  189
Liu Yangdeng  189
Liu Yuanqing  173–174
Li Wentian  298
Li Wenzhao  112
Li Yunze  109
*Lixue zongzhuan (Ancestral Traditions of Lixue)*  409–410
Lizheng shuyuan  45–46, 54, 56–57, 62–65, 90
Lizong  39, 107, 258, 362
local elites  40, 70, 96, 201, 205, 214, 281, 293, 326, 333, 350–354, 458
local neighborhood (community) schools (*shexue*)  227, 244
local schools  14, 93, 226–228, 231–232, 236–237, 247, 256, 387, 440–441
  in Ming China  159, 176, 179, 188, 191–192, 242
  in Qing China  245, 305, 315, 443, 443n15, 451
  in Song China  238–241, 254, 257, 258, 443
  in Japan  129–130
  in Korea  69–70, 74, 87, 206, 260, 273, 275–277, 322–327, 329, 336, 462, 464, 470, 477, 481–485
  in Vietnam  95–97, 120–121,
Longshan Academy  105–106
Longqing  160, 167
Lu Heshan  372
Lu Jiuling  240
Lu Jiuyuan  13, 32, 177, 187, 240, 371, 374
Lu Kejiu  168, 370, 374–377, 379, 382–384, 389
*Lunyu (Analects)*  26, 174n41, 175n45, 178n54, 229n6, 242, 257n16, 258n20, 264, 267, 273n66, 381n63, 412n73
  commentary on  255
  and curriculum  138, 148, 184
  lectures on  32–33, 176, 178, 337
Luo Hongxian  359
Luo Rufang  171, 177
Luoqing Academy  446, 451
Luo Tianxiang  61
Luoyang  45, 47, 49, 52–59, 402, 404, 417, 427, 430

Lü Ben  168
Lü Chengzhang  377
Lü Dalin  402
Lü Hao  367–368
Lü Yuan  368, 372
Lü Zuqian  2, 41, 254n6, 255, 366–371, 374, 378. 397n1
  and White Deer Grotto Academy  23–24, 31–32, 34
Lü Zujian  367–368
Lykeion  65
Lý Văn Phức  102

Ma Huaisu  53
Manchus  84–85, 99, 207
  and Manchu conquest  406, 409–410
Maoshan (Shangqing) School  399
Mao Yuanyi  244
Mao Zedong  11
Martial Temples (*wumiao*)  299, 450
Matsudaira Sadanobu  129–130
Ma Ŭigyŏng  82
medical doctor  89, 475
medicine  101, 404
Mencius  84, 407, 472
  veneration of  39, 340, 441
*Mencius (Mengzi)*  136, 212–213, 242, 255–256, 258n20, 264, 265, 412
  commentary on  255–256
  and curriculum  138, 148, 184, 240n47
  lecture on  177–178, 407
merchants  85–86, 170, 180, 188, 296, 313, 360
military  263–264
  military education  70–71, 128–130, 149, 185, 230–245
  enshrinement of military figures  73–74, 351, 459
  military service  471–477
Min Chŏngjung  73, 77–78
Mingdao Academy  34
Mingfu Gate (Mingfumen)  54–57, 58
Mingjing Academy  169
Mingluntang  246, 261–262, 273, 448
*Ming ruxue an (Records of Ming Scholars)*  168, 171, 177, 369
Mingzhi Academy  445–446
Min Sun  82
Min Yujung  73, 77
Mishima Chūshū  134, 143, 145, 150

Miwada Masako   134
Mongols   404, 450
   and building of academies   35–36, 176–177, 227
   and destruction of academies   30
Mount Lu (Lushan)   9, 31, 252, 271, 279, 281
Mount Song (Songshan)   11, 12, 61, 397–400, 414, 416–419, 421, 423, 428–431
Mouseion   65
Munhoe Academy   76, 459, 462
Munhŏn Academy   76, 85, 320, 320n5, 325, 329, 330–342, 348, 350, 354–356
music   151–152, 226, 230–231, 264
Munp'o Academy   78, 462
Murakami Butsusan   134, 139
Myŏnggok Academy   217, 329
Myŏngjong   207, 482

Nam Chihun   218
Namgye Academy   198n2, 222
name plaque. *See* plaque
Nam Ŭngun   74
Nam Yihŭng   459
Nanhu Academy   445
Nanshe Academy   437–438
Nasen   404
National Academy. *See* Sŏnggyun'gwan
National University. *See* Sŏnggyun'gwan
Ngô Sĩ Liên   99, 115
Nguyễn Công Thịnh   97
Nguyễn Đình Trụ   97
Nguyễn Huy Oánh   5, 6n13, 100–112, 121
   and Phúc Giang Academy   112–119
Nguyễn Huy Vượng   111, 117
Nguyễn Thiếp   94
Nguyễn Trung Ngạn   106
Nguyễn Văn Siêu   102
Nishō Gakusha   145–150
Ni Si   428
Nogang Academy   217
No In   24, 41
No Kyŏngnin   321
*Nup'an ko* (*Survey of Print Matrices*)   217–218

observatory   58, 60–64
O Changhwan   480, 483–487
offerings. *See* sacrifices
Ogyū Sorai   136

Ōhashi Totsuan   136
Oksan Academy   7, 12n25, 197–223, 273, 465

Paegundong Academy. *See* White Cloud Grotto Academy
Pak Sangch'ung   72
Pak Sech'ae   75–76, 459
Pak Sun   82
Pak Yŏng   263–267
Pak Yŏryong   346
Pan Yantong   298
paper tablets   339, 441, *See also* spirit tablets
Penghu Academy   8, 438
petitions   25, 32, 39, 71, 72, 184, 200, 326, 376, 402, 450
Phan Huy Chú   98–99
Phúc Giang Academy   5, 12, 94, 99, 102, 110–119, 120–121
P'iram Academy   201, 279–280
plaques   23, 25, 30–31, 39, 71, 74, 79–80, 85, 107, 199, 206, 326, 330, 401n18, 469n26
Poch'ang School (Poch'ang hakkyo)   85
poetry   102, 106, 214, 236, 344, 425n115
   in academies   107, 179, 218, 278–279, 301, 348
   on academies   79, 101, 104–110, 253n3, 278–279, 326, 405, 424–425, 429, 426n123
   and curriculum   131, 137, 146–147, 178, 182–185, 301–302, 311
political factions   6, 9, *See also* academy networks
   in Korea   72–73, 74, 83, 207, 214, 268, 275, 324, 346, 472, 477, 482–483
   in China   166, 377, 402
Pokch'ŏn local school (Pokch'ŏn hyanggyo)   273
Pongyang Academy   76, 85n10, 459
portraits   28, 218, 353, 372, 415, 426, 441, 444
popular religions   7–9, 310, 351, 362–363, 438–439, 442, 451–453
popular education   164, 174, 186–191, 244–245
private study. *See* jingshe
public space   27, 92, 186–191, 228, 246–247, 246n64, 307, 340, 344
printing   91, 117, 121, 202, 362
   in academies   94, 114–117, 199, 201, 208–209, 217–223
punishment. *See* discipline of students

INDEX    501

purges   78–79, 263, 324, 471,
Pyŏktong Academy   73, 77
Pyŏngsan Academy   198n2, 201, 210

Qian Dehong   166–167, 168–169, 375, 382
Qianlong   30, 362, 385, 386, 414, 420, 431, 440–448
Qi Jiguang   244
Quang Trung   94
*Quốc sử toản yếu* (*A Brief Survey of National History*)   101, 115, 116, 117

Rai San'yō   147
Ran Jinzu   407, 412–413
*Record of Rites*. *See* Liji
refuge. *See* hermitry
regulations. *See* academy regulations
Renjuku   131
Renwen Academy   182, 187–188
retreat. *See* jingshe
Ricci, Matteo   1
Risseisha   139
rituals   22, 28, 30, 116, 128, 197, 205, 226, 246–247, 314–315, 355, 453
    and academies   111, 116, 178–179, 187–189, 205, 211–212, 290, 294, 299, 308–311, 347, 350, 438, 440–444, 447
    and archery   228–234, 245
    in Korea   71, 84, 276–277, 340–341
    and Mingtang   51, 58
roster of academy directors   207, 489
roster of lectures. *See* lecture register
royal book donations   206–207, 215
royal plaque. *See* plaque
royal charter. *See* chartering
Ruan Yuan   312, 313
Ruilin   299
Ruizong   52, 57
Runan Academy   36
Ryonggok Academy   71, 77, 461, 464, 467–469, 475
Ryongjin Academy   462
Ryu Sŏngnyong   214

sacrifices   51, 57–58, 85, 200, 206, 208, 211–212, 221, 299, 351, 363, 371, 381, 426, 441, 451, 459, 465, 479, 481, 488
    academy prescriptions for   28–30, 211, 277, 334, 340

    to Confucius   9, 340–341
    to Zhu Xi   35–36, 40, 411n71, 353, 371, 374
    to Wang Yangming   187
    imperial *feng* and *shan* sacrifices   398–399
Saigō Takamori   136
Saionji Kinkazu   126
salaries of directors. *See* director of academy
*Samguk sagi* (*Historical Records of Three Kingdoms*)   202, 210, 216
*sarim*   78, 268, 321, 324, 348, 352, 471, 473–474, 478, 481
Satō Issai   136
school lands. *See* study fields
Seikei Shoin   131n17, 135–137, 139–141
Seitatsu Shoin   144
Sejong   38, 260, 480n52
Sekino Tadashi   11, 416–417
Shao Baowen   176
Shaolin Monastery (Shaolin si)   400, 420, 427
Shao Yong   36, 81, 176, 441
*Shenbao* (*Shanghai News*)   292, 299, 303–304, 312, 313
Shen Gulin   169
*shengyuan*. *See* classics licentiate
Shenzong   236, 402, 427
Shi Cheng   303
Shigeno Yasutsugu   143, 150
Shigu Academy   104, 106
*Shijing* (*Classic of Poetry*)   48, 138, 148, 184, 412, 452
Shiren Academy   109
Shi Xing   459
Shi Xizai   400
Shizong (Jin)   403
Shizutani Gakkō   130
Shōheizaka Gakumonjo   129–130, 136
Shoushan Academy   174
Shoushan Monastery   361, 362–366, 375–379, 382–386, 389–390
shrine   8, 65, 70–71, 362–364, 369–371, 378, 405, 438, 450, 457–459, 466, 489
    in academies   8–9, 11, 28, 39, 82, 187, 197–198, 206–207, 270–271, 274, 276, 281, 340–343, 350–353, 405–407, 412–413

shrine (cont.)
  enshrinement in academies   30, 37, 71–78, 198, 275, 277, 321, 330, 350–353, 438, 442–443, 449, 459, 483, 484
  enshrinement of Zhu Xi   30, 354, 354n84, 445–448
Shuixi jingshe   169
*Shujing* (*Classic of Documents*)   38, 148, 174n41, 184, 205, 412
Shu Qi   72, 459
Shu Yuan   400
Shu Zhibai   400
Sima Guang   402, 426–427, 430, 432, 441
Sim Cho   274
Simgok Academy   349
Sim T'ŏngwŏn   322, 324
six arts   226, 229, 236
*Six Classics*   79, 83, 187
slaves. *See* academy slaves
Sōma Kyūhō   135–136
state examinations   89, 95–99, 244, 300–308, 437–439
  training for   39, 170, 180–181, 290–292, 445
  critique of   83–84, 341
state schools. *See* local schools
statues   65, 362, 363, 438, 440, 441n9, 448
stelae   26, 27, 32, 107, 113, 118, 351, 378, 399, 404, 415, 417, 419–420, 423, 427, 462, 464, 489
students   14, 21, 26, 74, 94, 99, 139–140, 149, 179, 180, 187, 200, 263, 281, 302
  numbers   23, 25, 70, 135–136, 139, 145, 149, 304, 323, 402, 416, 483–485
  and masters   22, 28–30, 120, 121, 130, 141, 168
  and examinations   32–34, 39, 41, 180–181, 186, 200, 208, 227, 290, 301, 448, *See also* examinations
  selection of   7, 131, 138–139, 188, 294, 300, 304, 306, 323, 331–333, 335, 355, *See also* admission of students
  disicipline of   34, 40, 137, 144, 273, 276, 328–329, 331, 337, 344, *See also* discipline of students
study fields   10
  in Korea   199, 203, 206, 220, 270, 276n77, 473–474, 477, 480–486
  in Ming China   174, 187, 192, 384–386
  in Qing China   305, 407, 413, 445–446
  in Song China   368, 401
  in Vietnam   96, 118, 121
study regulations. *See* academy regulations
Sŏak Academy   205, 217, 273–274, 275, 351
*Sohak ŏnhae* (*Vernacular Explanation of the Lesser Learning*)   199, 207
*Sơ học chỉ nam* (*Guides for Primary Learning*)   101, 115, 116
Sohyŏn Academy   75, 320n5, 337, 350, 356, 461–462, 465, 467–468, 489
Soksil Academy   83, 277
Sŏ Kyŏn   74
Sŏ Kyŏngdŏk   74, 81–82
Song Chun'gil   261–262
Sŏnggyun'gwan   38–39, 71, 93, 260–263, 273, 277, 323–324, 334, 446, 484–485
Sŏng Hon   72, 75–76, 327
Song Qi   236
Song Siyŏl   72, 75, 77–78, 84, 274, 275, 483–484
Song Ŭlgae   260
Songyang Academy   11, 12, 74n25, 397, 400–422, 423–423
Sŏnjo   74, 79, 204, 268, 323, 327, 353, 482
Sŏnu Hyŏp   71, 77
Sosu Academy   39, 189n2, 201–202, 206, 270–271, 326, 462, 467, 469n26, *See also* White Cloud Grotto Academy
spirit tablets   30–31, 79, 187, 271, 339, 441, 443n15, 445, 450
spirit writing (*fuji*)   442
stipends   180–181, 303–305, 325, 473
study hall. *See* jingshe
study lodge. *See* jingshe
Sukchong   70, 85, 481–482
Sun Fengji   55
Sun Fu   445
Sùng Chính Academy   94
Sungnyŏl Academy   464
Sungyang Academy   10, 12n25, 68–69, 72–87, 461–463, 467–468, 489
Sun He   234
Sun Qifeng   409–410
Sun Taichong   399
Suiyang Academy   23, 397n1, 418

suppression of academies 9–10, 69–71, 86, 159–160, 166
Suyang Academy 330

T'aejong 78
Taewŏngun 10, 85, 459, 461
Taiji Academy 35–36
Taishi Academy. *See* Taiyi Academy
Taiyi Academy 400–402
Taizong (Tang) 53
Taizong (Song) 235
Tang Bin 408–411, 430
taxes
  exemption for academies 201, 206, 276n77, 471, 477, 485–486
Tianqi 172
tobacco 221, 311
Tobong Academy 274–275, 276n77, 341, 347
T'oegye 79, 81, 83, 214, 275n76, 277, 319, 347–349, 353–354, 476
  and *Articles of Learning* 267–270
  enshrinement 72, 77–75, 483–484
  and Isan Academy 272, 320n4, 334
  and Sosu Academy 39, 272–274, 324, 326, 350
  and Tosan Academy 204–205, 321–322, 467
  and Yŏktong Academy 325
Todong Academy 75, 198n2, 208
Tohoe Academy 72
Tŏkch'ŏn Academy 222
Tokugawa Ieyasu 129
Tokugawa Iemitsu 129
Tonam Academy 77, 198n2, 201
Tonggang Academy 217
Tongtian Palace 46, 48, 58
Tosan Academy 198n2, 201, 204–205, 208, 210, 217, 222, 465, 467
Tosan Study Hall 321, 348–349, *See also* Tosan Academy
tourism 11, 15, 140n41, 314, 397, 420–421, 461, 467–469
Trần Thái Tông 95
trees
  in academies 60, 85, 398, 405–406, 415, 417, 442
  logging of 368, 386
tributary missions. *See* envoys

Tsunetō Seisō 134, 139
tuition 96, 118, 128–129, 133, 138, 173, 175, 306

Uesugi Norizane 128
U Hyŏnbo 78
Ŭlchi Mundŏk 73, 76
Ŭnbyŏng chŏngsa 274, 320, 329–338, 345–350, 354–356
UNESCO 12, 119, 198n2, 421–423, 431–432, *See also* cultural heritage

vernacular editions (*ŏnhae*) 199, 214, 339, 341n46, 346n57
Village Libation Ceremony (*xiang yinjiu*) 230–234, 236–237, 245
village school. *See* local school
visitors 15, 35, 41, 137, 163, 178, 184, 199, 295, 298, 347, 467
  etiquette for 178, 187–188
  and visitors book 188, 207

Wang Anshi 402, 426, 427
Wang Bai 368
Wang Chengyu 181
Wang Fuzhi 109
Wang Gen 188, 188n72
Wang Ji (1498–1583) 167, 169–170, 171, 360, 375, 377
Wang Ji (1636–1689) 407
Wang Kaiyun 109
Wang Keshou 174
Wang Mang 49
Wang Rizao 407
Wang Rumei 428–429
Wang Shangjiong 405, 405n41, 429
Wang Shihuai 170–171, 190–191
Wang Sŏngsun 81
Wang Wenqing 105, 109–110, 112
Wang Xianqian 109
Wang Yangming 9, 136, 160, 175n43, 189, 192, 240n45, 244, 361, 367–375, 380, 383, 410
  and academies 160, 179, 186, 242–243, 377, 389
  enshrinement of 37, 104, 187
  and lectures 38, 163–168
Wang Yinglin 55
Wang Youdan 407
Wang Zeng 401

Wang Zhaosheng   444
Wang Ziying   173
Wang Zongmu   169, 172
Wanli   160, 169, 172, 174, 190, 203, 363, 366, 382–384
Wanxiang Shrine (Wanxiang shengong)   46, 48, 50, 58
war   96, 99, 235–236, 270, 418,
    Second World War   11
    Korean War   11, 198, 216, 462, 466,
    Civil War in China   11, 419
    Sino-Japanese War   149
Wei Liaoweng   241
Wei Shu   55, 57, 64
Wenchang (Wenchang dijun)   8, 299, 405, 437–445, 446–453, 437n1
Wenlan Academy   292, 313
Wen of Zhou, Duke   51, 265, 412
Wenshi Academy   440, 444, 445, 446–449, 452–453
Western Inscription   295
Western knowledge   7, 10, 127, 143–152
White Cloud Grotto Academy   39–40, 270–272, 320n4, 321–322, 324, 330, 350, 355, 469, 471, 480, See also Sosu Academy
White Deer Grotto Academy   1–3, 23–24, 37, 40, 176n50, 180, 182, 190, 252, 289, 418, 440
    Articles of Learning   9, 33–34, 39, 83, 112, 187, 253–260, 261–283, 349, See also Diagram of the White Deer Grotto Regulations
    as model academy   4, 31–32, 35–36, 39, 172, 197, 252–253, 411, 424, 425n115,
women education   101, 115–116, 134
woodblock printing   114–117, 209, 217–218, 221, See also printing
wooden boards   214, 218, 261–263, 261n31, 273–275, 279–280, 282, 350, 378, See also plaques
Wu Bingjian   296, 313
Wu Changzuo   437
Wu, Emperor (Han)   49, 398, 402, 418
Wufeng Academy   8, 167–168, 361, 362–390
Wuhua Academy   171, 178
Wu Lanxiu   298

Wu Sansi   61
Wuyi jingshe   258, 344–346
Wu Yubi   188
Wu Zetian   46, 47–52, 65, 398
Wu Ziyun   407, 413

Xiaolushan Academy   37
*Xiaojing (Classic of Filial Piety)*   48, 417
    and curriculum   138, 148
Xiaowen   399
*Xiaoxue (Elementary Learning)*. See Elementary Learning
Xiaozong   239
Xidingfang Academy   437
Xie Jinluan   449
Xie Lansheng   293–295, 296–298, 304
Xihu Academy   291–292, 304
Xilin Temple (Xilin siyuan)   359
*Xingli daquan* 性理大全 (*Great Collection of Works on Human Nature and Principles*)   115–117, 185–186, 207, 253n3
*Xinjing (Classic of the Mind)*   201, 218, 325
Xuan Xue   187
Xuanzong   45–46, 52–60, 61–65, 234, 398–399
Xue Juzhong   429
Xuegu Academy   172–173
Xuehai Academy   445–446
Xuehaitang (Sea of Learning Hall)   291–292, 298–299, 301–305, 308, 311, 312–315
Xu Fuyuan   178
Xu Heng   261, 263
Xu Jie   167
*Xunhuan ribao* (*Universal Circulating Herald*)   292, 298–300, 310
Xu Qian   368–369
Xu Xiake   405, 429
Xu Zan   376–377

Yang Eryou   448–449
Yang Maoyuan   109
Yang Na   400
Yang Shi   175, 402, 425, 427–428
Yang Xiong   61
*yangban*   461, 465, 470–474, 481, 484
Yangcheng Academy   8, 290–291, 293–296, 298–305, 309

INDEX

Yangming school   160, 163–164, 167, 168, 171, 187, 189, 192, , 369–370, 373–374, 377, 390, 410, *See also* Wang Yangming
Yan Xingbang   407
Yan Yuan   29, 61, 178, 264, 340, 410n8, 411, 412
Yao Wenzhao   372, 378, 387–388
Yasui Sokken   134, 150
Ye Feng   406–407, 411
Ye Shi   367–368
Yi Chae   82, 84, 349
Yi Chehyŏn   75, 204, 218–219
Yi Chemin   199, 203
Yi Chŏng   202–203
Yi Chŏngbo   69
Yi Chŏnggyi   347
Yi Chonyŏn   353
Yide Academy   173
Yi Haeng   272
Yi Hangbok   78, 459
Yi Hwang. *See* T'oegye
Yi Hyŏnil   214
Yi I. *See* Yulgok
*Yijing* (*Book of Changes*)   47, 64, 71, 82, 257n17, 412
　commentary on   48n10, 61–62, 64n56, 136, 255
　and curriculum   138, 149
　lectures on   184
Yi Kyebok   202
Yi Kyŏngch'ang   82
Yi Man'gyu   69, 475–478, 479
Yi Mansu   212
Yin Chong   61
Yin Dun   402
Ying Dian   369–373, 375, 378–384, 387, 389–390
Ying Jian   383
Ying Liang   380–383, 389–390
Ying Qing   377
Ying Tingyu   383, 387
Yingyuan Academy   291–292, 298–299, 301
Yi Ŏnjŏk   73, 214, 221
　enshrinement   77, 80–81, 199, 484
　and Oksan Academy   198, 201–205, 207–210, 213, 219, 222–223
Yi Tŏkhyŏng   205
Yi Tonghwi   85

Yi Wŏnik   74, 76
Yixing   46, 58, 60–65
Yŏktong Academy   325
Yŏngbong Academy. *See* Ch'ŏn'gok Academy
Yonggok Academy. *See* Ryonggok Academy
Yŏnggwang hyanggyo (Yŏnggwang local school)   277
Yŏngjo   69–70, 71n7, 73, 85, 482
Yongsan Academy   217, 273
Yongzheng   109, 437, 444
Yoshida Shōin   136
You Jujing   376
You Zuo   425
Yu Maoheng   171
Yu Yang   169
Yuan Haowen   403, 429
Yue Hesheng   178
Yue Yuansheng   187
Yuehua Academy   290, 291–292, 293, 296–301, 303–306, 309
Yuelu Academy   6n13, 21, 23, 118, 259, 289, 360, 397n1, 418, 439n5, 440, 441n9, 453
　and lectures   161–162, 177–178
　as model academy   25–31, 35–36, 105–112, 114, 121
Yuexiu Academy   290, 291–292, 293, 296–314
Yulgok   7, 81, 83, 262n33, 274–277, 487
　and academies   320–356, 489
　enshrinement   72, 75–77, 459, 483–484
Yun Sŏn'gŏ   349
Yushan Academy (Guangzhou)   291–292, 293, 297, 298–299, 303, 311
Yushan Academy (Jiangsu)   180, 182, 188–189
Yu Hŭich'un   73, 78

Zeng Fengyi   177
Zengzi   29, 340, 412, 441
Zhai Jinguan   296
Zhan Ruoshui   160, 166–167, 179, 192, 315, 372, 376–377, 380, 389
Zhang Boduan   189
Zhang Mao   369–372
Zhang Mu   407, 411
Zhang Qian   428–429
Zhang Shi   26–28, 30, 31, 107, 161–162, 371, 374
Zhang Shusheng   298
Zhang Sui   60

Zhang Xun   407, 411
Zhang Yue (667–730)   61, 234
Zhang Yue (?–?)   378, 387
Zhang Zai   81, 255, 402, 412, 441, 446–448
Zhang Zhidong   298–299, 301–304, 313–314
Zhao Peng   403–404
Zhao Shikong   173
Zhou Shuyuan   174
Zhen Dexiu   201, 240, 241n48, 325
Zheng Zhenxian   187
Zhengde   160, 366, 369, 370, 378
Zhengxue Academy   172, 180
Zhenzong   25, 235, 236, 402, 426
Zhixue Academy   171
Zhongshe Academy   437–438
*Zhongyong* (*Doctrine of the Mean*)   26, 33, 257, 276, 411
  commentary on   136, 204, 257n15
  and curriculum   138, 148, 184
  lectures on   26, 172, 209
Zhongzong   52
Zhou Deji   370–371
Zhou Dunyi   81, 255, 268, 271n59, 278n84, 412n72
  enshrinement   28, 30, 35, 104, 340, 441, 446–447
Zhou Shi   25, 109
Zhou Tong   375, 383
Zhou Ying   375
*Zhouli* (*Rites of Zhou*)   48, 185, 229, 242, 451
*Zhouyi*. *See Yijing*

Zhu Dong   106, 109
Zhu Xi   9, 22–25, 40, 81, 204, 412, 344, 355, 368, 428, 441, 478
  and White Deer Grotto Academy   2, 4, 31–33, 175n50, 239–241, 252
  and *Articles of Learning*   33–35, 39, 252–260, 349, 354
  and Yuelu Academy   26–27, 107, 161–162
  and academy model   5, 6n13, 270–272, 326
  relics of   21, 27, 107, 363–366
  enshrinement in academies   30–31, 35–36, 40, 75–77, 104–105, 340, 345, 348, 411–412, 445–448
  enshrinement in Confucian temple   30, 277
  shrine for   369–372, 374
  teachings in Korea   38–39, 263, 273, 279, 479
  teachings in Japan   136
  and community compact   339–340, 343
  and Buddhism   359
Zhuge Liang   272, 459
Zhulin jingshe   28–30, 258, 344, 441
Zisi   29, 412, 441
Zitong (Zitong dijun). *See* Wenchang
Ziyang Academy   102, 181
Zou Deyong   171
Zou Shouyi   170, 172, 189–190, 375
Zou Yuanbiao   171
*Zuozhuan*   26
  and curriculum   138, 148